COMPUTER-BASED CONSTRUCTION PROJECT MANAGEMENT

TAREK HEGAZY

University of Waterloo
Ontario

Prentice Hall

Upper Saddle River, New Jersey
Columbus, Ohio

Library of Congress Cataloging-in-Publication Data
Hegazy, Tarek.
    Computer-based construction project management / Tarek Hegazy.
        p. cm.
    Includes bibliographical references and index.
    ISBN 0-13-088859-1
    1. Building—Superintendence—Data processing. I. Title.

TH438.H42 2002
690'.068—dc21

                                                            2001021379

Editor in Chief: Stephen Helba
Executive Editor: Ed Francis
Production Editor: Christine M. Buckendahl
Production Coordination: Carlisle Publishers Services
Design Coordinator: Robin G. Chukes
Cover Designer: Diane Ernsberger
Cover photo: Stone Images
Production Manager: Matt Ottenweller
Marketing Manager: Jamie Van Voorhis

This book was set in Palatino by Carlisle Communications, Ltd., and was printed and bound by Courier Kendallville, Inc. The cover was printed by Phoenix Color Corp.

Prentice-Hall International (UK) Limited, *London*
Prentice-Hall of Australia Pty. Limited, *Sydney*
Prentice-Hall Canada, Inc., *Toronto*
Prentice-Hall Hispanoamericana, S.A., *Mexico*
Prentice-Hall of India Private Limited, *New Delhi*
Prentice-Hall of Japan, Inc., *Toyko*
Prentice-Hall Singapore Pte. Ltd.
Editora Prentice-Hall do Brasil, Ltda., *Rio de Janeiro*

10 9 8 7 6 5 4 3 2 1
ISBN: 0-13-088859-1

Preface

This book is first about improving the efficiency in managing construction projects through the use of computers. Second, it is about coping with increasing challenges of tight budgets, strict deadlines, and limited resources of construction projects. Third, it is about the modeling and utilization of construction information to support construction operations. With computer use so prevalent at the university and industry levels, this book focuses on the efficient use of computers in project management, as an important domain in which information technology can achieve substantial benefits.

The book introduces the basic quantitative methods for construction project management with hands-on computer application. Users will develop skills to analyze projects and use computers to optimize resource use and meet various project challenges during their planning and control. A variety of computer applications (spreadsheet templates, commercial software, and custom applications) are incorporated into the CD that comes with this book. These computer applications are not only for demonstration purposes but also for actual use in real-life project management.

In this book, computer-aided construction project management is described in a collective and practical manner that is not a software vendor's point of view. It includes topics such as construction contracts, integrated estimating and scheduling, resource management, bidding strategies, cash flow analysis, and project control. Whereas the book deals with the basics of these topics, the handling of these topics is current and reflects on recent research and developments in these areas. Early chapters (2, 3, and 4) use simple spreadsheets, and the reader is given detailed steps on how these spreadsheets are implemented and how they fit within a firm's information management system. Starting from Chapter 5, the reader will be using Microsoft Project and Primavera P3 software systems, powerful commercial programs for project management. Some chapters will also utilize custom applications and macro programs in Microsoft Project. The reader, however, will not be exposed to the complex code but to the relevant mathematical basics and the details of using the program. The last chapter also discusses advanced topics such as the application of artificial intelligence and the Internet in construction.

Main Features:

- Comprehensive coverage of quantitative construction management techniques for planning, estimating, scheduling, project crashing, cost optimization, cash flow analysis, bidding, and project control;
- All underlying concepts are presented both manually and on computer applications;
- A unified case study is used, and its development evolves with the concepts covered in the successive chapters;

- Another complete case study is included in Appendix B to present all concepts together in one place;
- The latest versions of industry-standard software for project management (Microsoft Project and Primavera P3) are covered in the book;
- Various tips and tricks are included to fully utilize the simple and powerful features of Excel and project management software to organize project information and efficiently manage construction;
- A simple step-by-step process to optimize project cost under time, resource, and cash flow constraints is explained and demonstrated in case studies;
- A fully working Excel template is included on the CD with a comprehensive model for estimating, scheduling, cash flow analysis, bid unbalancing, cost optimization, and project control, with automated links to Microsoft Project. This template is ready for use in your next project;
- Comprehensive coverage of resource management topics with various Microsoft Project templates for repetitive construction, multiskilled resources, and resource optimization;
- Newly emerging concepts such as Critical Chain Project Management are covered;
- A class game is included in Chapter 12 to demonstrate the impact of uncertainty;
- Many manual and computer-based exercises are included after each chapter to supplement the students' educational experience. Also, case study exercise projects in Appendix C can be used for student group projects;
- All Excel and Microsoft Project files that relate to the various chapters are included on the CD;
- A working version of Evolver (a commercial Genetic Algorithm software) is included on the CD and is used for cost optimization;
- A fully working version of ProBID software for competitive bidding is included on the CD; and
- Appendix A lists Web resources that supplement the material in various chapters.

Although this book is intended mainly for a senior undergraduate course in construction project management, the material also can be used for a course at the graduate level and for specialized workshops for trade engineers. The book assumes familiarity with basic computer operation and the use of word processing and spreadsheets in the Microsoft Windows environment.

Thanks to the reviewers of this book for their helpful comments and suggestions: David Bilbo, Texas A&M University; Burl George, Bradley University; Madan Mehta, University of Texas, Arlington; and John Schaufelberger, University of Washington.

Tarek Hegazy, Ph.D., P.Eng.
University of Waterloo

Contents

Chapter 8   Resource Management: Part 2 – Time-Cost Tradeoff   211

Construction Project Initiation

In this chapter, you will be introduced to:

- The unique characteristics and challenges of the construction industry.
- The life-cycle phases of projects.
- The various decisions involved in initiating a project: project delivery methods, contract types, and contractual relations among project participants.
- The competitive bidding process for project acquisition.
- Recent trends in contract strategies.

1.1   Introduction

A construction project is defined as a planned undertaking to construct a facility or group of facilities. The principal participants in construction projects are the owner, the architect/engineer, the consultant, the general contractor, and the subcontractors. Usually, there are many ways in which some or all of the participants join their efforts in a project. A suitable arrangement of these participants depends on the nature of the project, the size and strength of each participant, and the project objectives and constraints. It is important, therefore, to understand the environment in which a construction project is initiated so as to clearly define the roles and responsibilities of the various participants and to bring the project to fruition and success with respect to all of them. This chapter provides the background material regarding the organizational aspects of selecting the project participants, the contract type, and the project delivery approach that suit the environment of a project under consideration.

1.2   Construction: A Magnificent Creativity

Since the beginning of time, humans have been fascinated by large-scale objects in nature such as mountains, landscape, and the endless oceans. As humans grew more sophisticated over the years, some groups began to build large-size monuments of their own to glorify their civilization. The great pyramids of Giza are early examples of these monuments. Undoubtedly, the effort spent on building such huge monuments is a witness to the human ability to make creative and challenging construction. The impact of such large structures on human development has been tremendous on all fronts, including social, economic, and cultural.

In recent history, the human fascination with developing large-scale structures remains unchanged. The twentieth century was marked by its far leap in terms of technology, materials, and human sophistication. No wonder it is the greatest century in which humans have developed so many structures of unique scale and creativity that impacted the lives of almost all humans. The century also witnessed a rapid pace of developments in science and technology made by so many people in different places on our planet that it is seemingly becoming a single village. Despite some of the drawbacks of the rapid industrial developments on the environment and on the personal lives of humans, the achievements made in this century are remarkable. No doubt one of the major achievements that made everything else possible is the development of the existing huge infrastructure. This includes the highways we travel on, the buildings and factories in which we live and conduct our business, and the facilities that deliver all utilities easily to our reach.

It is beneficial before we embark on a book on construction to briefly recognize those individuals and also the landmark projects that were constructed during the twentieth century. Worth mentioning are three particular issues of the *ENR* (*Engineering News Record*) weekly construction magazine that were published during 1999, which marked the magazine's 125th anniversary. The July 26th issue selected the notable 125 projects that were constructed all over the world and covered in the magazine during its 125 years of service. These are:

1874 Eads Bridge	1937 Golden Gate Bridge	1973 Sydney Opera House
1875 Hoosac Tunnel	1940 Rockefeller Center	1974 Sears Tower
1883 Brooklyn Bridge	1940 Pennsylv. Turnpike	1974 Snowy Mountain Hydro
1885 Home Insur. Building	1940 Mississippi Dam	1975 Louisiana Superdome
1886 Lawrence Station	1941 Colorado Aqueduct	1975 CN Tower
1886 Statue of Liberty	1942 Grande Coulee Dam	1976 Quincy Market
1888 Homestead Steel	1942 Alaskan Highway	1976 Washington D.C. Metro
1889 Eiffel Tower	1943 The Pentagon	1977 Nurek Dam
1890 London Deep Tunnel	1944 Project Mulberry	1977 Trans Alaska Pipeline
1890 Firth of Forth Bridge	1944 Tennessee Dams	1980 Haj Terminal
1894 Union Station	1945 Oak Ridge Weapon	1980 Crystal Cathedral
1895 Folsom Power	1947 Levittown Housing	1980 St. Gotthard Tunnel
1900 Chicago Ship Canal	1950 Walnut Lane Bridge	1981 Statfjord B Platform
1902 Ingalls Building	1955 Disneyland	1981 Humber Bridge
1904 Trans-Siberian Rail	1957 Shippingport N.P. Plant	1982 Sasol
1904 New York Subway	1957 Mackinac Bridge	1982 Camp David Airbases
1907 NY Corton Dam	1959 St. Lawrence Seaway	1982 Thames Barrier
1909 Spiral Tunnels	1959 Guggenheim Museum	1982 Spaceship Earth
1909 Bayway Refinery	1960 Kuwait Desalination	1985 Hyperion Treat. Plant
1913 L.A. Aqueduct	1960 Brasilia	1985 James Bay Hydro
1913 Woolworth Tower	1962 Port Elizabeth Terminal	1985 Chicago Tunnel
1914 Panama Canal	1962 TWA Airport Terminal	1986 Hongkong-Shanghai
1916 Jones Island Treatment	1964 Verrazano Bridge	Bank
1917 Ford Rouge Plant	1964 Japanese Bullet Trains	1986 Jubail Industrial City
1920 Lincoln Highway	1964 Kennedy Space Center	1986 Holland's Delta Project
1922 Miami District	1965 St. Louis Gateway Arch	1986 Sunshine Stillwater Dam
1925 Cleveland Airport	1965 Houston Astrodome	1987 Upper Stillwater Dam
1927 Holland Tunnel	1966 Severn Bridge	1988 Seikan Rail Tunnel
1928 The Cascade Tunnel	1968 Guri Dam and Plant	1988 Canberra Parliament
1931 The Empire State Bldg	1970 Aswan High Dam	1988 Love Canal Cleanup
1931 George Wash. Bridge	1970 U.S. Pavilion - Expo 70	1989 Toronto Skydome
1932 Magnitogorsk	1973 Eisenhower Tunnel	1989 Salt Lake City Building
1935 Hoover Dam	1973 California Water Project	1989 European Atom
1936 S.F. Bay Bridge	1973 World Trade Center	Smasher

1989 Grande Arche
    Monument
1991 Itaipu Dam
1992 Georgia Dome
1993 General Plaza
1993 Natchez Trace Bridge
1994 Channel Tunnel
1995 Boston Harbor Cleanup
1995 Normandy Bridge
1995 Denver Airport

1995 NRDC's Building
1996 Interstate Highway
1996 H-3 Highway
1996 Northumberland Strait
1997 Guggenheim Museum
1997 Kuala Lumpur
1997 San Joaquin Hills Corridor
1997 Hibernia Offshore
    Platform

1998 Baldpate Platform
1998 Great Belt East Bridge
1998 Akashi Kaikyo
1998 Chek Lap Kok Airport
1999 Millennium Dome
1999 Tatara Bridge
1999 URSA Tension-Leg
    Platform

The *ENR*'s August 30th issue identified 125 people with the most outstanding contributions to the construction industry during the 125 years from 1874 to 1999. Their efforts, singularly and collectively, helped shape the world. Each pioneered in his territory, developing new analytical tools, equipment, engineering, or architectural designs. Through their companies, they also invented new means and methods for constructing the built environment. Examples of builders are Stephen Bechtel (1900–1989), John Dunn (1893–1964), Peter Kiewit (1900–1979), and John Fluor (1923–1984). Examples of architects are Albert Kahn (1869–1942) and Henry Richardson (1838–1886). Examples of structural engineers are Gustave Eiffel (1832–1923), Alan Davenport (1932), Karl Terzaghi (1883–1963), and Horst Berger (1928). Examples of technology and materials innovators are Omer Blodgett (1917), Willis Carrier (1887–1950), and Paul Teicholz (1937). Examples of educators are Robert Peurifoy (1902–1995) and Clarkson Oglesby (1908–1992).

Worth mentioning also is the *ENR*'s October 18th issue that listed the most important innovations that have been introduced to the construction industry during the 125 years between 1874 to 1999. These innovations are in fact solutions provided by the industry pioneers to respond to the challenges they faced in their projects. The results have been a glorious record of admirable and effective solutions to old problems, as well as new methods and materials for today's challenges and for the projects in the new millennium we have just embarked on. A listing of these innovations is as follows:

Transportation

High Speed Highways
Bridge Cantilevered Forms
Steel Framing in Bridges
Pneumatic Caissons
Jersey Barriers
Precast Bridge Segments
Mechanically Reinforced
    Earth
Asphalt Paving
Cloverleafs
Cable-Stayed Bridges
Concrete Paving
High-Speed Rail

Design, Testing, & Info. Tech.

Finite Element Analysis
Computer-Aided Design
Shear Walls
Nonlinear Analysis
Limit-State Design
Performance-Based Design
Wind-Tunnel Analysis
Seismic Engineering
Concrete Strength Testing
Nondestructive Testing

Photogrammetry
Computerized Project
    Management
Project Websites
Computerized Takeoffs

Management & Finance

Critical Path Method
Design Review by Peers
Privatized Public Works
Surety Bonds
Wrap-Up Insurance
Safety Programs

Equipment & Tools

Hydraulic Excavators
Self-Erecting Tower Cranes
Bulldozers
Safety Devices
Cordless-Tool Technology
Mobile Lift Platforms
Material Conveyors
Material Hoists
Directional Drilling Machines
Backhoe Loaders
Automatic Paving Machines
In-Place Milling Machines

Concrete Pumps
Concrete Mixers
Skid-Steer Loaders
Pneumatic Tools
Power Tools
Lasers in Construction
Theodolites
Global Positioning Systems
Dump Trucks

Materials & Processes

Engineered Wood Products
High-Strength Bolted
    Connections
Rotary Cement Kilns
Reinforced Concrete
Precast Concrete
Rebar
Underwater Concrete
Concrete Admixtures
Gypsum Wallboard
Slurry Walls
Geotextiles
High-Performance Metals
Fiber-Reinforced Polymers
Hot-Rolled Steel
Cold-Formed Steel

ARC Welding	**Power, Industrial, &**	Retractable Roofs
PVC Pipes	**Communication**	Space Frames
Standardized Sizing of	Nuclear Powerplants	Thin-Shell Concrete
Materials	Alternative Power Sources	Composite Structural Systems
Soil and Rock Anchors	Combined-Cycle Generation	Moment-Resisting Frames
Steel Decks	Fluidized-Bed Boilers	Fire-Resistant Construction
Sheet Piles	Pulverized-Coal Combustion	High-Performance Buildings
Modular Construction	Coal Gasification	Flat-Slab Design
High-Strength Concrete	Improved Instrumentation /	Air Conditioning
Driven Piles & Drilled Shafts	P&IDS	Integrated Systems
Cofferdams & Caissons	Zero Discharge Production	
	Telecommunications Cable	**Tunnel & Dams**
Environmental		Tunnel Boring Machine
Wastewater Treatment	**Buildings**	Drill Jumbo
Bioremediation	Tensioned Fabric Structures	Arch Dams
Water-Quality Modeling	Model Building Codes	Ground Freezing
Wastewater Digestion	Base Isolation	Austrian Tunneling Method
Drinking Water Treatment	Dampers	Vehicle Tunnel Ventilation
Environmental Impact Review	Slipforms	Embankment Dams
Waste-to-Energy Power	Flying Forms	Rolled-Compacted Concrete
Engineered Landfill	Tilt-Up Construction	Shield Tunneling
Pump-and-Treat Technology	Curtain Walls	Water-Cooled Mass Concrete
Microfiltration		

1.3   Need for Scientific Project Management in Construction

The construction industry is the largest industry in North America and the world. Although products are made, the construction industry is more of a service than a manufacturing industry. In Canada and the United States, investments in the construction industry amount to about 10% of the total investments in all industries. Growth in this industry in fact is an indicator of the economic conditions of a country. This is because the industry cuts across a large number of trades that consume a wide employment circle of labor. Construction also feeds and interacts with the manufacturing industry, which exports a large portion of its products to the construction industry.

In our daily life, we use various services from various industries, including the airline industry, publishing, railways, manufacturing, and the construction industry, which produces the facilities in which we live and do business. Many of these industries generally exhibit high-quality products, timeliness of service delivery, reasonable cost of service, and low failure rates. The construction industry, on the other hand, is generally the opposite. Most projects exhibit cost overruns, time extensions, and conflicts among parties. The reasons for the widespread use of these problems can generally be attributed to three main factors (Figure 1–1): (1) the unique and

Figure 1-1.
Reasons for Poor
Performance in
Construction

Nature of Projects	Industry Characteristics	Increasing Challenges
• Projects are unique and unrepeatable; • Projects are temporary; • Projects are constrained by time, money, & quality; • Projects involve many conflicting parties; and • Many decisions are made based solely on experience.	• Extremely fragmented, with many small specialties involved; • Intense competition and high failure rates; • Rapidly affected by recessions; • Little R&D expenditures; • Confidentiality and lack of information sharing; and • Slow to adopt new technologies.	• Global market competition; • Increasing regulations (e.g., environmental and safety); • New advances in materials and equipment; • Tight budget, less time, yet better quality is demanded; • Rising costs; and • Lack of skilled resources.

Figure 1–2.
Total Quality
Management
Objectives

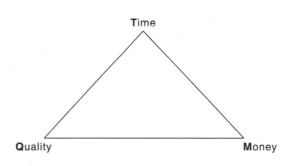

highly uncertain nature of construction projects; (2) the fragmented and highly competitive nature of the construction industry; and (3) the ever-increasing challenges facing the industry as a whole. In view of these increasing challenges, efficient management becomes a key to the success of any construction organization.

A scientific approach to construction project management can help construction participants in many ways, including:

- Cope with the increasing complexity of modern projects.
- Utilize resources (4 Ms) efficiently: Manpower, Materials, Machinery, and Money.
- Meet fiscal requirements and deadlines.
- Communicate effectively among the participants and avoid adverse relations.
- Improve construction quality and safety record.
- Achieve higher productivity.
- Document and utilize past experience to improve future construction.

In order for these benefits to be materialized, construction project management as a discipline has as its objective the control of three main aspects of construction: Time (T), Quality (Q), and Money (M). The (TQM) acronym is also in rhythm with the principles of "Total Quality Management" (Figure 1–2) which is a wide umbrella for quality in business and manufacturing. The specific discipline of construction project management, therefore, involves a wide spectrum of techniques and approaches that are discussed in this book and attempt to achieve its objectives through systematic application of: (1) contract management; (2) information management; (3) cost management; (4) time management; (5) resource management; (6) financial management; and (7) execution management.

1.4   Construction Project Participants

1. **Owner:**   The owner (also referred to as the **Client**) is the individual or organization for whom a facility or project is to be built or a service furnished under a contract. The owner, whether public or private, owns and finances the facility or project. Depending on the owner's in-house capabilities, he, she, or they may handle all or portions of basic planning, budgeting, project management, design, engineering, procurement, and construction. The owner engages architects, engineering firms, and contractors as necessary to accomplish the desired work.

   Public owners are public bodies of some kind ranging from agencies of the federal government down through the state, county, and municipal entities including boards, commissions, and authorities. Most public projects or facilities are built for public use and not sold to others. Private owners may be individuals, partnerships, corporations, or various combinations thereof. Most private owners have facilities or projects built for their own use (e.g., business, habitation) or to be sold, operated, leased, or rented to others.

2. **Architect:**   An architect is an individual who plans, programs, and designs buildings and their associated landscaping. Sometimes the architect also provides the aesthetics of the whole envelope or concept of the whole project. Since most architects have only limited capabilities in structural, electrical, and other specialized design, they mostly rely on consulting engineers for such work. The architect may be obligated by contract to make field visits to the construction site during the progress of the project. Such periodic visits are for the purpose of observing materials and completed work to evaluate their general compliance with plans and specifications. These visits can be interpreted neither as full-time inspection for quality control on the work nor as supervision on project progress.

3. **Architect/Engineer (A/E):**   The architect/engineer (also known as the design professional) is part of the business firm that employs both architects and engineers and has the capability to do complete design work. The A/E firm also may have the capability to perform construction management services.

4. **Construction Manager:**   The construction manager is a specialized firm or organization which furnishes the administrative and management services for on-site erection activities and may provide the consulting services necessary and as required by the owner from planning through design and construction to commissioning. The construction manager has a professional services contract with the owner and provides consulting and/or managerial functions. The construction manager, as the construction professional on the project team, is responsible for design coordination, liaison in the proper selection of materials and methods of construction, contracts preparation for award by the owner, cost and scheduling information and control, as well as quality. He or she is also responsible for managing operations normally associated with a contractor organization. One construction manager can handle more than one project.

5. **Engineer:**   The term *engineer* usually refers to an individual and/or a firm engaged in specialized design or other work associated with design or construction. Design engineers are usually classified as civil, electrical, mechanical, environmental, and so on, depending upon their specialty. There are also scheduling, estimating, cost, and construction engineers who originated from any of the basic engineering disciplines but have specialized in a particular area.

6. **Engineering-Construction Firm:**   An engineering-construction firm is a type of organization that combines both architect/engineering and construction contracting. The engineering-construction firm has the capability of executing a complete design-build sequence, or any portion of it. Sometimes this firm does the procurement of the equipment and materials needed to construct the project. This capability is usually found only among the largest firms.

7. **General Contractor (G.C.):**   The general contractor (also known as the *prime contractor*) is the business firm that is under contract to the owner for the construction of the project, or for a major portion of the project. The prime contractor brings together all of the diverse elements and inputs of the construction process into a single, coordinated effort for the purpose of management and control of the construction process. The prime contractor generally performs common construction operations such as site preparation, concrete placement, mechanical work, electrical work, and finishes. Subcontractors are frequently engaged, although the prime contractor retains the responsibility for the satisfactory performance of these subcontractors.

8. **Project Manager:** The project manager is the individual charged with the overall coordination of all the facets of a construction program—planning, design, procurement, and construction—for the owner.

9. **Project Engineer:** The project engineer exercises liaison with field and home office engineering. He or she also supervises and coordinates the work of all the engineers working on the project and performs these functions and responsibilities for the owner, the construction manager, or the contractor. He or she may also relieve the project manager of such administrative functions as management of change orders, updating progress schedules, conventional engineering practices, and monitoring delivery schedules.

10. **Subcontractor:** A subcontractor is under contract to another contractor, as opposed to an owner, to perform a portion on the contractor's work. A general contractor who is under contract with an owner may engage subcontractors for portions of the project, the type and amount depending on the nature of the project and the contractor's own organization. These subcontractors, in turn, may engage other subcontractors. Thus, there can be several levels of subcontracting to a general contractor.

11. **Specialty Contractor:** This contractor performs only specialized construction, like plumbing, electrical, and painting, either as a subcontractor or as a prime contractor.

1.5   Types of Construction

There is no universal agreement on the categories or types of construction and their inclusive elements. One simple classification is shown in Figure 1–3 with the three main categories of residential buildings, nonresidential buildings, and nonbuilding construction. The numbers shown in the figure are approximate and generally apply to the United States and Canada.

A more detailed classification of construction types is as follows:

1. **Residential Building Construction:** This category, also known as housing, includes all single-family homes, condominiums, multi-unit town houses, and low-rise and high-rise apartments. For some purposes, residential construction is divided into homes, townhouses, low-rise buildings (four stories or less), and high-rise buildings. Design of this construction type is done by owners, architects, or the builders themselves. Construction may be performed by the owner or independent contractors under contract with the owner. The backbone of the building construction profession has been, and always will be, the residential builder.

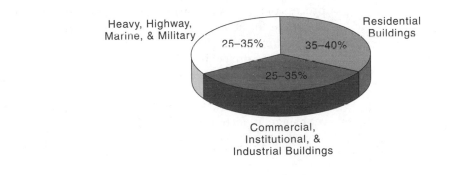

Figure 1-3. Simple Classification of Construction Types

Heavy, Highway, Marine, & Military — 25–35%

Residential Buildings — 35–40%

Commercial, Institutional, & Industrial Buildings — 25–35%

2. **Nonresidential Building Construction:** Nonresidential building construction includes buildings, other than housing, that are erected for commercial and industrial purposes. Typical commercial buildings are stores, office buildings, warehouses, small manufacturing facilities, hospitals, service stations, shopping centers, educational buildings, and institutional buildings (banks, churches, nursing homes, and the like). Industrial buildings are buildings reserved for major factories, power plants, petrochemical plants, and other process plants. Design of this construction type is predominantly done by architects, with engineering design services being obtained as required. Construction of this type is generally accomplished by prime contractors or construction managers who subcontract substantial portions of the work to specialty contractors.

3. **Nonbuildings:**

   Heavy and Highway Construction: This is, in general, the largest category in volume of work, though not in number of projects. Streets, highways, railroads, airports, tunnels, subways, bridges, dams, canals, hydroelectric work, refineries, chemical plants, power plants, industrial plants, and pipelines are typical examples of heavy and highway construction.

   Marine Construction: Marine construction, also known as waterfront construction, includes aqueous and subaqueous projects. Examples are dredging, jetties, piers, breakwaters, offshore platforms, submarine pipelines, and structures related to navigation and ocean commerce.

   Military Construction: These are federally funded projects that directly support the defense effort. Military construction includes everything from military housing to missile bases.

1.6   Life-Cycle Stages of Projects

The development of a construction project, from its initiation into its operation, may be divided into the following consecutive stages, as shown in Figure 1–4:

Figure 1–4. Project Life-Cycle Phases

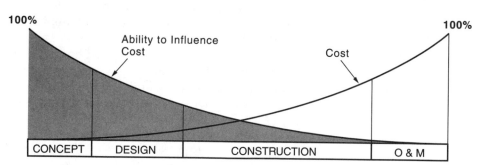

1. **Concept Stage:** When the need to build a new project is identified, the process of appraising various alternatives commences. This study, which is known as feasibility study, can in some cases take several years, particularly if environmental assessments need to be made. The study determines whether the project is truly viable and which of the various alternatives for carrying it out will be best. The master schedule using approximate durations of various operations is then prepared in order that the owner may know how long and how much it would take to reach the objective. The concept stage, in fact, is one of the major steps in a project life cycle, as it has the largest impact on cost and performance, as shown in Figure 1–4.

2. **Design Stage:** In this stage, decisions are taken concerning the sizes and types of structures required and the conceptual design is prepared. This involves preparing outline drawings and details of all services. This conceptual design should then be reviewed, as this is the main opportunity for cost saving and for ensuring that it meets the owner's objectives. At this stage also, a suitable project contract strategy that satisfies project objectives and constraints (such as a target completion date) is proposed. This strategy (dealt with in detail later) includes type of contract, interaction between design and construction, and method of selecting contractors. The contract strategy proposal is then submitted to the owner and is accompanied by a cost estimate, a schedule, and a plan for risk management. Upon reviewing the proposal, the owner may then proceed with investment in the project.

   Upon owner approval of the conceptual design, a detailed design and other steps are carried out to prepare specification and quantities of work, prepare tender documents, and implement the project contract strategy to procure bids and award the construction contract.

3. **Construction Stage:** The chosen project completion date will determine the overlap between the design and construction stages. The general contractor will carry out site construction. A mechanical and or electrical installation may be subcontracted under the supervision of the general contractor. The consultants will be deployed for contract administration and construction supervision. The contractor would seek the most efficient use of his resources using construction management techniques, such as those described in the various chapters of this book. Commissioning is then made and performance tests conducted, leading to project acceptance.

4. **Operation & Maintenance (O & M):** The operational maintenance of the project may be carried out by the owner's own employees. Project review may be required for future interests. Demolition occurs at the end of service life.

1.7   Project Contract Strategy

At the early stage of a project, and once a project manager is selected, the main issue that faces the owner is to decide on the contract strategy that best suits the project objectives. Contract strategy means selecting organizational and contractual policies required for executing a specific project. The development of the contract strategy comprises a complete assessment of the choices available for the management of design and construction to maximize the likelihood of achieving project objectives.

A road map to selecting a proper contract strategy for a project is illustrated in Figure 1–5, involving five key decisions related to:

1. Setting the project objectives and constraints.
2. Selecting a proper project delivery method.
3. Selecting a proper design/construction interaction scheme.
4. Selecting a proper contract form/type.
5. Contract administration practices.

Details on these five broad aspects are given in the following subsections.

As shown in Figure 1–5, a large number of possibilities exist for a contracting strategy. Often, the project manager or another consultant may help the owner in the five-step process of deciding a suitable contracting strategy. Such decisions, however, are not an exact science. In many cases, there is no one single best strategy, but several that are appropriate. The selection process often follows an "elimination" approach of rejecting obviously unsuitable strategies until reasonable alternatives remain. This process can also lead to new innovative strategies that suit the needs of

Figure 1-5. Key
Considerations in
a Contracting
Strategy

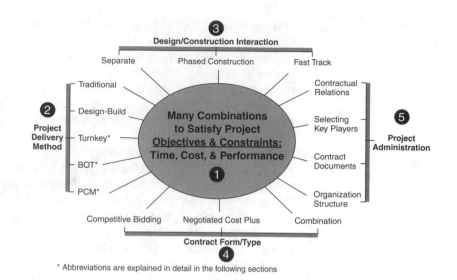

modern complex projects. Such innovative strategies can achieve various benefits, including: Shortening project duration by overlapping design and construction; providing flexibility for changes during construction; creating more designer/contractor teamwork to reduce adverse relationships; allowing a contractor to participate in the design process, thus augmenting the designer's construction experience; providing incentives for the contractor to save the owner money; and providing alternative financing methods.

1.7.1 Project Objectives and Constraints

Before owners can begin to choose a contracting strategy, they must gain an understanding of the project and the top-ranked objectives during its construction. A summary of various project objectives and constraints are as follows:

1.7.1.1 Time Objective   There may be a need for an early start to the construction phase for political reasons and/or a need for minimum project duration to maximize economic return. If this objective is top-ranked by the owner, the contracting strategies that allow speedy project delivery, such as overlapping design and construction, may become desirable.

1.7.1.2 Cost Objective   There may be a need for minimum project cost to ensure adequate economic return, a need for minimum total cost incorporating operation and maintenance costs, or a need to observe a maximum limit on monthly expenditure. The selected contracting strategy, therefore, should be flexible to the owner's cost requirement, while also maintaining the other objectives.

1.7.1.3 Performance Objective   An appropriate functional performance of each component in a project can be defined as the minimum acceptable to the owner and to society. To attain this objective, a "Value Engineering" program may be adopted by the project management team at the design stage to reevaluate the design components, thus introducing changes that save cost without sacrificing performance. If this objective is top-ranked by the owner, a contracting strategy that accommodates changes and a teamwork approach may become desirable.

1.7.1.4 Secondary Objectives   These objectives could arise on a construction project and would majorly influence contract strategy decisions. Examples include:

- Risk sharing between the owner and the contractor.
- Project requirement of staff training or transfer of technology.
- Involving the contractor in the design stage to reduce construction problems.
- Involving the owner in contract management.
- Choice of labor-intensive construction.
- Use of local materials and resources.
- Protection of the environment.

1.7.1.5 Project Constraints   All construction projects have constraints that influence the achievement of project objectives. These constraints should therefore be considered when choosing an appropriate contract strategy. Some of the project constraints are:

- Conditions of contract.
- Method of tender.
- Project size and duration.
- Project location.
- Relationship to other projects.
- Possession of land.
- Number of work packages.
- Target dates of the project.
- Possibility of design changes.
- Availability of construction resources.
- Freedom to choose designers and contractors.
- Adequacy of site investigation.
- Seasonal working.
- Access to the site.
- Number of contractors willing to tender.
- Inflation.
- Exchange rate.
- Union regulations.

1.7.2   Project Delivery Methods

The choice of a project delivery method should be related to project objectives and constraints, and also to the scope or the portion of the project tasks—design, construction, and finance—that is assigned to the contractor. The various project delivery methods are summarized as follows:

1.7.2.1 Traditional Approach   This is the most common approach in civil engineering projects in which the design has to be completed before construction can start. Design and construction are usually performed by two different parties who interact directly and separately with the owner. This approach takes two common forms:

  a. **Owner direct force:** In this approach, owners are responsible for the design, construction, and management of the work using their own forces. This approach is mostly used by developers who utilize typical designs and then use employed labor, hired labor, or subcontractors for the construction. Despite the cost saving in the use of direct force, it may result in a higher total cost if the owner lacks construction experience or managerial skills.

  b. **General Contractor (G.C.):** This is by far the most widely used (traditional) approach in construction. An A/E firm is hired by the owner to complete the design, then a general contractor is hired by the owner for the construction. Most often, the A/E firm will act as owner-representative in selecting and further supervising the general contractor who is usually selected based on a competition among interested bidders. Some of the pros and cons of this approach are summarized in Table 1–1.

Therefore, this method is fine in many cases where the project is clearly definable, design is completed, time need not be shortened, and changes are unlikely to occur during construction.

1.7.2.2 Design-Build   In this approach, a single organization is responsible for performing both design and construction and, in some cases, providing a certain "know-how" for the project. Within the design-build organization, parts of the design may be subcontracted to specialist consultants. Being responsible for both design and construction, the design-build contractor carries most of the project risks, and this can mean additional cost to owner. The owner's role in this approach is minimal and is only to express his or her objectives and specifications precisely before detailed design is started. Some of the pros and cons of this approach are summarized in Table 1–2.

The use of this approach, therefore, should be considered when contractors offer specialized design/construction/know-how expertise or when design is strongly influenced by the method of construction.

1.7.2.3 Turnkey   This approach is similar to the design-build approach, but the organization is responsible for performing design, construction, know-how (if any), and project financing. Owner payment is then made at the completion (when the contractor turns over the "key"). An example is franchise projects in which a new branch of a restaurant chain needs to maintain the same design, construction quality, and food-service quality.

Table 1-1. Pros and Cons of the Traditional Approach

Advantages	Disadvantages
• Price competition • Total cost is known before construction starts • Well-documented approach used in most government projects done for public works	• The approach takes a long time • Design does not benefit from construction experience • Conflicts between owner & G.C. and between A/E & G.C. • Changes may lead to disputes and claims

Table 1-2. Pros and Cons of the Design-Build Approach

Advantages	Disadvantages
• One contract that may include know-how • Minimum owner involvement • Time can be reduced if the design-build company overlaps design and construction • Possible coordination between design and construction • Easier implementation of changes • Less adversary relationships	• Cost may not be known until the end of design • High risk to contractor and more cost to owner • Design-build company may reduce quality to save cost • Due to minimal owner involvement, result may not be to his satisfaction

1.7.2.4 Build-Operate-Transfer (BOT)   In this approach, a business entity is responsible for performing the design, construction, long-term financing, and temporary operation of the project. At the end of the operation period, which can be many years, operation of the project is transferred to the owner. This approach has been extensively used in recent years and is expected to continue. An example of its use is in express routes and turnpikes. A consortium of companies shares the cost (design, construction, financing, operation, and maintenance) and the profits gained from user fees, for a stipulated number of years. Afterwards, the project returns to the government to become publicly owned. This approach has also been used extensively in large infrastructure projects financed by the World Bank in parts of the world that cannot afford the high investment cost of such projects.

1.7.2.5 Professional Construction Management (PCM)   In this approach, the owner appoints a PCM organization (also known as construction management organization) to manage and coordinate the design and construction phases of a project using a teamwork approach. The design may be provided by specialist design firms and in some cases by the PCM organization. With a high level of coordination between the participants, innovative approaches of overlapping design and construction (i.e., fast-tracking) can be adopted. The PCM organization aims at holding a friendly position similar to that of the consultants in the traditional approach.

The services offered by the PCM organization overlap those traditionally performed by the architect, the engineer, and the contractor. This may include: management and programming of design; cost forecasting and financial arrangements; preparation of tender documents; tender analysis and selection of contractors; selection of methods of construction; recommendations on construction economics; planning and scheduling construction works; materials procurement and delivery expedition; provision for site security, cleanup, and temporary utilities; supervision of control of construction contractors; construction quality assurance; cost control; costing of variations and assessment of claims; and certification of interim and final payments to contractors.

Although this approach is likely to prove marginally more expensive than the traditional approach, it offers greater guarantee of performance and the potential to avoid time overruns and to reduce the cost of claims. The payment to the PCM organization is usually a fixed fee or a percentage of the total project cost. The construction contract is usually a lump sum or a unit price (explained later). Some of the pros and cons of this approach are summarized in Table 1–3.

The use of PCM approach, therefore, should be considered when there is a need for time saving and flexibility for design changes, and the owner has insufficient management resources.

Table 1-3. Pros and Cons of the PCM Approach

Advantages	Disadvantages
• Utilization of construction skills at all stages with no conflict among participants • Independent evaluation of cost and schedule to the best owner interest • Time could be much less • Principals such as "value engineering" could be applied in all phases	• Higher owner involvement and responsibilities • Need skilled construction managers • PCM fees (up to 4%)

1.7.3 Design/Construction Interaction

In conjunction with decisions related to a suitable project delivery approach, the owner generally has three basic choices for the management of design and construction, as illustrated in Figure 1–6:

Figure 1–6.
Different Design/
Construction
Interaction Schemes

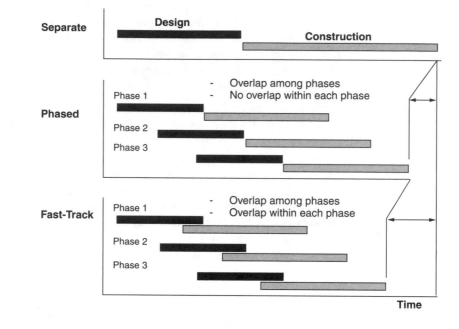

a. **Separate:** In this scheme, design is completed in full before bidding and construction of the whole project starts.

b. **Phased:** In this scheme, design is divided into phases that are dealt with as a separate package. Phases can be foundations, ground floor, repetitive floors, etc. These packages can overlap and, as such, some time can be saved since a contractor for the foundation phase, for example, can be employed even before the design for the remaining phases are completed. Within each phase, however, the design of that phase is completed before bidding and construction can begin.

c. **Fast-Track:** This scheme is similar to the previous one with the exception that a greater overlap is exercised between design and construction even within each phase. As such, a contractor can be employed early in each phase and is considered as an important team member who can start the construction as soon as a group of design details is finalized. In this approach, the potential for greater time savings becomes high, as illustrated in Figure 1–6.

Phased and fast-track approaches certainly require high levels of coordination and management to bring them to success. A PCM project delivery approach, therefore, may become desirable if time saving is a top-ranked objective to the owner. In general, therefore, decisions regarding the level of design/construction interaction required for a project can be facilitated by considering the following aspects:

- Extent to which construction is to be separated from or integrated with design.
- Size and nature of the work packages within the project.
- Appropriate number of design teams to suit the nature of the work.
- Selection of the design teams from in-house resources or external consultants.
- Process of supervision of construction.
- Restrictions on using a combination of contracting strategies within the project.

1.7.4   Construction Contract Form/Type

Construction contracts can be broadly grouped into two categories: (1) competitive bidding contracts and (2) negotiated cost-plus contracts. Specific contract types are classified according to the method of payment to the contractor. For example, the two common forms of competitive bidding contracts, lump sum and unit price, explicitly specify the method by which the contractor's submitted price is paid to him or her. Similarly, the various types of negotiated cost-plus contracts differ in the way in which the contractor is reimbursed for his or her cost (rather than price). The various contract forms are illustrated in Figure 1–7. The three basic factors that favor the use of a particular type of contract are:

- The need to provide an adequate incentive for efficient performance.
- The ability to introduce changes during construction.
- The allocation of risks between owner and contractor and the cost implication.

Figure 1–7.
Construction
Contract Forms

Construction Contract Forms		
1. Competitive Bidding	**2. Negotiated Cost-Plus**	**3. Combination**
Two Main Types:	Many Types:	New Innovative Types:
- Lump Sum (Buildings) - Unit Price (Heavy)	- Cost + % of Cost - Cost + Fixed Fee - Cost + Fee + Profit Sharing - Cost + Sliding Fee - Cost + GMP Complex projects, tunnels, power plants, process plants	- Use a combination of contract types in a single project - Teamwork
- High risk to contractor - Low risk to owner	Risk sharing	CM administered

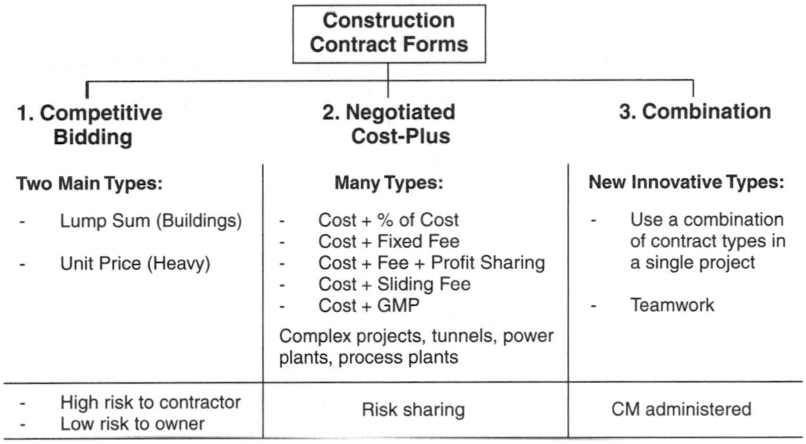

1.7.4.1 Competitive Bidding Contracts   Competitive bidding is the main process for selecting contractors, particularly for government projects. The process itself is discussed in detail in section 1.7.5.2(d). Two types of contracts are used under this process, as follows:

a. **Lump Sum:**   A single tender price is given to the contractor for the completion of a specified work to the satisfaction of the owner. Payment may be staged at intervals of time, with the completion of milestones. Since the contractor is committed to a fixed price, this type of contract has very limited flexibility for design changes. In addition, the tender price, expectedly, includes a high level of financing and high undisclosed risk contingency. One benefit to the owner, however, is that the contract final price is known at tender. But, an important risk to the owner is when not receiving competitive bids from a reasonable number of contractors who avoid higher risks on lump sum contract. Generally, this contract is appropriate when the work is defined in detail, limited variation is needed, and level of risk is low and quantifiable. It can be used for traditional, design-build, and turnkey projects. Lump sum contracts are also suitable for building projects since many items of the work, such as electrical, do not have detailed quantities associated with them.

b. **Unit Price:**   In this contract type, bidders enter rates against the estimated quantities of work. The quantities are remeasured during the course of the contract, valued at the tendered rates, and the contract price adjusted accordingly. The rates include risk contingency. Payment is made monthly for all quantities of work completed during the month. The contract allows the owner to introduce variations in the work defined in the tender documents. The contractor can claim additional payment for any changes in the work content of the contract, but this often leads to disputes and disagreements. One variation of this type is called a *schedule of rates* contract, which contains inaccurate quantities of work, possibly with upper and lower probable limits. Therefore, instead of submitting one total rate for each item of work, contractors submit separate rates for the labor hour, plant hour, and materials rates. The contract price is then devised by measuring the man-hours, plant hours, and quantities of materials actually consumed, and then pricing them at the tendered rates. Unit price contracts are best suited for heavy civil and repetitive work in which work quantities can be easily estimated from design documents.

1.7.4.2 Negotiated Cost-Plus Contracts In this category of contract types, project risks are high and can discourage contractors from being committed to lump sum or fixed-unit prices. Therefore, the owner shares the project risks by reimbursing the contractor for his or her actual costs plus a specified fee for head office overheads and profit. To allow for that, the contractor makes all his or her accounts available for inspection by the owner or by some agreed-upon third party. This category of contracts offers a high level of flexibility for design changes. The contractor is usually appointed early in the project and is encouraged to propose design changes in the context of value engineering. The final price, thus, depends on the changes and the extent to which risks materialize. The circumstances that lead to the adoption of this category of contracts are:

- Inadequate definition of the work at time of tender.
- Need for design to proceed concurrently with construction.
- Work involves exceptional technical complexity.
- Situations involving unquantifiable risks to the contractor such as work below ground level and the effect of inflation.
- Owner wishes to be involved in the management of his or her project.

Some of the common types of cost-plus contracts, classified by the method of payment to the contractor, are as follows:

a. **Cost + Fixed Percentage:** While this contract is simple to administer, it has no incentive for the contractor to save owner's money or time. Also, problems may occur if the contractor engages his or her resources in other projects and delays the work.

b. **Cost + Fixed Fee:** The fee is a fixed amount of money. As such, the contractor's fee will not increase if costly changes are introduced. While the contractor may desire to finish the project earlier, he or she still has no incentive to save owner's money.

c. **Cost + Fixed Fee + Profit Sharing:** In addition to the reimbursement of actual costs plus a fixed fee, the contractor is paid a share of any cost saving that the contractor introduces into the work.

d. **Cost + Sliding Fee:** The sliding fee is a fee that increases linearly with the amount of cost saving that the contractor introduces between the actual cost and a preset target cost, as shown in Figure 1–8. The fee can also be reduced when the actual cost exceeds the target.

It is noted that the target tender should be realistic and the incentive must be sufficient to generate the desired motivation. Specific risks can be excluded from the tendered target cost; when these risks occur, the target cost is adjusted accordingly.

Figure 1-8. Sliding Fee

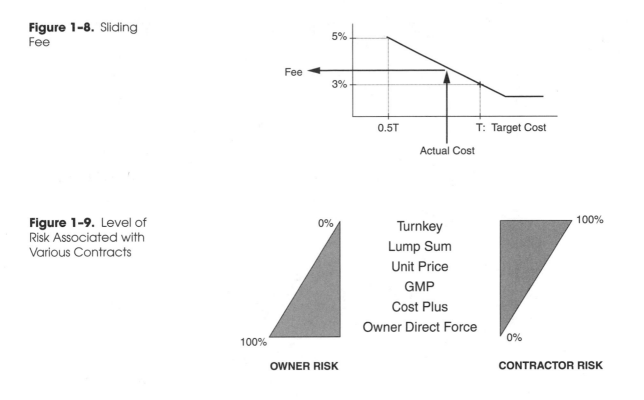

Figure 1-9. Level of Risk Associated with Various Contracts

e. **Cost + Guaranteed Maximum Price (GMP):** The contractor's cost in this case is reimbursed with the contractor giving a cap on the total price not to exceed a preset value.

A brief summary of the level of risk exposed by each of the discussed contract forms is illustrated in Figure 1–9. As shown in the figure, competitive bidding contracts (Lump Sum and Unit Price) are among the top risky contracts to contractors and thus present a challenge in estimating their cost and schedule at the bidding stage and before a commitment is made.

1.7.5 Project Administration Practices

Construction projects no doubt involve many administrative issues that project managers have to be familiar with. These include: contractual relationships among various parties, selecting key project participants, contract documents, and project organization structures. Some details related to these issues are as follows.

1.7.5.1 Contractual Relationships Within each project delivery method, the contractual relationships among the project participants can take various arrangements, and the owner needs to make a decision regarding the proper arrangement that suits the project and the parties involved. The two basic contractual relationships with an owner are: agent relationship, referred to as (A); and nonagent relationship, referred to as ($). The agent relationship is a contract, such as that between the owner and an A/E firm. In this case, the agent organization performs some service (e.g., design), in addition to possibly representing the owner in front of other parties (e.g., supervision over the contractor). The nonagent relationship, on the other hand, is a regular legally binding contract to perform a service, such as the contract between the owner and the contractor. The different contractual relationships associated with various project delivery methods are illustrated in Figures 1–10 and 1–11.

Figure 1-10.
Contractual
Relations in
Traditional and
Design-Build Projects

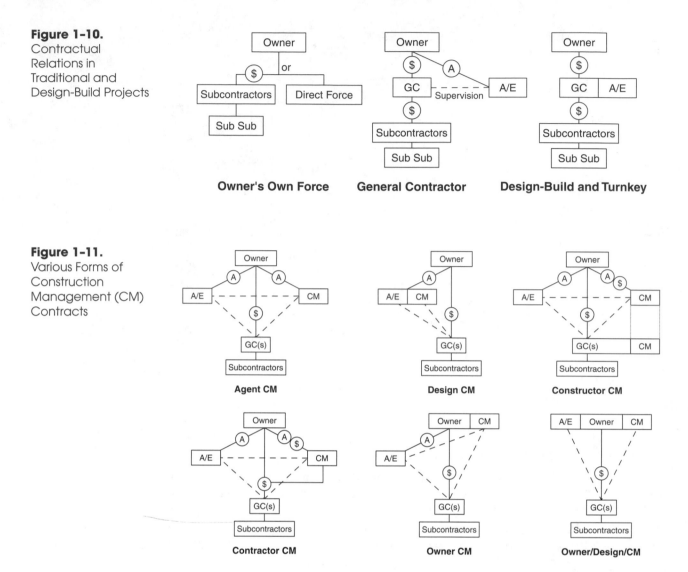

Figure 1-11.
Various Forms of
Construction
Management (CM)
Contracts

1.7.5.2 Selecting Key Players   Selecting key personnel and organizations that will participate in a project is a major step for the owner and can mean the success or failure of a project. The selection process depends on the delivery method selected for the project.

   a. **The Project Manager:**   A good project manager is an important ingredient for a successful project. He or she should have sufficient seniority to exercise effective control both within and outside the owner organization. The responsibilities of the project manager normally span design, construction, and commissioning. His or her function is to control the sequence of events and decisions leading to the completion of the project. For many projects, the manager will be supported by a small team experienced in engineering management. The project management team is responsible for:
   - Overseeing the owner's diverse interests.
   - Coordinating design and construction.
   - Forecasting project cash flow.
   - Appointing consultants and contractors.
   - Solving problems with local authorities and inhabitants.

- Coordinating the work of different contractors.
- Project commissioning.
- Transfer of responsibility for completed work from contractor to operator.
- On turnkey contracts, controlling quality of construction.
- On cost-plus contracts, examining construction actual cost.

b. **The A/E firm:**   The owner and his or her project management team will appoint a consulting firm in order to prepare the design details, specification of work, and bills of quantities. Supervision and administration of the construction contract will be the job of a senior engineer in the firm. On small projects, the engineer may act as a project manager. The engineer must guard the owner, through his or her field inspection forces, against deficiencies in the work. Continuous on-site inspection should be performed during progress of work to provide quality assurance on the job. The engineer also acts as agent for the owner in performing the following duties:

- Pre-tender evaluation of contractors.
- Preparation of tender documents.
- Evaluation of bids.
- Recommendation of appointment of contractors.
- Approval of the contractor's plan.
- Review of shop drawings.
- Construction quality assurance.
- Issuing of variation orders.
- Assessment of variations and claims.
- Forecast final cost.
- Evaluation of completed work.
- Certification of contractor's payment requests.
- Final inspection of work.

c. **The Resident Engineer:**   This is the engineer's or construction manager's representative on-site. The resident engineer has authority to administer the field operations of a construction project and he or she should be the sole spokesperson representing the owner's interests. Representatives, known also as quality assurance supervisors (inspectors), are needed for different aspects of the work. The job of the inspector is identical in all respects to that of the resident engineer, except for the responsibility of field administration. An inspector may be involved in several small projects at the same time. The responsibilities of the resident engineer can be summarized as follows:

- Be familiar with the contract documents.
- Be familiar with the construction schedule.
- Prepare a daily report of the contractor's activities, as-built details, instructions given to the contractor, any agreements made, and any dangerous conditions observed on-site.
- Check materials soon after delivery.
- Inspect work as it progresses and give decision on acceptance.
- Notify the contractor if any material or portion of work does not conform with the requirements and advise the engineer if the contractor ignores the notice.
- Seek advice from the engineer to solve any problem.
- Assist in obtaining any information required for proper execution of the work.
- Consider and evaluate the contract suggestions for modification in drawings and specifications and report them to the engineer.
- Report to the engineer any unrealistic tolerance in the contractor's work and any situation which appears to cause a delay in the completion of the contract.

- Control site testing laboratory and observes all contractor's tests.
- Follow up daily on any work to be corrected by the contractor.
- Review the application for payment with the contractor.

d. **The Contractor:** Contractor selection is an important decision for any project. By and large, the competitive bidding process has been the main vehicle for contractors to obtain jobs. The process is required by law for public projects, which has been the largest percentage of all projects, except in emergencies, such as war or natural disasters. Under this process, a simple quantitative criteria is used to award the bid to the "lowest responsible bidder," thus potentially obtaining the lowest construction cost. The process, however, has its drawbacks, including: (1) overlooking important criteria such as contractor's experience and strength; (2) potentially causing construction delays and problems if the contractor bids below cost to win the job; and (3) contributing to adverse relationships between the owner and the contractor.

The competitive bidding process encompasses three main steps (Figure 1–12): (1) owner announcement for the bid; (2) contractors' preparation and submission of their bids; and (3) owner evaluation and selection of a prospective contractor.

To announce for a project, the owner should have the design completed and a bid package prepared with all design information. The owner then announces a general call for bidders or sends a limited invitation to a list of prequalified contractors. Through the limited invitation, the owner organization can reduce potential construction problems by avoiding unknown contractors who intentionally reduce their bids to win jobs, particularly if the project requires certain experience. Owners, therefore, need to maintain a list of qualified contractors with whom they had successful experience or by advertising a call for prequalification.

Having decided to tender on a certain work, the contractor shall prepare a realistic and competitive bid. Following the description in Figure 1–12, a winner will be selected to be the contractor for the project. Once a contractor is selected and construction has started, the contractor becomes responsible for all work on the project whether constructed by the firm's own forces or by subcontractors. The contractor's senior representative on site is called the *site superintendent*. He or she is to be constantly on the site and shall give his or her full charge to the works. The site superintendent should have adequate knowledge of the methods and techniques required for the work. He or she is responsible for:

- Ensuring maximum cooperation of site staff in all matters affecting the efficiency, economy, and smooth running of the construction operation.
- Reviewing proposed design changes to suit particular methods of working which will result in cost savings.
- Reviewing any requirements of additional resources.
- Identifying and dealing with problems arising at site level which will result in delays or increase in cost.
- Ensuring compliance with contract documents and the engineer's instructions.
- Organizing and deploying the contractor's site staff, plant, labor, and all other resources.
- Operating and maintaining site-testing lab.
- Billing.
- Providing and updating all the schedules, budgets, expenditures, and other records required by the engineer.
- Administering purchases for the supply of materials and services.
- Coordinating subcontractors' work.
- Protecting persons and property on, and adjacent to, the construction site.

Figure 1-12 diagram content:

Step

1 ANNOUNCEMENT
Owner
A/E
CM

2 PREPARATIOIN & SUBMISSION
Contractor

3 EVALUATION & SELECTION
Owner, A/E, CM

Site Hand-over to start Construction

Notice to Proceed

Time

Notice to Bidders | Buy Bid Package | Bid Opening | Formal Contract

Bidding Period | Acceptance Period (30, 60, or 90 days)

Announcement	Announcement includes the following information:
	• Subject/scope of work, location, type of project;
	• Dates: purchase of bid package, bid submission, bid opening, etc;
	• Required prequalification documents;
	• Bid bond and its amount (0 to 10%) to ensure seriousness;
	• Performance bond and its amount (e.g., 100%) to ensure quality;
	• Price of bid package; and
	• Conditions for acceptance/rejection.
Bid Preparation	Contractor responsibilities:
	• Receive bid package from the owner. It may contain: drawings; specifications; bill of quantities; bid proposal form; general conditions; soil report; and addenda (changes to the bid package);
	• Inspect the site and its weather, services, bylaws, and resources;
	• Detailed planning, estimating, scheduling, and cash flow;
	• Prepare bid bond;
	• Complete all forms including bid proposal form;
	• Prepare data regarding contractor's organization structure (if needed); and
	• Submit bid.
	Owner's responsibilities:
	• Inform all bidders of any changes in dates or regulations; and
	• Answer any questions.
Bid Evaluation	• Options for selecting the winner: lowest responsible bidder; average bidder; bidder closer but below average; or weighted multicriteria.
	• Negotiation among top-ranked bidders.
	• Analysis of all bids to be passed to the decision committee.

Figure 1-12. The Competitive Bidding Process

The superintendent may be supported by *site engineers*. Each one of them has a particular responsibility, such as labor relations or technical matters. Each site engineer will be allocated a different section of the work. Site engineers may be involved in the design and installation of temporary works, detailed planning, and managing the day-to-day operations.

Specialist engineers or *quantity surveyors* will be employed to value the completed works. A general *foreman*, who is an experienced tradesperson, will be employed to organize the allocation of tradesmen, labor, machines, and materials to the various sections of the job on a day-to-day basis. He or she may contribute expertise in plant operation and methods of construction.

The site superintendent may also be supported by an *office manager* to manage stores and workshops, plant manager and fitters for maintenance of the plant, and experienced staff to provide site facilities.

Under a contract requiring a contractor quality control program, a contractor *quality control representative* is also required. His or her primary function is to assure that all inspections and tests are made and to prevent defective work. This includes checking all material and equipment delivered to the site.

1.7.5.3 Contract Documents   Once the parties that will be involved in a project are identified, their legal binding is a set of contract documents. The main goals of the contract documents are to enable fair payment for the work done by the contractor, to facilitate evaluation of changes, and to set standards for quality control. Typical contract documents needed for this purpose are:

- Conditions of contract.
- Specifications.
- Working drawings.
- Priced bills of quantities or schedules of rates.
- Signed form of agreement, which confirms the intent of the parties.
- Contract minutes of correspondence.

The basis of a successful contract is the preparation of the conditions of contract to clearly define the responsibilities of the parties. These conditions form much of the legal basis of the contract on which any decision by the courts would be made. The interests of all parties to a construction contract would be best served if the contractor is required to carry only those risks that he or she can reasonably be expected to foresee at the time of bidding. This will be less costly to the owner and better suited to the efficiency of the construction industry.

The general conditions of contract should prove suitable for the majority of conventional construction contracts, but the owner must satisfy himself or herself that they are relevant to the owner's particular job. Special conditions of contract can be added to satisfy the owner's special requirements. Some of the legally binding aspects included in the conditions of contract are briefly discussed in this section. The *contract period, liquidated damages,* and *incentives* clearly define that if the contractor fails to complete the works within the contract period, the contractor will pay the liquidated damages. In case of early completion, the contractor is paid the incentive amount. A *retention amount* is an amount that is held back by the owner for each certificate of payment due to the contractor. Its value is about 5% of each payment as insurance against defective work and to ensure the contractor has incentive to complete all aspects of work. The retention money is paid at the end of the contract. *Maintenance period* is usually specified as 52 weeks after the contract is completed, in which the contractor must remedy any defects that may appear in the work. Two types of *bonds* are required from the contractor in the form of letters of guarantee given by an approved surety, a bank, or a company that agrees to discharge the legal duties of the contractor if he or she fails to do so. The *bid bond* ranges from 0 to 10% of the tender price to ensure that the bidder is serious and will maintain his offer when selected. The *performance bond,* on the other hand, is required from the selected contractor after award of the contract to ensure that he or she faithfully performs his or her obligations under the contract. This bond may be 5 to 100% of the total contract price. Conditions for a *valid claim* can also be specified in the conditions of contract. The contractor should read the conditions of contract to ascertain which category of claim is applicable. Construction managers are advised, immediately after the event that is likely to produce extra cost or delay, to negotiate with the owner the basis for the claim.

1.7.5.4 Project Organization Structure   At the early stage of project initiation, one important decision has to be made by owners on how best to tie the project to the owner's parent firm. To address this issue, we look at the major organizational forms commonly used to house projects and discuss some of the critical factors that might lead us to choose one form over the other.

As shown in Figure 1–13(a), the two extreme ways of organizing a project are the functional and the project organizations. In between these two extremes are various forms of matrix (mixed) organization structures. The functional structure is shown in Figure 1–13(b). It utilizes the firm's normal functional channels, with each functional manager responsible for a segment of the project. At the other extreme, the project structure is formed by pulling a team of experts from relevant functional areas and then assigning them to every project manager (Figure 1–13c). Each of the two extremes has its advantages and drawbacks. With the full authority in the functional structure with the functional managers, an urgent work that is needed for a specific project might be delayed if functional managers are busy with other projects. On the other hand, while the project structure is more responsive to the needs of a construction project, it requires a lot of owner resources since each project has all the resources it needs. Also, the project structure is likely to exhibit a stressful work environment and anxiety as compared to the functional structure. The matrix structure, therefore, is a sort of tradeoff that ensures efficient utilization of owner resources.

The general form of a matrix organization is illustrated in Figure 1–13(d). Among the various matrix variations, several studies have reported that project-matrix is most suited to the dynamic nature of construction projects. Its requirement of resources is not a purely project structure and, as such, does not require a large amount of resources. However, the matrix structure has some potential problems that are a result of the fact that several project managers are competing to have the pool of technical experts under the various functional areas work on their projects before others. In some cases, political problems may occur between various project managers. In other cases, there could be a doubt as to who is in command, the project manager or the functional manager. Careful assignment of the responsibilities, in addition to proper management practices, are, therefore, important issues for the success of owner organization.

1.8   Emerging Trends

In North America, 85% of the total construction expenditures are typically spent on new projects while the remaining 15% are spent on repair and rehabilitation. In recent years, however, a larger portion of all construction work has been shifting from new to reconstruction projects. With a currently aging infrastructure, the market for rehabilitation and renewal has been growing in North America. On the other hand, the market for new construction has been growing internationally as various developing countries around the world, particularly in Asia, Africa, and South America are in need of a lot of new infrastructure projects. It is, therefore, expected that with the whole world being converted into a one large village, successfully competing at the international level is not expected to be easy and requires adapting of the firm's management practices to new, possibly risky, environments. Contractors need not only to use efficient tools to improve the productivity of their resources, but also to consider the cultural and political environments associated with projects.

Figure 1-13.
Common Forms of
Organization
Structure

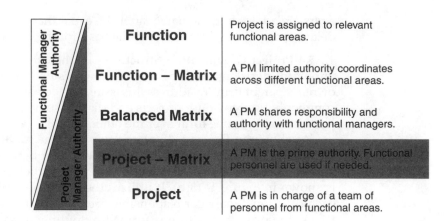

Function	Project is assigned to relevant functional areas.
Function – Matrix	A PM limited authority coordinates across different functional areas.
Balanced Matrix	A PM shares responsibility and authority with functional managers.
Project – Matrix	A PM is the prime authority. Functional personnel are used if needed.
Project	A PM is in charge of a team of personnel from functional areas.

(a) Comparison of Organization Structures

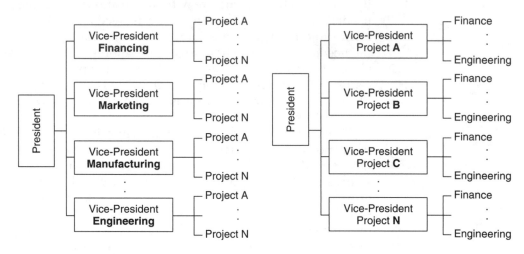

(b) Function Organization   **(c)** Project Organization

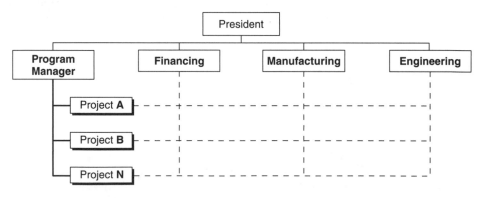

(d) Matrix Organization

In terms of contract management, various trends that have evolved over the last decade and are expected to grow in the North American construction industry and everywhere are:

- Growing design/build.
- Growing BOT (includes financing).
- Project partnering.
- Mergers between contractors and engineering firms.
- Internet use: send invitations to bidders, quotation or qualification requests, linking site to head office.
- Innovative contract practices:
  - A + B bidding method for cost and time;
  - Lane rental for highway construction; and
  - Incentive/disincentive clauses for contractors.

A lot of information can be found on each of these items either in journal publications or on websites. Some of the interesting web resources are listed in Appendix II, "Web Resources."

1.9 Where Do We Go from Here ?

This chapter has provided background material on the construction industry and the various aspects related to project initiation. As discussed in this chapter, a suitable contract strategy is one that considers the level of risk associated with the project and how the various parties can share that risk so that no one party is excessively exposed and the project runs smoothly with few problems during construction. The traditional design-bid-build remains a major project delivery method in which competitive bidding contracts (lump sum and unit price) are common. These types of contracts represent a major challenge to contractors as they have to prepare a detailed bid that is both accurate and competitive and, if lucky enough to win the job, and efficiently manage the construction to attain a fair profit. The life cycle of a traditional project is shown in Figure 1–14 with the various functions performed by various parties at each phase summarized on the figure. Special emphasis is made to the functions performed by the contractor in the bidding and construction stages as these are the main

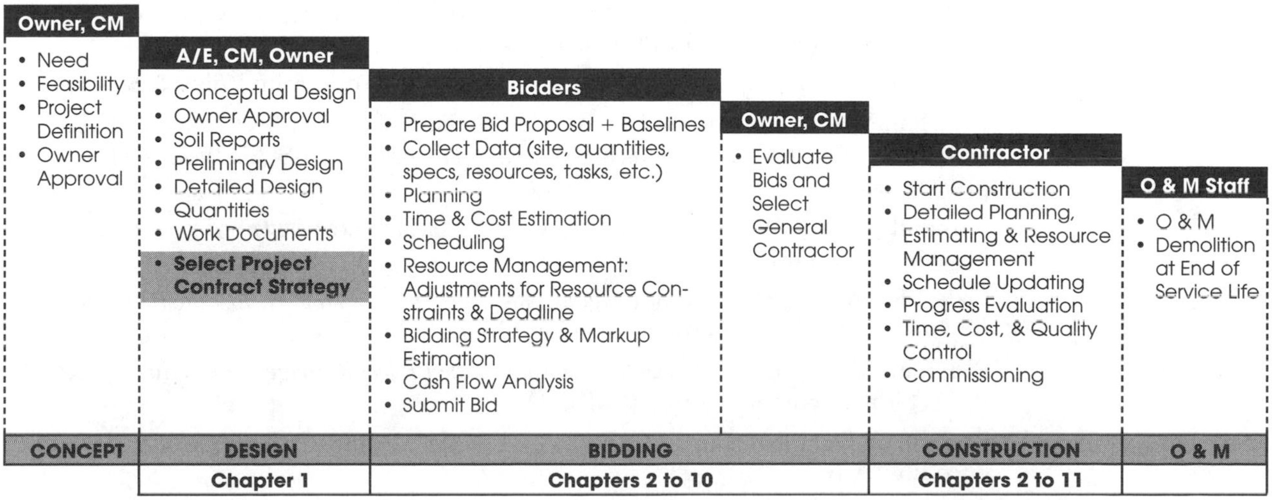

Owner, CM	A/E, CM, Owner	Bidders	Owner, CM	Contractor	O & M Staff
• Need • Feasibility • Project Definition • Owner Approval	• Conceptual Design • Owner Approval • Soil Reports • Preliminary Design • Detailed Design • Quantities • Work Documents • **Select Project Contract Strategy**	• Prepare Bid Proposal + Baselines • Collect Data (site, quantities, specs, resources, tasks, etc.) • Planning • Time & Cost Estimation • Scheduling • Resource Management: Adjustments for Resource Constraints & Deadline • Bidding Strategy & Markup Estimation • Cash Flow Analysis • Submit Bid	• Evaluate Bids and Select General Contractor	• Start Construction • Detailed Planning, Estimating & Resource Management • Schedule Updating • Progress Evaluation • Time, Cost, & Quality Control • Commissioning	• O & M • Demolition at End of Service Life
CONCEPT	DESIGN	BIDDING		CONSTRUCTION	O & M
Chapter 1		Chapters 2 to 10		Chapters 2 to 11	

Figure 1-14. Management Functions Made at the Different Phases of a Project Life Cycle

aspects discussed in the remaining chapters of the book. The ultimate goal is again the TQM (less time, higher quality, and less cost) in construction projects. In the following chapters, Figure 1–14 will act as our road map, which shows where the material in that chapter is applicable in the project. For interested readers, Appendix A lists many Internet websites with information related to the material in this chapter.

1.10 Bibliography

Cartey, G. (1995). "Construction," *Journal of Construction Engineering and Management*, ASCE, Vol. 121, No. 3, pp. 319–328.

Clough, R. H. and Sears, E. (1979). *Construction Project Management*, 2nd ed. Toronto: John Wiley & Sons.

Cook, L. and Hancher, D. (1990). "Partnering: Contracting for the Future," *Journal of Management in Engineering*, ASCE, Vol. 6, No. 4, pp. 431–446.

Fisk, E. (1992). *Construction Project Administration.* Englewood, New Jersey: Prentice Hall Inc.

Goldsmith, I. (1976). *Canadian Building Contracts*, 2nd ed. Toronto: The Carswell Comp. Ltd.

Gould, Frederick and Joyce, Nancy (1999). *Construction Project Management*, Upper Saddle River, New Jersey: Prentice Hall Inc.

Halpin, D. and Woodhead, R. (1998). *Construction Management*, 2nd ed. John Wiley & Sons.

Harris, F. and Srinivasan, R. (1991). "Lane Rental Contracting," *Journal of Construction Engineering and Economics*, Vol. 9, pp. 151–155.

Hendrickson, C. and Au, T. (1989). *Project Management for Construction: Fundamental Concepts for Owners, Engineers, Architects, and Builders.* Englewood, New Jersey: Prentice Hall,.

Herbsman, Z. (1995). "A+B Bidding Method-Hidden Success Story for Highway Construction," *Journal of Construction Engineering and Management*, ASCE, Vol. 121, No. 4, pp. 430–437.

Jaraiedi, M., Plummer, R., and Aber, M. (1995). "Incentive/Disincentive Guidelines for Highway Construction Contracts," *Journal of Construction Engineering and Management*, ASCE, Vol. 121, No. 1, pp. 112–120.

Kerridge, A. E. and Vervalin, C. H. (Eds.) (1986). *Engineering and Construction Project Management*, Houston: Gulf Publ. Co.

Kerzner, H. (2000). *Applied Project Management.* New York: John Wiley & Sons.

Konchar, M. and Sanvido, V. (1998). "Comparison of U.S. Project Delivery Systems," *Journal of Construction Engineering and Management*, ASCE, Vol. 124, No. 6, pp. 435–444.

Nunnally, S. W. (1993). *Construction Methods and Management*, 3rd ed., Englewood, New Jersey: Prentice Hall.

Oxley, R. and Poskitt, J. (1986). *Management Techniques Applied to Construction Industry*, 3rd ed. Rexdale, Ontario: Granada Publ. Ltd.

PMI Standards Committee (1996). *A Guide to the Project Management Body of Knowledge* Project Management Institute (PMI), PA.

Roman, D. D. (1986). *Managing Projects: A Systems Approach.* New York: Elsevier Science Publ. Co.

Tenah, K. and Guevara, T. (1985). *Fundamentals of Construction Management and Organization.* Reston Publishing Co., Inc.

Teplitz, C. and Worley, C. (1992). "Project Managers are Gaining Power Within Matrix Organizations," *PmNetwork*, PMI, Vol. 3, No. 2, pp. 33–35.

Tiong, R. (1990). "Comparative Study of BOT Projects," *Journal of Management in Engineering*, ASCE, Vol. 6, No. 1, pp. 107–122.

1.11 Exercises

1. Briefly explain the main types of construction.

2. What are the circumstances that favor the use of: (a) unit price contracts; and (b) cost-plus contracts? Compare these two types of contracts in terms of: flexibility to owner changes, and the financial objectives of owner and contractor?

3. Briefly explain the various forms of negotiated cost-plus contracts.

4. Briefly differentiate among the various project delivery approaches.

5. What are some of the challenges in fast-track projects?

6. What is the difference between a bid bond and a performance bond?

7. a. Outline the decisions taken by the project manager during the development of a contract strategy for the execution of a specific project.

   b. Explain why a consideration of incentives, flexibility, and risk sharing is vital when choosing a type of contract for civil engineering work.

   c. Comment on the following statement: "The interests of all parties to a construction contract will be best served if the contractor is required to carry only those risks that he/she can reasonably be expected to foresee at the time of bidding."

8. Sketch the various contractual relationships by which an owner organization may be engaged in the management of projects.

9. Briefly explain five roles of the project manager and the site superintendent.

10. What are the important elements to be included in a call for bidders? Attach a sample call for bidders from a newspaper.

11. What are the components of a bid package?

12. Explain the purpose of the site investigation made by prospective contractors during the bidding stage. What data do they obtain?

13. What are the various forms of matrix organizations? Which forms most suit construction projects?

14. Compare and contrast the use of a performance bond with that of retention money in terms of the protection given to the owner.

15. Explain the purpose of prequalification and outline what it involves.

16. List 10 subcontractors that can be engaged in a building project.

17. The use of a cost-based contract has a fundamental effect on the relationship between the owner and the contractor when compared with a price-based contract. Explain why this is the case.

18. a. Give three examples of secondary objectives on a construction project that would exert a major influence over contract strategy decisions.

    b. What are the circumstances that favor the use of turnkey contracts?

    c. Compare the following types of contract from the point of view of flexibility for design change and variation: lump sum, unit price, and cost-plus.

19. Conduct an Internet search on one of the project delivery methods and report the most interesting and informative sites.

20. Conduct an Internet search and discuss the following types of contracts: BOT, A+B, and lane rental.

Chapter 2

INFORMATION MANAGEMENT TOOLS

A fter studying this chapter, you will be able to:

- Manage your company's information using Excel data management tools.
- Understand the simple and powerful spreadsheet functions for managing information.
- Use Excel pivot tables for summarizing and reporting data.
- Use Excel mathematical optimization tool, the Solver program.
- Use other add-in programs for optimization based on genetic algorithms.
- Experiment with the Microsoft Project and Primavera P3 software.

Owner, CM	A/E, CM, Owner	Bidders	Owner, CM	Contractor	O & M Staff
• Need • Feasibility • Project Definition • Owner Approval	• Conceptual Design • Owner Approval • Soil Reports • Preliminary Design • Detailed Design • Quantities • Work Documents • Select Project Contract Strategy	• Prepare Bid Proposal + Baselines • **Collect Data (site, quantities, specs, resources, tasks, etc.)** • Planning • Time & Cost Estimation • Scheduling • Resource Management: Adjustments for Resource Constraints & Deadline • Bidding Strategy & Markup Estimation • Cash Flow Analysis • Submit Bid	• Evaluate Bids and Select General Contractor	• Start Construction • Detailed Planning, Estimating & Resource Management • Schedule Updating • Progress Evaluation • Time, Cost, & Quality Control • Commissioning	• O & M • Demolition at End of Service Life
CONCEPT	DESIGN	BIDDING		CONSTRUCTION	O & M

2.1 Introduction

The construction process is heavily information dependent. Well-maintained and organized data is crucial to support the timely and cost-effective planning, bidding, and control of projects. With the large amount of information related to resources and operations, it is sometimes difficult to obtain and organize such information either because of the limited time available or the inefficient methods of data collection and organization. Thus, improving the quality, integrity, and timeliness of construction data is a well-recognized need. This chapter, therefore, introduces the basic tools that can be used to manage construction data. Special emphasis is made on spreadsheet programs as simple-to-use tools that are customary to almost all construction practitioners and also have all the power functions that satisfy the need of construction applications. Some of the database capabilities in Excel are presented in addition to some add-in programs that provide optimization capabilities. Two project management software (Microsoft Project and Primavera P3) programs are then introduced before being used in the various chapters of this book.

2.2 Excel Data Management Tools

Spreadsheets are among the earliest software innovations that had a profound effect on the widespread use of personal computers. Among their strong features are their intuitive cell-based structure and the simple interface that is easy to use even for the first-time user. Underneath the structure and the interface is a host of powerful and versatile features, from data entry and manipulation to a large number of functions, charts, and word processing capabilities. Newer spreadsheet versions have also added many productivity features for Internet connectivity, workgroup sharing, programmability options, and a number of add-in programs. With their wide use, spreadsheets have proved suitable as a tool for developing computer models in domains such as construction, for which ease of use, versatility, and productivity are main issues.

Since the core of any management system, such as the one we intend to develop for construction, is a storage of the data and information for management operations, a brief review of the database capabilities in spreadsheet programs is presented. A few basic, but infrequently used, spreadsheet features need to be known and can be used to develop practical and powerful models for construction applications: data lists, data menu options, basic spreadsheet functions such as "VLOOKUP", and pivot table reports.

> **Note:** In Excel, a *data list* is the basic structure of columns and rows that contain data. The list works as a database that can be managed easily using built-in functions. It is basically a *table* of data in which the rows are data records and the columns are data fields, headed by field names. The characteristics of a data list are:
>
> - Its top row is termed a header row, consisting of one or more column labels.
> - All rows in the list below the header row contain records. The records are values that describe various items.

The data list in Figure 2–1 shows an example of an estimate sheet with each row representing one item in the estimate and its quantity of work, unit, cost, etc. shown in the various columns. Once the list is formed, the data management tools provided under Excel's **Data** menu, such as **Sort, Filter,** and **Outline** can be directly used to

One row of data headings →

Data arranged with each record in one row

	A	B	C	D	E	F	G	H
1	Item	Description	WBS	Quantity	Unit	Unit Cost	Total	
2	Item1	Layout	Layout	1.00	day	613.67	614	
3	Item2	Excavate Foundation & Utility Trench	Excavation	379.00	m3	3.10	1,175	
4	Item3	Backfill Utility Trench	Backfill	26.00	m3	1.22	32	
5	Item4	Compact Utility Trench	Compaction	26.00	m3	0.61	16	
6	Item5	Install Weeping Tile	Backfill	52.00	m	4.60	239	
7	Item6	Place Granular	Backfill	4.90	m3	41.66	204	
8	Item7	Backfill Around Foundation	Backfill	88.00	m3	1.22	107	
9	Item8	Compact Around Foundation	Compaction	88.00	m3	0.61	54	
10	Item9	Lot Grading	Excavation	266.00	m3	1.22	324	
11	Item10	Forms, Footing	Formwork	30.40	m2	58.28	1,772	
12	Item11	Removal of Form, Footing	Formwork	30.40	m2	2.91	88	
13	Item12	Keyway, 50mm x 100mm	Formwork	76.00	m	2.82	215	
14	Item13	Placing Concrete, Direct Chute	Concrete	6.10	m3	113.19	690	
15	Item14	Forms, Walls	Formwork	266.70	m2	78.76	21,006	
16	Item15	Removal of Form, Walls	Formwork	266.70	m2	2.91	775	
17	Item16	Anchor Bolts, 12mm diameter	Formwork	65.00	ea	9.65	627	
18	Item17	Reinforcing, Light, Footing	Reinforcing	0.08	ton	8,869.57	710	
19	Item18	Reinforcing, Light, Walls	Reinforcing	0.19	ton	8,869.57	1,685	
20	Item19	Placing Concrete, Walls	Concrete	26.67	m3	148.73	3,967	
21	Item20	Bank Run Gravel, Floor:200mm deep	Backfill	31.00	m3	6.13	190	
22	Item21	End Forms	Formwork	76.20	m	10.50	800	
23	Item22	Polyethylene Vapor Barrier	Insulation	154.00	m2	1.09	168	
24	Item23	Placing Concrete, Floor	Concrete	11.50	m3	110.54	1,271	
25	Item24	Steel Trowel Finish	Reinforcing	154.00	m2	0.27	42	
26	Item25	Damp Proofing, Foundation	Insulation	107.00	m2	5.43	581	
27	Item26	Insulation of Foundation	Insulation	58.00	m2	27.21	1,578	
28								

Figure 2–1. Excel Data List (Database)

manage the data in these lists. The data list, as such, becomes an intuitive and simple way of storing data related to each other. A separate list can thus be used to store separate data. One list, for example, can be used to store labor categories; another list can be used to store equipment categories, and so on. Later we can learn how to link all these separate data lists to use all their data together.

> **Note:** The software tools used in this book are Excel 97, Microsoft Project 98 and Primavera P3. While vendors may introduce newer versions from time to time, the features used in this book are mostly standard and available in any updates. Most of these features are also available in other software products. The reader can consult with the Help system of his or her software to search for desired features.

> **Note:** File **Chapter2.xls** on the CD includes all the spreadsheets used in this chapter.

2.2.1 Sorting Lists

Sorting is a valuable way of managing the data in an Excel data list. It helps you bring similar records together for visual inspection or other purposes such as preparing reports and charting the data. You can arrange the list's data in an order that you choose by sorting the records. Suppose you have the estimate data shown in Figure 2–1. You want to view the data in Figure 2–1 arranged according to the total cost. To do so, follow the steps in Figure 2–2.

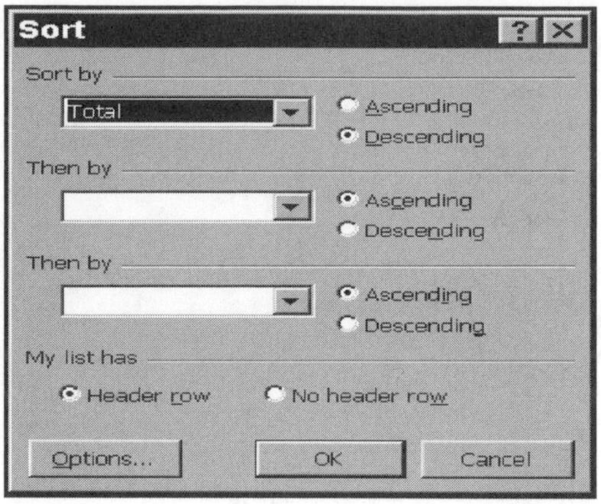

Figure 2-2. Data Sorting

1. Select one or more cells in the data list range A1:G27;
2. Choose **Data-Sort** menu option. The **Sort** dialog box appears as shown;
3. Because you want to sort by total cost, click the column label **Total** in the **Sort by** drop-down box;
4. Because you want the record with the highest total cost to appear first, choose the **Descending** option button, as shown. The result is shown in Figure 2–3.

	A	B	C	D	E	F	G	H
1	Item	Description	WBS	Quantity	Unit	Unit Cost	Total	
2	Item14	Forms, Walls	Formwork	266.70	m2	78.76	21,006	
3	Item19	Placing Concrete, Walls	Concrete	26.67	m3	148.73	3,967	
4	Item10	Forms, Footing	Formwork	30.40	m2	58.28	1,772	
5	Item18	Reinforcing, Light, Walls	Reinforcing	0.19	ton	8,869.57	1,685	
6	Item26	Insulation of Foundation	Insulation	58.00	m2	27.21	1,578	
7	Item23	Placing Concrete, Floor	Concrete	11.50	m3	110.54	1,271	
8	Item2	Excavate Foundation & Utility Trench	Excavation	379.00	m3	3.10	1,175	
9	Item21	End Forms	Formwork	76.20	m	10.50	800	
10	Item15	Removal of Form, Walls	Formwork	266.70	m2	2.91	775	
11	Item17	Reinforcing, Light, Footing	Reinforcing	0.08	ton	8,869.57	710	
12	Item13	Placing Concrete, Direct Chute	Concrete	6.10	m3	113.19	690	
13	Item16	Anchor Bolts, 12mm diameter	Formwork	65.00	ea	9.65	627	
14	Item1	Layout	Layout	1.00	day	613.87	614	
15	Item25	Damp Proofing, Foundation	Insulation	107.00	m2	5.43	581	
16	Item9	Lot Grading	Excavation	266.00	m3	1.22	324	
17	Item5	Install Weeping Tile	Backfill	52.00	m	4.60	239	
18	Item12	Keyway, 50mm x 100mm	Formwork	76.00	m	2.82	215	
19	Item6	Place Granular	Backfill	4.90	m3	41.66	204	
20	Item20	Bank Run Gravel, Floor:200mm deep	Backfill	31.00	m3	6.13	190	
21	Item22	Polyethylene Vapor Barrier	Insulation	154.00	m2	1.09	168	
22	Item7	Backfill Around Foundation	Backfill	88.00	m3	1.22	107	
23	Item11	Removal of Form, Footing	Formwork	30.40	m2	2.91	88	
24	Item8	Compact Around Foundation	Compaction	88.00	m3	0.61	54	
25	Item24	Steel Trowel Finish	Reinforcing	154.00	m2	0.27	42	
26	Item3	Backfill Utility Trench	Backfill	26.00	m3	1.22	32	
27	Item4	Compact Utility Trench	Compaction	26.00	m3	0.61	16	
28								

Figure 2-3. Result of Sorting by "Total" Value

After you choose **OK,** the range A1:G27 appears as shown.

Usually, the order in which the records are sorted is ascending (1, 2, 3, etc.) or descending (Excavation, Compaction, Backfill, etc.). But there are some custom sorting orders that you can access by choosing the **Options** button on the **Sort** dialog box. For example, if a list contains the names of the months of the year, you can sort it so that September (month 9) records precede October (month 10) records, even though alphabetic order calls for the reverse. The **Sort** options enable you to choose a custom sort order and change the orientation of the sort.

2.2.2 Filtering Lists

Filtering the data in a worksheet list is a useful way to view a subset of the records that compose a list. To filter a list is to extract records from it, based on criteria that you set. You can extract records visually, by causing Excel to temporarily hide records that do not meet your criteria, or you can extract them structurally, by causing Excel to move records that do meet the criteria to another part of the worksheet. There are two menu commands to filter a list, both found in the **Filter** menu that cascades from the **Data** menu: **AutoFilter** and **Advanced Filter,** as explained in Figures 2–4 to 2–9.

In **Advanced Filter**, the *List Range* edit box defines the list that is subject to the filtering process. Also, if you check the *Unique Records Only* check box, the **Advanced Filter** ignores duplicate records in the list identified by the *List Range* edit box.

The Advanced Filter allows you to create more complicated criteria than does the AutoFilter. In particular, you can use the Advanced Filter to specify:

- More than two criteria, which is the limit of the AutoFilter.
- Computed criteria: For example, "Display only those records whose total cost value is greater than the average total cost value." This is termed a computed criterion because Excel must compute, in this case, the average total cost in order to determine whether a record meets the criterion.

You must enter the criteria for record selection in a range on the worksheet, and refer to that range in the Advanced Filter dialog box's *Criteria Range* edit box. Additionally, in all but one situation, you need to repeat the column's headers as the first line in the criteria range. This is so that Excel knows which column to compare with which criterion. It is convenient to put the criteria in the same column as their associated list.

	A	B	C	D	E	
1	**Project Code** ▼	**Region** ▼	**Project Type** ▼	**Project Manage** ▼	**Project Value** ▼	
2	C-01	(All)	Residential	Bill	$ 200,000	
3	W-03	(Top 10...)	Residential	Thomas	$ 170,000	
4	C-03	(Custom...)	Residential	Smith	$ 325,000	
5	E-05	Central	Office Building	Smith	$ 145,000	
6	C-05	East	Restaurant	Smith	$ 180,000	
7	C-06	West	Office Building	Green	$ 420,000	
8	C-07	Central	Office Building	Jones	$ 600,000	
9	E-01	East	Residential	Thomas	$ 185,000	
10	E-02	East	Residential	Thomas	$ 210,000	
11	C-02	Central	Residential	Bill	$ 225,000	
12	E-03	East	Office Building	Bill	$ 160,000	
13	E-04	East	Office Building	Jones	$ 210,000	
14	W-01	West	Residential	Green	$ 210,000	
15	C-04	Central	Residential	Smith	$ 360,000	
16	W-02	West	Office Building	Green	$ 300,000	
17	E-06	East	Restaurant	Davis	$ 225,000	
18	W-04	West	Office Building	Jones	$ 300,000	
19	W-05	West	Restaurant	Davis	$ 140,000	
20						

Figure 2-4. Using AutoFilter

While any cell inside the data list is selected, choose the **Data-Filter-AutoFilter** menu option. The AutoFilter puts arrows (called AutoFilter control) beside the column labels in the header row to display filtering criteria. Notice in this figure, the drop-down box that appears when you click the control on cell B1, which contains several options in order to define the filtering criteria.

	A	B	C	D	E
1	Project Code ▼	Region ▼	Project Type ▼	Project Manage ▼	Project Value ▼
2	C-01	Central	Residential	Bill	$ 200,000
4	C-03	Central	Residential	Smith	$ 325,000
6	C-05	Central	Restaurant	Smith	$ 180,000
7	C-06	Central	Office Building	Green	$ 420,000
8	C-07	Central	Office Building	Jones	$ 600,000
11	C-02	Central	Residential	Bill	$ 225,000
15	C-04	Central	Residential	Smith	$ 360,000
20					

Figure 2-5. AutoFilter Results

Selecting the Central region brings only the subset of the list that meets this criterion (only the records from the Central Region). When you choose a criterion for two or more columns, the criteria are treated as connected by an AND. The entries that are displayed must meet all criteria that have been set.

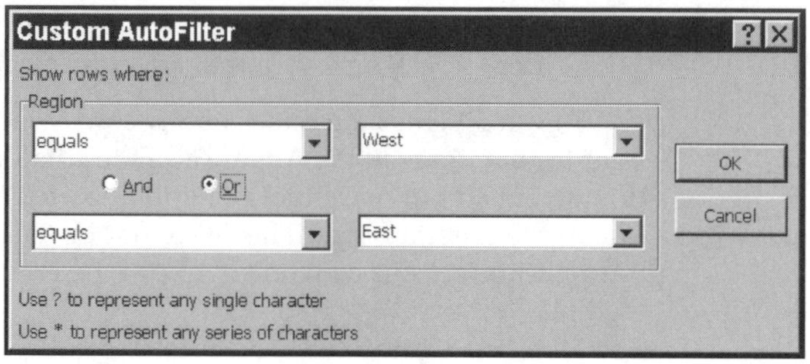

Figure 2-6. Custom AutoFilter

You can also use the **Custom** option in AutoFilter if you have no more than two criteria to apply. These criteria can be treated as connected by an AND or by an OR (a record is displayed if it meets either criterion).

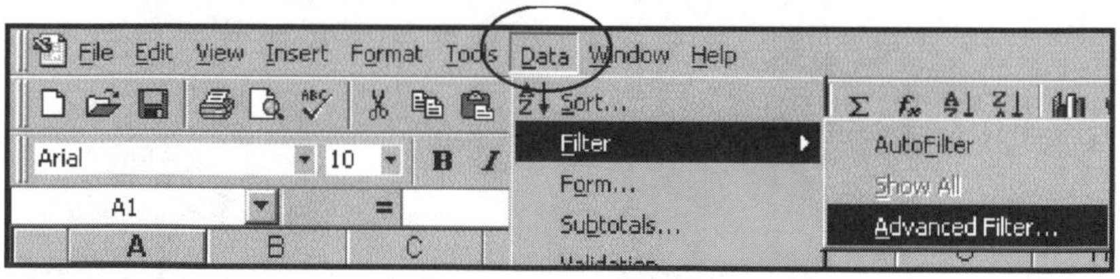

Figure 2-7. Using the Advanced Filter

The **Advanced Filter** command gives you more options than the AutoFilter command. Choose the **Data-Filter-Advanced Filter** menu option to activate it.

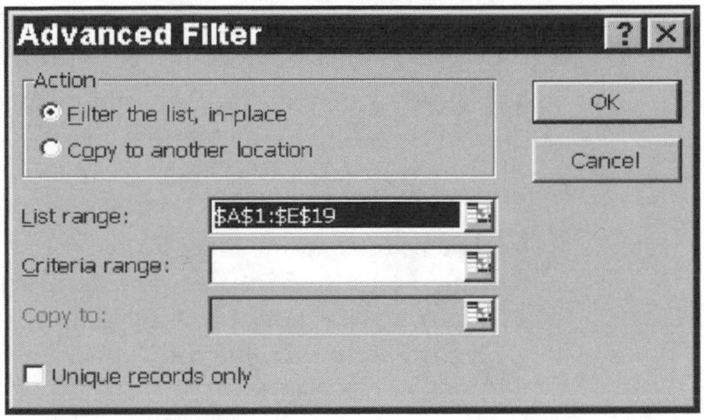

Figure 2-8. Advanced Filter Options

If you choose the **Filter the List In-place** option, the Advanced Filter hides rows containing records that do not meet your criteria, just as the AutoFilter does. If you choose the **Copy to Another Location** option, the *Copy to* edit box becomes enabled, and you can click in a worksheet cell to establish the first cell to contain the copied data.

Figure 2-9.
Applying Advanced Filter

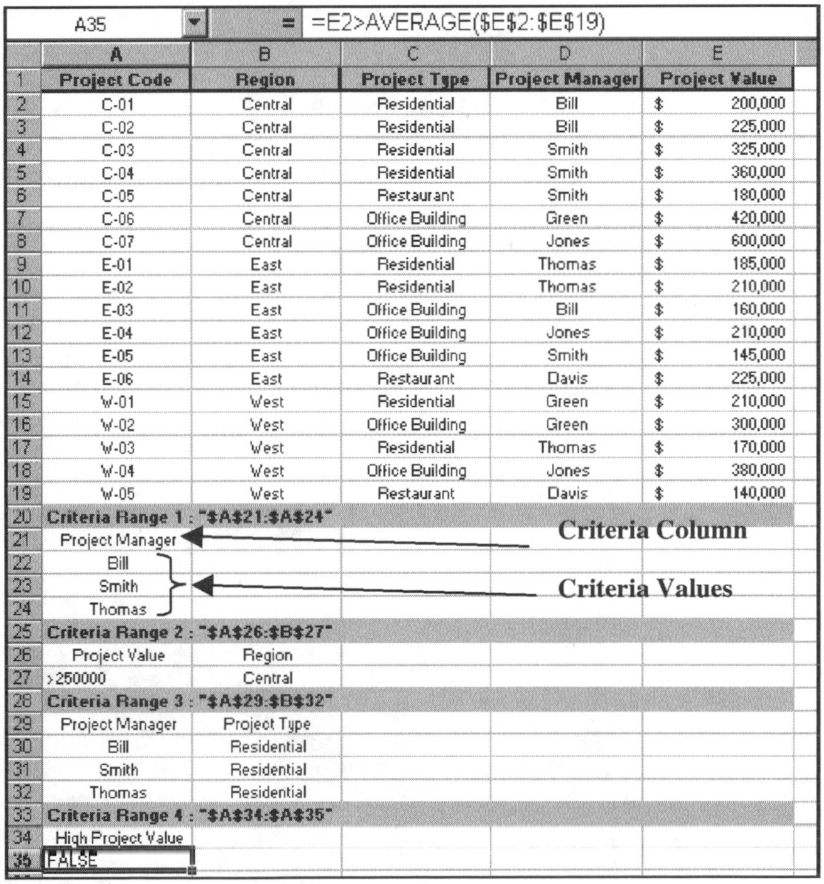

A35 = =E2>AVERAGE($E$2:$E$19)

	A	B	C	D	E
1	**Project Code**	**Region**	**Project Type**	**Project Manager**	**Project Value**
2	C-01	Central	Residential	Bill	$ 200,000
3	C-02	Central	Residential	Bill	$ 225,000
4	C-03	Central	Residential	Smith	$ 325,000
5	C-04	Central	Residential	Smith	$ 360,000
6	C-05	Central	Restaurant	Smith	$ 180,000
7	C-06	Central	Office Building	Green	$ 420,000
8	C-07	Central	Office Building	Jones	$ 600,000
9	E-01	East	Residential	Thomas	$ 185,000
10	E-02	East	Residential	Thomas	$ 210,000
11	E-03	East	Office Building	Bill	$ 160,000
12	E-04	East	Office Building	Jones	$ 210,000
13	E-05	East	Office Building	Smith	$ 145,000
14	E-06	East	Restaurant	Davis	$ 225,000
15	W-01	West	Residential	Green	$ 210,000
16	W-02	West	Office Building	Green	$ 300,000
17	W-03	West	Residential	Thomas	$ 170,000
18	W-04	West	Office Building	Jones	$ 380,000
19	W-05	West	Restaurant	Davis	$ 140,000
20	**Criteria Range 1 : "$A$21:$A$24"**				
21	Project Manager				◄ **Criteria Column**
22	Bill				
23	Smith				◄ **Criteria Values**
24	Thomas				
25	**Criteria Range 2 : "$A$26:$B$27"**				
26	Project Value	Region			
27	>250000	Central			
28	**Criteria Range 3 : "$A$29:$B$32"**				
29	Project Manager	Project Type			
30	Bill	Residential			
31	Smith	Residential			
32	Thomas	Residential			
33	**Criteria Range 4 : "$A$34:$A$35"**				
34	High Project Value				
35	FALSE				

Figure 2–9 displays four options for setting the Advanced Filter criteria. None of these criteria is possible through the AutoFilter:

a. Criteria range **A21: A24** contains three criteria connected by ORs. The three criteria relate to the column Project Manager and are put in different rows, as shown in A21: A24. The Advanced Filter would display only those records whose value on Project Manager is Bill or Smith or Thomas.

b. The criteria range **A26: B27** makes reference to two different columns: Project Value and Region. To connect multiple criteria by AND, enter them in different rows, as shown in A26: B27. Advanced Filter would display only those records whose value for Project Value is over $250,000 and which belong to the Central region.

c. The criteria range **A29: B32** is an example for connecting multiple criteria by both AND and OR, as both different columns and different rows are used. Advanced Filter would display only those records that matched (Bill and Residential) or (Smith and Residential) or (Thomas and Residential).

d. The criteria range **A34: A35** contains a *computed criterion*. The formula that returns FALSE in **cell A35** is =**E2 > AVERAGE ($E$2:$E$19).** The criterion specifies that only those records whose values on Project Value exceed the average project value are to be displayed. Notice about this criterion that:

- The use of E2 is a relative reference. As the Advanced Filter scans the records in the range E2: E19, it adjusts the relative reference to E3, E4, . . ., E19. On the other hand, the range $E$2: $E$19 is an absolute reference (shown by the $ sign) which specifies a constant value that does not change with the records.

- Cell A34's label is not *Project Value* but *High Project Value*. It is important to use a label that is not identical to any column label in the list's row header.

2.2.3 Using Data Forms

One of the trickiest parts of data management with Excel is seemingly the most trivial: getting the data into a workbook. But entering data into the spreadsheet's native row-and-column grid is extremely tedious and prone to error. The data form available within Excel provides a solid way for you to enter, view, and filter data. Figure 2–10 shows one such form, which was generated for the estimate data list behind the form.

Figure 2-10. Built-in Data Form

You can activate the form from any point in the list using the **Data-Form** menu option.

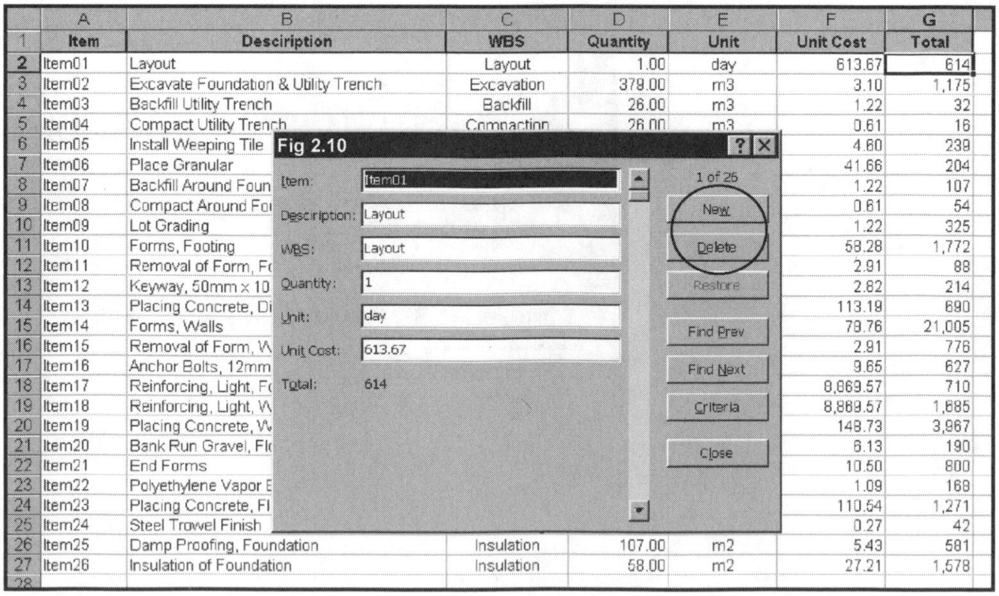

Using this built-in form, we can edit or delete the existing records in the list or add new records.

If the list contains calculated fields (e.g., column G), the calculations will not appear in the form but will be automatically added to all new records in the list.

In addition to entering, editing, and deleting records, you can also use an Excel data form as a filtering tool by following the steps in Figure 2–11.

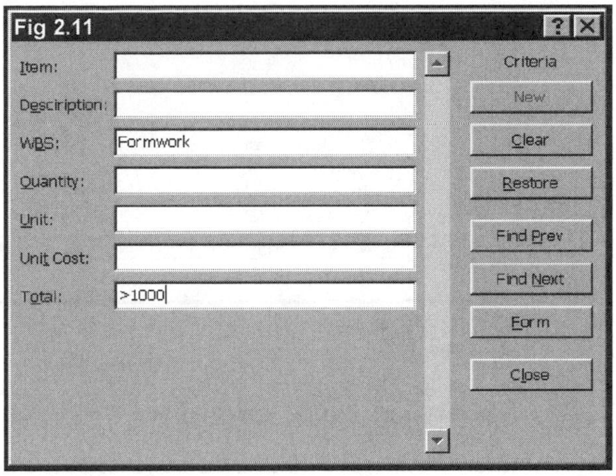

Figure 2-11. Filtering Data Using the Data Form

- Choose the **Criteria** command button on the form. Excel displays a blank record.
- Enter your criteria in the appropriate fields. You can enter criteria for as many fields as you like. The criteria shown here, for example, will find all records that meet the Formwork in the WBS field with its Total greater than 1000.
- Choose the **Find Next** and **Find Prev** command buttons to display the records that match the criteria. When you choose the Find Next command, Excel will display the next record in the list that meets the criteria. (The next record is determined by the current record. If the form displays the fourth record after you enter the criteria, Excel will search from that point forward when matching records.)

Since you can view only one filtered record at a time, this alternative to filtering data generally is not as efficient as the AutoFilter or the Advanced Filter. However, it still can be a useful tool, especially when you are in the middle of a data-entry task and want to ask some quick questions of your list.

2.3   Useful Excel Functions for Retrieving List Information

Getting data out of a list in a clear and efficient manner is an important part of the data-management process. Excel has several tools that help you accomplish that task. The Advanced Filter dialog box has already been introduced, having an option to copy records that match the criteria you specify to another part of the sheet, where you can manipulate them without affecting the original list.

In addition to extracting selected data from a list, you can create formulas that return specific information from the list. The built-in **Statistical List Functions** calculate statistics for only the records in the list that meet the criteria that you specify. The LOOKUP functions help you manage large lists of reference data by returning information for specific records from specific fields. The MATCH and INDEX functions give you further control over the data by allowing you to identify a given entry's position in a list or an array. The OFFSET function extends the capabilities of the Index function by reaching into a worksheet range and returning any number of values from that range.

Figure 2-12. Excel Statistical Functions for Data Lists

	A	B	C	D	E	F	G	H
					H2 ▾ = =DSUM(A1:E19,"Project Value",A21:E22)			
1	Project Code	Region	Project Type	Project Manager	Project Value			
2	C-01	Central	Residential	Bill	$ 200,000		DSUM:	2,310,000
3	W-03	West	Residential	Thomas	$ 170,000			
4	C-03	Central	Residential	Smith	$ 325,000			
5	E-05	East	Office Building	Smith	$ 145,000			
6	C-05	Central	Restaurant	Smith	$ 180,000			
7	C-06	Central	Office Building	Green	$ 420,000			
8	C-07	Central	Office Building	Jones	$ 600,000			
9	E-01	East	Residential	Thomas	$ 185,000			
10	E-02	East	Residential	Thomas	$ 210,000			
11	C-02	Central	Residential	Bill	$ 225,000			
12	E-03	East	Office Building	Bill	$ 160,000			
13	E-04	East	Office Building	Jones	$ 210,000			
14	W-01	West	Residential	Green	$ 210,000			
15	C-04	Central	Residential	Smith	$ 360,000			
16	W-02	West	Office Building	Green	$ 300,000			
17	E-06	East	Restaurant	Davis	$ 225,000			
18	W-04	West	Office Building	Jones	$ 380,000			
19	W-05	West	Restaurant	Davis	$ 140,000			
20								
21	Project Code	Region	Project Type	Project Manager	Project Value			
22		Central						
23								

2.3.1   Statistical List Functions

Excel's statistical list functions, sometimes referred to as the "D" functions (Database functions), provide an instantaneous way to measure a number of important list statistics, such as sums, averages, and standard deviations.

As shown in Figure 2–12, the most commonly used statistical list function, DSUM, formula in cell H2 uses the criterion range A21: E22 to calculate the total project value in the Central region.

The syntax of the DSUM function is =**DSUM(list range, calculation field, criteria range)**.

Because these functions use criteria ranges, you can specify that the calculation includes only certain records from the list by entering the appropriate criteria. This structure allows you to make the same formula quickly yield statistics for a number of different sets of records simply by changing the criteria in the criteria range. For example, if you entered the criterion "West" in cell B22, the DSUM formula would immediately reflect the total project value in the West region.

Table 2–1 includes a list of Excel's statistical functions that deal with data lists. Each of these functions has the same syntax as the DSUM formula in cell H2; each uses the same list, field, and criteria arguments.

Table 2-1. Statistical List Functions

Function	Returns
DAVERAGE	Average
DCOUNT	Count of cells containing numbers
DCOUNTA	Count of nonblank cells
DMAX	Maximum
DMIN	Minimum
DPRODUCT	Product
DSTDEV	Standard deviation
DSTDEVP	Population standard deviation
DSUM	Sum
DVAR	Variance
DVARP	Population variance

You can use these statistical functions to interpret list data and spot potential problems such as data-entry errors. You can check maximum and minimum values, compare maximum and minimum values to average, and compare the population standard deviation and population variance for different criteria.

2.3.2 Looking up Data

Referencing and searching a list is another important part of the data management process. In realistic systems, where several lists of data are available, a link needs to be established among them (similar to the relational database concept). One simple and important spreadsheet function, VLOOKUP, can be used to link separate lists of information by making a reference to where the original data is.

a. VLOOKUP Function: In Figure 2–13, for example, the top sheet includes a list that contains various labor categories and their hourly rates. Now consider the situation when a new list is used for estimating purposes (bottom), and this list refers to the Code of the labor being used. Accordingly, it is possible to determine the cost by using a VLOOKUP function to search the original labor list and determine its associated Rate/hr value, as shown. If the resource code specified in cell A4 of the estimate is changed (e.g., L9 is used), the costs will be adjusted automatically in cells C4 and D4 of the estimate. The VLOOKUP function, as such, provide a convenient means of linking the data stored in various separate lists.

Excel's lookup functions, VLOOKUP, HLOOKUP, and LOOKUP, provide you with different (and sometimes overlapping) ways of finding a specific piece of information within a structured list of unique records. The match

Figure 2-13.
VLOOKUP Function

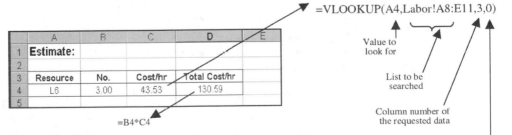

and index functions give you further control over the data by allowing you to identify a given entry's position in a list or an array. OFFSET function is particularly useful when you want to deal with a subset of data in a range by means of an array formula. The Help system of Excel can be used to obtain information about the syntax and use of these important functions.

b. **Using the MATCH Function to Aid Lookups:** When a lookup list grows, it becomes quite easy to calculate the column offset, thus returning incorrect information from the list. To avoid this problem, you can use Excel's MATCH function (Figure 2–14) to calculate the column offset. The syntax of the MATCH function is:

$$=MATCH(lookup\_value,lookup\_array,match\_type)$$

The function returns lookup_value's position within the lookup_array. If the lookup_value is the fourth item in the lookup_array, for example, the match function returns 4. The implication for the Vlookup and Hlookup function is straightforward. Using the match function, you can specify both the lookup_value and the column argument as they naturally occur in the list, rather than figuring out for yourself what integer you should be using for the column argument.

c. **LOOKUP Function:** The LOOKUP function (Figure 2–15) comes in handy in the event that you want to use a lookup_value in one list, yet return a value from another list. The syntax of the LOOKUP function is:

$$LOOKUP(lookup\_value, lookup\_range, result\_range)$$

- Here, the lookup_value and lookup_range arguments function similarly to the VLOOKUP function. But instead of comprising an entire list, the lookup_range includes only one column or row of a list.
- The result_range has the same size and dimension as the lookup_range, but it is usually located in a different list.

	A	B	C	D	E	F	G	H	I
	B14		= =MATCH(B13,A1:I1,0)						
1	**Project**	**Jan.**	**Feb.**	**March**	**April**	**May**	**June**	**July**	**Aug.**
2	Project1		$22,800	$30,450	$39,800	$38,550	$28,900	$29,350	$27,400
3	Project2	$10,500	$12,600	$13,800	$12,900	$13,250	$10,850		
4	Project3	$14,600	$14,900	$13,600	$14,200	$14,350	$14,500	$13,750	$13,800
5	Project4	$5,600	$4,800	$5,200	$6,300				
6	Project5				$21,500	$25,800	$26,900	$26,500	$27,100
7	Total	$30,700	$55,100	$63,050	$94,700	$91,950	$81,150	$69,600	$68,300
8									
9									
10	**Lookup Formula :**	**$14,200**	=VLOOKUP(B11,A1:I7,B14,FALSE)						
11	**Lookup_Value:**	Project3							
12									
13	**Column:**	April							
14	**Matching Index:**	5	=MATCH(B13,A1:I1,0)						
15									

Figure 2–14. Using the MATCH Function

Figure 2–14 shows a function to return the April's expenditures for Project3. Cell B14 holds the match formula that returns 5, which is the column position of April in the header row (range A1: I1). The VLOOKUP formula in cell B10 relies on the MATCH function to determine the column argument.

B16	▼	=	=LOOKUP("Item09",A2:A13,I2:I13)						
	A	B	C	D	E	F	G	H	I
1	**Item**	**Descirption**	**WBS**	**Quantity**	**Unit**	**Unit Cost**	**Total**		**Actual**
2	Item01	Layout	Layout	1.00	day	613.67	614		602
3	Item02	Excavate Foundation & Utility Trench	Excavation	379.00	m3	3.10	1,175		1,125
4	Item03	Backfill Utility Trench	Backfill	26.00	m3	1.22	32		32
5	Item04	Compact Utility Trench	compactio	26.00	m3	0.61	16		16
6	Item05	Install Weeping Tile	Backfill	52.00	m	4.60	239		245
7	Item06	Place Granular	Backfill	4.90	m3	41.66	204		215
8	Item07	Backfill Around Foundation	Backfill	88.00	m3	1.22	107		104
9	Item08	Compact Around Foundation	compactio	88.00	m3	0.61	54		54
10	Item09	Lot Grading	Excavation	266.00	m3	1.22	324		310
11	Item10	Forms, Footing	Formwork	30.40	m2	58.28	1,772		1,802
12	Item11	Removal of Form, Footing	Formwork	30.40	m2	2.91	88		85
13	Item12	Keyway, 50mm x 100mm	Formwork	76.00	m	2.82	215		218
14									
15									
16	**Lookup formula :**	310			=LOOKUP("Item09",A2:A27,I2:I27)				
17									

Figure 2–15. The LOOKUP Function

This example contains two lists. The first list is an estimate list, and the second list defines the actual cost of the tasks. The formula in cell B16, finds the Item09 position in the lookup range (range A2: A13) then returns the value from the corresponding position in the result range (actual cost, range I2: I13). Note here that the first range (A2:A13) has to be sorted ascendingly for the function to work properly.

In real life, of course, these lists are likely to be located on the separate sheets of a workbook or even separate workbooks. The lookup function makes it easy to look up information that is stored in different workbooks. Since the LOOKUP formula returns its result based on the relative values in the lookup range and the result range, the two ranges obviously must be of the same dimension and sorted in the same order.

Figure 2–16. The INDEX Function

The formula in cell B14 returns the value in the second row and the sixth column of range A2: F11 (the total cost of excavation).

B14	▼	=	=INDEX(A2:F11,2,6)			
	A	B	C	D	E	F
1	**Item**	**Description**	**Quantity**	**Unit**	**Unit Cost**	**Total Cost**
2	Layout	Layout	1.00	day	613.67	614
3	Excavation-1	Excavate Foundation & Utility Trench	379.00	m3	3.10	1,175
4	Backfill-1	Backfill Utility Trench	26.00	m3	1.22	32
5	Compact-1	Compact Utility Trench	26.00	m3	0.61	16
6	Weep-tile	Install Weeping Tile	52.00	m	4.60	239
7	Fill-1	Place Granular	4.90	m3	41.66	204
8	Backfill-2	Backfill Around Foundation	88.00	m3	1.22	107
9	Compact-2	Compact Around Foundation	88.00	m3	0.61	54
10	Grade	Lot Grading	266.00	m3	1.22	324
11	Fill-2	Bank Run Gravel, Floor:200mm dee	31.00	m3	6.13	190
12						
13						
14	**Index formula :**	1,175		=INDEX(A2:F11,2,6)		
15						

d. **INDEX Function:** The INDEX function (Figure 2–16) returns a value from a list based on the value's position in the list, rather than on a lookup value. The syntax of the index function is

$$=INDEX \ (range, \ row, \ column, \ which\_range)$$

The optional *which_range* argument gives you the opportunity to specify more than one range in the range argument. (You group multiple ranges inside parentheses.) For example, the formula =**INDEX((A4:B8,H4:I8),3,1,1)** returns the value from the third row and first column of range A4:B8. If you

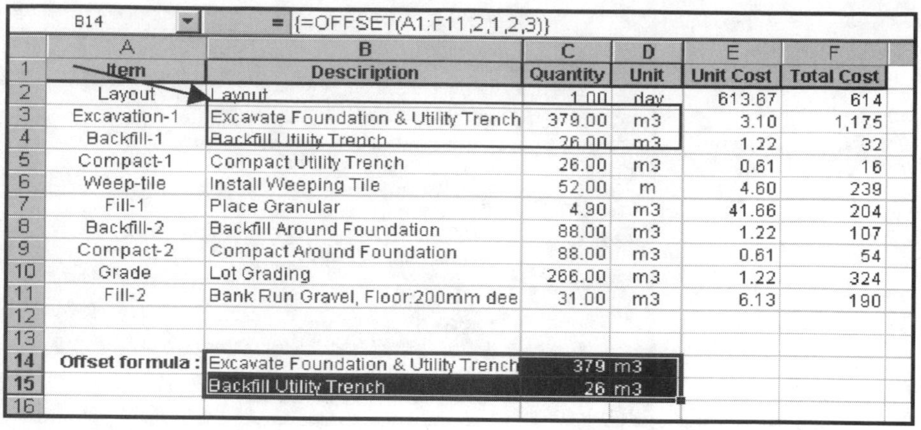

Figure 2–17. The OFFSET Function

The formula in cell B14 is shown here. It returns the values in a range that is two rows high and three columns wide. The upper-left cell of the result range (B3) is determined by an offset of two rows down and one column right of the upper-left cell of the original range (A1). So the formula returns the values in cells B3:D4.

change the last argument to 2, it will return the value from the third row and first column of range H4:I8.

e. **OFFSET Function:** OFFSET is similar to INDEX, but it identifies rows and columns slightly differently, and it can return more than one cell in an array (Figure 2–17). The syntax of the offset function is:

$$OFFSET(range,\ rows,\ columns,\ height,\ width)$$

- *Range* refers to the original range of data.
- *Rows* is the number of rows to offset, up or down, that you want the upper-left cell of the result to refer to.
- *Columns* is the number of columns to offset, left or right, that you want the upper-left cell of the result to refer to.
- *Height* is the height of the result range, in number of rows, the same height as the Range if omitted.
- *Width* is the width of the result range, in number of columns, the same width as Range if omitted.

You can enter a formula that returns multiple values by means of a special type of entry that is termed an *array formula*. To return the offset range in Figure 2–17, you would begin by highlighting the range that will contain the formula. Then, type the formula as given, but as you press Enter you should simultaneously hold down Ctrl+Shift. This instructs Excel to interpret what you have typed as an array formula, and to return the results to all the cells that you highlighted before entering the formula. More explanation can be found in Excel's Help system.

2.4 Excel Reporting Features: Pivot Tables

Reporting is another essential requirement for obtaining summary data on resources and operations. In Excel, the pivot table wizard provides an automated and powerful report generator. Pivot tables enable the user to:

- Summarize long lists in a compact format.
- Find relationships within lists that are hidden by all the details.

- See differences in one variable that are associated with differences in another variable.
- Display data in the form of subtotals, averages, percentages, standard deviations, and so on.

1. **Understanding Row and Column Fields:** A row field in a pivot table is a variable that takes on different values. For example, in Figure 2–18, the row field is the variable called Region, whose values are East and West. For each value of Region, the pivot table displays a summary of its data field. The same is true of a column field, which is a variable called Project Type in the given example.

   The basic effect of row and column fields on a pivot table is that each value, or item, that the field takes on defines a different row or column. So, if a pivot table has a row field that takes on four items and a column field that takes on two items, the pivot table has four rows, two columns, and therefore eight summary cells, exclusive of cells that contain labels, subtotals, and grand totals.

   After creating the pivot table, you can easily change a row field to a column field, or a column field to a row field, which is called *pivoting the table.* You just have to hold down the mouse button on the field you want to move (shaded cells in the pivot table) and release the mouse button when you move the pointer into the proper area.

   You can specify more than one row or column field in a pivot table; additional fields are called *inner fields.* Within one category, or value of the outer field, there can be several values for the inner field. The data field is summarized first by the value of outer field and then further summarized by the corresponding values of the inner field, as shown in Figure 2–19.

2. **Understanding the Data Field:** The data field is the variable that the pivot table summarizes. For each combination of values in the row and column fields, the data field takes on a different value: It is this value that appears in the pivot table's cells. Most frequently, the way the pivot table summarizes the data field is by its sum, as seen in the previous examples. Or, if it is not a variable that can be totaled, the summary statistic might be a count or percentage of the observations in a list.

Figure 2-18. Simple Pivot Table

To create a pivot table, as shown, all you need is a data field and a row and/or column field. *Data field* is the variable that is to be summarized, and the *row/column field* is the variable that controls the summary.

	A	B	C	D
1	**Region**	**Project Type**	**Project Value**	
2	East	Residential	$185,000	
3	West	Residential	$215,000	**Data**
4	East	Residential	$210,000	**List**
5	East	Office Building	$160,000	
6	West	Office Building	$240,000	
7	East	Office Building	$245,000	
8	West	Residential	$165,000	
9				
10	**Pivot Table**		**Column Field**	
11				
12	Sum of Project Value	Project Type		
13	Region	Office Building	Residential	Grand Total
14	East	405000	395000	800000
15	West	240000	380000	620000
16	Grand Total	645000	775000	1420000
17				

Row Field   Data Field

Figure 2–19. Using Inner Fields in a Pivot Table

Here, a pivot table was created by using Year as an outer-row field, Region as an inner-row field, and Project Type as column field.

	A	B	C	D	E
1	Region	Project Type	Year	Project Value	
2	East	Residential	1999	$185,000	
3	West	Residential	1998	$215,000	
4	East	Residential	1998	$210,000	
5	East	Office Building	1999	$160,000	
6	West	Office Building	1998	$240,000	
7	East	Office Building	1998	$245,000	
8	West	Residential	1999	$165,000	
9					
10					
11					
12	Sum of Project Value		Project Type		
13	Year	Region	Office Building	Residential	Grand Total
14	1998	East	$245,000	$210,000	$455,000
15		West	$240,000	$215,000	$455,000
16	1998 Total		$485,000	$425,000	$910,000
17	1999	East	$160,000	$185,000	$345,000
18		West		$165,000	$165,000
19	1999 Total		$160,000	$350,000	$510,000
20	Grand Total		$645,000	$775,000	$1,420,000
21					

Figure 2–20. Pivot Table with a Page Field

	A	B	C	D
1	Region	Project Type	Year	Project Value
2	East	Residential	1999	$185,000
3	West	Residential	1998	$215,000
4	East	Residential	1998	$210,000
5	East	Office Building	1999	$160,000
6	West	Office Building	1998	$240,000
7	East	Office Building	1998	$245,000
8	West	Residential	1999	$165,000
9				
10				
11				
12	Year	(All)		
13		(All)		
		1998		
14	Sum of Project Value	1999		
15	Region	Office Building	Residential	Grand Total
16	East	$405,000	$395,000	$800,000
17	West	$240,000	$380,000	$620,000
18	Grand Total	$645,000	$775,000	$1,420,000
19				

3. **Understanding the Page Field:** A page field is useful for adding another variable to the pivot table without necessarily viewing all its values at once. Suppose, for example, that you want to focus on project values for different project types, in different regions, over several years. If you define year as a page field, you can display project values within project type and region for all years or for any given year, as shown in Figure 2–20. By choosing different values from the page field, you can display different subsets of the data in the pivot table or all the data if you choose the (All) item in the page field's drop-down box.

2.4.1 Using the Pivot Table Wizard to Create a Report

There are two main ways to start the wizard: either by selecting Pivot Table Wizard from the **Data** menu (Figure 2–21), or by using the Pivot Table Wizard toolbar button. To install the Pivot Table toolbar, use **View-Toolbars** menu option and then check the **Query** and **Pivot** checkbox in the **Toolbars** list box.

When you activate the Pivot Table wizard, the first of the four steps in the wizard appears. Let's follow these four steps for creating the same report as that in Figure 2–20.

Figure 2–21
Activating Pivot
Table Wizard

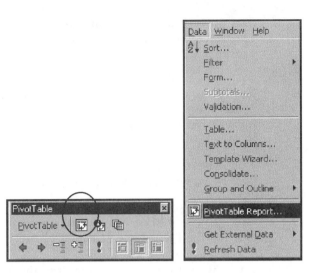

Figure 2–22.
Starting a Pivot
Table

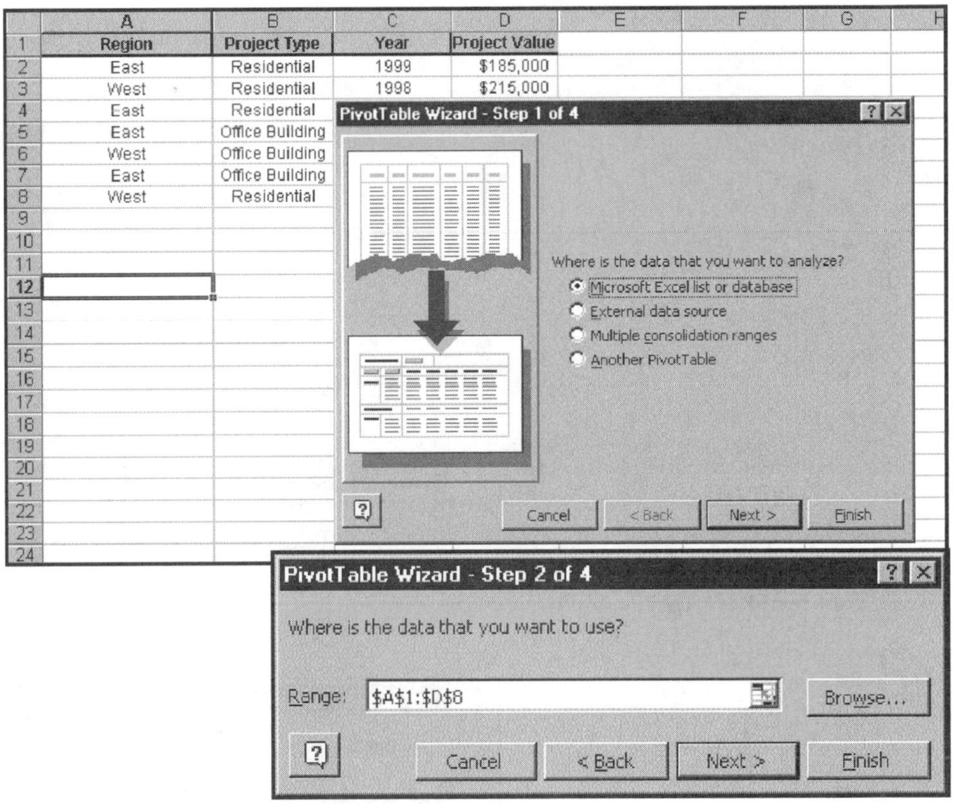

Step 1: Choosing the Type of Data Source

Having the data list on the sheet, select cell A12 and then start the Pivot Table Wizard.

First we define the source of the data as an Excel list, as shown. Hit the **Next >** button. Notice the variety of data sources that can be used to generate a Pivot Table.

Step 2: Specifying the Data Source

We then specify the range of the data source (A1: D8) and hit the **Next >** button, as shown in Figure 2–22.

Step 3: Designing the Pivot Table

This is the most critical step in creating the table: At this point, you determine which variables will act as row, column, page, and data fields. Figure 2–23 shows the fields used to prepare the pivot table in the Figure 2–20.

To drag a field button into one of the field areas, move your mouse pointer over the field button, hold down the mouse button, and continue to hold it down as you move the pointer into proper area. Then release the mouse button. Once finished, hit the **Next >** button.

Note that while the box in Figure 2–23 is active, you can double-click any field button (whether or not you have moved it into a field area) to set its options.

Step 4: Setting the Report Location

First of all, you have to choose where to put the pivot table, as shown in Figure 2–24. Leaving the Pivot Table Starting Cell box blank causes Excel to begin the pivot table in cell A1 of a new sheet.

If you want to change the default settings, you have to click on the **Options** button in the dialog box shown here. A new dialog box appears with the options seen in Figure 2–25.

Figure 2–23.
Designing the Pivot
Table

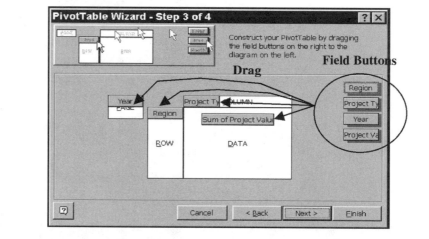

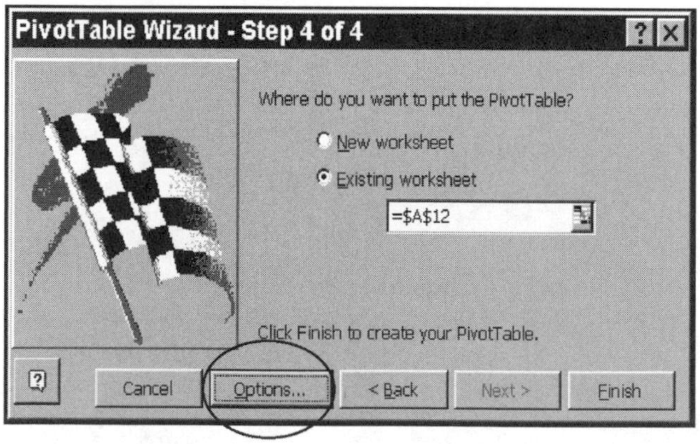

Figure 2–24. Pivot
Table Location

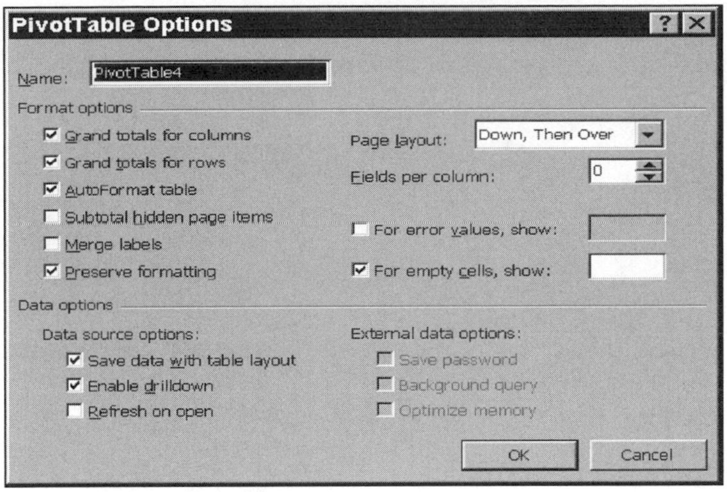

Figure 2-25. Pivot
Table Options

Figure 2-25. Pivot
Table Options

2.4.2 Using the Pivot Table Toolbar

When Excel completes the pivot table on a worksheet, it automatically displays the Query and Pivot toolbar (Figure 2–26). While any cell inside the report is selected, you can use the toolbar to:

- Choose the **Pivot Table Wizard** button to start the Wizard, either to create a new table or to modify an existing pivot table.
- Choose the **Pivot Table Field** button to change the characteristics of an existing pivot table field.
- Choose the **Ungroup** or **Group** button to expand or collapse a pivot table control field.
- Choose the **Hide** or **Show** buttons to display or suppress detail items in a control or data field.
- Choose the **Refresh Data** button to show changes that might have occurred in the underlying data source.

2.4.3 Customizing a Data Field

If you double-click the data field in Step 3 of the Wizard, a dialog box appears as shown in Figure 2–27. Notice the various summary functions and calculation methods in which the data can appear in the report. Details on each of these can be found in the Excel Help system.

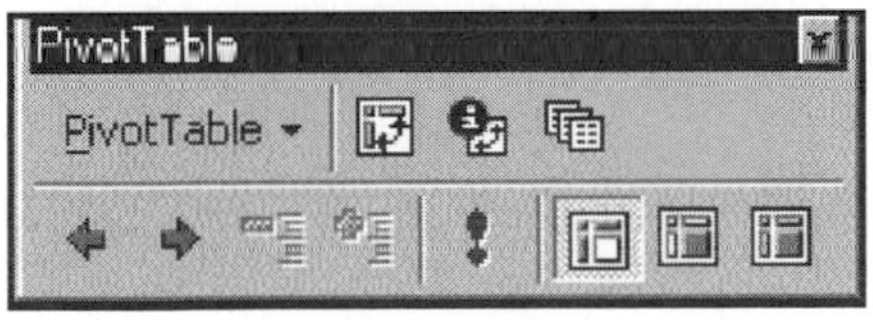

Figure 2-26. Pivot
Table Toolbar

Figure 2–27.
Changing Field
Options

2.5 Excel Optimization Tools

Operations research tools such as linear/nonlinear programming are quantitative methods that can be used to enhance decision making and foster effectiveness in the management of projects. Such techniques are beneficial because:

- They are applicable to a large variety of practical problems.
- Many software systems like Excel are available inexpensively and have these capabilities built in.
- These tools can be effectively applied, hiding all the underlying complexities of the theory and mathematical computations.

2.5.1 Goal-Seek

This Excel feature can be used to determine the proper values for the variables in any application so that a goal is met.

Example:

Suppose your goal is to limit spending on a certain work item to $1,200 and you would like to determine the proper amount of that item that you can afford to buy given that labor, equipment, and transportation costs per unit are $100, $140, and $5, respectively.

This simple example has a single objective, which is minimum cost and a single variable, which is quantity. The systematic approach for solving this type of problems is as follows:

- Develop a calculation model of this problem using spreadsheets. Basically, we always represent each variable in a separate cell and give it an initial quantity of 1.
- Always represent each data element in a separate cell. Use another adjacent cell to type a label for each data item.
- Write the worksheet formulas to do intermediate calculations.
- Set a single separate cell to represent the Goal.
- Activate **Goal-Seek** from the **Tools** menu and define the cells for the variable (changing cell) and the **Goal.**

Figure 2–28 shows the implementation model and the results of **Goal-Seek**. Notice that the Goal cell is linked to the variable by formulas.

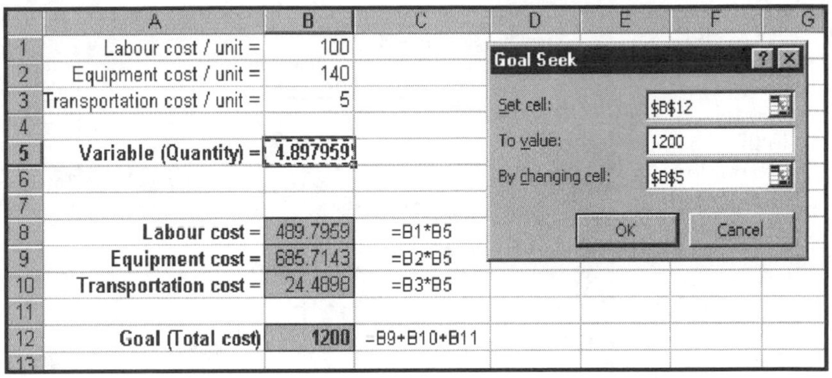

Figure 2–28. Using Goal-Seek

2.5.2 Excel Solver for Mathematical Optimization

Goal-Seek, as explained, is a simple tool which can be used to solve problems that involve one variable and that involve no constraints on the solution. Another Excel tool, Solver, which is an add-in program for general linear and nonlinear integer programming, is very useful for solving multivariable optimization problems. It uses the Simplex and branch-and-bound mathematical techniques for the optimization.

> **Note:** If **Solver** is not found under the Tools menu, **select Tools, Add-Ins,** and **install Solver.** Then look for the file **Solvsamp.xls** in your system, which has several interesting applications of the Solver program.

Using Solver to formulate optimization problems is a simple and straightforward process. Optimization, in general, tries to maximize or minimize an objective function (a goal) by determining the optimum values (quantities) for a set of decision variables so as to meet certain constraints. Using Solver, the user needs to establish the calculations sheet and then simply define the cells that represent the objective function, the variables, and the constraints.

> *Example:*
>
> This example involves the shipment of aggregates from three quarries to five projects. The aggregates can be shipped from any plant to any project, but it obviously costs more to ship over long distances than over short distances. The problem is to determine the amounts to ship from each quarry to each project at minimum shipping cost in order to meet the demand, while not exceeding the supply limit.
>
> *Data:*
>
> - The three quarries A, B, and C can produce a maximum of 310, 260, and 280 truckloads per day, respectively.
> - The five projects PR1, PR2, PR3, PR4, and PR5 have daily demands of 180, 80, 200, 160, and 220 truckloads, respectively.
> - The shipping costs ($) from any quarry to any project are as shown in Figure 2–29.

Figure 2-29.
Optimization Model

To verify the spreadsheet model, any change in the values of the variables should result in appropriated changes in the objective function.

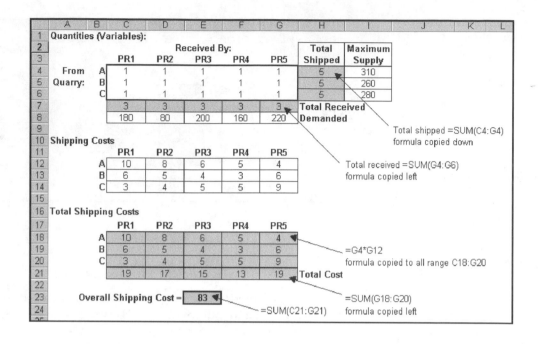

Solution:

The solution has to follow the four steps of the systematic approach described before:

1. Variables are represented in separate cells (C4: G6) with initial values of 1s. The variables represent the amount to be shipped from each quarry to each project.
2. Each data element is represented in a separate cell. These include the maximum supply of each quarry (H4: H6); demand amount of each project (C8: G8); and shipping costs (C12: G14).
3. Worksheet formulas are written to perform intermediate calculations (see Figure 2–29). This includes actual amount delivered to each project, actual amount shipped from each quarry, and the associated shipping cost.
4. Formulate a single cell for the Goal or objective function, in our example, the sum of overall shipping costs (cell E23).

The Solver program can then be activated from the **Tools** menu and the optimization parameters can be set as shown in Figure 2–30. The optimization objective is to minimize the total shipping cost (cell E23). The optimization variables are the quantities in the range C4: G6. The optimization constraints were also set to limit the values of the variables to positive integers, not to exceed the maximum available truckloads per day, and to meet the demand for each project. Using Solver, a solution was reached, achieving a minimum total shipping cost of $3,200, as shown in Figure 2–30.

The variables take their optimum values that result in lowest shipping cost.

2.5.3 Nontraditional Optimization Tool

While Solver is a convenient tool for mathematical optimization, in some situations it gets stuck and fails to solve the problem, or it gets trapped in local optimum. Alternatively, new software programs have recently been introduced as a result of advancements in the artificial intelligence branch of computer science. For optimization applications, a new technique, called Genetic Algorithms (GAs) has recently emerged with random optimization capabilities inspired by the biological systems' improved fitness

Figure 2–30. Solver
Solution

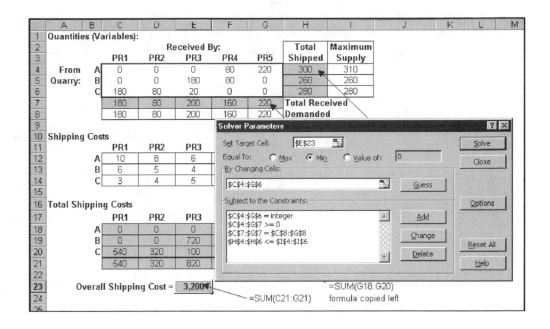

through evolution. Typically, GAs require a representation scheme to encode feasible solutions to an optimization problem. Usually this is done in the form of a string called a chromosome (or gene). Each gene represents one member (i.e., one solution) that is better or worse than other members in a population. The fitness of each gene is determined by evaluating its performance with respect to an objective function. To simulate the natural "survival of the fittest" process, best genes exchange information to produce offspring that are evaluated in turn and can be retained only if they are more fit than others in the population. Usually, the process is continued for a large number of offspring generations until an optimum gene (solution) is arrived at.

The powerful optimization capabilities of the GAs technique are potentially applicable in situations where traditional mathematical optimization does not work. Accordingly, the technique has recently been widely used by many researchers in various science and engineering applications. Without much details on the mathematics of the GAs technique, various software systems have recently been available commercially as simplified add-in programs to Excel that hide the underlying complexity. One well known software for GA-based optimization is the **Evolver** software from Palisade Corp. (working copy is included with the CD accompanying this book). More information on this software can be found on their websites (Appendix A, on web resources). This software, and others that you may find through a web search, works as an add-on to Excel, is very user friendly, and is nicely integrated into the Excel environment.

Usually most of the Genetic Algorithm software provides you with an interface that is similar to the Excel Solver. The main screen of Evolver, for example, is shown in Figure 2–31. You need to select the cells that represent the objective function, variables, and constraints, and can be identical to those that you specify for the Excel Solver.

The various Genetic Algorithm software products, however, differ in their solution mechanisms, their options, and their speed. The Evolver software, for example, is known for its fast processing. It also gives you the option to specify soft and hard constraints. From experimentation, however, it requires you to start the optimization with carefully decided initial values for the variables (can be easily done for the types of problems dealt with in this book). For example, you may use initial values that meet the constraints but do not necessarily optimize the objective function. The GeneHunter

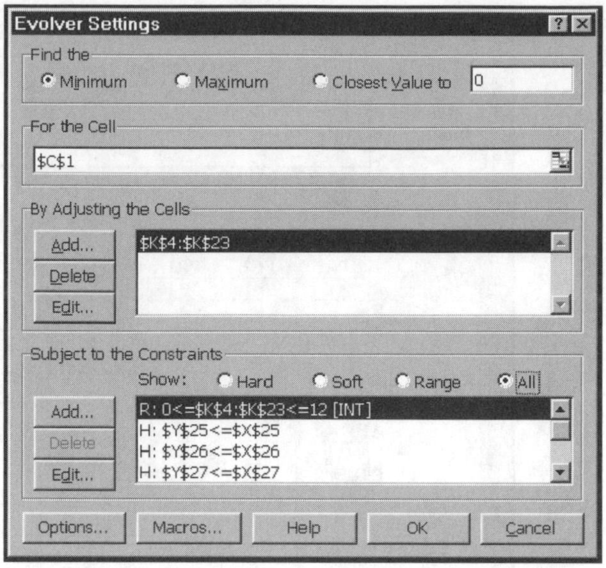

Figure 2-31. Using the Evolver Program

software from Ward Systems Group, Inc., on the other hand, gives you the option to specify a priority level for your constraints (High, Medium, or Low) and can work without presetting any values for the variables, but is slower than Evolver.

To enable a hands-on experimentation with GA software, an evaluation version of Evolver is provided with the CD of this book, courtesy of Palisade Corp. This version comes with a three-month and 80-variable limit (enough time for experimenting with the case studies of this book). A full working copy of their powerful industrial version is also available at the company's website and comes with 10-day limit (enough time for you to perform a case study of your own). After installing Evolver, the first thing you want to do is activate the tutorial session that comes with the software to get a quick tour of its capabilities and how to start working with the software. The interface looks similar to the Excel Solver program.

2.6 Project Management Software

Proper planning and scheduling, as integral parts of this book, are key factors to completing a construction project within budget, on time, and with few problems. Along the course of this book, we will be using one of the common software systems that support project management functions, Microsoft Project 98 and Primavera P3. Evaluation versions of both software systems are available from their websites (see Appendix A). Basically, Microsoft Project is a popular easy-to-use project management software, and P3 is a high-end software for project management. Both software systems allow you to put together a project plan, organize resources, assign responsibilities, and follow up during construction.

Neither software, nor any other project management software, cannot guarantee a successful project plan, but they are invaluable planning tools for:

- Organizing the plan and thinking through the details of what must be done.
- Scheduling deadlines that must be met.
- Scheduling the tasks in the appropriate sequence.
- Assigning resources and costs to tasks and scheduling tasks around resource availability.
- Fine-tuning the plan to satisfy time and budget constraints or to accommodate changes.

Note: Newer versions may have a different Welcome screen.

- Preparing professional-looking reports to explain the project to owners, top management, supervisors, workers, subcontractors, and the public.

Once work begins on the project, you can use the project management software to:

- Track progress and analyze the evolving "real" schedule to see if it looks like you will finish on time and within budget.
- Revise the schedule to accommodate changes and unforeseen circumstances.
- Try out different what-if scenarios before modifying the plan.
- Communicate with team members about changes in the schedule (even automatically notify those who are affected by changes!) and solicit feedback about their progress.
- Post automatically updated progress reports on an Internet website or a company intranet.
- Produce final reports on the success of the project and evaluate problem areas for consideration in future projects.

2.6.1 Microsoft Project Software

When you install Microsoft Project in the Windows environment, the Setup program places Microsoft Project on the Start menu, under programs. To start Microsoft, **choose Start, Programs, Microsoft Project.** The program first displays a new project window in the background, as shown in Figure 2–32. The following list describes the choices in the **Welcome!** dialog box:

- Choose **Learn While You Work** for a tutorial that displays cue cards from the online Help system to guide you through setting up a new project document. This tutorial is divided into 12 basic lessons for creating a project and seven advanced lessons for managing a project.
- Choose **Watch a Quick Preview** for a demonstration and tutorial of the major features of project scheduling with Microsoft Project.
- Choose **Navigate with a Map** to close the Welcome! window and begin working in Microsoft Project on your own.

Figure 2–32.
Microsoft Project 98
Welcome Screen

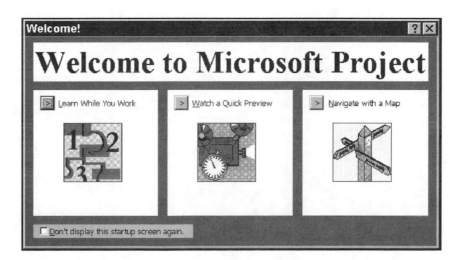

Once you move past the Welcome screen, you see the Microsoft Project title bar at the top of the screen, along with the Microsoft Project menu, two toolbars, and an entry bar. On the left side of the screen are the active split bar and the View bar to assist you in moving quickly between views. The status bar is visible at the bottom of the screen, and the data area in the center of the screen displays the project data, which can be arranged in a hierarchy (Figure 2–33). On the right side is the default Gantt chart (or Bar chart), which displays the time scale and shows the start and finish times of all tasks in the project.

2.6.1.1 The Tool Bar Appearing below the menu bar are the toolbars that contain buttons you activate with the mouse to provide shortcut access to frequently used menu choices or special functions. For complete descriptions of the toolbar buttons, use the Microsoft Project Help menu. Choose **Help**, **What's This?** By choosing this option, your mouse pointer now has a question mark attached to it. Simply click the tool you are interested in, and a mini–help screen will provide you information on that tool.

There are 12 toolbars provided in Microsoft Project. The two displayed initially are the Standard toolbar and the Formatting toolbar. You can add and remove toolbars to the display and create your own custom toolbars, by simply choosing **View**, **Toolbars.**

2.6.1.2 The Entry Bar The entry bar performs several functions:

- The left end of the entry bar displays progress messages that let you know when Microsoft Project is engaged in calculating, opening, and saving files, leveling resources, and so on.
- The center of the entry bar contains an entry area where data entry and editing takes place. During Entry and Editing modes, **Cancel** and **Enter** buttons also appear.

Figure 2–33.
Microsoft Project Screen

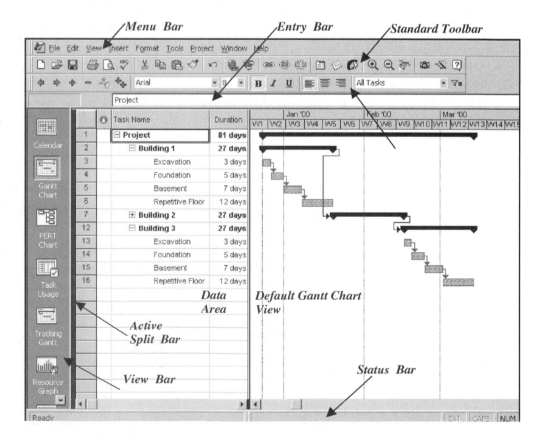

2.6.1.3 The View Bar The display in the data area is known as a *view*. The term view refers to the way the project data appears. The default view is the Gantt chart, which is divided into two parts: a table on the left shows a list of task names, and a time scale on the right displays a bar chart showing the beginning and ending of each task. As there are more than 25 views you can work with in Microsoft Project, the View bar and the active split bar will help you to quickly access the most commonly used view, switch between the views, and keep track of which view is being displayed. Scroll arrows on the View bar let you see additional views. At the bottom of the list is the **More Views** option, which takes you to a dialog box listing all the views in Microsoft Project.

2.6.1.4 A Guided Tour to Microsoft Project Microsoft Project has an extensive online help facility, with many new special aids to help you learn how to use its features. The learning aids range in complexity from the immediate and brief ScreenTips to the analytical suggestions provided by the Planning Wizard and the step-by-step instructions contained in the Getting Started tutorials.

2.6.1.5 Accessing Online Help There are many sources of Help in Microsoft Project:

- The **Help menu** offers access to the online help topics as well as access to the Office Assistant, a set of online tutorials featured in Getting Started, and Microsoft on the Web (if you are connected to Internet).
- To access context-sensitive help, choose **Help, What's This?** Or press **Shift+F1.** The mouse pointer changes into a question mark and an arrow. Choose a menu command or point on an area of the screen about which you want help and click the mouse button.
- Many dialog boxes feature a **Help** button in the title bar to explain parts of the dialog box. When you click this **Help** button, the mouse pointer becomes a question mark with an arrow. Click a feature of the dialog box to see the explanation of that feature.
- If you access the Internet, Microsoft on the Web offers quick access to the Microsoft website. Free Software, New Product Information, and Frequently Asked Questions are among the topics available online from Microsoft.

2.6.1.6 Using Contents and Index As shown in Figure 2–34, with the **Contents** and **Index** options on the **Help** menu, you can browse or search the entire contents of

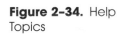

Figure 2–34. Help Topics

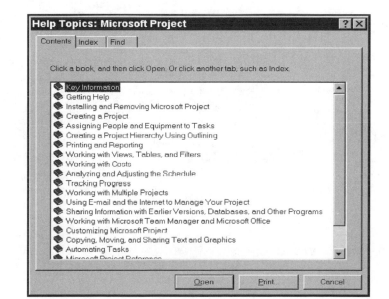

Note:	Newer versions may have comparable help features with a different interface.

Microsoft Project Help. Microsoft Project dialog box has three avenues for getting help: a table of contents, an alphabetical index, and a text search capability.

2.6.1.7 Getting Started   Microsoft has added three new help features for new users to Microsoft Project and project management. To access the new help option, you can use the options on the welcome screen of Figure 2–32 or select the **Help, Getting Started** menu option. A submenu appears with three menu choices, as follows:

- *Quick Preview:*   Choose **Quick Preview** to access a brief tutorial that provides an overview of the capabilities of Microsoft Project (Figure 2–35a). This tutorial is an excellent way to introduce new users to Microsoft Project.

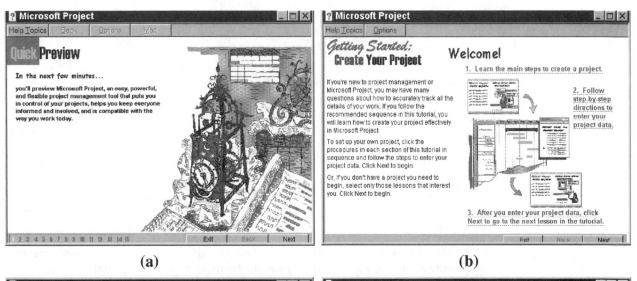

(a)   (b)

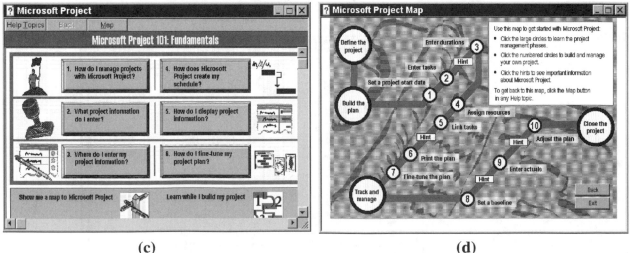

(c)   (d)

Figure 2–35. Planning Wizard Screens

■ *Create Your Project:* Choose **Create Your Project** to access a step-by-step tutorial to assist you in creating your first project (Figure 2–35b). This tutorial provides 12 lessons guiding you through the creation process. It also includes seven advanced lessons for managing your project.

■ *Microsoft Project 101: Fundamentals:* This feature is designed to assist new users in working with the software and designed to answer six specific questions (Figure 2–35 c&d). The screens are interactive. When you click a caption, more information appears on the screen.

2.6.1.8 Working with the Planning Wizard   There are still more learning aids than those accessed with the **Help** menu. The Planning wizard continuously monitors your use of the program and offers tips of techniques that might be more efficient or warns you about potential problems you might create for yourself as a result of current action. The Planning wizard is automatically turned on in Microsoft Project, and its options are controlled on the General tab of the Options dialog box. To access the Options dialog box, choose **Tools, Options.**

2.6.2   Primavera P3 Software

After installing Primavera software, as shown in Figures 2–36 and 2–37, you activate the P3 software and load one of the existing project examples. The main screen of Primavera P3 is similar to the main screen of Microsoft Project. Before actually working with the software, it is a good idea to activate the tutorial session under the main help menu, shown in Figure 2–38. This will give you a good idea on the software capabilities and features that we will use in later chapters.

Figure 2–36.
Primavera Files

The MPX Conversion program under Primavera group can convert to and from Microsoft Project files.

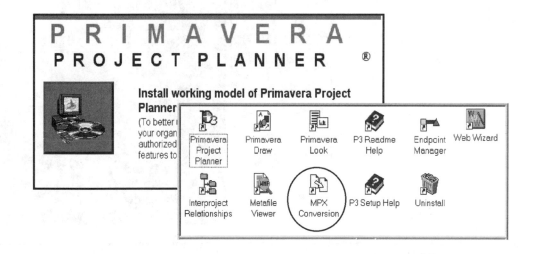

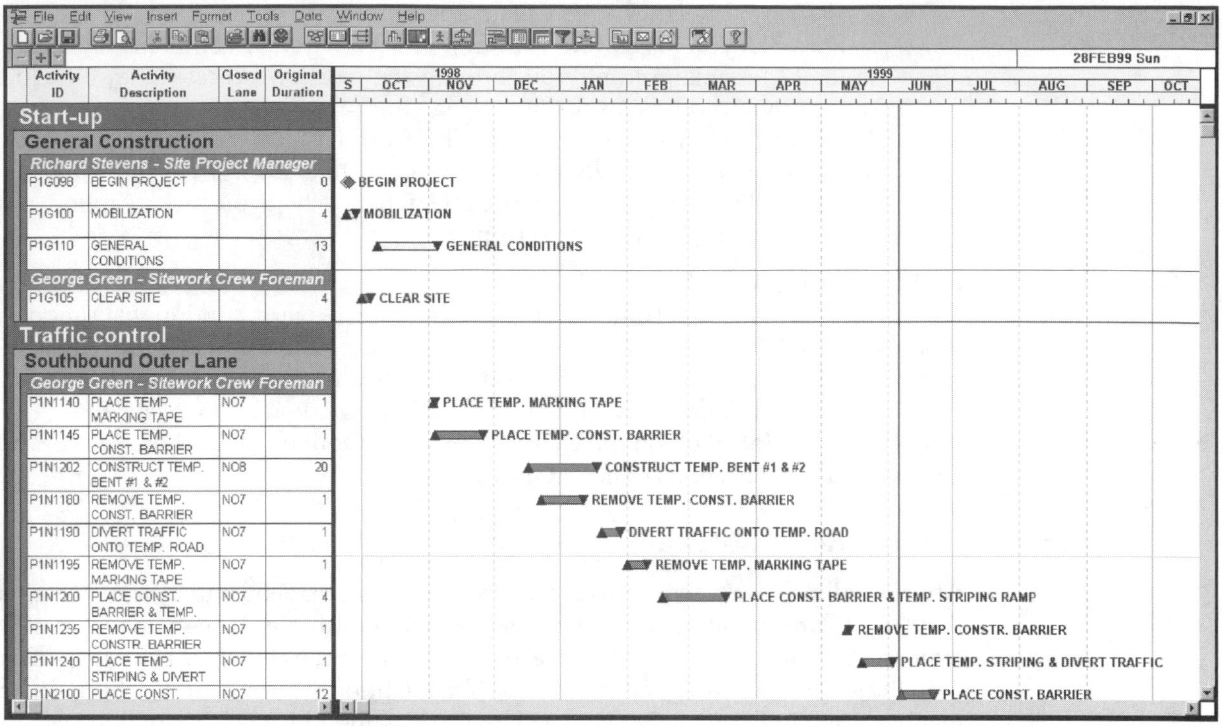

Figure 2-37. Primavera P3 Main Screen

Figure 2-38. Help Options and Tutorial Screen

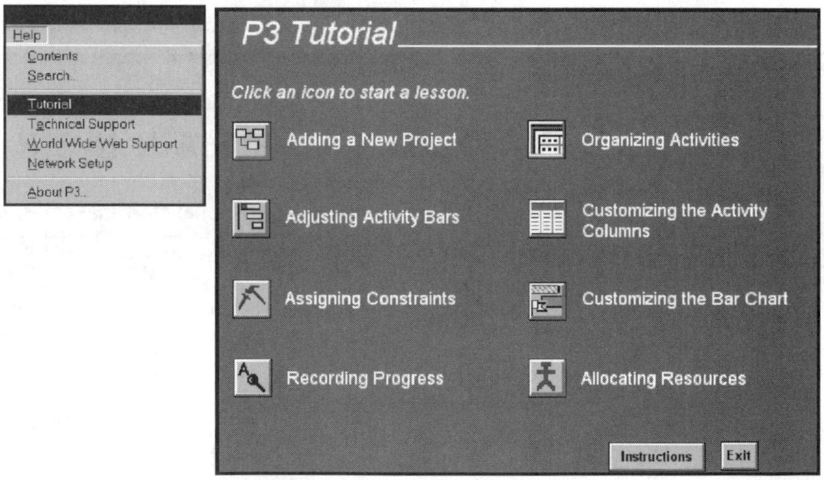

Note: Newer versions may have comparable help features with a different interface.

2.7 Summary

In this chapter, spreadsheets have been presented as an ideal platform with diverse tools that can be used for creating comprehensive models in construction. Many of the simple yet powerful features of Excel have been introduced, in addition to some add-in programs for optimization capabilities. In addition to Excel, one commonly used software for project management, Microsoft Project, has been briefly introduced so that both tools can be used in the remaining chapters of this book. For interested readers, Appendix A lists several Internet websites with information related to the material in this chapter.

2.8 Bibliography

Evolver reference manual (1998). Newfield, NY: Palisade Corp.

Microsoft Excel (1997). *Reference Manual, Project 98 Windows*. Microsoft Corporation, One Microsoft Way, Redmond, WA.

Microsoft Project (1998). *Reference Manual, Project 98 Windows*. Microsoft Corporation, One Microsoft Way, Redmond, WA.

Premavera (1995). *Reference Manual, Ver. 1.0 for Windows*. Primavera, Two Bala Plaza, Bala Cynwyd, PA 19004.

2.9 Exercises

1. Use the **Advanced Filter** option of Excel on the data of Figure 2–39 and apply the following criteria:

   a. Project Type is Office Building or Restaurant
   b. Project Value is less than $200,000 in East Region
   c. Project Value is greater than twice the minimum project value

   Print a screen capture of the criteria range and the resulting data. Note: use the **Print Screen** button to capture the Excel screen and then use **Edit-Paste** in a Word document.

2. a. Sort the data of Figure 2–39 by the Project Value using a descending sort.

   b. Use the VLOOKUP and MATCH functions to look for the project value of the project coded W-02.

   c. Find the value of the project coded C-06 using the INDEX function. Print the formulas and the result spreadsheet.

3. Use the following statistical features of Excel and apply these functions on the data of Figure 2–39:

   DSTDEV: Find the standard deviation of the project value for the residential projects in all the regions.

   DSUM: Find the summation of the project value for the office building projects in the central region.

Figure 2-39. Excel List for Exercises 2 and 3.

	A	B	C	D	E
1	**Project Code**	**Region**	**Project Type**	**Project Manager**	**Project Value**
2	C-01	Central	Residential	Bill	$ 200,000
3	C-02	Central	Residential	Bill	$ 225,000
4	C-03	Central	Residential	Smith	$ 325,000
5	C-04	Central	Residential	Smith	$ 360,000
6	C-05	Central	Restaurant	Smith	$ 180,000
7	C-06	Central	Office Building	Green	$ 420,000
8	C-07	Central	Office Building	Jones	$ 600,000
9	E-01	East	Residential	Thomas	$ 185,000
10	E-02	East	Residential	Thomas	$ 210,000
11	E-03	East	Office Building	Bill	$ 160,000
12	E-04	East	Office Building	Jones	$ 210,000
13	E-05	East	Office Building	Smith	$ 145,000
14	E-06	East	Restaurant	Davis	$ 225,000
15	W-01	West	Residential	Green	$ 210,000
16	W-02	West	Office Building	Green	$ 300,000
17	W-03	West	Residential	Thomas	$ 170,000
18	W-04	West	Office Building	Jones	$ 380,000
19	W-05	West	Restaurant	Davis	$ 140,000

DMAX: Find the maximum project value for all projects in the central region that have Mr. Smith as the project manager.

Print and submit the Excel spreadsheet showing the formulas used and the results of each case.

4. Given the cost data in the top part of Figure 2–40, answer the following:

a. Add formulas to the column, Total.

b. Write a VLOOKUP function in cell F10 so that when the reference (cell E10) is changed, the appropriate material cost is shown.

c. Write a VLOOKUP function in cell F14 so that when the reference or the type of cost (cells D14 and E14) is changed, the appropriate cost is shown.

d. What is the value that results from the formula shown in cell F17?

e. Write the two missing parameters in the formula of cell F20 so that it produces a result of 10000.

5. Prepare an Excel sheet with the data as shown in Figure 2–41.

a. Write MATCH and VLOOKUP functions in cells K2 and K3. The MATCH function returns the column number of the field Actual. The VLOOKUP function then returns the actual cost of Item6 (Backfill Around Foundation).

Figure 2-40. Excel Sheet for Exercise 4.

	A	B	C	D	E	F	
1	Code	Description	Labor	Equipment	Material	Total	
2	Task1	Excavation	2000	10000	0		(a)
3	Task2	Foundation	15500	22000	20000		
4	Task3	Backfill	4000	2000	5000		
5							
6							
7							
8							
9			Possible Values:		Reference	Material_Cost	(b)
10			Task1		Task2		
11			Task2				
12			Task3				
13				Reference	Type of Cost	Cost	(c)
14				Task1	Equipment		
15							
16							
17			Possible Values:			=VLOOKUP("Foundation",B1:F4,5,0)	(d)
18			Labor				
19			Equipment				
20			Material			=VLOOKUP(,C1:F4, ,0)	(e)
21							

Figure 2-41. Excel Sheet for Exercise 5.

	A	B	C	D	E	F	G	H	I	J	K	
1	Item	Descirption	WBS	Quantity	Unit	Unit Cost	Total Cost	Planned	Actual			
2	Item1	Layout	Layout	1.00	day	613.67	613.67	613.67	602	MATCH:		**(a)**
3	Item2	Excavate Foundation & Utility Trench	Excavation	379.00	m3	3.10	1,174.89	1,174.89	1,125	VLOOKUP:		
4	Item3	Backfill Utility Trench	Backfill	26.00	m3	1.22	31.69	31.69	32	INDEX:		**(b)**
5	Item4	Compact Utility Trench	Compaction	26.00	m3	0.61	15.86	15.86	16			
6	Item5	Place Granular	Backfill	4.90	m3	41.66	204.15	204.15	215			
7	Item6	Backfill Around Foundation	Backfill	88.00	m3	1.22	107.24	107.24	104			
8	Item7	Compact Around Foundation	Compaction	88.00	m3	0.61	53.68	53.68	54			
9	Item8	Lot Grading	Excavation	266.00	m3	1.22	324.16	324.16	310			
10	Item9	Forms, Footing	Formwork	30.40	m2	58.28	1,771.72	1,771.72	1,802			
11	Item10	Removal of Form, Footing	Formwork	30.40	m2	2.91	88.38	88.38	85			
12	Item11	Forms, Walls	Formwork	110.70	m2	35.76	3,959	3,959	4,200			
13	Item12	Removal of Form, Walls	Formwork	266.70	m2	2.91	775	775	760			**(c)**
14												
15	Item	Descirption	WBS	Quantity	Unit	Unit Cost	Total Cost	Planned	Actual	DMIN:		
16			Formwork	>100								
17												**(d)**
18	Item	Descirption	WBS	Quantity	Unit	Unit Cost	Total Cost	Planned	Actual	DSUM:		
19			Formwork			>10						
20												**(e)**
21	Item	Descirption	WBS	Quantity	Unit	Unit Cost	Total Cost	Planned	Actual1	DSTDEV:		
22					m3							
23												**(f)**
24									Offset Function:			
25												
26												
27												
28												

Figure 2–41. Excel Sheet for Exercise 5.

b. Use the INDEX function in cell K4 to find the Planned Cost of Item11.

c. Use the DMIN function in cell K15 to find the minimum Total Cost for all items that apply to the criteria range in cells A15:I16 (WBS is Formwork and Quantity is more than 100 m^2).

d. Use the DSUM function in cell K18 to find the summation of the Actual Cost of all items that apply to the criteria range in cells A18:I19 (WBS is Formwork and Unit Cost is more than 10).

e. Use the DSTDEV function in cell K20 to find the standard deviation of the Planned Cost for all items that apply to the criteria range in cells A20: I21.

f. Use the OFFSET function in the shaded range (G23:K25) to return the same values shown in the shaded range (D8:H10).

6. Summarize the data shown in Figure 2–42 using the **Pivot Table** option in Excel. Use the Year and Project Type as row fields, the Region as a column field, and the Project Value as a data field.

Show and print the following data on the pivot table:

a. The sum of project value for the 1998-East Region-Office Building projects.

b. The sum of project value for the 1999-Residential projects.

c. The total value of all projects.

d. The average value of the 1998 Office Building projects.

e. The average value of all projects.

f. Modify the pivot table by using the Year as a page field. Display the project value for all years and for the year 1999 only.

7. Prepare three Excel sheets as shown in Figure 2–43.

a. In Sheet 3, write VLOOKUP formulas in columns I and J (Problem and Cause) to show the corresponding data from sheets 1 and 2. Print the sheet and show the formulas.

Figure 2–42. Excel List for Exercise 6.

	A	B	C	D
1	Region	Project Type	Year	Project Value
2	East	Residential	1999	$185,000
3	West	Residential	1998	$215,000
4	East	Residential	1998	$210,000
5	East	Office Building	1999	$160,000
6	West	Office Building	1998	$240,000
7	East	Office Building	1998	$245,000
8	West	Residential	1999	$165,000

Figure 2–43. Excel Sheets for Exercise 7.

Sheet 1

	A	B
1	Problem ID	Problem Description
2	4	Wrong discount
3	6	Incorrect Ship To
4	8	Wrong product

Sheet 2

	A	B
1	Cause ID	Cause Description
2	S1	Error in shipping system
3	S2	Customer database error
4	S3	Error in order system
5	T3	Discount calculation error
6	T4	Lack of product knowledge

Sheet 3

	A	B	C	D	E	F	G	H	I	J
1	Office	Rep	Date	Order_No.	Product	Problem ID	Cause ID	Cost	Problem	Cause
2	2	John	10/1/95	1745	Cement	6	S2	$500		
3	1	Peter	7/10/95	1467	Timber	4	T3	$50		
4	2	John	6/25/95	1330	Timber	4	S3	$50		
5	1	Ric	5/1/95	1024	Cement	6	S1	$400		
6	2	Ramzy	8/1/95	1564	Cement	6	S1	$200		
7	1	Peter	6/15/95	1056	Timber	8	T4	$200		
8										

b. Construct a pivot table in a separate sheet using the Date as a column field, the Problem ID and the Cause ID as row fields, the Office, Rep, and Product as page fields, and the Cost as a data field. Experiment with the resulting pivot table and print the following:
1. The grand total cost of Office2 in which John is the Rep.
2. The grand total cost of all the offices, all products, and all reps.
3. The grand total cost of product Timber on 6/15/95 in Office1 with Peter as the Rep.

8. Develop an Excel model of the following optimization problem and use Excel Solver to determine the optimum values of the variables x_1 and x_2 and the value of the objective function:

Maximize $6 X_1 + 4 X_2$

Constraints: $(2 X_1 + 4 X_2)$ less than or equal to 13;

$(2 X_1 + X_2)$ less than or equal to 7; and

X_1 and X_2 are integer and nonnegative values.

9. The equipment workshop for a large earth-moving company has a backlog of five trucks (A, B, C, D, and E) needing engine overhaul. The five trucks are expected to take 22, 16, 35, 12, and 28 hours of work, respectively. Only a single crew can work on one job at a time. The service manager's performance is judged, in part, on the average time a truck spends in the shop awaiting or receiving maintenance. The service manager, therefore, needs to properly sequence available jobs so as to minimize the average time spent on the job. Prepare an Excel model of the problem and use Solver to determine the proper sequence of the jobs.

10. A concrete manufacturer is concerned about how many units of two types of concrete elements should be produced during the next time period to maximize profit. Each concrete element of type I generates a profit of $60, while each element of type II generates a profit of $40. Two and three units of raw materials are needed to produce one concrete element of type I and II, respectively. Also, four and two units of time are required to produce one concrete element of type I and II, respectively.

   If 100 units of raw materials and 120 units of time are available, how many units of each type of concrete element should be produced to maximize profit and satisfy all constraints? Use Excel Solver for the solution.

11. A building contractor produces two types of houses: detached and semidetached. The customer is offered several choices of architectural design and layout for each type. The proportion of each type of design sold in the past is shown in the following table. The profit on a detached house and a semidetached house is $1,000 and $800, respectively.

Design	Detached	Semidetached
Type A	0.1	0.33
Type B	0.4	0.67
Type C	0.5	——

The builder has the capacity to build 400 houses per year. However, an estate of housing is not allowed to contain more than 75% of the total housing as detached. Furthermore, because of the limited supply of bricks available for type B designs, a 200-house limit with this design is imposed. Use Excel to develop a model of this problem, and then use Solver to determine how many detached and semidetached houses should be constructed in order to maximize profits. State the optimum profit.

Chapter 3

PLANNING
Part 1—Network Diagrams

A fter studying this chapter, you will be able to:

- Understand the basic requirements of good project planning.
- Break down the project into activities.
- Identify the logical relationships among project activities.
- Draw a project network.
- Understand the difference between Activity-on-Arrow (AOA) and Activity-on-Node (AON) representations of project networks.

Owner, CM	A/E, CM, Owner	Bidders	Owner, CM	Contractor	O & M Staff
• Need • Feasibility • Project Definition • Owner Approval	• Conceptual Design • Owner Approval • Soil Reports • Preliminary Design • Detailed Design • Quantities • Work Documents • Select Project Contract Strategy	• Prepare Bid Proposal + Baselines • Collect Data (site, quantities, specs, resources, tasks, etc) • **Planning** • Time & Cost Estimation • Scheduling • Resource Management: Adjustments for Resource Constraints & Deadline • Bidding Strategy & Markup Estimation • Cash Flow Analysis • Submit Bid	• Evaluate Bids and Select General Contractor	• Start Construction • Detailed Planning, estimating & Resource Management • Schedule Updating • Progress Evaluation • Time, Cost, & Quality Control • Commissioning	• O & M • Demolition at End of Service Life
CONCEPT	**DESIGN**	**BIDDING**		**CONSTRUCTION**	**O & M**

3.1   Introduction

In the previous chapter, you learned simple ways to set up a basic information system for storing resource data and various methods of construction. In this chapter, you will be introduced to the project planning process. *Planning*, in fact, is a general term that sets a clear road map that should be followed to reach a destination. The term, therefore, has been used at different levels to mean different things. In construction, for example, plans may exist at several levels: corporate strategic plans, pretender plans, precontract plans, short-term construction plans, and long-term construction plans. These plans are, in fact, different from each other; their inputs are different and so are the computations needed to produce their outcome and the final usage of these plans. All these plans, however, involve *four steps:*

1. Performing a breakdown of major work items involved in the project (called activities or tasks).
2. Identifying the proper sequence by which the activities are to be executed.
3. Representing this information in a simple manner.
4. Estimating the resource, cost, and time needs of the individual activities.

The fourth step, in fact, deals with the estimating function that is a necessary part of planning. Because estimating can be applied differently according to the type of plan being generated, it is a large subject by itself and deserves one chapter of its own. In this book, therefore, this chapter is concerned only with the first three steps of planning mentioned above and is considered as part 1 of planning. In essence, this chapter deals with the individual ingredients of a project plan. Chapter 4 will then be dedicated to "Estimating" to determine the time and cost associated with the individual activities of a project plan, as part 2 of planning. Chapter 5 will deal with "scheduling" computations that are applied on the project plan as a whole. Chapters 6, 7, and 8 will also deal with important topics that help in modifying the schedule under resource constraints and other conditions.

3.2 Planning: A Challenge

Planning is, certainly, the most crucial, knowledge-intensive, ill-structured, and challenging phase in the project development cycle. It is highly sensitive to the project environment, the technology used, and the existing management and industry practices. Planning is the process of representing the project scope by its identifiable components. It involves the breakdown of the project into definable, measurable, and identifiable work tasks/activities, and then establishes the logical interdependence among them. Planning answers three main questions:

1. What is to be done?
2. How to do it (logical order)?
3. Who does it?

It accomplishes the definition of work tasks/activities and their sequence. Planning could be viewed as detective work, starting with an end (i.e., a project) and synthesizing the means or the steps required to yield this end.

Planning is a difficult task that can only be efficiently done through a good work team. The creative and highly experience-based nature of this task restricts it to human planners, with little or no help being provided by even the fastest computer available. Systematic and structured planning techniques are, therefore, important for:

- Minimizing the potential to overlook something.
- Sharing of team-work ideas.
- Having a clear definition of project scope and desired level of detail.
- Building confidence and commitment into team workers.
- Effectively communicating the plan to site personnel.

Detailed planning for tendering purposes and the preparation of construction needs to be conducted through brainstorming sessions among the planning team. The inputs and outputs of the planning process are shown in Figure 3–1.

Figure 3–1.
Detailed Pre-Tender
Planning

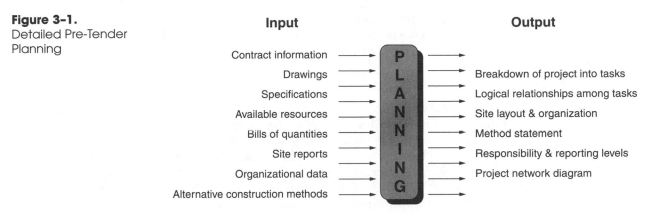

Planning requires a rigorous effort by the planning team. It is not expected that each member of the team knows every aspect of the project; however, a planner must know the different categories of work and be familiar with the terminology and knowledge used in general practice. The team should include or solicit the opinion of experts in all aspects including actual construction experience. This helps produce a realistic plan and avoids problems later on site. Along the course of planning, the team may consider some assumptions and has to have an open mind with regard to alternative construction methods. The most useful planning tool available to the planning team is the experience gained in previous projects. In addition to the planning team experience, the work breakdown structure, checklists, handbooks, software programs, and standard company procedures are also useful tools that can support planning and help prevent overlooking key items that may have cost or schedule implications.

3.3 Planning Steps

As mentioned in the introduction, the first part of planning, covered in this chapter, involves three main steps, as shown in Figure 3–2:

Figure 3–2.
Planning Steps

The details of these steps are described in the following subsections.

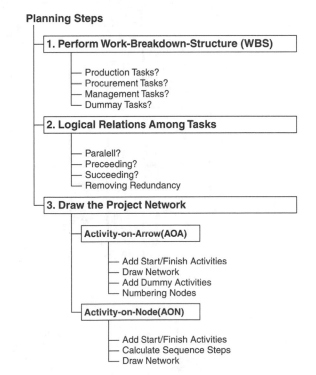

1. Breakdown of project activities.
2. Identifying the logical relationships among activities.
3. Drawing the project network.

3.3.1 Step 1: Project Breakdown

Project breakdown determines what is referred to as a project's ***work breakdown structure (WBS),*** which is basically a breakdown of the whole project into component parts. The WBS is created as a logical hierarchical decomposition of the project into different levels of detail, from a broad level (definable areas), down to a very detailed level (work packages), usually of reasonable and manageable size and duration (Figure 3–3). The smallest element in the decomposition is the "activity" or "task." An example activity is to install column formwork in Area2 of the project shown in Figure 3–3.

As shown in Figure 3–3, WBS elements at various levels relate to the contractor's organization breakdown structure (OBS), which defines the different responsibility levels and their appropriate reporting needs. The figure also shows that work packages are tied to the company unified code of accounts and the databases of resources, unit cost, and productivity data. The unified code of accounts allows cataloging, sorting, and summarizing of all information. It is also suitable for computerized processing and can be used by typical operating personnel. The activity of installing columns formwork of Area 2, for example, which is the responsibility of the general contractor's formwork foreman, has a unique code that represents all its data. This activity has a quantity of 1,200 m^2, an estimated duration of five days, an estimated cost of

Figure 3-3. Work Breakdown Structure (WBS) Linked to the Organization Breakdown Structure (OBS)

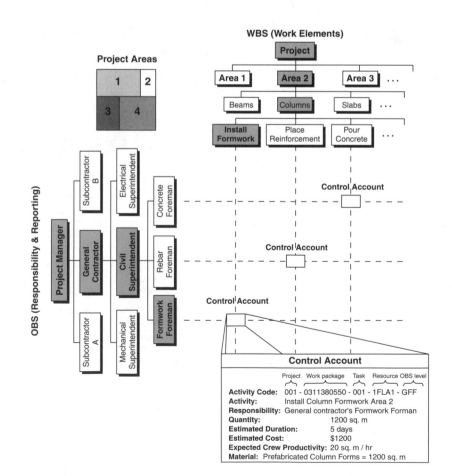

$1,200, and an expected crew productivity of 20 m^2/hr. The WBS, as such, facilitates integration of cost and schedule information for planning, budgeting, and controlling operations.

- **Guidelines for Constructing a WBS:** The building block of a WBS is the *activity*, which is a unique unit of the project that has a specified duration. In other words, an activity can be any function or decision in a project that consumes time. In performing a WBS for a construction project, we need to be especially concerned with five types of activities:
- **Production activities:** activities that involve the use of resources such as labor, material, equipment, or subcontractors. This type of activities can be easily identified by reading the project's drawings and specifications. Some examples are: excavation, formwork, reinforcement work, concreting, and so on. Each production activity can have a certain quantity of work, resource needs, costs, and duration.
- **Procurement activities:** activities that specify the time needed to procure for materials and/or manufacture equipment that are needed for any production activity of the project. Special attention paid to these activities ensures that the work is not delayed waiting for materials or equipment. To facilitate the identification of these activities, the list of production activities may be reviewed along with the drawings and specifications. Examples of such activities are brick procurement, boiler manufacturing and delivery, etc.
- **Management decision activities:** activities that are related to management decisions such as vacations, special delays, approvals, etc. For example, an "Approval" activity of one week may be used to delay the pile cap concreting activity until the client approves the results of a pile test.
- **Hammock activities:** activities that depend on other activities and are not needed for themselves. An example of this type of activities is a dewatering activity that is required as long as excavation and subsurface activities are progressing.
- **Dummy activities:** activities needed for presentation purposes to maintain logical relationships among activities. These are explained later in detail.

Among these types of activities, production activities are usually the first to be identified. Having a list of these production activities, the planning team can then review them and define their requirements of the other types of activities. Accordingly, a complete list of the activities in the project is defined.

To help planners in performing the WBS and identifying the project activities, checklists based on past company records may prove beneficial in preventing omissions. Also, for building projects, the MasterFormat list developed by the Construction Specifications Institute (CSI) is very useful and includes almost all tasks that may be encountered in building construction. The CSI list (Figure 3–4) incorporates 16 main divisions covering tasks from general requirements to mechanical and electrical

Division 1: General Requirements	Division 9: Finishes
Division 2: Site Work	Division 10: Specialties
Division 3: Concrete	Division 11: Equipment
Division 4: Masonry	Division 12: Furnishings
Division 5: Metals	Division 13: Special Construction
Division 6: Wood and Plastics	Division 14: Conveying Systems
Division 7: Thermal Moisture Protection	Division 15: Mechanical
Division 8: Doors and Windows	Division 16: Electrical

Figure 3–4. The Main Divisions in the MasterFormat List for Building Projects

work. Each division has many subitems (a detailed list is included in Appendix E) and can be used as a useful checklist that prevents omissions of necessary items.

In general, there are no firm rules that determine the proper level of detail for a WBS. Planners must decide for themselves what is appropriate and what is not. There are, however, some *guidelines,* which might be used to assist in this task:

1. Define the type of breakdown, whether it is by definable project areas or by definable functions such as civil, architectural, electrical, and mechanical.
2. Break down activities according to the job classifications of resources. For instance, activities such as concrete block masonry and exterior brick masonry might represent two activities.
3. Break down a project according to its various elements. Examples of this procedure are activities such as construct footings, construct columns, install machine base, or prepare budget.
4. Define and separate the areas on site that are repetitive in nature. An example WBS for a typical high-rise building is shown in Figure 3–5.

Although all projects contain activities of the types discussed in this section, the degree of breakdown of the project is controlled by the intended purpose of the plan and who is going to use it. At the working or production level, the detail must be extensive. Upper levels of management, on the other hand, will find rather broad activities acceptable.

For the purpose of demonstrating the process followed by a planner to establish a satisfactory set of activities, consider the following project:

Example:

A contractor has the bidding documents, including the drawings and specifications, for a certain project. Within a certain area in the project's WBS, a concrete foundation work package is included and the planning exercise for it is considered here. The first list of activities that might be put together for this work package is shown in Table 3–1. The activities shown in the list are representative of the production activity category.

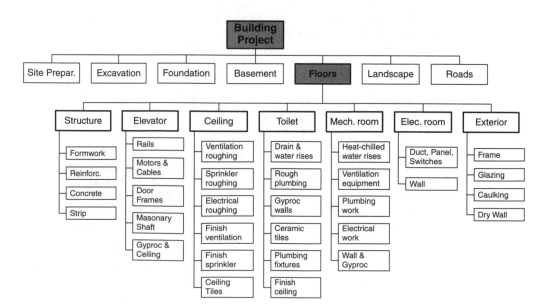

Figure 3–5. Typical WBS for a High-rise Building

Table 3-1. Initial Activity List for Example Project

Activity	Description
A	Site clearing
B	Removal of Trees
C	General Excavation
D	Grading general area
E	Excavation for utility trenches
F	Placing formwork and reinforcement for concrete
G	Installing sewer lines
H	Pouring concrete

Table 3-2. Preliminary Activity List for Example Project

	Activity	Description	
	A	Site clearing	Production activities
	B	Removal of Trees	
	C	Excavation	
	D	Grading	
	E	Excavation for utility trenches	
	F	Placing formwork and reinforcement for concrete	
	G	Installing sewer lines	
	H	Pouring concrete	
Additional activities	**J**	**Obtain formwork and reinforcing steel**	Material Procurement activities
	K	**Obtain sewer lines**	
	L	**Obtain concrete**	
	M	**Steelworker availability**	Labor procurement activity

This list is then reviewed to make sure it includes all the activities needed to accomplish the work. The activity "placing formwork and reinforcement for concrete" suggests that there will be some formwork and reinforcing steel to lay. An additional activity, "obtain formwork," is therefore added to the list. Similarly, the activities "obtain sewer line," "obtain other utilities," and "obtain concrete" are also added to the list. All these activities are of the *procurement* type. The contractor may also realize that all the steelworkers are occupied on another project and, therefore, another activity "Steelworker availability" is also added, representing a *labor procurement* activity. Table 3–2 shows the revised list after incorporating these changes.

3.3.2 Step 2: Identifying Logical Relationships Among Activities

In order to identify the logical relationships among activities, the planning team needs to answer the following questions for each activity in the list:

1. What activities must be finished before the current one can start?
2. What activity(ies) may be constructed concurrently with the current one?
3. What activity(ies) must follow the current one?

The answers to these questions will help establish the activity interdependencies and, accordingly, identify the logical relationships. To illustrate how the logical relationships among activities are identified, let us consider the preliminary activity list of the previous example (Table 3–2). The first activity (A) of Table 3–2 does not depend on any other activity and, therefore, can start right away. Activity B also can start

Table 3–3. Activity List with Dependencies for Example Project

Activity	Description	Depends Upon
A	Site clearing	——
B	Removal of trees	——
C	Excavation	A
D	Grading	A, B, C
E	Excavation for utility trenches	A, B, C
F	Placing formwork and reinforcement for concrete	B, C, J, M
G	Installing sewer lines	B, C, D, E, K
H	Pouring concrete	D, E, F, G, L
J	Obtain formwork and reinforcing steel	——
K	Obtain sewer lines	——
L	Obtain concrete	——
M	Steelworker availability	——

independently from site clearing. It is assumed that activity C (excavation) cannot start until activities A and B have been completed. Also, activity D (grading) can start only when activities A, B, and C are complete. Similarly, activity E (excavation of utility trenches), can not start before the site is cleared, trees are removed, and the excavation is completed. These preceding activities (A, B, and C) are thus inserted after activity E in the list. This process continues until the dependency for each activity has been identified, as illustrated in Table 3–3.

3.3.2.1 Removing Redundant Relationships   When the planning team defines all the logical relationships among the various project activities, sometimes some duplicate or unnecessary relationships may exist in the list. It is desirable, therefore, to identify these redundant relationships and remove them. A typical situation causing a redundant relationship is shown in Figure 3–6. The figure shows a situation in which the list of relationships (second column) includes one redundant relationship. Since A, B, and C are in sequence, only two relationships: "B depends on A," and "C depends on B" are necessary, while the relationship "C depends on A" is redundant. Although the last relationship is true, it is implied in the two relationships specified earlier. By removing this redundant relationship, therefore, we can define what is called the list of Immediately Preceding Activities (IPAs), as shown in the third column.

Defining redundant relationships in a systematic manner is straightforward and begins with the original activity list such as that shown in Table 3–3 or the first two columns of the table in Figure 3–6. We proceed by taking each activity in the list one by one. Starting from activity A, we look at its list of dependents. Since activity A has no dependents, we skip it. We then proceed to activity B, which has A as a dependent. Since that dependent has nothing in its list, we also skip it. We then come to activity C, which has two dependents in its original list: A and B. We look at those dependents one by one. The first dependent (A) has nothing in its list, so we skip it. The second dependent (B) has A in its own list. Since A also appears in the list of C (the ac-

Figure 3–6.
Removing
Redundant
Relationships

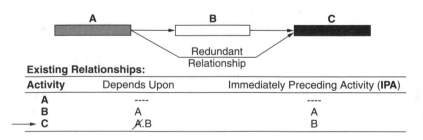

Table 3-4 Activity List After Removing Redundant Relationships

Activity	Description	IPAs
A	Site clearing	——
B	Removal of trees	
C	Excavation	A
D	Grading	~~A~~, B, C
E	Excavation for utility trenches	~~A~~, B, C
F	Placing formwork and reinforcement for concrete	B, C, J, M
G	Installing sewer lines	~~B~~, ~~C~~, D, E, K
H	Pouring concrete	~~D~~, ~~E~~, F, G, L
J	Obtain formwork and reinforcing steel	——
K	Obtain sewer lines	——
L	Obtain concrete	——
M	Steelworker	——

tivity being considered), we remove A from the list of C, leaving B only. The result of this process is the IPAs list.

Following the process of removing redundant relationships for the example project we have, we can obtain the list of IPAs shown in Table 3–4.

3.3.3 Step 3: Drawing the Project Network

The next step after identifying the logical relationships among activities is to represent these activities in a network diagram. Before doing that, we do one more step to ensure that the project has a unified starting point and a unified end point. These are as follows:

- **Checking the Need for a Start Activity:** We may need to add a dummy Start activity to unify the beginning of the project. The need for this dummy activity arises only when there is more than one activity in the project that has no predecessors (i.e., no IPAs). For example, in our foundation project, activities A, B, J, K, L, and M (Table 3–4) are all at the beginning of the project and thus, more than one starting point needs to be unified by a Start activity. To add this new activity at the beginning of the project, we need to change the data in Table 3–4 to reflect the new logical relationships. In our case, each of the activities A, B, J, K, L, and M will have, instead of no IPAs, one IPA which is the Start activity, as shown in Table 3–5.

Table 3-5. Adding Start and Finish Activities

Activity	Description	IPAs
ST	**Start Activity**	——
A	Site clearing	**ST**
B	Removal of trees	**ST**
C	Excavation	A
D	Grading	B, C
E	Excavation for utility trenches	B, C
F	Placing formwork and reinforcement for concrete	B, C, J, M
G	Installing sewer lines	D, E, K
H	Pouring concrete	F, G, L
J	Obtain formwork and reinforcing steel	**ST**
K	Obtain sewer lines	**ST**
L	Obtain concrete	**ST**
M	Steelworker availability	**ST**
FN	**Finish Activity**	**H**

- **Checking the Need for a Finish Activity:** We may need to add a dummy Finish activity to unify the end of the project. The need for this dummy activity arises only when more than one activity at the end of the project. For example, in our foundation project, only activity H in Table 3–4 does not show at all in the IPAs column, meaning it is never a predecessor to other activities. Since H is only one activity, we can conclude that we do have a unified end to the project and no need for a dummy Finish activity. However, for demonstration purposes, if we still add a Finish activity, as shown in Figure 3–5, then its predecessors (IPAs) should be set as the identified list of activities with no predecessors.

Once the activity list is finalized, there are two ways that are commonly used to draw a network diagram for a project:

1. Activity on Arrow (AOA) representation.
2. Activity on Node (AON) representation.

Each method is discussed in detail in the following subsections followed by an explanation of how a network is constructed for the small project example we have.

3.3.3.1 Activity on Arrow (AOA) Method of Network Drawing   This method of drawing a network diagram uses nodes that are linked with arrows. The arrows represent activities while the nodes represent the start and the end of an activity. The following are some basics that must be known before starting the drawing of a project network using the AOA method (Figure 3–7):

- The length of the arrow has no significance and may be straight, curved, or bent.
- Each activity has a definite beginning and end represented by *nodes* that are commonly called *events*.
- For a given activity, the event at the head of an arrow is called the *j event* while that at the tail is the *i event*, as shown in Figure 3–7(a).
- Two activities that are independent of each other will be indicated as two separate arrows having no connection [Figure 3–7(a)].
- When one activity depends upon another, both appear in the diagram as two arrows having a common node. For example, activity B of Figure 3–7(b) depends upon the completion of activity A. Other dependency situations are illustrated in Figure 3–7(c), (d), and (e). In Figure 3–7(c), activity C depends upon the completion of both activities A and B, which appears in the diagram as a *merge*. Similarly, both activities B and C cannot start until activity A is completed, forming a *burst* in the diagram, as shown in Figure 3–7(d). Figure 3–7(e), on the other hand, illustrates a *cross* situation where activities A and B must be completed before activities C and D can start.

In addition to the above, the following are some rules that need to be followed while constructing an AOA network diagram:

- Each activity must have a unique $i - j$ reference numbers, where the number at the tail of the arrow (i) is smaller than that at the head (j) (i.e., $i < j$).
- It is recommended to leave a gap between numbers (e.g., 5, 10, 15, etc.). This will allow for the accommodation of forgotten activities.
- Use horizontal parallel lines (preferably time scaled).
- Avoid back arrows and crossing of arrows, where possible.
- If the network size is large and cannot fit in a single sheet, preferably cut at a "milestone."
- Use subnetworks if needed.

Figure 3-7. Basic
Logic Patterns for
AOA Diagrams

(a) Independent Activities

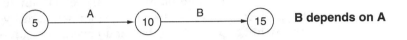

(b) Dependent Activities

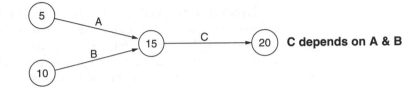

(c) A Merge

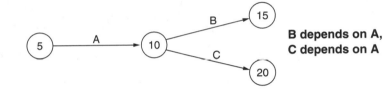

(d) A Burst

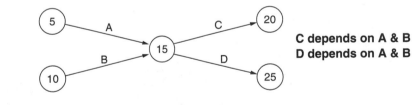

(e) A Cross

While constructing an AOA diagram, a number of situations will need special treatment, particularly adding dummy activities to preserve the required logical relationships. Examples of these situations are:

- When one activity depends upon two preceding activities and another activity depends upon only one of the preceding activities, the cross is not an accurate representation of the logic. Let us assume that activity C depends upon completing activities A and B and activity D depends only upon activity B. The logic can be represented using a dummy activity, as shown in Figure 3–8. A *dummy activity* is a fictitious activity that has no time duration and requires no resources.

- When two or more activities have the same predecessors and the same successors also. Figure 3–9(a) shows an example of two activities, A and B, that begin and end on common events numbered 10 and 20. To describe both activities by the numbers 10–20 is against the rules defined earlier. The solution for this problem is to establish a new event with a dummy activity connecting the new and original events Figure 3–9(b).

When all the redundancies have been eliminated, the AOA network diagram for the project can then be drawn. The planner starts by putting down the activities in an approximate order. Both the *i* and *j* events are added for each activity (numbering). The dependencies are then established by connected all related events with dummies. The resulting diagram is then reviewed and all unnecessary dummies are removed. The resulting AOA diagram for the example project is shown in Figure 3–10.

3.3.3.2 Activity on Node (AON) Method of Network Drawing   This method is also called the *precedence diagram method*. An activity in an AON diagram is represented by a name, to identify the activity, and a corresponding number enclosed in some kind of a symbol. The symbols are usually circular, but they may also be square, hexagonal, or any other convenient shape. The relationships among activities are expressed by a connecting line or a link from one symbol to another.

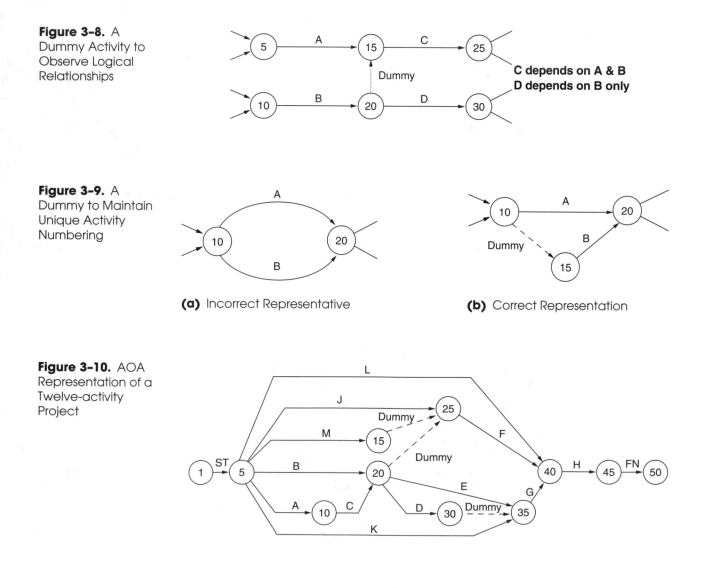

Figure 3-8. A Dummy Activity to Observe Logical Relationships

Figure 3-9. A Dummy to Maintain Unique Activity Numbering

(a) Incorrect Representative   **(b)** Correct Representation

Figure 3-10. AOA Representation of a Twelve-activity Project

Using the AON method, some basics must be known before starting to draw a project network (Figure 3–11):

Figure 3-11. Basic Logic Patterns for AON Diagrams

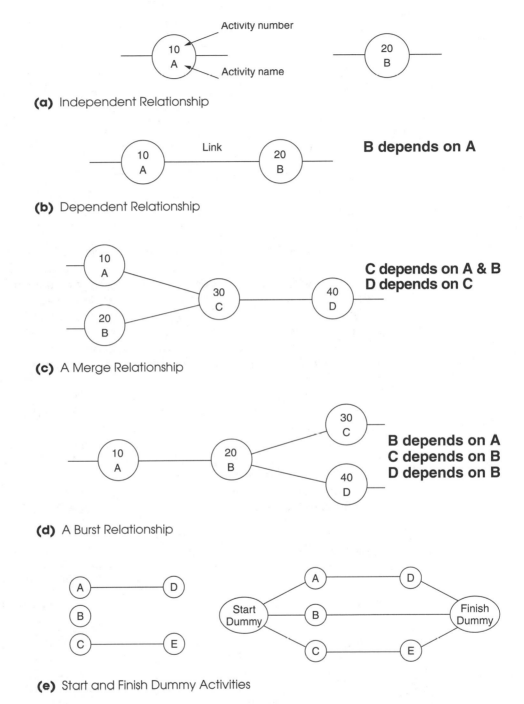

(a) Independent Relationship

(b) Dependent Relationship

(c) A Merge Relationship

(d) A Burst Relationship

(e) Start and Finish Dummy Activities

- Independent activities appear on the diagram as a separate symbols without a connecting line [Figure 3–11(a)].
- If the two activities are related, their symbols should be linked. Figure 3–11(b) illustrates a case where activity A is to be completed before activity B can start.
- The diagram can contain a merge relationship, as in Figure 3–11(c) and a burst relationship as in Figure 3–11(d).

Figure 3-12. A Rough Network Diagram for the Example Project

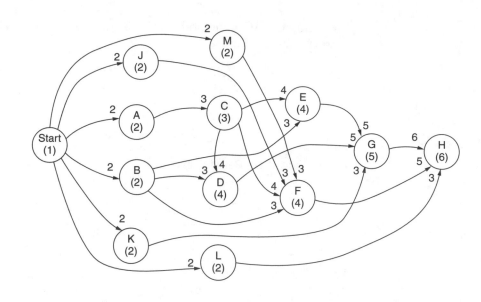

To clearly understand the logic of the AON network before drawing it, some kind of ordering for the activities becomes necessary. This objective is met by placing the activities in sequence step order. A *sequence step* may then be defined as "the earliest logical position in the network that an activity can occupy while maintaining its proper dependencies." Once the sequence step number for each activity is determined (as explained next), we can easily assemble the finished network with the activities arranged in their sequence step order. Afterwards, the activities can be numbered.

To illustrate the process of placing activities in sequence step order and drawing the AON diagram, let us consider our small project. Given the information in Table 3–5, a rough diagram is first drawn from the available activity list, as shown in Figure 3–12. Sequence step 1 (shown between brackets in the figure) is assigned to the start activity. The sequence step number is then increased by one and put as a label at the end of the links leaving an activity. When all the links entering an activity have been labeled, the largest step number from the entering links is chosen as the sequence step number for that activity.

It is also possible to determine the sequence steps without drawing a rough diagram for activities. Using a table format such as that of Table 3–6, the sequence steps

Table 3-6. Determining the Sequence Steps

Activity	IPAs	Sequence Step (SS) Cycle 1
ST	—	SS(ST) = 1
A	ST	2 = 1 + SS(ST)
B	ST	2 = 1 + SS(ST)
C	A	3 = 1 + SS(A)
D	B, C	4 = 1 + Highest of [SS(B), SS(C)]
E	B, C	4 = 1 + Highest of [SS(B), SS(C)]
F	B, C, J, M	4 = 1 + Highest of [SS(B), SS(C), SS(J), SS(M)]
G	D, E, K	5 = 1 + Highest of [SS(D), SS(E), SS(K)]
H	F, G, L	6 = 1 + Highest of [SS(F), SS(G), SS(L)]
J	ST	2 = 1 + SS(ST)
K	ST	2 = 1 + SS(ST)
L	ST	2 = 1 + SS(ST)
M	ST	2 = 1 + SS(ST)
FN	H	7 = 1 + SS(H)

Figure 3-13. The Final AON Diagram for the Example Project

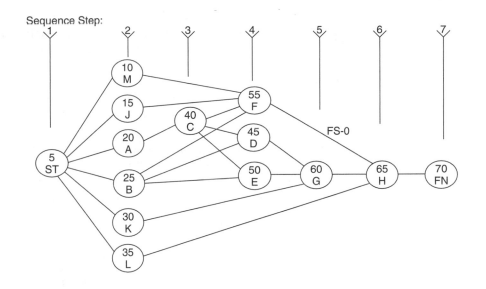

are calculated through cycles. At the first cycle, the start activity is assigned a sequence step 1. We then take all the activities one by one on the list, look at their IPAs, and then assign a sequence step that equals to the highest sequence step of all IPAs plus one. When every activity in the list has been considered, the process is repeated until no changes to the sequence steps are made. In our example project, no changes in number will occur after the first cycle and, therefore, there is no need for any further cycles.

After all the sequence step numbers have been assigned, the final AON diagram can be drawn and permanently numbered. In Table 3-6, the largest sequence step number was 7, which was assigned to the Finish activity and, therefore, the diagram is arranged in seven vertical columns, one for each sequence step. Each activity is positioned on its individual sequence step to allow for drawing the connecting links with as few crossed lines as possible. The last step is to assign the permanent activity numbers. Figure 3-13 shows the final AON diagram for the example with activity numbers assigned in intervals of five.

Difference Between AOA and AON   While both the AOA and the AON representations can be easily performed, it is worthwhile noting the major differences between the two, particularly the benefits of AON representation. In terms of presentation, you may have noticed in AON representation that the use of dummy activities to control the logical relationships was not needed. The sequence step calculation also made the AON to look more organized and clearer to read. The technique is also well suited to computer implementation. On the technical side also, the AON has a major advantage in terms of the types of logical relationships it allows. In AOA networks, any activity (arrow) can only Start after all its predecessors have Finished, which is called a *Finish-to-Start* relationships among activities. In practical situations, however, sometimes we need more diversity in the relationships. For example, we may need to specify that an activity can Start after two days from the start of its predecessor (i.e., a *Start-to-Start* relationship with a two-day lag time). Another example is when an activity can Finish after five days from the Finish time of its predecessor. In all these situations, the AOA representation can hardly be adapted to allow the relationship to be specified on the network. Therefore, while the AOA representation works well for the Finish-to-Start type of relationships among activities only, the AON allows for any of the four types of relationships Finish-to-Start, Start-to-Start, Start-to-Finish, and Finish-to-Finish. Simply, the links in the AON diagram can be labeled with its relationship type and the lag time between each two activities. The relationship between activities F and H in Figure 3–13, for example, shows a Finish-to-Start relationship with zero lag time (default relationship). This feature is simply not possible in AOA representation.

3.4   Case Study Project

Let's now consider a small case study project and apply the planning concepts to it. In the following chapters, we will also continue on the same case study and apply the various project management concepts, following the systematic procedure in Figure 3–14.

In this section, we will deal with the first step of the process which is planning. (highlighted box in Figure 3–14). In the following, a description of the case study project is given and detailed planning is then performed.

Figure 3–14.
Analysis Procedure

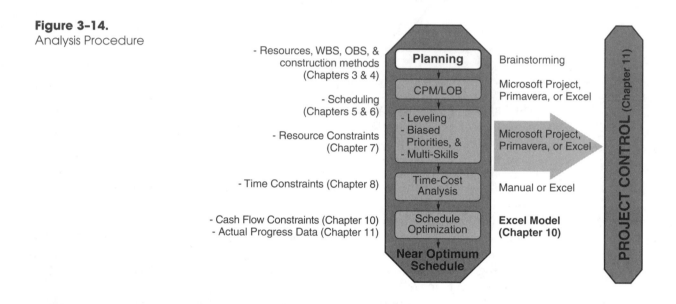

| **Note 1:** | The procedure of Figure 3–14 is straightforward. In each of the following chapters, new concepts will be added and the tools we will use in each chapter will change as appropriate to the material in the chapter. In addition to the various computer tools, an Excel model will be developed and expanded as new concepts are added to it. When we reach Chapter 10, the Excel model will become sophisticated enough to address all management needs simultaneously. At that time, you will be able to automatically import data from your Microsoft Project file and accordingly set up the spreadsheet model for project optimization. At that time also, we will tie all concepts related to estimating and scheduling together. |

| **Note 2:** | The analysis of our case study is scattered in various chapters to demonstrate the application of the various concepts. To bring all these analysis components together, a *new case study* is presented in Appendix B. The new case study will show how the concepts evolve and how to apply various methods to optimize the project. |

Note 3:	In addition to the two case studies solved in the book, Appendix C provides information regarding to other *exercise projects* that students can attempt to solve either individually or in groups.

Please note that the CD accompanying the book has an evaluation version of the Evolver software that comes with a three-month and 80-variable limit (enough time for experimenting with the case studies of this book). A full working copy of Evolver industrial version is also available at the company's website (see Appendix A) and comes with 10-day limit (enough time for experimenting with an example project).

3.4.1   Project Description:

The case study is a small multihouse project. The project management team identified the main segments of a single house (house1), the levels of responsibilities, and the logical relationships between the activities as follows:

Project description:

- 11 work packages (activities) are involved: A, B, C, D, E, F, G, H, I, J, and K.
- Civil activities are: A and B (Substructure) and C, D, E, and F (Superstructure).
- Electrical activities are: G (Interior work) and H (Exterior work).
- Mechanical activities are: I (HVAC), J (Elevator), and K (Plumbing).

Supervision personnel:

- Substructure is supervised by Mark (activity A) and Peter (activity B).
- Superstructure is supervised by Hossam (activities C and F) and Sam (activities D and E).
- All electrical work is supervised by George.
- Adam is responsible for all HVAC and plumbing work; and Wang is responsible for the elevator work.

Logical relationships:

- Activities E and F follow activity B.
- Activity C precedes activity G.
- Activity I follows the completion of activity E.
- The predecessors to activity K are activities H and I.
- Activity D follows activity A and precedes activity H.
- Activity J is preceded by activities F and G.

The questions that relate to planning and we need to answer in this chapter are:
   a. Construct an AON and an AOA network of the project.
   b. Use an Excel list to input the WBS and OBS data.
   c. If the cost of each task is assumed to be $1,000, construct a pivot table report that can show a summary of the costs.

3.4.2   Planning

   a. From the planning information available to us, we can form the relationship table and the network diagrams as shown in Table 3–7, Figure 3–15, and Figure 3–16.
   b. From the project information, the WBS and its link to the OBS are shown in Figure 3–17. A simple Excel list that shows all the information about the activities, the WBS, the OBS, and cost information is shown in Figure 3–18.

Table 3-7. Activity Dependency Table and Sequence Step Calculation.

Activity	IPAs	Sequence Step (SS) Cycle 1
ST	—	SS(ST) = 1
A	ST	SS(A) = 2
B	ST	SS(B) = 2
C	ST	SS(C) = 2
D	A	SS(D) = 3
E	B	SS(E) = 3
F	B	SS(F) = 3
G	C	SS(G) = 3
H	D	SS(H) = 4
I	E	SS(I) = 4
J	F, G	SS(J) = Highest of [SS(F), SS(G)] + 1 = 4
K	H, I	SS(K) = Highest of [SS(H), SS(I)] + 1 = 5
FN	J, K	SS(FN) = 6

Note: A Start (ST) and a Finish (FN) activities have been added.

Figure 3-15. AOA Network of the Case Study

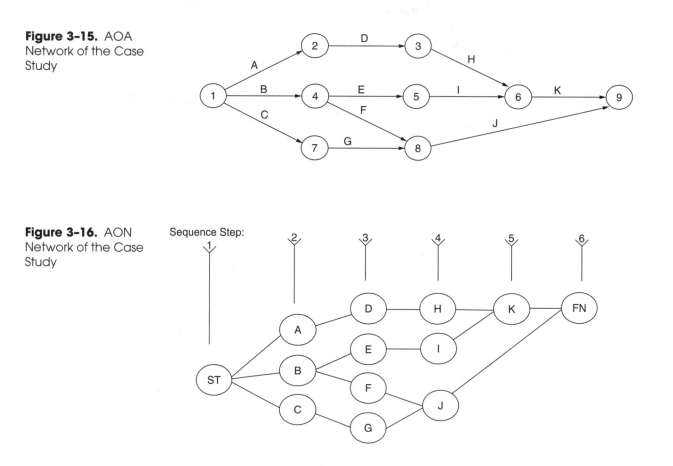

Figure 3-16. AON Network of the Case Study

Figure 3-17. WBS and OBS of the Case Study

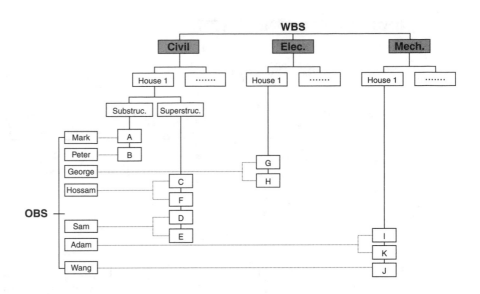

Figure 3-18. An Excel List That Links the WBS to the OBS

	A	B	C	D	E	F	G	H	I	J
1	Item	Desc.	WBS1	WBS2	WBS3	OBS	COST			
2	1	A	Civil	House1	Substruct.	Mark	1000			
3	2	B	Civil	House1	Substruct.	Peter	1000			
4	3	C	Civil	House1	Superstruct.	Hosam	1000			
5	4	D	Civil	House1	Superstruct.	Sam	1000			
6	5	E	Civil	House1	Superstruct.	Sam	1000			
7	6	F	Civil	House1	Superstruct.	Hosam	1000			
8	7	G	Electrical	House1	Interior	George	1000			
9	8	H	Electrical	House1	Exterior	George	1000			
10	9	I	Mechanical	House1	HVAC	Adam	1000			
11	10	J	Mechanical	House1	Elevator	Wang	1000			
12	11	K	Mechanical	House1	Plumbing	Adam	1000			
13										
14										
15				**Notice the**					WBS1	Civil
16				**arrangement of the**			**Page**		WBS2	House1
17				**data in columns: 3**			**Fields**		WBS3	Superstruct.
18				**levels of WBS and one**					OBS	Sam
19				**level of OBS**						
20									Sum of COST	
21									Desc.	Total
22									D	1000
23									E	1000
24									Grand Total	2000
25										

c. A pivot table is shown in Figure 3–18. By selecting the appropriate values from the comboboxes (page fields), the appropriate costs are summed and shown in the pivot table. This Excel feature, therefore, can be used to provide various cost reports at all levels of the WBS and OBS of the project. Other Excel options to summarize the data is the **Data-Subtotals** menu option, which provides the screen shown in Figure 3–19 and can automatically adjust the data list to show cell total costs.

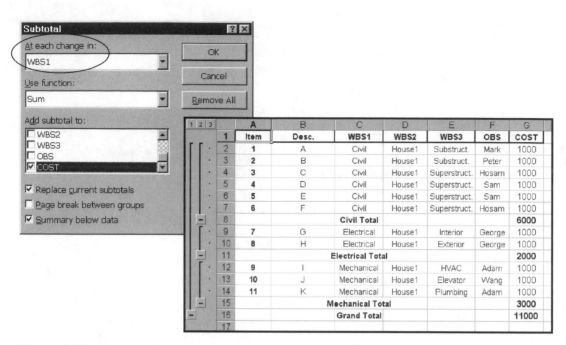

Figure 3–19. Using the **Data-Subtotals** Menu Option to Summarize Data

3.5 Summary

In this chapter, we have started to get deeply involved into the planning process. The end product of the information in this chapter is that you are able to draw a network diagram such as that of Figure 3–13 for any project and link it to a complete work-breakdown structure and the organization breakdown structure. In subsequent chapters, the use of project plans in estimating, scheduling, resource management, and project control will be discussed.

3.6 Bibliography

Ahuja, H. N. (1976). *Construction Performance Control by Networks*. New York: John Wiley & Sons.

Halpin, D. and Woodhead, R. (1998). Construction Management, 2nd ed. John Wiley & Sons.

Harris, R. (1978). *Resource and Arrow Networking Techniques for Construction*. New York: John Wiley & Sons.

Rasdorf, W. and Abudayyeh, O. (1991). Cost and Schedule-Control Integration: Issues and Needs, *Journal of Construction Engineering and Management*, ASCE, Vol. 117, No. 3, pp. 486–501.

Postula, F. (1991). WBS Criteria for Effective Project Control, *1991 AACE Transactions*, AACE, pp. I.6.1–I.6.7.

3.7 Exercises

1. Remove the redundant dummies from the following AOA diagrams, without changing the logical relationships:

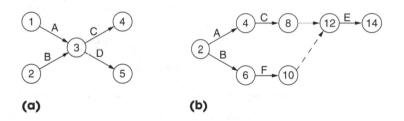

2. Make any necessary corrections to the following AOA representation:
   a. C depends on A and B, while D depends on B only.
   b. E depends on A and B. C depends on A. F depends on B.

(a)   **(b)**

3. Calculate the sequence step numbers for the following project:

Activity	Depends on	Sequence Steps		
A	J, I, P			
B	H			
C	B, G			
D	H, L			
E	A, C, K			
F	—			
G	O			
H	—			
I	N, Q			
J	B, N			
K	J, M, P			
L	—			
M	D			
N	F			
O	—			
P	H, N			
Q	F			

4. Construct AOA and AON networks according to the activity descriptions below. Remove redundant relationships. For the AON network, arrange activities in proper sequence steps. Show all calculations.

   Activity B depends on activity A.

   Activity G follows activities E, F, and D.

   Activity E depends on activities B and A.

   Activity F can start when activities D and B are completed.

   Activity C is followed by activity F and follows activity A.

   Activity D depends upon activities A and B.

5. The set of activities to be considered in the plan for the construction of a concrete foundation is as follows:

Activity	Description
A	Layout foundation
B	Earth excavation
C	Obtain concrete materials
D	Place concrete
E	Obtain steel reinforcement
F1	Cut and bend reinforcement part 1
F2	Cut and bend reinforcement part 2
G1	Place reinforcement part 1
G2	Place reinforcement part 2
H	Obtain formwork
I	Erect formwork
J	Remove formwork
K	Cleanup

   In this project, a crew of steel fixers is used for cutting and bending reinforcement and another crew is used for placing reinforcement. The first part of reinforcement can be placed during formwork erection while the second part should wait for completion of formwork erection. Tabulate the predecessors of each activity and draw an AON network of the work.

6. Construct an AON network according to the activity description below. Label activities by their letters and node numbers. Remove redundant relationships and arrange activities in proper sequence steps. Show all calculations.

   Activity H is followed by activities V, X, L and Z.

   Activity C precedes activity P and follows the completion of activities Q, J, and E.

   The predecessors to activity N are activities E, K, and F.

   Activity O follows activities D and N, and precedes activity P.

   Activity J is preceded by activities T, D, and L.

   Activity I follows activity U and precedes activity Q.

   Activity U can start when activities V and X are completed.

   Activity D follows activity U.

   Activity E depends on activity L and H and precedes activities T, N, and J.

   Activity M is preceded by activities X, L, and Z and is followed by activities K and F.

7. Consider the construction for a reinforced concrete culvert together with the grading of the approaches to the culvert on either side. The culvert consists of a base slab carrying wing walls and a roof. The list of activities to be considered in the plan of the works together with their durations is as follows:

Activity	Duration (weeks)
Construct base slab	4
Construct north apron slab	4
Construct south apron slab	4
Construct north section of side walls	7
Construct south section of side walls	7
Construct north wing walls	6
Construct south wing walls	7
Construct north section of roof	14
Construct south section of roof	14
Grade north approaches	15
Grade south approaches	10

The following information is extracted from the contract method statement:

■ Aprons will be constructed after construction of the base slab and before grading of the approaches.
■ Side walls, wing walls, and roof slabs will be constructed in the north side and then in the south side to economize with formwork.
■ Wing walls will be constructed after side walls.

Prepare the complete plan of the works using the precedence diagram method.

8. Consider the WBS-OBS shown in Figure 3–3. Develop an Excel list containing the WBS elements shown. The list should be a good representation of the WBS hierarchy and involves fields to specify all the data associated with each element as a control account (code, description, responsibility, quantity, . . . etc.). Once the list is developed, design a pivot table that summarizes the data. Print the data list and two pivot table screens showing: the total estimated cost for Area2; and total estimated cost of all the work supervised by the Concrete Foreman. Make reasonable assumptions of missing data.

9. Consider the WBS shown in Figure 3–5. Develop an Excel list containing the WBS elements shown. Assume that the building has 10 repetitive floors. Make reasonable assumptions about a cost value for each element in the WBS and design the list to be a good representation of the WBS hierarchy. Once the list is developed, design a pivot table that summarizes the data. Print the data list and a pivot table that allows the user to select and view the total cost associated with any level in the WBS.

Chapter 4

PLANNING
Part 2—Time & Cost Estimation

After studying this chapter, you will be able to:

- Understand the basics of cost estimation.
- Identify with standard references for cost estimation.
- Establish a simplified estimating system on Excel.
- Modify the project network to show resources, costs, and durations of activities.

Owner, CM	A/E, CM, Owner	Bidders	Owner, CM	Contractor	O & M Staff
• Need • Feasibility • Project Definition • Owner Approval	• Conceptual Design • Owner Approval • Soil Reports • Preliminary Design • Detailed Design • Quantities • Work Documents • Select Project Contract Strategy	• Prepare Bid Proposal + Baselines • Collect Data (site, quantities, specs, resources, tasks, etc) • **Planning** • **Time & Cost Estimation** • Scheduling • Resource Management: deadline, resource constraints, ICI, etc • Bidding Strategy & Markup Estimation • Cash flow analysis • Submit Bid	• Evaluate Bids and Select General Contractor	• Start Construction • Detailed Planning, Estimating & Resource Management • Schedule Updating • Progress Evaluation • Time, Cost, & Quality Control • Commissioning	• O & M • Demolition at End of Service Life
CONCEPT	DESIGN	BIDDING		CONSTRUCTION	O & M

4.1 Introduction

To complete the planning task, in this chapter we will estimate the resources, costs, and time requirements of the individual activities of a project. The objective of this step is to refine our network diagram by adding information related to the resources, time, and cost associated with the activities of a project network. Activity D of our case study project (shown in the figure below), for example, shows the estimate data for a given method of construction, indicating that it can be constructed in eight days by a crew that involves two L1 (labor category) and one E3 (equipment category), for the total direct cost of $18,000. One possibility during the estimation process is to define for each activity a set of possible methods of construction with different resources, durations, and costs. The various construction methods may provide us with options to choose from if we need to speed certain activities to meet a given deadline or resource constraints. These topics will be dealt with in detail in Chapters 7 and 8.

Expected Result of This Chapter after Applying Cost Estimation Concepts

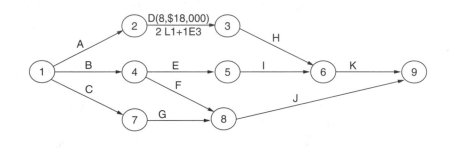

4.2 Construction Estimating: Types and Challenges

Cost estimation is probably the most crucial function to the success of construction organizations. Cost estimating needs to be done in different manners at different stages of a project (Figure 4–1). At the early stages where project budgets are to be decided, detailed information is not available and **parametric** cost estimating techniques are most applicable. With the ever increasing budget restrictions, accurate estimating becomes crucial to the setting of appropriate project budgets. Despite its great importance, the estimating task is neither simple nor straightforward because of the lack of information at this early project stage and to the existence of many external factors that affect a project including political, site, environmental, and technological risks. Once budgets have been approved and project scope becomes well defined, *detailed* cost estimating methods become necessary for construction bidding and project control. On the one hand, accurate bid proposals maintain contractor's success and establish his potential profits while inaccurate estimates could result in either significant monetary losses, if the estimates are too low, or no jobs at all if too high. On the other hand, estimating realistic costs and schedule baselines is certainly important for efficient job control.

The main differences between parametric and detailed estimating methods are summarized in Table 4–1. Essentially, parametric estimating (either preliminary or elemental) is made without working drawings or detailed specifications. The estimator, who often works on behalf of the owner or the designer, may have to make such an estimate from rough design sketches, without dimensions or details and from an outline specification and schedule of the owner's space requirements. The

Figure 4-1.
Estimate Types
Through Project
Phases

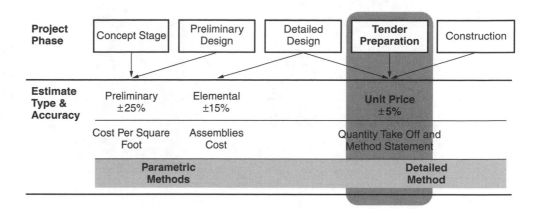

Table 4-1. Parametric Versus Detailed Estimating

Parametric Estimate	Detailed Estimate
• At the early stage of the project • A rough estimate • Easy to perform • More important to the owner • Less expensive than detailed estimate • Based on two or more project parameters • Accuracy can be improved by applying variation factors • Suitable for decisions related to budgeting and the (go / no-go) decision for the project.	• During the planning and scheduling of a project • An accurate estimate • Requires a lot of effort • More important to the contractor • Can cost from 0.5% to 2% of total project cost • Based on quantity take off from drawings and specifications • Based mainly on real cost data of work items • Suitable at the bidding stage

preliminary cost estimate, as such, can serve several purposes, including feasibility analysis, budgeting, preparing owner's funding, and a baseline for evaluating contractors' bids.

The preliminary estimate can price the whole project as a function of some project parameters such as the square footage of floor area or linear foot, etc. In the elemental estimate, on the other hand, the project is first divided into convenient functional elements that are separately priced to improve accuracy. As such, the elemental estimate can reveal the costs distribution of the project components to enable a cost comparison of each element in different projects. This enables the owner to determine how costs could be allocated to obtain a better project. The approach used to conduct a preliminary or elemental estimating is illustrated in Figure 4–2. Basically, we start from stored cost data (e.g., $/floor area) related to some existing projects that most closely resemble the one at hand and then modify these costs, by means of variation factors, to suit the environment of the new project. It is essential, therefore, to keep detailed historical cost records related to past projects or use one of the published references such as R.S. Means, which includes cost data relevant to almost all types of projects in North America.

R.S. Means publishes two notable reference books: *Square Foot Costs*, which can be used for preliminary estimating; and *Assemblies Costs*, which can be used for elemental estimating. Both references were developed based on an average of over 11,500 actual projects reported to R.S. Means from contractors, designers, and owners. The two references are easy to use and can generate an estimate within minutes.

Figure 4-2.
Parametric
Estimating
Approach

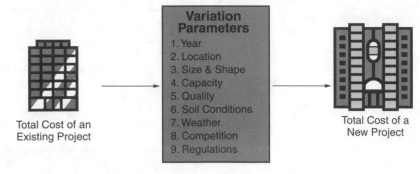

They simply provide tables for the cost per square foot of various projects, in addition to cost adjustment factors for project size and city indexes.

The main difference between parametric and detailed estimating is that detailed estimating can be performed only when work items are identified and a take off of their quantities is possible. A detailed estimate requires analysis of the method of construction to be used, the quantity of work, the production rates of resources, and the factors that affect each subitem. The key to the quantity take off is a structured work-breakdown structure (WBS) with a proper code of accounts for all work items. The most common code, as discussed in Chapter 3, is the 16 divisions of the MasterFormat. It should be noted that job planning has a great influence on the detailed estimate. For example, estimating an accurate unit price (e.g., cost per cubic yard) for an excavation task, to be used for bidding purposes, requires careful consideration of all the details such as dewatering, available excavators, drivers, weather conditions, and so on. As such, detailed cost estimating is feasible only in conjunction with the overall planning and scheduling of the project. It is the purpose of this chapter, therefore, to focus on detailed estimating and its relationship with the overall planning, scheduling, and control of projects.

In general, estimating is not a simple task and the different estimating methods have different associated degrees of accuracy (Figure 4–1). Many mistakes and errors in judgment can happen during the process. Added to the limited time usually available for estimating and bidding, there are three main reasons for the difficulties associated with detailed cost estimation. First, collecting cost data is a difficult task because such information is the confidential property of each construction firm. Second, each construction firm uses its own unique cost estimation approach and most firms do not like to share their approaches or their experience and cost data with other competing construction firms. Third, most firms believe that such information usually makes a difference in being more competitive in the market. Under such environment, contractors devise their own methods for cost estimation based solely on their own experience and, as such, are often inaccurate and unstructured. There is a need, therefore, for a simplified methodology for organizing cost data and effectively utilizing it to develop accurate cost estimates. With cost estimating being one of the major functions in project management, many professional engineering societies had established expert groups specialized in cost estimation, like the American Association of Cost Engineers (AACE).

4.3 Cost Components

Before describing the process of detailed cost estimation for a project, let's have a look at a contractor's point of view of the various cost categories associated with a project and its relation to the bid price that he/she decides. Figure 4–3 shows the main components of a bid price being the direct cost, indirect cost, and markup. These are as follows:

Figure 4–3.
Anatomy of a Bid
Price.

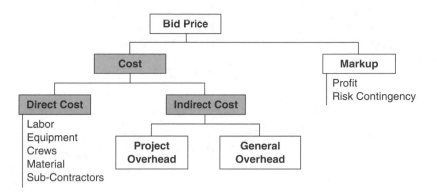

4.3.1 Direct Costs (70 to 90% of total cost)

Direct costs are the costs attributed to the production activities of a project. They are estimated based on detailed analysis of the contract, the site conditions, resource productivity data, and the method of construction being used for every activity. The direct costs are the summation of the cost of the labor, equipment, crews, materials, and subcontractors used in all the activities in a project's WBS. The estimation of the direct costs are discussed in the next sections in detail.

4.3.2 Indirect Costs

These costs are of two categories:

4.3.2.1 Project Overhead (5 to 30% of total cost)   These include the cost of items which cannot be directly charged to a specific work element. These include the costs of utilities, permits, supervisors . . . etc., which service many elements in the project's WBS.

4.3.2.2 General Overhead (0 to 15% of total cost)   These are costs that cannot be directly attributed to a single project and include items such as head office expenses, taxes, etc. The current project's share of these costs can be estimated to be proportional to the project's value as compared to the total yearly volume of the contractor's organization.

4.3.3 Markup (0 to 20% of total cost)

This bid component represents the contractor's added fees (percentage of direct plus indirect costs) that cover two aspects:

Profit: Depending on the business objectives of the contractor organization. This item can be decided based on the level of competition and the contractor's need for winning this particular project.

Risk Contingency: Used to provide a safeguard against uncertain circumstances that are anticipated to affect the project such as weather, labor problems, soil conditions, changes . . . etc.

In estimating these bid components, contractors are faced with various degrees of difficulties. The relative difficulty in estimating appears to be combined with the level of uncertainty involved in the process, being lowest in estimating the direct cost and highest in estimating the markup, as shown in the dotted line of Figure 4–4. As the estimating difficulties increase from direct cost to markup, so does the expected variability among bidders' estimates of these cost items. The solid black range on the figure shows the approximate contribution of each cost element to a total bid. It is

Figure 4-4.
Difficulties
Associated with
Estimating Bid
Components

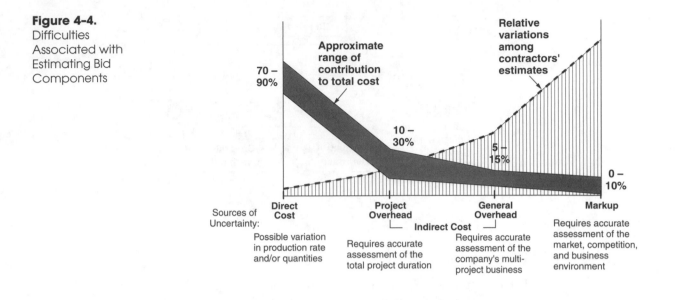

evident that the direct cost, which has the largest contribution to the total bid, exhibits the least variation among contractors' estimates of this item. This is a consequence of the low level of difficulty involved, the well-developed procedures available, and the possibility that all bidders have access to the same resource pool. On the other extreme, contractors' markup estimates, which often have the smallest contribution to total bid, exhibit a high degree of variability among bidders, probably because they include a number of qualitative factors that are difficult to assess. As such, it is likely that the contractors' bid prices, and accordingly their chances of achieving profit/loss, are functions of the markup strategy they select to cope with anticipated project uncertainties. With the markup properly estimated, it can make the bid low enough to win the job and still high enough to ensure a fair profit. Many researchers in the literature, therefore, have been interested in developing bidding strategy models to help contractors decide on the optimum markup value to allocate to a project.

4.4 Detailed Estimating

Detailed estimating for large jobs takes weeks and involves many people from many different disciplines. A general contractor who is preparing a bid will request proposals from subcontractors and material suppliers, and will quantify "take off" and price work that will be done by its own work forces. Where quotes cannot be obtained, contractors will utilize company records and published cost data. The estimate preparation process is shown in Figure 4–5.

Detailed cost estimation, therefore, is as much of an art as it is a science. A good estimator is a person who can use his or her communication and negotiation skills to get the cheapest quotes from suppliers and subcontractors. Good estimators are also the ones who use their experience on past projects to anticipate the impact of a new project situation on the production rates of resources. They are also the ones who are organized and can simplify and possibly computerize or automate some of the tasks involved to facilitate speedy production of estimates without omissions or errors. Details on estimating the various cost components are discussed in the next subsections.

Figure 4-5.
Detailed Estimating
for Bidding Purposes

4.4.1 Direct Cost

The steps needed to estimate the direct costs associated with project activities are shown in Figure 4–5. In this process, however, it is important to understand the basic relationships among the three elements that constitute a *method of construction* for an activity: resources, time, and direct cost. Let's describe these relationships through simple examples. From there, we can understand the characteristics of a good estimate and determine the important estimate-related information that we need to store and organize.

Example 1

If the daily production rate of the crew (CR-06) that works in activity D of our case study project is 175 units/day (e.g., ft^2/day) and the total crew cost per day is \$1,800. The material needed for daily work is 4.5 units of M1 (\$100/unit).

a. Calculate the time and cost it takes the crew to finish 1,400 units.
b. Calculate the total unit cost. Consider an eight hour work day.

Solution:

a. Duration (Units of time) $= \dfrac{\textbf{Quantity}}{\textbf{Production} \text{ per Unit of time}} = \dfrac{\text{ft}^2}{\text{ft}^2/\text{day}}$ **(4.1)**

$$= \frac{1,400}{175} = 8 \text{ days}$$

Cost (\$) **= Duration** (Units of time) $\times$ **Cost** per Unit of time **(4.2)**
$= 8 \text{ days} \times \$1,800 \text{ \$/day} = \$14,400$

Then, **Total Cost** $= \$14,400 + 4.5 \text{ M1 units} \times 8 \text{ days} \times \$100/\text{unit} = \$18,000$

b. Unit Cost $= \dfrac{\textbf{Total Cost}}{\textbf{Quantity}} = \dfrac{\$}{\text{unit}}$ **(4.3)**

$$= \frac{\$18,000}{1400} = \$12.86/\text{unit} \quad (\text{e.g., } \$/\text{ft}^2)$$

Equations 4.1 to 4.3 become the basic relationships we need in detailed estimating based on quantity take off. They give us the duration, total cost, and the unit cost. While Equation 4.2 directly relates time and cost, all equations include variables that directly relate to the resources. The production rate per unit of time in Equation 4.1, for example, depends upon the size of the crew being used. Also, the cost per unit of time in Equation 4.2 is a function of the hourly rates of the resources that constitute the crew. Now, let's take a more detailed example to emphasize the important relationships involved.

Example 2

A small concreting subcontractor keeps track of his resources by creating tables to store information related to his labor, equipment, material, and crew resources. In a separate table, the subcontractor also keeps information related to his frequently used concreting methods, as shown in Figure 4–6.

The subcontractor is currently preparing an estimate for a new concreting job in which he has to pour 500 cubic feet (cu ft) of concrete using pumps. A normal working day is eight hours. The rate for the labor overtime per hour is considered to be 1.5 × normal rate. The crew production during an overtime hour is 90% of their production in a regular hour.

If the subcontractor is free to use either of the two methods of construction, Md4 and Md6, calculate the following:

a. Total cost and time required to finish the job in both cases.

b. Plot a graph showing the duration versus total cost for the two methods of construction.

Solution:

a. Estimating Direct Cost and Duration:

a.1 <u>Method Md4:</u>   One of crew C16 in addition to material M12 are used under normal working conditions to produce 100 cu ft/day. The daily costs relate to the crew hourly rates and the amount of material needed for the production. Then,

$$\text{Duration (days)} = \frac{\text{Quantity}}{\text{Production per unit of time}} = \frac{\text{Cu ft}}{\text{Cu ft/day}} = \frac{500}{100} = 5 \text{ days}$$

Total Cost (\$) = Duration (days) × Cost per day

$$= 5 \text{ days} \times (\text{daily cost of crew C16} + \text{cost of 100 M12 material})$$

$$= 5 \text{ days} \times \quad 2L1 \times \$15 \times 8 = \$240$$
$$3L4 \times \$25 \times 8 = \$600$$
$$1E2 \times (\$40+\$10) \times 8 = \$400$$
$$2E14 \times (\$15+\$5) \times 8 = \$320 + 100 \times \$17$$

$$= 5 \times (\$1560 + \$1,700) = \$16,300$$

Code	Description	Rate/hr
L1	General Laborer	15
L4	Concrete Worker	25

Equipment:

Code	Description	Rental $/hr	Operational $/hr
E2	Crane & Bucket	40	10
E14	Pump & Tool	15	5

Crews:

Code	Description	Unit	Composition
C16	Concrete Crew	cu ft	2L1 + 3L4 + 1E2 + 2E14

Materials:

Code	Description	Unit	Cost/Unit
M12	Ready-mixed concrete	cu ft	17

Methods of Construction:

Code	Description	Unit	Resources	Production/d	Notes
Md4	Concreting by Pump - 8 hrs/day	cu ft	1 **C16** + M12	100	Normal Hours
Md6	Concreting by Pump - 14 hrs/day	cu ft	1 **C16** + M12	?	6 overtime hours/day

Figure 4–6. Resources Used by a Concreting Subcontractor

<u>a.2 Method Md6:</u> One of crew C16 and one of M12 are used under a 14-hour day (six overtime hours). The daily costs relate to the crew hourly rates and the amount of material needed for the production. Then,

Production per day = 100 for working hours + $(0.9 \times 100/8) \times 6$ for overtime
$$= 100 + 67.5 = 167.5 \text{ cu ft/day (note the ``?'' in Figure 4--6)}$$

Then, Duration (days) $= \dfrac{\text{Quantity}}{\text{Production per unit of time}} = \dfrac{500}{167.5} = 3 \text{ days}$

Total Cost ($) = Duration (days) $\times$ Cost per day

= 3 days $\times$ (daily cost of crew C16 + cost of 167.5 M12 material)

= 3 days $\times$ 2L1 $\times$ \$15 (8 + 1.5 $\times$ 6) = \$510

                                      3L4 $\times$ \$25 (8 + 1.5 $\times$ 6) = \$1275

                                      1E2 $\times$ (\$40+\$10) $\times$ 14 = \$700

                                      2E14 $\times$ (\$15+\$5) $\times$ 14 = \$560 + 167.5 $\times$ \$17

= 3 $\times$ (\$3,045 + \$2,847.5) = \$17,677.5

b. Cost and Time Relationship:

Figure 4-7. Activity Direct Cost Versus Activity Duration

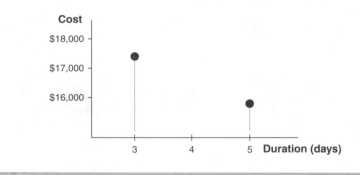

The two examples above serve to demonstrate several important points:

- We can change our resource types, working hours, or the construction technology associated with a certain activity and will obtain a different method of construction that has specific resources, time, and cost.
- The more resources we use in an activity, the less time it takes to construct the activity, but the more costly it becomes (as depicted in Figure 4–7).
- Organizing our resource and estimate data in the form of tables facilitates the estimating task and speeds the process.
- The *essential data* needed for detailed estimating are the resources' rates, the composition of various construction methods, and the production rates of the resources in various construction methods. All this information is project independent and can be collected and stored based on historical records. To estimate the cost for a new job, a reference to one or more of the stored methods of construction is the only thing needed along with the quantity of work to be done. The rest is simple calculations, as presented in Example 2.
- Using a proper coding system for the resources and methods of construction is important in organizing the estimate. The code also facilitates the link between the estimate and the project's WBS and OBS.

One important note to generalize the basic Equation (4.1) for detailed estimating is to introduce a unitless productivity factor (f), as follows:

$$\text{Duration} = \frac{\text{Quantity}}{\text{Production rate} \times f} \tag{4.4}$$

The productivity factor (f) adjusts the duration estimate for an activity to account for many of the practical aspects that describe the environment under which the activity resources have to perform the work. Some of these aspects are:

- Local weather conditions.
- Learning curve.
- Labor unrest.
- Crew absenteeism.
- Economic activity level (recession vs. boom).
- Space congestion.
- Regulatory rules and cultural habits.
- Design changes and rework.
- Overtime.
- Uncertainty (owner attitude, project location, management conditions, etc).

It is very difficult, however, to assess the impact of these individual aspects, or a combination of them, on the production rate of a working crew. Estimating the factor (f), therefore, has concerned a large number of researchers who studied the impact of these aspects, particularly local weather conditions, as the most influential aspect. One simple approach to use for weather-sensitive activities is a different value for (f) associated with each month of the year (e.g., 0.7 for January to represent bad weather conditions and 1.0 for August to represent favorable conditions, etc.). As such, the factor (f) in Equation 4.4, reduces the production rate under bad weather conditions, resulting in increased duration of the activity. To use this simple adjustment, however, the month in which the activity takes place must be estimated.

4.4.2 Using Published Cost Data

A lot of published cost data is available commercially and can provide support during the estimating process. One important source is R.S. Means references, which publishes several publications, including:

- *R.S. Means Forms Book.*
- *R.S. Means Building Construction Cost Data Book.*
- *R.S. Means Heavy Construction Cost Data Book.*

The forms book provides various forms that can be used during the estimating and construction stages. For example, a "Site Analysis Form" can be used to collect data from the site to ensure that no items with cost implications are overlooked. The latter two cost books are very important pricing guides and provide data related to crew formations, hourly rates, and production rates of crews in various tasks related to buildings and heavy construction, respectively.

The R.S. Means cost books are readily usable for estimating purposes. The books are organized in accordance with the Construction Specifications Institute's 16 Divisions of the Masterformat. Under these 16 main divisions, the book contains information about more than 21,000 items (construction methods). These items use a total of 345 predefined crew configurations provided in the book. An example page of some of the items in the *Building Construction Cost Book* is shown in Figure 4–8.

The coding system is composed of three sets of numbers to classify items. Considering one of the items in Figure 4–8, for example, 022-246-0100, which represents:

022   Earth work (part of CSI coding 02 for site work)
246   Excavation, bulk, scrapers
0100 Elevating scraper 8.4 m3, sand and gravel 450-m haul

Each item in the list of Figure 4–8 includes information related to the crew code, which describes the crew composition in terms of labor and equipment categories. Crew production rate is also included with the item. It is noted that crew production is represented in two types of information in separate columns: the daily production in *units/day*; and alternatively, *labor hours/unit* of production. Both representations can be derived from each other (example shown in Figure 4–9). The basic difference between the two representations is that the daily production in units/day can be achieved only by a prespecified crew configuration. In the estimating job, therefore, the estimator can develop the estimate very easily (as demonstrated in Example 2 earlier) given that he or she is using the exact crew configurations. The labor hours per unit, on the other hand, is more general and can be used with various crew configurations that can be decided at the time of the estimate. For example, if a concreting job requires 0.5 labor hours per cubic feet, then, the estimator may estimate the duration to pour 100 cu ft (requiring a total of $100 \times 0.5 = 50$ labor hours) in various ways: a) using a crew of 4 labors, 8 hours/day will take a duration of about 1.5 days; or b) using 5 labors, 10 hours/day will take a duration of 1 day.

Figure 4–8. Typical Building Construction Cost Data

Coding System

022 | Earthwork

2 SITE WORK

	Code	022 200 Excav./Backfill/Compact.		CREW	DAILY OUTPUT	LABOR HOURS	UNIT	1998 BARE COSTS MAT.	LABOR	EQUIP.	TOTAL	TOTAL INCL O&P	
242	3040	Clay		B-10W	294	.041	m3		1.03	1.41	2.44	3.13	242
	3200	45 m haul, sand & gravel			237	.051			1.28	1.75	3.03	3.88	
	3220	Common earth			206	0.058			1.47	2.01	3.48	4.47	
	3240	Clay			130	0.092			2.33	3.18	5.51	7.10	
	3300	90 m haul, sand & gravel			107	.112			2.83	3.87	6.70	8.6	
	3320	Common earth			91.75	.131			303.	4.51	7.81	10	
	3340	Clay			76.46	.157			3.96	5.40	9.36	12.05	
	4000	149 KW, 15 m haul, sand & gravel		B-10B	1,070	.011			.28	.78	1.06	1.29	
	4020	Common earth			940	.013			.32	.89	1.21	1.46	
	4040	Clay			589	.020			.51	1.41	1.92	2.34	
246	0010	**EXCAVATION, BULK, SCRAPERS**	R022 -240										246
	0100	Elevating scraper 8.4 m3, sand & gravel 450 m haul		B-33F	528	.027	m3		.68	1.79	2.47	3.01	
	0150	900 m haul			466	.030			.77	2.03	2.80	3.42	
	0200	1500 m haul			386	.036			.93	2.46	3.39	4.12	
	0300	Common earth			459	.031			.78	2.06	2.84	3.47	
	0350	900 m haul			405	.035			.88	2.34	3.22	3.93	
	0400	1500 m haul			336	.042			1.07	2.82	3.89	4.73	
	0500	Clay, 450 m haul			287	.049			1.25	3.30	4.55	5.55	
	0550	900 m haul			252	.056			1.42	3.76	5.18	6.30	
	0600	1500 m haul			210	.067			1.71	4.51	6.22	7.55	
	1000	Self propelled scraper, 10.7 m 3¼ push dozer, sand											
	1050	And gravel, 450 m haul		B-33D	703	.020	m3		.51	2.64	3.15	3.68	

Important: See the Reference Section for critical supporting data – Reference Nos., Crews & City Cost Indexes

Code for Material & Supporting Info. — Crew Code — Crew Production Rate/day — Labor hrs/Unit — Detailed Unit Costs

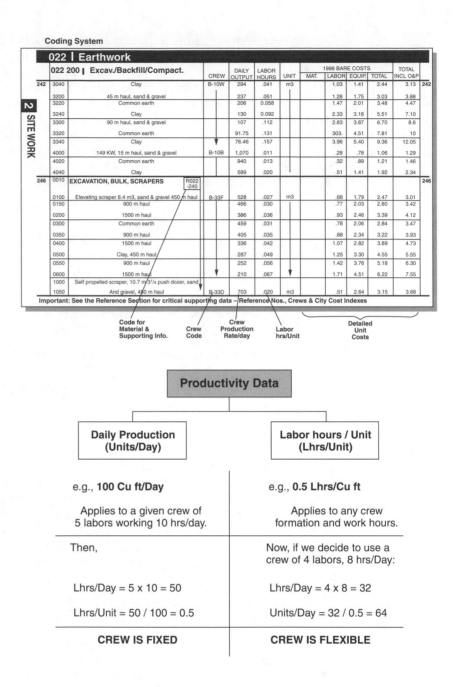

Figure 4–9. Two Alternative Representations of Production Information

In addition to work items and their crews and production rates, the R.S. Means cost data books include details on the cost of labor, equipment, and material of each item, as shown in Figure 4–8. Added to that are various cost adjustments such as indexes for cost adjustment for 305 cities in North America.

Example on Estimating:

As shown in Figure 4–10, various construction methods for rough carpentry are listed.

We assume that the method with code 061-114-2720 is used for carpentry. This method uses crew F-2 which produces a daily production of 1.49 units/day. The composition of the F-2 crew and the hourly rates are shown in Figure 4–11.

Figure 4–10.
Construction
Methods for Rough
Carpentry

		061 100 | Wood Framing		CREW	DAILY OUTPUT	LABOR-HOURS	UNIT	BARE COSTS MAT.	LABOR	EQUIP.	TOTAL	TOTAL INCL O&P	
114	0100 2650	FRAMING, JOISTS Joists, 2" x 4"	R061 -010	F-2	.83	19.277	M.B.F.	550	485	22	1,057	1,400	114
	2655 2680	Pneumatic nailed 2" x 6"	R061 -030	F-2A F-2	.96 1.25	16.667 12.800		550 525	420 325	78 14.70	1,048 864.70	1,350 1,100	
	2685 2700	Pneumatic nailed 2" x 8"		F-2A F-2	1.44 1.46	11.111 10.959		525 565	280 276	52 12.60	857 853.60	1,075 1,075	
	2705 2720	Pneumatic nailed 2" x 10"		F-2A F-2	1.68 1.49	9.524 10.738		565 655	240 271	44.50 12.35	849.50 938.35	1,050 1,175	
	2725 2740	Pneumatic nailed 2" x 12"		F-2A F-2	1.71 1.75	9.357 9.143		655 705	236 230	44 10.50	935 945.50	1,150 1,150	
	2745 2760	Pneumatic nailed 2" x 14"		F-2A F-2	2.01 1.79	7.960 8.939		705 730	201 225	37.50 10.30	943.50 965.30	1,125 1,175	
	2765 2780	Pneumatic nailed 3" x 6"		F-2A F-2	2.06 1.39	7.767 11.511		730 1,200	196 290	36.50 13.25	962.50 1,503.25	1,150 1,800	

061 | Rough Carpentry

Figure 4–11. Data
for Crew F-2

Crew No.	Bare Costs		Incl. Subs O & P		Cost Per Labor-Hour	
Crew F-2	Hr.	Daily	Hr.	Daily	Bare Costs	Incl. O&P
2 Carpenters	$25.20	$403.20	$40.25	$644.00	$25.20	$40.25
2 Power Tools		18.40		20.25	1.15	1.27
16 L.H., Daily Totals		$421.60		$664.25	$26.35	$41.52

For the purpose of estimating direct costs, we divide the quantity of the work by the production (1.49/day) to determine the duration in days. Also, quantity multiplied by unit cost ($1,175) determines the total direct cost.

4.4.3 Indirect Cost

As explained earlier, the two components that comprise the indirect costs for a project are the project overhead and the general (head office overhead). According to the CSI format, which is followed by R.S. Means, overhead is classified as general requirements and is covered in the Division 1 (see Figure 3–4 in Chapter 3, and Appendix E). The R.S. Means approach to estimating overhead and profit is basically to add 10% on all materials, 10% on equipment, 10% on subcontractor costs, and an average of 58.8% on labor bare costs. As such, the overhead associated with labor is the greatest of any of the cost categories. The bare costs covers the worker's take-home pay plus fringe benefits, vacation, and paid sick days. The 58% overhead charges will then cover workers' compensation insurance (19%); federal and state unemployment costs, social security taxes, builder's risk insurance, and public liability insurance (16.8%); general overhead (13%); and profit (10%).

With the O&P added to the estimate as a percentage of labor, equipment, material, and subcontractors costs, the O&P become roughly estimated. Alternatively, we can estimate detailed project overhead and general overhead costs as follows:

4.4.3.1 Project Overhead These are field-related costs that are incurred in achieving contract completion, but which do not apply directly to any specific work item. A detailed analysis of the particular demand of the contract is a reliable way to arrive at an accurate estimate of these costs. Companies develop their own forms and checklist for estimating these costs. One example is included on the CD of this book as an

Excel template. The file **Indirect.xls** has a user-friendly interface and formulas that help the user estimate the five main components that comprise the project overhead (Figure 4–12):

- Variable Indirects:
  i.e., costs that depend on project duration, including wages and salaries of supervisors, medical and safety personnel, etc.
- Fixed Indirects:
  A. Project office expenses (equipment, supplies, etc.);
  B. Site installations (cranes, temporary facilities, etc.); and
  C. Operations of site installations (to maintain the operation of part B).

Each of these components includes many subitems (see Table 4–2). The variable part of the indirect cost (e.g., supervisors, cranes, and financing costs) is highly dependent on the project duration and as such requires accurate assessment of the project schedule. It is important, therefore, to finalize the indirect costs after accurate assessment of the project schedule and its impact on direct cost (will be covered in detail in Chapters 8 to 10).

4.4.3.2 General Overhead These are fixed indirect costs unrelated to a specific contract, rather to the operation of the contractor's head office. These costs can be estimated using the following formula:

$$\text{General Overhead} = \frac{\text{Project Direct Costs} \times \text{Total Head-Office Overhead in a Year}}{\text{Expected Sum of Direct Costs of All Projects during the Year}}$$

In the template of Figure 4.12, also Table 4.2, these costs can be added under item *D. Others*.

It is noted that the equation used here is a direct function of proper estimation of direct costs.

Figure 4-12. Excel Template For Indirect Cost Estimation

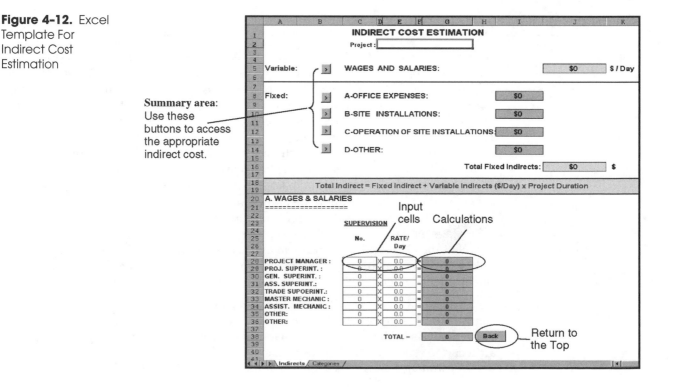

Table 4–2. List of Project Overhead Costs

Variable Cost ($/day): WAGES & SALARIES	Fixed Cost: A. OFFICE EXPENSES	Fixed Cost: B. SITE INSTALLATIONS	Fixed Cost: C. OPERATION OF SITE INSTALLATIONS
SUPERVISION • PROJECT MANAGER • PROJ. SUPERINT. • GEN. SUPERINT. • ASS. SUPERINT. • TRADE SUPOERINT. • MASTER MECHANIC • ASSIST. MECHANIC **ENGINEERING** • PROJECT ENGINEER • OFFICE ENGINEER • COST ENGINEER • SCHEDULE ENGR. • DESIGN ENGINEER • FIELD ENGINEER • ENGR. TECHNICIAN **OFFICE & CLERICAL** • PERSONNEL MANAGER • PURCHASING AGENT • ACCOUNTANTS • PAYMASTER • WAREHOUSE CHIEF • GENERAL HELP • EQUIPMENT CLERK **MEDICAL & SAFETY** • SAFETY SUPERVIS. • FIRST AID MEN • NURSES • SECURITY MEN **EMPLOYEE BENEFITS** • WORKMEN'S COMPENS. • SOCIAL SEC. & PEN. PLAN • UNEMPLOYMENT INS. • HEALTH, WELFARE, GROUP INS. • VACATION/HOLIDAY PAY **TRAVEL TIME PAY** • TRAVELLING EMPLOYEES **LABOR ADJUSTMENTS** • SHIFT PREMIUMS • HIGHT PREMIUMS • UNDERGROUND PREMIUMS • COMPRESSED AIR PREMIUMS • PRODUCTION BONUS • EQUIPMENT PREMIUM	**OFFICE EQUIPMENT/ SUPPLIES** • FURNITURE & FURNISHINGS • EQUIPMENT (e.g., COMPUTERS) • SUPPLIES & STATIONARY • POSTAGE • BADGES, TENCILS • PAYROLL & ACC. COMPUTER **ENGIN. EQUIPMENT/SUPPLIES** • SURVEYING EQUIP. & SUPPLIES • REPRODUCTION EQUIP. & SUPPL. • DRAFTING EQUIP./SUPPLIES • COMPUTER EXPENSES • PHOTOGRAPHIC EQUIP. & SUPPL. • CONSULTING, TESTING & INSP. **LEGAL & PUBLIC RELATIONS** • LEGAL/AUDIT FEES • DONATIONS / PR **MEDICAL & SAFETY SUPPLIES** • MEDICAL EXAMINATIONS • MEDICAL SUPPLIES • SAFETY & WEATHER WEAR • SIGNS & BARRICADES • FIRE PROTECTION • SUPPLIES **EMPLOYEE MOVE IN, MOVE OUT** • HOURLY EMPLOYEES • SALARIED EMPLOYEES • HEAD OFFICE VISITS • EXECUTIVES • FAMILY MOVE IN/OUT **CATERING COST** • ROOM AND BOARD • ALLOWANCE • LIVING EXPENSES **NONRECOVERABLE INS. COSTS** • INSURANCE CLAIMS (e.g., AUTO) **INSURANCE, TAXES & BONDS** • INSURANCE • TAX (PROPERTY & BUSINESS) • BONDS (PERFORMANCE) • EQUIPMENT TAXES • EQUIP. & VEHICLE LICENSE **COMMUNICATION EXPENSES** • LONG DISTANCE CHARGES • TELEX, FAX LINE CHARGES **FREIGHT EXPENSES** • FREIGHT AND EXPRESS COST • HANDLING, PACKING **MISCELLANEOUS** • PARTIES/ENTERTAINMENT • DUES, LICENSES, PERMITS • YARD, OFFICE RENTALS	**EQUIPMENT ERECTION NONPAY ROADS & YARDS** • CONSTRUCTION OF SITE HAUL • PREPARATION OF CAMP SITES • YARD AREAS, & STORAGE SITES • CONSTRUC. OF DOCKS, PIERS • LOADING PLATFORMS, etc. • CONSTRUCTION OF FENCES **BUILDING ERECTION & DISMANT** • OFFICE, WAREHOUSE, etc. • CAMP AND HOUSE TRAILERS • WORKSHOPS • EXPLOSIVES MAGAZINES • WORK PLATFORMS • MATERIAL WEIGH SCALES **SERVICES INSTALL. & REMOVAL** • WATER SYSTEM • SEWAGE SYSTEM • DRAINAGE SYSTEM • AIR SUPPLY AND DISTRIBUTION • HEATING AND DISTRIB. SYSTEM • STANDBY GENERATORS • POWERLINES, LIGHTING SYSTEM • ELECTRICAL HOOK UPS • COMMUNICATIONS • INSTALLATION **SHOP EQUIP, & SHOP TOOLS** • PURCHASE/INSTALL. OF HOISTS • SMALL TOOLS, WINCHES, JACKS, etc. **FINAL CLEAN UP** • COST OF LABOR, EQUIP., OR MATERIAL TO CLEAN UP THE SITE AT COMPLETION	**ROAD & YARD MAINTENANCE** • COST OF SURFACE MAINTENANCE, DUST CONTROL, SNOW REMOVAL, DRAINAGE MAINTENANCE **PROJECT OPERATION & MAINT.** • TRAILOR LOT RENTALS • BUILDING REPAIRS & MAINT. • BUILDING INTERNAL SERVICES • JANITORIAL SERVICES • GARBAGE PICKUP • FUEL SUPPLY **SERVICES, OPERATION & MAINT.** • WATER SYSTEM • SEWAGE SYSTEM • DRAINAGE SYSTEM • AIR SUPPLY AND DISTRIBUTION • HEATING AND DISTRIB. SYSTEM • STANDBY GENERATORS • POWERLINES, LIGHTING SYSTEM • ELECTRICAL HOOK UPS • COMMUNICATIONS INSTALLATION **INDIRECT TRANSPORTATION** • PICKUPS, CREW CABS, CREW TRANSPORT, CREW BUSES, etc. **WAREHOUSE OPERATIONS** • VEHICLE AND DRIVER • PICK UP SERVICES • YARD EQUIPMENT **SERVICE & MAINT. EQUIPMENT** • SHOP SUPPLIES (e.g., BOLTS) • WELDING SUPPLIES • GENERAL SHOP LABOR **EXPENDABLES** • COST OF MACHINE ATTACHMENTS THAT UNDERGO WEAR (e.g., BITS) **ELECTRICAL POWER CHARGES** **PROJECT SMALL TOOLS**

Fixed Cost: D. OTHERS

FINANCING
• COST OF FINANCING THE JOB CALCULATED AT CURRENT INTEREST RATE

HEAD OFFICE SUPPORT
• MONTHLY OR % CONTRIBUTION TO MAINTENANCE OF HEAD OFFICE FACILITIES & STAFF

CONTINGENCIES
• ESTIMATED COST OF INTERFERENCES INCLUDING FLOODS, TAX INCREASE, EARTHQUAKES, STRIKES

BONUS OR PENALTY

ESCALATION

4.4.3.3 Total Indirect Cost   Once the template of Figure 4.12 is filled, the total indirect cost is obtained by adding up the project overhead and the general overhead components. The total indirect cost can then be expressed in the following straight line relationship:

> Total Indirect = **a + b X**
>
> = **Fixed Indirects + Variable Indirects ($/day) x Project Duration**

4.4.4   Finalizing a Bid Proposal

When the O&P is added to the estimate as percentages for labor, equipment, material, and subcontractors costs, as in the R.S. Means approach, the O&P become fairly distributed among the contract items and the final bid can be easily summed. On the other hand, when the direct and indirect costs are calculated separately, as explained in the previous section, two more steps are needed to finalize the bid: (a) estimating a proper markup percentage to cover for profit and risk contingency; and (b) adding all the cost components to formulate the final bid.

The markup is usually assessed at what is considered to be possible in the prevailing market conditions. However, the following factors should be taken into consideration when deciding the markup:

- Competition.
- Contractor's desire for work.
- Level of project uncertainty.
- Project type, size, and complexity.
- Contractor's experience on similar projects.
- Market conditions.

Estimating a percent markup is more of an art than it is science and relies heavily on experience and the gut feeling of contractors. Many statistic-based models have been developed in the literature to support contractors' decision on bid/no-bid and markup estimation (covered in Chapter 9). The key to theses models is storing information related to past bids and analyzing the bidding behavior of competing companies. One approach is also to analyze the behavior of the lowest bidder in past bids. This analysis helps in determining an optimum markup value that makes the bid low enough to win the job, yet high enough to attain a fair profit.

Once a markup percentage is decided, the total of direct cost, indirect cost, and markup form the total bid price. This works fine for lump-sum contracts because the contractor is obliged to submit only one figure of his final bid. However, in unit price contracts, the contractor is required to submit unit prices associated with the bid items, which embed all the costs. While direct cost are estimated for each item independently, contractors need to distribute the total of the indirect cost plus markup among the items to determine the final unit prices. Generally, there are two ways by which the contractor can allocate the indirect cost and markup to the bid items. A straightforward method is to distribute these costs to all items according to their relative direct costs. This is known as "balanced bidding." Alternatively, a contractor can perform "unbalanced bidding" by raising the prices on certain bid items and decreasing the prices on others so that the total bid price remains the same. There are two main reasons for unbalancing:

1. Improving project financing; and
2. Adjusting the bid under expected quantity change.

To improve project financing, a contractor can raise the unit prices for the bid items that come early in the schedule and also reduce the prices for later items. This enables the contractor to charge more for early work and accordingly will receive a higher owner payment such that his own financing cost is less. Also, when the contractor knows by experience that the bid quantities are inaccurate, he or she can adjust his or her prices to attain a competitive edge and possibly a more potential profit. For example, when a certain item is expected to have much less quantity than stated in the bid package, the contractor may reduce the bid price on this item to produce a competitive bid, yet without much loss since the item is going to have less quantity than specified. Also, when the contractor expects that a certain item will increase in quantity, he or she may increase the unit price on such an item to increase his or her potential profit. In all cases, however, bid unbalancing is a risky task to the contractor. Some owners analyze the bids to detect bid unbalancing and disqualify the bidders who employ this approach.

4.5   Commercial Estimating Software

Computers have clearly added speed, power, and accuracy to construction cost estimation. A wide variety of software systems for estimation have been developed for commercial use (Table 4–3). Many of these systems also provide integration with various modules for quantity take off, scheduling, and CAD.

These software tools can organize the estimate, link it to resource databases, provide reports, and possibly integrate with other systems. In principal, they do the same functions as the Excel estimating system presented in this chapter. They, however, vary in their strengths and weaknesses. Also, in many situations, they involve a rigid structure that is different from what the user is familiar with. A thorough investigation of their capabilities is, therefore, highly recommended before purchasing software. Experimenting with a working demo version may be a good evaluation for the suitability of certain software to the requirements of the user. A good Internet search can also be helpful in this regard (see Appendix A of web resources).

Table 4–3. Cost Estimation Software Systems

Computer Software	Description
Win Estimate	Building construction estimator assigns WBS tags to each item.
Success	Cost estimation and cost management with a link to scheduling software.
Design 4/Cost	Preliminary estimate based on square foot system.
Microfusion for Windows	An advanced integrated planning, estimating, proposal preparation, and performance management system.
Timberline	A cost estimating software with modules for CAD and scheduling.
G2 Estimator	Cost estimation based on previous experience.
Best Estimate	Cost estimation software.

4.6   Back to Our Case Study Project

In terms of the road map to our case study, the material in this chapter continues the planning (shaded box) by estimating the resources, durations, and costs of the activities' methods of construction.

Figure 4–13. Case Study Outline

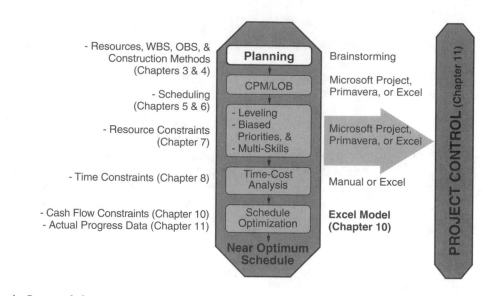

4.6.1   A Spreadsheet-Based System

With our knowledge of the basic equations for cost and time estimation, this section presents you with a simplified Excel system that uses the Excel functions discussed in Chapter 2. The system represents an integrated approach for planning, estimating, schedule optimization, and project control (see Figure 4–14). The whole system fits into a single Excel file **Case-Study.xls,** which comes on the CD of this book. All the data in this file belong to our case study project but you can use the same file as a template for other projects. You can experiment with the various sheets of this Excel file and view the underlying formulas (shaded cells). The two main components of the system are:

a. a depository of project-independent data.
b. a project management system for estimating, scheduling, and project control.

Figure 4–14.
Components of the
Excel Project
Management
System

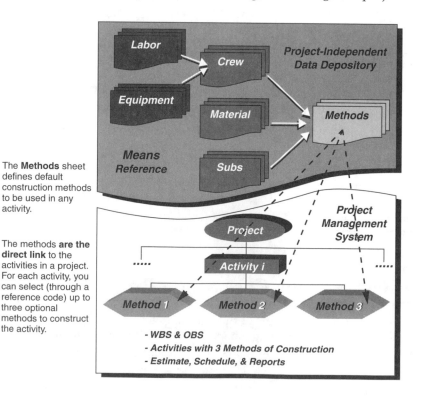

The **Methods** sheet defines default construction methods to be used in any activity.

The methods **are the direct link** to the activities in a project. For each activity, you can select (through a reference code) up to three optional methods to construct the activity.

4.6.1.1 Data Depository The data depository of the system is needed to provide data for the project management system in a manner that reduces redundancy, saves time and cost, and increases productivity. Similar to the way we did in Example 2 before, the design of the data depository in Excel involved setting up several data lists, establishing relationships among them, and designing related reports. As shown in Figure 4–14, it incorporates the following six worksheets. A description is these sheets is provided next along with various screen shots:

- **5 Resource Sheets:** Labor, Equipment, Crews (combination of labor and equipment), Materials, and Subcontractors;
- **1 Construction Methods Sheet.**

Labor: The *labor list* (Figure 4–15) contains five fields: code; description; total hourly rate (Rate/hr); basic hourly rate; And availability constraints (not used here). Basic rates are obtained by a means-based average of wage rates from 30 major U.S. cities. The total rate (rate/hr) is then calculated by multiplying the basic rate with a constant, 1.58, which is an average of the adjustments used by means to the basic rate for workers' compensation, overhead, and profit (O&P).

Equipment: The equipment basic rate (Figure 4–16) includes not only rental cost, but also operating costs such as fuel, oil, and routine maintenance. An average of 10% is added to the basic rate for O&P to calculate the rate/hr.

Crews: Crews were defined by assigning up to five labor and equipment resources, using their codes as reference (Figure 4–17). Accordingly, the calculations in columns N to R use the VLOOKUP function to determine the individual costs per day of the five resources. These costs are then summed in column C to determine the total crew rate per day, Rate/d.

Material: The material basic unit cost (Figure 4–18) includes delivery to the site, without including the sales tax or allowance for wasted material. An average 10% is added to the basic unit cost for O&P to calculate the Cost/Unit.

Figure 4–15. Labor Sheet

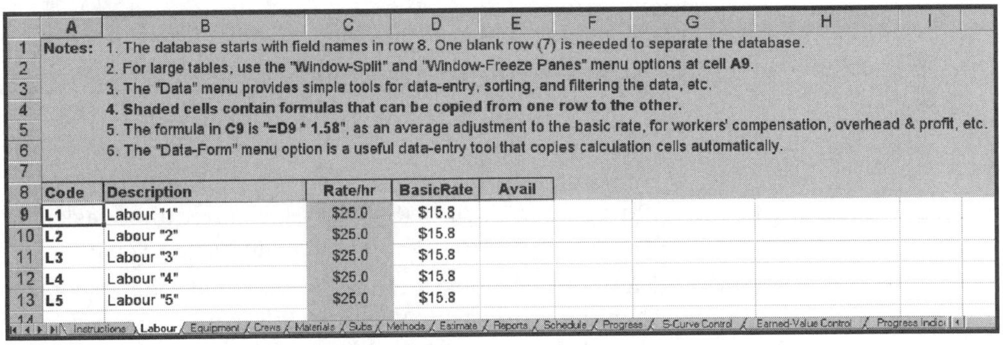

Notes: 1. The database starts with field names in row 8. One blank row (7) is needed to separate the database.
2. For large tables, use the "Window-Split" and "Window-Freeze Panes" menu options at cell **A9**.
3. The "Data" menu provides simple tools for data-entry, sorting, and filtering the data, etc.
4. Shaded cells contain formulas that can be copied from one row to the other.
5. The formula in **C9** is "**=D9 * 1.58**", as an average adjustment to the basic rate, for workers' compensation, overhead & profit, etc.
6. The "Data-Form" menu option is a useful data-entry tool that copies calculation cells automatically.

Code	Description	Rate/hr	BasicRate	Avail
L1	Labour "1"	$25.0	$15.8	
L2	Labour "2"	$25.0	$15.8	
L3	Labour "3"	$25.0	$15.8	
L4	Labour "4"	$25.0	$15.8	
L5	Labour "5"	$25.0	$15.8	

Figure 4–16. Equipment Sheet

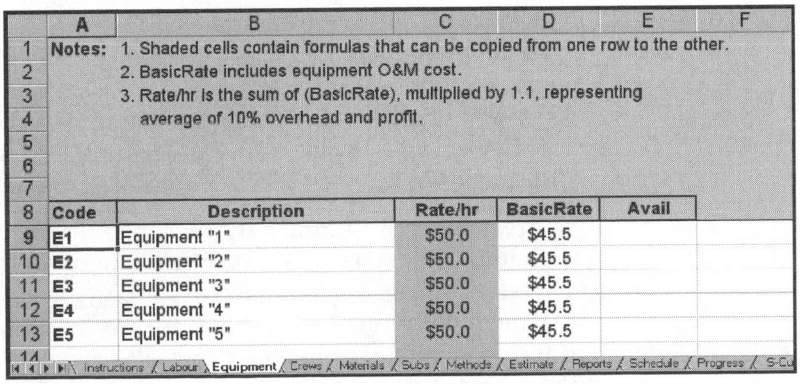

Notes: 1. Shaded cells contain formulas that can be copied from one row to the other.
2. BasicRate includes equipment O&M cost.
3. Rate/hr is the sum of (BasicRate), multiplied by 1.1, representing average of 10% overhead and profit.

Code	Description	Rate/hr	BasicRate	Avail
E1	Equipment "1"	$50.0	$45.5	
E2	Equipment "2"	$50.0	$45.5	
E3	Equipment "3"	$50.0	$45.5	
E4	Equipment "4"	$50.0	$45.5	
E5	Equipment "5"	$50.0	$45.5	

Figure 4–17.
Crews Sheet

The easiest approach to add new crews is to copy the last row to a new one and then modify its data.

Code	Description	Rate/d	NoR1	Res1	NoR2	Res2	NoR3	Res3	NoR4	Res4	NoR5	Res5	$Res1	$Res2	$Res3	$Res4	$Res5	Avail
CR-01	Crew "1"	$500	0.25	E1	2.00	L1							$12.5	$50.0				
CR-02	Crew "2"	$800	0.50	E2	0.50	E3	2.00	L1					$25.0	$25.0	$50.0			
CR-03	Crew "3"	$1,400	2.00	E1	2.00	L1	1.00	L4					$100.0	$50.0	$25.0			
CR-04	Crew "4"	$2,600	3.00	E2	3.00	L2	4.00	L1					$150.0	$75.0	$100.0			
CR-05	Crew "5"	$800	2.00	L1	2.00	L5							$50.0	$50.0				
CR-06	Crew "6"	$1,800	2.00	L1	2.50	E5	1.00	E3					$50.0	$125.0	$50.0			
CR-07	Crew "7"	$1,400	2.00	L1	1.00	L2	2.00	E5					$50.0	$25.0	$100.0			
CR-08	Crew "8"	$2,000	2.00	L1	1.00	L2	1.00	L3	3.00	E5			$50.0	$25.0	$25.0	$150.0		
CR-09	Crew "9"	$700	2.00	L1	0.50	L5	0.50	L4	0.25	E3			$50.0	$12.5	$12.5	$12.5		
CR-10	Crew "10"	$686	1.00	L2	2.00	L1	0.21	E4					$25.0	$50.0	$10.7			
CR-11	Crew "11"	$3,000	2.00	E1	3.00	E3	4.00	L1	1.00	L3			$100.0	$150.0	$100.0	$25.0		
CR-12	Crew "12"	$2,000	1.00	E2	2.00	E3	2.00	L1	2.00	L2			$50.0	$100.0	$50.0	$50.0		
CR-13	Crew "13"	$1,800	2.00	E1	4.00	L1	1.00	L4					$100.0	$100.0	$25.0			
CR-14	Crew "14"	$2,200	2.00	E2	3.00	L2	4.00	L1					$100.0	$75.0	$100.0			
CR-15	Crew "15"	$200	1.00	L1									$25.0					
CR-16	Crew "16"	$400	2.00	L1									$50.0					
CR-17	Crew "17"	$600	3.00	L1									$75.0					
CR-18	Crew "18"	$800	4.00	L1									$100.0					

Notes: 1. A crew contains up to five labour and equipment resources;
2. Select LABOUR or EQUIPMENT using the comboboxes and then copy their codes from cells O2 or O3 to resource fields **Res1** to **Res5**; and
3. Shaded cells contain formulas that can be copied from one row to the other.

Selection: L5 / E1

Instructions / Labour / Equipment / **Crews** / Materials / Subs / Methods / Estimate / Reports / Schedule / Progress / S-Curve Control / Earned-Value Control / Progress Indic

Figure 4–18.
Materials Sheet

	Code	Description	Cost/Unit	Basic$/Unit	Unit	Avail
9	M1	Material "1"	$100.0	$90.9	unit	
10	M2	Material "2"	$100.0	$90.9	unit	
11	M3	Material "3"	$100.0	$90.9	unit	
12	M4	Material "4"	$100.0	$90.9	unit	
13	M5	Material "5"	$100.0	$90.9	unit	

Notes: 1. The "Avail" field can be used to link this table to other inventory sheets.
2. An average 10% is added to the Basic$/Unit for overhead and profit.
3. Material costs include delivery to the site. No sales tax included or allowance for wasted material.

Instructions / Labour / Equipment / Crews / **Materials** / Subs / Methods / Estimate / Reports / Schedule / Progress / S-Curve Control / Earned-Value Control

Subcontractors: The subs sheet (Figure 4–19) defines various subcontractors, providing their unit cost (SubCost) for the required tasks. An average of 10% is added to the SubCost for O&P to calculate the Cost/Unit.

Methods of Construction: Various methods of construction were defined in a separate worksheet, Methods, following the R.S. Means approach (Figure 4–20) so that they become ready for use in any project estimate. The Methods sheet defines the resources used in each construction method (crews and material, or subcontractor), the overtime strategy they use, daily production rate, and assumed seasonal productivity factors. To facilitate user input of the resources used in each method, some screen elements such as combo boxes are used on the sheet, as shown in Figure 4–20. The same coding system of the means can be used in this worksheet. The regular daily production rate **RegPr/d** is obtained directly from the means or input by the user according to experience and/or company records.

Three seasonal productivity rates (winter, spring, and fall) can be specified to each method. These factors adjust the daily production rates, depending on the season in which the activity planned to be constructed. For activities that are insensitive to weather conditions, the user can use a value of 1.0 for the three factors. It is noted that the use of these factors becomes advantageous when the estimate is integrated with a scheduling module. These factors, as such, make it possible to refine the cost based on the scheduled time of the activities.

Figure 4–19. Subcontractors Sheet

The lump sum values can be quoted directly from local subcontractors.

Notes: 1. An average 10% is added to the SubCost for overhead and profit.

Code	Description	Cost/Unit	Sub-Contractor	SubCost/Unit	Unit
S1	Type of Work 1	$4,000.7	Sub-contractor "1"	$3,637.0	LSUM
S2	Type of Work 2	$3,601.0	Sub-contractor "2"	$3,273.6	LSUM
S3	Type of Work 3	$21.3	Sub-contractor "3"	$19.4	LSUM
S4	Type of Work 4	$5,601.3	Sub-contractor "4"	$5,092.1	LSUM
S5	Type of Work 5	$20.0	Sub-contractor "5"	$18.2	LSUM
S6	Type of Work 6	$12,800.6	Sub-contractor "6"	$11,636.9	LSUM
S7	Type of Work 7	$12,600.6	Sub-contractor "7"	$11,455.1	LSUM
S8	Type of Work 8	$15,800.2	Sub-contractor "8"	$14,363.8	LSUM
S9	Type of Work 9	$7,600.4	Sub-contractor "9"	$6,909.5	LSUM

Instructions / Labour / Equipment / Crews / Materials / Subs / Methods / Estimate / Reports / Schedule / Progress / S-Curve Control / Earned-Value Control / Progress Ind

Notes:
1. Select a CREW (or a SUB) and a MATERIAL using the comboboxes, then copy their code from cells J2, J3, & J4 to fields **Crew/SUB/Material**;
2. Shaded cells contain formulas that can be copied from one row to the other.
3. **Assumptions**: Week is 5days, 8hours Overtime hour is 90% productivity; and First 4 overtime hours, rate is 1.2 of normal rate, afterwards, 1.5 times.

Selection:

CR-03	CR-03	Crew
M2	M2	Material
S2	S2	Sub

Code	Description	Cost /d	TotPr /d	Unit Cost	Units	Crew	Sub	RegPr/d
CSI-01-1	Md 1	$500	100.00	$5	unit	CR-01		100.000
CSI-01-2	Md 2	$1,667	100.00	$17	unit	CR-02		100.000
CSI-01-3	Md 3	$3,000	150.00	$20	unit	CR-03		122.450
CSI-02-1	Md 4	$5,533	200.00	$28	unit	CR-18	S3	200.000
CSI-02-2	Md 5	$2,000	125.00	$16	unit	CR-05		125.000
CSI-02-3	Md 6	$2,250	175.00	$13	unit	CR-06		175.000
CSI-03-1	Md 7	$5,000	125.00	$40	unit	CR-07		125.000
CSI-03-2	Md 8	$1,500	5.00	$300	unit	CR-16	S5	5.000
CSI-04-1	Md 9	$750	0.06	$12,000	unit	CR-09		0.063
CSI-04-2	Md 10	$886	0.07	$12,400	unit	CR-10		0.071
CSI-05-1	Md 11	$1,067	0.08	$12,800	unit	CR-17	S4	0.083
CSI-06-1	Md 12	$2,000	0.13	$16,000	unit	CR-16	S6	0.125
CSI-06-2	Md 13	$2,700	0.17	$16,200	unit	CR-17	S7	0.167
CSI-07-1	Md 14	$8,500	0.50	$17,000	unit	CR-17	S8	0.500
CSI-07-2	Md 15	$1,667	0.17	$10,000	unit	CR-16	S9	0.167
CSI-08-1	Md 16	$1,667	0.17	$10,000	unit	CR-16	S1	0.167
CSI-08-2	Md 17	$800	0.10	$8,000	unit	CR-16	S1	0.100
CSI-08-3	Md 18	$1,000	0.11	$9,000	unit	CR-17	S2	0.111

Code	MatQ/d	Material	Hrs/d	OTadj	MatCost	CrewCost	SubCost	WinProd	SprProd	FallProd
CSI-01-1			8.00	8.00		499.93		1.00	1.00	1.00
CSI-01-2	8.67	M2	8.00	8.00	866.67	799.93		1.00	1.00	1.00
CSI-01-3	11.80	M3	10.00	10.40	1,180.16	1,819.86		1.00	1.00	1.00
CSI-02-1	4.73	M1	8.00	8.00	472.66	799.86	4,260.81	1.00	1.00	1.00
CSI-02-2	12.00	M1	8.00	8.00	1,200.00	799.86		1.00	1.00	1.00
CSI-02-3	4.50	M1	8.00	8.00	450.07	1,799.93		1.00	1.00	1.00
CSI-03-1	36.00	M2	8.00	8.00	3,600.11	1,399.89		1.00	1.00	1.00
CSI-03-2	10.00	M3	8.00	8.00	1,000.00	399.93	100.07	1.00	1.00	1.00
CSI-04-1	0.50	M4	8.00	8.00	50.00	700.01		1.00	1.00	1.00
CSI-04-2	2.00	M4	8.00	8.00	199.97	685.75		1.00	1.00	1.00
CSI-05-1			8.00	8.00		599.89	466.77	1.00	1.00	1.00
CSI-06-1			8.00	8.00		399.93	1,600.07	1.00	1.00	1.00
CSI-06-2			8.00	8.00		599.89	2,100.11	1.00	1.00	1.00
CSI-07-1			8.00	8.00		599.89	7,900.11	1.00	1.00	1.00
CSI-07-2			8.00	8.00		399.93	1,266.74	1.00	1.00	1.00
CSI-08-1	6.00	M5	8.00	8.00	599.95	399.93	666.78	1.00	1.00	1.00
CSI-08-2			8.00	8.00		399.93	400.07	1.00	1.00	1.00
CSI-08-3			8.00	8.00		599.89	400.11	1.00	1.00	1.00

Instructions / Labour / Equipment / Crews / Materials / Subs / Methods / Estimate / Reports / Schedule / Progress / S-Curve Control / Earned-Value Control / Progress Indic

Figure 4–20. Construction Methods Sheet

When the user specifies working hours per day (**hrs/d** field) that are greater than 8, the total daily production, **TotPr/d,** and the total daily cost, **Cost/d,** are automatically adjusted for the overtime. The assumptions made are as follows:

- Normal working hours are 8 hours/day.
- Overtime hour has 90% productivity of a regular hour.
- The hourly rate of the first 4 overtime hours is 1.2 the normal hourly rate, Afterwards it is 1.5 of the normal hourly rate.
- Two methods can be identical except work hours are different.

It is noted that the methods that involve subcontractors may need special care. As shown, the regular production rate, **RegPr/d,** is a fraction that is determined based on the duration quoted for the job. For example, if the subcontractor is doing a lump sum job (i.e., quantity = 1) that takes him 10 days to finish, then his production should be 1/10 or 0.1 units per day. Here, Regular Production = 1 / Duration.

4.6.1.2 Project Management System Added to the six worksheets of the data depository, the **Case-Study.xls** file incorporates various other sheets that form a comprehensive system for estimating, schedule optimization, and project control. The latter sheets relate to the specific project being analyzed. The first sheet that needs to be set up is the Estimate sheet. This sheet, in addition to the Reports sheet, are described in this chapter while the others will be described in the various chapters that come.

The "Estimate" Sheet   This sheet defines the activities of the project being studied and their data related to: the work breakdown structure (WBS) of the project, the contract items, and the responsibility levels of the organization breakdown structure (OBS). The row data that we need to input into this sheet was discussed previously in Chapter 3. The project network, the WBS, and the OBS are shown in Figures 3–15 and 3–17. Using this data, in the Estimate sheet we add each activity in a new row and then enter its data in the white cells, as shown in Figure 4–21, including a reference to the methods of construction for each activity.

For indirect cost estimation, we will use the equation: **Indirect cost = a + b X,** where (a) is the fixed indirects and (b) is the variable indirects. For simplicity in our case study, we will use a = 0 and b = $500/day. Therefore, **indirect costs = $500/day.**

Once done with data entry, automatic calculations are made for the cost, duration, and resource amounts for each activity, as a function of its selected method of construction (column O in Figure 4–21). As shown, column O shows values of 1 for all activities, indicating that the first method (cheapest) is selected for all activities. For example, activity D has one method of construction **md6**. Its total cost is $18,000 and duration of 8 days (columns R and AH in Figure 4–23), which are the same values determined by the manual calculation of Example 1 of section 4.4.1.

Part of user inputs

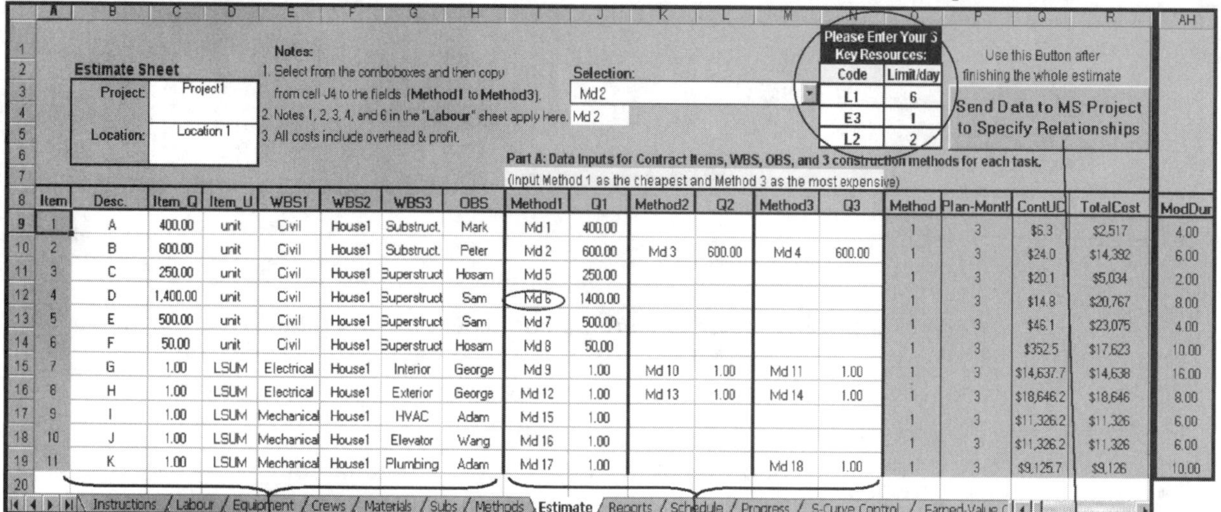

Item	Desc.	Item_Q	Item_U	WBS1	WBS2	WBS3	OBS	Method1	Q1	Method2	Q2	Method3	Q3	Method	Plan-Month	ContUC	TotalCost	ModDur
1	A	400.00	unit	Civil	House1	Substruct.	Mark	Md 1	400.00					1	3	$6.3	$2,517	4.00
2	B	600.00	unit	Civil	House1	Substruct.	Peter	Md 2	600.00	Md 3	600.00	Md 4	600.00	1	3	$24.0	$14,392	6.00
3	C	250.00	unit	Civil	House1	Superstruct	Hosam	Md 5	250.00					1	3	$20.1	$5,034	2.00
4	D	1,400.00	unit	Civil	House1	Superstruct	Sam	Md 6	1400.00					1	3	$14.8	$20,767	8.00
5	E	500.00	unit	Civil	House1	Superstruct	Sam	Md 7	500.00					1	3	$46.1	$23,075	4.00
6	F	50.00	unit	Civil	House1	Superstruct	Hosam	Md 8	50.00					1	3	$352.5	$17,623	10.00
7	G	1.00	LSUM	Electrical	House1	Interior	George	Md 9	1.00	Md 10	1.00	Md 11	1.00	1	3	$14,637.7	$14,638	16.00
8	H	1.00	LSUM	Electrical	House1	Exterior	George	Md 12	1.00	Md 13	1.00	Md 14	1.00	1	3	$18,646.2	$18,646	8.00
9	I	1.00	LSUM	Mechanical	House1	HVAC	Adam	Md 15	1.00					1	3	$11,326.2	$11,326	6.00
10	J	1.00	LSUM	Mechanical	House1	Elevator	Wang	Md 16	1.00					1	3	$11,326.2	$11,326	6.00
11	K	1.00	LSUM	Mechanical	House1	Plumbing	Adam	Md 17	1.00			Md 18	1.00	1	3	$9,125.7	$9,126	10.00

WBS of the case study, as discussed in Chapter 3. To add new items, last row is copied to a new one and then modified.

3 methods of construction for every activity. For example, activity K can be constructed by either of: **method md17** or **md18**. Quantity is 1 because it is a subcontracted Lump Sum activity.

Button to automatically send the estimate data to a scheduling software (used in Chapters 5 & 10).

Going backward to the Methods sheet, we can copy and add two rows for **methods md17** and **md18**. We then specify what resources will be employed in these methods. Therefore, we may need to go back to the resource sheets and add these resources if they are not included yet, e.g., a new subcontractor, crew, or equipment etc. Notice here that method **m18** employs **subcontractor S2** and crew **CR-17**. The composition of the crew can also be found in the crews, labor, and equipment sheets.

Figure 4–21. The "Estimate" Sheet

The Estimate sheet is a large one, involving five parts and Figure 4–21 shows only the first part. The formulas used in this estimating sheet are complex due to their link with all other sheets, however, they are based on the same data management tools of Excel described in Chapter 2. The various parts of the sheet are:

Part A: Data Input (Columns A to R): This part is the part that relate to Figure 4–21 and discussed. Based on this part, a pivot table can be easily constructed to automatically generate the bid proposal form of the project. It can also be used to provide summary reports pertaining to unit costs, cost of resources, and the total costs at the different WBS levels, as explained later.

Part B: Calculations for the Selected Methods of Construction (Columns T to AJ): The cells in this part automatically calculate the cost and duration of the construction method being selected for each activity. This part has links to the resources' sheets and the Methods sheet to calculate the time and cost of activities, considering the seasonal productivity factor (PrFactor). The PrFactor (column AG of the Estimate sheet) references the productivity factor of the selected construction method based on the season in which the activity is planned to be executed (the season indicated by the PlanMonth value in Part A).

Part C: Time and Cost Calculations for Three Construction Methods (Columns AK to AQ): In this part, the cost and duration of three candidate construction methods for each activity are calculated. This part, therefore, allows for quick what-if analysis regarding time and cost. By simply changing the value in the method index (column O in Part A), related calculations can also be viewed in Part B. Also, the calculations related to the time and cost of the various methods of construction give an indication of the time-cost relationship within each activity.

Part D: Daily Demand of three Key Resources (Columns AR to AU): This part calculates the daily amount of three user-defined key resources that are needed to perform the selected methods of construction for the activities. This resource calculation may help the user forecast the problems that may arise if some of these key resources are limited. Furthermore, this part can be used for resource scheduling purposes (subject of Chapters 7 and 8).

Part E: Tasks Planned versus Actual Performance (Columns AW to BJ): This part provides the planned versus actual performance, regarding time, cost, and quality of the selected method of construction for an activity. This analysis may help the contractor not only in updating the production data of the resources based on the actual performance, but also in investigating the factors that contributed to any failure/lack of performance.

The "Reports" Sheet Reporting plays a vital role in the efficiency of any management system. Different levels of reports that summarize the data stored in the system become essential for supporting decision and for identifying important trends that can be used as basis for corrective actions. In our Excel system, the pivot table feature of Excel was used for reporting purposes. Using the data stored in various sheets, such as those of the resources and the estimate sheet, various sample reports were generated to provide the contractor/subcontractor with summary information related to time, cost, and resource use. The Reports sheet provides the following three reports to summarize the data in the Estimate sheet (Figure 4–22):

a. **Bid Proposal Report:** This report [Figure 4–22a] summarizes the data in Part A of the estimate sheet, providing details of the direct cost estimation of the various items: item number; item description; quantity; unit; unit price; and the total bid price. At this stage when indirect costs are not yet estimated and

Useful Pivot Table reports.

Note: If data is changed, you need to refresh the pivot tables (from the pivot tables toolbar).

(a) Pivot Table Report For Bid Proposal. **(b)** Summary WBS Report. **(c)** Methods of Construction Report.

Sum of TotalCost

Item	Desc.	Item_Q	Item_U	Unit Cost	Total
1.00	A	400.00	unit	5.00	$2,000
2.00	B	600.00	unit	16.67	$10,000
3.00	C	250.00	unit	16.00	$4,000
4.00	D	1400.00	unit	12.86	$18,000
5.00	E	500.00	unit	40.00	$20,000
6.00	F	50.00	unit	300.00	$15,000
7.00	G	1.00	LSUM	12000.23	$12,000
8.00	H	1.00	LSUM	16000.00	$16,000
9.00	I	1.00	LSUM	10000.00	$10,000
10.00	J	1.00	LSUM	10000.00	$10,000
11.00	K	1.00	LSUM	8000.00	$8,000
Grand Total					$124,999

Part (b):

WBS1	Civil
WBS2	House1
WBS3	Superstruct.
OBS	Hosam

Sum of TotalCost

Item	Desc.	Item_Q	Item_U	Total
3.00	C	250.00	unit	$4,000
6.00	F	50.00	unit	$15,000
Grand Total				$19,000

Part (c):

Task	B

Data	Total
Duration1	6.00
Duration2	4.00
Duration3	3.00
Cost($)1	9999.57
Cost($)2	12000.00
Cost($)3	16600.00

Instructions / Labour / Equipment / Crews / Materials / Subs / Methods / Estimate / Reports / Schedule / Progress / S-Curve Control / Earned-Value Control / Progress Indici

Figure 4-22. Pivot Table Reports in the "Reports" Sheet

the schedule sheet is not used, the report automatically sums the direct costs associated with each contract item and the overall project total cost (cell BT21). When these issues are addressed (by the end of Chapter 10), this report will provide the bid prices that can be readily used for bid submission purposes.

b. **Summary WBS Report:** This report [Figure 4–22b] summarizes the data in Part A of the estimate sheet, considering user-defined WBS and OBS data. For that purpose, the report was configured with four fields (3 WBS and 1 OBS), shown as drop-down boxes created by the pivot table wizard (cells BO26 to BP29). By choosing different values from the drop-down boxes, different subsets of the data are aggregated and displayed. For example, the total direct cost for the Civil-Superstructure work in House1 supervised by "Hosam" is shown to be $19,000. Similarly, the sum of the cost associated with the various areas in a project can be presented and may also be graphed to facilitate decision making.

c. **Methods of Construction Report:** This report [Figure 4–22(c)] summarizes the data in Part C of the Estimate sheet, providing the time-cost relationship between the three methods of construction associated with the selected activity (Activity B). This may be used to facilitate time-cost trade off analysis (discussed later in Chapter 8).

In addition to these reports, the powerful capabilities of pivot tables can be utilized for automatically generating multiproject reports. When data for several projects are available, pivot tables can be designed to analyze various aspects such as unit price deviation in contract items from one project to the other.

4.7 Summary

In this chapter, you have been introduced to the basics of cost estimation with emphasis on detailed estimating. By the end of this chapter, we are now able to use industry-standard references for cost estimation and accordingly modify our project network to show resources, costs, and durations of activities.

In this chapter, you have also been presented with a simplified estimating system on Excel. This system can support small/medium subcontractors and possibly contractors in effectively managing their resource and cost information of various projects. In addition to facilitating the estimating process, one of the benefits of the spreadsheet system is its being transparent, yet including powerful capabilities that can satisfy the needs of most users. At the end of this chapter, the resources, costs, and durations of the activities in our case study project were determined. As such, the project network showing the activities' durations associated with the cheapest methods of construction is shown in Figure 4–23.

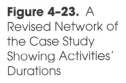

Figure 4-23. A Revised Network of the Case Study Showing Activities' Durations

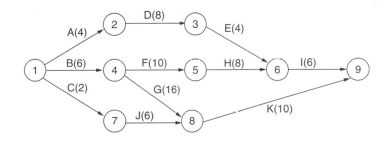

4.8 Bibliography

Black, J. (1982). Cost Engineering Planning Techniques for Management. New York: M. Dekker Inc.

Campbell, W. and Ahuja, H. (1994). *Estimating: From concept to completion.* Englewood Cliffs, NJ: Prentice-Hall Inc.

Clark, F. (1978). *Applied Cost Engineering.* New York: M. Dekker Inc.

Ellis, M. (1989). "A Model for Prediction of Highway Construction Production Rates." Ph.D. thesis, University of Florida.

Fayek, A., Duffield, C., and Young, D. (1994). "A Review of Commercially Available Cost-estimating Software Systems for Construction Industry." *Engineering Management Journal.* 6(4), 23–33.

Goldman, J. (1990). *Means Estimating Handbook* Kingston, MA: R. S. Means Co.

Gould, F. (1997). *Managing the Construction Process: Estimating, Scheduling, and Project Control.* Upper Saddle River, NJ: Prentice Hall Inc.

Greer, W. (1990). *Cost analysis and estimating: tools and techniques.* New York: Springer-Verlag.

Hegazy T. and Ayed, A., (1998). "A Neural Network Model for Parametric Cost Estimation of Highway Projects," *Journal of Construction Engineering and Management,* ASCE, Vol. 24, No. 3, pp. 210–218.

Hegazy, T. and Moselhi, O. (1995). "Elements of Cost Estimation: A Survey in Canada and The United States," *Cost Engineering*, AACE International, Vol. 37, No. 5, pp. 27–33.

Hegazy, T. and Moselhi, O. (1994). "ESTIMATOR: A Prototype of An Integrated Bid Preparation System," *Journal of Engineering Construction and Architectural Management*, Vol. 1, No. 1, pp. 51–57.

Hollman, J. (1994). "A parametric building cost estimating system." *AACE Transactions.* EST.4,1–7.

Lee, H. (1992). "Automated Interactive Cost Estimating System for Reinforced Concrete Building Structures." Ph.D. thesis, The University of Michigan.

Lopez, O. (1993). "Forecasting Construction costs in Hyper-inflated Economies." Ph.D. thesis, The University of Texas at Austin.

Melin, J. (1994). "Parametric estimation." *Cost Engineering*, AACE International, 36(1), 19–23.

Neil, J. M. (1982) *Construction Cost Estimating for Project Control.* Prentice-Hall Inc., N.J., 1982.

R.S. Means (1999). *Building Construction Cost Data.* Kingston, MA: R. S. Means Co.

4.9 Exercises

1. a. Why should the estimator visit the construction site before producing the cost estimate?

   b. Discuss the procedures which might be followed with respect to adding time contingency allowances into construction networks.

   c. Comment on the following statement: "If the contractor adds a cost contingency allowance into his tender price, he will lose the tender."

2. The following table gives the work items of a certain contract together with their estimated quantities and total direct cost. Total of indirect cost and markup is $140,000.

Work Item	Estimated Quantity	Unit	Estimated Direct Cost
Common excavation	500,000	m^3	$475,000
Rock excavation	200,000	m^3	$2,400,000
Structures	——	Lump Sum	$400,000

   a. Develop a balanced bid.
   b. If you, as a contractor, have a reason to think that rock excavation quantities are considerably less than estimated and common excavation is higher, develop an unbalanced bid to maximize profit.

3. Enter the data of Figure 4–6 into a spreadsheet program and print the answer to the example. Use separate sheets for the labor, equipment, material, crews, methods, and the estimate.

4. A grout curtain is to be formed underneath a dam. This involves drilling through the underlying rock. A total of 388 grout holes will be drilled with a total depth of 21,390 meters. The following table shows the work divided into five activities together with the resources used.

Activity	Description	No. of Holes	Total Depth (m)	No. of Drill Units per Rig
100	Grout 1	154	7400	4
200	Grout 2	53	2870	2
300	Grout 3	55	3130	3
400	Grout 4	79	4510	4
500	Grout 5	47	3480	3

Assume that the drilling rate is 20 m/day and the grouting rate approximately equals the drilling rate. The drilling rig can drill more than one hole at a given position; however, it must be moved from the hole position before grouting and this requires 0.5 day for each move. With a six-day week, estimate activity durations in weeks. Also, estimate the unit cost of drilling and grouting given that the cost of drilling is $2,300/week/drill-unit and the cost of grouting is $5.80/m.

5. a. Give a reason why minimum material content does not necessarily result in minimum cost.

b. In the process of producing a cost estimate for bidding purpose the contractor should identify the risks he is going to carry and give responses to deal with them. Give your views, as a contractor, on the possible responses to the following risks:
   - Client's indecisions or delays.
   - Troubles encountered with different public services.
   - Late supply of materials.
   - Equipment breakdown.

c. Determine the duration and the direct cost rate for an excavation activity. The material to be excavated is estimated to be 3360 m^3. Use an excavator with an output of 1200 m^3/week loading three trucks. A small bulldozer will be needed at the dump site to spread excavated material. Two helpers will be used to guide the operators. Use the following weekly rates:

   rate of one excavator - $1,000/week
   rate of one bulldozer - $750/week
   rate of one truck - $450/week
   rate of one driver - $120/week
   rate of one helper - $100/week.

6. Consider a single activity "Wood Gym Floor" under the "Finishing" item of a certain project. Assume that the quantity of this activity is **1250** m^2. Use the following data for item CSI 095 801 0100 from the R.S. Means cost book to estimate the construction *cost* and *time* to finish this activity. It is noted that using local labor, you estimate the bare hourly rates for a tile layer and a tile layer helper to be $30 and $23, respectively.

095 Acoustical Treatment & Wood Flooring

095 800	Wood Comp. Flooring		CREW	DAILY OUTPUT	LABOR HOURS	UNIT	MAT.	LABOR	EQUP.	TOTAL	TOTAL INCL O&P
							1998 BARE COSTS				
801	0010	**WOOD COMPOSITION**									
	0100	Gym floors 57 mm × 175 mm × 100 mm,	D-7	13.9	1.148	m2	48.5	27		75.5	93.50
	0200	Thin set, on concrete	"	23.23	0.689	↓	44	16.20		60.20	72.50
	0300	Sanding and finishing, add on 51 mm grout setting bed	1 Carp	18.58	0.431		6.45	11.40		17.85	25

The details of the crew D-7 are:

Crew no.	Bare costs		Incl. Subs O&P		Cost per labor-hour	
Crew D-7	Hr.	Daily	Hr.	Daily	Bare Costs	Incl. O&P
1 Tile Layer	$26.10	$208.80	$38.60	$308.80	$22.55	$34.83
1 Tile Layer Helper	$21.00	168.00	31.05	248.40		
16 L.H., Daily Totals		$376.80		$557.20	$23.55	$34.83

7. a. Comment on the following statement: "The existence of a realistic cost estimate against which tenders can be compared is a vital factor in the quality of a decision made by the engineer with respect to selection of the best bid."

   b. Suggest a regime for evaluation of bids when the contractors are invited to specify their preferred contract duration.

8. Set up spreadsheets to model the data in Question 5(c) using functions to perform the calculations and to provide the answers to the question. Use separate lists for labor, equipment, crews, methods, and estimate.

Chapter 5

CRITICAL-PATH ANALYSIS FOR NETWORK SCHEDULING

A fter studying this chapter, you will be able to:

- Perform CPM and PDM analyses for AOA and AON networks.
- Calculate the early / late times that an activity can start/finish.
- Determine the total project duration, activity floats, and the path of critical activities.
- Represent the schedule using bar charts (Gantt charts).
- Use Microsoft Project Software to schedule projects.
- Experiment with a spreadsheet model for network analysis.

Owner, CM
- Need
- Feasibility
- Project Definition
- Owner Approval

A/E, CM, Owner
- Conceptual Design
- Owner Approval
- Soil Reports
- Preliminary Design
- Detailed Design
- Quantities
- Work Documents
- Select Project Contract Strategy

Bidders
- Prepare Bid Proposal + Baselines
- Collect Data (site, quantities, specs, Resources, tasks, etc)
- Planning
- Time & Cost Estimation
- Scheduling
- Resource Management: Deadline, Resource Constraints, TCT, etc
- Bidding Strategy & Markup Estimation
- Cash Flow Analysis
- Submit Bid

Owner, CM
- Evaluate Bids and Select General Contractor

Contractor
- Start Construction
- Detailed Planning, Estimating & Resource Management
- Schedule Updating
- Progress Evaluation
- Time, Cost, & Quality Control
- Commissioning

O & M Staff
- O & M
- Demolition at End of Service Life

| CONCEPT | DESIGN | BIDDING | CONSTRUCTION | O & M |

5.1 Scheduling Objectives

In the last two chapters, you were introduced to the project planning process. In Chapter 3, we used AOA and AON representations to develop a picture of the interrelationships within a project. In Chapter 4, also, we calculated the time and cost of individual activities based on our estimation of the resources and methods of construction to be used. However, we do not know how long the total project duration is. Also, we need to evaluate the early and late times at which activities start and finish. In addition, since real-life projects involve hundreds of activities, it is important to identify the group of critical activities so that special care is taken to make sure they are not delayed. In addition, since the construction environment is always exposed to constraints and changes, it is important to be able to evaluate the implications of changes in start and/or finish times of activities on the overall project duration. All these statements, in fact, are the basic objectives of the scheduling process, which, in essence, adds a time dimension to the planning process. In other words, we can briefly state that: Scheduling = Planning + Time. In fact, the schedule is very important for the contractor to know when and how much labor is needed; vendors to know when to deliver materials; and subcontractors to know when they can do their work.

5.2 Network Scheduling

The inputs to network scheduling of any project are simply the AOA or the AON networks with the individual activity duration defined. The network scheduling process follows the Critical Path Method (CPM) technique. Applying the CPM technique for AOA and AON networks, however, is slightly different. In AOA networks, we use the traditional CPM and in AON networks, we use the CPM with slight modifications and will refer to it as the Precedence Diagram Method (PDM). To demonstrate CPM and PDM analyses, let's consider a simple five-activity project, with activity A at the start, followed by three parallel activities B, C, and D, which are then succeeded by activity E. The AOA or the AON networks of this example are presented in Figure 5–1. Detailed description of the CPM and PDM analyses of theses AOA or the AON networks are presented in the following subsections. It is noted that the example at hand involves only simple finish-to-start relationships among activities.

Figure 5-1. Network Example: (a) Activity on arrow (AOA); (b) Activity on node (AON)

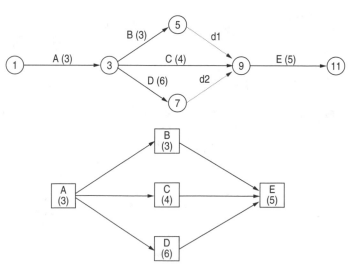

5.2.1 Critical Path Method (CPM)

The CPM is a systematic scheduling method for AOA network. The CPM involves four main steps:

- A forward pass to determine activities early-start times.
- A backward pass to determine activities late-finish times.
- Float calculations.
- Identifying critical activities.

5.2.1.1 Forward Pass The forward pass determines the early-start times of activities. Before explaining the detailed calculations involved, let's add two boxes on each node to put the calculations inside them, as shown in Figure 5–2. The forward pass proceeds from the left-most node in the network (node 1) and moves to the right, putting the calculations inside the shaded boxes to the left.

Each node in the network, in fact, is a point at which some activities end (head arrows coming into the node), as shown in Figure 5–3. That node is also a point at which some activities start (tail arrows of successor activities). Certainly, all successor activities can start only after the latest predecessor is finished. Therefore, for the forward pass to determine the early-start (ES) time of an activity, we have to look at the head arrows coming into the start node of the activity. We then have to set the activity ES time as the latest finish time of all predecessors.

In our example, the forward pass calculations are as follows:

1. We begin at node 1, the start node of the project, and assign it an early-start time of zero. Here, all activity times use an end-of-day notation. Therefore, the ES of activity A being zero means that activity starts at end of day zero, or the beginning of day 1 in the project. Using this notation, as well, the calculations are performed irrespective of the actual project start on the calendar.

2. We now move to node 3. This node receives one head arrow, and as such, it has one predecessor, activity A. Since the predecessor started on time zero and has 3 days duration, then, it ends early at time 3 [Early-Finish (EF) = Early-Start (ES) + d]. Accordingly, the ES time of all successor activities to node 3 (activities B, C, and D) is time 3. This value is, therefore, put in the shaded box on top of node 3, as shown in Figure 5–4.

Figure 5-2
Preparation for the
Forward Pass

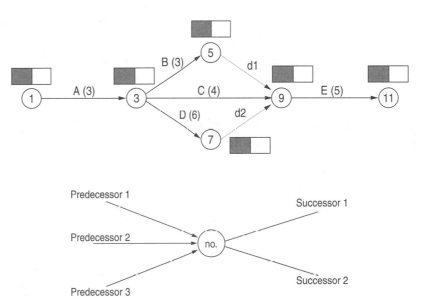

Figure 5-3. A Node
in an AOA Network

Figure 5-4. Forward Pass Calculations in AOA Networks

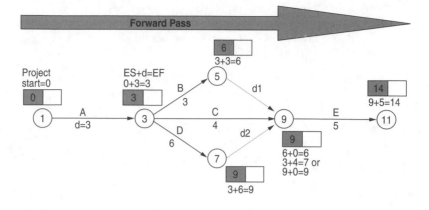

3. We now move forward to successor nodes 5, 7, and 9. However, since node 9 is linked to nodes 5 and 7 by dummy activities, we begin with nodes 5 and 7. Node 5 receives one head arrow from its predecessor activity B, and we evaluate the EF time of B as 6 [ES (3) + d (3)]. Successor activities to node 5, therefore, can have an ES time of 6. Similarly, the ES time at node 7 is calculated as time 9.

4. Moving to node 9, we evaluate the EF times of its three predecessors (d1, C, and d2) as time 6, 7, and 9, respectively. Accordingly, the ES time of successor activities is the largest value 9. Notice that only the largest EF value of predecessor activities is used to calculate the ES of successor activities, and all other values are not used. As such, only ES values can be directly read from the calculations in Figure 5–4. EF values, on the other hand, can be calculated as EF = ES + d.

5. We now move to the last node 11. It receives one head arrow, activity E, which has an ES value of 9. The EF time of activity E, therefore, equals 9 + 5 = time 14. Since node 11 is the last node, the EF of this node becomes the end of the project, reaching a total project duration of 14 days.

5.2.1.2 Backward Pass The backward pass determines the late-finish (LF) times of activities by proceeding backward from the end node to the starting node of the AOA network. We put the LF values in the right side boxes adjacent to the nodes, as shown in Figure 5–5. Putting Figure 5–3 in mind again, certainly, we can allow predecessor activities to be delayed so that they finish no later than the earliest late-start (LS) time of successor activities. Therefore, for the backward pass to determine the late-finish (LF) times of activities and put them on the shaded squares of Figure 5–5, we look at

Figure 5-5. Backward Pass Calculations in AOA Networks

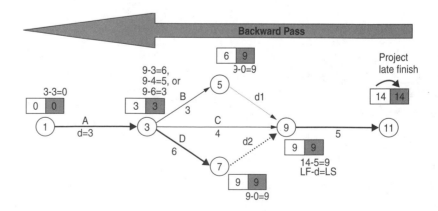

the successors (tail arrows) going out of the node, evaluate their smallest late-start (LS) value, and then use this value as the LF time of predecessors. For the example at hand, we do the following:

1. We begin at the last node of the network (node 11) and we transfer the early-finish value from the left box to be the late-finish (LF) value at the right-side box.
2. We then move backward to node 9, which has only one tail arrow of activity E. With the LF time of E being time 14, its LS time becomes LS = LF – d = 14 – 5 = time 9. At node 9, therefore, time 9 becomes the LF time of the predecessor activities of this node.
3. Move backward to predecessor nodes 5, and 7. Node 5 has one tail arrow of the dummy activity d1, and, as such, the LF time value to be used at node 5 becomes 9. Similarly, the LF time value of node 7 becomes 9.
4. Moving to node 3, we evaluate the LS time of its three successor activities B, C, and D as 6, 5, and 3, respectively. The LF time at node 3, therefore, becomes the smallest value 3. With other LS values not used, the values in the calculation boxes, as such, directly show the LF times of activities. LS times can be calculated as LS = LF – d.
5. We now proceed to the first node in the network (node 1). It connects to one tail arrow of activity A. The LS time of A, therefore, is LS = LF – d = 3 – 3 = 0, a necessary check to ensure the correctness of the calculation.

5.2.1.3 Float Calculations Once forward-pass and backward-pass calculations are complete, it is possible to analyze the activity times and find interesting conclusions. First, let's tabulate the information we have as shown in Table 5–1. One important aspect is Total-Float (TF) calculations, which determine the flexibility of an activity to be delayed. Notice in Table 5–1 that some activities, such as activity A, has ES time = LS time, and also its EF time = LF time, indicating no slack time for the activity. Other activities, such as B, can start early at time 3 and late at time 6, indicating a three-day total float. Float calculations can be illustrated as shown in Figure 5–6 for any activity.

Figure 5–6 shows two ways of scheduling each activity using its activity times. One way is to schedule its as early as possible (using its ES time). The other way is as late as possible (using its LS time). The activity float can, therefore, be represented by the following relationships:

$$\text{Total Float (TF)} = \text{Total Slack} = \text{LF} - \text{EF}$$
$$= \text{LF} - \text{ES}$$

Figure 5–6. Float Calculations

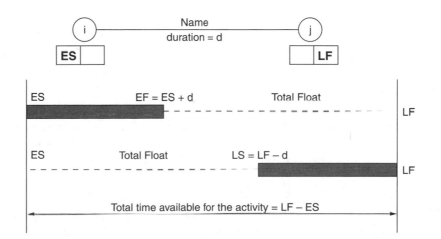

Table 5–1. CPM Results

Activity	Duration (d)	Results of Forward and Backward Pass		Calculations of Other Activity Times		Float Calculations	
		Early Start (ES)	Late Finish (LF)	Late Start LS = LF – d	Early Finish EF = ES + d	Total Float TF = LF – ES – d	Critical Activity
A	3	0	3	0	3	0	Yes
B	3	3	9	6	6	3	No
C	4	3	9	5	7	2	No
D	6	3	9	3	9	0	Yes
E	5	9	14	9	14	0	Yes

Also, with the ES and LF times directly read from the boxes used in forward and backward pass calculations, the total time available for the activity is LF – ES, as shown in the figure. Subtracting the activity duration, the activity total float becomes TF = LF – ES – d. Using these relationships, activities total floats are calculated as shown in Table 5–1.

Another type of float often used in network analysis is the Free Float, which can be calculated as:

Free Float = ES (of succeeding activity) – EF (of activity in question)

The free float defines the amount of time that an activity can be delayed without taking float away from any other activity. With free float available for an activity, a project manager knows that the float can be used without changes in the status of any noncritical activity to become critical.

5.2.1.4 Identifying Critical Activities   The total float values of activities are very useful for practical scheduling of the activities and in responding to the many changes that occur on site. Activities with zero floats mean that they have to be constructed right at the their schedule times, without delays. These activities, as such, are considered to be critical. They deserve the special attention of the project manager because any delay in critical activities causes a delay in the project duration.

One interesting observation in the results of CPM analysis is that critical activities form a continuous path that spans from the beginning to the end of the network. In our example, activities A, D, and E (excluding dummy activities) are critical and the critical path is indicated by bold lines on Figure 5–5. Notice that among the three paths in this example (A-B-E; A-C-E; and A-D-E), the critical path is the longest one, an important characteristic of the critical path. In real-life projects with many activities, it is possible that more than one critical path are formed. By definition, the length of these critical paths is the same. It is noted that the example we used here to demonstrate the CPM analysis is very simple and involves only finish-to-start relationships. More involved examples will be given in Section 5.3.

5.2.2   Precedence Diagram Method (PDM)

Precedence Diagram Method (PDM) is the scheduling method used for AON networks. It basically follows the CPM method, however, with slight variation to suit AON networks. The PDM follows the same four steps of the CPM.

5.2.2.1 Forward Pass
To prepare for the forward pass, the AON network of Figure 5–1 can be modified by adding four boxes to each activity to put their related calculations, as shown in Figure 5–7. The top two boxes are used in the forward pass.

Figure 5-7. Forward Pass in PDM Analysis

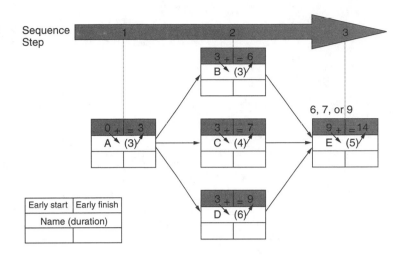

To generalize the calculations and make them suitable for computerization, forward pass can proceed from one sequence step in the network to the other. In our example, the process is as follow:

1. At sequence step 1 is activity A (first activity in the network). We give it an early-start (ES) of 0 in the left top box. Adding the activity duration, we determine the EF time of the activity, and we put it in the top right box.
2. We move forward to sequence step 2 with activities B, C, and D. These three activities have only A as a predecessor with time 3 as its EF. As such, all three activities can start as early as time 3 (ES = 3). Each activity, accordingly, calculates its own EF time based on its duration.
3. Moving forward to sequence step 3 is activity E. This activity has three predecessors (3 head arrows) of activities B, C, and D with their largest EF time being 9. The ES of activity E, thus, becomes time 9. Adding its duration, the EF becomes time 14.

5.2.2.2 Backward Pass Once the forward pass is finished, the backward pass can start, moving from the last sequence step backward to the first, putting the calculations in the bottom two boxes of each activity, as shown in Figure 5–8. The process is:

1. We start at the last sequence step, activity E and we transfer the early-finish value to become the activity's late-finish (LF) time. Then, subtracting the activity's own duration, the late-start (LS) time is calculated as time 9 and put in the bottom left box of the activity.
2. Moving backward to sequence step 2, activities B, C, and D all have one successor (activity E) with LS time of 9. The LF of all these activities becomes time 9. Each activity then calculates its own LS time, as shown in Figure 5-8.
3. Moving to sequence step 1 is activity A. The activity is linked to 3 tail arrows (i.e., has 3 successors) of activities B, C, and D. The LF of activity A, thus, is the smallest of its successors' LS times, or time 3. Activity A then calculates its own LS as time zero.

5.2.2.3 Float Calculations Notice that by the end of the backward pass, all activity times can be read directly from the boxes of information on the activity, without additional calculations. This also makes it simple to calculate the total float of each activity using the same relationships used in the CPM analysis, basically,

$$\text{Total Float} = \text{LS} - \text{ES} = \text{LF} - \text{EF} = \text{LF} - \text{ES} - \text{d}.$$

5.2.2.4 Identifying Critical Activities Critical activities can also be easily determined as the ones having zero float times, activities A, D, and E. The critical path is

Figure 5-8.
Backward Pass in
PDM Analysis

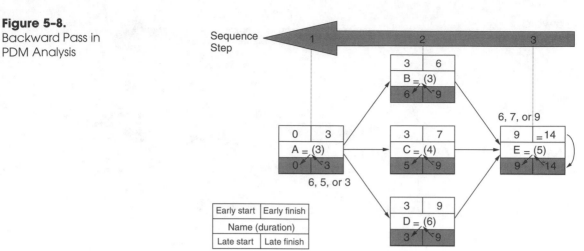

then shown in bold as Figure 5–8. The PDM analysis, as explained, is a straightforward process in which each activity is considered as an entity that stores its own information. The analysis in fact lends itself very well to the recent advancements in object-oriented programming (OOP). In OOP concepts, objects are independent entities that store information and values, incorporate calculation procedures, and can send messages to other objects.

Using OOP concepts, forward pass, for example, can be implemented by letting each object (activity) wait until it receives messages from all its predecessors about the time they finished. The activity, as such, calculates its own start time as the largest predecessor finish time. The activity also can calculate its own duration at that time using its stored information about resources and production rates. Then, it calculates its own finish time and then sends that time to its predecessors so that they can start their own calculations. One major benefit of OOP concepts is that it lets the programmer focus more on problem-solving issues related to his or her problem and less on programming issues.

5.2.3 Schedule Presentation

After the CPM and PDM calculations are made, it is important to present their results in a format that is clear and understandable to all the parties involved in the project. The simplest form that has been used for decades is the bar chart or Gantt chart, named after the person who first used it. A Gantt chart is plotted using either early or late activity times, as shown in Figures 5–9 and 5–10. The early Gantt chart is drawn using the ES times of activities, while the late Gantt chart is drawn using the LF times. The chart in fact shows various interesting details. Float times of activities, for example, can be shown, thus informing practitioners of the range of permissible changes to the schedule. Critical activities can be shown in a different color or pattern, as shown in Figure 5–9 and 5–10. The Gantt chart can also be used for accumulating total daily resources and/or costs, as shown at the bottom part of Figure 5–11. One additional benefit of the Gantt chart is its use on site to plot and compare the actual progress in the various activities to their scheduled times, as shown in Figure 5–11 with actual bars plotted at the bottom.

Figure 5-9. Early Bar Chart

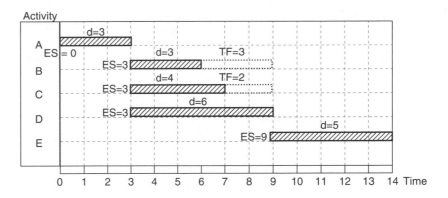

Figure 5-10. Late Bar Chart

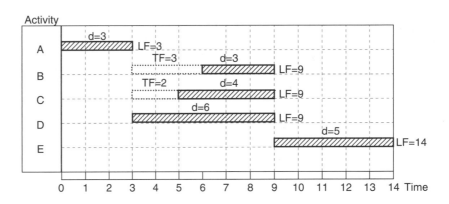

Figure 5-11. Using a Bar Chart to Accumulate Resources

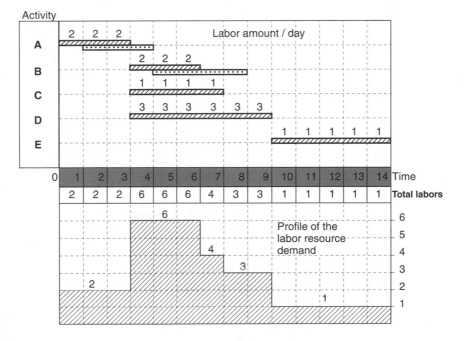

5.3 Manually Solved Examples

For the project data shown in Table 5–2, complete the following steps or answer the questions:

a. Draw an AOA network of the project.
b. Perform forward pass and backward pass calculations?
c. What is the effect of delaying activity D by three days?

Table 5–2. Data for Example 1

Activity	Duration	Immediate Predecessor
A	2	—
B	6	A
C	3	A
D	1	B
E	6	B
F	3	C, D
G	2	E, F

Solution

a, b. The solution is shown in Figure 5–12.
c. Total float of activity D = LF – ES – d
$$= 11 - 8 - 1 = 2.$$

Then delaying activity D by 1 day more than its total float will cause a net delay in the whole project by 1 day to become 17 days.

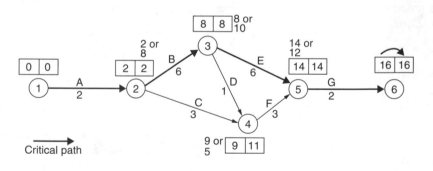

Figure 5-12. Solution to Example 1

Example 2

Perform PDM calculations for the small project below and determine activity times. Durations are shown on the activities. The solution is shown in Figure 5–13.

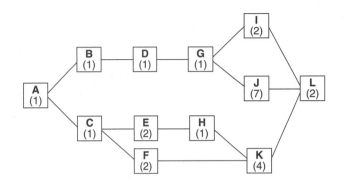

Solution

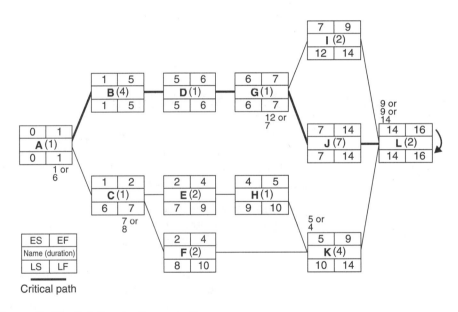

Critical path

Figure 5-13. Solution to Example 2

Example 3

Perform PDM calculations for the small AON network shown here. Pay special attention to the different relationships and the lag times shown on them.

Solution

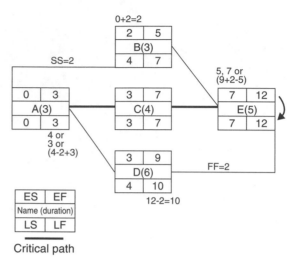

Figure 5-14. Solution to Example 3

5.4   Criticisms to Network Techniques

The CPM and PDM analyses for network scheduling provide very important information that can be used to bring the project to success. Both methods, however, share some drawbacks that require special attention from the project manager. These drawbacks can be summarized as follow:

- Assume all required resources are available: The forward pass and backward pass calculations do not incorporate resources into their formulation. Dealing with limited resources, therefore, has to be done separately after the analysis, as described in Chapter 8.

- Large resource fluctuations can result: Since CPM and PDM formulations deal mainly with activities durations, not resources, most often they result in large fluctuations in the total resources, from one day to the other. Special resource-leveling effort has to be done, therefore, to reduce the hiring and firing of resources. This is covered in Chapter 8.

- Ignore project deadline: The formulations of CPM and PDM methods do not incorporate a deadline duration to constrain project duration. This aspect is covered in Chapter 9.

- Ignore project costs: Since CPM and PDM methods deal mainly with activities durations, they do not deal with any aspects related to cost minimization of the project. This is covered in Chapter 9.

- Use deterministic durations: The basic assumption in CPM and PDM formulations is that activity durations are deterministic. In reality, however, activity durations take certain probability distribution that reflect the effect of project conditions on resource productivity and the level of uncertainty involved in the project.
- Do not consider realistic productivity factors: With CPM and PDM analyses determining the start times of activities, it is possible to convert these start times to calendar days and accordingly identify the time of the year in which each activity is planned for construction. Based on that, it is possible to modify activity durations and costs to reflect the impact of productivity related factors such as weather conditions. For example, if January productivity is 0.7, an activity constructed in January can be modified so that its duration becomes:

d1 (modified duration) = d (original duration)/productivity factor

c1 (modified cost) = c (original cost)/productivity factor

Accordingly, total project duration becomes longer but more closely reflects actual construction conditions. This is covered in Chapter 9.

5.5   Scheduling with Microsoft Project Software

Let's now use the commercial scheduling software (Microsoft Project) and apply it to our case study project which resulted from the planning stage in Chapter 3. We first activate Microsoft Project to start a new project. In starting any project, let's follow the systematic steps shown in Figure 5–15 to 5–26.

Figure 5–15. Initial Setup of Microsoft Project

Once a new file is open, use the **Tools-Options** menu item to start setting up the Microsoft Project software.

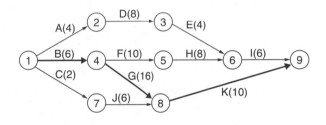

Figure 5-16. Setup Default Options

With the Schedule tab, adjust default options as shown. Important ones are: scheduling from start date, duration entered in days, default task type is "Fixed Duration", and new tasks are *not* effort driven.

The last two options will not let the duration change automatically when resources are added or removed.

Click the **Set as Default** button, then the **OK** button.

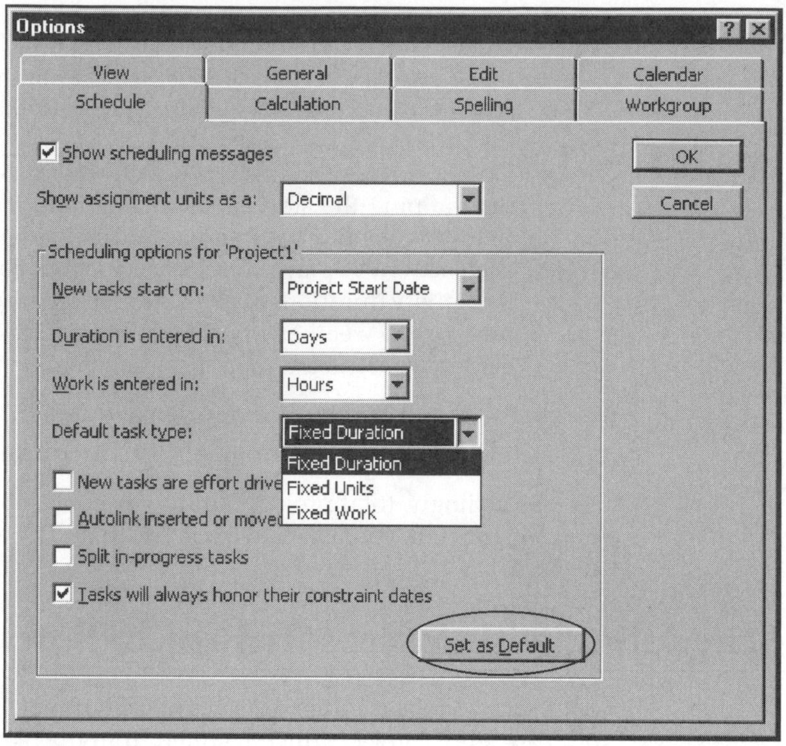

Figure 5-17. Setup Project Start Date

Now, use the **Project-Project Information** menu option to specify the project start date as August 1. When finished, click the **OK** button.

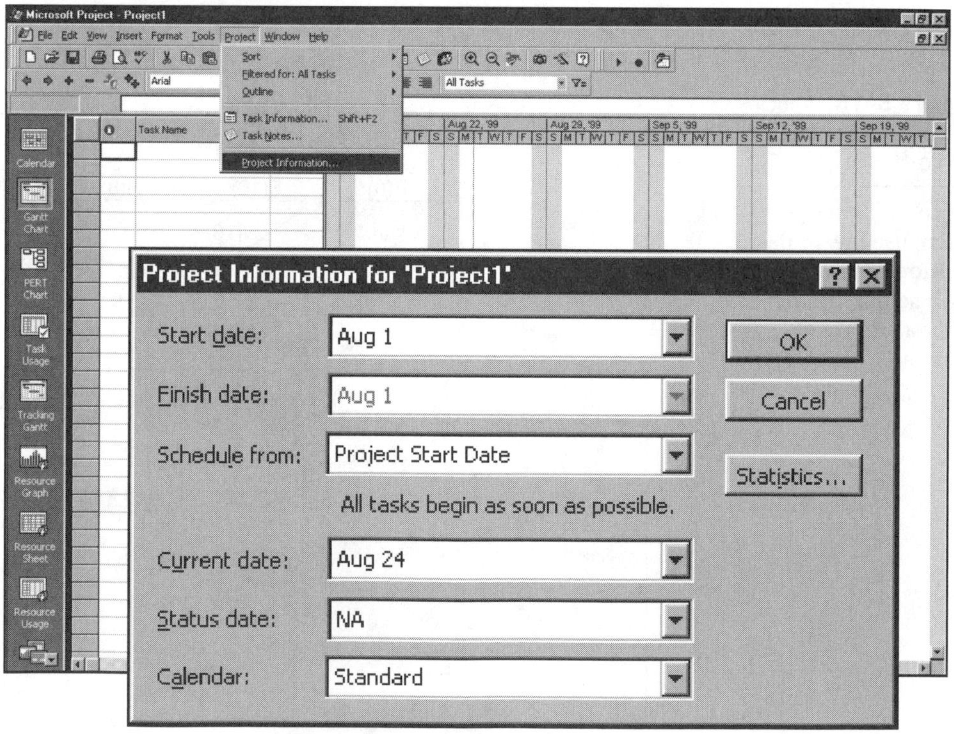

Figure 5-18. Setup Working Times

Use the right mouse button on the Gantt chart calendar and select **Change Working Time.** Then, as shown, select the Saturday and Sunday columns and specify them as **Working Time.** This gives us a 7-day working week. You may also specify any day as off or change the work hours on any day. Then, click **OK.**

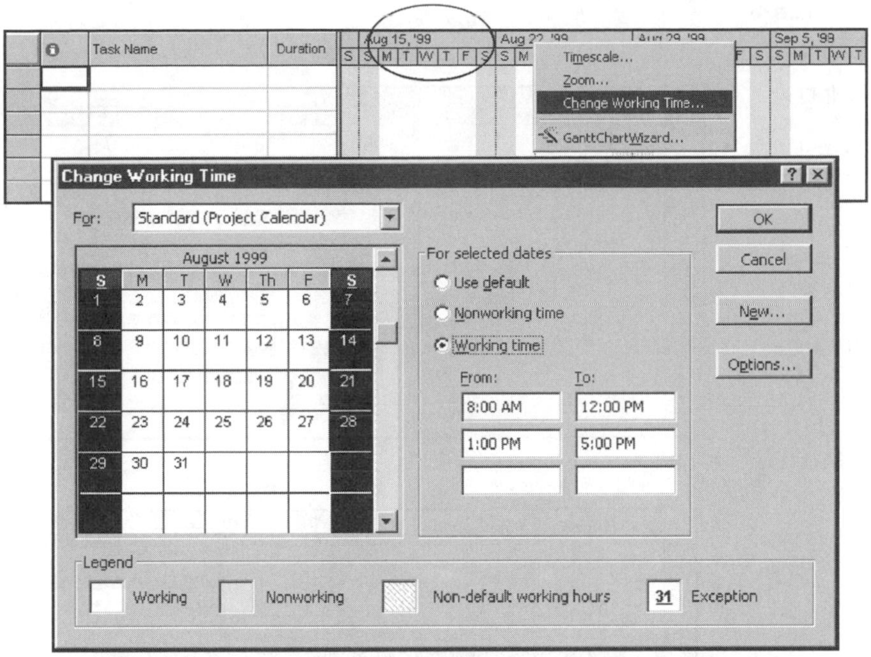

Figure 5-19. Setup Time Scale

Use the right mouse button on the Gantt chart calendar and select **Time Scale.** Set the major scale units as months labeled as shown. Also, set the Minor scale units as days labeled as shown. Use the Enlarge text box to adjust the view of the Gantt chart as desired.

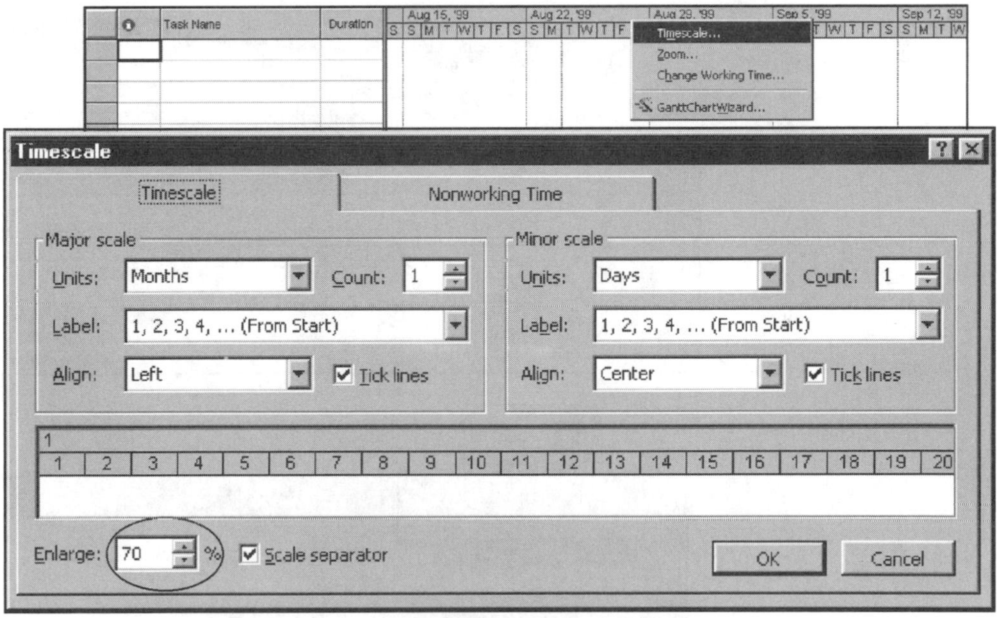

Figure 5-20. Set up the Layout

Use the **Format-Layout** menu option to select how the bar chart will look.

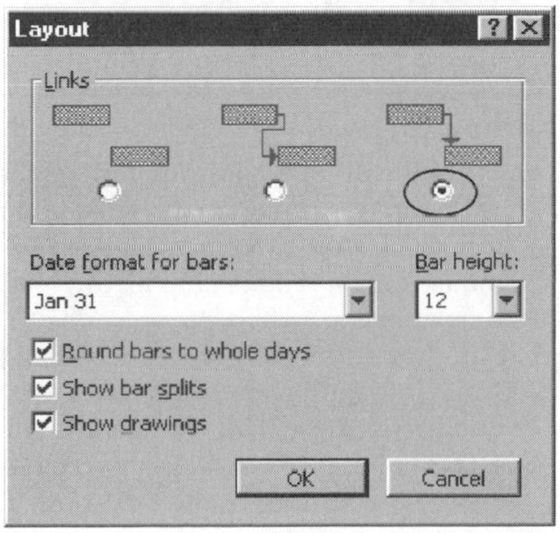

Figure 5-21. Input Project Activities into Gantt Sheet

To input the activities of the project, let's enter their names one-by-one in the Gantt sheet with their durations in the two columns shown.

	ⓘ	Task Name	Duration
1		A	4 days
2		B	6 days
3		C	2 days
4		D	8 days
5		E	4 days
6		F	10 days
7		G	16 days
8		H	8 days
9		I	6 days
10		J	6 days
11		K	10 days

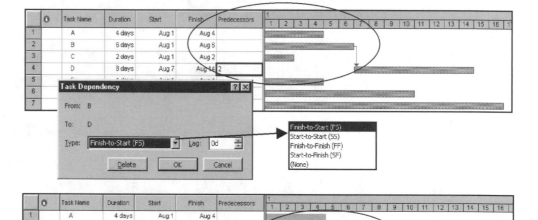

(a)

(b)

(c)

Figure 5-22. Specifying Relationships

There are several ways to specify the relationships among the tasks.

a. Move the divider bar until you see the Predecessors column. Then type the row numbers of the predecessors separated by commas and hit the Enter key. A relationship will be inserted (arrow) and task 2 is made to follow task 1, as shown. If you double-click the mouse on the relationship arrow, a window for specifying the relationship type and lag time appears.

b. Another simple way to insert a relationship is to drag from the middle of one task (Course turns into four arrows) into another task. Automatically, a relationship will be inserted and predecessor ID is written into the Predecessors column.

c. A third approach is to select two tasks using (use the Ctrl key) and then link them using the toolbar buttons or the **Edit-Link Tasks** menu option.

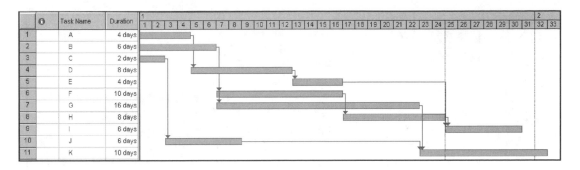

Figure 5–23. The Schedule

Once relationships are entered by any method, a 32-day schedule will result. You can adjust the project data to fit the screen as described before.

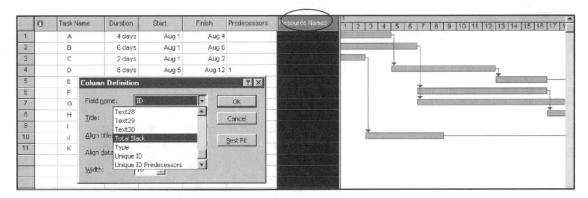

(a)

(b)

Figure 5-24. The Schedule Data

To view activity times such as Early-Start or the Total Float (called Total Slack), you have two options:

a. Use the divider bars to view all the columns in the Gantt sheet. Select the top part of any column and then use **Insert-Column** menu option to add a column in the selected position. Now, select the type of information you would like to view. Here, we select the **Total Slack** and hit **OK.** Continue doing the same to view all desired data.

b. View one of the software's preset tables. Use the **View-Table-Schedule** menu option to show all schedule data, as shown here.

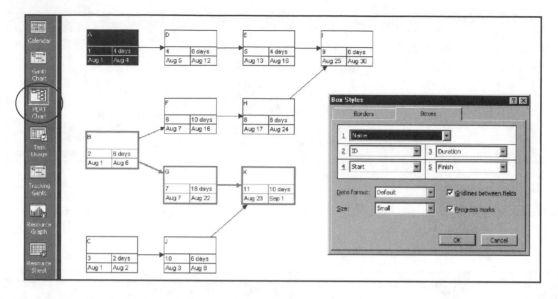

Figure 5-25. Viewing the Project Network

Use **View-PERT Chart** menu option to view the project network. Notice that critical activities have bold borders. To specify what data to view in the box of each task, use **Format-Box Styles** menu option. Experiment with this option and then view the project Gantt chart.

> **Note:** You can use the PERT chart view to insert tasks (use **Insert-New Task**) and link them by dragging from one to the other. Also, double-click the mouse on each task to specify its duration.

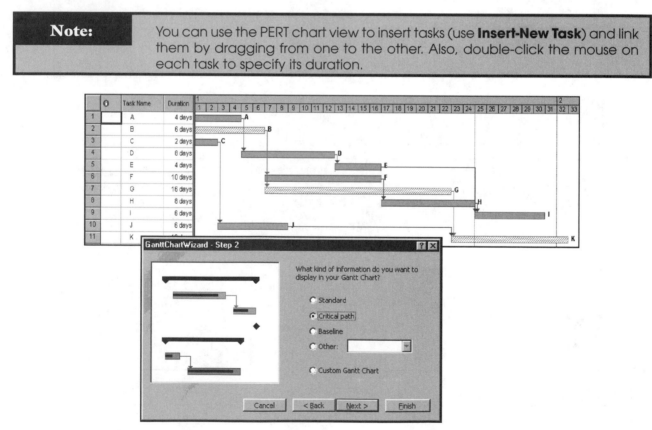

Figure 5-26. Modifying the Bar Chart

Use the **Format-GanttChartWizard** menu option to format the bar chart. Show the critical path, and put custom task information (task name) on the right side of the bars. You can also use **Format-Bar Styles** to change the pattern of critical tasks as shown. Now you can print your schedule and save the file. Compare the results with our manual solution of Example 3. The file of this example (**CPM-Ch05.mpp**) is provided on the CD accompanying this book.

5.6   Scheduling with P3 Software

We can use P3 software on the case study project by either starting a new P3 file or converting the Microsoft file we generated in the previous step into P3 format. In performing these options, we will follow the steps shown in Figures 5–27 to 5–29.

Figure 5–27.
Starting a New P3 Project

From the P3 main **File** menu, start a new project. Note that the process of creating a project is well described in the tutorial under the Help menu.

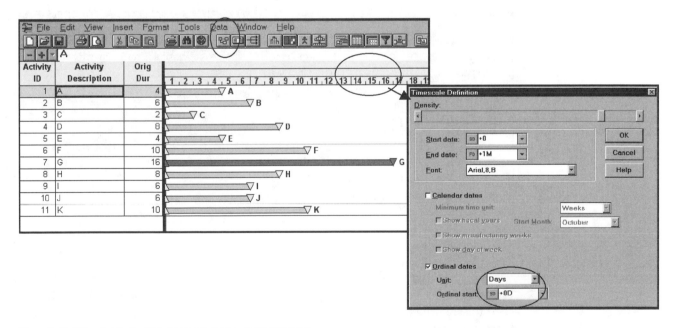

Figure 5–28. Activity IDs, Descriptions, & Durations

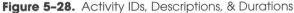

Now, add activity IDs, descriptions, and durations as shown and the bars will all look parallel. To adjust the time scale, right-click the mouse on it and adjust the options as shown. Now, to add the logical relationships, we can simply access the PERT view (Network diagram) from the toolbar and add them by dragging from each predecessor task to its successor.

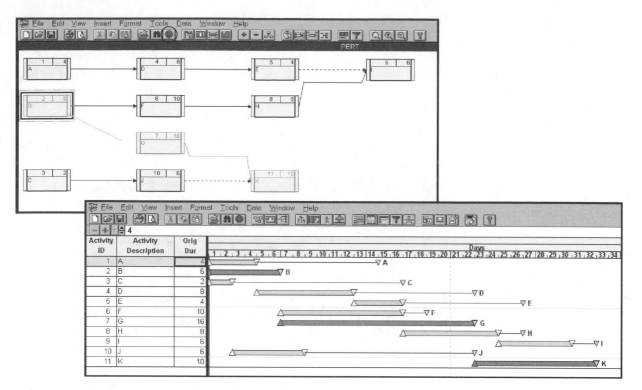

Figure 5-29. Adding Relationships and Calculating the Schedule

After adding the relationships, the schedule button on the toolbar calculates the schedule. Then, we can view the bar chart which shows critical activities and float times as lines. Total project duration is 32 days.

Importing Microsoft Project Files:

As an alternative to creating a new P3 file, it is possible to import the file from Microsoft Project. Three simple steps are involved:

1. Open the Microsoft Project file and use the **Save As** feature and save the file MPX format.

2. Activate the MPX conversion program that comes with the P3 package, select the option to convert from MPX to P3, choose the MPX file we saved in the previous step, assign a P3 file name, and then confirm the conversion.

3. Activate P3 software and load the newly created P3 file.

5.7 Back to Our Case Study Project

Following the case study road map, we will consider the result of planning and proceed to schedule the project (shaded box) by performing critical-path analysis on the project network.

5.7.1 Manual Solution

For the AOA network of our case study project in which each activity uses its cheapest method of construction, we need to do the following:

Figure 5–30.
Network
Calculations for the
Case Study

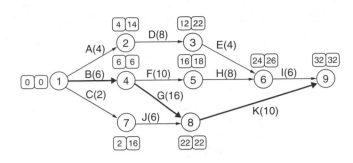

Table 5–3. Activity Times

Activity	Duration	ES	LF	TF = LF − ES − d	Critical
A	4	0	15	10	
B	6	0	6	10	*
C	2	0	16	14	
D	8	4	22	10	
E	4	12	26	10	
F	10	6	18	2	
G	16	6	22	0	*
H	8	16	26	2	
I	6	24	32	2	
J	6	2	22	14	
K	10	22	32	0	*

Figure 5–31. Early
Bar Chart

ACTIVITY	1	2	3	4	5	6	7	8	9	10	11	12	13	14	15	16	17	18	19	20	21	22	23	24	25	26	27	28	29	30	31	32
A																																
B																																
C																																
D																																
E																																
F																																
G																																
H																																
I																																
J																																
K																																

- Calculate ES, LF, & TF for all activities. Identify critical ones.
- Draw an early bar chart for the project.
- Ascertain the effect of delaying activity H by two days on project duration.

Solution

First, we perform forward and backward pass calculations as shown in Figure 5–30. Critical activities are highlighted with dark arrows. Project duration is 32 days, similar to MS Project and P3 solutions. The calculations related to activity times and total floats are shown in Table 5–3, and an early bar chart for the Case Study is shown in Figure 5–31.

Since the total float of activity H is 2 days, delaying its start two days will not affect the project duration.

5.7.2 Critical Path Model on a Spreadsheet

To experiment with critical path analysis in a transparent manner, let's try to model it on the familiar spreadsheet format. Using a small four-activity network (Figure 5–32), forward pass and backward pass calculations can be modeled using spreadsheet functions. We will introduce one small change to the calculations for the purpose of becoming more general. Each activity has a delay time, which can originally be set to zero. The benefit of these delay values is to allow any desired adjustments to the schedule as will be explained in Chapter 8. Considering these delays, forward pass calculation determines the early-start time of each activity. Activity E in Figure 5–32, for example, has three predecessors (P1 = A, P2 = B, and P3 = C). Accordingly, activity E can start only after the latest of those predecessors has finished and the Delay$_E$ time has passed. Thus, the early-start (ES$_E$) of activity E becomes the largest of F1, F2, and F3 values calculated in the forward pass table of Figure 5–32.

Backward pass calculation, on the other hand, determines the late-finish time of each activity. Activity A in Figure 5–32, for example, has three successors (S1 = B, S2 = C, and S3 = D). Accordingly, activity A may finish no later than the earliest of its successor's late-start times. Thus, the late-finish (LF$_A$) of the current activity A becomes the smallest of T1, T2, and T3 values calculated in the backward pass table of Figure 5–32. Putting the forward pass and backward pass calculations together, a complete CPM model is obtained. In fact, the calculations in the cells of the forward pass and backward pass tables lend themselves well to application on a spreadsheet. Developing such a spreadsheet model for CPM analysis will be demonstrated on our case study project that was calculated manually under Example 3 of the solved examples discussed earlier. A CPM model of the case study was implemented on Microsoft Excel, as shown in the spreadsheet of Figure 5–33. The spreadsheet file

Figure 5-32. Table Format for CPM Calculations Considering Activity Delay

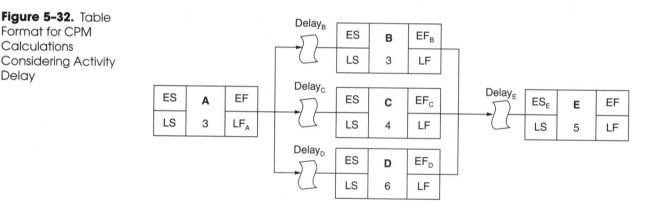

Forward Pass: ES$_E$ = Largest of (EF$_B$+Delay$_E$, EF$_C$+Delay$_E$ or EF$_D$+Delay$_E$)

ID	Duration	Predecessors			F1	F2	F3	Delay	ES$_E$
		P1	P2	P3					
E	5	B	C	D	EF$_B$+Delay$_E$	EF$_C$+Delay$_E$	EF$_D$+Delay$_E$	0	Largest of (F1, F2, or F3)

Backward Pass: LF$_A$ = Smallest of (LS$_B$–Delay$_B$, LS$_C$–Delay$_C$, or LS$_D$–Delay$_D$)

ID	Duration	Successors			T1	T2	T3	Delay	LF$_A$
		S1	S2	S3					
A	3	B	C	D	LS$_B$–Delay$_B$	LS$_C$–Delay$_C$	LS$_D$–Delay$_D$	0	Smallest of (T1, T2, or T3)

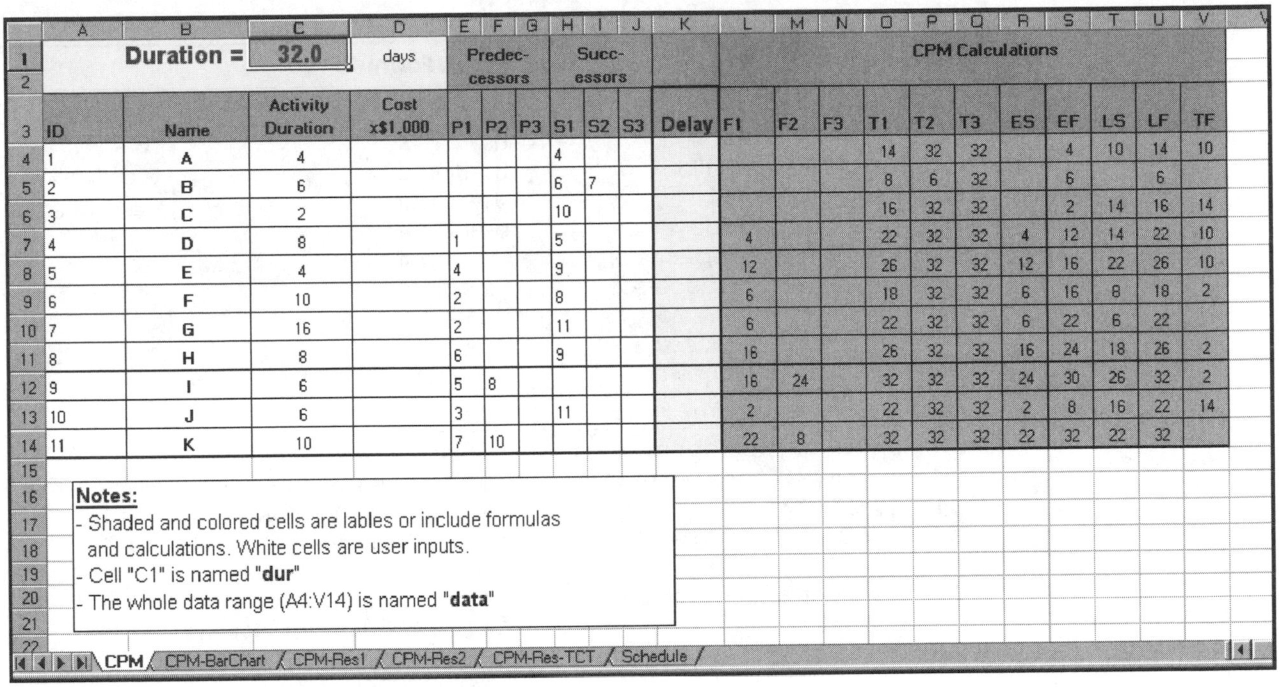

ID	Name	Activity Duration	Cost x$1,000	P1	P2	P3	S1	S2	S3	Delay	F1	F2	F3	T1	T2	T3	ES	EF	LS	LF	TF
1	A	4					4							14	32	32		4	10	14	10
2	B	6					6	7						8	6	32		6		6	
3	C	2					10							16	32	32		2	14	16	14
4	D	8		1			5				4			22	32	32	4	12	14	22	10
5	E	4		4			9				12			26	32	32	12	16	22	26	10
6	F	10		2			8				6			18	32	32	6	16	8	18	2
7	G	16		2			11				6			22	32	32	6	22	6	22	
8	H	8		6			9				16			26	32	32	16	24	18	26	2
9	I	6		5	8						16	24		32	32	32	24	30	26	32	2
10	J	6		3			11				2			22	32	32	2	8	16	22	14
11	K	10		7	10						22	8		32	32	32	22	32	22	32	

Duration = 32.0 days — Predecessors — Successors — CPM Calculations

Notes:
- Shaded and colored cells are lables or include formulas and calculations. White cells are user inputs.
- Cell "C1" is named **dur**
- The whole data range (A4:V14) is named **data**

Sheet tabs: CPM / CPM-BarChart / CPM-Res1 / CPM-Res2 / CPM-Res-TCT / Schedule

Figure 5–33. Excel CPM Model of the Case Study Project

(**CPM.xls**) comes with the CD of the book and represents a template for CPM analysis with one row for each activity. The data for an activity are represented in columns. The shaded cells include formulas, while the white cells are user inputs pertaining to the activity ID, Name, Duration, Cost, IDs of three predecessors, IDs of three successors, and a Delay value. The total project duration (32 days) is also included in a separate cell at the top of the spreadsheet.

The spreadsheet formulas for a typical activity in the CPM model of Figure 5–33 are shown in Table 5–4. The formulas are simple and use the VLOOKUP function to identify activity-related data in the whole table. These formulas are written once in the cells of one row and then copied several times according to the number of activities in the project. The spreadsheet, as such, represents a transparent CPM model that allows for quick what-if analysis. Any change in the duration of any activity or the logical relationships automatically changes the project duration along with all the CPM data regarding the activities' early and late times as well as the total floats, which identify critical and noncritical activities. Experiment with different options and see their impact on the schedule.

We can benefit a great deal by using the CPM model on Excel and we can expand it in various ways. One way is to include a bar chart with the schedule, as given in the second sheet of the **CPM.xls** file (Figure 5–34). Another way of expanding this model is to use the Delay values in column K to intentionally delay the start times of some values. This can be a helpful feature to avoid overallocation of our resources (this topic is discussed in Chapter 7).

Most importantly, we can add a schedule sheet to our Excel-based project management file **Case-Study.xls** and, as such, we can link the estimate data to a scheduling sheet, as discussed in the next subsection.

Table 5-4. Spreadsheet Formulas for Activity 1 in Row 4

Cell	Description	Data/Formula
A4	Activity ID	User Input
B4	Activity description	User Input
C4	Activity duration	User Input
D4	Activity Cost	User Input
E4	ID of 1st predecessor	User Input
F4	ID of 2nd predecessor	User Input
G4	ID of 3rd predecessor	User Input
H4	ID of 1st successor	User Input
I4	ID of 2nd successor	User Input
J4	ID of 3rd successor	User Input
K4	Delay (lag time in days)	User Input
L4	EF*of 1st predecessor	=IF(E4="", K4,VLOOKUP(E4,data,19) + K4)
M4	EF of 2nd predecessor	=IF(F4="", K4,VLOOKUP(F4,data,19) + K4)
N4	EF of 3rd predecessor	=IF(G4="", K4,VLOOKUP(G4,data,19) + K4)
O4	LS of 1st successor	=IF(H4="",dur,VLOOKUP(H4,data,20)-VLOOKUP(H4,data,11))
P4	LS of 2nd successor	=IF(I4="",dur,VLOOKUP(I4,data,20)-VLOOKUP(I4,data,11))
Q4	LS of 3rd successor	=IF(J4="",dur,VLOOKUP(J4,data,20)-VLOOKUP(J4,data,11))
R4	ES of current activity	=MAX(L4:N4)
S4	EF of current activity	=R4+C4
T4	LS of current activity	=U4-C4
U4	LF of current activity	=MIN(O4:Q4)
V4	TF of current activity	=U4-R4-C4

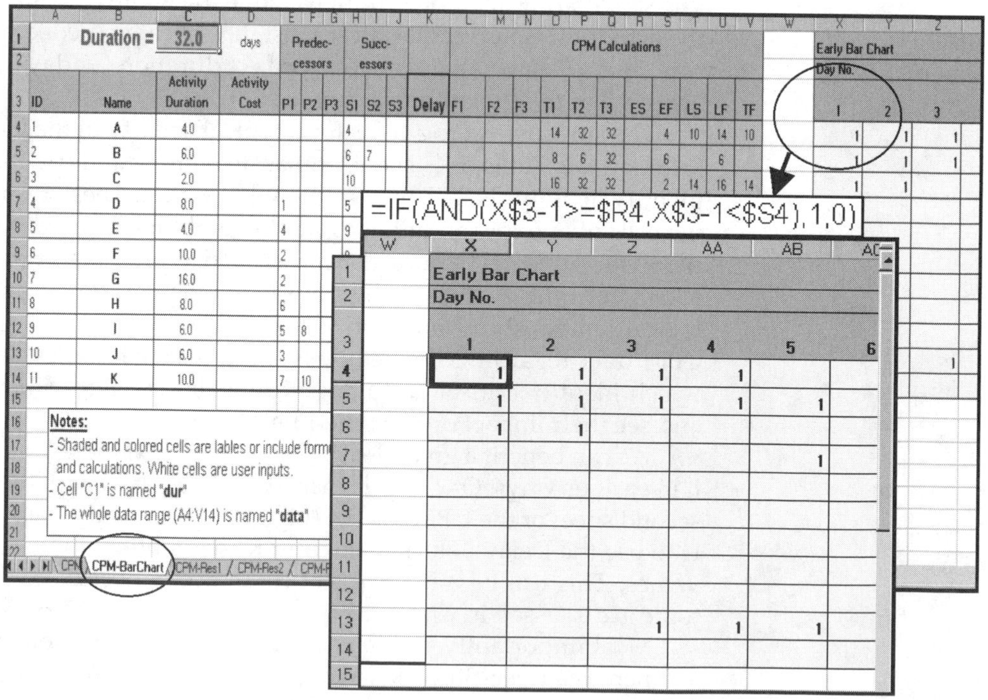

Figure 5-34. CPM Model with Bar Chart

The sheet CPM-BarChart extends the CPM to view a bar chart of the schedule. The formula in cell X4, shown, is made once and then copied to all the bar chart range. Row 3 indicates the working days in the project and a "1" in the bar chart indicates that the activity is scheduled in this day.

Note:

- The full data Range (A4:V21) is named **data**.
- Cell (C1) representing project duration is named **dur** and contains the equation =MAX(S:S).
- EF: Early-Finish; ES: Early-Start; LS: Late-Start; LF: Late-Finish; TF: Total-Float

5.7.3 Tying the Estimate to the Schedule

In Chapter 3, we entered all the activity data in the Excel system for Project Management (**Case-Study.xls file**). Now, it is possible to build upon this estimate data and generate a schedule for the case study project without reentering the tasks and their durations. We can do this as illustrated in Figures 5–35 to 5–38.

In the Estimate sheet we make sure that: various construction methods are specified for the various activities, three key resources are identified with their daily limits, and the cheapest construction method selected. Afterwards, we are ready to send the estimate data to Microsoft Project automatically using the **Up** button.

Activities' names, durations, and resources are automatically entered into a new Microsoft Project file and become ready for you to specify the logical relationships, as

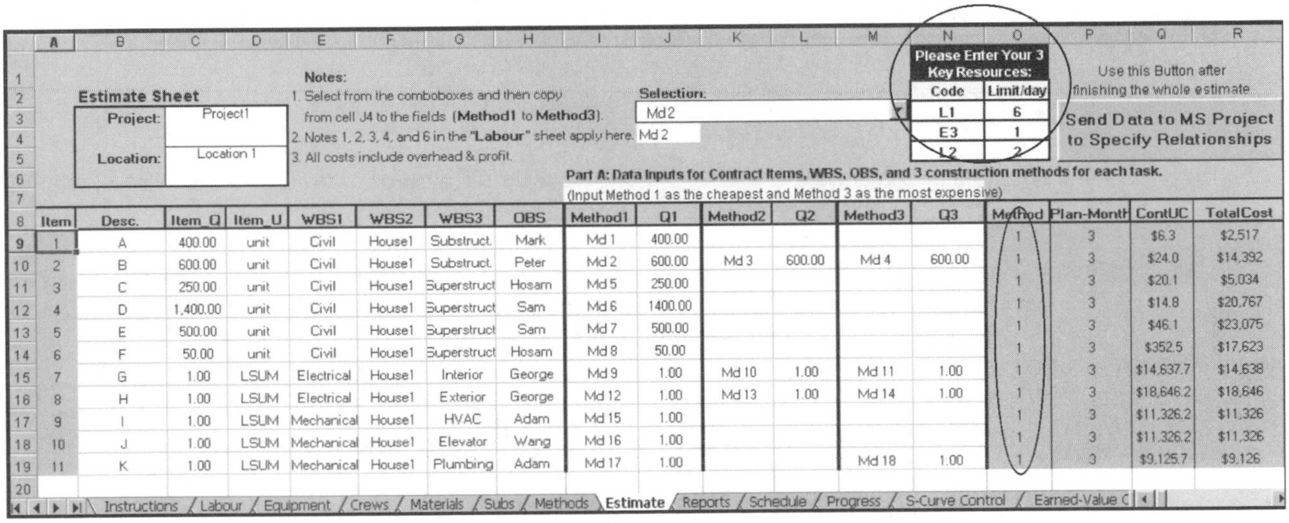

Item	Desc.	Item_Q	Item_U	WBS1	WBS2	WBS3	OBS	Method1	Q1	Method2	Q2	Method3	Q3	Method	Plan-Month	ContUC	TotalCost
1	A	400.00	unit	Civil	House1	Substruct.	Mark	Md 1	400.00					1	3	$6.3	$2,517
2	B	600.00	unit	Civil	House1	Substruct.	Peter	Md 2	600.00	Md 3	600.00	Md 4	600.00	1	3	$24.0	$14,392
3	C	250.00	unit	Civil	House1	Superstruct	Hosam	Md 5	250.00					1	3	$20.1	$5,034
4	D	1,400.00	unit	Civil	House1	Superstruct	Sam	Md 6	1400.00					1	3	$14.8	$20,767
5	E	500.00	unit	Civil	House1	Superstruct	Sam	Md 7	500.00					1	3	$46.1	$23,075
6	F	50.00	unit	Civil	House1	Superstruct	Hosam	Md 8	50.00					1	3	$352.5	$17,623
7	G	1.00	LSUM	Electrical	House1	Interior	George	Md 9	1.00	Md 10	1.00	Md 11	1.00	1	3	$14,637.7	$14,638
8	H	1.00	LSUM	Electrical	House1	Exterior	George	Md 12	1.00	Md 13	1.00	Md 14	1.00	1	3	$18,646.2	$18,646
9	I	1.00	LSUM	Mechanical	House1	HVAC	Adam	Md 15	1.00					1	3	$11,326.2	$11,326
10	J	1.00	LSUM	Mechanical	House1	Elevator	Wang	Md 16	1.00					1	3	$11,326.2	$11,326
11	K	1.00	LSUM	Mechanical	House1	Plumbing	Adam	Md 17	1.00			Md 18	1.00	1	3	$9,125.7	$9,126

Figure 5–35. Finalizing the Estimate Data

Figure 5–36. Automatically Generated Microsoft Project File Based on the Estimate Sheet

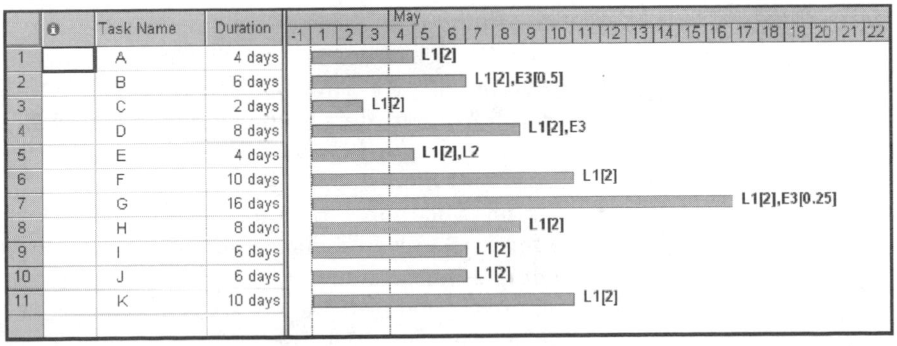

	Task Name	Duration
1	A	4 days
2	B	6 days
3	C	2 days
4	D	8 days
5	E	4 days
6	F	10 days
7	G	16 days
8	H	8 days
9	I	6 days
10	J	6 days
11	K	10 days

Figure 5-37.
Adding Activity
Relationships to the
Activities in MS
Project

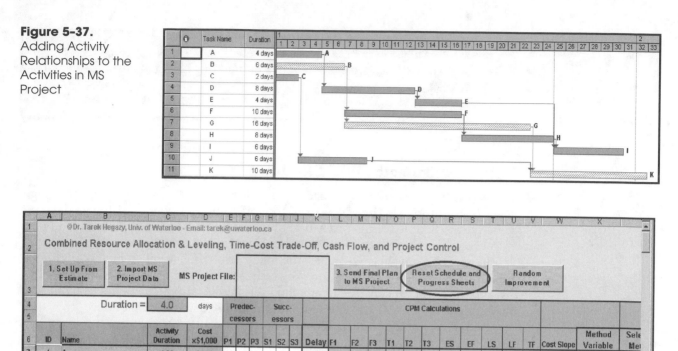

Figure 5-38. The Schedule Sheet with Automated Setup Buttons

discussed earlier in Figure 5–22. If we follow the steps in Figures 5–22 to 5–26, we will end with the project network shown in Figure 5–37.

We are not yet finished with the Microsoft Project file, and we can still continue using the software features to improve the schedule under resource constraints. This issue is covered in Chapter 7. In that chapter, we will obtain the best schedule of the software, then transfer that schedule back to the Schedule sheet of the Excel system using automated buttons that link the schedule to the estimate (Figure 5–38). The Schedule sheet follows the CPM model described in Section 5.7.2 and will be used to optimize the schedule under various work constraints.

5.8   Advanced Topics

In addition to the basic scheduling concepts we experimented with in this chapter, Microsoft Project, and other software systems, provide you with other advanced features that you might need in the management of your projects. Some of these include:

- Scheduling from the end date. In this case, you input the project deadline and select the Schedule From End Date option under project information;
- Experiment with Effort-Driven tasks (refer to the help system of Microsoft Project for more details on using this option).
- Experimenting with activity constraints (refer to the help system of Microsoft Project for more details on using this option).
- Use the Microsoft Project toolbar for PERT (Program Evaluation and Review Technique) to consider uncertainty in activity duration. PERT uses three duration estimates for each activity (optimistic, pessimistic, and most-likely) to schedule the project and provide probabilistic assessment of project completion (refer to the help system of Microsoft Project for more details on using this option).

5.9 Summary

Time in construction means money and the best way to manage time is through scheduling. The schedule is both a powerful management and communication tool among project participants. Without a schedule, it becomes almost impossible to coordinate the diverse activities in a project. Through network scheduling, we can determine the start and finish times of activities, determine which activities are critical and need not be delayed, and the amount of freedom or slack we have in case a delay has to be introduced. No doubt, network scheduling is becoming a standard practice in almost all projects, not only at the preconstruction phase but also during construction. In addition, a comparison of as-planned versus as-built schedules can show the impact of various delays on the project and thus can be used for claim analysis.

5.10 Bibliography

Ahuja, H. N. (1976). *Construction Performance Control by Networks.* New York: John Wiley & Sons.

Harris, R. (1978). *Resource and Arrow Networking Techniques for Construction.* New York: John Wiley & Sons.

Hendrickson, C. and Au, T. (1989). *Project Management for Construction: Fundamental Concepts for Owners, Engineers, Architects, and Builders.* Englewood Cliffs, NJ: Prentice Hall.

5.11 Exercises

1. For each of the project networks shown below (activity durations in brackets):
   - Calculate ES, LF, & TF for all activities. What are the critical activities?
   - Draw an early bar chart for the project.
   - What is the effect of delaying activity H by two days on the total project duration?

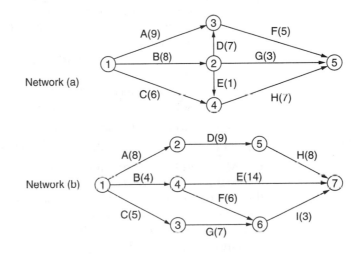

Network (a)

Network (b)

2. Calculate the schedule for the following network:

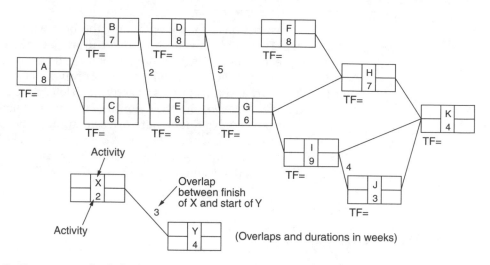

Activity

X
2

Activity

Overlap between finish of X and start of Y

Y
4

(Overlaps and durations in weeks)

3. Prepare a schedule for the small project in Exercise 7 of Chapter 3.

4. Draw an AON network for the following activities, showing all planning and scheduling steps. Calculate the ES, EF, LF, and TF for all activities and show the critical path.

Activity	Duration	Depends Upon
A	2	
B	6	A
C	3	A
D	1	B, A
E	6	B, A
F	3	A, D, B, C
G	2	C, D, F, E

5. Using Microsoft Project software (or Primavera), follow the guidelines in this chapter to set up a new project file. Enter the data for the solved Example 1 in Section 5.3 into the software, then:

   ■ Show critical activities with a different pattern. Put the duration of each activity on the right side of its bar.
   ■ Show columns for task ID, Name, Start, Finish, Predecessors, Successors, and Total float.
   ■ On the network (PERT chart), show tasks' start times, tasks' finish times, durations, and total floats.

   Print two sheets: one sheet for Gantt chart showing the activity data and the bar chart, and another sheet for the PDM network.

6. Repeat question 5 for the solved Example 2 in Section 5.3.

7. Repeat question 5 for the solved Example 3 in Section 5.3.

8. Use Microsoft Project software and follow the guidelines in this chapter to set up a new project file. Add two tasks, "Part 1" and "Part 2," to the project then enter the data of networks (a) and (b) in question 1 as subtasks of Part 1 and Part 2, respectively. Part 2 has a finish-to-start relationship with Part 1 with a five-day lag time. Print two sheets: Gantt chart and the PDM network showing project duration and critical activities.

9. Modify the spreadsheet file for CPM calculations, **CPM.xls**, for the data of the solved Example 1 in Section 5.3. Print the spreadsheet showing project duration and critical activities.

10. Repeat exercise 9 for the solved Example 2 in Section 5.3.

Chapter 6

SCHEDULING OF LINEAR AND REPETITIVE PROJECTS

After studying this chapter, you will be able to:

- Identify the unique requirements of projects that involve repetitive activities.
- Differentiate between a resource-driven and a duration-driven schedule.
- Understand the basics of the Line-of-Balance (LOB) technique.
- Determine a balanced mix of resources and keep them fully employed.
- Perform integrated CPM-LOB calculations.
- Experiment with the BAL program.

Owner, CM					
• Need • Feasibility • Project Definition • Owner Approval	**A/E, CM, Owner**		**Owner, CM**		
	• Conceptual Design • Owner Approval • Soil Reports • Preliminary Design • Detailed Design • Quantities • Work Documents • Select Project Contract Strategy	**Bidders**		**Contractor**	
		Prepare Bid Proposal + Baseines • Collect Data (site, quantities, specs, resources, tasks, etc.) • Planning • Time & Cost Estimation • **Scheduling** • Resource Management:deadline resource constraints, TCT, etc. • Bidding Strategy & Markup Estimation • Cash Flow Analysis • Submit Bid	• Evaluate Bids and Select General Contractor	• Start Construction • Detailed Planning, Estimating & Resource Management • **Schedule Updating** • Progress Evaluation • Time, Cost, & Quality Control • Commissioning	**O & M Staff** • O & M • Demolition at End of Service Life
CONCEPT	**DESIGN**	**BIDDING**		**CONSTRUCTION**	**O & M**

6.1 Introduction

In the previous chapter, you were introduced to the network techniques (CPM and PDM) for project scheduling. In this chapter, we will learn a new technique, Line-of-Balance (LOB) for scheduling linear projects that involve a recognizable number of repetitive activities. Examples of this category of projects include highways, pipelines, and high-rise buildings. Being a resource-driven technique, the objective of the LOB technique is to determine a balanced mix of resources and synchronize their work so that they are fully employed and non interrupted. As such, it is possible to benefit from repetition, and the crews will likely be able to spend less time and money on later units once they develop a learning momentum. Another benefit of the LOB technique is its interesting representation of the schedule, given the large amount of data for the repetitive units. This chapter introduces integrated CPM-LOB calculations that combine the benefits of CPM network analysis of a single unit and the resource-driven LOB analysis and representation. This enables us to effectively schedule projects with repetitive activities.

6.2 Linear Projects

Linear projects are projects involving repetitive activities. They take their name from either: (a) involving several uniform units of work such as multiple houses or typical floors in a building; or (b) being geometrically linear such as highway, pipeline, and utility projects. In both categories, however, some nontypical units could be involved such as a nontypical floor in a high-rise building or a nonstandard station in a highway project. The activities in these nontypical units may certainly involve higher or lower quantity of work than their counterparts in the typical units. To simplify the scheduling task in these situations, we can assume that the project is comprised of (n) typical units, with the activities in each unit having average quantity of the work in all units. As the number of units in a project increases, eventually the project becomes more complex and more challenging.

6.3 Resource-Driven Scheduling: How Is It Different

As we have seen in network scheduling, the basic inputs to critical-path analysis are the individual project activities, their durations, and their dependency relationships. Accordingly, the forward-path and backward-path calculations determine the start and finish times of the activities. The CPM algorithm, therefore, is *duration driven*. Activities' durations here are functions of the resources that are required (rather than available) to complete each activity. The CPM formulation, therefore, assumes that resources are in abundance and cannot be used to determine what resources are needed in order to meet a known project deadline duration.

Resource-driven scheduling, on the other hand, is different and is more focused on resources. Its objective is to schedule the activities (determine their start and finish times) so that a project deadline is met using predefined resource availability limits. The LOB technique dealt with in this chapter is resource driven.

6.4 Basic LOB Representation

Let's consider a medium-sized high-rise building of 40 typical floors. The construction of each typical floor, undoubtedly, involves various interrelated activities. If a CPM network is to be developed for the whole project, certainly it will be so complex and will be composed of copies of the activities in a single floor. A bar chart of the proj-

Figure 6-1. Basic LOB Representation

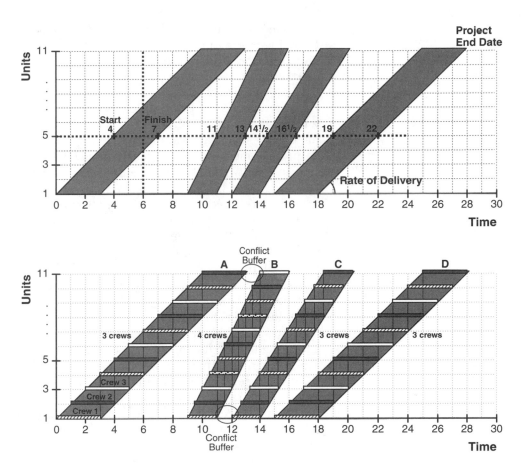

Figure 6-2. LOB Schedule with Crew Details

ect will still be so complex and will not serve the purpose of a good communication tool between planners and execution personnel.

A schedule representation that suits projects with repetitive activities is shown in Figure 6–1 between time on the horizontal axis and units on the vertical axis. This representation shows the following information:

- Each sloping bar represents one activity (A, B, C, or D) in the project and the width of the bar is the activity duration of one unit, which is uniform along all units.
- Activities (slopped bars) are sequential with no interference or overlapping. This is dictated by the sequential logical relationships involved. These sequential activities could be the activities of any continuous path in a CPM network that is repeated for several units.
- A horizontal line at any unit intersects with the activity bars at the planned start and finish times of the work in that unit.
- A vertical line at any date (time) shows the planned work that should be completed/started before and on that date.
- The slope of each activity represents its planned rate of progress and this is the direct function of the number of crews involved in the activity. The slope of the last activity is the rate of delivery of the various units.
- The finish time of the last unit in the last activity represents the end date of the project.

It is possible also to add more details to the basic LOB schedule as shown in Figure 6–2. The modified figure shows interesting information, as follows:

- The number of crews employed in each task is graphically represented with each crew indicated by a different pattern. As such, the movement of the crews from one unit to the other is shown.

- The three crews employed in activity (A) have different work assignments. Crew 1 works in four units (numbers 1, 4, 7, and 10) and leaves site on day 12. Similarly, Crew 2 works on four units (numbers 2, 5, 8, and 11) then leaves site on day 13. Crew 3, on the other hand, works on three units only (numbers 3, 6, and 9) and leaves site on day 11.
- Each crew moves to a new unit as soon as it finishes with the previous one, without interruption. As such, work continuity is maintained and the learning phenomenon can lead to some savings in cost and time.
- To prevent interference among the sequential tasks of the LOB schedule in case an activity is slightly delayed, a buffer time may be introduced as shown, to act as float.
- When a slower activity is to follow a faster activity (e.g., C follows B), the activity C can be scheduled starting from unit 1, immediately following the predecessor B. Because interference can happen at unit 1, buffer time may be added to the start of unit 1 (potential conflict is at the bottom unit) to avoid any overlap.
- When a faster activity is to follow a slower activity (e.g., B follows A), the activity B needs to be scheduled starting at the top unit. If buffer time is to be added, it will be added at the top. Notice that the start of unit 1 in activity B has been delayed to allow the task to proceed at its desired high rate without interruption.
- Changing the production rate (slope) of any activity changes the project duration. Even speeding one task may prove to be harmful to the project when the conflict point changes from bottom to top.
- If speeding an activity or relaxing it may result in a delay in the project, a good scheduling strategy is to schedule the activities as parallel as possible to each other and also parallel to a desired project delivery. This, in fact, is one of the objectives of LOB scheduling.

6.5 CPM-LOB Calculations

Having the LOB representation in mind, the objective is to achieve a *resource-balanced* schedule by determining the suitable crew size and number of crews to employ in each repetitive activity. This is done such that: (1) the units are delivered with a rate that meets a prespecified deadline; (2) the logical CPM network of each unit is respected; and (3) crews' work continuity is maintained. The analysis also involves determining the start and finish times of all activities in all units and the crews' assignments.

The CPM-LOB formulation that achieves the above objective involves four main issues, which are discussed in the next sections:

- Crew synchronization and work continuity equation.
- Computation of a project delivery rate that meets a given deadline duration.
- Calculating resource needs for critical and noncritical activities.
- Drawing the LOB schedule.

6.5.1 Crew Synchronization

A simple relationship between the duration taken by a crew in one unit (D) and the number of crews (C) to employ in a repetitive activity can be derived from the illustration in Figure 6–3. In this figure, we have a five-unit activity and three crews to use. Only one crew is assumed to work in a single unit and the crew spends time (D) on the unit before moving to another unit. Certainly, the duration (D) is a direct function

Figure 6–3. Crew Synchronization

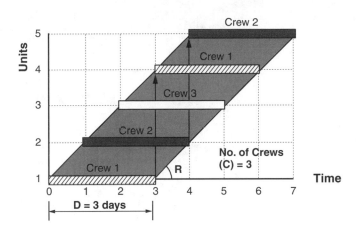

of the quantity of work (in man-hours) needed for each unit and the number of resources forming the crew, as follows:

$$D \ (days) = \frac{Quantity \ of \ work \ in \ one \ unit}{(Number \ of \ crew \ members \times hours \ per \ day)} = \frac{Man \ hours}{Man \ hours/day} \quad \textbf{(6.1)}$$

Using Equation 6.1 and knowing that the quantity of work is the same for each unit (i.e., the numerator is constant), a different choice of crew formation (the denominator, number of crew members) results in a different duration (D) for the unit. The more people assigned to a crew, the less the time they take to finish the work of one unit.

Now, having three crews available for this activity, it is possible to schedule their movements in and out of each unit, as shown in the figure, so that they are not interrupted and the work progresses at a rate (R). For that work synchronization to happen, the following simple relationship applies:

$$Number \ of \ Crews \ (C) = D \times R \quad \textbf{(6.2)}$$

In the example shown, $C = 3$; $D = 3$ days; then, R becomes 1 unit/day, according to Equation 6.2. Therefore, it is possible to achieve work continuity given any change in the number of crews (C) or crew formation (affects D) by adjusting the rate of progress (R). For example, if four crews become available, we can apply the same Equation 6.2 to determine a faster progress rate of 1.25 units/day will be achieved.

Driving the relationship of Equation 6.2 is simple. By enlarging part of Figure 6–3 and dividing the duration (D) among the (C) crews, the slope of the shaded triangle in Figure 6–4 becomes:

$$R = \frac{1}{(D/C)} \quad \textbf{(6.3)}$$

and the time D/C becomes:

$$D/C = \frac{1}{R} \quad \textbf{(6.4)}$$

Both equations lead to our formulation of $C = D \times R$. Equation 6.4 also means that work continuity is achieved by shifting the start of each unit from its previous one by a time D/C or $1/R$. This shift also has another practical meaning. Because each crew has part of its duration nonshared with other crews, the chances of work delay are reduced when two crews need the same equipment, or other resource, such as a crane on site.

Figure 6-4. Deriving
Equation 6.2

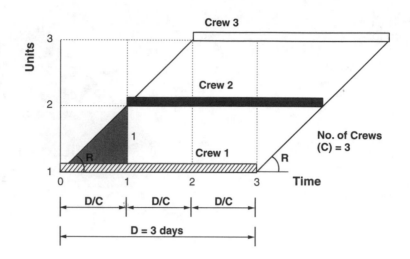

6.5.2 Meeting a Deadline Duration

A basic objective in CPM-LOB calculation is to meet a given deadline for finishing a number of (n) repetitive units, each having its own CPM network of component activities. Using the illustration in Figure 6–5, it is possible to formulate a strategy for meeting the deadline by calculating a desired rate of delivery (R_d) for the units, as follows:

$$R_d = \frac{n - 1}{T_L - T_1} \tag{6.5}$$

where T_L is the deadline duration of the project and T_1 is the CPM duration of the first unit. The delivery rate determined from Equation 6.5 is, in fact, the minimum rate required to meet the desired deadline. Any higher rate can expectedly produce a shorter project duration, however, more crews may need to be used and the schedule can be more costly.

Figure 6-5.
Calculating a
Desired Rate of
Delivery

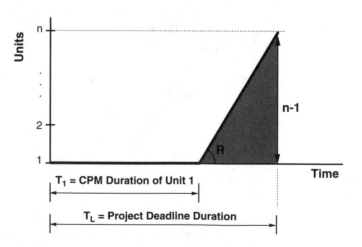

6.5.3 Calculating Resource Needs

Once a minimum delivery rate (R_d) is calculated, it is desirable to enforce this rate on the schedule of the repetitive activities to determine the resources needed to complete the project on time. Equation 6.2, therefore, needs to be applied particularly to the crit-

Figure 6–6.
Utilization of Float in
LOB Calculations

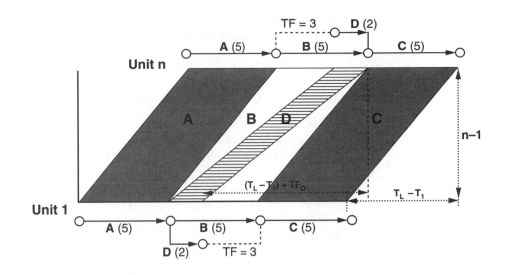

ical activities, which are the sequential tasks that take the longest path in the CPM network of each unit. Noncritical activities, on the other hand, have float (*TF*) times and as such, we can afford to relax them according to their float times to reduce cost. It is, therefore, possible to modify Equation 6.5 and generalize it to determine a desired rate (R_i) for any repetitive task (*i*), as follows:

$$R_i = \frac{n-1}{(T_L - T_1) + TF_i} \tag{6.6}$$

The formulation of Equation 6.6, therefore, applies to both critical and noncritical tasks, as a function of the activity's total float value. For critical activities, total floats are zeroes and Equation 6.6 is reduced to Equation 6.5. The physical meaning of Equation 6.6 is illustrated in Figure 6–6. In this figure, a five-unit project is shown with each unit consisting of a simple four-activity network. Three of the four activities, A, B, and C, are sequential and have five-day durations each. The fourth activity D runs parallel to B and has a duration of 2 days only. Accordingly, A, B, and C are critical activities where as activity D is noncritical with Total Float (*TF*) of three days. As shown in Figure 6–6, the slopes of activities A, B, and C are the same and are steep. The slope of activity D, on the other hand, has been relaxed by simply starting unit 1 of task D as early as possible while starting the last unit as late as possible (notice the difference in the CPM networks of the first and the last units). In this manner, simple analysis of the slope of activity D in the figure leads us to the formulation of Equation 6.6. Using this approach, the relaxation of noncritical activities can be performed without violating any logical relationships or crew work continuity requirements.

With the desired rates calculated for the individual activities, a generalized form of Equation 6.2 can be used to determine the necessary number of crews (C_i) to use in each activity (*i*), as follows:

$$C_i = D_i \times R_i \tag{6.7}$$

Another important consideration is that, in most cases, the number of crews calculated using Equation 6.7 is not an integer value. Because a fraction of a crew is not possible, the number of crews (C_i) has to be rounded up to determine the actual number of crews (C_{ai}). As a consequence to that, the actual rates of progress in the activities (R_{ai}) need to be adjusted, as follows:

$$C_{ai} = Round\ Up\ (C_i) \tag{6.8}$$

$$R_{ai} = \frac{C_{ai}}{D_i} \tag{6.9}$$

Equations 6.6 to 6.9, therefore, become the necessary and sufficient basis of integrated CPM-LOB calculations.

6.5.4 Drawing the LOB Schedule by Hand

A LOB schedule becomes simple to draw when all activities run with an exact similar rate (i.e., activities run parallel to each other). However, because of the rounding of number of crews in Equation 6.8, the activities' actual rates (R_{ai}) calculated using Equation 6.9 will not be parallel. Drawing the LOB schedule as such requires extra care, as conflict points, either at the top unit or at the first unit, will be introduced due to the difference in progress rates from one activity to the other. As explained earlier, sometimes speeding an activity will cause a net delay in the whole project, if work continuity is to be maintained. Therefore, some noncritical activities may end up being delayed in some situations, violating the logical relationships or becoming critical themselves. Also, in some situations, the end schedule may slightly extend beyond the deadline. In this case, a simple approach to use is to reschedule the project with a deadline duration that is slightly (one or two days) shorter than originally desired. Therefore, the LOB schedule should be carefully made.

To draw the LOB schedule using the activities' actual rates (R_{ai}), we need to proceed in a forward path, following the logical relationships in the CPM network. When an activity is considered, its predecessors are first examined to identify their largest finish times, which are then considered as a boundary on the start of the current activity. Drawing the schedule by hand is simple when the network is small and can be done with varying levels of detail, as shown in Figures 6–1 and 6–2.

In terms of presentation, showing all the activities on the same grid results in a crowded schedule and can be confusing even for a small network. Two interesting approaches can be used to circumvent this problem. One approach is to draw the critical path on one grid and draw the other paths, each on a different grid. The benefit of drawing these paths is to help visualize the successor/predecessor relations for any given task, and accordingly facilitate any desired changes to rates or crews. The second approach is to extend the LOB representation to show the noncritical activities on a mirrored grid as shown in Figure 6–7. From that schedule, the start and finish times of each unit in each activity can be read and crew assignments can be shown.

Figure 6–7.
Alternative LOB
Representation

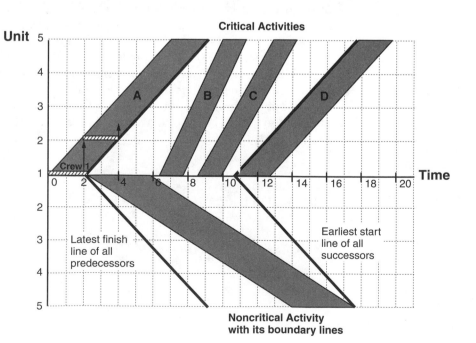

6.6   Back to Our Case Study Project

In terms of the road map to our case study, we will continue the effort towards establishing a realistic schedule of the project considering the activities with repetitive nature.

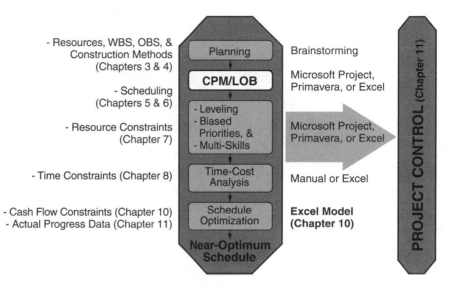

6.6.1   Detailed Calculation Procedure

Now, let's describe the systematic CPM-LOB procedure and apply it our case study project. Consider that the project involves five typical units. The CPM network of the activities in a single unit is shown in Figure 6–8, which is the one we determined based on our planning task in the previous chapters.

Activity durations, in days, are shown inside the brackets. The owner wants the contractor to finish all the work in 50 days. Calculate and draw a LOB schedule that helps the contractor meet the deadline. Also, determine how many crews are needed and show on the LOB schedule how the crews move from one unit to the other.

Solution:

The solution to this case study follows three typical steps, as follows:

Step 1: Perform CPM Calculations for a Single Unit
In this step, we determine the duration of a single unit and identify the critical path. As shown in Figure 6–9, the CPM duration (T_1) of a single unit is 32 days and the critical path is B-G-K.

Figure 6–8. CPM Network of a Single Unit

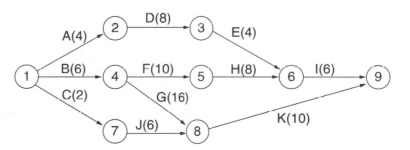

Figure 6-9. CPM
Calculations for a
Single Unit

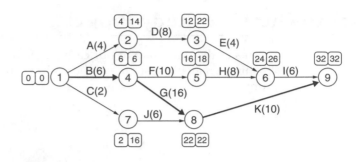

Step 2: Construct LOB Calculations Table

In this step, we construct a table for calculating the desired rate of progress in each activity, apply the continuity equation (Equation 6.2) to determine the number of crews, and then determine the actual rate of progress in each activity. The calculations are shown in Table 6–1.

Given that a project duration (T_L) of 50 days is desirable, the 32 days taken by the first unit (T_1) will leave only 18 days ($T_L – T_1$) to deliver the remaining four (i.e., $n –$ 1) units. This gives a rate of delivery (4/18 = 0.222 units per day), or simply one unit every 4.5 days. As discussed before, this rate will be applied to the critical activities as a desired rate required to meet the deadline. Noncritical activities, on the other hand, will have smaller rates depending on their float times (column 4 of Table 6–1). The two shaded columns in Table 6–1 represent the necessary calculations that enable us to draw a LOB schedule.

Table 6-1. LOB Calculations

Activity	Activity Duration (D)	Total Float (TF)	Desired Rate (R) = (n - 1) / (T_L - T_1 + TF)	Required Crews (C) = D × R	Actual Crews (C_a)	Actual Rate (R_a) = C_a / D
A	4	10	0.143	0.572	1	0.25
*B	6	0	0.222	1.332	2	0.333
C	2	14	0.125	0.250	1	0.5
D	8	10	0.143	1.144	2	0.25
E	4	10	0.143	0.572	1	0.25
F	10	2	0.200	2	2	0.2
*G	16	0	0.222	3.552	4	0.25
H	8	2	0.200	1.6	2	0.25
I	6	2	0.200	1.2	2	0.333
J	6	14	0.125	0.75	1	0.167
*K	10	0	0.222	2.22	3	0.3

T_L = deadline duration = 50 days; T_1 = CPM duration of a single unit; * = Critical activity

Step 3: Draw the LOB Schedule

In this step, we draw the LOB schedule, following the procedure described in Section 6.5.4, and accordingly determine the project completion date. Let's start with the critical path. First, we construct an empty grid and then plot the activities one by one as a four-point parallelogram (Figure 6–10). The two points on the left side represent the line connecting the start times of all units whereas the right side line connects the finish times. We start with activity B, the first critical activity. The first unit starts at time 0 (lower-left point) because this is the first activity in the path. The finish time of the

Figure 6-10. LOB Schedule for the Critical Path

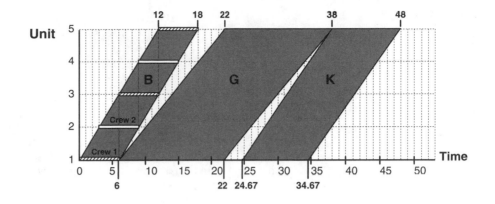

first unit (bottom-right point), therefore, is at time 6 because the activity has a duration of six days. Knowing the two bottom points of B, the top two points are then determined, considering the actual progress rate of this activity ($R = 0.333$, see Table 6–1). As discussed in Section 6.6, each unit starts after (1/R) days from the start of its previous unit. Therefore, the last unit (unit 5) starts after $4 \times (1/0.333)$ days from the start of unit 1 (0), or $12 + 0 =$ day 12, as shown in Figure 6–10. The finish time of unit 5 (top-right point) then becomes $12 + 6$ (duration) = day 18.

Once an activity is plotted, we proceed with its successor, activity G in our case. Because G depends only on B, its start is bounded only by the finish line of activity B, which is the line between day 6 on unit 1 and day 18 on unit 5. Now, because G has a slower progress rate (0.25) than the boundary line (0.333), we can start the first unit of G (lower-left point) right after the work in activity B has finished, which is day 6 (notice that conflict point is at bottom). The finish of unit 1 (lower-right point of G), then, becomes day 22 (starts at day 6 + a duration of 16 days). Following that, similar to what we did for activity B, we can plot the top two points, considering the progress rate of activity G.

After plotting activity G, we continue with the last activity on the critical path, activity K. Because K depends on both G and J, the start of K has to be bounded by the largest finish times of G and J. For G, the finish times are connected by the line between day 22 on unit 1 and day 38 on unit 5. For J, on the other hand, simple calculations have to be made to determine its finish times. As illustrated in Figure 6–11, J follows C and has a slower rate than C. Then, without doing any calculations for C, we sketch the duration of C as 2 days, then proceed with J at unit 1 with 6 days duration, then we draw the sloped line of J's finish times, from day 8 to day 32, which are smaller than those for activity G. As such, the start of activity K is bounded by day 22 on unit 1 and day 38 on unit 5.

Figure 6-11. Determining the Boundary Line on Activity K

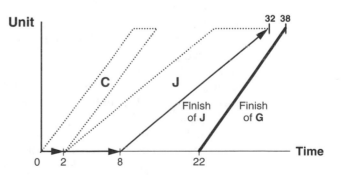

Figure 6-12. LOB Schedule for Path A-D-E-I

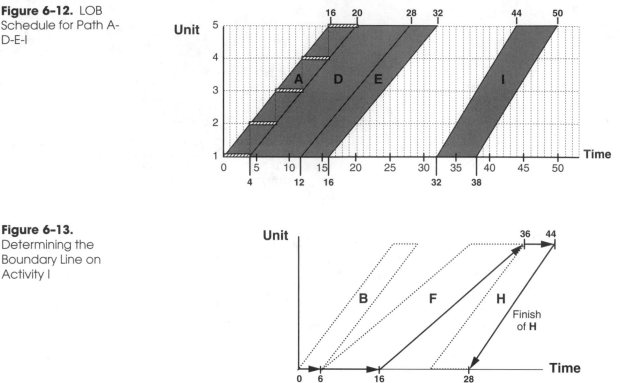

Figure 6-13. Determining the Boundary Line on Activity I

Activity K has a higher progress rate than that of its boundary line, and as such, is expected to have a conflict point at top unit. Therefore, we start plotting that activity starting from the top unit and then subtract the slope of this activity to determine the start of unit 1 (lower point), as shown on Figure 6–10. Following that process, we can see that the project is planned to end at day 48, thus meeting the 50-day deadline. Also, after drawing the lines representing the activities on the LOB schedule, it is possible to show the activities' crew assignments and their movement along the different units. Activity B in Figure 6–10, for example, shows the work assignments for its two crews. Each crew can be given a different pattern or color to be easily identified.

Let's now investigate other paths in the CPM of this example. We will consider the path connecting activities A-D-E-I and will use the same procedure described for drawing the LOB schedule of the critical path. Activities A, D, and E are sequential, have no more than one predecessor, and have identical progress rates. As such, they can be easily plotted as shown in Figure 6–12. Activity I, on the other hand, has two predecessors, E and H. The finish line of activity E is shown in Figure 6–12 and spans from day 16 till day 32. The finish line of activity H, however, can be calculated considering the B-F-H path, as illustrated in Figure 6–13. Accordingly, the start of activity I is bounded by activity H (not activity E). Now, because the activity being considered (I) has a higher progress rate (0.333) than its boundary line (0.25), we need to draw the activity starting from the top point at day 44. The resulting LOB schedule of this path (Figure 6–12) extends the project duration till day 50, which still meets the scheduling goal. The significance of this change in project duration is that the critical path has also changed for unit 5 (all other units end before day 48). This change in the critical path is caused by the relaxation of the slopes of noncritical activities and the unavoidable rounding of the crew numbers. As demonstrated by this example, extra care has to be taken when drawing the LOB schedule to determine the planned project duration.

6.6.2   Schedule Modifications

Whereas the relaxation of noncritical activities may cause a change in the critical path and extension to the project duration, one might question the feasibility of using the activity total floats to relax the slopes of noncritical activities. The expected cost savings, however, justify its use. The fewer crews that result from the relaxation are expected to cause less site congestion and avoid problems related to limited availability of resources. In view of these pros and cons, a compromising modification to Equation 6.6 may prove beneficial. Using the activities' free float values rather than the total floats is expected to relax noncritical activities moderately and reduce the impact on the critical path. In our example, when using the free floats to recalculate Table 6–1, only activity F has changed to involve three crews rather than two. Consequently, the project duration remained 48 days and the critical path remained the same.

Regardless of the formulation used to initiate a LOB schedule, many situations in practice may require changes to the schedule due to fewer available crews or even a tighter deadline. Let's, for example, consider some modifications to the 20-day schedule of Figure 6–7. Analysis of this schedule clearly indicates that the fast rate of progress in activity B and the slow rate of progress in activity D are responsible for the project duration being extended till day 20. If it is desired to reduce the project duration without completely rescheduling, several scheduling options are possible, including slowing activity B and/or speeding activity D by using different crews than originally decided. However, in some situations, changing crew sizes or number of crews may not be possible or may produce undesirable results. In these situations, it is still possible to improve the schedule by introducing interrupts into fast activities and increasing the rate of slower ones. These two strategies are illustrated in Figure 6–14.

To slow activity B, a layoff and recall strategy is applied to it. In this strategy, the start of unit 4 is delayed for two days (measured from the scheduled start determined by continuity equations). In this case, the crew is laid off after unit 3 and later recalled to start unit 4. This strategy is beneficial only when one or more fast activity(ies) (e.g., B) are trapped between two slower ones (A and C). This strategy makes it possible to start the first part of activity B earlier than its original schedule. Accordingly, activity C is possible to start earlier. The reduction of the project duration achieved through this strategy, however, comes at the expense of continuity and learning. This loss in

Figure 6–14.
Improving the LOB
Schedule

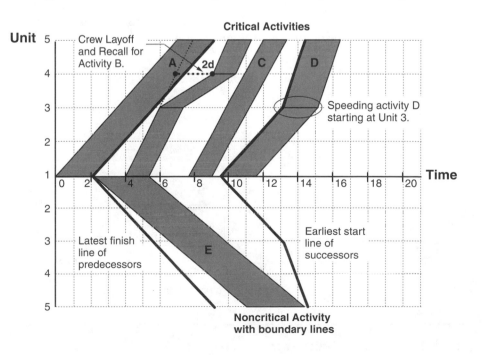

continuity may become negligible when a large number of units are involved and the layoff and recall strategy is not extensively applied. The second strategy that can reduce project duration is speeding the rate of progress in the slow activity D, starting after unit 3, by employing more crews in the activity. It is worth noting that the two strategies are most beneficial when applied to critical activities. It is also understandable that the changes caused by these strategies to the critical activities may consequently affect the start and finish times (boundary lines) of noncritical activities. Some changes to the progress rates of noncritical activities may thus become necessary.

6.6.3 The BAL Program

While it is simple to calculate and draw the LOB schedule by hand, performing these calculations for even a moderate-size project can be time consuming and complex. It is desirable, therefore, to automate the calculations and integrate them with a commercial scheduling software such as Microsoft Project. A program that does this task is included with the CD that comes with this book. The program BAL is a VBA macro attached to a Microsoft Project File (**CPM-LOB.mpp**). Some of BAL characteristics are:

- It works on a Microsoft Project file containing the CPM of a typical unit.
- The current version considers only finish-to-start activity relationships (zero lag).
- The LOB algorithm of BAL uses the free float rather than the total float in its implementation of Equation 6.6.
- It allows the user to specify the number of repetitive units and the desired deadline duration. It then automatically calculates and draws the LOB schedule.
- It uses color codes to show the different crews.
- It allows the user to easily change the number of crews for an activity to respect any crew constraints.
- It allows the user to apply a layoff-and-recall strategy at any unit.
- It allows the user to easily generate a Microsoft Project file with the start and finish times of all units taken from the finalized LOB schedule.

Using BAL, you can experiment with various options to optimize the schedule, determining optimum layoff and recall strategy, and accordingly minimize project cost. Also, once you generate a Microsoft Project file of your LOB schedule, you can use all the powerful tracking and control features of the software to bring the project to success. To demonstrate program BAL, a step-by-step guide is provided with the screen views shown in Figures 6–15 to 6–25.

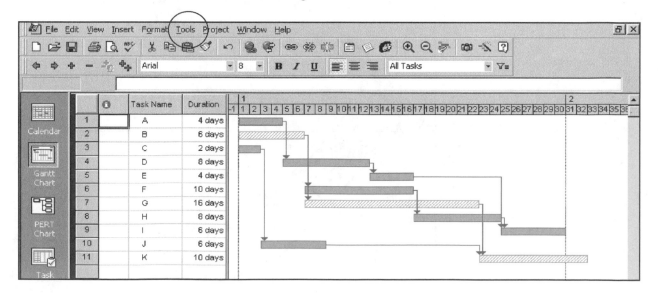

Figure 6-15. Activating BAL program

Figure 6-16. The LOB Schedule

Now, type in the number of units (**5**) and the deadline duration (**50**) into the two text boxes and then hit the **Start LOB** key to perform the calculations. With this very little input, the resulting schedule is automatically calculated and presented on the screen as shown in this figure. The top pane shows the critical path, and the bottom pane can show all the paths, one at a time, using the shown scroll bar.

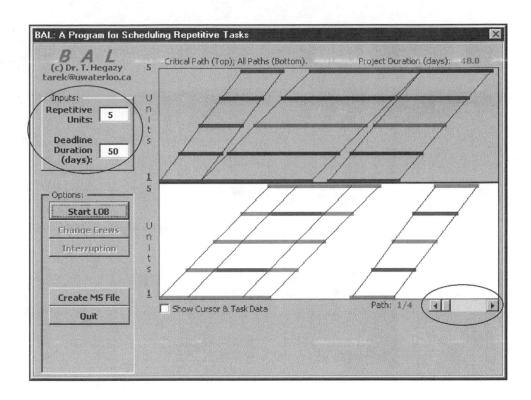

To experiment with program BAL, first copy the file **CPM-LOB.mpp** from the CD to your working directory. Then, run Microsoft Project and use the **File-Open** menu option to load the file. The Gantt chart shown is for the same example that we solved manually earlier. To activate the macro program, use the **Tools-Macro-Macros** menu option and select the macro **lob** from the list of macros and hit the **Run** key. The main screen will appear.

Now, add a third task called Finishing and specify a 50-day duration for it. With these three activities in our new project, let's add simple start-to-finish relationships among them. Automatically the repetitive subproject will adjusts itself to start on November 3, after the Basement is finished, as shown in this schedule. Using all the features of Microsoft Project, you have full access to the subproject, as shown here in expanded form.

Note: If you encounter an error when trying to run the **lob** macro, this means you have an error during the CD installation. Try reinstalling, but if problem persists, read the **LOB-Problem.txt** that comes on the CD.

Note: The BAL program works only on Microsoft Project software. P3 users, however, can convert the resulting schedule into P3 format using the MPX conversion program of P3, as discussed in Chapter 5.

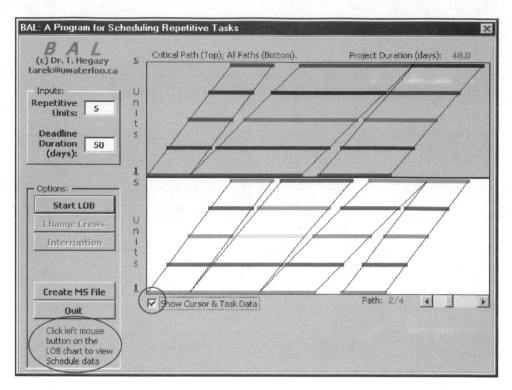

Figure 6-17. View Options

Using the scroll bar, the second path is shown in this figure. Also, the total project duration (48 days) is indicated on the top-right corner. The different colors indicate the number of crews in each activity. To view the data related to any activity, the small checkbox at the bottom of the LOB schedule is selected, as shown here. Notice the message that appears at the bottom-left corner asking the user to click on any activity to view its data.

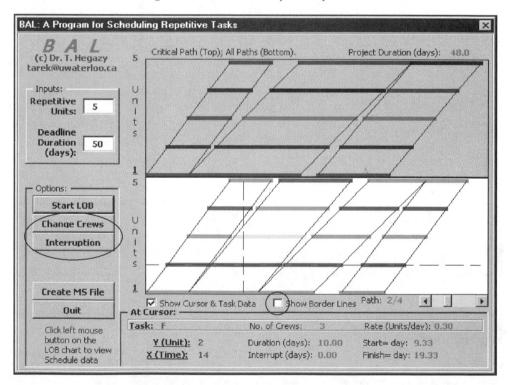

Figure 6-18. Showing Activity Data

By clicking on unit 2 of the second activity, as shown in this figure, the data of this activity appears at the bottom. Cursor location is also shown. Notice that two buttons become active and both apply to the selected activity: one to change the number of crews; and the other to introduce interrupt time (layoff-and-recall strategy). Also, a checkbox appears to show/hide the activity boundary lines.

Figure 6–19.
Showing Activity
Border Lines

In this figure, the
Show Border Lines
checkbox is selected.
Also, the **Change
Crews** button was
used to change the
crews for activity (F)
to 2 instead of 3. The
result, as shown, is a
50-day project
duration, similar to
the manual
calculations. Notice
that the top pane
shows 48 days for the
path B-G-K, which is
the original critical
path.

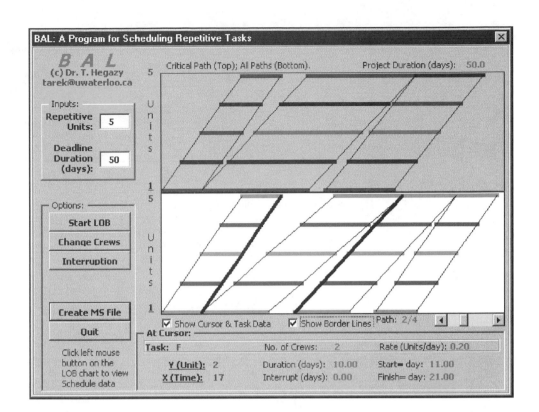

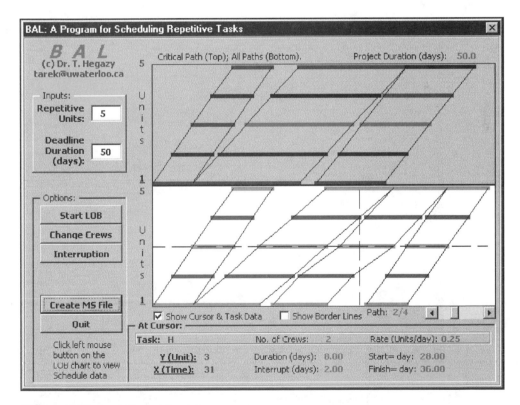

Figure 6–20. Layoff and Recall

Now, let's try the layoff-and-recall option. In all the paths of this example, you will not find a
fast task between two slower ones, which is a good candidate for this strategy. However, for
demonstration purposes, a 2-day interrupt to unit 3 of activity H has been introduced by
clicking on the **Interruption** button and entering the amount. The resulting schedule is still
50 days, as shown. Notice that the bottom part of activity H (units 1 and 2) is shifted to
the left, closer to the predecessor.

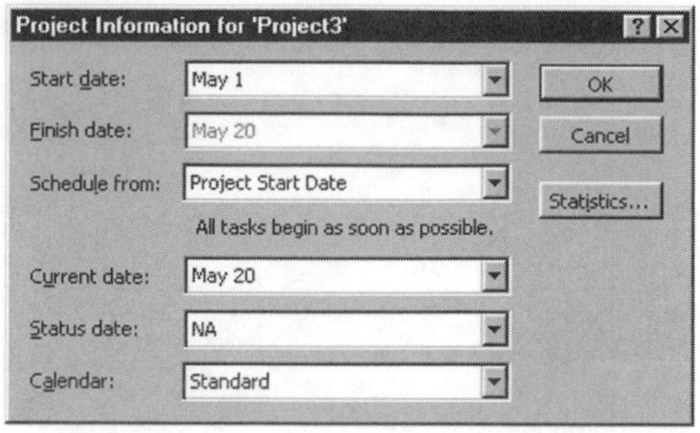

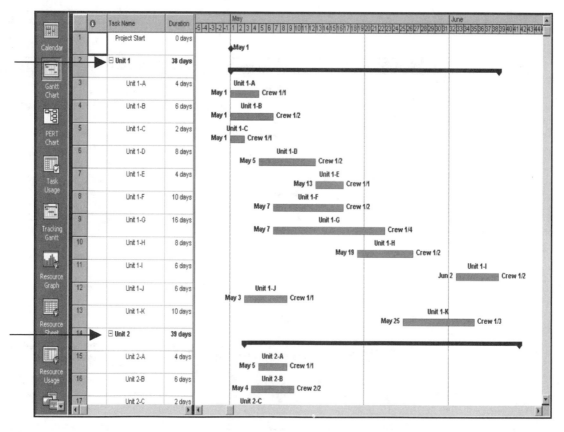

Figure 6–21. Generating a Microsoft Project File of the Resulting Schedule

To generate a Microsoft Project file, the user clicks on the **Create Microsoft File** button. A screen for the information about a new project file will be displayed, as shown. The user enters the start date of the project. In our case, we can start our project at May 1st, for example.

Figure 6–22. Looking at the Gantt Chart

According to the start date you specified, a complete schedule is generated for you, grouped by unit number. The start of each activity is derived from the LOB schedule, relative to your selected start date (May 1st). Notice that the schedule is generated with 7 working days per week. However, if you change the project start date and/or specify weekends as nonworking time, the schedule will adjust itself correctly.

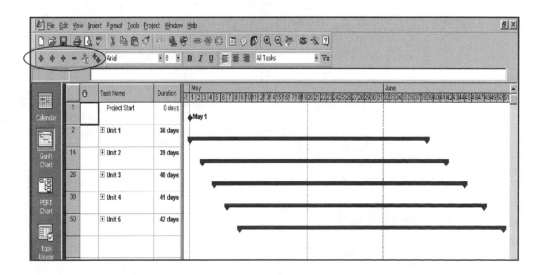

		O	Task Name	Duration	Start	Finish	Predecessors	Crew No.	Interrupt	
1			Project Start	0 days	May 1	May 1				◆May 1
2			⊟ Unit 1	38 days	May 1	Jun 7				
3			Unit 1-A	4 days	May 1	May 4	1	Crew 1/1	0	Unit 1-A Crew 1/1
4			Unit 1-B	6 days	May 1	May 6	1	Crew 1/2	0	Unit 1-B Crew 1/2
5			Unit 1-C	2 days	May 1	May 2	1	Crew 1/1	0	Unit 1-C Crew 1/1
6			Unit 1-D	8 days	May 5	May 12	1FS+4 days	Crew 1/2	0	Unit 1-D Crew 1/2
7			Unit 1-E	4 days	May 13	May 16	1FS+12 days	Crew 1/1	0	Unit 1-E Crew 1/1
8			Unit 1-F	10 days	May 7	May 16	1FS+6 days	Crew 1/2	0	Unit 1-F Crew 1/2
9			Unit 1-G	16 days	May 7	May 22	1FS+6 days	Crew 1/4	0	Unit 1-G
10			Unit 1-H	8 days	May 19	May 26	1FS+18 days	Crew 1/2	0	May 19
11			Unit 1-I	6 days	Jun 2	Jun 7	1FS+32 days	Crew 1/2	0	
12			Unit 1-J	6 days	May 3	May 8	1FS+2 days	Crew 1/1	0	Unit 1-J Crew 1/1
13			Unit 1-K	10 days	May 25	Jun 4	1FS+24.67 days	Crew 1/3	0	
14			⊟ Unit 2	39 days	May 3	Jun 10				
15			Unit 2-A	4 days	May 5	May 8	1FS+4 days	Crew 1/1	0	Unit 2-A Crew 1/1
16			Unit 2-B	6 days	May 4	May 9	1FS+3 days	Crew 2/2	0	Unit 2-B Crew 2/2
17			Unit 2-C	2 days	May 3	May 4	1FS+2 days	Crew 1/1	0	Unit 2-C

Figure 6–23. Looking at the Project Data

Now, let's have a look at the spreadsheet part at the left of the Gantt chart. By moving the vertical divider lines to the right, we find important schedule data. The two right-most columns, for example, show the crew number assigned to each activity and the interrupt time used. The predecessors column also shows a link between each activity and the project start date at row 1.

Figure 6–24.
Summarizing the Project View

Interestingly, we can use the outline buttons to view the summary tasks for each unit. Notice that the project duration is 50 days and that the units follow the LOB rate of delivery (slope). Once we are finished with viewing, let's save the project file.

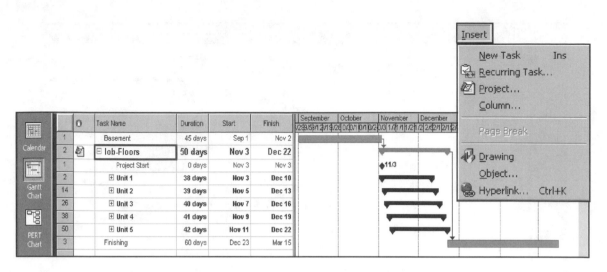

Figure 6-25. Utilizing the Generated Project

The project file we have is certainly the best schedule for the repetitive activities involved. We can utilize this schedule efficiently by incorporating it as a subproject of a larger project. To demonstrate that, let's make a new project file and give it a September 1st start, for example. Use the **Insert-New Task** option to add a Basement activity of 45-days' duration. Then use the **Insert-Project** option to add a subproject, which is the one we saved in the previous step. Automatically the project will be inserted, with May 1st being the start of this subproject.

6.7 Summary

The line-of-balance (LOB) technique introduced in this chapter is advantageous to bar charts and network techniques for planning and scheduling projects with repetitive activities. The calculations needed to merge the capabilities of the LOB technique with those of CPM network techniques are presented in this chapter to offer a better planning and scheduling tool for real-life construction projects. The CPM-LOB technique synchronizes the resources needed for the repetitive activities, maintains work continuity, preserves the logical relationships in every unit, achieves a desired production rate, and provides a legible presentation of the large data included in a schedule. A prototype PC-based computer program (BAL) is also presented to automate the CPM-LOB calculations and integrate it into Microsoft Project software. BAL calculates activities' start and finish times as well as the number of crews to be employed in each activity. It then presents the LOB schedule, showing crews' movements along the repetitive units and enables fast and simple updating of schedule data to meet the project deadline. The capabilities of the prototype are demonstrated through an example application.

6.8 Bibliography

Al Saraj, Z. (1990). "Formal Development of Line of Balance Technique." *Journal of Construction Engineering and Management*, ASCE, 116(4), 689–704.

Eldin, N., and Senouci, A. (1994). "Scheduling and Control of Linear Projects." *Canadian Journal of Civil Engineering*, 21, 219–230.

El-Rayes, K., and Moselhi, O. (1998). "Resource-Driven Scheduling of Repetitive Activities." *Journal of Construction Management and Economics*, 16, 433–446.

Harris F., and McCaffer R. (1989). *Modern Construction Management*, 3rd ed. Oxford: BSP Professional Books.

Hegazy, T., Moselhi, O., and Fazio P. (1993). *BAL: An Algorithm for Scheduling and Control of Linear Projects*. 1993 AACE Transactions, AACE International, C.8.1–C.8.14.

Laramee, J. (1983). "A Planning and Scheduling System for High-Rise Building Construction." Master Thesis, Center for Building Studies, Concordia University, Montreal, Canada.

Lumsden, P. (1968). *The Line of Balance Method.* London: Pergamon Press.

Moselhi, O., and El-Rayes, K. (1993). "Scheduling of Repetitive Projects with Cost Optimization." *Journal of Construction Engineering and Management*, ASCE, 119(4), 681–697.

Reda, R. (1990). "RPM: Repetitive Project Modeling." *Journal of Construction Engineering and Management*, ASCE, 116(2), 316–330.

Russell, A., and Wong, W. (1993). "New Generation of Planning Structures." *Journal of Construction Engineering and Management*, ASCE, 119(2), 196–214.

Senouci, A., and Eldin, N. (1996). "A Time-cost Trade-off Algorithm for Nonserial Linear Projects." *Canadian Journal of Civil Engineering*, 23, 134–149.

Suhail, S., and Neale R. (1994). "CPM/LOB: New Methodology to Integrate CPM and Line of Balance." *Journal of Construction Engineering and Management*, ASCE, 120(3), 667–684.

6.9 Exercises

1. The following network diagram represents the activities involved in a single house. Each activity shows the man-hours needed and the number of crew members. You are to construct five houses in 24 days.

   a. Manually calculate the number of crews that need to be involved in each activity. Draw the schedule and define the day numbers in which each crew enters and leaves the site;

   b. Solve the same problem using BAL program. Print the LOB schedule of BAL and the Microsoft Project schedule. Note: Use the Alt + Print Screen buttons to capture the screen of the LOB schedule and then paste it into any word processing program for printing; and

   c. Using program BAL, use only two crews for each activity. Afterwards, experiment with the layoff-and-recall option to determine the shortest project duration possible.

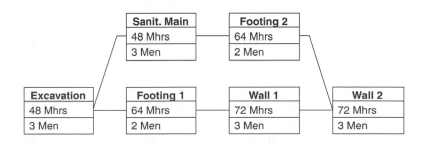

2. Answer questions (a), (b), and (c) in exercise 1, considering the following network diagram. Consider the construction of six units within 35 days.

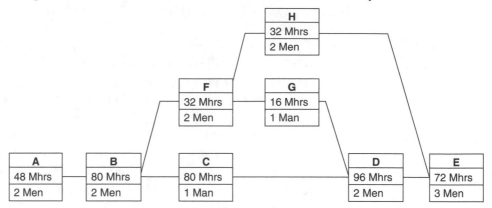

3. The construction plan for a house is as follows, with activities' durations in days:

   a. Calculate a weekly target rate to be used for scheduling a project of 30 repetitive houses, if all crews are working five 8-hour days per week and the project has to be delivered in 85 days.

   b. Given a desired target rate of four units per week, what is the number of crews to be employed in activity B.

   c. Using the same crews obtained in (b), activity B has to be sped-up to a target rate of five units per week. Calculate how much time a crew needs to cut from the duration of each unit. Work continuity and crew synchronization has to be maintained.

   d. Solve part (a) using BAL program.

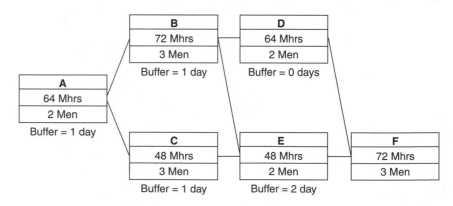

4. For the six-activity house shown below, each task in the network shows the man-hours needed, the number of crew members, and the end buffer times in days. If you are to construct these tasks for six houses in 27 days, calculate the number of crews to be involved in each task and draw the schedule. Assume eight work hours per day.

	B
	72 Mhrs
	3 Men
	Buffer = 1 day

(network diagram with nodes A, B, C, D, E, F as described)

A — 64 Mhrs, 2 Men, Buffer = 1 day
B — 72 Mhrs, 3 Men, Buffer = 1 day
D — 64 Mhrs, 2 Men, Buffer = 0 days
C — 48 Mhrs, 3 Men, Buffer = 1 day
E — 48 Mhrs, 2 Men, Buffer = 2 day
F — 72 Mhrs, 3 Men

5. Solve question 4 using BAL program, considering all buffers to be zeroes.

6. Use BAL program with the network of Exercise 1(a) of Chapter 5, using 20 units and a project duration that is 50% more than the duration of a single unit. Comment on the resulting schedule.

7. Use BAL program with the network of Exercise 1(b) of Chapter 5, using 100 units and a project duration that is twice the duration of a single unit. Comment on the resulting schedule.

Chapter 7

RESOURCE MANAGEMENT
Part 1—Resource Allocation and Leveling

After studying this chapter, you will be able to:

- Understand the resource management needs of projects.
- Use common heuristic techniques to reschedule projects that suffer from limited resources so that project delay is minimized.
- Utilize any multiskills of available resources to compensate for resource shortages.
- Understand the basis for leveling the fluctuation in daily resource demands.
- Use Microsoft Project software for resource allocation and leveling.
- Experiment with a spreadsheet model for resource allocation and leveling.

Owner, CM					
• Need • Feasibility • Project Definition • Owner Approval	**A/E, CM, Owner**				
	• Conceptual Design • Owner Approval • Soil Reports • Preliminary Design • Detailed Design • Quantities • Work Documents • Select Project Contract Strategy	**Bidders**			
		• Prepare Bid Proposal + Baselines • Collect Data (site, quantities, specs, resources, tasks, etc) • Planning • Time & Cost Estimation • Scheduling • **Resource Management: Adjustments for Resource Constraints & Deadline** • Bidding Strategy & Markup Estimation • Cash Flow Analysis • Submit Bid	**Owner, CM**		
			• Evaluate Bids and Select General Contractor	**Contractor**	
				• Start Construction • Detailed Planning, Estimating & **Resource Management** • Schedule Updating • Progress Evaluation • Time, Cost, & Quality Control • Commissioning	**O & M Staff**
					• O & M • Demolition at End of Service Life
CONCEPT	**DESIGN**	**BIDDING**		**CONSTRUCTION**	**O & M**

7.1   Resource Management Objectives

In Chapters 5 and 6, we dealt with the CPM and LOB analyses for scheduling projects. In these chapters, we discussed that one of the main assumptions used in the analyses is that we have all the resources needed for the schedule. This assumption, however, is not always true for construction projects. Under resource constraints, the schedule becomes impractical, cost and time are not accurate, and resources may not be available when needed. To bring the schedule to practical terms, special adjustments have to be made to the schedule to properly manage available resources and meet project constraints. Three types of analyses, therefore, may be applied:

1. *Smoothing Resource Profiles (Resource Leveling):* Applies when it is desired to reduce the hiring and firing of resources and to smooth the fluctuation in the daily demand of a resource, as shown in Figure 7–1.

    In this case, resources are not limited and project duration is not to be delayed. The objective in this case is to shift noncritical activities within their float times so that a better resource profile is obtained.

2. *Scheduling with Limited Resources (Resource Allocation):* Applies when the original schedule shows that several activities require a certain resource at the same time. If the resource is limited, one of the activities has to be delayed, thus delaying the whole project. The objective in this case is to properly select which activities to delay and which one to start so that the total project delay is minimized.

3. *Meeting a Deadline Duration (Time-Cost Tradeoff):* Applies when the project duration determined by the CPM and PDM analyses is unacceptably large and extends beyond a desired deadline. The objective in this case is to apply overtime strategy, or any other strategy, to crash the project duration so that the total project cost is minimized and the deadline is met.

It is noted that the second type of analysis, which deals with limited resources, has been referred to as "resource allocation," "resource-constrained scheduling," or "resource leveling." The latter name, however, has been used for both resource smoothing (first analysis) and resource allocation (second analysis) and resource smoothing. To prevent a mix-up of the terminology, the term "resource leveling" will only be used to refer to resource smoothing.

The first two types of analysis are dealt with in this chapter, and the time-cost tradeoff analysis is covered in Chapter 8, within the context of project time-cost optimization.

Figure 7-1.
Resource-Leveling
Objective

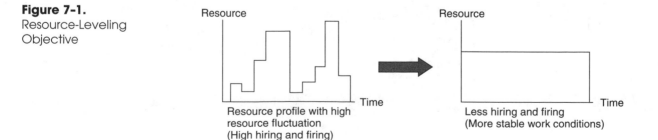

7.2 Smoothing Resource Profiles (Resource Leveling)

The problem of resource fluctuation appears after the initial CPM or PDM analysis is conducted and a bar chart is drawn. The peaks and valleys in the resource profile indicate high day-to-day fluctuation in resource demand (Figure 7–2). Although a project may not suffer from limited resources, our objective as project managers is to hire the minimum number of resources, to reduce daily resource fluctuation, and to ensure better utilization of our resources. Typical situations include the full utilization of a rented piece of equipment that needs to be returned early, also reducing the number of skilled workers who need to be hired for the job. To do that, various resource-leveling techniques have been applied in the industry with the sole objective of reducing peak requirements and smoothing out period-to-period fluctuations in resource assignment. With this specific scope, such techniques do not address resource limits and consider the project duration as satisfactory and does not require shortening. With the complexity of the resource-leveling problem particularly in a multiresource environment, however, optimal solutions that use mathematical programming such as the Simplex method could only work for small-sized construction projects. Heuristic algorithms based on rules of thumb and experience are therefore needed.

In essence, resource-leveling heuristics shift noncritical activities within their float times so as to move resources from the peaks to the valleys, without any project delay (i.e., area underneath the resource profile remains constant). Usually, project managers have desired resource profiles that they try to get their resource profiles to match. Desired resource profiles for human resources, however, differ from equipment and material profiles, as shown in Figure 7–3. Accordingly, the resource-leveling strategy becomes different. All strategies, however, will eventually produce a schedule that is somewhere between the early-start schedule and the late-start schedule (critical activities remain unchanged and noncritical ones shifted within their float times).

Figure 7–2. Daily Resource Fluctuation

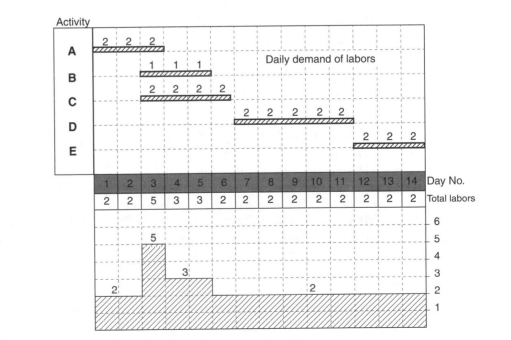

Figure 7-3.
Resource-Leveling
Strategies

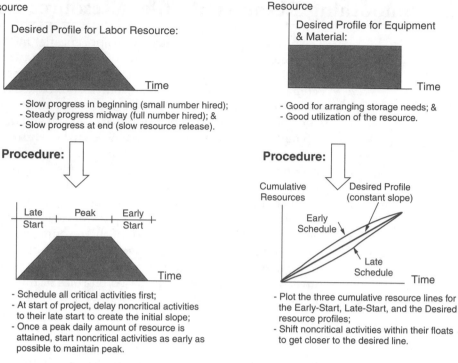

- Slow progress in beginning (small number hired);
- Steady progress midway (full number hired); &
- Slow progress at end (slow resource release).

- Good for arranging storage needs; &
- Good utilization of the resource.

Procedure:

Procedure:

- Schedule all critical activities first;
- At start of project, delay noncritical activities to their late start to create the initial slope;
- Once a peak daily amount of resource is attained, start noncritical activities as early as possible to maintain peak.

- Plot the three cumulative resource lines for the Early-Start, Late-Start, and the Desired resource profiles;
- Shift noncritical activities within their floats to get closer to the desired line.

> **Note:** Because resource-leveling techniques may end up reducing peak resource demands, in case of slight resource limits, one might use these techniques before using any resource-allocation techniques such as those described in Section 7.2. One essential benefit is that you are guaranteed not to cause project delays.

7.2.1 Manual Heuristic Solution: Method of Moments

A well-known heuristic algorithm is the Minimum Moment Algorithm. The objective in this algorithm is to minimize daily fluctuations in resource use. The algorithm uses the moment of the resource histogram around the horizontal axis (time) as a good heuristic measure of the fluctuations in daily resource demands. This is illustrated in Figure 7.4a, where Histogram 1 and Histogram 2 are two alternative resource histograms, both having a total area of 40 resource days (i.e., equal total resource demands). Histogram 1 is an ideal one with a constant daily demand of 4 resource units, no day-to-day resource fluctuations, and the resource will be released after day 10. Histogram 2, on the other hand, exhibits high resource fluctuation with daily demand in the range of 2 to 6 resource units, and the resource will not be released until the end of day 12. The moment (M_x) of both histograms around the horizontal axis (days) are 160 and 166, respectively, representing a better resource leveling of Histogram 1. The moment M_x is calculated by summing the daily moments, as follows:

$$M_x = \sum_{j=1}^{n} \left[(1 \times Resource\ Demand_j) \times \frac{1}{2}\ Resource\ Demand_j \right] \quad \text{(7.1)}$$

where n is the working-day number of the project's finish date. Or, for comparison reasons, Equation 7.1 becomes:

$$M_x = \sum_{j=1}^{n} (Resource\ Demand_j)^2 \quad \text{(7.2)}$$

Figure 7-4.
Resource Histogram
and Moment
Calculation

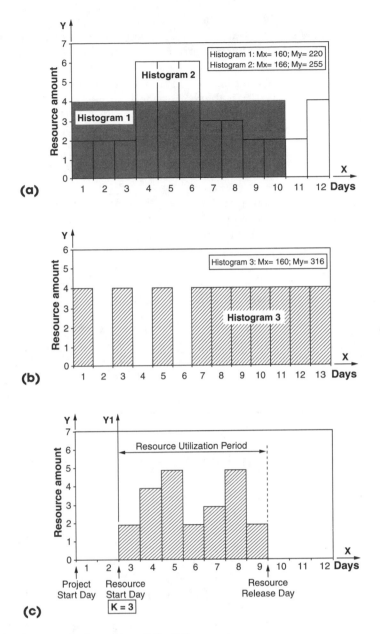

7.2.2 Modified Heuristics: Double Moments

Although the minimum moment (M_x) method can be used to compare among histograms in terms of resource fluctuation, it does not take into consideration the resource utilization period. The latter is very important to minimize, particularly for equipment resources that are shared among projects or rented from external sources. Figure 7–4b, for example, shows a resource histogram having the same 40 resource days (total area), a maximum resource demand of 4, and a utilization period that extends until the end of day 13. Its M_x is 160, the same as that of Histogram 1, indicating similar resource fluctuation as Histogram 1 and better than Histogram 2, regardless of its 3- and 1-day extensions beyond the two histograms, respectively. The single moment M_x, therefore, does not consider for the extended assignment of the resource. To overcome that, the moment M_y (around the vertical axis, resource amount) is computed as follows:

$$M_y = \sum_{j=l}^{n}[(1 \times Resource\ Demand_j) \times j)] \tag{7.3}$$

Using equation 7.3, the M_y values calculated for the three resource histograms of Figure 7.4a and b are 220, 255, and 316, respectively. The value of M_y, as such, gets higher as the resource remains employed in the project till a later date. Accordingly, M_y can be used as a good indicator of the resource release date in the project. Also, a simple modification to Equation 7.3 can be used to calculate the moment M_y around a vertical axis that corresponds to the first day the resource is employed in the project (k, Figure 7–4c). In this case, the value of M_y represents the resource utilization period, irrespective of when the resource is employed or released, expressed as follows:

$$M_y = \sum_{j=k}^{n}[(1 \times Resource\ Demand_j) \times (j - k)] \tag{7.4}$$

Having the moment calculations defined, a project manager may use them as modified heuristics in four ways, according to his or her resource management objectives: 1) minimize the M_x alone when the focus is on reducing daily resource fluctuations; 2) minimize the M_y of Equation 7.4 alone when the focus is on reducing the resource utilization period; 3) minimize the M_y of Equation 7.3 alone when the focus is on releasing the resource at an early date; or 4) minimize the double moments ($M_x + M_y$) when the focus in on both aspects.

Note: In most cases, applying resource leveling to smooth the profile of one resource may produce a more rough profile for another resource. Optimizing the resource leveling of all the resources in a project is, therefore, a complex task.

7.3 Scheduling with Limited Resources (Resource Allocation)

Shortage of resources is a major challenge for construction projects. Often, the number of skilled labor is limited, expensive equipment is shared among several projects, material quantity is limited, and/or a limited space is available for storage. Scheduling under these resource constraints becomes a complex problem, particularly when more than one resource is limited.

A resource conflict occurs when, at any point in the schedule, several activities run in parallel and the total amount of their required resource(s) exceeds the availability limit. The situation is illustrated in Figure 7–5, with activities A, B, and C requiring a total of 5 labors in day 3, while only 4 are available per day.

The simple solution to that situation is that we can prioritize the parallel activities, give the resource to higher priority activities, and delay the others until the earliest time the resource becomes available again, thus potentially delaying the whole project. Notice that if we delay an activity at time 3, we may end up with another resource conflict later in time. Continuing with identifying next conflict points and resolving them determines the new schedule and the new project duration.

Now, for efficient resource management, the essential question we have is:

> Is there an optimum way to prioritize the activities that compete for the limited resource at any time so that the net project delay is minimized?

In general, however, scheduling with limited resource is a difficult problem that mathematicians refer to as a "large combinatorial problem." Since the 1960s, various models were developed in an attempt to answer this question, and thus optimize re-

Figure 7–5.
Resource Conflict at Day 3

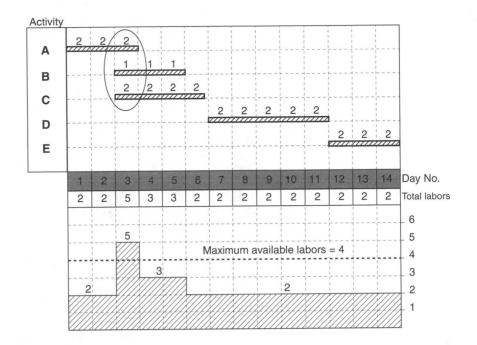

source allocation decisions. Early efforts used mathematical optimization, dynamic programming, and linear programming. These models, however, were applicable only to very small-size problems. Alternatively, heuristic solutions for this problem have been developed since the 1960s. Heuristic solutions, in general, use simple rules of thumb to provide approximate but good solutions that are usable for large-scale problems. An example of these rules of thumb is that the resource can be assigned to activity(ies) that have smaller total float values than others (indicating a desire not to delay the critical and close-to-critical activities). In this case, we are resolving resource conflicts using the *least total-float (LTF)* heuristic rule to prioritize the parallel activities that compete for the limited resource.

7.3.1 Manual Heuristic Solution for Our Case Study

Different heuristic rules have been used since the 1960s. Also, a single rule or a hierarchy of heuristic rules may be used to prioritize competing activities. Almost all heuristic rules are based mainly on an activity characteristic, such as duration, total float, number of successors, etc. The two most effective and commonly used heuristic rules are the least total-float (LTF) and the earliest late-start (ELS). These two rules have been proven to provide identical results, with the ELS rule being advantageous compared to the LTF rule. This is because the value of the late-start derived from the original CPM calculations, unlike the total-float values, need not be changed every time an activity is rescheduled due to insufficient resource availability. As such, the ELS rule can be applied with much less computational effort than the LTF rule. All heuristic rules, in general, have the advantage of being simple, easy to apply, and can be used for large-size projects.

The scheduling process using heuristic rules is outlined in Figure 7–6. It starts from the project start time and goes through cycles (shaded area) of identifying eligible activities according to the network logic and resolving the overrequirements of resources using the selected set of heuristic rules. Most commercially available scheduling software provide resource allocation capabilities (sometimes referred to as resource leveling) utilizing proprietary heuristic approaches.

Figure 7-6.
Resource Allocation
Procedure

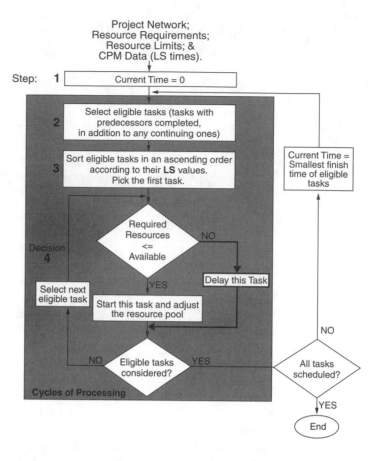

The heuristic procedure of Figure 7–6 for resource allocation is demonstrated on our case study project. Until now, we discussed planning and cost estimation in Chapter 4 and then performed scheduling in Chapters 5 and 6. As mentioned in Chapter 4, we are using the cheapest method of construction for each task because, at this stage, we have no reason to use more expensive ones. Accordingly, durations and costs of activities were calculated on the Estimate sheet of the **Case-Study.xls** file (Figure 4–21). The part of that sheet that shows the amount of resources needed per day is shown in Figure 7–7 and will be used in this chapter. The network in Figure 7–7 shows the activities' durations on top of activity arrows and amount of resources below the activity arrows. Initial schedule data, specifically the late-start times of activities, is also shown on the figures for use in the calculations.

Case Study Requirements

The project is scheduled to be 32 days (discussed in Chapter 5) when we did not consider any resource limits. With the current limit on the availability of the three key resources for this project, we need to determine how the resources are allocated to the various activities so that resource limits are not violated and the total project duration is minimized.

Solution

Applying the heuristic procedure of Figure 7–6, we will reschedule the project in a completely different manner than the CPM technique, with more focus on the resources. Calculations are performed manually in a table that is set up as shown in Figure 7–8. The first seven columns of the table represent activities' data, whereas the last two columns are the scheduling decisions made at each cycle. At the beginning of the project (current time = 0), the only

Key Resources

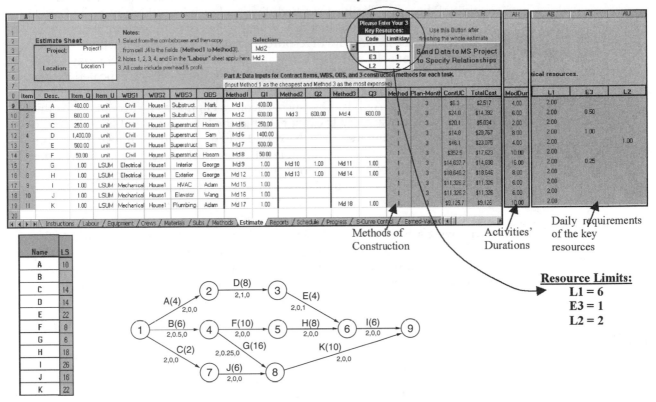

Figure 7-7. Case Study Data in the Estimate Sheet

Figure 7-8. Table Setup for the Manual Solution

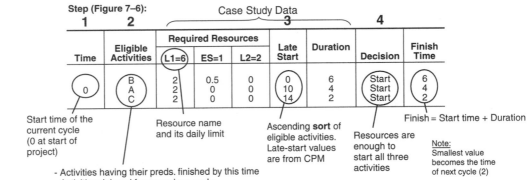

eligible tasks were A, B, and C, which were sorted by their late-start values, putting B on top, i.e., activity B has the smallest late-start and as such has a higher priority of getting the resource when the resource is limited.

Considering these three activities in their priority order, available resources were enough to start activity B, remaining resources were enough to start A (next in order), and the remaining resources were enough to start C. As such, activity B was scheduled to start at time 0 and to end at time 6 (duration = 6 days); activity A to start at time 0 and to end at time 4; and activity C to start at time 0 and to end at time 2. Having these decisions made and put in columns 8 and 9, the earliest time more resources became available is day 2, in which activity C finishes (i.e., the smallest finish time in this cycle). As noticed, the three activities A, B, and C run in parallel, and we have enough resources to start them all.

At day 2, activity C is finished, and as such, its immediate successor (activity J) becomes eligible for scheduling (unless it has other unfinished predecessors), in addition to B and A, which were continuing from the previous cycle. Because the amount of resources needed for the eligible activities at this cycle are available, activity J can start and is scheduled to end on day 8. The smallest finish time at this cycle is day 4, then the process is repeated at time 4. At this cycle are available, activity A is finished while activities B and J are still continuing. Activity D, a such, becomes eligible as it succeeds A. At this cycle, however, activity D cannot start as the total amount of E3 will exceed the limit (1.5 compared to 1). Next cycle then proceeds at time 6, right after the finish of B. Accordingly, eligible activities are: J (continuing from previous cycle); D (delayed from previous cycle); and G and F (successors of B). After sorting with respect to the late-start values and considering these tasks one by one, G and F could start, while D was delayed. The process, therefore, was continued from one cycle to the other as shown in Table 7–1 until all activities were scheduled. Activity I was the last activity and was scheduled to finish at day 40. Project duration, as such, becomes 40 days; an eight-day extension beyond the original CPM duration of 32 days. Notice that at any cycle, the total amount of resources used by the starting and continuing activities is less than or equal to the resource availability limit.

Table 7-1. Complete Manual Solution of the Case Study

Time	Eligible Activities	Required Resources			Priority Rule (Late-Start)	Duration	Decision	Finish Time
		L1 = 6	E3 = 1	L2 = 2				
0	B	2	0.5	0	0	6	Start	6
	A	2	0	0	10	4	Start	4
	C	2	0	0	14	2	Start	2
2	B	2	0.5	0	---	---	Continue	6
	A	2	0	0	---	---	Continue	4
	J	2	0	0	16	6	Start	8
4	B	2	0.5	0	---	---	Continue	6
	J	2	0	0	---	---	Continue	8
	D	2	1	0	14	8	Delay	---
6	J	2	0	0	---	---	Continue	8
	G	2	0.25	0	6	16	Start	22
	F	2	0	0	8	10	Start	16
	D	2	1	0	14	8	Delay	---
8	G	2	0.25	0	---	---	Continue	22
	F	2	0	0	---	---	Continue	16
	D	2	1	0	14	8	Delay	---
16	G	2	0.25	0	---	---	Continue	22
	D	2	1	0	14	8	Delay	---
	H	2	0	0	18	8	Start	24
22	H	2	0	0	---	---	Continue	24
	D	2	1	0	14	8	Start	30
	K	2	0	0	22	10	Start	32
24	D	2	1	0	---	---	Continue	30
	K	2	0	0	---	---	Continue	32
30	K	2	0	0	---	---	Continue	32
	E	2	0	1	22	4	Start	34
32	E	2	0	1	---	---	Continue	34
34	I	2	0	0	26	6	Start	40

Using the table format, as you have seen, simplified the solution process and made it very much systematic. The same table format can also be used with any heuristic rule. The only change you need to do is to replace the values in the "Late-Start" column with the values of the heuristic rule you choose, and accordingly sort the eligible activities before making decisions at each cycle. If, for example, you would like to give the resource to the activities with longer duration, you would put the duration values in that column and sort the eligible activities in a descending order (top activities have higher priority of getting the resource first). The rest of the calculations remain the same.

The question now is how to minimize the project extension. In the next subsections, we will try various methods: assigning biased priorities to activities, and multi-skill resource scheduling. To demonstrate such methods, we will discuss a bigger example so that the concepts become clear. Later, we will come back to our case study.

7.3.2 Another Example

Now, let's apply the same resource-allocation procedure on a project of 20 activities and six resources. The project data including activities' resource requirements and daily limits on the six resources is presented in Table 7–2. The CPM network of the case study is also shown in Figure 7–9, showing a project duration of 32 days, without considering the resource limits. Applying the heuristic procedure of Figure 7–6 to schedule the project considering the given resource constraints was performed manually in Table 7–3, showing a 49-day duration (17-day delay from the original CPM duration of 32 days).

Table 7-2. Project Data

Activity Name	Duration (days)	Predecessor Activities	Resource Requirements per Day					
			R1	R2	R3	R4	R5	R6
A	6	——	5	2	2	2	7	4
B	3	——	3	5	2	3	9	6
C	4	A	2	4	4	2	3	1
D	6	——	5	4	3	5	5	4
E	7	A, B	3	5	2	3	8	0
F	5	C	4	1	4	9	2	5
G	2	D	4	1	4	3	9	8
H	2	A, B	5	5	4	0	9	1
I	2	G, H	3	2	4	3	4	2
J	6	F	1	5	4	6	7	3
K	1	C, E	3	3	2	4	5	1
L	2	E, G, H	3	2	2	8	3	4
M	4	I, K	2	2	2	2	4	8
N	2	F, L	1	4	4	3	4	1
O	3	L	5	5	4	6	2	3
P	5	J, M, N	3	2	3	4	7	8
Q	8	O	4	5	4	2	3	4
R	2	D, O	5	3	3	3	7	8
S	6	P, R	2	4	6	2	3	4
T	2	Q	1	6	2	7	5	2
Daily Resource Limits			**7**	**10**	**10**	**16**	**18**	**13**

Table 7-3. Complete Manual Solution for the New Example

Time	Eligible Activities	R1=7	R2=10	R3=10	R4=16	R5=18	R6=13	Late Start	Duration	Decision	Finish Time
0	A	5	2	2	2	7	4	0	6	Start	6
	B	3	5	2	3	9	6	6	3	Delay	-
	D	5	4	3	5	5	4	7	6	Delay	-
6	B	3	5	2	3	9	6	6	3	Start	9
	C	2	4	4	2	3	1	6	4	Start	10
	D	5	4	3	5	5	4	7	6	Delay	-
9	C	2	4	4	2	3	1	---	---	Continue	10
	D	5	4	3	5	5	4	7	6	Start	15
	E	3	5	2	3	8	0	9	7	Delay	-
	H	5	5	4	0	9	1	13	2	Delay	-
10	D	5	4	3	5	5	4	---	---	Continue	15
	E	3	5	2	3	8	0	9	7	Delay	-
	F	4	1	4	9	2	5	10	5	Delay	-
	H	5	5	4	0	9	1	13	2	Delay	-
15	E	3	5	2	3	8	0	9	7	Start	22
	F	4	1	4	9	2	5	10	5	Start	20
	G	4	1	4	3	9	8	13	2	Delay	-
	H	5	5	4	0	9	1	13	2	Delay	-
20	E	3	5	2	3	8	0	---	---	Continue	22
	G	4	1	4	3	9	8	13	2	Start	22
	H	5	5	4	0	9	1	13	2	Delay	-
	J	1	5	4	6	7	3	15	6	Delay	-
22	H	5	5	4	0	9	1	13	2	Start	24
	J	1	5	4	6	7	3	15	6	Start	28
	K	3	3	2	4	5	1	16	1	Delay	-
24	J	1	5	4	6	7	3	---	---	Continue	28
	I	3	2	4	3	4	2	15	2	Start	26
	K	3	3	2	4	5	1	16	1	Start	25
	L	3	2	2	8	3	4	17	2	Delay	-
25	I	3	2	4	3	4	2	---	---	Continue	26
	J	1	5	4	6	7	3	---	---	Continue	28
	L	3	2	2	8	3	4	17	2	Delay	-
26	J	1	5	4	6	7	3	---	---	Continue	28
	L	3	2	2	8	3	4	17	2	Start	28
	M	2	2	2	2	4	8	17	4	Delay	-
28	M	2	2	2	2	4	8	17	4	Start	32
	N	1	4	4	3	4	1	19	2	Start	30
	O	5	5	4	6	2	3	19	3	Delay	-
30	M	2	2	2	2	4	8	---	---	Continue	32
	O	5	5	4	6	2	3	19	3	Start	33
32	O	5	5	4	6	2	3	---	---	Continue	33
	P	3	2	3	4	7	8	21	5	Delay	-
33	P	3	2	3	4	7	8	21	5	Start	38
	Q	4	5	4	2	3	4	22	8	Start	41
	R	5	3	3	3	2	8	24	2	Delay	-
38	Q	4	5	4	2	3	4	---	---	Continue	41
	R	5	3	3	3	2	8	24	2	Delay	-
41	R	5	3	3	3	7	8	24	2	Start	43
	T	1	6	2	7	5	2	30	2	Start	43
43	S	2	4	6	2	3	4	26	6	Start	49

Figure 7-9. Project Network

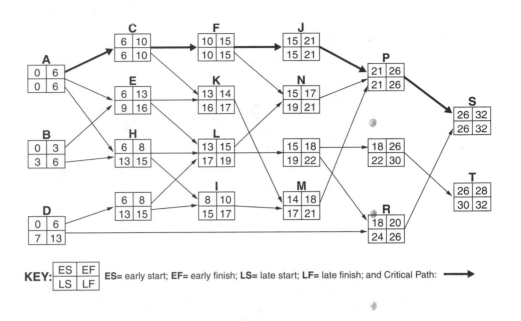

KEY: $\begin{array}{|c|c|} \hline ES & EF \\ \hline LS & LF \\ \hline \end{array}$ **ES**= early start; **EF**= early finish; **LS**= late start; **LF**= late finish; and Critical Path: ➡

7.4 Using Microsoft Project

Let's now use Microsoft Project on our example project. We need to start a new project and then enter the data of Table 7–2 into the software, following the same general steps described in Chapter 5. The project will look as shown in Figure 7–10, with a 32-day duration. The process used to assign resources, perform resource leveling, and perform resource allocation is shown in Figures 7–11 to 7–17. You can follow these steps or load the **Sch-Level.mpp** file from the CD.

If you do not want to redo the leveling options each time you make changes to the schedule, you can set the "Leveling Calculations" option in Figure 7–16 to "Automatic."

Figure 7-10. Microsoft Project Schedule with 32-day Duration

Now, to input our resource information and their daily limits, we use the **View-Resource Sheet** menu option.

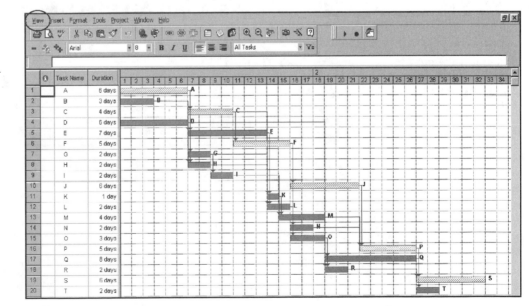

Figure 7-11.
Specifying
Resources

First, let's view the
resource sheet and
specify the resource
types. For resource-
leveling purposes, we
specify a high Max.
Units, indicating that
we have enough
resources.

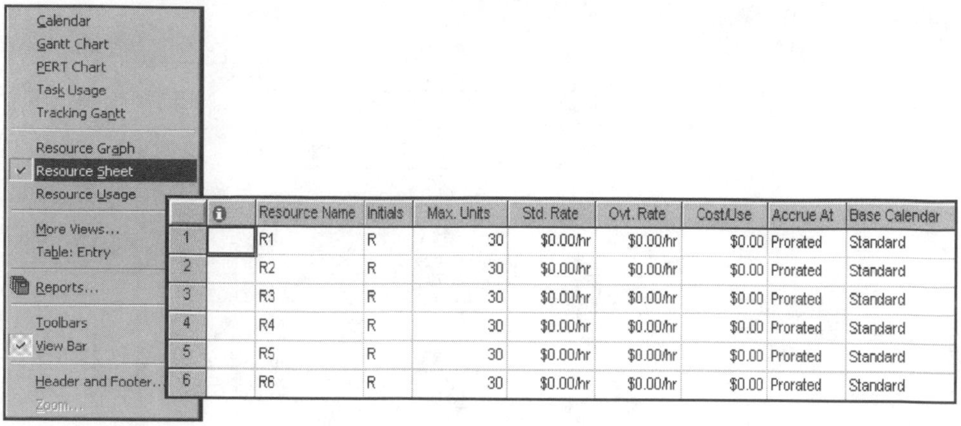

		🛈	Resource Name	Initials	Max. Units	Std. Rate	Ovt. Rate	Cost/Use	Accrue At	Base Calendar
1			R1	R	30	$0.00/hr	$0.00/hr	$0.00	Prorated	Standard
2			R2	R	30	$0.00/hr	$0.00/hr	$0.00	Prorated	Standard
3			R3	R	30	$0.00/hr	$0.00/hr	$0.00	Prorated	Standard
4			R4	R	30	$0.00/hr	$0.00/hr	$0.00	Prorated	Standard
5			R5	R	30	$0.00/hr	$0.00/hr	$0.00	Prorated	Standard
6			R6	R	30	$0.00/hr	$0.00/hr	$0.00	Prorated	Standard

Menu items:
Calendar
Gantt Chart
PERT Chart
Task Usage
Tracking Gantt

Resource Graph
✓ Resource Sheet
Resource Usage

More Views...
Table: Entry

Reports...

Toolbars
✓ View Bar

Header and Footer..
Zoom...

Note: Resource Leveling: In this option, we do not consider any resource limits, only the fluctuation of resource profiles.

Figure 7-12. Assign
Resources to Tasks

From the Gantt chart,
select each activity,
push on the toolbar
button shown, and
type the units of each
resource. Click on the
Assign button and
continue to next
activity, and so on.
Once finished, you
will notice that project
duration is still 32
days.

Assign Resources

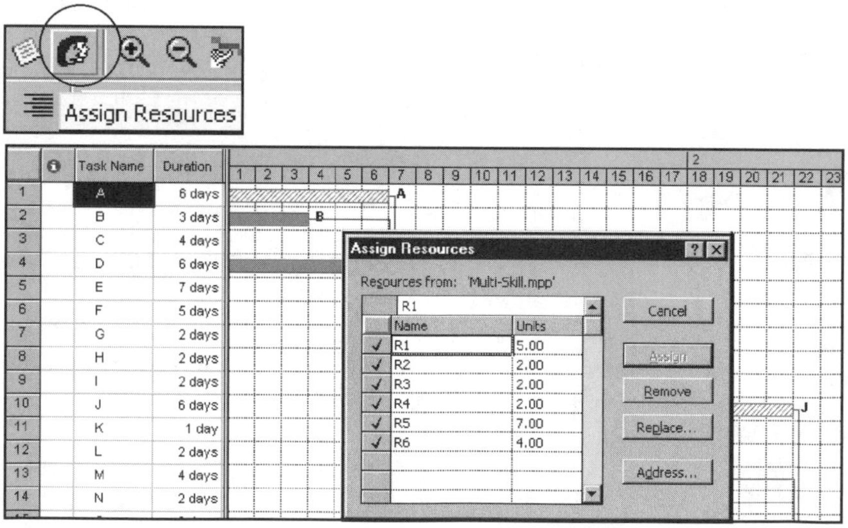

	🛈	Task Name	Duration
1		A	6 days
2		B	3 days
3		C	4 days
4		D	6 days
5		E	7 days
6		F	5 days
7		G	2 days
8		H	2 days
9		I	2 days
10		J	6 days
11		K	1 day
12		L	2 days
13		M	4 days
14		N	2 days

Assign Resources dialog:
Resources from: 'Multi-Skill.mpp'
R1

Name	Units
✓ R1	5.00
✓ R2	2.00
✓ R3	2.00
✓ R4	2.00
✓ R5	7.00
✓ R6	4.00

Buttons: Cancel, Assign, Remove, Replace..., Address...

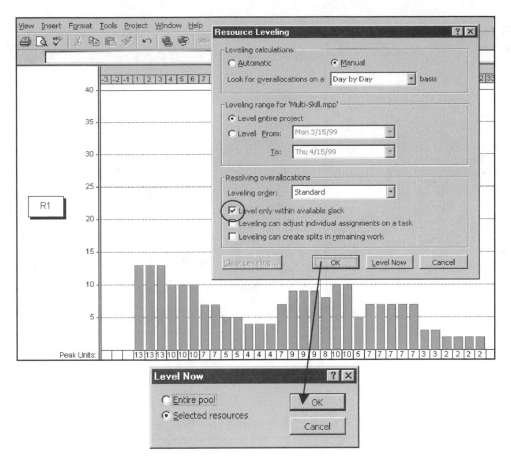

Figure 7-13. Using the Resource-Leveling Option

We now view the resource graph of R1 (use **View-Resource Graph**). The graph shows that R1 fluctuates between a minimum demand of 2 R1 units to a maximum of 13 units. We will now apply resource leveling and try to smooth this profile.

Now, we use the **Tools-Resource Leveling** menu option. Select the **Level only within available slack** option. This ensures that project duration remains unchanged. Push the **Level Now** button and then select the **Selected resources** option to smooth only the R1 resource.

Figure 7-14. Input Data for Resource Allocation

Now, let's view the resource sheet again and specify the resource limits we have. This is important before we start resource allocation to account for these limits. Once finished, return back to view the Gantt chart.

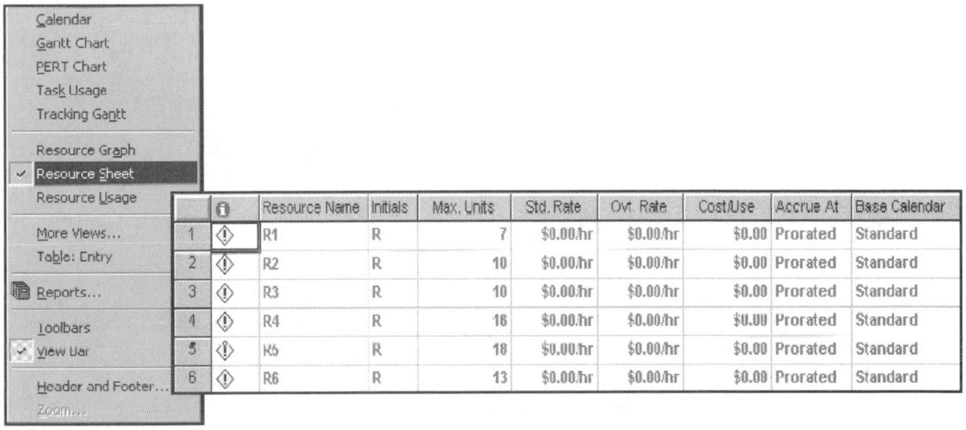

	ⓘ	Resource Name	Initials	Max. Units	Std. Rate	Ovt. Rate	Cost/Use	Accrue At	Base Calendar
1	◊	R1	R	7	$0.00/hr	$0.00/hr	$0.00	Prorated	Standard
2	◊	R2	R	10	$0.00/hr	$0.00/hr	$0.00	Prorated	Standard
3	◊	R3	R	10	$0.00/hr	$0.00/hr	$0.00	Prorated	Standard
4	◊	R4	R	16	$0.00/hr	$0.00/hr	$0.00	Prorated	Standard
5	◊	R5	R	18	$0.00/hr	$0.00/hr	$0.00	Prorated	Standard
6	◊	R6	R	13	$0.00/hr	$0.00/hr	$0.00	Prorated	Standard

Note: You may refer to the Help system to find detailed instructions on the steps shown.

Figure 7-15.
Viewing
Overallocated
Resources

With resources and
their limits specified
while the duration is
unchanged, let's view
the Resource Graph.
Notice the over-
allocation in R1,
indicating the need to
perform resource
allocation calculations
to resolve this
problem. After
viewing, return to the
Gantt chart.

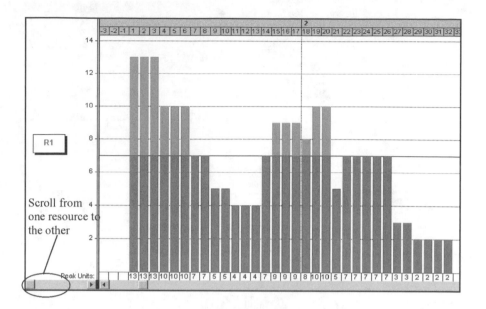

Figure 7-16.
Resource Allocation
Option

To use resource
allocation, we use the
**Tools-Resource
Leveling** menu
option. Select the
Standard leveling
order. Keep the option
boxes unselected and
push the **Level Now**
button to start.

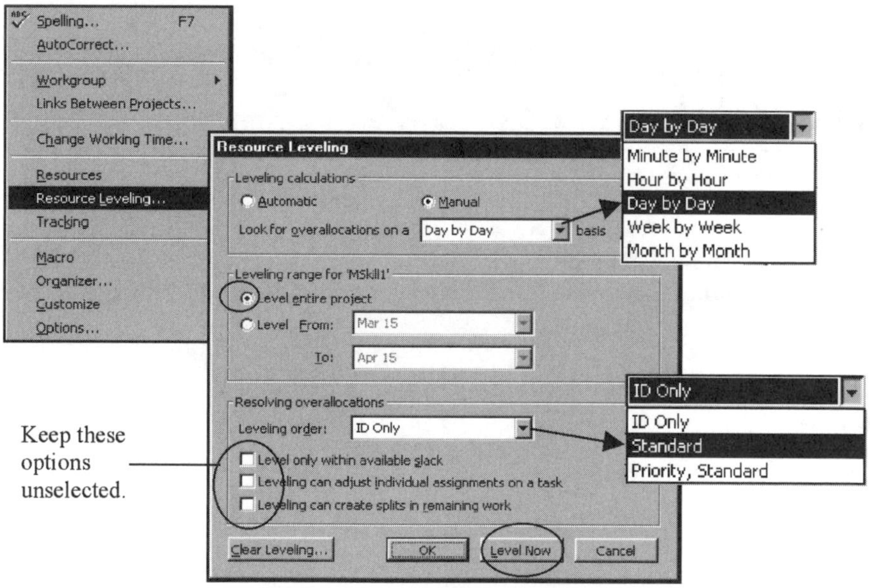

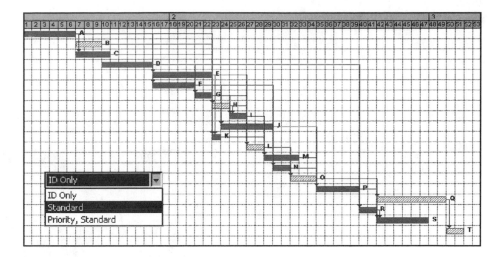

Figure 7-17. Extended Schedule due to Resource Limits

Project duration becomes 51 days. Now retry using the other **Leveling Order** options such as **ID Only** in Figure 7.16. It will give you a 54-day schedule. Thus, our best solution so far is the 51-day schedule shown here. Notice that this schedule is two days longer than the 49-day manual solution of Table 7–3, which shows that software systems do not exactly follow the manual approach.

7.5 Using Primavera P3

Now let's apply resource allocation and leveling options using Primavera P3 software. The simplest approach to enter the project data in P3 is through MPX conversion. First, we save the Microsoft file as a MPX format (Figure 7–18) and then use the conversion program that comes within the Primavera group to convert the MPX file into P3 format. Once conversion is done, the P3 project file looks as shown in Figure 7–19.

After conversion, the project is 32-days' duration before resource allocation or leveling are applied. The next steps are to specify the resources (Figure 7–20) and then assign these resources to the various activities (Figure 7–21).

We proceed with resource assignments by selecting the activity details form (bottom of bar chart) and selecting the resource tab. Now, we specify the resource category and the number of daily units.

As shown in Figure 7–22, we activate resource leveling from the toolbar and set the options. To apply resource smoothing, we set the **Smoothing** option to become **Time Constrained,** which does not allow extension or delay to the project. We also may extend the resource limits before smoothing.

To apply resource allocation, we set the **Smoothing** option to **Non-Time Constrained** to allow the project to be delayed as needed. We also select the prioritization rule (Late Start) and select all the resources to be leveled. Notice the diverse number of prioritization rules available in P3. The result of resource allocation (Figure 7–23) is a 49-day duration, similar to the manual calculations.

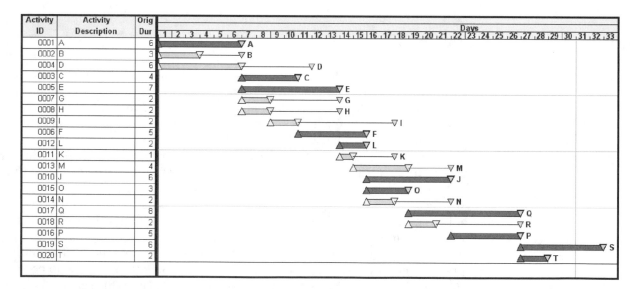

Figure 7-18. Converting Microsoft Project File into P3 Format

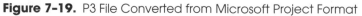

Figure 7-19. P3 File Converted from Microsoft Project Format

Figure 7-20.

Specifying
Resources

The MPX conversion
feature did not
properly convert the
resources, so we have
to respecify the six
resource categories of
this example.

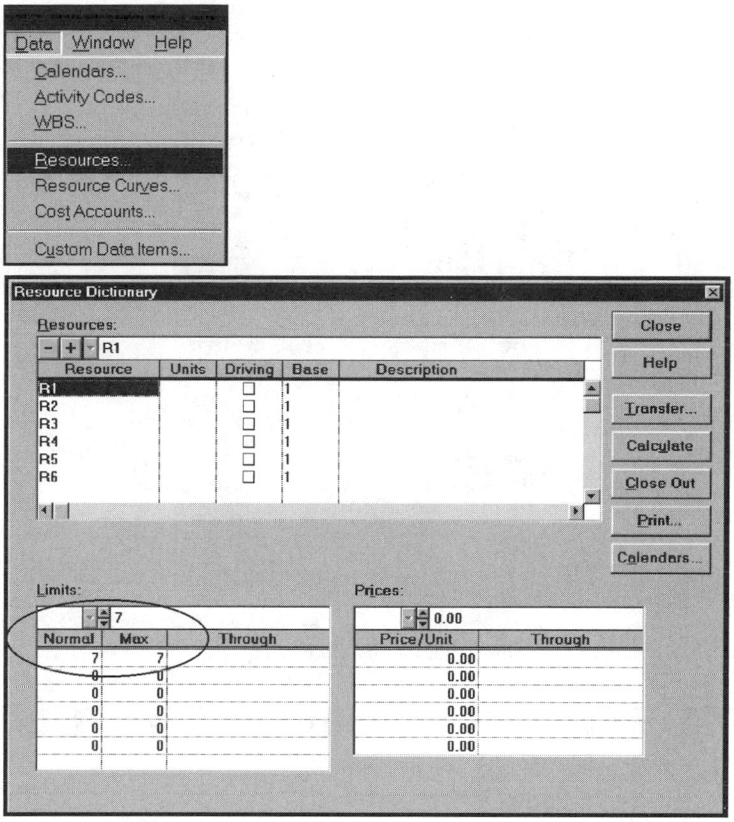

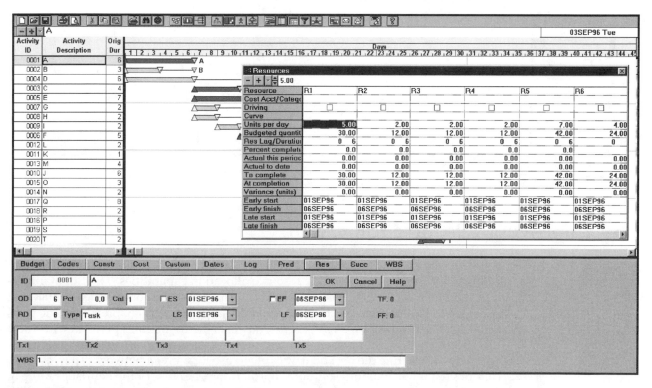

Figure 7-21. Assigning Resources to Activities

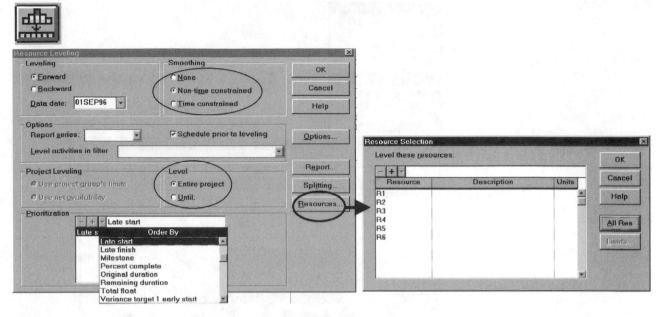

Figure 7-22. Activating Resource Allocation/Leveling

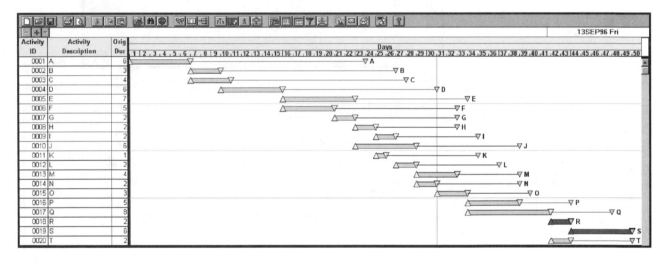

Figure 7-23. Result of Resource Allocation – Duration = 49 days

7.6 Improving Resource Allocation

As mentioned before, almost all commercial software for planning and scheduling utilizes heuristic rules to provide resource allocation capabilities. The **Standard** option used by Microsoft Project, for example, is based on the common least total-float (LTF) rule. As demonstrated by the various examples of this chapter, heuristic rules are easy to apply. Despite these benefits, however, heuristic rules perform with varying effectiveness when used on different networks and there are no hard guidelines that help in selecting the best heuristic rule to use for a given network. They, as such, cannot guarantee optimum solutions. Furthermore, because of the heuristic nature of the solution, there is a large inconsistency among the resource-constrained capabilities of commercial project management software, as reported in recent surveys, and demonstrated in this chapter. Although Primavera P3 provided a better solution than Microsoft Project 98, no one software always produces better results than others.

7.6.1 Using Biased Priorities

Because it is not possible to select an optimum heuristic rule for a given project network, one possible approach is to try a series of heuristic rules and then select the schedule with minimum duration. This procedure, however, has little diversity because the number of effective rules to enumerate is small and it is not expected that less effective rules will change much when effective rules are not improving the schedule. Therefore, without introducing new rules or changing the mechanics of heuristic procedures, a simple approach of forcing random activity priorities is used to improve the schedule. The concept is demonstrated on the example project we have.

First, let's set the "Leveling Calculation" option of Microsoft Project 98 (Figure 7–11) to "Automatic" to get the 51-day duration as in Figure 7–17, using the software's standard set of heuristic rules. It is noted that this solution was produced using the same default priority level for all project activities (set to Lowest). To view these priorities on Microsoft Project 98, let's insert a column on the Gantt chart left side, as shown in Figure 7–24.

Microsoft Project 98 software allows users to select among eight priority levels ("Highest" to "Lowest"), and assign it to every task. The software also provides a second set of heuristic rules for resource allocation in which activity priority takes precedence over its "standard" set of heuristic rules (Figure 7–25).

Let's then introduce some bias into some activities and consequently monitor their impact on the schedule. As an example, consider the case when only activity (R) in our case study is given Highest priority while all others are set to Lowest. With this limited change to the original schedule, the project duration decreased to 47 days (Figure 7–26). This simple approach can, therefore, be used to improve the results of existing heuristic procedures.

Surely, it is not possible to readily identify from a given network which activities to assign higher priorities than others to improve the schedule. Therefore, a simple iterative procedure may be used. First, we keep the software setup as shown in Figure 7–24. Afterwards, we manually pick an activity at random, change its priority level anywhere from Highest to Lowest and observe the consequent project duration. If the project duration decreases, we retain that change in priority level, otherwise we discard it. Through this process, the default schedule of commercial software systems can be much improved. Certainly with Microsoft Project 98, we can write a simple macro program and then assign the macro to a toolbar button for quick and automated access to this procedure.

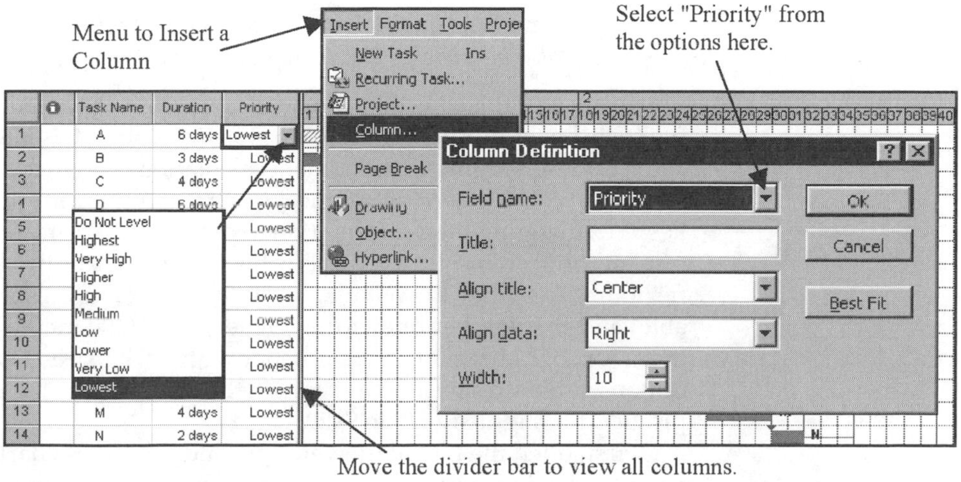

Figure 7–24. Insert "Priority" Column

To have **Priority** as the third column, highlight the third column and then use the **Inset-Column** menu option.

Move the divider bar to view all columns.

Figure 7-25.
Resource Allocation
Option under Biased
Priorities

Shown here are the
Resource Leveling
options to use when
changing the
priorities of some
activities. The
purpose is to
investigate if
changing the
priorities will provide
a better schedule.

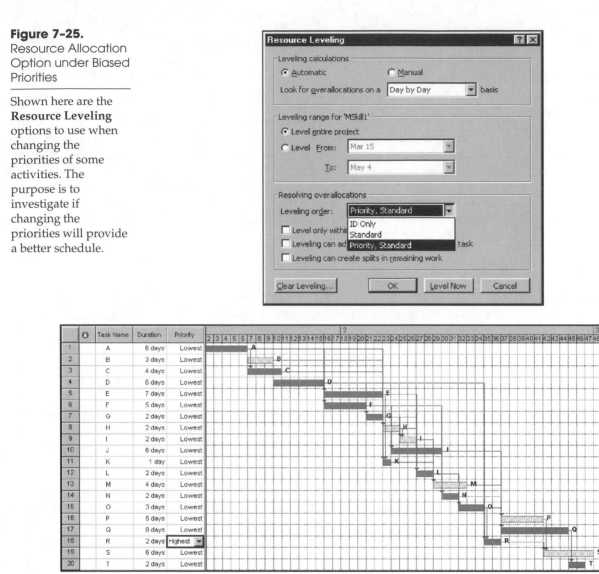

Figure 7-26. Improved 47-day Schedule with Highest Priority Assigned Only to Activity R

7.6.1.1 Optimizing the Process:

*Can we determine the optimum set of activities' priorities that
minimizes the total project duration under resource constraints while
also minimizing the appropriate moment(s) of selected resources?*

To answer this question, a macro program is included with the Microsoft Project
file (**Sch-Level.mpp**). The program was developed based on the concepts of genetic
algorithms to automate the moment calculations and incorporate them into Microsoft
Project. The GA macro, in essence, generates a random population of solutions and
keeps exchanging their information to produce offspring solutions that are evaluated
until an optimum solution is achieved. In the present program, the user is given the
flexibility to specify the population size (initial random solutions, 50 to 100 is reasonable) and the number of offspring generations (100 increments is reasonable). Using
the GA program, you can experiment with various resource allocation and leveling
options to obtain a desirable schedule. To demonstrate the program, some screens are
provided in Figures 7–27 to 7–29.

First, open the file **Sch-Level.mpp,** and the Gantt chart will appear. Notice that a
column of activity priorities is already inserted with only activity R having a Highest

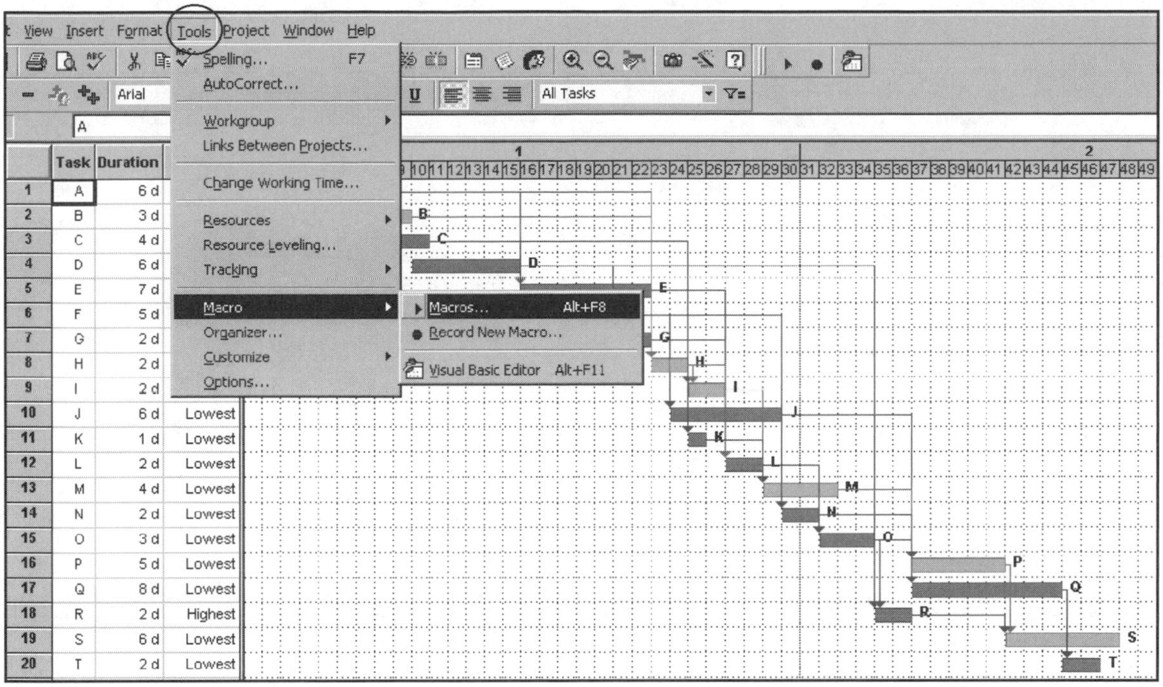

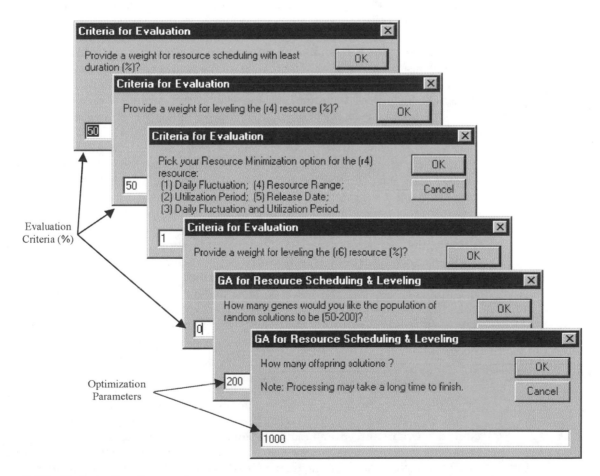

Figure 7-27. Activating the "Scheduling_Leveling" Macro

Figure 7-28. Optimization Parameters

	Task	Duration	Priority	Leveling Delay
1	A	6 d	Very High	0 ed
2	B	3 d	Very Low	12 ed
3	C	4 d	Medium	0 ed
4	D	6 d	Very High	6 ed
5	E	7 d	Lowest	4 ed
6	F	5 d	High	2 ed
7	G	2 d	Lowest	11 ed
8	H	2 d	High	2 ed
9	I	2 d	High	0 ed
10	J	6 d	High	0 ed
11	K	1 d	Higher	0 ed
12	L	2 d	High	1 ed
13	M	4 d	Very High	0 ed
14	N	2 d	Medium	2 ed
15	O	3 d	Very High	0 ed
16	P	5 d	Medium	1 ed
17	Q	8 d	Lowest	2 ed
18	R	2 d	Very High	0 ed
19	S	6 d	Low	0 ed
20	T	2 d	Higher	0 ed

Figure 7–29. Activities' Delay Values Associated with the Best Schedule (45 Days)

priority, thus producing a 47-day project duration. Now, use the **Tools-Macro-Macros** menu option and select the macro **Scheduling_Leveling** from the list of macros and click on the **Run** button. An introductory screen will appear.

For simplicity, only one resource (R4) of the six resources in the present project is assumed to be critical and requires smoothing of its profile, in addition to minimizing the project delay associated with the resource limits we have in this project. Therefore, we input our criteria for evaluating solutions (50% weight for reducing project duration and 50% for reducing R4 fluctuation) in the next set of windows shown in Figure 7–28. Notice that the weights for resources R1, R2, R3, R5, and R6 are set to zeroes. Accordingly, the process continues and the resulting schedule is shown in Figure 7–29.

A 45-day duration is obtained. The moment of R4 is also improved from 2405 to 2265. The process took almost 50 minutes on a Pentium 233 MHz machine. Note that because of the random nature of the process, exact results may not be obtained each time you try the program. This result shows a much improved schedule that is 4 days shorter than that produced by any software currently available on the market.

Applying the genetic algorithms technique to this complex problem has been demonstrated to be efficient because it arrives at solutions by searching only a small fraction of the total search space. With 20 activities, each having eight options for its priority, the total search space is 8^{20}. It may take about 1000 offspring solutions (involving a search space of 20,000) to arrive at near-optimum results.

After resource allocation is completed and the best schedule is determined (in this example a 45-day duration), it is possible to see how the software could resolve resource overallocation. Let's insert a column into the Gantt chart called **Leveling Delay**, as shown in Figure 7–29. As shown in the figure, the values in this column specify a start delay for each activity so that daily resources do not exceed the availability limits. These values will be used later in our spreadsheet model that tries to improve the schedule even further.

The use of the biased-priority procedure on Microsoft Project 98 software benefited from the software's feature of allowing user-specified priorities to activities. Other software, such as Primavera P3, for example, does not directly allow for that and, as such, requires some manipulation. The user, for example, can specify a custom activity code called "priority" to contain a number representing the priority level of each activity. This code can then be used as the leading heuristic rule to implement the procedure, as shown in Figure 7–30.

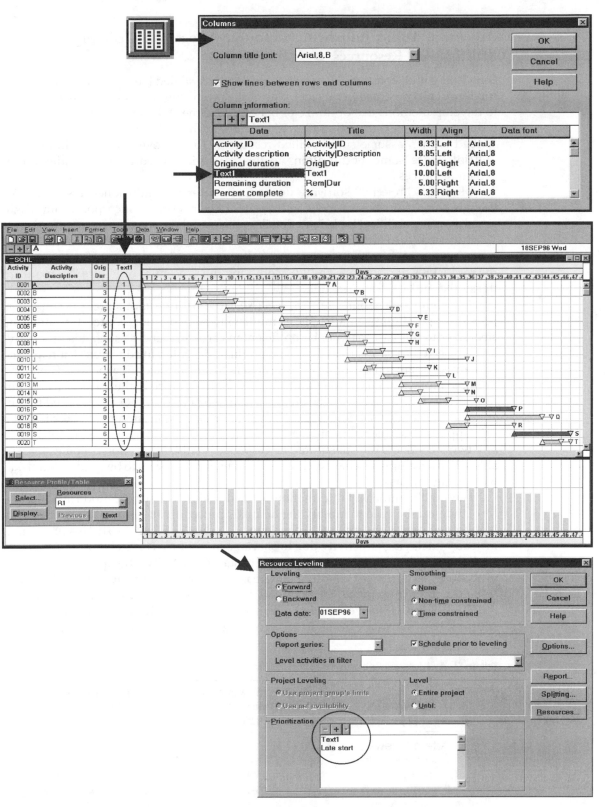

Figure 7-30. Adding Biasness to Resource Allocation Using P3

Using the **Format Column** toolbar, we insert a column for the **Text1** field, which can contain user-defined data. Then, we specify values of 1 for low-priority activities and values of zero for higher priority (e.g., activity R only). Afterwards, we change the rules used for resource allocation to become **Text1**, then **Late Start**, thus forcing the priority levels to take precedence. Accordingly, when resource allocation was performed, a *46-day schedule was obtained*, as shown in the bar chart.

7.6.2 Advanced Topic: Improving Resource Allocation Utilizing Multiskilled Resources

Scheduling with constrained resources, particularly skilled labor, is a major challenge for almost all construction projects. One of the promising solutions to this problem is to develop methods that optimize or better utilize the skilled workers already in the industry. Most resource allocation techniques, such as the heuristic procedure described earlier, assume single-skilled resources. To improve existing solutions, we will introduce some modifications to this heuristic procedure to consider multi-skilled resources.

Microsoft Project 98 software does not consider for multiskilled resources. Although some software vendors indicate that their systems incorporate multiskill scheduling capabilities (Table 7–4), details on most of their procedures are proprietary.

Two steps are carried out to modify the described single-skill resource allocation process to be used for multiskill resource allocation: (1) Storing the information about the multiskills of resources; and (2) Modifying the procedure of Figure 7–6 to utilize the stored multiskill information.

The ability of a resource (e.g., a steel fixer) to substitute another (e.g., a carpenter) provides a good representation of the multiskill ability of this resource. Certainly, the steel fixer in this case may not be proficient in carpentry, and as such, his productivity is expected to be less than that of an original carpenter. In some cases, it may take two, three, or any other number of steel fixers to substitute one carpenter. Therefore, a simple representation of the multiskill of resources can be in the form of a substitution rule, as follows: 2 R4 = 1 R2; meaning that two of resource R4 are required to substitute a shortage of one R2 resource. One important assumption made here is that a rule applies to all members of its resources (e.g., if 2 steel fixers = 1 carpenter, then any two steel fixers can substitute one carpenter). This assumption becomes reasonable when a training mechanism is implemented for resources to be used in multiskill work assignments.

Having the multiskill information defined in terms of substitution rules, this information can be used to modify the heuristic procedure of Figure 7–6, replacing its highlighted part with a multiskill checking procedure of Figure 7–31. This procedure, instead of delaying an activity due to shortage in resources (as in Figure 7–6), checks to see if enough substitute resources exist to start the activity. The multiskill checking procedure starts, first, by checking if there is one or more substitution rule(s) that can solve the resource conflict. For example, if the shortage in resource R1 = 2, and 2R2 = 1R1; 3R3 = 1R1, then either 4 (2 × 2) units of resource R1 or 6 (3 × 2) units of resource R3 can substitute the shortage in resource R1. Also, in case the free amount of

Table 7–4. Multiskill Scheduling Capabilities of Software Systems

Software (1)	Single-skill Resource Allocation (2)	Multiskill Resource Allocation (3)
Artemis Views	Yes	Yes
Autoplan	Yes	Yes
Micro Planner X*	Yes	No
Microsoft Project	Yes	No
MPS-Team Mgmt.	Yes	No
Perception	Yes	Yes
Primavera P3	Yes	No
Project Scheduler 7	Yes	No
Project Workbench	Yes	No
SAS/OR*	Yes	Yes

* Examined from a trial version

Figure 7-31. Multi-Skill Checking Procedure

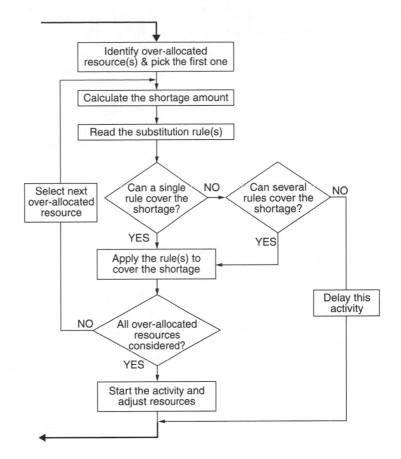

either resource (R2 and R3) is not enough to substitute for the whole shortage, a combination of resources R2 and R3 together, according to their availability, can be used to substitute the shortage in R1. When a substitution takes place, the resource pool is adjusted accordingly and the resource allocation procedure is continued without delaying the activity in question, thus saving project time. If, during the multiskill checking procedure, a resource conflict could not be solved, then the activity will be delayed.

Case 1

We now apply the multiskill procedure on the project using one substitution rule (2 R5 = 1 R1). Applying the proposed procedure manually is shown in Table 7–5, resulting in a 39-day project duration, with a single substitution rule. The last column in Table 7–5 indicates when the substitution rule was used to schedule the activities. At the beginning of the project (current time = 0), the only eligible activities were A, B, and D, which were sorted by their late-start values (column 9). Considering these three activities in order, activity A could start and accordingly, not enough resources will be available for either B or D. As such, activity A was started at time 0 and could end at time 6 (duration = 6 days). Before delaying activities B and D, the multiskill checking procedure of Figure 7–31 was applied using the substitution rule (2 R5 = 1 R1).

Accordingly, activity B could start at time 0 because the shortage of one resource in R1 (out of the 7 available, 5 were used by A and 3 are required for B) could be covered by two free R5 resources. Notice here that the substitution information of activity B is shown in columns 3–8 of Table 7–5. In column

Table 7-5. Manual Scheduling of Case 1 Using Multiskilled Resources

Time	Eligible Activity	R1=7	R2=10	R3=10	R4=16	R5=18	R6=13	Late Start	Duration	Decision	Finish Time	Substitution Rule Used
0	A	5	2	2	2	7	4	0	6	Start	6	
	B	3–1	5	2	3	9+2	6	6	3	Start	3	2 **R5** = 1 **R1**
	D	5	4	3	5	5	4	7	6	Delay	-	
3	A	5	2	2	2	7	4	0	6	Continue	6	2 **R5** = 1 **R1**
	D	5–3	4	3	5	5+6	4	7	6	Start	9	
6	D	5	4	3	5	5	4	7	6	Continue	9	
	C	2	4	4	2	3	1	6	4	Start	10	
	E	3	5	2	3	8	0	9	7	Delay	-	
	H	5	5	4	0	9	1	13	2	Delay	-	
9	C	2	4	4	2	3	1	6	4	Continue	10	
	E	3	5	2	3	8	0	9	7	Start	16	
	H	5	5	4	0	9	1	13	2	Delay	-	
	G	4	1	4	3	9	8	13	2	Delay	-	
10	E	3	5	2	3	8	0	9	7	Continue	16	
	F	4	1	4	9	2	5	10	5	Start	15	
	G	4	1	4	3	9	8	13	2	Delay	-	
	H	5	5	4	0	9	1	13	2	Delay	-	
15	E	3	5	2	3	8	0	9	7	Continue	16	
	G	4	1	4	3	9	8	13	2	Start	17	
	H	5	5	4	0	9	1	13	2	Delay	-	
	J	1	5	4	6	7	3	15	6	Delay	-	
16	G	4	1	4	3	9	8	13	2	Continue	17	
	H	5	5	4	0	9	1	13	2	Delay	-	
	J	1	5	4	6	7	3	15	6	Start	-	
	K	3	3	2	4	5	1	16	1	Delay	22	
17	J	1	5	4	6	7	3	15	6	Continue	22	
	H	5	5	4	0	9	1	13	2	Start	19	
	K	3	3	2	4	5	1	16	1	Delay	-	
19	J	1	5	4	6	7	3	15	6	Continue	22	
	I	3	2	4	3	4	2	15	2	Start	21	
	K	3	3	2	4	5	1	16	1	Start	20	
	L	3	2	2	8	3	4	17	2	Delay	-	
20	I	3	2	4	3	4	2	15	2	Continue	21	
	J	1	5	4	6	7	3	15	6	Continue	22	
	L	3	2	2	8	3	4	17	2	Delay	-	
21	J	1	5	4	6	7	3	15	6	Continue	22	
	L	3	2	2	8	3	4	17	2	Start	23	
	M	2	2	2	2	4	8	17	4	Delay	-	
22	L	3	2	2	8	3	4	17	2	Continue	23	
	M	2	2	2	2	4	8	17	4	Start	26	
23	M	2	2	2	2	4	8	17	4	Continue	26	
	N	1	4	4	3	4	1	19	2	Start	25	
	O	5	5	4	6	2	3	19	3	Delay	-	
25	M	2	2	2	2	4	8	17	4	Continue	26	
	O	5	5	4	6	2	3	19	3	Start	28	
26	O	5	5	4	6	2	3	19	3	Continue	28	2 **R5** = 1 **R1**
	P	3–1	2	3	4	7+2	8	21	5	Start	31	
28	P	3	2	3	4	7	8	21	5	Continue	31	
	Q	4	5	4	2	3	4	22	8	Start	36	
	R	5	3	3	3	7	8	24	2	Delay	-	
31	Q	4	5	4	2	3	4	22	8	Continue	36	2 **R5** = 1 **R1**
	R	5–2	3	3	3	7+4	8	24	2	Start	33	
33	Q	4	5	4	2	3	4	22	8	Continue	36	
	S	2	4	6	2	3	4	26	6	Start	39	
36	S	2	4	6	2	3	4	26	6	Continue	39	
	T	1	6	2	7	5	2	30	2	Start	38	

3, the shortage in one R1 resource was subtracted, and two of R5 resources were added to column 7. This approach made it possible to maintain a total amount of used resources at any cycle that is less than or equal to the resource availability limit.

After scheduling activity B, the multiskill checking procedure was used for activity D but failed to resolve the conflict in resources R1, R2, R5, and R6, thus delaying D until the earliest time more resources became available (day 3). At day 3, activity B was finished, and the eligible activities were A (continued from previous cycle) and D (delayed from previous cycle). After sorting and considering these activities one by one, D could start only after the given substitution rule was applied. Accordingly, the shortage of three R1 resources could be covered by six R5 resources. The process was then continued until all activities were scheduled (project duration = 39 days). As shown, using just one rule of substitution resulted in a 12-day saving in project duration (from 51 to 39 days).

The manual process shown in Table 7–5 undoubtedly indicates the benefit of utilizing the multiskills of resources to minimize project duration. It also shows that the calculations add little computational burden on the scheduling process. Once the multiskill scheduling procedure is finished, the calculation table can be used to read the multiskill strategy that specifies when, how long, and what resource substitutions should take place. Table 7–5, for example, directly shows the strategy used in case 1 as follows:

- Two of the free R5 resources are to join R1 resources in the period from time 0 to time 3, to help in activity B.
- Six of the free R5 resources are to join R1 resources in the period from time 3 to time 6, to help in activity D.
- Two of the free R5 resources are to join R1 resources in the period from time 26 to time 28, to help in activity P.
- Four of the free R5 resources are to join R1 resources in the period from time 31 to time 33, to help in activity R.

Case 2

Let's now apply the multiskill scheduling process to a more involved situation with several resource substitution rules. We will use the following substitution rules on the project (*2 R5 = 1 R1; 2 R4 = 1 R2; 2 R5 = 1 R4; 2 R4 = 1 R5; and 2 R6 = 1 R5*). The manual solution of this case is shown in Table 7–6. The first two cycles are similar to those in Table 7–5. Afterwards, the process continues to the third cycle (day 6), which includes four eligible activities: activity D (continuing till day 9); and three more activities: C, E, and H. Activity C could start because enough resources were available. As such, activities C and D consumed a total of 7, 8, 7, 7, 8, and 5 of resources R1 through R6, respectively. Now, considering activity E, its resources are checked one by one. Activity E requires three of R1 resource while none were available because all 7 R1 resources were used in D and C. The multiskill checking procedure was then used and a substitution rule (2R5 = 1 R1) was applied to utilize six free R5 resources to replace the missing 3 R1 resources. Accordingly, the substitution amount of 3 was subtracted from column 3, and at the same time, an amount of 6 was added to R5 (column 7). Using this substitution, the total amount of R5 requirement becomes 22 (5 for activity D; 3 for activity C; 8 originally required for activity E; and 6 for the substitution), thus leaving a

Table 7-6. Manual Scheduling of Case 2 Using Multiskilled Resources

Time	Eligible Activity	R1=7	R2=10	R3=10	R4=16	R5=18	R6=13	Late Start	Duration	Decision	Finish Time	Substitution Rule Used
0	A	5	2	2	2	7	4	0	6	Start	6	
	B	3–1	5	2	3	9+2	6	6	3	Start	3	2 **R5** = 1 **R1**
	D	5	4	3	5	5	4	7	6	Delay	-	
3	A	5	2	2	2	7	4	0	6	Continue	6	2 **R5** = 1 **R1**
	D	5–3	4	3	5	5+6	4	7	6	Start	9	
6	D	5	4	3	5	5	4	7	6	Continue	9	2 **R5** = 1 **R1**
	C	2	4	4	5	3	1	6	4	Start	10	2 **R6** = 1 **R5**
	E	3–3	5–3	2	2	8+6–4	0+8	9	7	Start	13	2 **R4** = 1 **R2**
	H	5	5	4	3+6	4	1	13	2	Delay	13	
9	C	2	4	4	2	3	1	6	4	Continue	10	2 **R5** = 1 **R1**
	E	3	5	2	3	8	0	9	7	Continue	13	2 **R4** = 1 **R5**
	G	4–2	1	4	3+8	9+4–6	8+4	13	2	Start	11	2 **R6** = 1 **R5**
	H	5	5	4	0	9	1	13	2	Delay	-	
10	E	3	5	2	3	8	0	9	7	Continue	13	
	G	4	1	4	3	9	8	13	2	Continue	11	
	F	4	1	4	9	2	5	10	5	Delay	-	
	H	5	5	4	0	9	1	13	2	Delay	-	
11	E	3	5	2	3	8	0	9	7	Continue	13	
	F	4	1	4	9	2	5	10	5	Start	16	
	H	5	5	4	0	9	1	13	2	Delay	-	
13	F	4	1	4	9	2	5	10	5	Continue	16	
	H	5–2	5	4	0	9+4	1	13	2	Start	15	2 **R5** = 1 **R1**
	K	3	3	2	4	5	1	16	1	Delay	-	
15	F	4	1	4	9	2	5	10	5	Continue	16	
	I	3	2	4	3	4	2	15	2	Start	17	2 **R5** = 1 **R1**
	K	3–3	3	2	4	5+6	1	16	1	Start	16	
	L	3	2	2	8	3	4	17	2	Delay	-	
16	I	3	2	4	3	4	2	15	2	Continue	17	
	J	1	5	4	6	7	3	15	6	Start	22	2 **R5** = 1 **R4**
	L	3	2	2	8–1	3+2	4	17	2	Start	18	
17	J	1	5	4	6	7	3	15	6	Continue	22	
	L	3	2	2	8	3	4	17	2	Continue	18	
	M	2	2	2	2	4	8	17	4	Delay	-	
18	J	1	5	4	6	7	3	15	6	Continue	22	
	M	2	2	2	2	4	8	17	4	Start	22	2 **R4** = 1 **R2**
	N	1	4–1	4	3+2	4	1	19	2	Start	20	
	O	5	5	4	6	2	3	19	3	Delay	-	
20	J	1	5	4	6	7	3	15	6	Continue	22	
	M	2	2	2	2	4	8	17	4	Continue	22	
	O	5	5	4	6	2	3	19	3	Delay	-	
22	O	5	5	4	6	2	3	19	3	Start	25	2 **R5** = 1 **R1**
	P	3–1	2	3	4	7+2	8	21	5	Start	27	
25	P	3	2	3	4	7	8	21	5	Continue	27	
	Q	4	5	4	2	3	4	22	8	Start	33	
	R	5	3	3	3	2	8	24	2	Delay	-	
27	Q	4	5	4	2	3	4	22	8	Continue	33	2 **R5** = 1 **R1**
	R	5–2	3	3	3	2+4	8	24	2	Start	29	
29	Q	4	5	4	2	3	4	22	8	Continue	33	
	S	2	4	6	2	3	4	26	6	Start	35	
33	S	2	4	6	2	3	4	26	6	Continue	35	
	T	1	6	2	7	5	2	30	2	Start	35	

shortage of 4 in resource R5 (limit is 18). To substitute for the missing R5 resources, a search through available rules reveals that rule (2 R6 = 1 R5) can be used and requires the use of eight free R6 resources. Adding these eight to the resource requirements of R6 makes a total of 13, which is the resource availability limit, thus making the substitution possible. Once the assignment conflict of R1 is resolved through the two nested rules, the process is continued with R2, which also exhibited a shortage of 3 that was substituted by the rule (2 R4 = 1 R2). Activity E can then start. Moving to activity H, the substitution rules did not solve the conflicts in R1, R2, R3, R5, and R6 and thus activity H has to be delayed till the earliest time more resources become available (day 9). It is noted that at the beginning of a new cycle (e.g., at time 9), all the resource substitutions that took place at the previous cycle are released so that the activities can be scheduled using the original resources.

The fourth cycle at day 9 includes four eligible activities: C and E (continued from previous cycle till days 10 and 13, respectively); H (delayed from previous cycle); and one more new activity (G). The resources used by activities C and E were 5, 9, 6, 5, 11, and 1 for R1 through R6, respectively. Activity G can start because the available substitution rules can solve the conflicts in R1 (4 of R5 substituted 2 of R1) and R5 (8 of R4 plus 4 of R6 substituted 6 of R5). It is worthwhile to note that the shortage of 6 R5 resources is covered by two resources (8 from R4 and 4 from R6) as long as there is not a single resource that can cover the shortage totally. Activity H is delayed because the available substitution rules still could not solve the conflicts in R1, R2, R3, R5, and R6. The process is continued through all the cycles of Table 7–5 until all activities are scheduled (project duration = 35 days; only 3 days' extension beyond the original CPM duration of 32 days).

7.6.3   A Macro Program for Multiskill Resource Allocation

Performing the multiskill scheduling calculations can be tedious when the project size gets bigger. It is desirable, therefore, to automate the calculations and incorporate it into Microsoft Project. A macro program was developed for that purpose and is included in the CD accompanying this book. The program name is **MURSA**, which is an abbreviation **MU**ltiskill **ReS**ource allocation **A**lgorithm. MURSA is a VBA macro attached to a Microsoft Project file (**Multi-Skill.mpp**). This program uses the ELS heuristic rule and follows the manual steps described earlier. Using MURSA, you can experiment with various resource substitution rules to obtain a desirable schedule. To demonstrate program MURSA, step-by-step screens are provided in Figures 7–32 to 7–37.

It is noted that to clear the schedule and return to the original CPM analysis of Microsoft Project, you can activate the macro "Clear_Leveling."

Note:	It is very important for every project manager to consult with trade unions to make sure they approve the suggested multiskill strategy before putting it into action on site.

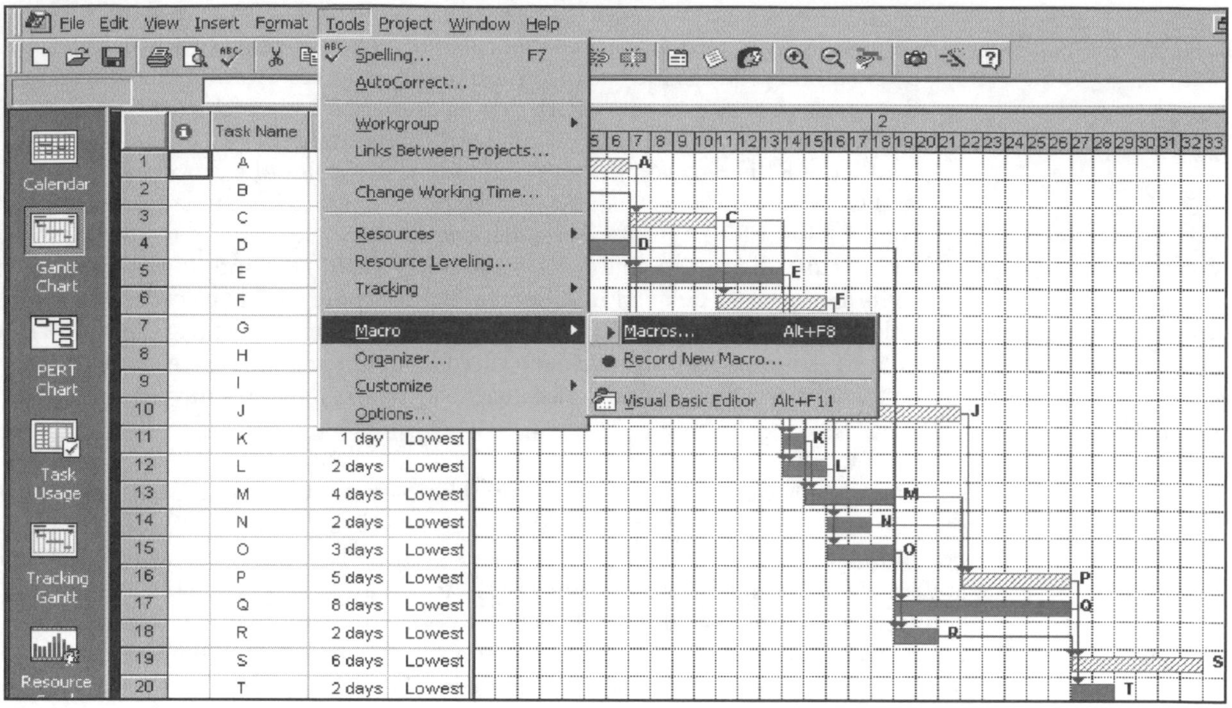

Figure 7–32. Activating MURSA Program

First, open the file **Multi-Skill.mpp** from where you installed the CD; use the **File-Open** menu option to load the file (Figure 7–32), and the Gantt chart of our case study will appear. Notice that a column of activity priorities is already inserted. In fact, you can use this file to experiment with the various scheduling options described earlier. Now, use the **Tools-Macro-Macros** menu option and select the macro **MURSA** from the list of macros and click the **Run** button. An introductory screen will appear.

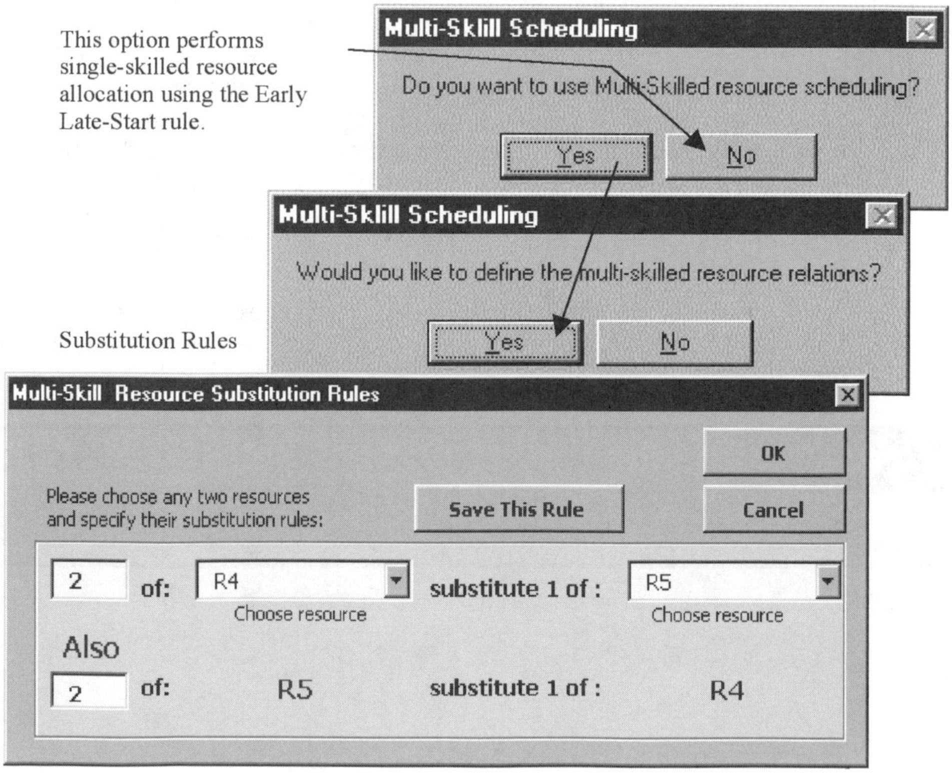

Figure 7–33.
Defining Resource
Substitution Rules

If you choose the multiskilled resource allocation, you need to specify the resource substitution rules from the shown screen. Choose two resources from the two combo boxes, then type the substitution amounts in the text boxes, then use the **Save This Rule** button each time. The five substitution rules used in case 2 are already input. When finished click on the **OK** button.

This option performs single-skilled resource allocation using the Early Late-Start rule.

Substitution Rules

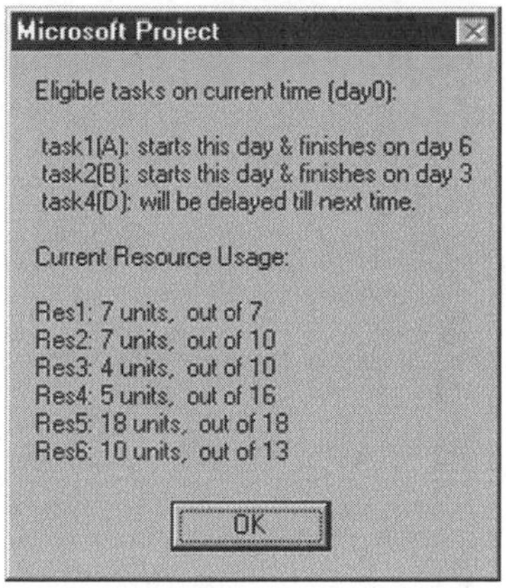

Figure 7-34. Multiskill Resource Allocation Calculations

The calculations proceed and provide you with a message box of the decision made at each cycle of the process. Starting at time 0, this figure shows that activities A and B are started, while activity D is delayed. The calculations follow the manual process shown in Table 7–6. Click on the **OK** button to continue to the next cycles. After the last step, some background processing will take a little while before a message appears.

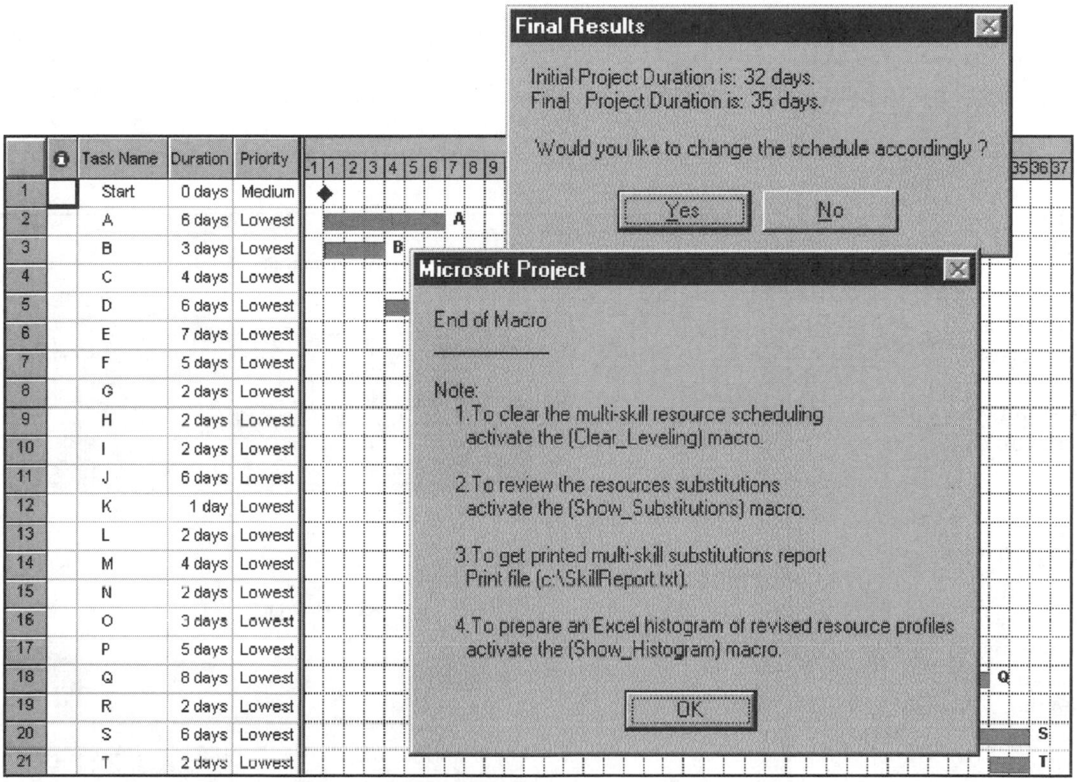

Figure 7-35. Multiskill Resource Allocation Results

The calculations result in a 35-day duration, as shown here. You may now change the schedule accordingly. The final note refers you to other macros you may use.

Multi-Skilled Resource Substitution Report

Substitution for activity:

(5/20)   OK

E

6 units of res. Res5 substitute 3 units of res. Res1 in task E, from day 6 to day 9.
6 units of res. Res4 substitute 3 units of res. Res2 in task E, from day 6 to day 9.
8 units of res. Res6 substitute 4 units of res. Res5 in task E, from day 6 to day 9.

Figure 7–36. Report on Resource Substitutions

After the multiskill resource allocation process is ended, you may activate the **Show_Substitutions** macro to view the window shown here. You can scroll to view all activities and their related substitution strategy. A complete report can also be obtained by printing the file **c:\SkillReport.txt**.

Figure 7-37.
Revised Resource
Histograms

Because the multiskill scheduling process has changed the resource assignments on activities, you can not depend on the default resource histograms of Microsoft Project. To view the revised histogram of any resource (showing no overallocation), You can activate the **Show_Histogram** macro to view an Excel sheet **c:\rveshistogram.xls** generated by the scheduling process.

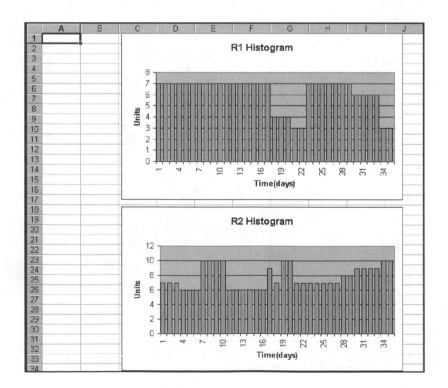

198

7.7 Optimization of Resource Allocation and Leveling on Excel

To consolidate our understanding of the resource allocation and leveling concepts, let's try some experiments on a spreadsheet model for CPM analysis. We will follow the steps shown in Figures 7–38 to 7–41. First, activate Microsoft Excel and use the **File-Open** menu option to load the spreadsheet file **Sch-Level.xls** from where you installed the CD of this book. The file is a workbook containing three sheets that will take us step by step to developing an optimization model for resource allocation and leveling combined.

With few changes to the Excel bar chart sheet, it is possible to add calculations for accumulating daily resources so that resource profiles can be plotted and total demand is compared with the maximum available. In addition, moment calculations can be incorporated as shown in the CPM-Res sheet (Figure 7–39).

To resolve the resource overallocation of the original CPM analysis, we need to change the schedule so that resource limits are not exceeded. We do that by specifying proper values in the Delay column. If we specify any value of delay to any activity, the bar chart automatically changes, and accordingly, so do the resource usage and profile. As shown in Figure 7–39, we can directly copy the delay values from Microsoft Project (Figure 7–29) as the values that achieve a 45-day duration without exceeding resource limits.

Duration = 32.0 days

				Predecessors			Successors				CPM Calculations											Early Bar Chart Day No.			
ID	Name	Activity Duration	Activity Cost	P1	P2	P3	S1	S2	S3	Delay	F1	F2	F3	T1	T2	T3	ES	EF	LS	LF	TF	1	2	3	4
1	A	6					3	8	5					6	13	9		6		6		1	1	1	1
2	B	3					5	8						9	13	32		3	6	9	6	1	1	1	
3	C	4		1			6	11			6			10	16	32	6	10	6	10					
4	D	6					7	18						13	24	32		6	7	13	7	1	1	1	1
5	E	7		1	2		11	12			6	3		16	17	32	6	13	9	16	3				
6	F	5		3			10	14			10			15	19	32	10	15	10	15					
7	G	2		4			9	12			6			15	17	32	6	8	13	15	7				
8	H	2		1	2		9	12			6	3		15	17	32	6	8	13	15	7				
9	I	2		7	8		13				8	8		17	32	32	8	10	15	17	7				
10	J	6		6			16				15			21	32	32	15	21	15	21					
11	K	1		3	5		13				10	13		17	32	32	13	14	16	17	3				
12	L	2		5	7	8	14	15			13	8	8	19	19	32	13	15	17	19	4				
13	M	4		9	11		16				10	14		21	32	32	14	18	17	21	3				
14	N	2		6	12		16				15	15		21	32	32	15	17	19	21	4				
15	O	3		12			17	18			15			22	24	32	15	18	19	22	4				
16	P	5		10	13	14	19				21	18	17	26	32	32	21	26	21	26					
17	Q	8		15			20				18			30	32	32	18	26	22	30	4				
18	R	2		4	15		19				6	18		26	32	32	18	20	24	26	6				
19	S	6		16	18						26	20		32	32	32	26	32	26	32					
20	T	2		17							26			32	32	32	26	28	30	32	4				

CPM | CPM-BarChart | CPM-Res

Figure 7–38. CPM Model

The second sheet, shown here, is a CPM model with a bar chart of the example project. Notice that the Delay column shows zero values, meaning that activities are to start exactly at their Early-Start times.

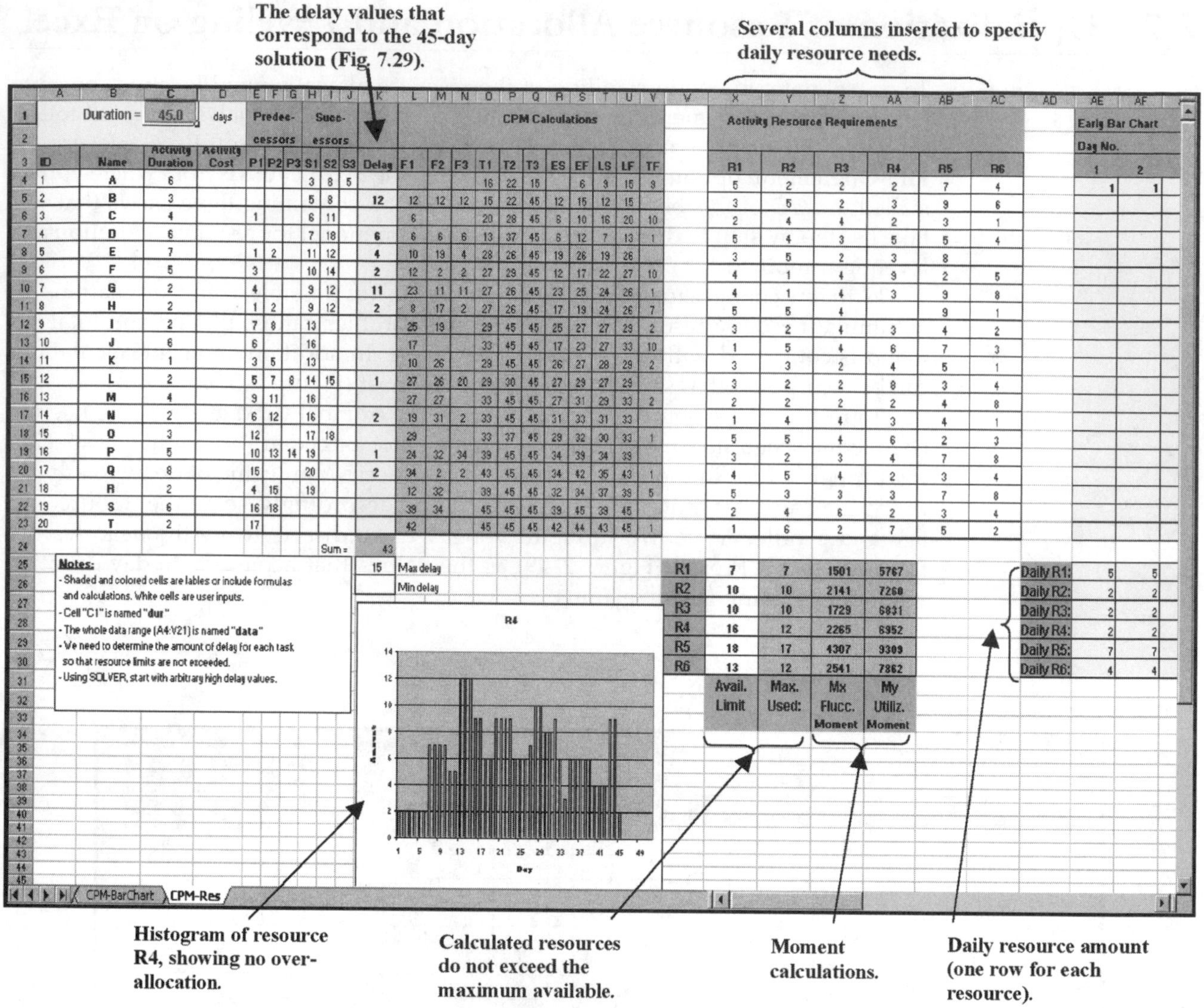

The delay values that correspond to the 45-day solution (Fig. 7.29).

Several columns inserted to specify daily resource needs.

ID	Name	Activity Duration	Activity Cost	P1	P2	P3	S1	S2	S3	Delay	F1	F2	F3	T1	T2	T3	ES	EF	LS	LF	TF	R1	R2	R3	R4	R5	R6	Day 1	Day 2
1	A	6					3	8	5					16	22	15		6	9	15	9	5	2	2	2	7	4	1	1
2	B	3					5	8		12	12	12	12	15	22	45	12	15	12	15		3	5	2	3	9	6		
3	C	4		1			6	11			6			20	28	45	6	10	16	20	10	2	4	4	2	3	1		
4	D	6					7	18		6	6	6	6	13	37	45	6	12	7	13	1	5	4	3	5	5	4		
5	E	7		1	2		11	12		4	10	19	4	28	26	45	19	26	19	26		3	5	2	3	8			
6	F	5		3			10	14		2	12	2	2	27	29	45	12	17	22	27	10	4	1	4	9	2	5		
7	G	2		4			9	12		11	23	11	11	27	26	45	23	25	24	26	1	4	1	4	3	9	8		
8	H	2		1	2		9	12		2	8	17	2	27	26	45	17	19	24	26	7	5	5	4		9	1		
9	I	2		7	8		13				25	19		29	45	45	25	27	27	29	2	3	2	4	3	4	2		
10	J	6		6			16				17			33	45	45	17	23	27	33	10	1	5	4	6	7	3		
11	K	1		3	5		13				10	26		29	45	45	26	27	28	29	2	3	3	2	4	5	1		
12	L	2		5	7	8	14	15		1	27			29	30	45	27	29	27	29		3	2	2	8	3	4		
13	M	4		9	11		16				27	27		33	45	45	27	31	29	33	2	2	2	2	2	4	8		
14	N	2		6	12		16			2	19	31	2	33	45	45	31	33	31	33		1	4	4	3	4	1		
15	O	3		12			17	18			29			33	37	45	29	32	30	33	1	5	5	4	6	2	3		
16	P	5		10	13	14	19			1	24	32	34	39	45	45	34	39	34	39		3	2	3	4	7	8		
17	Q	8		15			20			2	34	2	2	43	45	45	34	42	35	43		4	5	4	2	3	4		
18	R	2		4	15		19				12	32		38	45	45	32	34	37	39	5	5	3	3	3	7	8		
19	S	6		16	18						39	34		45	45	45	39	45	39	45		2	4	6	2	3	4		
20	T	2		17							42			45	45	45	42	44	43	45		1	6	2	7	5	2		

Sum = 43

Max delay 15
Min delay

Duration = 45.0 days

Predecessors • Successors • CPM Calculations • Activity Resource Requirements • Early Bar Chart • Day No.

Notes:
- Shaded and colored cells are labels or include formulas and calculations. White cells are user inputs.
- Cell "C1" is named "dur"
- The whole data range (A4:V21) is named "data"
- We need to determine the amount of delay for each task so that resource limits are not exceeded.
- Using SOLVER, start with arbitrary high delay values.

R4 (histogram)

	Avail. Limit	Max. Used:	Mx Fluct. Moment	My Utiliz. Moment
R1	7	7	1501	5767
R2	10	10	2141	7268
R3	10	10	1729	6831
R4	16	12	2265	6952
R5	18	17	4307	9309
R6	13	12	2541	7862

Daily R1:	5	5
Daily R2:	2	2
Daily R3:	2	2
Daily R4:	2	2
Daily R5:	7	7
Daily R6:	4	4

CPM-BarChart / CPM-Res

Histogram of resource R4, showing no over-allocation.

Calculated resources do not exceed the maximum available.

Moment calculations.

Daily resource amount (one row for each resource).

Figure 7–39. Excel Model for Resource Allocation and Leveling

Figure 7.40. Solver Failed to Provide a Solution

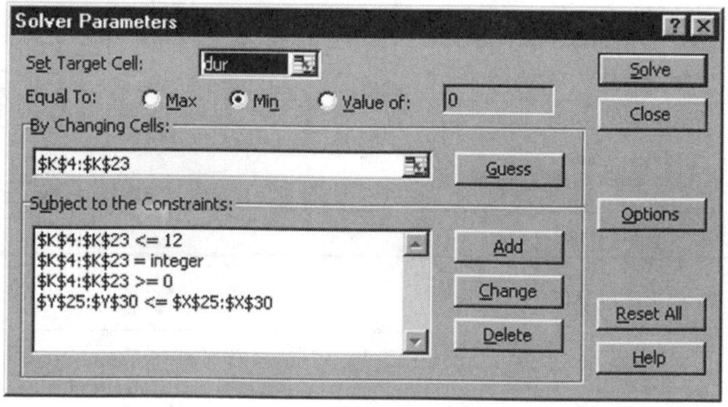

Solver Parameters

Set Target Cell: dur

Equal To: ○ Max ● Min ○ Value of: 0

By Changing Cells:
$K$4:$K$23

Subject to the Constraints:
$K$4:$K$23 <= 12
$K$4:$K$23 = integer
$K$4:$K$23 >= 0
$Y$25:$Y$30 <= $X$25:$X$30

[Solve] [Close] [Guess] [Options] [Add] [Change] [Delete] [Reset All] [Help]

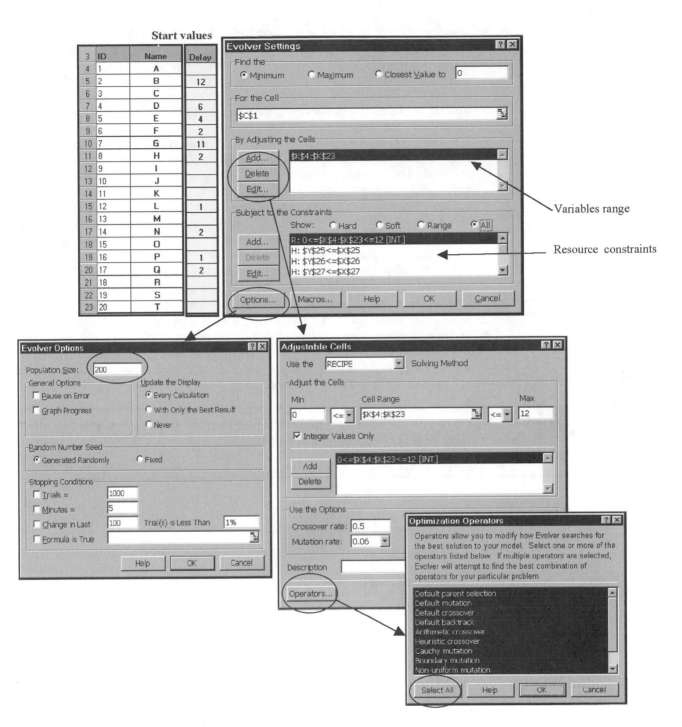

Start values

3	ID	Name	Delay
4	1	A	
5	2	B	12
6	3	C	
7	4	D	6
8	5	E	4
9	6	F	2
10	7	G	11
11	8	H	2
12	9	I	
13	10	J	
14	11	K	
15	12	L	1
16	13	M	
17	14	N	2
18	15	O	
19	16	P	1
20	17	Q	2
21	18	R	
22	19	S	
23	20	T	

Figure 7–41. Evolver Optimization Setup

In fact, this sheet becomes an interesting model for performing resource allocation and leveling. Now we can carry out several experiments:

- **Resource Leveling:** manually introduce delay values only to noncritical activities (activities with zero values for their total floats) and monitor changes to the shape of the resource profile. Project duration will not change.

- **Resource Allocation:** manually introduce delay values to any activity (critical and noncritical) and monitor the peak resources used compared to the limit. Monitor also the project duration. Can you arrive at the least duration without exceeding resource limits?

- Use the Excel Solver tool to try arriving at the optimum delay values. In fact, if you activate Solver, you will see that the parameters have already been input (Figure 7–40) and ready to solve. Before starting Solver, however, it is recommended that you put arbitrary values (0 to 15) for the delay so that project duration is extended. Afterwards, let Solver minimize project duration for you. It is highly likely, however, that Solver will stop without being able to solve this problem.

- Use the Evolver tool to try arriving at the **optimum delay values and accordingly the minimum-duration schedule.** In Evolver, for example, you may set the optimization parameters as shown in Figure 7–41. The objective function is to minimize the duration cell and the variables are the values in the delay column (should be an integer from (0 to 12). The constraints, on the other hand, are to limit the daily resources used to the maximum available. One addition constraint is also used to minimize the sum of delays. Once these are set, you can let the optimization proceed for some time. One possible option is to add other constraints to minimize the moment of any resource and as such the optimization can run with multiple objectives: resource allocation and leveling. It is noted that because the 45-day schedule is a near-optimum solution, optimization may take a long time to reach a better solution.

- To view the optimum solution of this particular example, copy the delay values given at the far right side of this sheet (column CE, after the bar chart) to the variables in column K. A 43-day solution will result (our manual heuristic solution of Table 7–3 gave 49 days).

> **Note:** You can experiment with the trial version of Evolver to replicate this experiment and others covered in the next chapters. The standard version is valid for three months.

7.8 Back to Our Case Study Project

Based on the various approaches we discussed in this chapter regarding resource allocation and leveling, we can follow the systematic approach and apply it to our case study project, as follows:

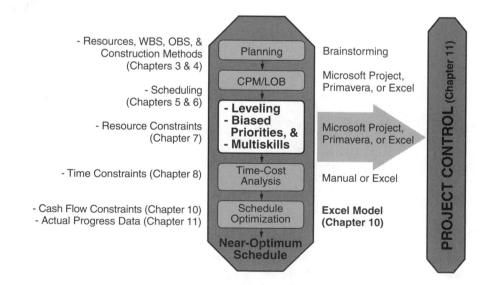

7.8.1 CPM / LOB Analysis

The CPM analysis was discussed thoroughly in Chapter 5 and the project duration of the case study is 32 days. We will assume that the project is not repetitive and thus the LOB schedule of Chapter 6 is not required for the sake of simplicity.

7.8.2 Dealing with Resources

This part involved the following steps in sequence:

- We continue working on the **Case-Study.xls** file after generating a Microsoft Project file and specifying the activity relationships (Section 5.7.3 in Chapter 5).
- In Microsoft Project, resource limits will be automatically transferred to the Resource Sheet from the Estimate (Figure 7–7). The 32-day schedule will have resource overallocations. The Microsoft Project file name of our case study is **CPM-Ch07.mpp.**
- We now try resource leveling on Microsoft Project with *delays limited to float* times (similar to Figure 7–13). This resulted in no improvement to the schedule nor solved the resource overallocation.
- We consider the manual resource allocation solution we did in Table 7–1. This resulted in a 40-day duration with all our resources being within their availability limits.
- We try resource allocation on Microsoft Project, similar to what we did in Figures 7–14 and 7–17, still resulting in a 40-day duration;
- We then try using biased priorities in some tasks and see if this can improve the schedule and produce a shorter one without violating the resource limits (similar to Figures 7–24 to 7–26). For our small case study, however, this process still did not improve the 40-day duration of our schedule. In larger networks, such as the 20-activity example discussed earlier, substantial improvements can be achieved.
- One last option we can try is to see if we have multiskilled resources that can be used to improve the schedule (as discussed in Section 7.6.2). For our case study, however, we will not consider this option for simplicity.
- Lastly, we finalize the best schedule we can get out of Microsoft Project and the experimentation with the various options in this chapter. The result is a schedule of **40-day duration** (Figure 7–42). Notice that the leveling delay values that resolved the resource conflicts are shown in the figure.

7.8.3 What is Next?

We are now ready to send the best solution found so far to our Excel project management system (the **Case-Study.xls** file). By proceeding to the Schedule sheet of the Excel file, we can use the first two buttons. Button 1 automatically sets up the Schedule sheet based on the estimate data, and button 2 imports your saved Microsoft Project file of your resource-leveled schedule (Figure 7–43).

During the file import, you can automatically activate resource leveling and resource allocation with biased priorities if you have not done that manually in Microsoft Project.

After using the first two buttons, the schedule sheet is shown in Figure 7–44. We will try to use optimization tools to see if we can improve the schedule even further.

Figure 7-42. Best Solution of Microsoft Project

Case study project (**CPM-Ch07.mpp**). Notice the leveling delay values of the activities (2 days in D and 8 days in G).

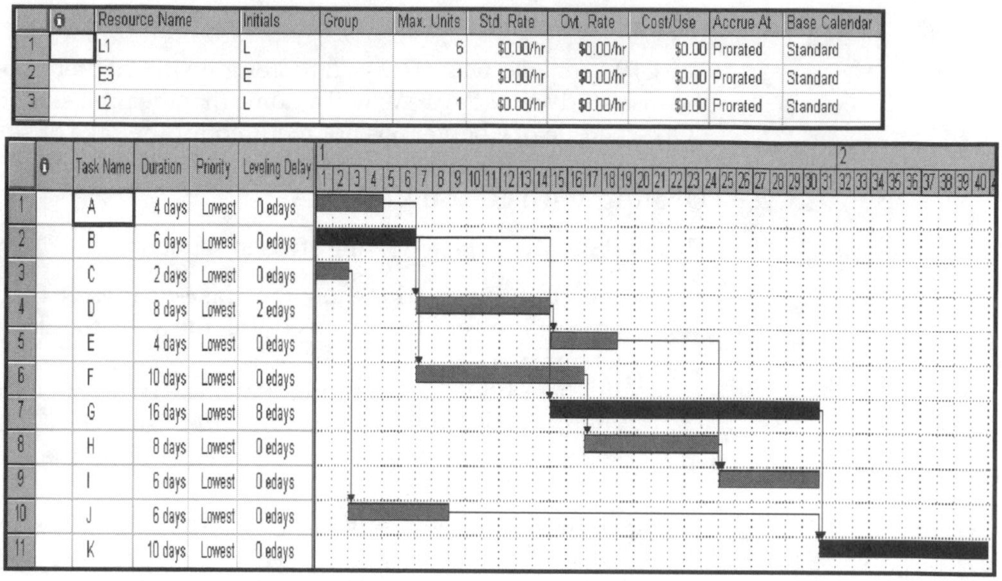

	Resource Name	Initials	Group	Max. Units	Std. Rate	Ovt. Rate	Cost/Use	Accrue At	Base Calendar
1	L1	L		6	$0.00/hr	$0.00/hr	$0.00	Prorated	Standard
2	E3	E		1	$0.00/hr	$0.00/hr	$0.00	Prorated	Standard
3	L2	L		1	$0.00/hr	$0.00/hr	$0.00	Prorated	Standard

	Task Name	Duration	Priority	Leveling Delay
1	A	4 days	Lowest	0 edays
2	B	6 days	Lowest	0 edays
3	C	2 days	Lowest	0 edays
4	D	8 days	Lowest	2 edays
5	E	4 days	Lowest	0 edays
6	F	10 days	Lowest	0 edays
7	G	16 days	Lowest	8 edays
8	H	8 days	Lowest	0 edays
9	I	6 days	Lowest	0 edays
10	J	6 days	Lowest	0 edays
11	K	10 days	Lowest	0 edays

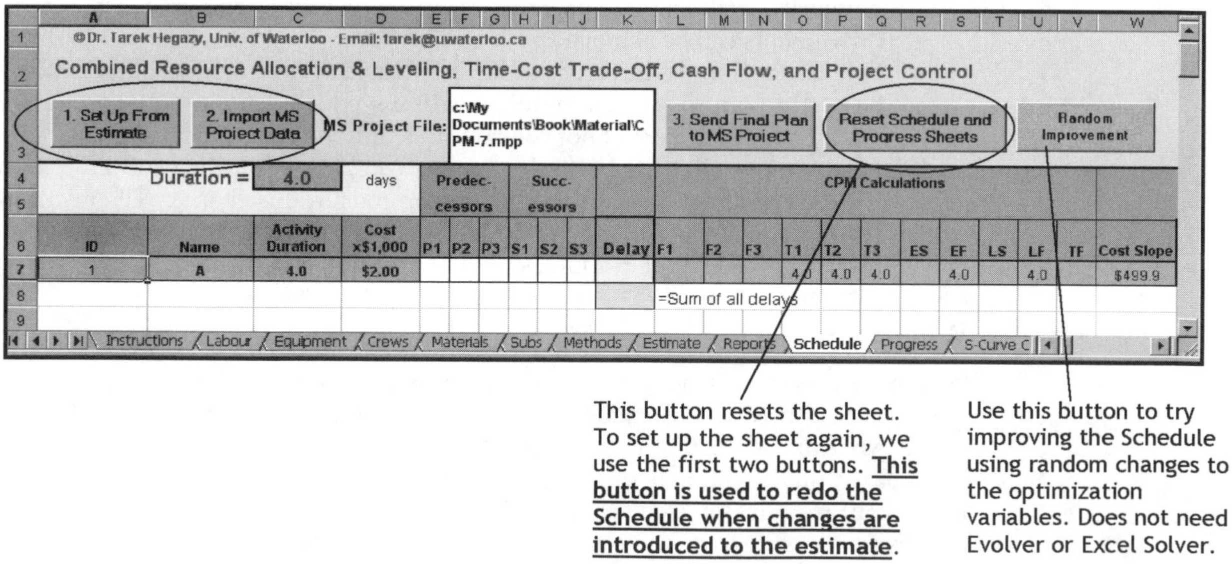
©Dr. Tarek Hegazy, Univ. of Waterloo - Email: tarek@uwaterloo.ca
Combined Resource Allocation & Leveling, Time-Cost Trade-Off, Cash Flow, and Project Control
1. Set Up From Estimate
2. Import MS Project Data
MS Project File:
c:\My Documents\Book\Material\CPM-7.mpp
3. Send Final Plan to MS Project
Reset Schedule and Progress Sheets
Random Improvement
Duration = 4.0 days
Predecessors
Successors
CPM Calculations
ID
Name
Activity Duration
Cost x$1,000
P1 P2 P3 S1 S2 S3 Delay F1 F2 F3 T1 T2 T3 ES EF LS LF TF Cost Slope
1 A 4.0 $2.00 4.0 4.0 4.0 4.0 4.0 $499.9
=Sum of all delays
Instructions Labour Equipment Crews Materials Subs Methods Estimate Reports Schedule Progress S-Curve
This button resets the sheet. To set up the sheet again, we use the first two buttons. This button is used to redo the Schedule when changes are introduced to the estimate.
Use this button to try improving the Schedule using random changes to the optimization variables. Does not need Evolver or Excel Solver.

Figure 7-43. Schedule Sheet Automated Setup Buttons

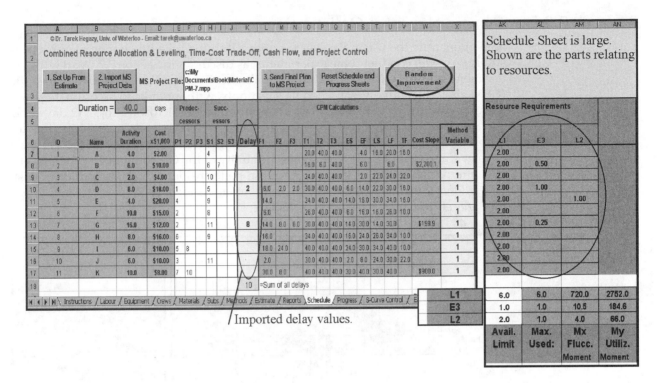

Figure 7–44. Schedule Sheet after Importing Microsoft Project File

7.8.4 Random Improvements

Let's now try to improve the schedule using the automated button on top of the Schedule sheet. Select the proper optimization objective (as shown) and then let the program introduce random values in the delay column. Although this process may not arrive at the optimum result, it substitutes manual process and, if used with large number of random trials, can produce excellent results. After some experimentation, various good solutions were obtained.

7.8.5 Genetic Algorithm Optimization

To demonstrate the use of Evolver for optimizing the schedule under resource constraints, we can conduct some experiments, as discusses in Section 7.7. We do this experiment on the **Case-Study.xls** file in Figure 7–44 or the simplified Excel file (**CPM.xls**) which involves a schedule sheet only, without links to an estimate sheet. Starting with the leveling delay values imported from Microsoft Project (2 days in D and 8 days in G), the Evolver program produced a 40-day schedule. Although the duration is not reduced, the final solution is different from the initial one (delays are 2 days in A and 8 days in G). This shows the ability of the GA software to generate various alternative solutions that may result in better resource profiles and lower cost. *This solution certainly assumes that a 40-day duration is acceptable. In Chapter 8, we will deal with project crashing to a meet a given deadline.*

© Dr. Tarek Hegazy, Univ. of Waterloo - Email: tarek@uwaterloo.ca

Combined Resource Allocation & Leveling, Time-Cost Trade-Off, Cash Flow, and Project Control

| 1. Set Up From Estimate | 2. Import MS Project Data | MS Project File: | c:\My Documents\Book\Material\CPM-7.mpp | 3. Send Final Plan to MS Project | Reset Schedule and Progress Sheets | Plan Improv |

Duration = 40.0 days

CPM Calculations — Resource Requirements

ID	Name	Activity Duration	Cost x$1,000	P1	P2	P3	S1	S2	S3	Delay	F1	F2	F3	T1	T2	T3	ES	EF	LS	LF	TF	L1	E3	L2
1	A	4.0	$2.00				4			2	2.0	2.0	2.0	22.0	40.0	40.0	2.0	6.0	18.0	22.0	16.0	2.00		
2	B	6.0	$10.00				6	7						18.0	6.0	40.0		6.0		6.0		2.00	0.50	
3	C	2.0	$4.00				10							24.0	40.0	40.0	2.0	22.0	24.0	22.0		2.00		
4	D	8.0	$18.00	1			5				6.0			30.0	40.0	40.0	6.0	14.0	22.0	30.0	16.0	2.00	1.00	
5	E	4.0	$20.00	4			9				14.0			34.0	40.0	40.0	14.0	18.0	30.0	34.0	16.0	2.00		1.00
6	F	10.0	$15.00	2			8				6.0			26.0	40.0	40.0	6.0	16.0	16.0	26.0	10.0	2.00		
7	G	16.0	$12.00	2			11			8	14.0	8.0	8.0	30.0	40.0	40.0	14.0	30.0	14.0	30.0		2.00	0.25	
8	H	8.0	$16.00	6			9				18.0			34.0	40.0	40.0	18.0	24.0	28.0	34.0	10.0	2.00		
9	I	6.0	$10.00	5	8						18.0	24.0		40.0	40.0	40.0	24.0	30.0	34.0	40.0	10.0	2.00		
10	J	6.0	$10.00	3			11				2.0			30.0	40.0	40.0	2.0	8.0	24.0	30.0	22.0	2.00		
11	K	10.0	$8.00	7	10						30.0	8.0		40.0	40.0	40.0	30.0	40.0	30.0	40.0		2.00		
										10	=Sum of all delays													

◄◄ ◄ ► ►◄ \ Instructions / Labour / Equipment / Crews / Materials / Subs / Methods / Estimate / Reports \ Schedule / Progress / S...

	Avail. Limit	Max. Used:	Mx Flucc. Moment	My Utiliz. Moment
L1	6.0	6.0	720.0	2768.0
E3	1.0	1.0	10.5	184.6
L2	2.0	1.0	4.0	66.0

Figure 7-45. Alternative Solution Provided by Evolver: Duration = 40 Days (best solution so far)

7.9 Advanced Topics

In dealing with resources and trying to optimize their use, project managers may encounter special circumstances that require the use of more advanced strategies. Some of these situations include:

- Scheduling resources in a multiproject environment. In this regard, Microsoft Project provides some guidelines and tools for sharing resources across projects. You may refer to the Help system or a dedicated book on the software for more information.
- Using resource calendars to specify unusual work hours for the resources. This may also be used to consider a variable resource availability limit, which is assumed constant per day in all the calculations made in this chapter. Most scheduling software; including Microsoft Project, provides this capability.
- Applying resource allocation and/or leveling for only a group of activities or between two specified dates (a feature in most scheduling software).
- Resolving resource constraints by allowing tasks to split (a feature in some scheduling software).

7.10   Summary

In this chapter, you have been introduced to the basics of resource allocation and leveling. You also have learned four ways to improve the resource management of projects: 1) an improvement to resource allocation heuristics using random activity priorities; 2) a procedure for utilizing multiskilled resources; 3) a modification to resource leveling heuristics using double moments; and 3) a multiobjective optimization of both resource allocation and leveling using the Genetic Algorithms technique. The final objective is to keep refining our schedule, solving its problems, and making it as realistic as possible so that it can be followed on site. Without this much structured planning and scheduling, execution may neither proceed on time nor on budget.

7.11   Bibliography

Allam, S.I.G. (1998). Multi-project scheduling: a new categorization for heuristic scheduling rules in construction scheduling problems. *Journal Construction Management and Economics*, E&F.N. Spon Ltd., 6(2), pp. 93–115.

Chan, W., Chau, D., and Kannan, G. (1996). Construction resource scheduling with genetic algorithms. *Journal of Construction Engineering and Management*, ASCE, 122(2): pp. 125–132.

Davis, E. W., and Patterson, J. H. (1975). A comparison of heuristic and optimum solutions in resource-constrained project scheduling. *Management Science*, 21(8), pp. 944–955.

Easa, S. (1989). Resource leveling in construction by optimization. *Journal Construction Engineering and Management*, ASCE, 115(2), pp. 302–316.

Gavish, B., and Pirkul, H. (1991). Algorithms for multi-resource generalized assignment problem. Management Science, 37(6), pp. 695–713.

Harris, R. (1978). *Resource and Arrow Networking Techniques for Construction.* New York: John Wiley & Sons.

Hegazy, T., and El-Zamzamy, H. (1998). Project management software that meet the challenge, Construction Engineering Journal, AACE International, 4(5), pp. 25–33.

Moselhi, A., and Lorterapong, P. (1993). Least impact algorithm for resource allocation. Canadian Journal Civil Engineering., CSCE, 20(2), pp. 180–188.

Shah, K., Farid, F., and Baugh, J. (1993). Optimal resource leveling using integer-linear programming. Proc. 5th International Conference in Computing in Civil & Building Engineering, ASCE, 1, pp. 501–508.

Talbot, F. and Patterson, J. (Dec. 1979). Optimal methods for scheduling projects under resource constrains. Project Management Quarterly, pp. 26–33.

Wiest, D. (1964). "Some properties of schedules for large projects with limited resource." Operations Research, 12, pp. 395–416.

7.12   Exercises

1. State briefly what is meant by resource constraints.
2. The program of a small contract is given in the table below. Each activity requires the continuous use of a mechanical excavator throughout its duration. What will be the minimum contract duration if no more than two excavators can be made available for the work and if it is assumed that having started an activity, it must be completed without a break? Compare manual versus Microsoft Project solutions.

Activity	Duration (weeks)	Depends upon
A	1	—
B	2	A
C	2	A
D	3	A
E	4	B
F	5	C
G	4	D
H	1	C,E
I	3	G
J	1	F,H,I

3. Two schedule alternatives have associated resource profiles as shown below. Which alternative would you choose and why? Also calculate the total *worker-weeks* needed for both cases.

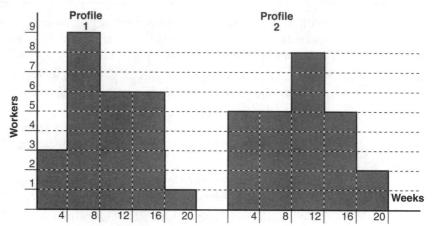

4. The data for a small project are as follows:

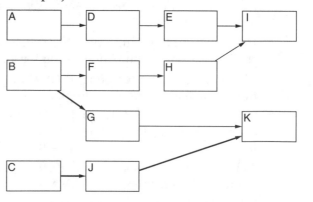

	Duration	Resources Requirements		
Activity	(days)	Men	Equip. 1	Equip. 2
A	4	3	0	1
B	6	6	1	0
C	2	4	0	1
D	8	0	1	0
E	4	4	1	0
F	10	0	1	0
G	16	4	0	0
H	8	2	0	1
I	6	4	1	0
J	6	5	0	1
K	10	2	0	1

Maximum Resources: Men = 8; Equip.1 = 1; and Equip.2 = 1

a. Do the following manually:
  ▪ Use the early-late start rule to schedule the project, respecting resource constraints.
  ▪ Use the early-late start rule to schedule the project, respecting resource constraints and utilizing the following multiskill rule (1R2 = 1R3).
  ▪ Show the tables of calculations and draw the resource aggregation charts in both cases after resource allocation.
b. Do the following using Microsoft Project software:
  ▪ Solve the problem using Microsoft Project and show total project duration.
  ▪ Attempt to reduce project duration by assigning random priorities to the tasks.
  ▪ Print the resulting schedule and resource profile.

5. The following project is considered for multiresource scheduling.

Activity i - j	Description	Duration (Weeks)	Resources Required A	B	C
1 - 2	A	3	4	4	2
1 - 3	B	4	3	4	1
1 - 5	C	5	1	3	2
2 - 4	D	2	1	0	0
2 - 6	E	3	2	1	0
3 - 4	F	4	2	2	1
4 - 7	G	3	3	1	2
5 - 6	H	6	4	4	4
5 - 7	I	4	3	2	1
6 - 7	J	3	1	4	5

a. Develop a resource schedule using a limit of seven Resource A, seven Resource B, and six Resource C.
b. Solve the problem using Microsoft Project and show total project duration. Attempt to reduce project duration by assigning random priorities to the tasks.
c. If the project deadline duration is 14 weeks, estimate the minimum resource level required for each resource.
d. Briefly describe the benefits of using the double moments approach in managing the resources of a project.

6. Consider the following project.

Activity	Predecessor	Duration	Resources Plumbers	Labors
A	-	4	2	3
B	-	3	1	-
C	-	6	1	3
D	B	8	3	4
E	B	7	-	1
F	C	2	3	5
G	A, D	9	1	2
H	E	5	2	4
I	E	4	-	2
J	F, I	4	2	3

a. Eleven plumbers and nine labors are available for the project. Both resources must work at the same time when assigned to the same activity. Prepare an activity schedule that satisfies the resource constraints.
b. Solve the problem using Microsoft Project and show total project duration. Attempt to reduce project duration by assigning random priorities to the tasks.

7. A network for a small project is shown below with activity duration and required number of laborers. During the first 10 days of the project, the contractor has a maximum of four laborers. Afterwards, a subcontractor will be employed to relieve the work force.

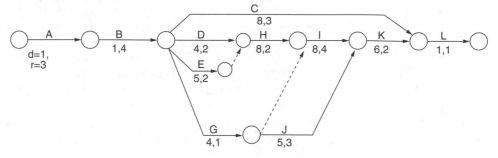

a. Use the early late-start rule (ELS) to resolve any resource conflicts in the first 10 days and calculate the consequent project extension.
b. Briefly describe a suitable strategy for smoothing the labor resource used, assuming the contractor has no resource constraints.

8. A network for a small project is shown below.

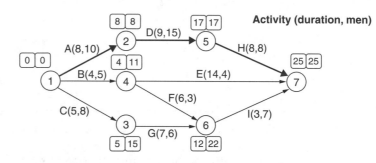

a. Develop a resource schedule using a limit of 20 men.
b. Solve the problem using Microsoft Project and show total project duration. Attempt to reduce project duration by assigning random priorities to the tasks.
c. Modify the **Sch-Level.xls** file to consider the data of this exercise. Use Evolver to solve the problem and print your Excel model. Draw a modified network that corresponds to your optimum solution.

9. A network for a small project is shown below.

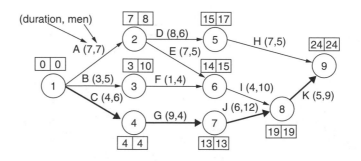

a. Develop a resource schedule using a limit of 15 men/day.
b. Solve the problem using Microsoft Project and show total project duration. Attempt to reduce project duration by assigning random priorities to the tasks.
c. Modify the **Sch-Level.xls** file to consider the data of this exercise. Use Evolver to solve the problem and print your Excel model. Draw a modified network that corresponds to your optimum solution.

Chapter 8

RESOURCE MANAGEMENT
Part 2—Time-Cost Tradeoff

After studying this chapter, you will be able to:

- Understand the basic relationship between project cost and project duration.
- Perform simple time-cost tradeoff (TCT) calculations to crash project duration.
- Model the time-cost tradeoff as an optimization problem.
- Use nontraditional optimization technique for TCT optimization.
- Experiment with an all-in-one spreadsheet model for schedule optimization under time, cost, and resource constraints.

Owner, CM	A/E, CM, Owner	Bidders	Owner, CM	Contractor	O & M Staff
• Need • Feasibility • Project Definition • Owner Approval	• Conceptual Design • Owner Approval • Soil Reports • Preliminary Design • Detailed Design • Quantities • Work Documents • Select Project Contract Strategy	• Prepare Bid Proposal + Baselines • Collect Data (site, quantities, specs, resources, tasks, etc) • Planning • Time & Cost Estimation • Scheduling • **Resource Management: Adjustments for Resource Constraints & Deadline** • Bidding Strategy & Markup Estimation • Cash Flow Analysis • Submit Bid	• Evaluate Bids and Select General Contractor	• Start Construction • Detailed Planning, Estimating & **Resource Management** • Schedule Updating • Progress Evaluation • Time, Cost, & Quality Control • Commissioning	• O & M • Demolition at End of Service Life
CONCEPT	**DESIGN**	**BIDDING**		**CONSTRUCTION**	**O & M**

8.1 Resource Management Continued

This chapter continues the discussion made in the previous chapter related to project resource management and deals with what is referred to as the *Time-Cost Tradeoff (TCT)* analysis. TCT analysis is, in fact, an important management tool for overcoming a serious CPM limitation of being unable to confine the schedule to a specified duration. The objective of the analysis is to reduce the original CPM duration of a project to meet a specific deadline, in the least costly manner. In addition to meeting the deadline, reducing project duration is also desirable to avoid adverse weather conditions, receive an early-completion bonus, free key resources early, and avoid liquidated damages. Later in this chapter, also, we will combine all resource management aspects into an integrated model so that the schedule can be optimized under time, cost, and resource constraints.

8.2 Project Time-Cost Relationship

In general, there is a tradeoff between the time and the direct cost to complete an activity: the less expensive the resources, the larger duration they take to complete an activity. For example, using more productive equipment or hiring more workers may save time, but the cost could increase. This time-cost relationship for a single activity is illustrated in Figure 8–1(a), where the activity can be constructed by option A, B, or C. As shown in the figure, the least-direct cost required for completing an activity is called normal cost, and the corresponding duration is called the normal duration. The shortest possible duration required for completing the activity is called the crash duration, and the corresponding cost is called the crash cost. Similar to the example covered in Chapter 4 (Figure 4–7), each option (A, B, and C) represents a different construction method in which some of the resources are changed (e.g., overtime hours, faster installed material, multiple shifts, more resources) or a different technology is used. Ultimately, resource assignment decisions made at the activity level control the overall duration and cost of a project.

Figure 8-1. Activity Time/Direct-Cost Relationships

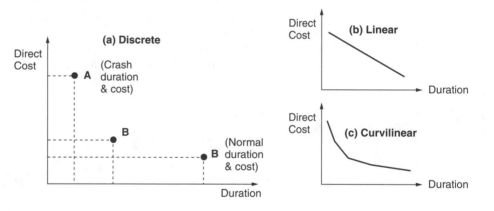

Usually, we start the estimating and scheduling processes by assuming the least costly option for all activities (option C). Because this strategy may lead to a project duration that is longer than desired, planners can perform the so-called time-cost tradeoff (TCT) analysis. The analysis involves selecting some of the critical activities (on the longest path in the network) to shorten their duration even at extra cost (i.e., using a more costly construction method). To offset the increase in cost, the noncritical activities can then be relaxed by selecting less costly methods of construction. With projects involving a large number of activities with various construction options, large numbers of combinations can be formed, each resulting in a certain project duration and direct cost. It is possible, therefore, to plot these various scenarios as shown in Figure 8–2 to try finding the optimum TCT decision for the project. By plotting the direct cost and indirect cost curves individually, the total-cost curve can be formed by adding these two components. The minimum total-cost point on this curve thus presents the set of activities' optimum construction methods associated with optimal balance of project duration and cost.

Finding optimal TCT decisions is difficult and time-consuming, considering the number of permutations involved. For example, a project of only 10 activities, each

Figure 8-2. Project Time-Cost Relationship

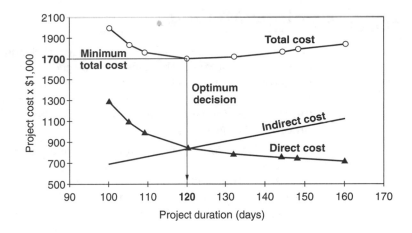

having three possible construction options, a total of 3^{10} (59,049) combinations can be formed and the number of combinations increases exponentially with the number of activities. Evaluating each combination requires recalculating of the schedule using the CPM and assessing of total project cost. Exhaustive enumeration is, therefore, not economically feasible even with fast computers. This is, although the TCT analysis is traditionally performed in isolation from other computations, related to resource allocation and leveling.

8.3 Existing TCT Techniques

A brief overview of existing techniques for solving the TCT problem, along with their advantages and drawbacks, is compiled in Figure 8–3. Since the early 1960s, heuristic methods and mathematical programming models have been used as two distinct categories of solutions. In the literature, various models of both categories have been developed and their performance compared. The main criticisms to mathematical programming models have been their complex formulations, computational-intensive nature, applicability to small-size problems, and local minimum solutions. Heuristic approaches, on the other hand, have been criticized for not being able to guarantee optimum solutions, despite their easy-to-understand formulation and acceptable solutions for most CPM networks.

Figure 8-3. Existing TCT Approaches

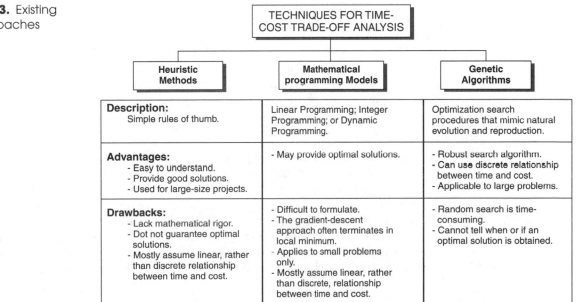

	TECHNIQUES FOR TIME-COST TRADE-OFF ANALYSIS	
Heuristic Methods	**Mathematical programming Models**	**Genetic Algorithms**
Description: Simple rules of thumb.	Linear Programming; Integer Programming; or Dynamic Programming.	Optimization search procedures that mimic natural evolution and reproduction.
Advantages: - Easy to understand. - Provide good solutions. - Used for large-size projects.	- May provide optimal solutions.	- Robust search algorithm. - Can use discrete relationship between time and cost. - Applicable to large problems.
Drawbacks: - Lack mathematical rigor. - Dot not guarantee optimal solutions. - Mostly assume linear, rather than discrete relationship between time and cost.	- Difficult to formulate. - The gradient-descent approach often terminates in local minimum. - Applies to small problems only. - Mostly assume linear, rather than discrete, relationship between time and cost.	- Random search is time-consuming. - Cannot tell when or if an optimal solution is obtained.

8.4 The Cost-Slope Method

One of the simple heuristic approaches for TCT analysis is known as the cost-slope approach. The analysis shortens the project duration based on the assumption that all the activities' direct-cost/time relationships are linear, as shown in Figure 8–1(b). According to this assumption, the cost slope of an activity is defined as the rate at which the direct cost increases when its duration is shortened by a unit of time. The detailed procedure is as follows:

1. Use normal durations and costs for all activities.
2. Calculate the CPM and identify the critical path.
3. Eliminate all noncritical activities.
4. Tabulate normal/crash durations and costs for all critical activities.
5. Compute and tabulate the *cost slope* of each critical activity:

$$\text{Cost Slope} = \frac{\text{Crash Cost} - \text{Normal Cost}}{\text{Normal Duration} - \text{Crash Duration}} \qquad (8.1)$$

6. Identify the critical activity with the least-cost slope and possible duration shortening.
7. Reduce the duration of this activity until its crash duration is reached or until the critical path changes.
8. If the network has more than one critical path, we need to shorten all of them simultaneously. This can be done by shortening a single activity that lies on all paths or by shortening one activity from each path. The option to choose is determined by comparing the cost slope of the single activity versus the sum of cost slopes for the individual activities on all critical paths.
9. Calculate the direct cost increase caused by activity shortening by multiplying the cost slope by the time units shortened. Add the additional cost to the total direct cost.
10. If float times are introduced into any activity, relax them to reduce cost.
11. Plot one point (project duration versus total direct cost) on a figure such in Figure 8–2.
12. Continue from Step 2 until no further shortening is possible to the project.
13. Plot indirect project costs on the same figure. Add the direct cost and indirect cost and plot the total cost curve.
14. Get the optimum TCT strategy as the one with minimum total cost.

8.5 Back to Our Case Study Project

This chapter continues the efforts toward improving the schedule, considering deadline duration. Later in this chapter, we will integrate all resource aspects together, including resource fluctuation, resource limits, and time-cost analysis.

8.5.1 Manual Cost-Slope Method

Let's take our small case study project as an example of cost-slope calculations. In Chapter 7, we dealt with the situation of given availability limits for the three main resources used in the case study, L1, E3, and L2. Under these resource limits, the project duration was determined to be 40 days. It is possible now to take the case study one step further and assume a certain deadline. However, even for this simple example, the involved calculations can be complicated. Therefore, in this section we will deal only with TCT analysis separately to demonstrate the basic computations involved. Later, in Section 8.5.4, we will combine both approaches to try meeting a

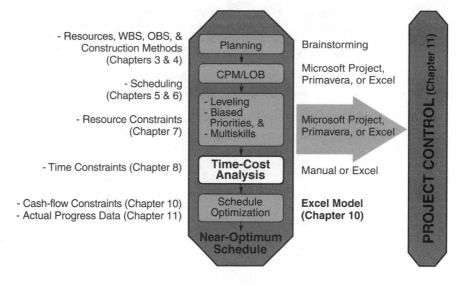

deadline and, at the same time, respect resource availability limits and resource fluctuation needs.

Now, we need to use the cost-slope method to determine the optimum project duration and cost under the following assumptions:

- Resources are not constrained.
- Relationship between time and cost of each activity is linear. The relationship is defined by two points: the normal point (construction method with longest duration and cheapest cost) and the crash point (construction method with shortest duration).
- Activities' data are shown in Table 8–1.
- The daily indirect cost is assumed to be $500, as per our estimate that we discussed in Chapter 4.

Table 8-1. Case Study Data

Activity	Normal Duration	Normal Cost	Crash Duration	Crash Cost
A	4	2,000	No Crashing	
B	6	10,000	3	16,600
C	2	4,000	No Crashing	
D	8	18,000	No Crashing	
E	4	20,000	No Crashing	
F	10	15,000	No Crashing	
G	16	12,000	12	12,800
H	8	16,000	4	17,000
I	6	10,000	No Crashing	
J	6	10,000	No Crashing	
K	10	8,000	9	9,000

Solution

Our solution will follow the cost-slope procedure described earlier. First, we calculate the cost slope of the various activities, as shown in Table 8–2.

Table 8-2. Cost-slope Calculation

Activity	Cost Slope ($/day) Equation 8.1	Normal Duration	Normal Cost	Crash Duration	Crash Cost
A	——	4	2,000	No Crashing	
B	(16,600-10,000)/(6-3) = **2,200**	6	10,000	3	16,600
C	——	2	4,000	No Crashing	
D	——	8	18,000	No Crashing	
E	——	4	20,000	No Crashing	
F	——	10	15,000	No Crashing	
G	(12,800-12,000)/(16-12) = **200**	16	12,000	12	12,800
H	(17,000-16,000)/(8-4) = **250**	8	16,000	4	17,000
I	——	6	10,000	No Crashing	
J	——	6	10,000	No Crashing	
K	(9,000-8,000)/(10-9) = **1,000**	10	8,000	9	9,000
			Total Cost = 125,000		

Afterwards, we perform cycles of modifications to the schedule and cost. Each cycle provides us with a crashing strategy with certain total cost and project duration. All these strategies will then be plotted as shown later in Figure 8–9. Detailed analysis is as follows:

- *Cycle 1:* Using the initial CPM data (Figure 8–4), we determine:

Total Project Duration	= **32 days**
Indirect Cost	= 32 × 500 = 16,000
Total Direct Cost	= 125,000
Total Cost	= 125,000 + 16,000 = 141,000

Figure 8-4. Case Study Network

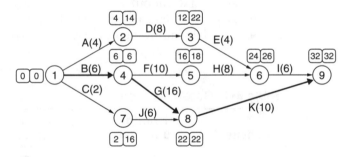

- *Cycle 2:* Using the initial CPM data (Figure 8–4), we determine:

Number of Critical Paths	= One path of 32 days. Next path is 30 days.
Critical Activities	= B-G-K
Activity with Lowest Cost Slope	= G (200)
Maximum Shortening Possible	= 2 days (smaller of the 4-day allowable shortening for G; or the 2-day difference between the critical path and the next path).
Action	= G becomes 14 days.
CPM Recalculation	= Figure 8–5
Total Project Duration	= 30 days
Indirect Cost	= 30 × 500 = 15,000
Total Direct Cost	= 125,000 + 2 × 200 = 125,400
Total Cost	= 125,400 + 15,000 = 140,400

Figure 8–5.
G Reduced 2 days.
Project Duration =
30 days.

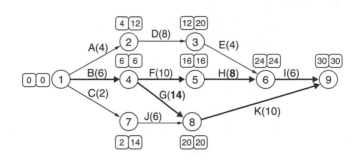

■ *Cycle 3:* Using the revised CPM data (Figure 8–5), we determine:

Number of Critical Paths	= Two paths of 30 days. Next path is 22 days.
Critical Activities	= Path 1: B-G-K; and Path 2: B-F-H-I
Activity with Lowest Cost Slope	= G on Path 1 and H on Path 2, simultaneously. (smaller of: the 2,200 slope of B, which lies on both paths; and the 450 sum of (200 slope of G and 250 slope of H).
Maximum Shortening Possible	= 2 days (2-day allowable shortening for G and H; afterwards, G reaches its 12-day crash duration. No change in critical paths is expected.)
Action	= G becomes 12 days; H becomes 6 days.
CPM Recalculation	= Figure 8–6
Total Project Duration	= 28 days
Indirect Cost	= 28 × 500 = 14,000
Total Direct Cost	= 125,400 + 2 × 450 = 126,300
Total Cost	= 126,300 + 14,000 = 140,300

Figure 8–6.
G and H Reduced 2
days. Project
Duration = 28 days.

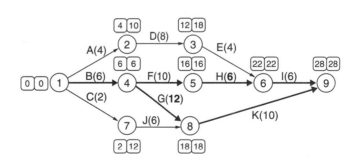

■ *Cycle 4:* Using the revised CPM data (Figure 8–6), we determine:

Number of Critical Paths	= Two paths of 28 days. Next path is 22 days.
Critical Activities	= Path 1: B-G-K; Path 2: B-F-H-I
Activity with Lowest Cost Slope	= K on Path 1 and H on Path 2, simultaneously. (smaller of the 2,200 slope of B, which lies on both paths; and the 1,250 sum of 1000 slope of K and 250 slope of H.)

Maximum Shortening Possible	= 1 day (1-day allowable shortening for K and H; afterwards, K reaches its 9-day crash duration. No change in critical paths is expected.)
Action	= K becomes 9 days; H becomes 5 days.
CPM Recalculation	= Figure 8–7
Total Project Duration	= 27 days
Indirect Cost	= 27 × 500 = 13,500
Total Direct Cost	= 126,300 + 1 × 1250 = 127,550
Total Cost	= 127,550 + 13,500 = 141,050

Figure 8-7.
K and H Reduced 1 day. Project Duration = 27 days.

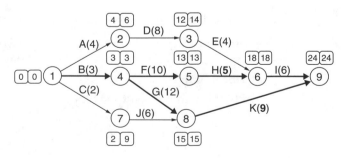

- *Cycle 5:* Using the revised CPM data (Figure 8–7), we determine:

Number of Critical Paths	= Two paths of 27 days. Next path is 22 days.
Critical Activities	= Path 1: B-G-K; Path 2: B-F-H-I
Activity with Lowest Cost Slope	= B on both paths. (B is the only activity that can crash both paths simultaneously. Slope = 2,200.)
Maximum Shortening Possible	= 3 days (All the allowable shortening time for B. No change in critical paths is expected.)
Action	= B becomes 3 days.
CPM Recalculation	= Figure 8–8
Total Project Duration	= 24 days
Indirect Cost	= 24 × 500 = 12,000
Total Direct Cost	= 127,550 + 3 × 2,200 = 134,150
Total Cost	= 134,150 + 12,000 = 146,150

Figure 8-8.
B Reduced 3 days. Project Duration = 24 days.

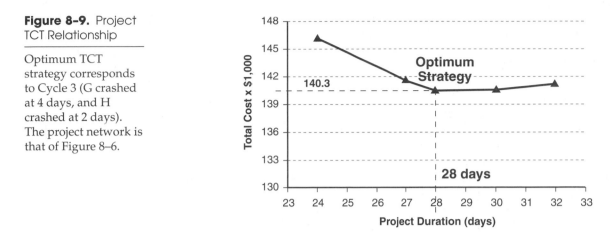

Figure 8-9. Project TCT Relationship

Optimum TCT strategy corresponds to Cycle 3 (G crashed at 4 days, and H crashed at 2 days). The project network is that of Figure 8–6.

8.5.2 Cost-Slope Method on Excel

As mentioned earlier, the comprehensive Excel model of the case study is included in the **Case-Study.xls** file. Let's now load this file, proceed to the Schedule sheet and then apply the cost-slope analysis to it, as shown in Figures 8–10 to 8–12. Now, let's assume that it is desired to shorten the project to meet a 28-day deadline (ignoring resource limits and thus setting all the delay column to zeroes).

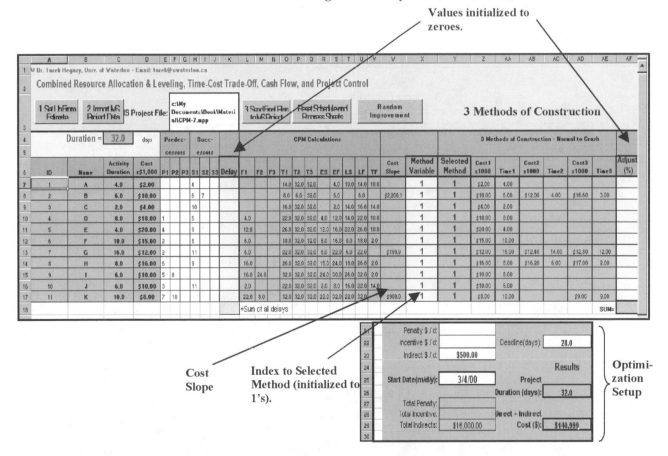

Figure 8-10. The CPM-TCT Model of the Case Study with Some Activities Having up to Three Construction Methods

Note: The Schedule sheet is set up automatically from the Estimate sheet using the buttons at the top. We may later reset this sheet and reuse the first two buttons to set up the sheet again.

As shown in Figure 8–11 in the Schedule sheet, columns Z to AE are used to allow user input of three methods of construction for each activity. Column X specifies the user selection of the method used in the activity (index 1, 2, or 3). Accordingly, formulas are included in columns C and D to determine the duration and cost of each activity. As shown here, method 1 (cheapest) has been selected for all activities. Any change in the method variable of any activity automatically changes the activity duration and cost and accordingly all related CPM calculations. The model as such allows the project manager to examine various scenarios of project execution and their impact on total cost and time.

One column (W) has also been added with equations to calculate the cost slope of critical activities (assuming linear relationship between normal and most crashed strategy). Any change in the method of any activity changes the project duration, cost, and the CPM critical activities. At the bottom of the CPM analysis section, all the information related to TCT optimization is included. This part allows user input of daily penalty, daily incentive, daily indirect cost, and the deadline duration. As shown in this figure, the project duration of 32 days is four days beyond the 28-day deadline and the total cost is $141,000. Our task now is to try to meet the deadline in the least costly manner.

With this TCT model, all the ingredients for the analysis become clear and simple. The objective is to set the values in the Method Variable column so that the project duration cell is less than the deadline duration cell, while the total cost cell is minimized.

Variable (any value >= 0).

Automatically set between 1 to 3.

Duration = 32.0 days

3 Methods of Construction - Normal to Crash

	A	B	C	D	V	W	X	Y	Z	AA	AB	AC	AD	AE
6	ID	Name	Activity Duration	Cost x$1,000	TF	Cost Slope	Method Variable	Selected Method	Cost1 x1000	Time1	Cost2 x1000	Time2	Cost3 x1000	Time3
7	1	A	4.0	$2.00	10.0		1	1	$2.00	4.00				
8	2	B	6.0	$10.00		$2,200.1	1	1	$10.00	6.00	$12.00	4.00	$16.60	3.00
9	3	C	2.0	$4.00	14.0		1	1	$4.00	2.00				
10	4	D	8.0	$18.00	10.0		1	1	$18.00	8.00				
11	5	E	4.0	$20.00	10.0		1	1	$20.00	4.00				
12	6	F	10.0	$15.00	2.0		1	1	$15.00	10.00				
13	7	G	16.0	$12.00		$199.9	1	1	$12.00	16.00	$12.40	14.00	$12.80	12.00
14	8	H	8.0	$16.00	2.0		1	1	$16.00	8.00	$16.20	6.00	$17.00	2.00
15	9	I	6.0	$10.00	2.0		1	1	$10.00	6.00				
16	10	J	6.0	$10.00	14.0		1	1	$10.00	6.00				
17	11	K	10.0	$8.00		$900.0	1	1	$8.00	10.00			$9.00	9.00
18														SUM=

21	Penalty $ / d:			
22	Incentive $ / d:		Deadline(days):	28.0
23	Indirect $ / d:	$500.00		
24			Results	
25	Start Date(m/d/y):	3/4/00	Project	
26			Duration (days):	32.0
27	Total Penalty:			
28	Total Incentive:		Direct + Indirect	
29	Total Indirects:	$16,000.00	Cost ($):	$140,999
30				

Figure 8-11. Setup for TCT Analysis

It is possible to apply the TCT analysis by simply changing the Method Variable of critical activities to select different construction methods with faster duration and least cost increase. Our guide in this process is the Cost Slope column. Figure 8–11 shows the starting point in the schedule with activity G being the critical activity with least cost slope. It is possible, therefore, to change the method of construction of G to 3 (faster, but more costly). Accordingly, the schedule improves to become 30 days and $140,800. The critical activities also change. Following that, we continue looking at the new critical activities, selecting the one with smallest cost slope, and crashing that activity. Accordingly, after G was crashed, activity H was crashed by setting its method to 3. Accordingly, the duration became 28 days, thus meeting the deadline. The total cost of the project in this case remained $140,800.

The manual solution obtained on Excel is shown in Figure 8–12. Although the process is simple, some observations are as follows:

1. The cost-slope approach produces different results when the activity time-cost relationships are either linear or discrete. The discrete case, however, is more close to reality.
2. It is difficult to optimize TCT decisions manually. As demonstrated by the spreadsheet analysis, we could meet the project deadline, however, we do not know if a better solution exists for the simple project at hand. Also, in larger projects the manual process can be time consuming.
3. It is possible to try spreadsheet-based optimization tools such as linear programming (Solver) and genetic algorithms optimization (Evolver) to optimize TCT decisions. Because Solver will not operate on this type of problem, the use of GA tools is described in the following subsection.

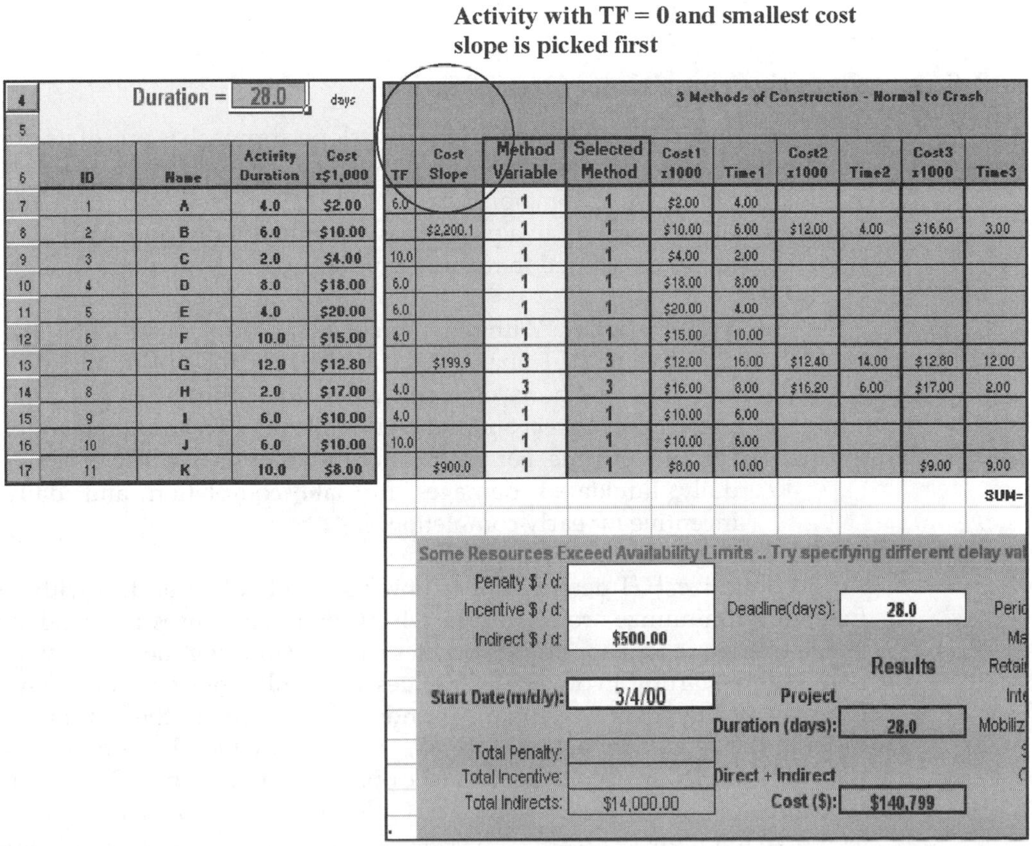

	ID	Name	Activity Duration	Cost x$1,000	TF	Cost Slope	Method Variable	Selected Method	Cost1 x1000	Time1	Cost2 x1000	Time2	Cost3 x1000	Time3
7	1	A	4.0	$2.00	6.0		1	1	$2.00	4.00				
8	2	B	6.0	$10.00		$2,200.1	1	1	$10.00	6.00	$12.00	4.00	$16.60	3.00
9	3	C	2.0	$4.00	10.0		1	1	$4.00	2.00				
10	4	D	8.0	$18.00	6.0		1	1	$18.00	8.00				
11	5	E	4.0	$20.00	6.0		1	1	$20.00	4.00				
12	6	F	10.0	$15.00	4.0		1	1	$15.00	10.00				
13	7	G	12.0	$12.80		$199.9	3	3	$12.00	16.00	$12.40	14.00	$12.80	12.00
14	8	H	2.0	$17.00	4.0		3	3	$16.00	8.00	$16.20	6.00	$17.00	2.00
15	9	I	6.0	$10.00	4.0		1	1	$10.00	6.00				
16	10	J	6.0	$10.00	10.0		1	1	$10.00	6.00				
17	11	K	10.0	$8.00		$900.0	1	1	$8.00	10.00			$9.00	9.00
														SUM=

Figure 8–12. Application of the Cost-slope Method

Meets the deadline with a cost of $140,799

8.5.2.1 Random Improvements   Let's now try to improve the schedule using the automated button on top of the Schedule sheet. Selecting the proper optimization objective (as shown) and then letting the program introduce random changes in the methods of construction column, the experiment produced a better solution that meets the 28-day deadline with a total cost of $140,000.

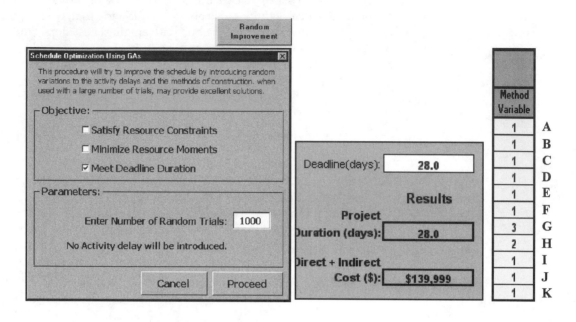

8.5.3   Genetic Algorithms Optimization

The linear relationship assumed in the cost-slope approach is one of its drawbacks. In addition, it is not guaranteed to determine the global minimum cost for the project. To illustrate how a more general and practical TCT analysis is formulated, we need to consider that each activity in a project has a number of discrete methods of construction (three methods defined in the Schedule sheet).

> **TCT Objective:** With the discrete methods of construction, the objective of TCT analysis is to search for the optimum set of activities' methods of construction that minimizes the total project cost (direct and indirect) while not exceeding the target completion time. For practicality, the analysis needs to consider daily liquidated damages for late completion and daily incentive for early completion.

To optimize TCT decisions, let's now use the Evolver add-in with the objective function to minimize project cost in cell AC26. Evolver uses the genetic algorithms (GAs) technique that applies a random search for locating the globally optimal solution. Before starting Evolver, all activities with only one construction method were given a fixed index of 1 in column Y and were not used in the optimization. The indices to the remaining activities (B, G, H, and K), which have more than one construction method, was considered as the optimization variables. These variables were then initialized with integer values of 3 (index to the shortest method of construction), as shown in Figure 8–13. This can be a most expensive solution but is a good start for Evolver. Also, all delay values for the activities (column K) are set to zeros.

Figure 8–13.
Initialization of
Optimization
Variables

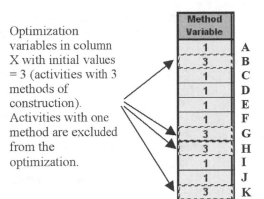

Optimization
variables in column
X with initial values
= 3 (activities with 3
methods of
construction).
Activities with one
method are excluded
from the
optimization.

Figure 8–13 shows a good starting point for Evolver with variables set to 3 (shortest method of construction). This gives a short project duration (meeting the deadline constraint), but it is more expensive than desirable. Evolver then can optimize this solution by finding a cheaper one.

Evolver is set up as shown in Figure 8–14. One constraint is needed that limits project duration to the specified deadline. The Evolver optimization process ran smoothly and an optimum solution was found (Figure 8–14), which is better than the manual solution obtained by the cost-slope approach.

It is noted that for this particular example, the cost-slope heuristic approach was able to obtain a close-to-optimum solution. The good solution of this approach, however, is in most cases accidental. Remarkably, the GA model is able to provide several equally good solutions compared to the single solution by the heuristic approach. In

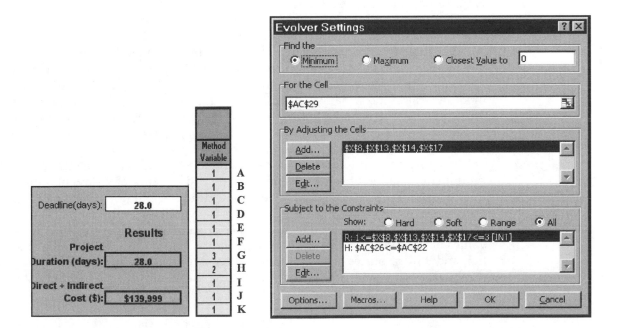

Figure 8–14. Evolver Optimization Results

(Construction methods that meet the 28-day deadline with minimum cost of $140,000.) This solution is identical to the one generated by random improvements.

addition, the cost-slope approach becomes obsolete when the TCT analysis is combined with other aspects related to resource allocation and leveling, as discussed later in this chapter.

8.5.3.1 Comments on the TCT Model Based on its application on our project, the TCT model has been demonstrated to have several interesting characteristics, including:

- The model considers discrete time-cost relationships within activities.
- The GA optimization proved to be efficient at finding solutions by searching only a small fraction of the total search space.
- The model considers project deadline, daily incentive, daily liquidated damages, and daily indirect cost into its formulation and uses total project cost as the objective function.
- The model accounts for the formation of multiple critical paths during the process.

8.5.4 Integration of TCT, Resource Allocation, and Resource Leveling

At this stage, we discussed the problem of meeting a project deadline in isolation from other aspects related to resource constraints. Let's now use the Excel model to address all aspects of resource management simultaneously. Later, in Chapter 10, we can also add aspects related to cash-flow management. Ultimately, we will be able to optimize the schedule development in consideration of time, cost, and resource constraints so as to achieve the best economic benefit for a project.

For simplicity, let's assume that the project manager is concerned with one key resource, L1, for which he has a limit of 6 per day, as discussed in Chapter 7, meanwhile trying to meet the 28-day deadline. The model that incorporates both TCT and resource calculations is included in the Schedule sheet of the **Case-Study.xls** file. In this sheet, to the right of the data for the methods of construction, columns AK to AN (in Figure 8–15) show the resource data and their related calculations.

The spreadsheet in Figure 8–15 is set up so that the amount of L1 resource used by every activity (column AK) is a function of the construction method index (column X). Also, three rows of calculations are added at the bottom of the bar chart to calculate the daily amount of resources needed for the project. Calculations for resource moments (discussed in the previous chapter) are also included. All shaded cells in this model are calculations that you can check how their underlying formulas are written. This sheet now becomes very flexible. If we change the index to the method of construction used in any activity, the activity duration, cost, and resource amount will change. Accordingly, project duration and cost will change.

It is possible now to use the model of Figure 8–15 and try to determine the optimum combination of construction methods and the proper delay amounts that minimize total project cost while meeting the deadline and not exceeding the limit on L1 resource. As such, Figure 8–15 shows the variables in the model as the two columns K and X (variables in column AF are dealt with in Chapter 10). The initial values of these columns are shown on the figure, leading to a 24-day project duration and 9 L1 resources per day. Our objective now is to try meeting the maximum availability limit of 6 L1 resources per day and the 28-day deadline with least project cost.

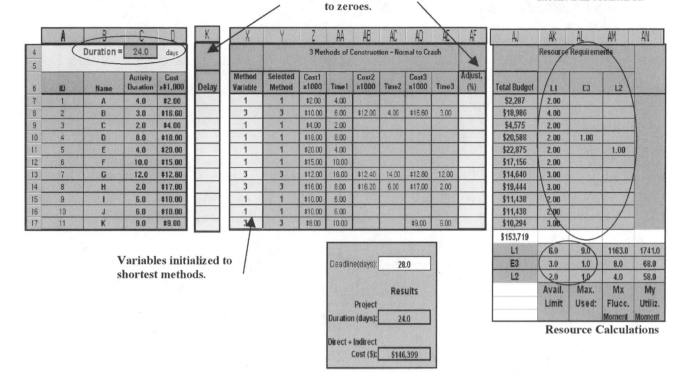

Figure 8–15. Initialization for Combined TCT and Resource Analyses

8.5.5 Solution Approach 1

To solve the problem, we can use the Evolver program and set it up for the combined TCT and resource optimization, as shown in Figure 8–16. Once the optimization parameters are specified, optimization can be started. Because the process is essentially a random process, it might not readily arrive at the optimum solution. In some situations, a rerun of Evolver may become necessary to avoid a stagnant solution, particularly if the problem is much larger in size. We can, in this case, start the optimization giving the variables different initial starting values. After the processing is stopped, we can manually manipulate the values of the variables to try improving it. For example, if we arrive at the solution shown in Figure 8–17, we may check if all the four days of delay in activity D are absolutely needed. We then set that value to 3 and check the impact on project cost, duration, and daily resource amount. You will see that it increased the daily demand of L1 resource to 8 (thus violating its limit of 6 per day). Therefore, we return the value back to 4. Following this manual check, the solution shown in Figure 8–17, which meets all constraints at minimum cost, becomes the optimum for this case study.

One set of construction methods and a 4-day delay in Activity D meet the 28-day deadline, do not exceed the 6 L1 resource limit, and are at a minimize cost of $141,400.

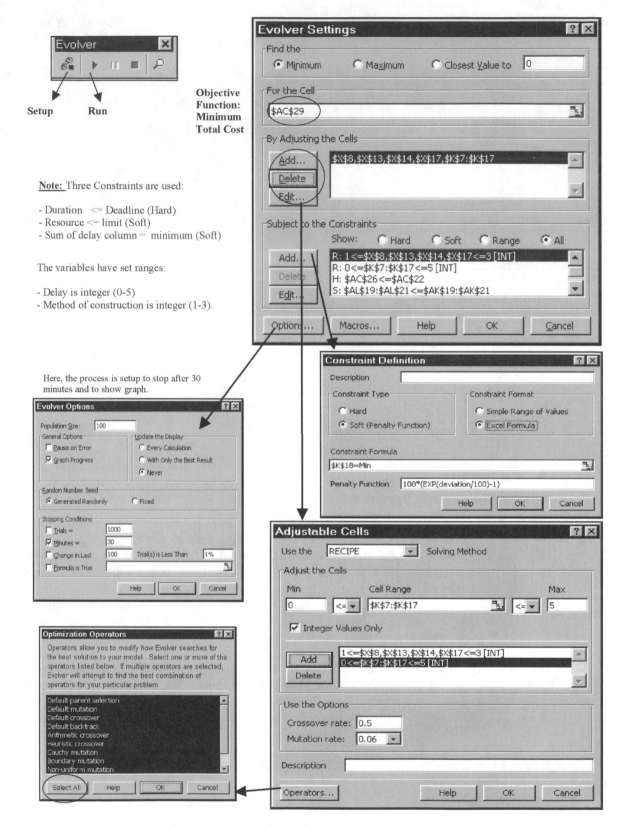

Figure 8-16. Evolver Setup for Combined TCT and Resource Allocation

	ID	Name	Activity Duration	Cost x$1,000	P1	P2	P3	S1	S2	S3	Delay	F1	F2	F3	T1	T2	T3	ES	EF	LS	LF	TF	Cost Slope	Method Variable	Total Budget	L1	E3	L2
7	1	A	4.0	$2.00				4							6.0	28.0	28.0		4.0	2.0	6.0	2.0		1	$2,330	2.00		
8	2	B	4.0	$12.00				6	7						4.0	4.0	28.0		4.0		4.0		$2,200.1	2	$13,985	2.00		
9	3	C	2.0	$4.00				10							12.0	28.0	28.0		2.0	10.0	12.0	10.0		1	$4,661	2.00		
10	4	D	8.0	$18.00	1			5			4	8.0	4.0	4.0	16.0	28.0	28.0	8.0	16.0	10.0	18.0	2.0		1	$20,977	2.00	1.00	
11	5	E	4.0	$20.00	4			9				16.0			22.0	28.0	28.0	16.0	20.0	18.0	22.0	2.0		1	$23,308	2.00		1.00
12	6	F	10.0	$15.00	2			0				4.0			14.0	28.0	28.0	4.0	14.0	4.0	14.0		$1,500.0	1	$17,181	2.00		
13	7	G	14.0	$12.40	2			11				4.0			16.0	28.0	28.0	4.0	18.0	4.0	18.0		$199.9	2	$14,451	2.00		1.00
14	8	H	8.0	$16.00	6			9				14.0			22.0	28.0	28.0	14.0	22.0	14.0	22.0		$166.7	1	$18,646	2.00		
15	9	I	6.0	$10.00	5	8						20.0	22.0		26.0	28.0	28.0	22.0	28.0	22.0	28.0		$1,666.7	1	$11,654	2.00		
16	10	J	6.0	$10.00	3			11				2.0			18.0	28.0	28.0	2.0	8.0	12.0	18.0	10.0		1	$11,654	2.00		
17	11	K	10.0	$8.00	7	10						18.0	0.0		20.0	20.0	20.0	10.0	20.0	10.0	20.0		$900.0	1	$9,323	2.00		

Total Budget: $148,469

	Avail. Limit	Max. Used	Mx Fluc. Moment	My Utiliz. Moment
L1	6.0	6.0	848.0	2044.0
E3	3.0	1.0	8.0	100.0
L2	2.0	2.0	22.0	235.0

Penalty $/d:
Incentive $/d: Deadline(days): 28.0
Indirect $/d: $500.00

Results

Start Date(m/d/y): 3/4/00
Project Duration (days): 28.0

Total Penalty:
Total Incentive:
Total Indirects: $13,999.98   Direct + Indirect Cost ($): $141,399

Figure 8-17. Evolver Solution

> **Note:** With the simple nature of this case study, the benefit of the GA optimization, as compared to processing time and the little schedule/cost improvements, may not be apparent. In realistic small/medium projects, however, it is advantageous to use these tools because they are not sensitive to problem size. You can stop processing at any time to examine near-optimum solutions, set all constraints as soft constraints to determine near-optimum solutions fast, use your experience to minimize the number of variables in the problem, and configure the software to save a history of best solutions. Also, it is worthwhile at the planning stage to set up the model, make sure all data are correct, and then as a last step, leave it overnight for optimization. Next morning, they most likely come up with a solution that meets most of your project constraints and can be the key to a profitable job. After all, what other tools do we have to support our decisions for managing projects?

8.5.6   Solution Approach 2

Instead of setting up Evolver to solve the combined problem, it is possible in some cases to set Evolver to solve the problem incrementally. In this approach, a smaller model is set up to solve the resource constraints problem, as explained in Chapter 7 in which only the delay column is the variable. After reaching a solution for this part, Evolver can be set up again to solve the TCT problem, as explained in this chapter, with the methods of construction as variables. The benefit of this approach is that the number of optimization variables at each step is small and the optimization setup is much easier. This approach, as such, can suit large problems, which may take a long time for the optimization.

8.5.7 Other Experiments

Without using the Evolver software, we can try to improve the schedule using the **Random Improvement** button on top of the Schedule sheet. Selecting the proper optimization objective (as shown) and then letting the program introduce random changes in both the delay column and the methods of construction column. Using one experiment with 1,000 trials, a good solution was obtained, deadline was met with a total cost of $141,799, which is very close to the optimum. Still, however, this solution can be improved if the other experiments are tried.

The results of this example show that the scheduling model and the Evolver program are able to optimize the schedule as desired by the user. Also, the random improvement procedure also produces good results. The Excel model can still be used with some variations in the objective functions and constraints. For example, the user may set the objective function to minimize the fluctuation in the demand profile of a certain resource and so on. Moment calculations can be used as soft constraints so that it can be minimized to reduce resource fluctuation (M_x) or resource utilization time (M_y), or both. A summary of these experiments is discussed in Chapter 10.

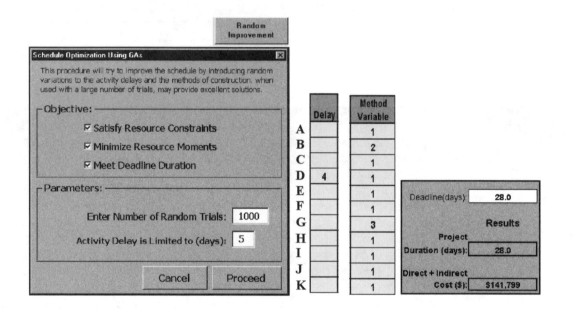

8.6 Another Solved Example

Now let's experiment with a little bigger example of a project with 18 activities as shown in Figure 8–18.

The model of this example is included in a spreadsheet file **TCT.xls** that comes with the CD of this book. The file shows, in three separate sheets, the stages in developing the model: CPM, CPM-BarChart, and the CPM-TCT analysis. To start creating this model, three spreadsheets of the previous example **CPM.xls** were duplicated into an empty spreadsheet. To do that, we click the right mouse button on the spreadsheet tab and use the option **Move or Copy,** as shown in Figure 8–19. The new file is then adjusted for the new case study and renamed **TCT.xls.** Details of the model are in Figures 8–20 and 8–21.

Figure 8-18. Network of Case Study

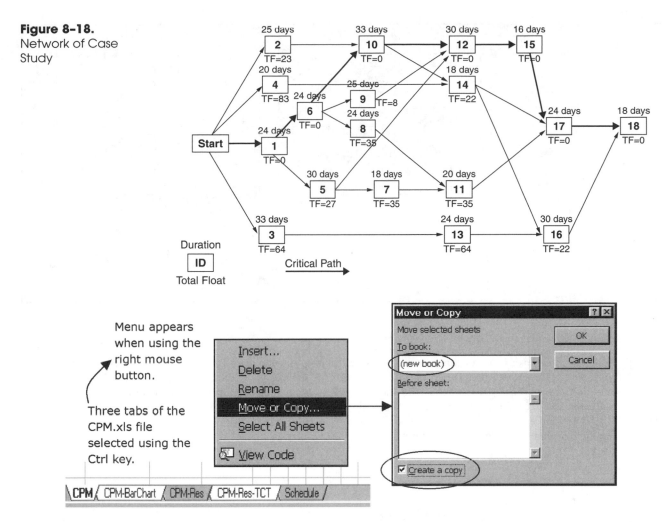

Figure 8-19. Creating a Model for the New Example

Menu appears when using the right mouse button.

Three tabs of the CPM.xls file selected using the Ctrl key.

Figure 8-20. The CPM-BarChart Model of the New Example

The model shows a 169-day duration for the project. Activities' durations in Column D are user-input values and represent the normal durations of activities.

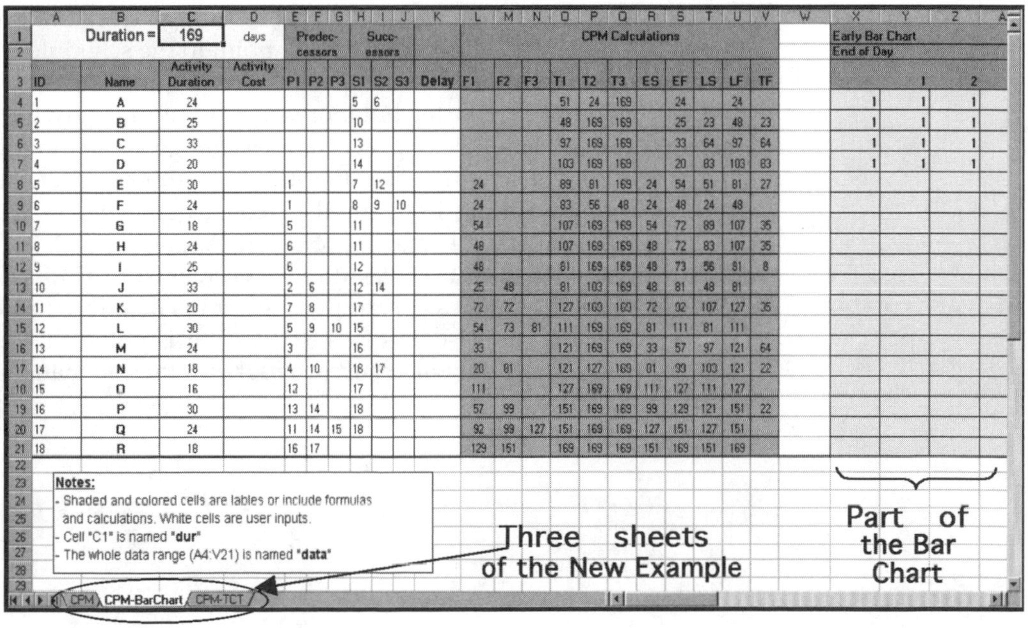

229

ID	Name	Activity Duration	Activity Cost	P1	P2	P3	S1	S2	S3	Delay	F1	F2	F3	T1	T2	T3	ES	EF	LS	LF	TF	Cost Slope	Selected Method	Cost1 x1000	Time1	Cost2 x1000	Time2	Cost3 x1000	Time3	
1	A	24	$1.20				5	6						51	24	169		24		24		$120.0	1	$1.20	24	$1.50	21	$2.40	14	1
2	B	25	$1.00				10							48	169	169	25	23	48	23			1	$1.00	25	$1.50	23	$3.00	15	1
3	C	33	$3.20				13							97	169	169	33	64	97	64			1	$3.20	33	$3.20	33	$4.50	15	1
4	D	20	$30.00				14							103	169	169	20	63	103	83			1	$30.00	20	$30.00	20	$45.00	12	1
5	E	30	$10.00	1			7	12		24			89	61	169	24	54	51	61	27		1	$10.00	30	$10.00	30	$20.00	22	
6	F	24	$18.00	1			8	9	10	24			83	56	45	24	48	24	48		$2,200.0	1	$18.00	24	$18.00	24	$40.00	14	
7	G	18	$22.00	5			11			54			107	169	169	54	72	89	107	35		1	$22.00	18	$22.00	18	$30.00	9	
8	H	24	$0.12	6			11			48			107	169	169	48	72	83	107	35		1	$0.12	24	$0.21	21	$0.22	14	
9	I	25	$0.10	6			12			48			81	169	169	48	70	56	81	8		1	$0.10	25	$0.15	23	$0.30	15	
10	J	33	$0.32	2	6		12	14		25	48		81	103	169	48	81	48	81		$7.2	1	$0.32	33	$0.32	33	$0.45	15	
11	K	20	$0.30	7	8		17			72	72		127	169	169	72	92	107	127	35		1	$0.30	20	$0.30	20	$0.45	12	
12	L	30	$1.00	5	9	10	15			54	73	81	111	169	169	81	111	81	111		$125.0	1	$1.00	30	$1.00	30	$2.00	22	
13	M	24	$1.80	3			16			33			121	169	169	33	57	97	121	64		1	$1.80	24	$1.60	24	$4.00	14	
14	N	18	$2.20	4	10		16	17		20	81		121	127	169	81	99	103	121	22		1	$2.20	18	$2.20	18	$3.00		
15	O	16	$3.50	12			17			111			127	169	169	111	127	111	127		$250.0	1	$3.50	16	$3.50	16	$4.50	12	
16	P	30	$1.00	13	14		18			57	99		151	169	169	99	129	121	151	22		1	$1.00	30	$1.50	20	$3.00	20	
17	Q	24	$1.80	11	14	15	18			92	99	127	151	169	169	127	151	127	151		$220.0	1	$1.80	24	$1.80	24	$4.00	14	
18	R	18	$2.20	16	17					129	151		169	169	169	151	169	151	169		$88.9	1	$2.20	18	$2.20	18	$3.00	9	

Duration = 169.0 days

Notes:
- Shaded and colored cells are tables or include formulas and calculations. White cells are user inputs.
- Cell "C1" is named **"dur"**.
- The whole data range (A4:V21) is named **"data"**.
- We need to determine the proper indices for the "Selected Method" column (1 to 3) so that total cost is minimized.
- SOLVER will not work for this problem.
- GeneHunter will work with Enumerated Genes. Start with arbitrary values for the methods.

Optimization setup

Penalty $ / d:	$20,000.00
Incentive $ / d:	$10,000.00
Indirect $ / d:	$1,000.00
Deadline	110.0 days

Results

Project Duration: 169.0 days

Total Penalty:	$1,180,000.00
Total Incentive:	
Total Indirects:	$169,000.00
Total Project Cost ($):	$1,448,740.00

CPM / CPM-BarChart / CPM-TCT

Figure 8-21. The CPM-TCT Model of the New Example

Columns Z to AE allow user input of three methods of construction for each activity. Column Y also specifies the user selection of which of these three methods is used in the project (index 1, 2, or 3). As shown here, method 1 (cheapest) has been selected for all activities. Any change in the selected method of any activity automatically changes the activity duration and cost and accordingly all related CPM calculations. As shown in Figure 8–21, the project duration of 169 days is 59 days beyond a 110-day deadline, thus a total penalty of $1,180,000 is added to the total cost. Our task now is to try meeting the deadline in the least costly manner.

8.6.1 Cost-Slope Method

As demonstrated before, we can attempt the TCT analysis manually by simply changing the Selected Method of critical activities to select different construction methods with faster duration and least cost increase. Our guide in this process is the Cost Slope column. Figure 8–21 shows the starting point in the schedule with activity J being the critical activity with least cost slope. It is possible, therefore, to change the method of construction of J to 3 (faster, but more costly). Accordingly, the schedule improves to become 161 days and the critical activities change. Following that, we continue looking at the critical activities, selecting the one with smallest cost slope, and crashing that activity by setting its method of construction to 3. Accordingly, after J was crashed, the sequence of crashing was: I, R, A, L, Q, and O. In these steps, the project duration reduced from 161 days after J was crashed to 151, 142, 132, 124, 114, and 110 days for the subsequent steps, respectively, thus meeting the deadline. The total cost of the project in this case becomes $216,270. It is noted that further crashing of the schedule is possible but will result in a higher total cost than obtained by the solution obtained (Figure 8–22).

					3 Methods of Construction - Normal to Crash					
ID	Name	TF	Cost Slope	Selected Method	Cost1 x1000	Time1	Cost2 x1000	Time2	Cost3 x1000	Time3
1	A		$120.0	3	$1.20	24	$1.50	21	$2.40	14
2	B	13		1	$1.00	25	$1.50	23	$3.00	15
3	C	14		1	$3.20	33	$3.20	33	$4.50	15
4	D	33		1	$30.00	20	$30.00	20	$45.00	12
5	E	5		1	$10.00	30	$10.00	30	$20.00	22
6	F		$2,200.0	1	$18.00	24	$18.00	24	$40.00	14
7	G	5		1	$22.00	18	$22.00	18	$30.00	9
8	H	5		1	$0.12	24	$0.21	21	$0.22	14
9	I		$20.0	3	$0.10	25	$0.15	23	$0.30	15
10	J		$7.2	3	$0.32	33	$0.32	33	$0.45	15
11	K	5		1	$0.30	20	$0.30	20	$0.45	12
12	L		$125.0	3	$1.00	30	$1.00	30	$2.00	22
13	M	14		1	$1.80	24	$1.80	24	$4.00	14
14	N		$88.9	1	$2.20	18	$2.20	18	$3.00	9
15	O		$250.0	3	$3.50	16	$3.50	16	$4.50	12
16	P		$200.0	1	$1.00	30	$1.50	28	$3.00	20
17	Q		$220.0	3	$1.80	24	$1.80	24	$4.00	14
18	R		$88.9	3	$2.20	18	$2.20	18	$3.00	9

Figure 8-22. Cost Slope Solution Meeting a 110-day Deadline for $216,270

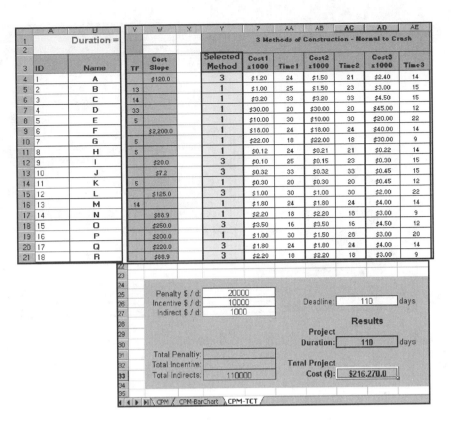

8.6.2 Genetic Algorithms Optimization

Both Solver and Evolver were applied to this example. The Solver screen for this example is shown in Figure 8–23. The optimization objective is to minimize the total project cost (cell AC33). The optimization variables are the values in the Selected Method column (cells V6 to V23). The optimization constraints were also set to limit the values of the variables to integers between 1 and 3. Experimenting with Solver, however, it failed to provide a solution for this problem.

Evolver was also used for this example. Before starting Evolver, the variables (index of construction methods) were initialized with integer = 3 (shortest methods). The objective function and variables (adjustable cells) are shown in the Evolver screen of Figure 8–24. No constraints needed to be specified, rather, an option in Evolver to enumerate the values in the variables was used. Upon completion of the process that ran smoothly for a few minutes, an optimum solution was found, achieving a solution identical to that in Figure 8–22 but using a different set of construction methods.

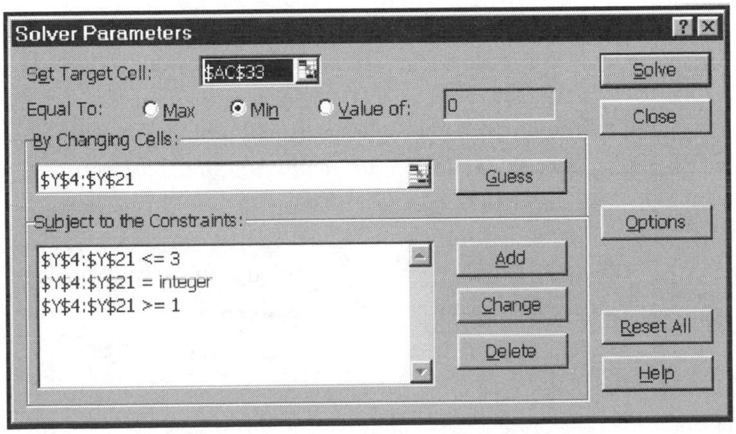

Figure 8-23. Excel Solver Failed to Provide a Solution

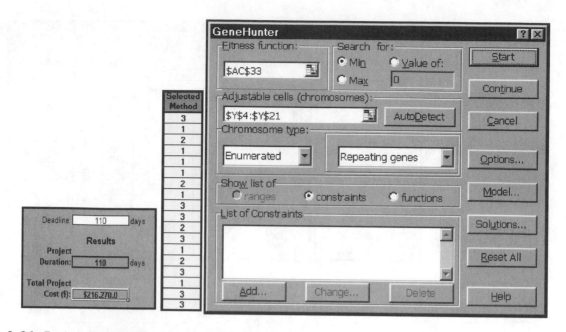

Figure 8-24. Evolver Provided Another Solution with Identical Results

8.7   Summary

In this chapter, a spreadsheet model for time-cost tradeoff analyses was introduced and a case study project was used to demonstrate its operation. For TCT optimization, the optimization attempts to find the optimum combination of construction methods for the different activities, considering deadline duration, late completion penalty, early completion incentive, and daily indirect cost. Based on the obtained results, the genetic algorithms technique was able to find an optimum solution to the problem. The model, as such, is preferably applicable at the aggregate, rather than the very detailed, activity level. The genetic algorithms technique also has been shown to hold a great promise as an optimization search mechanism that does not suffer from the drawbacks of traditional mathematical programming techniques. The TCT model is also expanded to include resource allocation and leveling.

8.8   Bibliography

Feng, C., Liu, L., and Burns, S. (1997). Using genetic algorithms to solve construction time-cost trade-off problems. *Journal of Computing in Civil Engineering*, ASCE, 11(3): pp. 184–189.

Hegazy, T., and Moselhi, O. (1994). Analogy-based solution to markup estimation problem. *Journal of Computing in Civil Engineering*, ASCE, 8(1): pp. 72–87.

Karshenas, S., and Haber, D. (1990). Economic optimization of construction project scheduling. *Construction Management and Economics*, 8(2): pp. 135–146.

Kelly, J. E. Jr. (1961). Critical path planning and scheduling: mathematical basis. *Operations Research*, 9(3): pp. 167–179.

Koumousis, V. K., and Georgiou, P. (1994). Genetic algorithms in discrete optimization of steel truss roofs. *Journal of Computing in Civil Engineering*, ASCE, 8(3): pp. 309–325.

Li, H., and Love, P. (1997). Using improved genetic algorithms to facilitate time-cost optimization. *Journal of Construction Engineering and Management*, ASCE, 123(3): pp. 233–237.

Liu, L., Burns, S., and Feng. C. (1995). Construction time-cost trade-off analysis using LP/IP. *Journal of Construction Engineering and Management*, ASCE, 121(4): pp. 446–454.

Mitchell, M. (1998). *An Introduction to Genetic Algorithms*. MIT Press.

Moselhi, O. (1993). Schedule compression using the direct stiffness method. *Canadian Journal of Civil Engineering*, 20: pp. 65–72.

Siemens, N. (1971). A simple CPM time-cost tradeoff algorithm. *Management Science*, 17(6): pp. B-354–363.

8.9   Exercises

1. Discuss, with the help of a simple diagram, the activity time-cost relationship.

2. If the *cost slope* of an activity is $100/day; the maximum crashing possible for the activity is 5 days; and its crash cost is $2,000, what is its normal cost?

3. The following tasks are part of a network and are the only ones available for crashing. Which one would you start with and why?

	ES	LF	Duration	Cost/day
A	5	20	10	$4
B	18	32	14	$8
C	15	21	6	$12

4. The following table gives the activities involved in a small contract under both normal and crash conditions. The indirect cost for this contract is $250/week. The contract conditions state that the contractor will pay $200/week for delays by his own fault.

Activity	Predecessors	Duration (week) Normal	Crash	Cost ($) Normal	Crash
A	—	7	3	1400	5400
B	—	9	5	4500	7500
C	A	8	5	2400	3900
D	B	14	9	1200	4200
E	C, D	4	2	800	2300
F	B	9	5	2700	5700
G	F	7	3	2100	5300
H	E, G	12	7	4900	6900

Determine the minimum contract cost for a 32-week project duration.

5. In performing the three aspects of resource management, individually, complete the following table to describe the characteristics of each technique:

	Allocation	TCT	Leveling
• Resources are limited.	Y	N	N
• Project can be delayed.			
• Activities can be delayed beyond their float.			
• Critical activities are affected.			
• Moments are calculated.			
• Noncritical activities are affected.			
• Objective is to reduce project delay.			
• Objective is to minimize total project cost (direct + indirect).			
• Objective is to reduce resource fluctuation.			
• Activities can split.			
• Critical activities can be shortened.			

6. The data of a small project is shown below. Assuming a $1,000/day indirect cost, determine: (a) the optimum project duration that minimizes total project cost; and (b) the optimum strategy to meet an 18-day deadline.

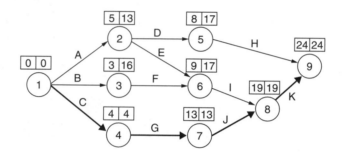

Activity	Normal Duration	Normal Cost	Crash Duration	Crash Cost	Cost Slope
A	7	15000	7	15000	
B	3	6000	3	6000	
C	4	8000	3	8500	
D	8	16000	8	16000	
E	7	15000	7	15000	
F	1	2000	1	2000	
G	9	18000	7	19000	
H	7	15000	7	15000	
I	4	8000	4	8000	
J	6	12000	4	15000	
K	5	10000	4	11000	

7. Cost and schedule data for a small project are given below. Assume an indirect cost of $200/day. Develop the time-cost curve for the project and determine the minimum contract duration.

Activity	Preceded by	Cost ($) Crash	Cost ($) Normal	Duration (days) Crash	Duration (days) Normal
A	—	3900	3600	6	7
B	A	6500	5500	3	5
C	B	7200	6350	7	9
D	B	4900	4700	18	19
E	B	2200	2050	9	10
F	C	1700	1200	6	8
G	F	7200	7200	5	5
H	E	10000	9450	10	11
I	D, G, H	4700	4500	6	7

8. Draw the precedence diagram for the following data:

Activity	Followed by	Duration (days) Normal	Duration (days) Minimum	Cost Slope $/day
A	B, E, F	7	5	200
B	K	9	5	450
C	H, D	8	7	400
D	I, N	11	4	100
E	G, M	9	6	400
F	L	8	7	500
G	C	7	5	200
H	I, N	6	2	200
I	—	12	9	200
J	E, F	10	8	600
K	G	14	10	350
L	M	18	16	700
M	C	9	8	550
N	—	12	9	200

It is required to compress the schedule to 65 days. Determine the resulting increase in the project's direct cost.

9. The duration and direct-cost data for an activity-on-arrow network is given in the following table. Any duration between the normal duration and the crash duration is possible for each activity. Indirect costs are equal to 200 cost units + 50 cost units per day. Draw the CPM network and establish the optimum (least total cost) project duration and the corresponding cost.

Activity	Normal		Crash	
	Dur. (days)	Cost (Units)	Dur. (days)	Cost (Units)
1-2	6	180	3	330
2-3	4	160	2	320
2-6	5	100	5	100
1-3	4	400	4	400
3-6	8	160	3	360
3-5	2	20	1	50
1-4	4	150	4	150
4-5	4	160	3	210
5-6	4	165	2	305

Chapter 9

BIDDING STRATEGY AND MARKUP ESTIMATION

A fter studying this chapter, you will be able to:

- Understand the factors that affect markup decision.
- Utilize the data of past bids to analyze the bidding behavior of key competitors.
- Analyze the probability of winning a bid at a given markup value.
- Estimate an optimum markup value as an allowance for risk and profit.

Owner, CM	A/E, CM, Owner	Bidders	Owner, CM	Contractor	O & M Staff
• Need • Feasibility • Project Definition • Owner Approval	• Conceptual Design • Owner Approval • Soil Reports • Preliminary Design • Detailed Design • Quantities • Work Documents • Select Project Contract Strategy	• Prepare Bid Proposal + Baselines • Collect Data (site, quantities, specs, resources, tasks, etc) • Planning • Time & Cost Estimation • Scheduling • Resource Management: Adjustments for Resource Constraints & Deadline • **Bidding Strategy & Markup Estimation** • Cash Flow Analysis • Submit Bid	• Evaluate Bids and Select General Contractor	• Start Construction • Detailed Planning, Estimating & Resource Management • Schedule Updating • Progress Evaluation • Time, Cost, & Quality Control • Commissioning	• O & M • Demolition at End of Service Life
CONCEPT	DESIGN	BIDDING		CONSTRUCTION	O & M

9.1 Accounting for Project Risks

At this stage in our project, we have calculated the direct and indirect costs, calculated project duration, resolved resource problems, and adjusted the schedule so that it meets the deadline. All these aspects establish a good baseline plan in terms of time and cost for the project. Now, it is time to put the final touches on the bid.

If you are much involved in the construction business, you must have experienced how difficult it is to decide on a suitable bidding strategy against the expected competitors. This bidding strategy is basically a fine-tuning of the bid by accounting for the level of uncertainty associated with the project and as an allowance for profit. In general, contractors often have two main methods of assessing and accounting for project risks: (1) estimating a single percentage markup to be added to the total cost; (2) detailed analysis of the risky components in the project, the probability of risk occurrence, and the expected damages so as to assign an appropriate contingency allowance for each of these components. The latter analysis, however, is lengthy and may not suit competitive bids; as such, it is beyond the scope of this book. Specific techniques that can account for the uncertainty associated with activities' durations and cost will be sufficiently described in Chapter 12. Our bidding strategy, therefore, will focus on estimating an optimum markup for a project.

Markup needs to be optimally decided for a project. We need to decide on the percentage that makes the bid low enough to win and, at the same time, high enough to make a reasonable profit. Despite the importance of these decisions to a costly commitment, you might have to decide on them while a lot of information is still lacking and under pressures to speed up the bid preparation. Often, many construction practitioners are left to their own intuition and "gut feeling," with little or no help from available tools. In this chapter, therefore, we will be introduced to the basics that will allow us to estimate an optimum markup value for the project. In the next chapter, we can then deal with project financing so that the bid becomes ready for submission.

9.2   Analyzing the Bidding Behavior of Key Competitors

For a contractor to sustain success in the construction business, he or she has to be the lowest bidder for a sufficient number of projects while that bid price is not too low, in order to make a reasonable profit. It is important, therefore, to strike a balance between profitability and the chances of winning. To enable us to establish a winning bidding strategy, we need to keep track of our past bids, analyze their information, and depict any bidding pattern our key competitors use. First, let's see what kind of information we have:

- Our cost estimate (C = direct cost + indirect cost) for any past bid is known to us. Because we cannot know the cost estimate of other competitors, let's assume that the cost estimates of all bidders are the same. This assumption is not true but can be realistic if we assume that all bidders have access to the same subcontractors and follow standard construction technology.
- The bid prices of competitors in past bids are known to us as a public information published by most owners after the bid is let. Government agencies such as public works (largest owner organizations) make this information public. Therefore, the relationship between the bid price and the cost estimate in any bid is as follows:

$$\text{Bid Price } (B_i) \text{ of competitor i} = C * (1 + \text{markup}) \tag{9.1}$$

$$\text{Thus, } B_i/C = 1 + \text{markup} \tag{9.2}$$

$$\text{And, markup} = B_i/C - 1. \tag{9.3}$$

The B_i/C ratio in Equations 9.2 and 9.3 is a representation of the markup used by competitor i in one bid. For example, in a past bid that we lost, our cost estimate was $1,000,000. For that project, we submitted a total bid of $1,150,000 while our key competitor, Company A, bid $1,100,000. Assuming cost estimate is constant, we used a markup of 15% (markup = B/C −1) while Company A used a 10% markup. Because we lost that bid, it is important for us to analyze if the 10% markup used by Company

A is a policy that is repeated in other bids. If this is true, then it is possible in the future to beat them by bidding with a markup less than 10%; otherwise we need to analyze how their markup policy changes from one bid to the other.

Let's now expand our analysis of Company A's bidding behavior by retrieving all our records of past bids in which we competed against them. Let's assume we found 31 past bids and we have all the information regarding our cost estimates and the bid prices. From that information, we can create a histogram as shown in Figure 9–1(a). The histogram in Figure 9–1(a) shows the frequency at which Company A bid at different markup levels. From the histogram, we can answer the following questions:

1. If the B/C ratio used by Company A in a past bid was 1.25, it means the company used a markup of _____% of cost.

   Answer: 25% because markup = B/C − 1 = 1.25 − 1 = 0.25 = 25%

2. If we decide to use a 10% markup in a new bid against Company A, how many times in the past did they underbid us at this level of markup?

   Answer: six times. From the histogram, the number of occurrences to the left of B/C = 1.1 are 3 + 2 + 1 = 6.

3. What are our chances of winning Company A using 25% markup?

   Answer: 6/31. From the histogram, the number of occurrences to the right of B/C = 1.25 are 3 + 2 + 1 = 6. Then the probability = 6 out of the total 31 past bids.

Figure 9–1.
Analyzing the
Bidding Behavior of
a Competitor

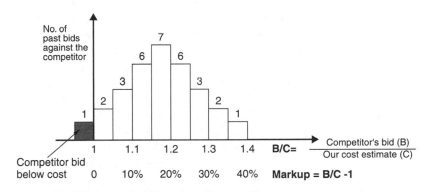

(a) Analyzing Past Bids against One Key Competitor

Calculate the mean (m) and standard deviation (s) of **B/C ratio** of this competitor, assuming a normal distribution and, repeat the analysis for a key competitors.

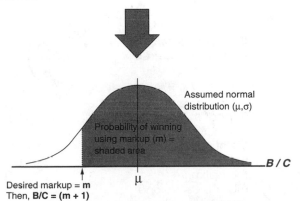

(b) Calculating the Probability of Winning This Competitor Using a Given Markup Value

4. If we bid right at cost (no profit), then our B/C becomes what?

   Answer: 1 because B = C, then B/C = 1.0 and markup = B/C − 1 = 0.

5. How many times did Company A bid below cost?

   Answer: 1 as read from the left part of the histogram.

6. What is the average markup used by Company A and how much does it vary?

   Answer: We can calculate the μ and σ of the B/C ratio from the histogram:

   $$\text{Mean } (\mu) = 1 \times 1.375 + 2 \times 1.325 + 3 \times 1.275 + 6 \times 1.225 + 7 \times 1.175$$
   $$+ 6 \times 1.125 + 3 \times 1.075 + 2 \times 1.025 + 1 \times 0.975 = 1.175$$

   $$\text{Standard Deviation } (\sigma) = \text{Sqrt } [(n \, (\Sigma X^2 - (\Sigma X)^2)/n(n-1)] = 0.0931$$

   The μ and σ of B/C ratio, therefore, represent the competitor's behavior and can be used to evaluate the probability of beating our competitor using any markup value, as shown in Figure 9–1(b).

9.3   Estimating Optimum Markup

9.3.1   What to Optimize?

In order to optimize our markup decision, we need to define what optimum means by providing a measure of optimality. Notice that we have two conflicting objectives: to reduce markup to improve the probability of winning; and to increase markup to improve profitability. If you recall what we did in Chapter 8, we were trying to optimize time-cost tradeoff (TCT) decisions. We also had two conflicting forces: direct cost and indirect cost. When we crashed the project, direct cost increased while the indirect cost decreased. In that case, we used a simple measure of optimality that is a *summation* of the two components, which is the total project cost. That measure of optimality is acceptable to use because both components have the same units (cost) and thus can be added together. Notice here that for TCT decisions, we needed to minimize the measure of optimality and determine the decision that brings minimum total cost for the project.

The markup case is apparently different. The probability of winning is unit-less, whereas profit is in dollars. In this case, it is logical to use multiplication instead of summation, and thus use what is called the *expected profit* as a measure of optimality. The expected profit can be viewed as a fictitious profit value that is weighed by the chances of attaining that profit. Certainly, in this case, our bidding strategy should focus on maximizing the expected profit and we can define our optimum markup as the one that maximizes it, as formulated in Figure 9–2.

Figure 9-2. Bidding Strategy Formulation

Expected profit of a given markup = 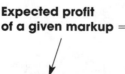 $\times$

Repeat the calculations using various markup values and find the optimum markup as the one associated with maximum expected profit.

Markup (%) × Cost

1. Calculate the probability of winning individual competitors, then

2. Combine these probabilities to determine the probability of winning all of them simultaneously.

Example: Winning a Single Competitor

You have kept good records of the bidding behavior of one competitor, Company A. The mean and standard deviation of the company's B/C ratio are calculated to be 1.1 and 0.1, respectively. Answer the following:

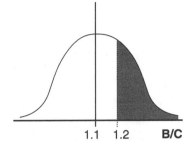

a. What is the probability of winning Company A in a new bid, using a 20% markup? Your cost estimate for the new project is $1,000,000.
b. What is the expected profit at this markup?

Solution:

a. At 20% markup, **B/C** = 1 + markup = 1.2
   We then use the standardized normal distribution table:
   $Z = (X - \mu)/\sigma = (1.2 - 1.1)/0.1 = 1.0$
   and from the table (provides left side area), probability = 0.8413
   Then, the probability of beating Company A at 20% markup = shaded area = $1 - 0.8413 = 0.1587$
b. Expected profit = Probability of winning × Profit
   = Probability of winning × Cost × Markup
   = $0.1587 × \$1,000,000 × 0.2 = \$31,740$

9.3.2 Beating All Competitors Simultaneously

Similar to the above example, it is simple to calculate the probability of winning each competitor separately from all others. To determine our probability of winning them all, however, is still simple but controversial and many formulations are available with various assumptions.

Friedman, in 1956, was the first to suggest a model that predicts the probability of winning a bid knowing the previous performance of other competitors (mean and standard deviation of B/C distributions). Friedman employed a basic assumption in his bidding model that different competitors' probability distributions are mutually independent. Accordingly, he suggested a multiplicative model to combine the probabilities of winning individual competitors, at a given markup, as follows:

a. Probability of winning (n) known competitors is:

$$P(Win_{all}) = P(Win_1) \times P(Win_2) \times \dots \times P(Win_n) \tag{9.4}$$

b. Probability of winning (n) unknown competitors is:

$$P(Win_{all}) = P(Win_{Typical\ Competitor})^n \tag{9.5}$$

Where, $P(Win_i)$ is the probability of winning competitor i. Also, the typical competitor is one who represents the average bidder who is experienced in the type of bid being analyzed.

The most notable model proposed a decade after Friedman's is that of Gates in 1967. Gates has criticized Friedman's basic assumption of independence and offered his own assessment. According to Gates, the probability of winning all competitors at a given markup is as follows:

a. Probability of winning (n) known competitors is:

$$P(Win_{all}) = \frac{1}{[(1 - P(Win_1) / P(Win_1)] + ... + [(1 - P(Win_n)) / P(Win_n)] + 1} \quad \textbf{(9.6)}$$

b. Probability of winning (n) unknown competitors is:

$$P(Win_{all}) = \frac{1}{n[(1 - P(Win_{Typical\ Competitor}) / P(Win_{Typical\ Competitor})] + 1} \quad \textbf{(9.7)}$$

Friedman's and Gates's models give different results, and debate over the years has not been able to resolve this conflict. Instead, these models have generated controversy and confusion about their application in the construction industry. A number of studies concluded that Friedman's model is more correct when the variability of bids is caused only by markup differences, while Gates's model is more correct when the variation in bids is caused only by variations in cost estimates. A comprehensive study of a contractor's application of both models over a period of several years showed that Gates's model produces higher markups than that of Friedman's. In this sense, Friedman's model could represent a pessimistic approach whereas Gates's represents an optimistic one. Despite their differences, however, over the study period, both models have led, approximately, to the same total of potential profits.

9.4   The Optimum-Markup Estimation Process

Let's now look at the detailed process for optimum markup estimation and apply it to an example. The following four steps will be followed:

1. Assume a percentage markup in the range from 1–20%, with 1% increments. Later we can repeat this process with finer increments to refine the calculations.
2. At each markup, we calculate the *expected profit*, as follows:
   - Profit = cost × markup (%).
   - Probability to win each competitor (from his past history);
   - Combined probability $P(win_{all})$, using Friedman's or Gates' models; then
   - Calculate expected profit = profit × $P(win_{all})$.
   - Tabulate the markup and expected profit values
   - Increment markup and repeat the calculations in this step.

3. Plot the tabulated markup versus expected profit values, as shown, where (X = markup; Y = expected profit).

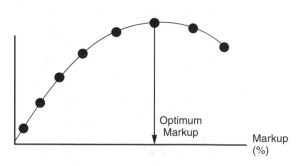

4. Choose the optimum markup from the plot.

Example

A contractor wants to determine the optimal bid to submit for a job with estimated cost $1,000,000, bidding against three key competitors with the following historical data.

Competitor	No. of Occurrences	B/C Mean (μ)	B/C Standard Deviation (σ)
A	5	1.081	0.052
B	6	1.032	0.044
C	8	1.067	0.061

Solution

1. Let us assume a range of markups from 1% to 7% with 1% increments.
2. At **markup = 1%,** we calculate the following:
   a. Probability of beating the first competitor, A:

   $X = B/C = 1 + \text{markup} = 1 + 0.01 = 1.01$

   $Z_A = (X - \mu_A)/\sigma_A = (1.01 - 1.081)/0.052 = -1.365$

   Then, from the table of standardized normal distribution, the probability $P(\text{Win}_A)$ at 1% markup $= 1 - F_z(-1.365)$
   $= 1 - 0.086 = 0.914$

   b. Probability of beating the second competitor, B:

   $X = B/C = 1 + \text{markup} = 1 + 0.01 = 1.01$
   $Z_B = (X - \mu_B)/\sigma_B = (1.01 - 1.032)/0.044 = -0.500$
   Then, from the table of standardized normal distribution, the probability $P(\text{Win}_B)$ at 1 % markup $= 1 - F_z(-0.500)$
   $= 1 - 0.309 = 0.691$

   c. Probability of beating the third competitor, C:

   $X = B/C = 1 + \text{markup} = 1 + 0.01 = 1.01$
   $Z_C = (X - \mu_C)/\sigma_C = (1.01 - 1.067)/0.061 = -0.934$
   Then, from the table of standardized normal distribution, the probability $P(\text{Win}_A)$ at 1% markup $= 1 - F_z(-0.934)$
   $= 1 - 0.175 = 0.825$

   d. Probability of beating A, B, and C, simultaneously and the expected profit:
   Using Friedman's model and 1% markup:

   $P(\text{Win}_{all})\text{-F} = 0.914 \times 0.691 \times 0.825 = 0.521$
   $\text{EP-F (expected profit)} = \$1,000,000 \times 0.01 \times 0.521 = \$5,213.3$

   Using Gates's model and 1% markup:

   $$P(\text{Win}_{all})\text{-G} = \frac{1}{[(1 - 0.914)/0.014 + (1 - 0.691) / 0.691 + (1 - 0.825) / 0.825 + 1]}$$
   $$= 0.571$$

   $\text{EP-G (expected profit)} = \$1,000,000 \times 0.01 \times 0.571 - \$5,705.9$

   e. Incrementing markup and repeating the calculation in a, b, c, and d above, as tabulated in Table 9–1.

Table 9-1. Markup versus Expected Profit: Friedman and Gates Models

Markup (%)	Z_A	P(Win$_A$)	Z_B	P(Win$_B$)	Z_C	P(Win$_C$)	P(win$_{all}$) Friedman	EP Friedman	P(win$_{all}$) Gates	EP Gates
1.0	−1.365	0.914	−0.500	0.691	−0.934	0.825	0.521	**$5,213.3**	0.571	**$5,705.9**
2.0	−1.173	0.880	−0.273	0.607	−0.770	0.779	0.417	**$8,330.3**	0.484	**$9,680.9**
3.0	−0.981	0.837	−0.045	0.518	−0.607	0.728	0.316	**$9,466.5**	0.400	**$12,004.6**
4.0	−0.788	0.785	0.182	0.428	−0.443	0.671	0.225	**$9,012.1**	0.322	**$12,895.8**
5.0	−0.596	0.724	0.409	0.341	−0.279	0.610	0.151	**$7,537.0**	0.253	**$12,655.5**
6.0	−0.404	0.657	0.636	0.262	−0.115	0.546	0.094	**$5,640.2**	0.194	**$11,610.1**
7.0	−0.212	0.584	0.864	0.194	0.049	0.480	0.054	**$3,806.2**	0.144	**$10,068.9**
3.1	−0.962	0.832	−0.023	0.509	−0.590	0.722	0.306	**$9,484.2**		
3.2	−0.942	0.827	0.000	0.500	−0.574	0.717	0.296	**$9,486.3**		
3.3	−0.923	0.822	0.023	0.491	−0.557	0.711	0.287	**$9,473.5**		
4.1	−0.769	0.779	0.205	0.419	−0.426	0.665			0.615	**$12,917.3**
4.2	−0.750	0.773	0.227	0.410	−0.410	0.659			0.308	**$12,927.9**
4.3	−0.731	0.768	0.250	0.401	−0.393	0.653			0.301	**$12,927.7**

Figure 9-3.
Optimum Markup Plot

From this plot, we can evaluate our probability of winning the bid at any markup value.
P(Win)
   = $\dfrac{\text{Expected Profit}}{\text{Markup} \times \text{Cost}}$

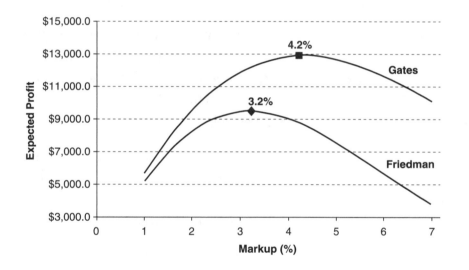

Notice that the top part of Table 9–1 shows that the highest expected profit for Friedman's model occurs around a markup of 3%, whereas it is around 4% for Gates model. Therefore, the second and third parts of Table 9–1 show refined calculations in which the markup is incremented by small values around the expected optimum. Accordingly, it is seen from the calculations that optimum markup is as follows:
Using Friedman's model, optimum markup = 3.2%.
Using Gates' model, optimum markup = 4.2%.

3. Plotting the markup versus expected profit relationship and confirming the optimum markup values, as shown in Figure 9–3:

9.4.1 Important Bidding Relationships

From the previous discussion and the solved example given, let's discuss some of the observed relationships:

- When the σ of the B/C ratio of a competitor is small, it indicates that this competitor uses a consistent markup policy. It is possible in this case to establish a markup to win over him or her.
- Friedman's model, in most cases, determines a lower optimum markup than that of Gates's (as shown in the solved example). In this sense, Gates's model is more optimistic as it assumes that you can still win the bid at a high markup.
- If you have entered only one bid against a competitor in the past, the σ of his or her B/C ratio becomes zero and the use of probability tables is not possible. Therefore, one bid against a competitor is not sufficient to determine your competitor's bidding behavior. In a new bid against this competitor, therefore, it is advisable to replace it with a typical one whose behavior is close to the type of project being analyzed.
- In case of high project risk, the chances of cost and schedule variations are high, thus their potential impact on project cost is high. In this case, therefore, it is wise to use higher markup as an allowance for unforeseen conditions. The use of Gates's model in this case is more advisable than Friedman's model.
- When the level of competition is high (large number of bidders) and the economic conditions are not favorable, winning bids becomes difficult and bidders reduce their bids to become more competitive.
- In construction, an average bidder behavior is exhibited as having a bid/cost ratio mean of 1.06 and a standard deviation of 0.065. For building construction, markup may vary from 2 to 10%, whereas for highway and heavy civil construction, it can reach up to 20%. The average number of competitors bidding for a job is around six. Accordingly, if no information is available regarding typical competitor behavior, numbers around these values can be assumed.
- The correlation between markup and number of competitors and between markup and project size has been studied by many researchers and can be expressed in the following simple relationship:

$$\frac{M2}{M1} = \left(\frac{N1}{N2}\right)^{0.7} \qquad \textbf{(9.8)}$$

where, $N1$ and $N2$ are the number of competitors on jobs 1 and 2; $M1$ and $M2$ are the markup on jobs 1 and 2, respectively. According to this inverse relationship, markup is reduced with increase in the level of competition associated with a larger number of competitors.

- Project size, as indicated by its cost estimate (C), has an important impact on the markup value, as expressed in the following relationship, which indicates that the percentage markup is less when project size increases.

$$\frac{M2}{M1} = \left(\frac{C1}{C2}\right)^{0.2} \qquad \textbf{(9.9)}$$

The use of this relationship becomes handy so that last-minute adjustments can be made to the bid at the negotiation table. If, for example, you received information that the winning bid has the potential for additional work to be awarded later, you may be willing to reduce your markup so that your bid becomes more competitive. In this case, this relationship can give you a rough figure on the revised markup to use.

- With Friedman's and Gates's models being viewed as pessimistic and optimistic, respectively, a moderate bidding strategy is to consider the average of their optimum markups.

9.5 Bidding Strategy Program on Excel

As seen in the earlier solved example, optimum markup calculations can be tedious particularly if a large number of competitors are involved. Let's now try an Excel sheet, **Bidding.xls**, developed to automate the calculations involved. For the purpose of using this spreadsheet, we will consider the following case study.

Example

The previous records of past bids against four key competitors is in the following table. Using Friedman's and Gates's models, determine the markup needed to optimize expected profit in bidding against competitors A, B, and C in a new job with an estimated total cost of $4,000,000.

Job No.	Contractor's Cost Estimate ($)	Bid Price of Competitors ($)		
		A	B	C
1	1,550,000	1,900,000	1,700,000	1,750,000
2	2,000,000	—	2,000,000	2,200,000
3	1,300,000	1,500,000	1,400,000	1,650,000
4	1,200,000	—	1,600,000	1,400,000

Solution:

The solution of this example is provided in the **Bidding.xls** spreadsheet. Detailed explanation on the use of this sheet as it applies to the example is made in Figures 9–4 to 9–6.

Names of Other Competitors Here
(Sheet is Set up for a total of 40)

	A	B	C	D	E	F	G	H
1			Analysis:	Company A	Company B	Company C		
2			Mean	1.19	1.13	1.17		
3			St.Dev.	0.04	0.12	0.06		
4	Row Data:		No. of Bids	2.00	4.00	4.00		
5								
6	Bid No.	Type of Project	Cost Estimate	Company A	Company B	Company C		
7	1	Building	$1,550,000.00	$1,900,000.00	$1,700,000.00	$1,750,000.00		
8	2	Building	$2,000,000.00		$2,000,000.00	$2,200,000.00		
9	3	Building	$1,300,000.00	$1,500,000.00	$1,400,000.00	$1,650,000.00		
10	4	Building	$1,200,000.00		$1,600,000.00	$1,400,000.00		
11								

Historical Bids, Each in One Row (sheet is set up for 1000 bids)

Instructions:
- Enter the names of your competitors in the yellow cells of Row 6.
- Enter Past bids, each in a single row, starting from Row 7.
- Select the "Bidding" sheet.
- Enter the Cost Estimate and Select competitors using the Combo Boxes.
- Watch Optimum Markup being calculated automatically.

 PastBids / Bidding / Internal_Calculations

Figure 9–4. Storing Historical Bids

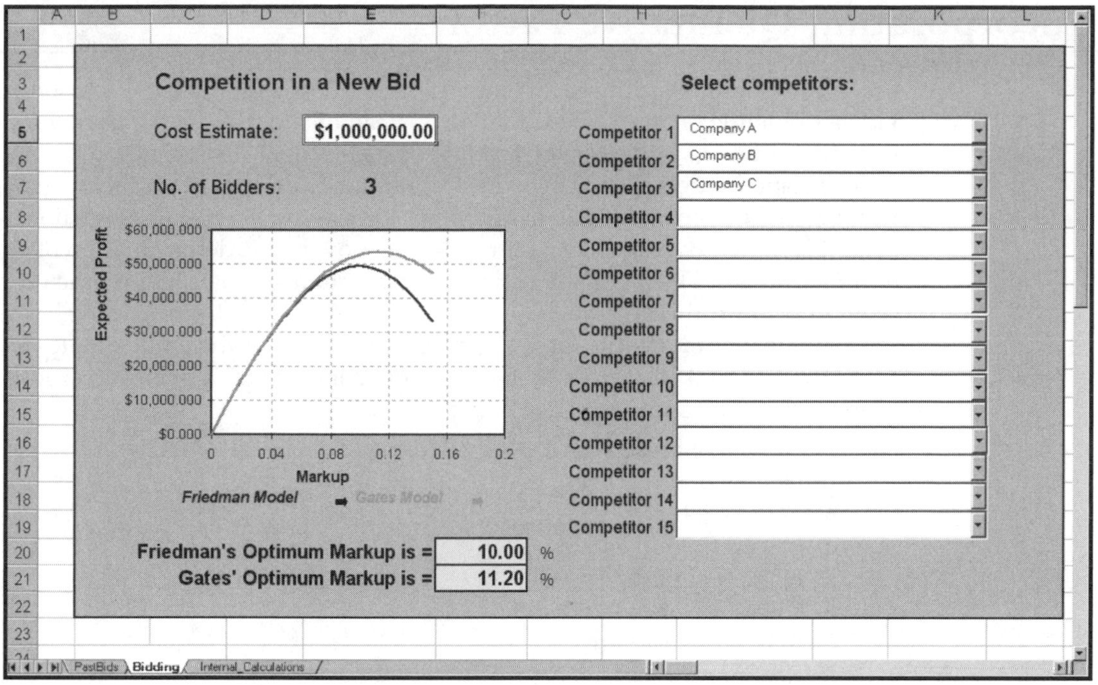

Figure 9-5. Bidding Sheet with Markup Calculations

Here you enter only the cost estimate and select the competitors (up to 15) from user-friendly combo boxes. Accordingly, optimum markup is calculated automatically (10% and 11.2% for Friedman and Gates, respectively).

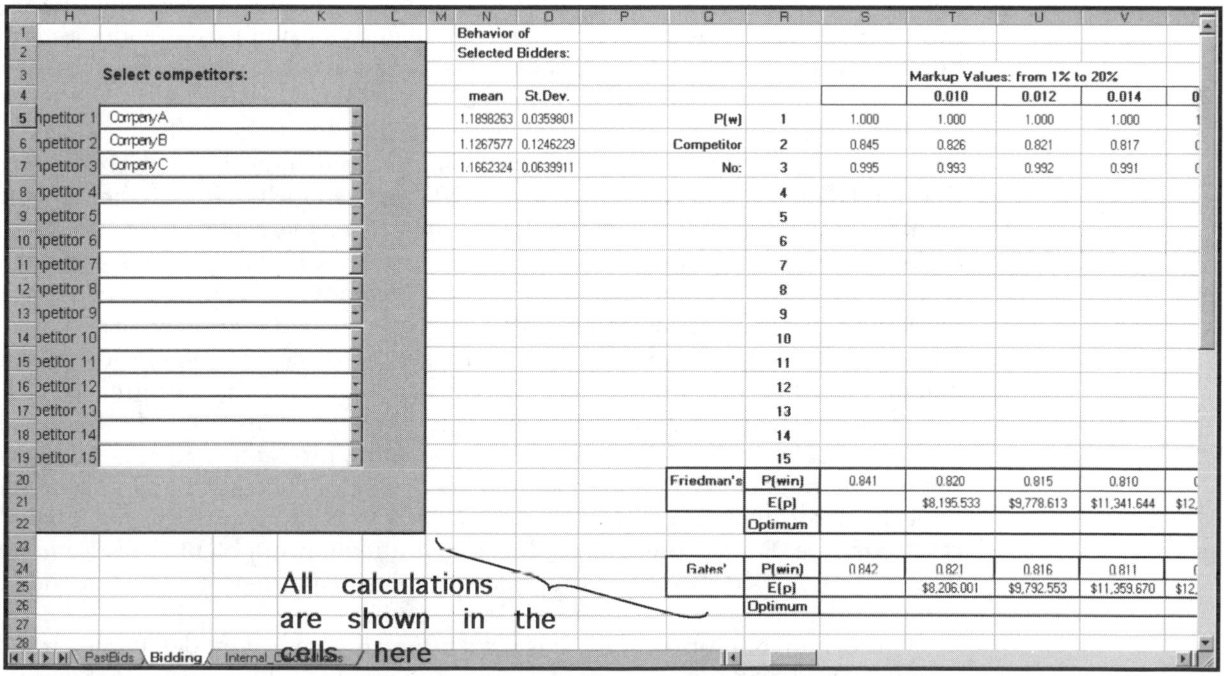

Figure 9-6. Detailed Optimum Markup Calculations

9.6 Incorporating Qualitative Factors

Probability-based bidding models such as Friedman's and Gates's are useful and provide a guideline on markup estimation, instead of shooting in the dark. From a practical point of view, however, the sole use of such probabilistic methods is inadequate. Probabilistic models do not account for a number of important factors, such as the keenness of the contractor to win the job, prevailing economic conditions, level of project complexity, and owner's attitude, that govern the determination of markup in current practice. The results of various surveys among construction practitioners also seem to support this argument.

One survey among the top 400 general contractors in the United States have identified the top-ranked factors that govern the contractors' markup decisions. The 10 top-ranked factors are:

1. Degree of hazard
2. Degree of difficulty
3. Type of job
4. Uncertainty in estimate
5. Historical profit
6. Current work load
7. Risk of investment
8. Rate of return
9. Owner
10. Location

Noted that *competition* and *profitability*, which are the only two factors considered in the formulation of probabilistic models, were not among the top-ranked factors. Other surveys have identified similar factors but with a different ranking order in which the contractor's workload and desirability of the job are at the top. Despite the dependence of Friedman's and Gates's models on quantitative factors only, the argument of their inapplicability is not true. Their underlying analysis provides a starting point for markup estimation and their analyses of past bids could disclose the essence of the factors that are implicit in the markup decided by a contractor.

The subject of incorporating qualitative factors into markup estimation has contributed to the development of nontraditional decision-support systems based on artificial intelligence. One such system, ProBID, has been included with the CD of this book for your experimentation. ProBID is a comprehensive system based on the concepts of artificial neural networks, which is capable of learning the ins and outs of real-life projects to become able to predict the outcomes of new projects. In a sense, it works as a sort of complex regression model that has good interpolative and extrapolative performance. In addition, ProBID organizes the contractor's historical information regarding past projects and past bids and analyzes the performance of key competitors. Therefore, in addition to suggesting a markup value, ProBID intelligently recognizes the risk pattern of your upcoming project and then matches your project environment with a number of stored cases of successful and unsuccessful projects. Accordingly, ProBID predicts some indicators of the project's potential success or failure. ProBID predictions direct your attention to potential problem areas that you may consider to adjust your estimate, think of alternative decisions, and take early countermeasures to help assure a successful bid.

One benefit of ProBID is that it is not a purely theoretical model. Rather, it is developed based on the experience of a large number of real-life projects that were collected from general contractors in the United States and Canada. Although ProBID was initially intended for building projects, it is designed with a powerful "Adaptation" option that builds on your own past projects' experience and enables you to develop custom predictors that suit your particular work environment, locality, and types of projects.

To experiment with ProBID, you need to install it from the CD to your hard disk. Afterwards, you can activate the **PB.bat** file to run the program. After the introductory screens, the main menu appears. Figures 9–7 to 9–13 show the main features of ProBID and its use.

Figure 9-7. ProBID Main Screen and Help Topics

You can follow the help topics to get a good idea about ProBID features.

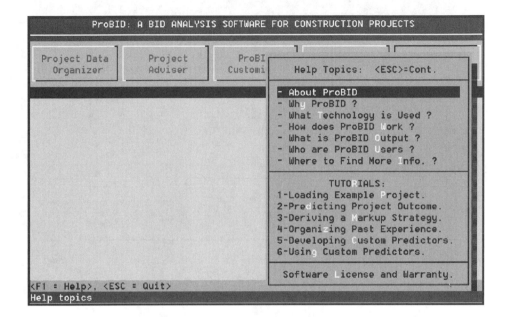

Figure 9-8. Loading an Example Project

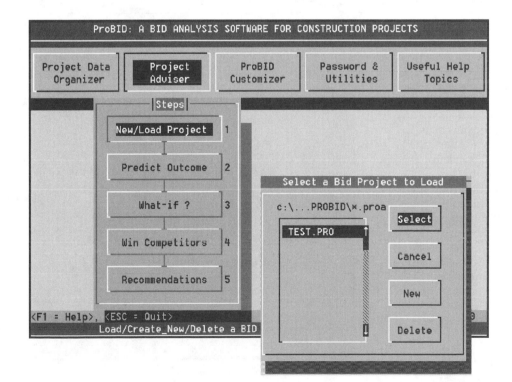

Figure 9-9. Data Inputs for a Project

You need to input various factors that describe the project in terms of: **a.** General information about the job type, owner, etc. **b.** Job uncertainty and complexity levels. **c.** Market condition. **d.** Your company's experience and need for the job.

Figure 9-10. ProBID Predictions

Predictions include:
- (%) Markup.
- Chance to win/lose.
- ($) left on the table.
- Change orders level.
- Claims level.
- Actual duration (months).
- Actual profitability.

```
┌─ PREDICTIONS ──────────────── Screen 5 ─┐
│       Based on the BID CASES stored      │
│          in ProBID, it seems that:       │
│                                          │
│  - If you use a markup of  4.9 % above   │
│    the job's $ 25.00 mil. estimated cost,│
│                                          │
│  - You are likely to  WIN  the bid, with │
│    $ 0.004 mil., Money left on the Table.│
│                                          │
│       Predicted execution outcomes are:  │
│                                          │
│  - Potential Change Orders    : High     │
│  - Potential Claims & Disputes : Low     │
│  - Project Duration (months)  : 10       │
│  - Actual Profitability level : Medium   │
│                                          │
│ ─────────────────────────── Screen 5 ─── │
└──────────────────────────────────────────┘
```

Steps
1 New/Load Project
2 Predict Outcome
3 What-if ?
4 Win Competitors
5 Recommendations

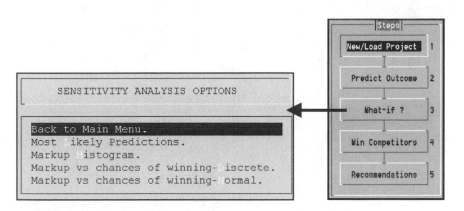

SENSITIVITY ANALYSIS OPTIONS

Back to Main Menu.
Most Likely Predictions.
Markup Histogram.
Markup vs chances of winning-Discrete.
Markup vs chances of winning-Normal.

Figure 9-11. Sensitivity Analysis Option

Sensitivity analysis examines how ProBID predictions may vary with changes in your assessment of the project factors. The simulation generates a number of scenarios (simulations) that are minor random variations of the assessment you provided during the editing of the project data. All simulations are then input to the prediction model you select, and predictions for all scenarios are produced. As a result, the mean and standard deviation in all scenarios will be reported as the most likely predictions for the project outcomes. Refer to the manual for guidelines on the number of simulations to use and how to interpret the results.

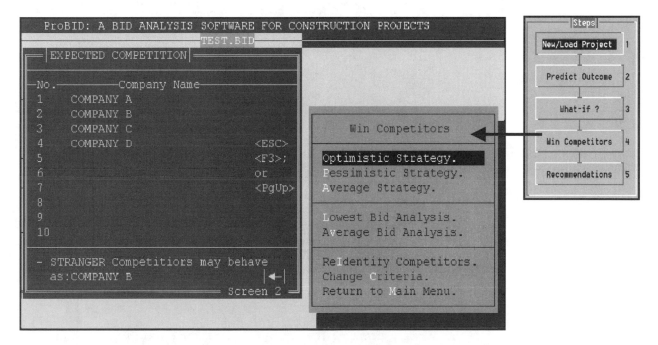

Figure 9-12. Using Friedman's and Gates's Models To Establish a Winning Strategy

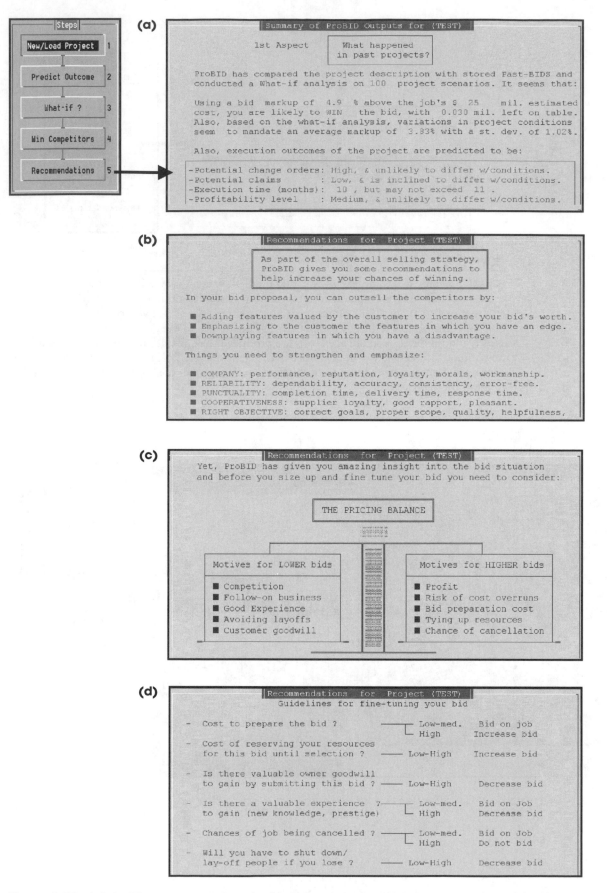

Figure 9-13. A Set of Recommendations for the Example Project **(a)** Summary of all project results; **(b), (c),** and **(d)** Guidelines for fine-tuning the markup and for providing a more attractive bid.

9.7   Back to Our Case Study Project

We can easily apply the concepts presented in this chapter to our case study project. For simplicity we will assume a 5% markup is most suited to the project at hand. In the next chapter, we will use this percentage in finalizing our bid proposal, considering the expected project cash flow.

9.8   Summary

Bidding strategy models are, basically, methodologies designed to maximize contractor's expected profit in a competitive environment, where expected profit is, for a given bid amount, the product of the profit that would be realized from the bid and the probability of winning the job with that bid. These models enable the contractor to organize his past experience on bids and use this experience to establish winning strategies against key competitors. Collectively, all bidding strategy models compromise between a contractor gaining a maximum profit and being the lowest bidder. In both Friedman's and Gates's models, optimum markup is determined in an iterative manner, within a practical range of markup. Incremental variations in markup are plotted against the expected profit and the optimum markup is determined as the markup corresponding to peak expected profit.

Despite the differences in assumptions and basic formulations between these models, they generally provide answers to three questions:

1. What is the probability of winning at a desired markup?
2. What is the optimum markup value?
3. What is the probability of winning at optimum markup?

In this chapter, a spreadsheet model, **Bidding.xls**, is used to automate the calculations involved in probability-based bidding strategies. A more sophisticated program, Pro-BID, is also used to consider the qualitative factors that affect markup decisions and provide guidelines on fine-tuning the markup estimate. After a markup is estimated, our bid for a project becomes close to being ready for submission. In the next chapter, we will consider project financing options and the final preparation of a bid proposal.

9.9   Bibliography

Ahmad, I., and Minkarah, I. (1988, July). "Questionnaire Survey on Bidding in Construction," *Journal of Management in Engineering*, American Society of Civil Engineers, Vol. 4, No. 3, pp. 229–243.

Benjamin, N. B. H., and Meador, R. C. (1979, March). "Comparison of Friedman and Gates Competitive Bidding Models," *Journal of the Construction Division*, American Society of Civil Engineers, Vol. 105, No. CO1, pp. 25–40.

Friedman, L. (1956). "A Competitive Bidding Strategy," *Operations Research*, Vol. 4, pp. 104–112.

Gates, M. (1967, March). "Bidding Strategies and Probabilities," *Journal of the Construction Division*, American Society of Civil Engineers, Vol. 93, No. CO1, pp. 75–107.

Ioannou, P. G. (1988, June). "Bidding Models-Symmetry and State of Information," *Journal of Construction Engineering and Management*, American Society of Civil Engineers, Vol. 114, No. 2, pp. 214–232.

Morin, T. L., and Clough, R. H. (1969, July). "OPBID: Competitive Bidding Strategy Model," *Journal of the Construction Division*, American Society of Civil Engineers, Vol. 95, No. CO1, pp. 85–106.

Moselhi, O., and Hegazy, T. (1990, April). "Optimum Markup Estimation: A Comparative Study," *Proceeding,* 11th International Cost Engineering Congress, 6th AFITEP Annual Meeting, Paris.

Park, W. R. (1968, June). "Bidders and Job Size Determine Your Optimum Markup," *Engineering News Record,* pp. 122–123.

Runeson, G. (1990, March). "Incorporation of Market Conditions into Tendering Models," *Proceeding,* International Symposium on Building Economics and Construction Management, CIB, Sydney, Australia, March, Vol. 6, 1990, pp. 393–404.

Sey, Y., and Dikbas, A. (1990, March). "A Study on Factors Affecting Tender Price of Contractors," *Proceeding,* International Symposium on Building Economics and Construction Management, CIB, Sydney, Australia, March, Vol. 6, 1990, pp. 451–464.

Van Der Meulen, G. J. R., and Money, A. H. (1984, June). "The Bidding Game," *Journal of Construction Engineering and Management,* American Society of Civil Engineers, Vol. 110, No. 2, pp. 153–164.

9.10   Exercises

1. The previous record of a contractor's bidding encounters against three competitors is:

Job No.	Contractor's Cost Estimate ($ millions)	Bid Price of Competitors ($ millions)		
		A	B	C
1	0.85	1.05	1.1	0.95
2	1.6	2.1	1.8	1.6
3	0.7	—	—	0.9
4	2.0	2.4	—	2.2

Using Friedman's and Gates's models, determine the markup needed to optimize expected profit in the following cases, and comment on the results:

   a. Bidding against A, B, and C in a new job with estimated total cost of $10,000.
   b. Bidding against A, B, and C in a new job with estimated total cost of $5,000,000.
   c. Comment on the impact of project size in (a) and (b) on the estimated optimum markup.
   d. Bidding against six typical competitors with behavior close to that of competitor B.

2. Briefly explain if the following statements are right or wrong and why?

   - When the σ of the B/C ratio of a competitor is small, winning this competitor becomes easier to predict.
   - Friedman's model uses a pessimistic strategy whereas Gates's model uses an optimistic strategy.
   - In case of high project risk, the use of Gates's model is more appropriate than Friedman's.
   - You should (increase/decrease) your bid markup when you bid against a larger number of competitors than you initially expected.
   - You should (increase/decrease) your bid markup when high risk is involved.
   - You should (increase/decrease) your bid markup when you need the job badly.

3. Your company is very keen on winning a job for which you submitted a bid of $1,100,000. Your cost estimate for the job is about $1,000,000. After the bid opening, your company, and two others, is selected for final negotiation with the owner. At

that meeting, you were asked if you are willing to reduce your final bid. You were also told that there is high chance of additional work that will be added, in the order of about 20% of the original volume of work. Based on this information, how much will you go down in your bid.

4. If a typical competitor has a B/C ratio with $\mu = 1.05$ and $\sigma = 0.09$, what is the markup associated with a 30% probability of beating four typical competitors?

5. Assume that a typical competitor has a B/C ratio with $\sigma = 0.07$. Also, assume that the markups associated with a 23% probability of beating seven typical competitors is 6.5% using Friedmans model. Calculate the average markup used by this competitor in any bid.

6. Analysis of the bidding behavior of a typical competitor against you, as a contractor, has revealed that *his bid/your cost* in ten previous bids take the following histogram.

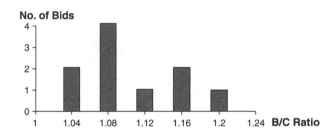

a. Based on that behavior, what is the markup value that this competitor uses on average? What is the your probability of winning this competitor if you use a markup of 14%?

b. In a new project with a $1,000,000 estimated cost, what is your optimum markup strategy against four typical competitors using Friedman's model? What is the expected profit at optimum markup?

c. Optimum markup generally _____(increases/decreases) with the number of competitors.

d. Which model (Friedman/Gates) is more sensitive to the number of competitors and why?

7. The previous records of past bids against four key competitors is in the following table:

Job No.	Contractor's Cost Estimate ($)	Bid Price of Competitors ($)			
		A	B	C	D
1	1,550,000	1,900,000	1,700,000	1,750,000	—
2	2,000,000	—	2,000,000	2,200,000	—
3	1,300,000	1,500,000	1,400,000	1,650,000	1,550,000
4	1,200,000	—	1,600,000	1,400,000	—
	Maine Experience	Hospitals	Town Houses	Office Buildings	Comm. Buildings

Using Friedman and Gates models, determine the markup needed to optimize expected profit in the following cases using an estimated total cost of $4,000,000:

a. Bidding against A, B, and C in a new job.

b. Bidding against six unknown competitors in an office building project.

c. You are bidding for a project that involves building several townhouses. Companies A, B, and C are also interested in bidding for that job, in addition to two unknown bidders.

  d. How will the optimum markup obtained in case (c), above, change if the unknown bidders are assumed to have a bidding behavior that is the average of all companies.

  e. Comment on the behavior of contractor D and how you can incorporate it in your bidding strategy.

8. Using the Excel program **Bidding.xls** for bidding strategy and the data of the solved problem in Section 9.5, try to determine the optimum markup using Solver to maximize the expected profit. Using the formulation on the sheet, set up Solver for optimizing the markup based on Friedman's and Gates' formulations, independently. Compare the results with those of the solved example.

Chapter 10

PROJECT FINANCING AND SCHEDULE INTEGRATION

A^{fter} After studying this chapter, you will be able to:

- Understand the various options of project financing.
- Graphically compare a project's cumulative cost and the owner's payment scheme.
- Perform overdraft calculations to determine the interest charges due to financing;
- Finalize a bid proposal in a manner that improves financing.
- Integrate cash flow calculations into an overall spreadsheet model for scheduling, resource management, and cash flow optimization.
- Experiment with various case studies.

Owner, CM	A/E, CM, Owner	Bidders	Owner, CM	Contractor	O & M Staff
• Need • Feasibility • Project Definition • Owner Approval	• Conceptual Design • Owner Approval • Soil Reports • Preliminary Design • Detailed Design • Quantities • Work Documents • Select Project Contract Strategy	• Prepare Bid Proposal + Baselines • Collect Data (site, quantities, specs, resources, tasks, etc) • Planning • Time & Cost Estimation • Scheduling • Resource Management: Adjustments for Resource Constraints & Deadline • Bidding Strategy & Markup Estimation • **Cash Flow Analysis** • Submit Bid	• Evaluate Bids and Select General Contractor	• Start Construction • Detailed Planning, Estimating & Resource Management • Schedule Updating • Progress Evaluation • Time, Cost, & Quality Control • Commissioning	• O & M • Demolition at End of Service Life
CONCEPT	DESIGN	BIDDING		CONSTRUCTION	O & M

10.1 Introduction

In the previous chapters, we learned techniques for scheduling and resource management so that our bid proposal is realistic and is close to being finalized. In this chapter, we will be introduced to project financing options and cash-flow calculations, which are very important, and in many cases are reasons for problems and even bankruptcies to contractors. The purpose of the analysis is to understand the financing needs of our project, determine the interest charges associated with our financing decisions, investigate various financial incentives in our bid that appeal to owners, and finalize our bid in a manner that improves project financing.

10.2 Project Cash Flow

At the project level, a *project's cash flow* is basically the difference between the project's expense and its income (shaded area in Figure 10–1). At the construction company level, on the other hand, the difference between a company's total expense and its total income over a period of time is the *company's cash flow*. Let's now consider the single project case.

**Figure 10-1.** Project Cash Flow Curves

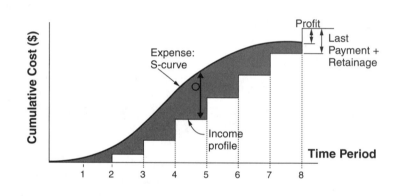

In Figure 10–1, a brief explanation of the terminology and the various elements included in preparing the contractor's cash flow for a project is as follows:

Time Period: This is the time at which changes in income or expenses occur. Usually, this period (often monthly or bimonthly) is stipulated in the contract as the time at which the contractor can submit an invoice of past period's work or receives an owner payment.

The Expense Profile (S-curve): The expense profile is a graphical presentation of the cumulative expenses (direct plus indirect) associated with executing the works, along the project duration. At each time period, the expenses of all the work completed till this period are accumulated from the project bar chart. In most cases, particularly at the planning stage, the contractor's direct and indirect *expenses* can be estimated to be equal to the direct and indirect *costs* estimated for the activities, as illustrated later by example.

The general "*S*" shape characteristic of the expense profile is shown in Figure 10–2 and can apply to most construction projects. Early in the project, activities are mobilizing and the expenditure curve is relatively flat. As many other activities come on line, the level of expenditure increases and the curve has a steeper middle section. Toward the end of a project, activities are winding down, finish-

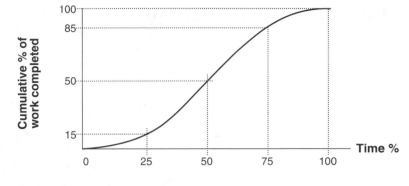

Figure 10-2. General Characteristics of the S-curve

The cost S-curve can be calculated from various points at the end of the time periods. For each point, the contractor sums the total costs of the planned work during that period and then draws a cumulative S-curve.

ing tasks take a long time but costs are small, and expenditures flatten again. It is noted also that when expenses on activities are not the same as their cost estimate, we can plot two S-curves, one for the expenses and one for the cost.

Retainage (%): This is the amount retained by the owner from every invoice, before a payment is made to the contractor. The purpose is to ensure that the contractor will continue the work and that no problems will arise after completion. This retainage amount (0 to 10%) is stipulated in the contract along with the time at which all the withheld amount will be repaid to the contractor. Owners have many options of deciding this amount, depending on their incentive policies and their relationship with the contractor. Examples are:

- A retainage amount of 5% is applied to all invoice payments, up to a maximum of $3000. All withheld amounts will be repaid to the contractor: 50% at substantial completions, and the other 50% three months later.
- A retainage amount of 10% is applied to all payments made before 50% of the work is completed. All withheld amounts are repaid to the contractor two months after substantial completion.

The Income Profile: The income profile is the ladder line in Figure 10–1 and represents the cumulative progress payments to be received by the contractor from the owner. In most cases, when owners receive an invoice for payment, the contractor receives his or her payment after a certain delay time (for processing and approvals) of one or more period(s), as stipulated in the contract.

As opposed to the expense S-curve, the contractor's income profile is a function of the contract price and is calculated as follows:

1. At each time period (i), the contractor sums the contract prices (incorporate direct cost, indirect cost, and markup) associated with the work of this period. This sum is often referred to as the *budget value* of the work. This amount is the invoice value to be billed to the owner.
2. The owner's payment is calculated by subtracting the stipulated retainage from the bill amount, and payment is expected to be made to the contractor after the delay period is passed.
3. Repeat these calculations for all periods and plot the ladder line.

10.3   Project Financing Options

Based on the discussion made on Figure 10–1, we can make several observations related to project financing, as follows:

- The shaded area in Figure 10–1 represents the difference between the contractor's expense and income curves, i.e., the amount that needs to be financed (overdraft amount). The larger the shaded area, the more money to be financed and the more interest charges are expected to cost the contractor.

- The amount of money to be financed in each month can be shown directly on the cash flow figure as the vertical difference between expense and income. For the case shown in Figure 10–1, the largest amount to be financed is the amount, O, right before receiving the owner payment in period 5. This value is sometimes referred to as *cash out-of-flow*.

- The contractor in the case of Figure 10–1 attained his profit only after the last owner payment, which included a payback of the retainage withheld during the previous progress payments.

- To *improve project financing*, i.e., minimizing the cash out-of-flow, we can get the expense and income curves closer together to reduce the shaded area. Various options are available to shift the expense curve to the right and/or the income curve to the left, as follows:

   a. **Subcontractors' Credit:** Subcontracting parts of the work with delayed payments to subcontractors reduces the direct expenses per period, thus shifting the expense curve to the right.

   b. **Arrangement with Material Suppliers:** This, similar to subcontractors' credit, can shift the expense curve to the right, closer to the income profile.

   c. **Owner Mobilization Payment:** This strategy substantially improves financing by asking owners for an advance payment for mobilization purposes. The mobilization payment can then be deducted from one or more progress payments. This strategy, however, may be used only in projects that require expensive site preparation, temporary facilities, etc. The effect of this strategy is shown schematically in Figure 10–3 in which no external financing is needed. In this case, the contract is fully financed by owner payments.

   d. **Front-end Loading (Bid Unbalancing):** In this strategy, the contractor inflates the bid prices of the items that are early in the schedule and deflates the bid prices of later items, so that the total bid remains unchanged. As such, the early invoices will be of higher value, thus attaining a larger income that can facilitate the financing of the remaining stages in the project. The effect of bid unbalancing on cash flow curves is shown in Figure 10–4, leading to some improvement as depicted in a lower monthly value to be financed and less shaded area (less interest charges). To perform bid unbalancing, contractors distribute the indirect cost plus markup unevenly among the contract items. However, because owners can detect unrealistic bids and can discredit them, contractors need to exercise care when doing the bid unbalancing. It is possible also to formulate the bid unbalancing situation as an optimization problem to determine the optimum unit prices that minimize the cash out-of-flow.

Other general guidelines that can be followed during construction to prevent undesirable or unexpected changes to project financing are:

   e. Accurate request for payments that is thoroughly checked for accurate progress measurements and free of errors.

   f. Proper planning of materials and large equipment delivery.

   g. Short-term loan, considering interest charges into account.

Figure 10-3. Effect of Mobilization Payment

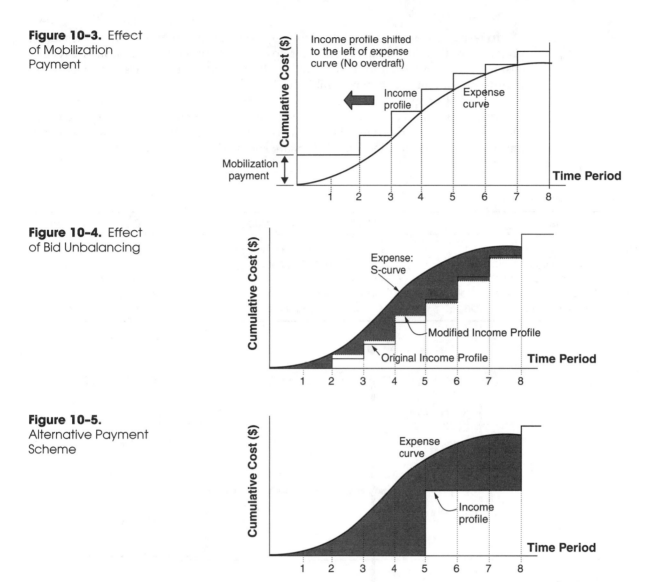

Figure 10-4. Effect of Bid Unbalancing

Figure 10-5. Alternative Payment Scheme

In the situation when project financing is not a major concern to the contractor, it is possible for the contractor to propose an alternative payment scheme that can be attractive to the owner, thus giving the contractor a competitive advantage. As shown in Figure 10–5, a two-payment scheme, rather than a period-by-period payment, is used to suit the budgetary constraints of an owner.

10.4   Calculating the S-curve

The S-curve of cumulative expenses is one of the main elements of cash-flow analysis. In general, however, an S-curve is a cumulative plot of costs or any other data that we would like to see how it accumulates along the project duration. In the next chapter, for example, we will plot an S-curve for the completion percentage of the project. That is to say, for example, that by the end of month 2, the project should be 45% complete. We can also plot various S-curves and use them for comparison purposes. For example, we can plot the S-curve of the planned versus actual percentage complete in the project. That is to say that by the end of month 2, our actual completion percentage is 38%, as opposed to the 45% on the plan. Various S-curves, therefore, can be used to view the overall picture of the project from different angles.

In terms of cost, we can plot various S-curves to show cumulative values along project duration. Each S-curve requires two essential types of information: the type of cost to be accumulated and the type of bar chart schedule. Examples of S-curves and their requirements are shown in Table 10–1.

Now, with a given type of cost and a given bar chart type, we can calculate the S-curve of cumulative costs. Consider, for example, an S-curve for the direct costs of planned work. The Estimated Direct Costs and the Planned Schedule are shown in Figure 10–6. The estimated direct costs are evenly distributed along the duration of

Table 10-1. Example S-curves

S-curve	Cost to be Accumulated	Bar Chart Type
• Direct Costs of Planned Work	• Estimated Direct Costs	• Planned Schedule
• Direct Expenses of Completed Work	• Actual Direct Expenses	• Actual Schedule
• Budget Value of Planned Work	• Contract Bid Prices	• Planned Schedule
• Budget Value of Completed Work	• Contract Bid Prices	• Actual Schedule
• Actual Cost of Completed Work	• Actual Direct + Indirect Expenses	• Actual Schedule

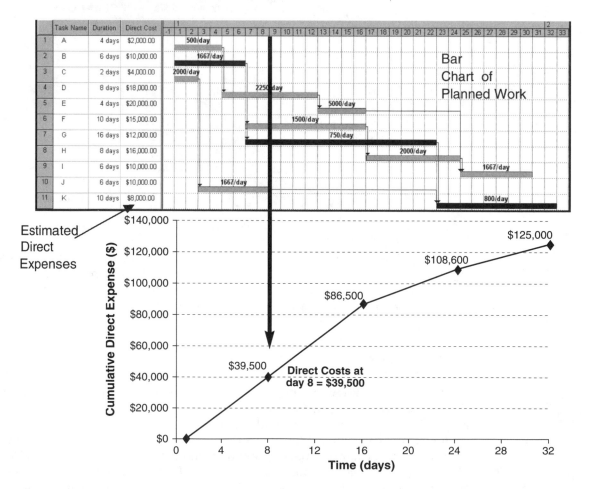

Figure 10-6. The Project Bar Chart and the S-curve of Cumulative Direct Costs

each activity and shown on the activity bars. The S-curve is then plotted from various points along the project duration. At any point of day i (e.g., i = day 8), cumulative costs are calculated by looking at the part of the bar chart to the left of that date and summing the costs of the activities (j's), as follows:

$$\text{Cumulative Costs} = \sum_{j=1}^{n} (\text{Days of activity } j \text{ at left of time } i \times \text{Cost/day of activity}$$

j) at time (i)

where, (j) is activity number 1, 2, . . . , n.

Therefore, at day 8, which is the first time period, the cumulative direct costs =

  4 days activity A × $500 /d
+ 6 days activity B × $1,667 /d
+ 2 days activity C × $2,000 /d
+ 4 days activity D × $2,250 /d
+ 2 days activity F × $1,500 /d
+ 2 days activity G × $750 /d
+ 6 days activity J × $1,667 /d = $39,500

We then repeat this calculation day by day, bi-daily, weekly, or monthly along the project duration, depending on the time period of the project. The result is the S-curve shown in Figure 10–6, with the cumulative costs at various time periods shown on the figure. Although this calculation is time consuming, it is necessary as the basis for cash flow analysis. Later, we will discuss how to get the S-curve directly from Microsoft Project, Primavera, or Excel.

10.5   Overdraft Calculations and Interest Charges

From the previous discussion on cash flow curves, a summary of the variables that affect project financing and need to be considered in overdraft calculations are:

- The project bar chart, which is developed considering project constraints.
- Activities' direct and indirect costs (function of the construction methods).
- Contractor method of paying his or her expenses (immediate or credit).
- Contractor's markup.
- Method of distributing indirect cost plus markup among activities.
- Retainage amount.
- Retainage payback time.
- Time of payment delay by owner.
- Owner mobilization payment.
- Interest rate on overdraft amount.

Now, let's demonstrate the detailed overdraft calculations considering all the cash flow variables. We will use our small project that we dealt with in the previous chapters, and we will consider two different financing scenarios to illustrate the various options.

10.5.1   Financing Scenario 1

The first scenario deals with the case study that we dealt with in previous chapters, but assuming we have no resource problems or deadline constraints.

Problem Variables:

- The 32-day network of the case study is shown in Figure 10–7.
- All activities use their cheapest method of construction (index 1), and the direct costs of activities are shown in Figure 10–7.
- Indirect cost is $500 per day (total of $16,000).
- Contractor's optimum markup is 5%.
- To determine bid prices, indirect costs are distributed in a balanced way among activities.
- Contractor will pay his expenses immediately, thus expenses equal costs.
- Time period = 8 days.
- Retainage amount is 10%.
- All withheld retainage money will be paid back with the last payment.
- Owner's payment delay of any invoice is one period. For example, the first invoice will be submitted at the end of the first period and payment (invoice minus retainage) will occur at the end of the second period.
- No mobilization payment is given to contractor.
- The interest rate applied to any overdraft money is 1% per period.

Solution

Calculations of overdraft amounts and interest charges incorporate five main steps, as follows:

Step 1: Project Network and Bar Chart

The network of the planned schedule is shown in Figure 10–7. Estimated direct costs are also shown in the same figure. The bar chart of the work plan is shown in Figure 10–6.

Step 2: Assessment of Costs, Expenses, and Bid Prices

Based on the assumptions used in this scenario, all costs of activities become immediate expenses to the contractor. The budget value or bid price of activities, on the other hand, is basically a summation of cost and markup. The distinction between the three items of costs, expenses, and bid prices is important. The calculations of costs (direct plus indirect) and bid prices (budget values) are shown in Table 10–2. Expenses, on the other hand, is the portion of the costs (0 to 100%) incurred at a given time. In this example, expenses equal costs.

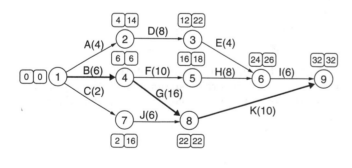

Activity	Duration	Direct Cost
A	4	$2,000
B	6	$10,000
C	2	$4,000
D	8	$18,000
E	4	$20,000
F	10	$15,000
G	16	$12,000
H	8	$16,000
I	6	$10,000
J	6	$10,000
K	10	$8,000

Total Direct Cost = **$125,000**

Figure 10–7. Network and Activity Data of Scenario 1

Table 10-2. Cost and Budget Calculations

Activity	Duration	Direct Cost	Indirect Cost (Balanced Bid)	Total Cost	Markup (5%)	Bid Price (Budget Value)
A	4	$2,000	= 16,000 * (2000/125,000) = $256	$2,256	$113	$2,369
B	6	$10,000	= 16,000 * (10000/125,000) = $1,280	$11,280	$564	$11,844
C	2	$4,000	= 16,000 * (4000/125,000) = $512	$4,512	$226	$4,738
D	8	$18,000	= 16,000 * (18000/125,000) = $2,304	$20,304	$1,015	$21,319
E	4	$20,000	= 16,000 * (20000/125,000) = $2,560	$22,560	$1,128	$23,688
F	10	$15,000	= 16,000 * (15000/125,000) = $1,920	$16,920	$846	$17,766
G	16	$12,000	= 16,000 * (12000/125,000) = $1,536	$13,536	$677	$14,213
H	8	$16,000	= 16,000 * (16000/125,000) = $2,048	$18,048	$902	$18,950
I	6	$10,000	= 16,000 * (10000/125,000) = $1,280	$11,280	$564	$11,844
J	6	$10,000	= 16,000 * (10000/125,000) = $1,280	$11,280	$564	$11,844
K	10	$8,000	= 16,000 * (8000/125,000) = $1,024	$9,024	$451	$9,475

Total Direct Cost = $125,000   Total Cost = $141,000   Total Bid = $148,050

Step 3: Cash Flow Calculations

Cash flow calculations are compiled in a table format (Table 10–3). In this table, five periods (each is eight days) are used along the project duration, including an extra period after project completion. We then perform the calculations, starting from row 1 in a systematic fashion. The table is basically divided into three sections: (1) the top section for S-curve computations of cumulative expenses; (2) the middle section calculating the owner cumulative payments; and (3) the bottom section for overdraft calculations and interest charges.

The calculations involved in the first two sections in Table 10–3 (cumulative expenses and cumulative owner payments) are straightforward. The direct cost values in row 1 are obtained from the calculations of S-curve for direct costs, as discussed in Section 10.4. Then, in row 1a, costs become immediate expenses to the contractor. Afterwards, we add indirect expenses and then accumulate the total expenses, thus forming an S-curve for total expenses.

The second part of the table deals with owner payments, and the essential part of this calculation is row 5 in which the budget value of the work is calculated. For that part, S-curve calculations were performed using the bar chart of the plan and the bid prices (budget values) in column 7 of Table 10–2. We then subtract retainage amounts and shift the payment by the amount of owner delay (one period). Notice that at the end of the last time period (period 5), two payments are planned to be received from the owner; $17,482 for the work done in period 4; and $14,805 as a payback of all retention withheld by owner. Here, the last period requires extra care for its calculations.

The calculations in the third section of Table 10–3 (overdraft) can be tricky. The simplest way to understand it is as a bank account. We start the project with a balance of zero and proceed to withdraw funds to cover the expenses needed for the work of the first period (–$43,500). By the end of the first period, the bank adds its interest charges and sends you the statement of –$43,935 as total overdraft balance. We then keep withdrawing money to cover the expenses during the second period ($51,000), and as such we accumulate an overdraft of –$94,935 = –($43,935 + $51,000). Interest charges are then added to increase the overdraft to –$95,884 and the second bank statement is sent to you. Right after sending the statement, a deposit of $42,106 owner payment is made, however, this will only appear in next month's statement. Notice here that owner payments are right aligned in Table 10–3 to remind you that the de-

Table 10-3. Cash Flow Calculations for Scenario 1

		Time Period				
		1st	2nd	3rd	4th (Last)	5th (End)	5th
(1)	Direct Costs	$39,500	$47,000	$22,100	$16,400	$0	Retainage Payback
(1a)	Direct Expenses = (1)	$39,500 +	$47,000 +	$22,100 +	$16,400 +	$0	
(2)	Indirect Expenses ($500/d)	$4,000	$4,000	$4,000	$4,000	$0	
(3)	Total Expenses = (1a) + (2)	$43,500	$51,000	$26,100	$20,400		
(4)	**Cumulative Expenses = Cumulative of Row 3**	**$43,500**	**$94,500**	**$120,600**	**$141,000**	**$141,000**	
(5)	Budget Value of Work	$46,784	$55,667	$26,175	$19,424		
(6)	Retainage (5) × 10%	$4,678	$5,567	$2,618	$1,942	$0	= Sum of (6) **$14,805**
(7)	Amount Payable = (5) − (6)	$42,106	$50,100	$23,558	$17,482	$0	
(8)	Payment Received = (7)		$42,106	$50,100	$23,558	$17,482	
(9)	**Cumulative Owner Payment = Cum. of (8)**		**$42,106**	**$92,206**	**$115,763**	**$133,245**	**$148,050**
(10)**	Overdraft Balance at End of Period, before Interest	− $43,500* +	− $94,935 +	− $79,879** +	− $50,977 +	− $27,930	− $28,209
(11)	Interest on Overdraft Balance = (10) × 1%	− $435	− $949	− $799	− $510	− $279	+ $17,482 + $14,805
(12)	**Total Overdraft Balance = (10) + (11)**	**− $43,935**	**− $95,884**	**− $80,678**	**− $51,487**	**− $28,209**	**$4,078**

* A negative sign represents an overdraft whereas a positive sign represents a positive balance.

** Overdraft balance at end of period can be calculated in two ways:

= Total overdraft balance (row 12) at previous period + Owner payment (row 8) made at previous period. e.g., at end of period 3 = (−$95,884) − (26,100) + ($42,106) = −$79,879; or

= Cumulative expenses (row 4) to this period + Sum of interest paid until previous period (row 11) + Cumulative payments received (row 9) until the previous period = (−$120,600) + (−$435 − $949) + $42,106 = −$79,879.

266

Figure 10-8. Cash Flow Plot of Scenario 1

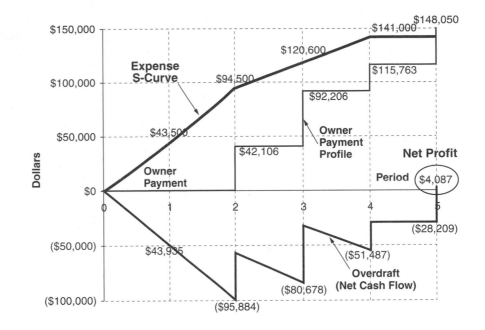

posit will show in next statement. The calculation is also logical from the bank's point of view because an end-of-period payment will not relieve you from interest on the current period. Continuing our progress on the project, we withdraw additional –$26,100 to spend on progress in the third period. At the end of the period, the overdraft is calculated as shown at the bottom of Table 10–3, then interest is added to calculate a total overdraft of –$80,678. The process then continues until the end of period 5, which is one period after the completion of the project. Immediately afterwards, all amounts withheld are repaid back and final adjustments are made in the last column of the table.

Step 4: Plotting the Overdraft Profile
The calculations in Table 10–3 are used to plot the cash flow plot as shown in Figure 10–8. The "Overdraft Profile" shows all the overdraft transactions and the financing amount needed each period. The values below the horizontal axis represent financing amounts that include interest charges whereas the values above the axis represent a positive balance (profit).

Step 5: Interpreting the Results
Various interesting observations can be made on the overdraft calculations and the associated tables and figures, as follows:

- The sum of interest charges is determined from row (11) in Table 10–3 as $435 + $949 + $799 + $510 + $279 = $2,972, representing the cost to the contractor due to project financing. Failing to add these costs to the indirect cost reduces the contractor's net profit;
- The area in Figure 10–8 enclosed between the expense S-curve and the owner payment profile is the area of financing. It is possible, therefore, to roughly estimate the interest charges directly from the graph. Notice that the area of one grid unit in the figure is ($50,000 × 1 period). Therefore, if we add the number of grid units that make the enclosed area, it is approximately 5 units and as such the interest charges are as follows:

    5 units × ($50,000 × 1 period) × 0.01 interest per period = $2,500

which is an underestimation of the actual interest charges since the effect of compounding is not considered.

- As given in the problem statement, the project's total direct plus indirect costs are $141,000. With markup being 5%, a profit of $7,050 is expected. If we subtract the interest charges, the net profit becomes $4,078, as shown in the last overdraft balance (row 12) of Table 10–3.
- The amount required to be financed (cash needed) for this project is shown in row 12 of Table 10–3 and the overdraft curve of Figure 10–8. For this project, therefore, the maximum finance amount is $95,884 and is needed in the second period. This information is important to be communicated to the financing institution.
- Multiproject financing is performed by adding the monthly overdraft amounts from several projects and presenting a combined overdraft diagram to the financing institution.

10.5.2   Financing Scenario 2

Let's now look at another scenario of project financing to investigate the effect of some of the financing options discussed in Section 10.3. We will use the same case study project again but with different assumptions. In this scenario, we will take the result of applying resource analysis and time-cost tradeoff analysis performed in Chapters 7 and 8. These analyses were necessary to meet a *28-day deadline* and to limit the amount of L1 resource needed for the project to 6. The schedule that resulted from the analysis was shown in Figure 8–17.

Problem Variables:

- Project network and activity data are shown in Figure 10–9. Project was crashed four days by selecting appropriate methods of construction for the activities, as discussed in Chapter 8. Also, a delay of four days was applied to activity D to account for L1 resource limit of six per day.
- Indirect cost is $14,000 ($500 per day).
- Contractor's optimum markup is 5%.
- Bid is *unbalanced* as shown in Figure 10–9. The indirect costs of early activities are increased by a positive adjustment while indirect costs of later activities are decreased by a negative adjustment. Total bid, however, does not change.
- *50% of the contractor's expenses in any period are credit by suppliers*, which will be paid in the following period.
- Time period = 8 days.
- Retainage amount is 10%.
- All withheld retainage money will be paid back with last payment.
- Owner's payment delay of any invoice is one period.
- A *20% mobilization* payment is given to the contractor at the beginning of the project and will be deducted from the first two payments.
- The interest rate applied to any overdraft money is 1% per period.

Solution

Step 1: Project Network and Bar Chart
Project network is shown in Figure 10–9. Notice the two critical paths in the network: Path B-G-K and Path B-F-H-I. Project duration is 28 days. The bar chart is also shown in Figure 10–10.

Step 2: Assessment of Costs, Expenses, and Bid Prices
Similar to the previous scenario, activities' direct costs, indirect costs, markup, and bid prices are calculated as shown in Table 10–4.

Figure 10-9.
Network and
Activity Data of
Scenario 2

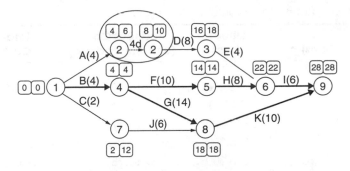

Activity	Delay	Duration	Direct Cost	Indirect Cost (unbalanced bid)			Total Cost
				Balanced	Adjust. (%)	Total*	
A		4	$2,000	$256	1.27	$398	$2,398
B		4	$12,000	$1,280	2.77	$1,707	$13,707
C		2	$4,000	$512	2.54	$795	$4,795
D	4	8	$18,000	$2,304	−1.43	$1,778	$19,778
E		4	$20,000	$2,560	−1.59	$1,976	$21,976
F		10	$15,000	$1,920	0.96	$1,783	$16,783
G		14	$12,400	$1,536	1.27	$1,541	$13,941
H		8	$16,000	$2,048	0	$1,758	$17,758
I		6	$10,000	$1,280	−2.23	$787	$10,787
J		6	$10,000	$1,280	−2.23	$787	$10,787
K		10	$8,000	$1,024	−1.34	$691	$8,691
		Total =	$127,400			$14,000	$141,400

* Total indirect = balanced indirect + adjustment (%) × $14,000
Note: Shaded activities are crashed to reduce project duration.

	Task Name	Duration	Direct Cost	Leveling Delay	
1	A	4 days	$2,000.00	0 edays	500/day
2	B	4 days	$12,000.00	0 edays	3000/day
3	C	2 days	$4,000.00	0 edays	2000/day
4	D	8 days	$18,000.00	4 edays	2250/day
5	E	4 days	$20,000.00	0 edays	5000/day
6	F	10 days	$15,000.00	0 edays	1500/day
7	G	14 days	$12,400.00	0 edays	886/day
8	H	8 days	$16,000.00	0 edays	2000/day
9	I	6 days	$10,000.00	0 edays	1667/day
10	J	6 days	$10,000.00	0 edays	1667/day
11	K	10 days	$8,000.00	0 edays	800/day

Figure 10-10. Bar Chart of Scenario 2 with Direct Costs

Table 10-4. Cost and Budget Calculations

Activity	Duration	Direct Cost	Indirect Cost (unbalanced bid)	Total Cost	Markup (5%)	Bid Price (budget value)
A	4	$2,000	$398	$2,398	$120	$2,518
B	4	$12,000	$1,707	$13,707	$685	$14,392
C	2	$4,000	$795	$4,795	$240	$5,034
D	8	$18,000	$1,778	$19,778	$989	$20,767
E	4	$20,000	$1,976	$21,976	$1,099	$23,075
F	10	$15,000	$1,783	$16,783	$839	$17,623
G	14	$12,400	$1,541	$13,941	$697	$14,638
H	8	$16,000	$1,758	$17,758	$888	$18,646
I	6	$10,000	$787	$10,787	$539	$11,326
J	6	$10,000	$787	$10,787	$539	$11,326
K	10	$8,000	$691	$8,691	$435	$9,126

Total Direct Cost = $127,400   Total Cost = $141,400   Total Bid = $148,470

Step 3: Cash Flow Calculations

Similar to Scenario 1, cash flow calculations are summarized in Table 10–5.

Compiling this table becomes simple given, that the values in rows 1 and 5 are computed from the bar chart. Row 1 is the calculation of the direct costs in every period, following S-curve calculations based on the bar chart and direct costs of Figure 10–10. Because direct expenses in this scenario are less than direct costs, due to suppliers' credit, we can accordingly calculate the direct expenses in each period. Afterwards, we add the indirect expenses in row 2 to determine the cumulative expenses in row 4.

To calculate the owner's payments, we need to consider the budget value of the work planned to be performed in each period. This can be calculated also from the planned bar chart in Figure 10–10 but considering the budget values of activities shown in the last column of Table 10–4. Overdraft calculations, on the other hand, are identical to those performed for Scenario 1.

Step 4: Plotting the Overdraft Profile

The calculations in Table 10–5 are used to plot the cash flow plot as shown. The "Overdraft Profile" shows all the overdraft transactions and the financing amount needed each period. The values below the horizontal axis represent financing amounts that include interest charges whereas the values above the axis represent a positive balance (profit).

Step 5: Interpreting the Results

The calculations in Table 10–5 and Figure 10–11 show a much-improved cash flow as a result of project crashing, mobilization payment, bid unbalancing, and suppliers' credit. Accordingly, the results of the second financing scenario are as follows:

- The sum of interest charges is $1,656, which is much less than the $2,972 of the first financing scenario.
- In addition to a lower bid and a shorter duration, the net profit is $5,414, which is higher than the $4,078 of the first scenario.
- To the contractor's benefit, the amount required to be financed for this project, has reduced substantially to a maximum of $57,949 and is required later in the project (period 3), as opposed to the $95,884 needed in period 2 in the first scenario.

Table 10-5. Cash Flow Calculations for Scenario 2

		Time Period					
		1st	**2nd**	**3rd**	**4th (Last)**	**5th (End)**	**5th Retainage Payback**
(1)	Direct Expenses	$37,543	$38,086	$41,905	$9,867	$0	
(1a)	**Direct Expense Considering** Supplier's Credit	$18,771	$37,814	$39,995	$25,886	$4,933	
(2)	Indirect Expenses ($500/d)	+ $4,000	+ $4,000	+ $4,000	+ $2,000	+ $0	
(3)	Total Expenses = (1a) + (2)	$22,771	$41,814	$43,995	$27,886	$4,993	
(4)	**Cumulative Expenses = Cumulative of Row 3**	**$22,771**	**$64,586**	**$108,581**	**$136,467**	**$141,400**	
(5)	Budget Value of Work	$44,501	$44,366	$48,401	$11,201	$0	
(6)	Retainage (5) × 10%	– $4,450	– $4,437	– $4,840	– $1,120	$0	
(7)	Amount Payable = (5) – (6)	$40,051	$39,930	$43,561	$10,081	$0	= Sum of (6)
(8)	Payment Received	29,694 (Mobil.)	$25,204 Half mobil. deducted	$25,083 Half mobil. deducted	$43,561	$10,081	**$14,847**
(9)	**Cumulative Owner Payment = Cum. of (8)**	**$29,694**	**$54,898**	**$79,981**	**$123,542**	**$133,623**	**$148,470**
(10)	Overdraft Balance at End of Period, before Interest	– $6,923	– $34,892	– $54,032	– $57,375	– $19,321	– $19,514 + $10,081 + $14,847
(11)	Interest on Overdraft Balance = (10) × 1%	+ $0	+ – $349	+ – $540	+ – $574	– $193	
(12)	**Total Overdraft Balance = (10) + (11)**	**– $6,923**	**– $35,241**	**– $54,572**	**– $57,949**	**– $19,514**	**$5,414**

271

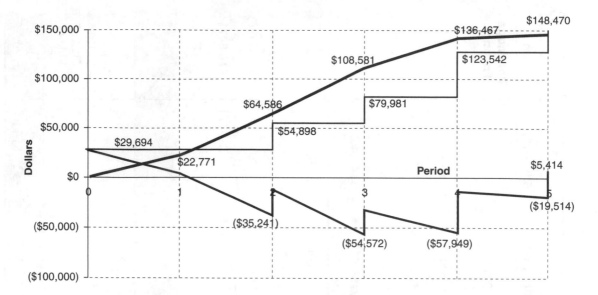

Figure 10-11. Cash Flow Plot of Scenario 2

10.6   Using Microsoft Project

In Microsoft Project alone, there is no direct way to perform overdraft analysis. However, it is possible to use the cash flow reports of the software as a basis for the analysis. For example, with some manipulation, we can use the software to determine the values of direct costs per period that we use in row 1 of our analysis table and also the budget values of the work per period that we use in row 5 of the analysis. Using these values, the rest of the table can be calculated easily on a spreadsheet program like Excel. The use of Microsoft Project is demonstrated in the Figures 10–12 to 10–15.

We first load the **CPM-Ch10.mpp** file of our case study project into Microsoft Project. Once loaded, we adjust the durations of tasks B and G as per the second scenario. Also, we specify the four days of leveling delay for activity D. This brings to us a 28-day duration and a schedule that does not require more than 6 L1 resources. Afterwards, we activate the Cost Table from the **View-Table-Cost** menu option.

In Figure 10–13, the Cost Table is shown and we can manually enter the Budget value of each activity from the data in Table 10–4 to the Fixed Cost column. Automatically, the Total Cost column is adjusted. Now, we need to save the schedule as our baseline by selecting **Tools-Tracking-Save Baseline** menu options. We are now ready to view Cash Flow reports associated with the saved baseline.

From the **View-Reports** menu option we can access various reports. We need to select the Costs reports, and then the **Cash Flow** option. We can adjust the way the report looks like by selecting the **Edit** button.

In Figure 10–15, we can set the time period for which the cash flow data is to be viewed (shown here as three days). Accordingly, a detailed report is presented with the cost per period calculated in the bottom row. This data can readily be used and plotted cumulatively as the S-curve of budget values for the project.

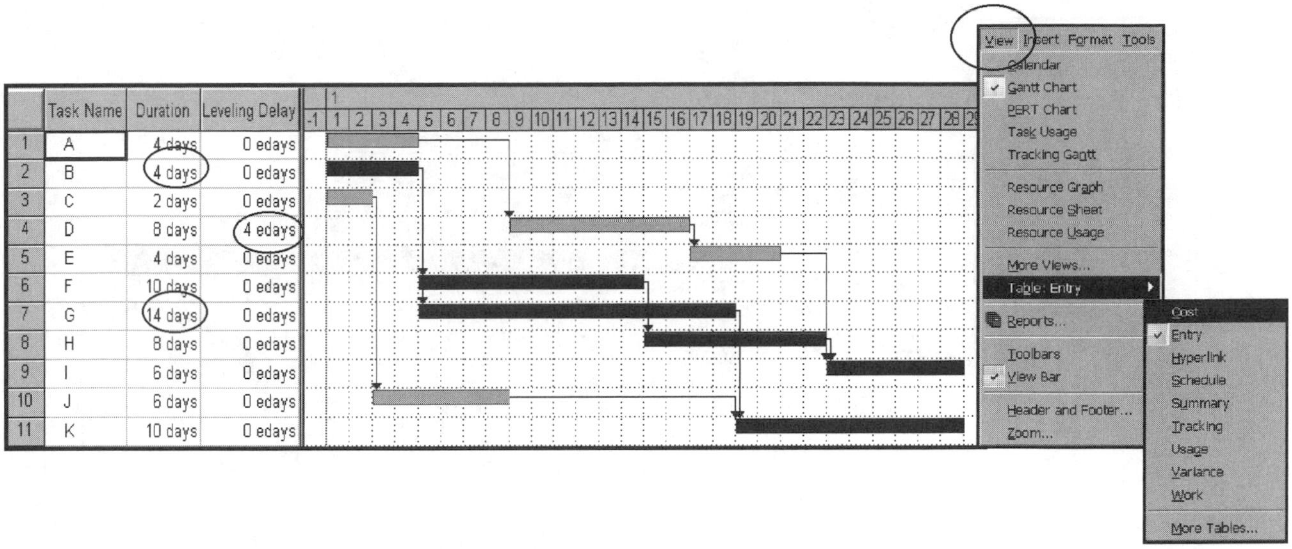

	Task Name	Duration	Leveling Delay
1	A	4 days	0 edays
2	B	4 days	0 edays
3	C	2 days	0 edays
4	D	8 days	4 edays
5	E	4 days	0 edays
6	F	10 days	0 edays
7	G	14 days	0 edays
8	H	8 days	0 edays
9	I	6 days	0 edays
10	J	6 days	0 edays
11	K	10 days	0 edays

View menu:
- Calendar
- ✓ Gantt Chart
- PERT Chart
- Task Usage
- Tracking Gantt
- Resource Graph
- Resource Sheet
- Resource Usage
- More Views...
- Table: Entry ▶
- Reports...
- Toolbars
- ✓ View Bar
- Header and Footer...
- Zoom...

Table submenu:
- Cost
- ✓ Entry
- Hyperlink
- Schedule
- Summary
- Tracking
- Usage
- Variance
- Work
- More Tables...

Figure 10-12. Loading Project File of Scenario 2

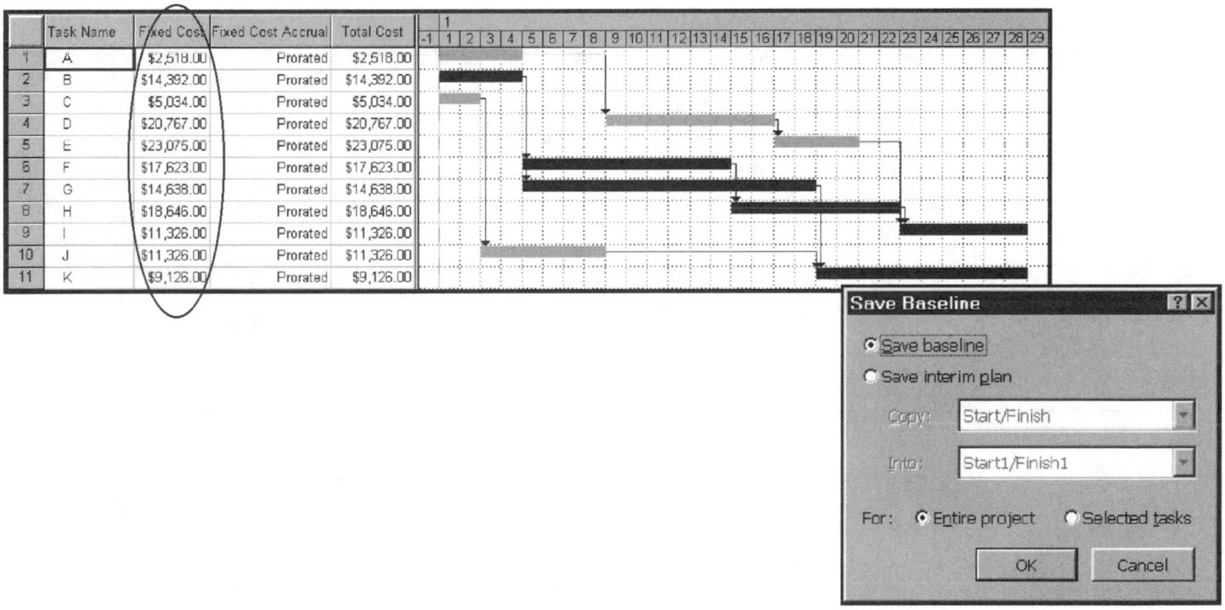

	Task Name	Fixed Cost	Fixed Cost Accrual	Total Cost
1	A	$2,518.00	Prorated	$2,518.00
2	B	$14,392.00	Prorated	$14,392.00
3	C	$5,034.00	Prorated	$5,034.00
4	D	$20,767.00	Prorated	$20,767.00
5	E	$23,075.00	Prorated	$23,075.00
6	F	$17,623.00	Prorated	$17,623.00
7	G	$14,638.00	Prorated	$14,638.00
8	H	$18,646.00	Prorated	$18,646.00
9	I	$11,326.00	Prorated	$11,326.00
10	J	$11,326.00	Prorated	$11,326.00
11	K	$9,126.00	Prorated	$9,126.00

Save Baseline dialog:
- ⊙ Save baseline
- ○ Save interim plan
- Copy: Start/Finish
- Into: Start1/Finish1
- For: ⊙ Entire project ○ Selected tasks
- [OK] [Cancel]

Figure 10-13. Input of Tasks' Cost Data

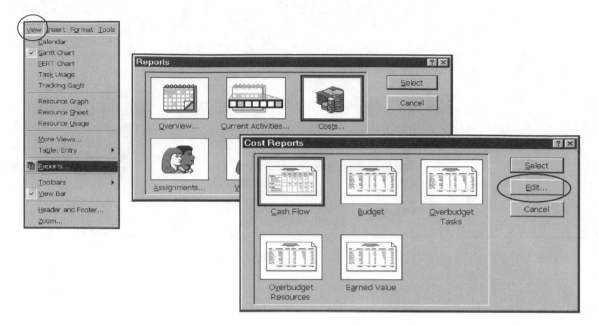

Figure 10-14. Viewing Cash Flow Reports

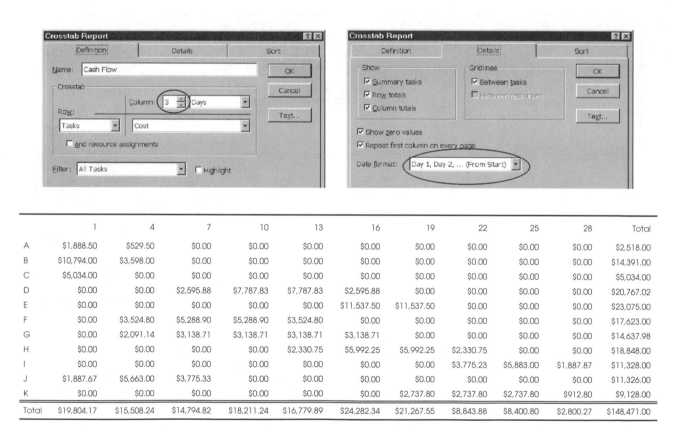

	1	4	7	10	13	16	19	22	25	28	Total
A	$1,888.50	$529.50	$0.00	$0.00	$0.00	$0.00	$0.00	$0.00	$0.00	$0.00	$2,518.00
B	$10,794.00	$3,598.00	$0.00	$0.00	$0.00	$0.00	$0.00	$0.00	$0.00	$0.00	$14,391.00
C	$5,034.00	$0.00	$0.00	$0.00	$0.00	$0.00	$0.00	$0.00	$0.00	$0.00	$5,034.00
D	$0.00	$0.00	$2,595.88	$7,787.83	$7,787.83	$2,595.88	$0.00	$0.00	$0.00	$0.00	$20,767.02
E	$0.00	$0.00	$0.00	$0.00	$0.00	$11,537.50	$11,537.50	$0.00	$0.00	$0.00	$23,075.00
F	$0.00	$3,524.80	$5,288.90	$5,288.90	$3,524.80	$0.00	$0.00	$0.00	$0.00	$0.00	$17,623.00
G	$0.00	$2,091.14	$3,138.71	$3,138.71	$3,138.71	$3,138.71	$0.00	$0.00	$0.00	$0.00	$14,637.98
H	$0.00	$0.00	$0.00	$0.00	$2,330.75	$5,992.25	$5,992.25	$2,330.75	$0.00	$0.00	$18,848.00
I	$0.00	$0.00	$0.00	$0.00	$0.00	$0.00	$0.00	$3,775.23	$5,883.00	$1,887.87	$11,328.00
J	$1,887.67	$5,663.00	$3,775.33	$0.00	$0.00	$0.00	$0.00	$0.00	$0.00	$0.00	$11,326.00
K	$0.00	$0.00	$0.00	$0.00	$0.00	$0.00	$2,737.80	$2,737.80	$2,737.80	$912.80	$9,128.00
Total	$19,804.17	$15,508.24	$14,794.82	$18,211.24	$16,779.89	$24,282.34	$21,267.55	$8,843.88	$8,400.80	$2,800.27	$148,471.00

Figure 10-15. Viewing Cash Flow Reports

10.7 Using Primavera P3

Similar to Microsoft Project, there is no direct way to perform overdraft analysis on Primavera P3. However, we can manipulate the software to determine the cumulative costs, which can then be transferred to Excel or other software to perform overdraft calculations. To use the P3 program, we follow the steps in Figures 10–16 to 10–20.

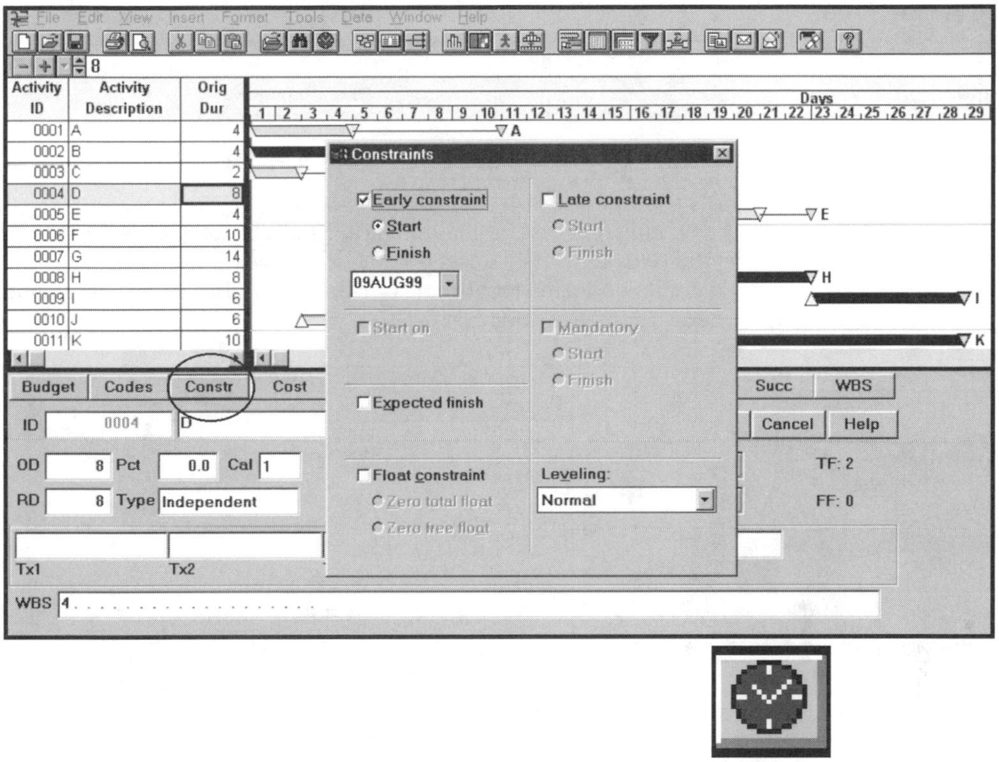

Figure 10-16. Input of Project Data

First we input the activity names, durations, and relationships. The durations correspond to the project crashing decisions. We then specify a delay of four days to the start of activity D. From the activity details window, we select the **Constr** tab to specify the delay as a start constraint. Once done, we schedule the project using the **Schedule** button.

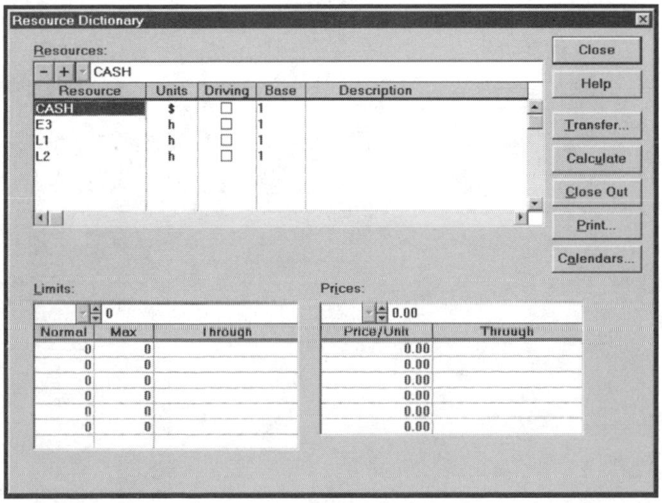

Figure 10-17. Specifying a Cost Code

Before entering costs for the activities, we need to add a Resource Code called Cash. We access that screen from the **Data-Resources** menu option.

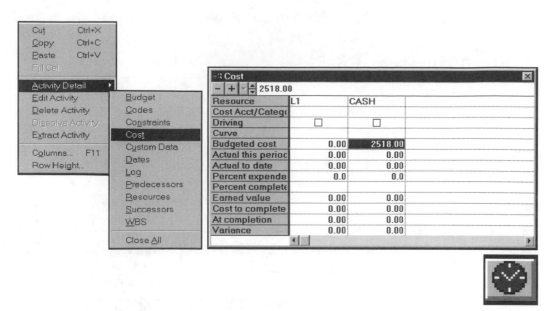

Figure 10-18. Entering Activities' Budgeted Costs

We now can start entering the budgeted cost for the activities. First the cost form is activated by a right click on any of the activities and selecting the **Activity Detail-Cost** option. Now we select the activities one by one, add the Cash resource and assign a value for its budgeted cost (from last column in Table 10–4). Once done, we need to reschedule the project again using the **Schedule** toolbar button.

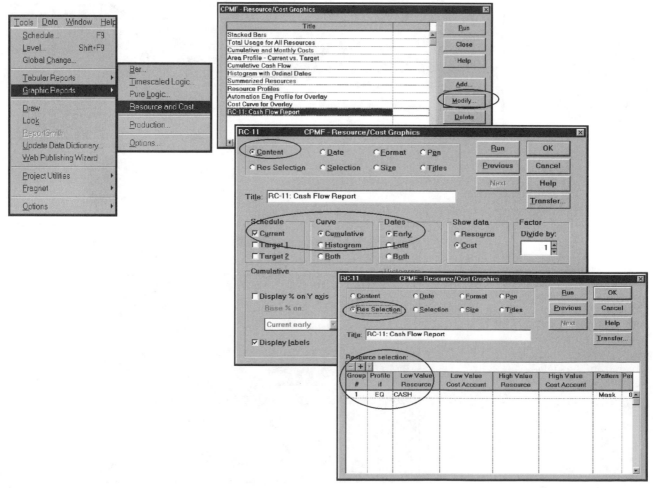

Figure 10-19. Preparing for Cash Flow Reports

From the **Tools** menu, we can access the many graphical reports on resources and costs. Let's add a new report and specify its options as shown.

Figure 10-20. Cash Flow Graph

After selecting the report options, the report shows the S-curve of budgeted costs as shown here.

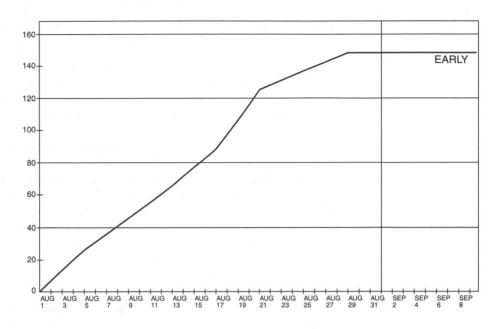

10.8   Back to Our Case Study Project

We now come to the last step of planning. We will try to optimize our schedule considering all project constraints related to time, cost, and resources together. Accordingly, we will have our bid proposal ready for submission.

Now that we have discussed the various financing options and the overdraft calculations, let's incorporate that into our spreadsheet model so that we can experiment with all the scheduling options in a transparent way. Let's now load the spreadsheet model of our case study project (the **Case-Study.xls** file). This file works as a template that we can use for other projects. The Schedule sheet is fairly simple and versatile. In the next few figures, let's see how the large Schedule sheet can be used.

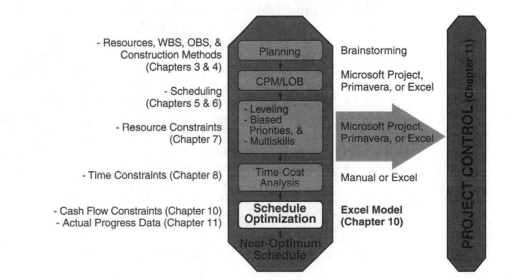

Some of the characteristics of the Schedule Sheet in Figure 10–21 are:

- The figure shows the solution of the second financing scenario of this chapter. Using the top two buttons, the Schedule sheet was automatically set up with the activities' data linked by formulas to the Estimate sheet, including three methods of construction and amounts of three key resources.
- The Schedule sheet is set up to allow you to distribute the total indirect cost among the various activities.
- Column AG, *Balanced Indirect Cost*, has formulas to automatically distribute the total indirect costs proportional to the activities' direct costs.
- Column AF is a user input of any adjustment (% of total indirect cost) positive or negative to cause bid unbalancing. Accordingly, the total indirect costs of the tasks are calculated by formulas in column AI and the total budget values (direct + indirect + markup) are calculated in column AJ.
- Cash flow calculations are set up underneath the bar chart of the project. Formulas are included to calculate the daily expenses and all other details of the cumulative expenses (S-curve), owner payments, and overdraft amounts at each time period, based on user inputs of the cash flow variable.
- Cash flow curves are plotted automatically, based on the values input by the user.
- The Estimate sheet has formulas to transfer the scheduled start times of the activities to the estimate and as such, season-based productivity factors are applied to activities' durations and costs (Figure 10–22).
- Any changes to the methods of construction, activity delays, adjustment amounts, financing options, resource data, project deadline, or any activity data, will automatically reflect on the total project duration and cost. As such, you can easily experiment with any combination of variables and examine the result. We can also use Evolver to try minimizing total project cost under constraints.

10.8.1 Cash Flow Optimization

With our **Case-Study.xls** file being so flexible, we can attempt to do one more refinement to the schedule in an attempt to optimize financing cost or the overdraft amount. Here, we will assume that other optimization experiments have taken place and accordingly the activities' delay values and methods of construction are set to meet the project deadline and resource limits. We then need not tamper with these values. Instead we will try the following:

- Objective is to minimize overdraft money (finance money, cell AG33).
- Variables are the activities' adjustment values (column AF), which lead to an increase or a decrease in the unit cost of the activities.
- The concept is to assign high positive adjustment percentages to the activities that are early in the schedule and high negative percentage to the ones that are late in the schedule. As such, total bid is not changed but our invoices to the owner are higher early in the project to facilitate financing.
- We need to be careful with this bid unbalancing process so that our unit prices are still within the practical range acceptable to owners. Therefore, a constraint on the maximum adjustment percentage can be assigned.
- Total of the adjustment values have to add up to zero.

For demonstration purposes, let's now apply this optimization experiment on our case study, as shown in Figures 10–23 to 10–25.

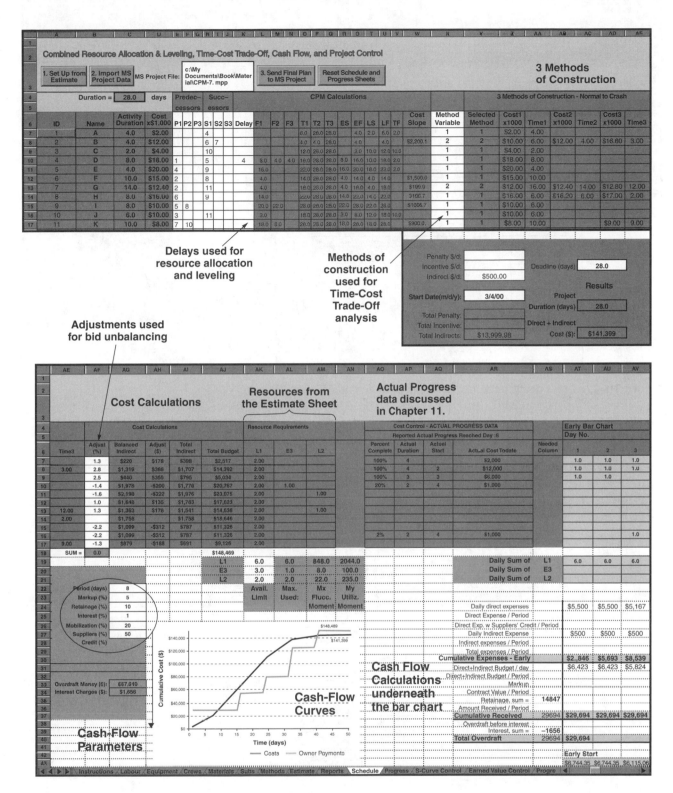

Figure 10–21. Overall Schedule Sheet for Financing Scenario 2

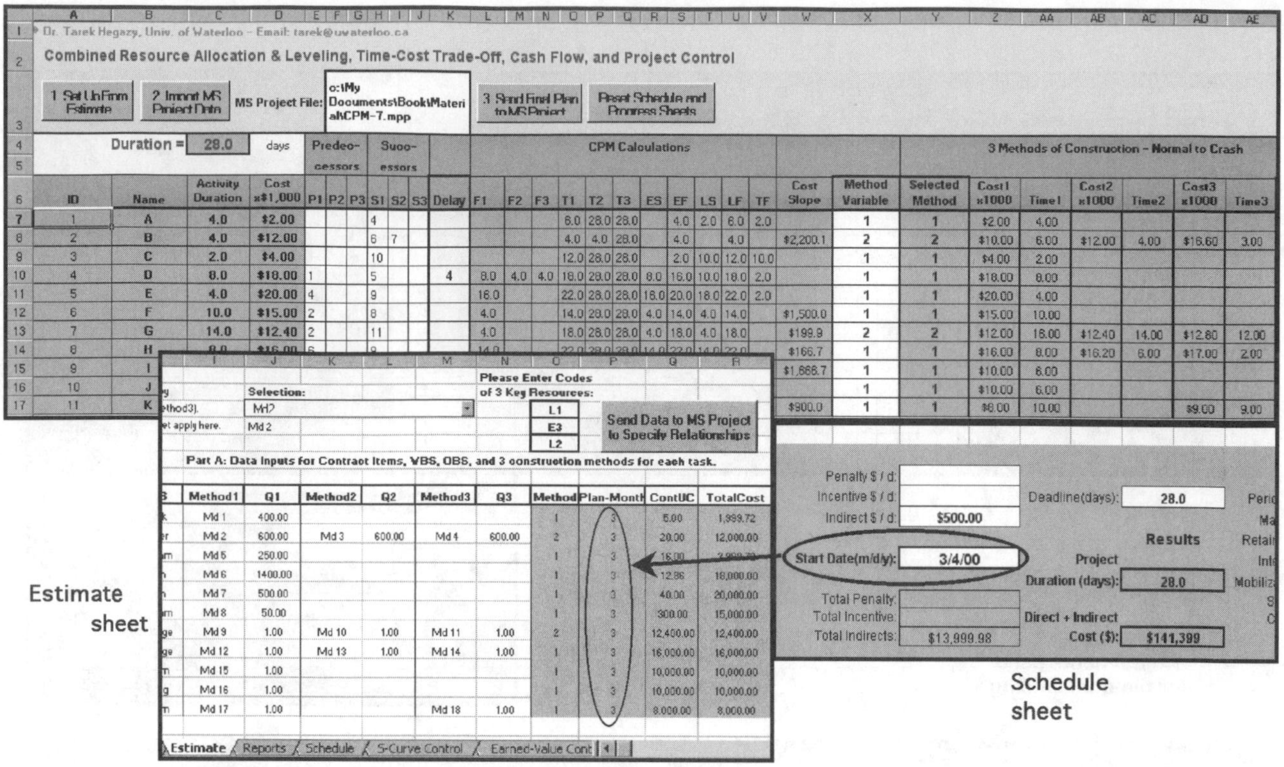

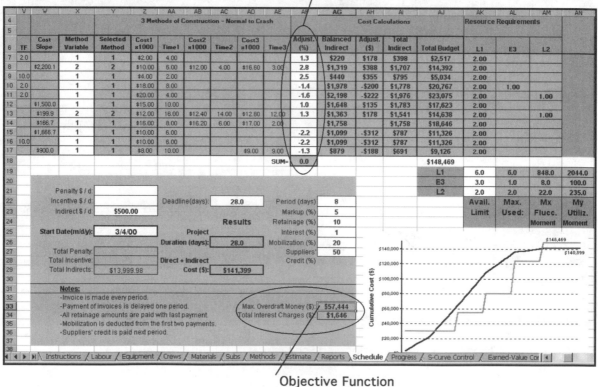

Figure 10-22. Link from the Schedule Sheet Back to the Estimate Sheet

Figure 10-23. Preparation for Cash Flow Optimization

Notice here that in our manual bid unbalancing that we discussed earlier, the resulting maximum overdraft amount is $57,444.

Figure 10-24.
Solver Screen with
Optimization Setup

Constraints are:
Adjustment
percentages are
limited to within
±5%; and total of all
adjustments = zero.

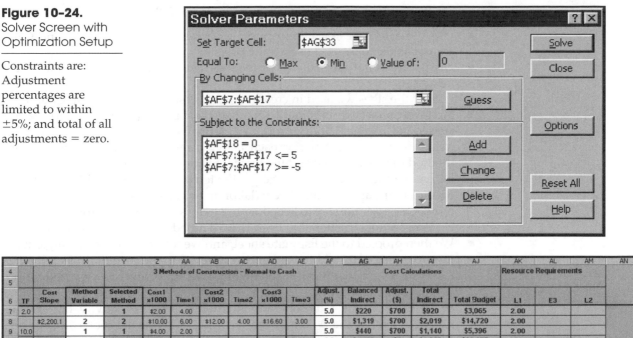

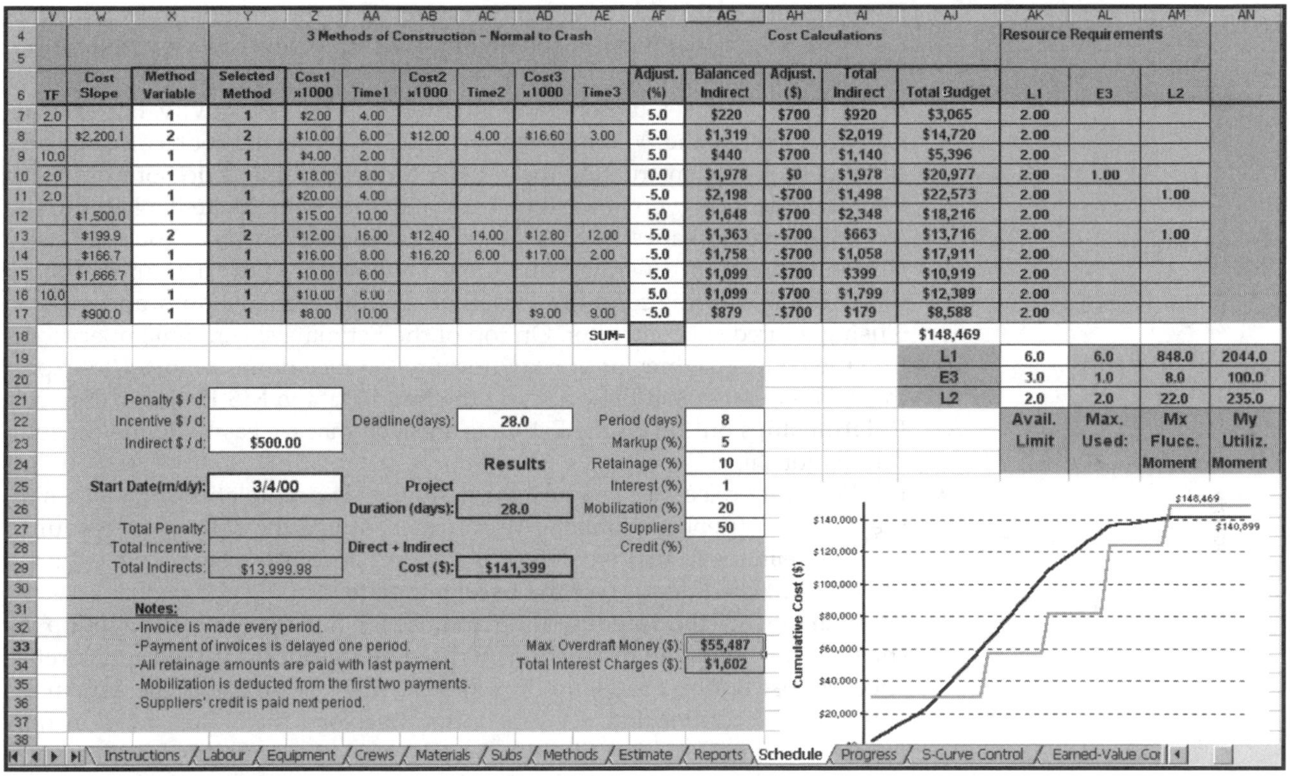

Figure 10-25. Cash Flow Optimization Result

Solver found an optimum solution with maximum overdraft amount of $55,487. This experiment shows that Solver can work easily for this problem. For consistency with the manual solution, however, in our case study we will adopt the schedule in Figure 10-23.

10.8.2 Using the Excel Template on Other Projects

The **Case-Study.xls** file works as a generalized model for resource data storage, estimating, scheduling, cash flow analysis, bidding, and project control. All elements of the schedule are variables that you can change, and its immediate effect on total project duration and cost is instantly shown. This sheet, as such, becomes a generalized model on which you can experiment with project cost optimization, under any set of constraints and variables. Later, in Chapter 11, we will continue using the template for progress evaluation and control during construction.

To use the file for a new project, we need to do the following:

- Use the **File-Save As** menu option of Excel to create a copy of the **Case-Study.xls** file to be used in the new project.
- Use the **Reset** button on the Schedule sheet to remove the data from the Schedule sheet.
- Follow the steps we used in creating our case study, starting from Chapter 3.
- First, the project team should finanlize their initial planning effort, as discussed in Chapters 3 and 4: project Work Breakdown Structure, three possible methods of construction for each activity, resource requirements for each method of construction, and the logical relationships between activities.
- Before we add project information to the template, you may add resource categories in the appropriate sheets (labor, material, etc) related to the project at hand. One essential step to keep in mind here is that activities are defined with methods of construction that need to be defined in the Methods sheet.
- We then proceed to the Estimate sheet, and we may overwrite existing data or remove some of the old rows that do not relate to the current project. Keep at least one row so that you can copy it and paste it to new rows with all formulas copied automatically.
- In the Estimate sheet, use one row to enter each project activity. For each activity, we specify the WBS information and we define the codes of three possible methods of constructing the activity (if these methods do not exist yet in the Methods sheet, you need to go back and add them. Make it a habit to use *method 1* as the cheapest and *method 3* as the most expensive. You may use a simple strategy to generate your three methods of construction: method 1 with normal working conditions, method 2 with overtime hours, and method 3 using a hired subcontractor. On top of the Estimate sheet, remember to define the codes for three of our key resources. Once done, we need to export their data to Microsoft Project using the **Send Data to MS Project to Specify Relationships** button on the Estimate sheet so that we easily define the logical relationships;
- In Microsoft Project, we can add the activities' logical relationships in a simple and user-friendly manner. We can then utilize the software's resource-leveling features so that we determine an initial solution before we export it back to the Schedule sheet of the Excel template.
- We then move to the Schedule sheet and use the first two buttons to set up the sheet. You will find all instructions written on the sheet for your quick reference. We use Button 1 to set up the schedule sheet according to the data in the Estimate sheet. After that, we use Button 2 to load the logical relationships from the Microsoft Project file. Afterwards, we can specify the deadline, indirect cost, and cash flow variables. During the sheet setup process, links are established from the Schedule sheet back to the Estimate sheet so that costs are modified depending on the time of year the activity is scheduled.
- Remember to estimate the project indirect cost using the **Indirect.xls** file and also to estimate the markup value to use in the project using the **Bidding.xls** file. These values are used as important parameters in schedule refinement.
- Once done, the model becomes ready for optimization. Similar to our discussion in this chapter and previous ones, the total cost becomes your objective function to minimize. Using a Genetic Optimization tool, you can specify the constraints and proceed with the optimization. A summary of the optimization experiments that you can conduct is given in the next section.
- Once a satisfactory project schedule is determined, you can proceed to the Reports sheet, refresh the pivot table data from the Pivot-Table toolbar and automatically a bid proposal form becomes ready for submission.
- If you successfully win the project, you can use the Progress sheet to enter actual performance data and then monitor the project progress during con-

struction (discussed in Chapter 11). Accordingly, cost control curves will adjust automatically.

- At any time, you may send the plan (and optionally actual progress data) to Microsoft Project (using Button 3) to utilize its powerful graphics and other project control features.
- It is noted that if you introduce changes to the number of activities in the project (has to be done in the Estimate sheet), you need to reset the schedule sheet using the fourth button. This will remove all data from the Schedule and Progress sheets, then you can repeat the process to adjust the template according to the new activities in the project.

10.8.3. Summary of Schedule Optimization Experiments

Table 10-6. Summary of Optimization Experiments

If You Want to:	Optimization Setup	
Resolve resource constraints	Objective function:	minimize project duration
	Variables:	values in the "delay" column
	Initial variable values:	delay values imported from Microsoft Project
	Constraints:	delay range (e.g., integers 0-5); daily resources <= maximum available (hard) sum of delays = minimum (soft).
Resolve resource constraints, reduce daily fluctuation, and release some resources early	Objective function:	minimize project duration
	Variables:	values in the "delay" column
	Initial variable values:	delay values imported from Microsoft Project
	Constraints:	delay range (e.g., integers 0-5); daily resources ™ = maximum available (hard); sum of delays = minimum (soft); (optional) moment M_x = minimum (soft); (optional) moment M_y = minimum (soft).
Meet deadline duration	Objective function:	minimize total project cost
	Variables:	the "Method Variable" column
	Initial variable values:	index to the shortest construction method
	Constraints:	variables range (integers 1-3); project duration <= deadline (hard).
Resolve resource constraints and meet deadline duration	Objective function:	minimize total project cost
	Variables:	"Delay" and "Method Variable" columns
	Initial variable values:	zero delays and shortest methods
	Constraints:	delay range (e.g., integers 0-5); Method variables (integers 1-3); Project duration <= deadline (hard); daily resources <= maximum available (soft); sum of delays = minimum (soft).

Table 10-6. Summary of Optimization Experiments (continued)

If You Want to:	Optimization Setup	
Resolve resource constraints, meet deadline duration, reduce daily fluctuation, and release some resources early	Objective function:	minimize total project cost
	Variables: Initial variable values:	"Delay" and "Method Variable" columns zero delays and shortest methods
	Constraints:	delay range (e.g., integers 0-5); method variables (integers 1-3); project duration <= deadline (hard); daily resources <= maximum available (soft); sum of delays = minimum (soft); (optional) moment M_x = minimum (soft); (optional) moment M_y = minimum (soft).
Optimize cash flow	Objective function:	minimize overdraft money (usually applied after one of the top experiments)
	Variables:	activities' adjustment column AF;
	Initial variable values:	zeroes
	Constraints:	adjustment range (integers –5 to +5); sum of the adjustment values = 0 (hard).
Optimize all aspects together: resources, deadline, and cash flow	Objective function:	minimize total project cost
	Variables:	"Delay" column, "Method Variable" column, and activities' adjustment column AF
	Initial variable values:	zero delays, shortest methods, & zero adjustment
	Constraints:	delay range (e.g., integers 0-5); method variables (integers 1-3); adjustment range (integers –5 to +5); project duration <= deadline (hard); daily resources <= maximum available (soft); sum of delays = minimum (soft); (optional) moment M_x = minimum (soft); (optional) moment M_y = minimum (soft); sum of the adjustment values = 0 (hard).

10.8.4   Finalizing Our Bid Proposal

Now, after we completed all planning and estimating steps and refined the schedule to account for resource constraints, deadline, and cash flow requirements, we can use the Reports sheet to show various important reports (Figure 10–26). The figure shows the three automated reports available. One important step is that we need to refresh the data in each report by selecting each report and selecting the Refresh button on the Pivot Table toolbar. The three reports are as follows:

a. A pivot table report of the *bid proposal* associated with the finalized plan. The report (Figure 10–26) shows the unit prices associated with the work items in the project, to be submitted to the owner.

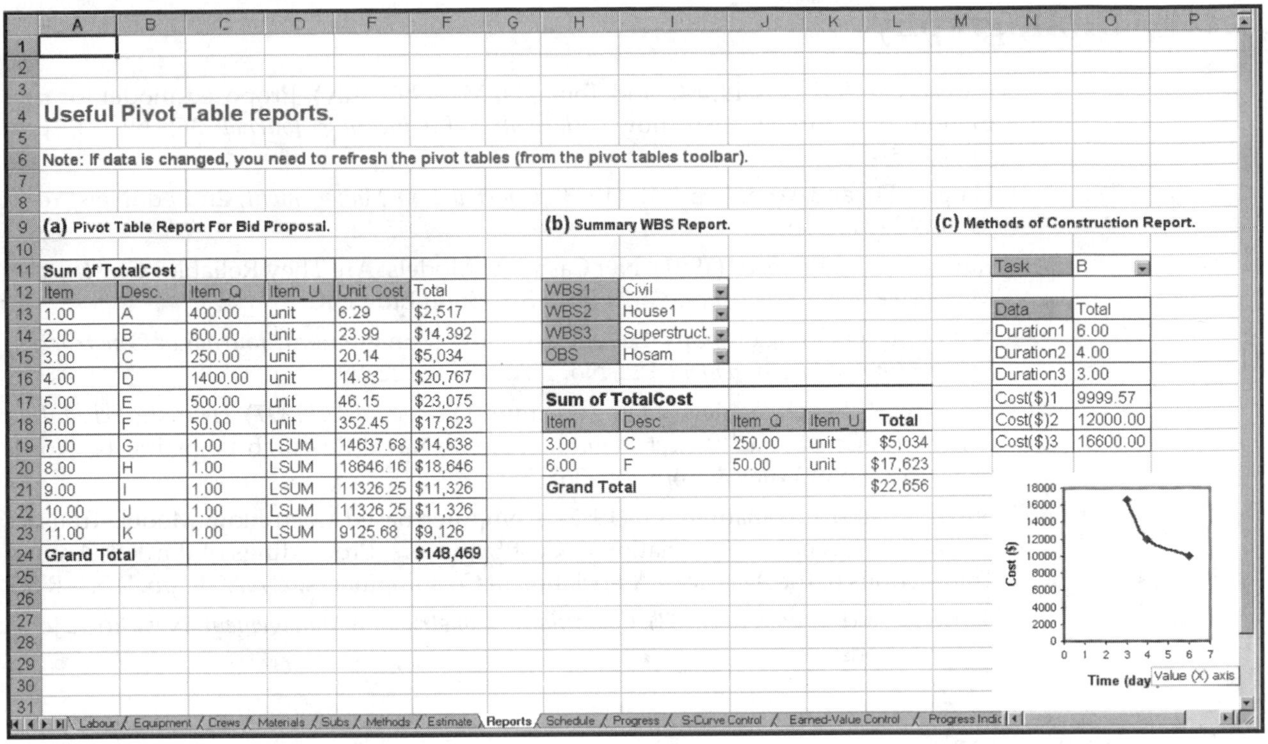

Sum of TotalCost

Item	Desc.	Item_Q	Item_U	Unit Cost	Total
1.00	A	400.00	unit	6.29	$2,517
2.00	B	600.00	unit	23.99	$14,392
3.00	C	250.00	unit	20.14	$5,034
4.00	D	1400.00	unit	14.83	$20,767
5.00	E	500.00	unit	46.15	$23,075
6.00	F	50.00	unit	352.45	$17,623
7.00	G	1.00	LSUM	14637.68	$14,638
8.00	H	1.00	LSUM	18646.16	$18,646
9.00	I	1.00	LSUM	11326.25	$11,326
10.00	J	1.00	LSUM	11326.25	$11,326
11.00	K	1.00	LSUM	9125.68	$9,126
Grand Total					$148,469

WBS1	Civil
WBS2	House1
WBS3	Superstruct.
OBS	Hosam

Sum of TotalCost

Item	Desc	Item_Q	Item_U	Total
3.00	C	250.00	unit	$5,034
6.00	F	50.00	unit	$17,623
Grand Total				$22,656

Task	B
Data	Total
Duration1	6.00
Duration2	4.00
Duration3	3.00
Cost($)1	9999.57
Cost($)2	12000.00
Cost($)3	16600.00

Figure 10-26 Automated Project Reports

b. A pivot table that summarizes the costs associated with the work breakdown structure items and the organization breakdown structure items of the project. In Figure 10–26, for example, the report shows the total budget of the Civil-Superstructure work supervised by Hosam as $22,656. Using this report, you can select the WBS and OBS levels you would like to have a report on.

c. A pivot table report on the time-cost relationships among the three methods of construction for any activity that you select in the report.

10.9 Summary

The flow of money from the owner to the contractor is in the form of progress payments. Estimates of work completed are made by the contractors periodically (usually monthly), and are verified by the owner's representative. Depending on the type of contract (e.g., lump sum, unit price, etc.), these estimates are based on evaluations of the percentage of total contract completion or actual field measurements of quantities placed. Owners usually retain 10% of all validated progress payment claims submitted by contractors. The accumulated retainage payments are usually paid to the contractor with the last payment.

Various options are available to the contractor to improve project financing, including: 1) realistic bid unbalancing; 2) subcontracting; and 3) owner mobilization payment. With project financing being costly to contractors, a scheduling model on Excel has been developed to allow us to optimize the schedule considering all our project management needs.

10.10 Bibliography

Eldosouky, A. I., Elsaid, M., and Toma, H. M. (1997, July). Proposed model for prediction of contract cash flow, *Alexandria Engineering Journal 36*, No. 4, July pp. C353–C364.

Halpin, D., and Woodhead, R. (1998). *Construction Management,* 2nd ed. New York: John Wiley & Sons.

KaKa, A., and Price, A. (1991). Net Cashflow Models: Are They Reliable? *Construction Management and Economics,* Vol. 9, E. & F.N. Spon Ltd., UK.

Navon, R. (1996). Company-Level Cash-Flow Management, *Journal of Construction Engineering and Management 122,* No. 1, ASCE, pp. 22–29.

Padman, R., Smith-Daniels., D.E., and Smith-Daniels, V. L. (1997). *Heuristic Scheduling of Resource-Constrained Projects with Cash Flows,* Naval Research Logistics, 44, No. 4, New York: John Wiley & Sons, pp. 365–381.

Singh, S., and Lokanathan, G. (1992). Computer-Based Cash-Flow Model, Transactions of the American Association of Cost Engineers, Proceedings of the 36th Annual Transactions of the American Association of Cost Engineers, 2, AACE, pp. R.5.1–R.5.1

Stark, R., and Mayer, R. (1983). *Quantitative Construction Management.* New York: John Wiley & Sons.

10.11 Exercises

1. The following table shows a contractor's project budget and profit for a new contract:

Month Number	1	2	3	4	5	6	7	8	9	10
Value of work each month (× $1000)	2	3	4	8	9	9	8	5	4	2
% Profit charged	6	6	6	6	6	6	6	10	10	10

Measurements are made monthly with payment delay of one month and 10% retention. Half the retention is paid on completion and the other half is released six months after completion. Draw the cumulative income and expense curves and determine the monthly net cash flow. Interest rate is 1% per period.

2. The data of a small project are as follows. The indirect cost for this contract is $250/week. Determine the schedule timing of the activities so that the weekly cost of the contract will not exceed $750/week.

Activity	Predecessors	Duration (week)	Cost ($)
A	-	7	1400
B	-	9	4500
C	A	8	2400
D	B	12	1200
E	C, D	4	800
F	B	9	2700
G	F	7	2100
H	E, G	7	4900

3. The table below lists the cumulative monthly expenses incurred by a contractor and the corresponding monthly payments received from the owner of a project. Calculate the cost to the contractor of providing the working capital necessary to finance the project if interest rate is 10%. If the owner makes his payments one month later than anticipated in the table, by what percentage will the financial charge increase?

End of Month	Cumulative Expense ($ × 1000)	Cumulative Income ($ × 1000)
0	0	0
1	12	0
2	20	0
3	54	0
4	90	14
5	130	40
6	180	100
7	220	130
8	240	190
9	260	210
10	290	300
11	290	320
12	290	340

4. Briefly discuss the factors that minimize the contractor's negative cash flow required to execute a construction contract.

5. The activities involved in the construction of a small building are given below. The price of the work contained in each activity is listed in the table. The contractor undertaking this project would like you to prepare graphs of cumulative expense and income to date against time for activities starting as early as possible. The markup is 10% of tender value and retention is 5%. Measurement is made monthly with a payment delay of one month. The retention is paid at the end of the contract. To simplify the calculations you may assume that all costs must be paid by the end of the month in which they are incurred. What is the maximum amount of cash the contractor needs to execute this contract and when does he require this amount?

No.	Activity	Duration (months)	Predecessors	Overlap	Value ($)
10	Excavation	2	-	-	9,000
20	Concrete bases	3	10	1	12,000
30	Erect frames	1.5	20	1	18,000
40	Concrete floor slab	1	20	1	15,000
50	Fix cladding	1.5	30	1	6,000
60	Install plant	1	40, 50	-	20,000

6. A simplified project is shown in the following figure. The direct costs associated with the individual activities are shown above the bars. It is assumed that project indirect cost will amount to $5,000 monthly. The contractor included a profit mark-up of $10,000 to his bid so that the total bid price was $210,000. The owner retains 10% of all validated progress payments until one half of the contract value (i.e., $105,000). The progress payments will be billed at the end of the month and the owner will transfer the billed amount minus any retains to the contractor's account 30 days later. Determine the expenses and income profile of this project.

Activity			
A	50000		
B		40000	
C		60000	
D			30000

Time →

7. A contractor's expected monthly cost (direct plus indirect) is shown in the following table. Find the highest amount of cash he or she needs and the month in which this amount is required. Contract conditions are as follows:

- The contractor adds a markup of 8% to the total cost before submitting an invoice.
- Owner retention is 10% of the requested amount.
- Average delay between a request for payment and making the payment is one month.
- A mobilization payment (20% of total contract value) is paid to the contractor and will be deducted from the first two owner payments (50% each).
- Bank interest rate is 14% per annum.

End of Month	0	1	2	3	4	5	6	7	8	9	10
Direct Cost		2400	2400	3400	5400	5400	7400	5400	3400	1400	–
Indirect Cost		600	600	600	600	600	600	600	600	600	–

8. Answer question 7 under the following changes in contract conditions:

- Half of the monthly direct costs shown in the table are credit given by suppliers who agreed to get their money one month after credit is made.
- There is no mobilization payment.

Chapter 11

CONSTRUCTION PROGRESS CONTROL

A fter studying this chapter, you will be able to:

- Understand the basics of project control and how to bring success to construction.
- Learn the site measurements needed to evaluate actual construction progress.
- Compare actual versus planned progress of work using the Earned Value technique.
- Determine schedule updating needs and the impact of changes.
- Forecast the actual cost at project completion based on the actual progress of work.
- Experiment with various software tools for project control.
- Understand the basis of the critical chain concept for project control.

Owner, CM	A/E, CM, Owner	Bidders	Owner, CM	Contractor	O & M Staff
• Need • Feasibility • Project Definition • Owner Approval	• Conceptual Design • Owner Approval • Soil Reports • Preliminary Design • Detailed Design • Quantities • Work Documents • Select Project Contract Strategy	• Prepare Bid Proposal + Baselines • Collect Data (site, quantities, specs, resources, tasks, etc) • Planning • Time & Cost Estimation • Scheduling • Resource Management: Adjustments for Resource Constraints & Deadline • Bidding Strategy & Markup Estimation • Cash Flow Analysis • Submit Bid	• Evaluate Bids and Select General Contractor	• Start Construction • Detailed Planning, Estimating & Resource Management • **Schedule Updating** • **Progress Evaluation** • **Time, Cost, & Quality Control** • Commissioning	• O & M • Demolition at End of Service Life
CONCEPT	DESIGN	BIDDING		CONSTRUCTION	O & M

11.1 Preparing for the Big Challenge: Construction

In the previous chapters, you have learned various techniques for scheduling and resource management so that your bid proposal is both competitive and realistic. In this chapter, we will assume the role of the contractor who won the job and is in the process of bringing the plan into action during construction. Before we embark on actual construction, however, let's look at the global picture and formulate reasonable expectations of the construction environment so that we can be more prepared to deal with its challenges.

11.1.1 Problems during Construction

Anyone who is involved in the construction business will be able to recognize various common factors in almost all projects:

- Construction is a dusty, dirty, and multifaceted operation. Material is delivered daily at the same time that tens to hundreds of workers must come together to complete their assignments. As construction proceeds, the site becomes congested.
- Despite the fact that the estimate and plans were made with a large factor of safety in each and every task, many activities consume more than their estimated time and cost. This is because trades tend to delay their start to the last minute, thus wasting float time (referred to as student syndrome).
- Even if one crew or trade works in a more productive way and finishes its work early, the following trades are not obliged to start earlier than initially planned. Thus, earlier work is not reflected on the project. Rather, the more productive crew may be penalized by cutting its estimates on new projects or even getting it dowsized.
- During construction, frequent changes are introduced to the scope of work, thus causing a lot of work disruption and cost overrun.
- In the midst of the work, some trades proceed slower than desired whereas others proceed faster than desired, and in both cases, delays occur.
- Dealing with suppliers and subcontractors also may not be easy.

11.1.2 Objectives of Project Control

During construction, our objective is to make sure that we execute the project as smoothly as possible so that the planned level of profit can be attained. This means we need to:

- Accurately follow the project plan.
- Update the project plan based on new circumstances.
- Monitor actual site execution and keep track of resources.
- Provide detailed progress reports, comparing actual versus planned progress.
- At any stage during construction, forecast the cost at completion.
- Take corrective actions at any stage to bring time and cost closer to the plan.

We can divide these responsibilities into four main aspects, as shown in Figure 11–1. Each of these is dealt with in a separate subsection.

Figure 11-1.
Elements of Project
Control

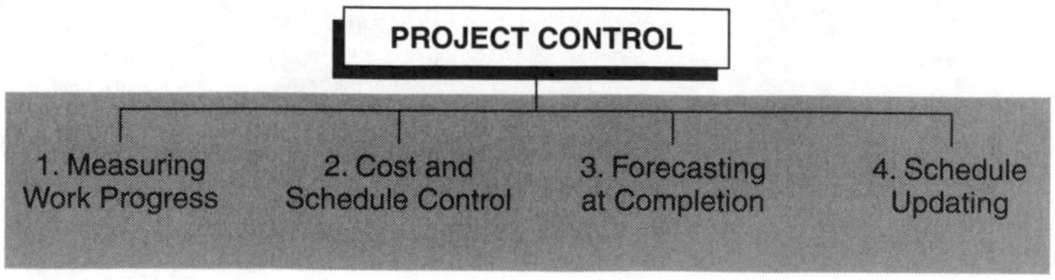

PROJECT CONTROL			
1. Measuring Work Progress	2. Cost and Schedule Control	3. Forecasting at Completion	4. Schedule Updating

11.2 Measuring Work Progress

During the course of construction, the individuals executing it must periodically report the progress on each activity. Because the nature of each activity varies, no single reporting method is suitable and several methods of measuring progress are required. The convenient measure of the work progress of each activity is in terms of the percentage of work done each day or within a given period, referred to as its *percent complete*.

11.2.1 Calculating Activities' Percent Complete

The most common six methods for calculating the activities' percent complete based on actual progress on site are presented as follows:

1. **Units Completed:** Applies to activities that involve repeated production of easily measured units of work (e.g., pile driving).

$$\% \text{ Complete} = \text{Units Completed} / \text{Total Units}$$

2. **Incremental Milestone:** Applies to activities that include subtasks that must be handled in sequence. Each milestone is assigned a certain percentage as a rule of credit.

   For example, Installation of Major Equipment:
Receive & Inspect	15%
Setting Complete	35%
Alignment Complete	50%
Internals Installed	75%
Testing Complete	90%
Accepted by Owner	100%

3. **Start/Finish:** Applies to activities that lack readily definable intermediate milestones or those for which the effort/time is difficult to estimate (e.g., planning activities). A percent complete is arbitrarily assigned to the start of a task, and 100% is recorded when the task is finished. The start and finish percentages are assigned depending on the duration and value of the activity, as shown here.

		Duration		
		V. Short	**Short**	**Long**
Value	**Low**	0, 100	50, 100	20, 100
	High	0, 100	30, 100	20, 100

4. **Supervisor Opinion:** Applies to minor activities and requires the subjective judgment of supervisors. Examples are dewatering, temporary construction, and landscaping.
5. **Cost Ratio:** Applies to activities that are budgeted based on a bulk allocation of dollars and involve a long time or are continuous during the life of a project (e.g., project management, quality assurance, and project controls).

$$\% \text{ Complete} = \frac{\text{Actual Cost (or hrs) of Work to Date}}{\text{Forecast at Completion}}$$

6. **Weighed or Equivalent Units:** Applies to activities that are composed of two or more overlapping subtasks, each with a different unit of work measurement. In essence, all the elements are converted into an equivalent amount of a unified measurement unit. In the following example, a structural steel with a total weight of 520 tons is used as an example. All subtasks are converted into their equivalent steel tons as a unified measurement unit.

Example: Structural Steel Erection

Weight (1) cost/total	Subtask	Unit	Total Quantity (2)	Quantity to Date (3)	Earned Tons (4)
0.02	Run Found. Bolts	Each	200	200	10.4
0.02	Shim	%	100	100	10.4
0.05	Shakeout	%	100	100	26
0.06	Columns	Each	84	74	27.5
0.11	Beams	Each	859	45	3
0.10	Cross Braces	Each	837	0	0
0.20	Girts & Sag Rods	Each	38	0	0
0.09	Plumb & Align	%	100	5	2.3
0.30	Connections	Each	2977	74	3.9
0.05	Punch List	%	100	0	0

Total Steel Tons = 520   **83.5**

$$\text{Earned Tons to Date (4)} = \frac{\text{Quantity to Date (3)}}{\text{Total Quantity (2)}} \times \text{Weight (1)} \times \text{Total Steel Tons}$$

$$= 74/84 \times 0.06 \times 520 = 27.5 \text{ Tons; and}$$

$$\% \text{ Complete} = \frac{\Sigma \text{ Earned Tons}}{\text{Total Steel Tons}}$$

$$= 83.5/520 = 16.1\%$$

11.2.2 Calculating the Project's Percent Complete

It is possible to measure the work progress done on a daily basis within each activity based on daily site reports. For the purpose of reporting to management and for submitting invoices to owners, progress is calculated at prespecified intervals (e.g., monthly). The end-of-period report can be easily obtained by accumulating the total percent complete in each activity for all work performed within the period.

Based on the activities' percentage complete, we can calculate the overall project percent complete, the budget value of the work done, and other information related to progress payments. The relationship between the individual activities' percent complete and the overall project percent complete can be illustrated in the following example.

Example

The planned versus actual bar charts of a completed project are shown in Figure 11–2. Each week, the planned amount of work is prorated according to the activity duration. The actual progress, however, is shown as percent complete done within each period (week) on the actual bar chart.

Figure 11–2.
Planned versus
Actual Bar Charts

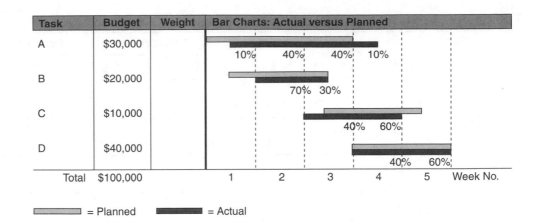

Task	Budget	Weight	Bar Charts: Actual versus Planned
A	$30,000		10% 40% 40% 10%
B	$20,000		70% 30%
C	$10,000		40% 60%
D	$40,000		40% 60%
Total	$100,000		1 2 3 4 5 Week No.

▭ = Planned   ▬ = Actual

a. Calculate the planned versus actual percent complete at the end of each week and draw the budget S-curves of planned versus actual progress.
b. Compare the actual versus planned progress of the project by end of week 4.
c. Calculate the Earned Value (i.e., the budgeted cost of the actual work) in the second period.

Solution

a. To calculate the percent complete, we proceed as follows:
   - We deal with planned separately from actual progress.
   - The planned percent complete at the end of each week is prorated with activity duration.
   - If you add the weekly percent completes of each activity in Figure 11–2, they add up to 100%. These percentages then are written cumulatively, as shown in Table 11–1.
   - We calculate the weight of each activity as the activity's total budget in proportion to the total project budget.
   - Now, we calculate the project percent complete at the end of each week (planned separately from actual), using the numbers in Table 11–1, as follows:

Project percent complete at any date

$$= \sum_{i=1}^{n} \textbf{Cumulative percent complete to date}_i \times \textbf{Weight}_i$$

Where, i = activity number 1, 2, . . . n.

For example, **Actual project percent complete at end of week 2** = 0.50×0.3 (A) + 0.70×0.2 (B) + 0×0.1 (C) + 0×0.4 (D) = 0.29 = **29%**

Following that, the project percent complete in all weeks is calculated as shown in Table 11–2.

   - *Interpretation:* Notice that the project proceeded in week 1 slower than planned but managed to get closer to planned in the following periods.
   - Now, we can plot the S curves (Figure 11–3) based on the data in Table 11–2.

b. By the end of week 4, planned progress (project percent complete) is 77.5% as compared to the actual percent complete of 76%.
c. The actual work done in the second period, as shown in Figure 11–2, is 40% of activity A and 70% of activity B. With (n) activities in the project,

Table 11-1. Cumulative Percent Complete in the Individual Activities

Task	Budget	Weight		Cumulative Percent Complete at End of Week No.				
				1	**2**	**3**	**4**	**5**
A	$30,000	30%*	Plan	0.333	0.666	1.0	1.0	1.0
			Actual	0.1	0.5	0.9	1.0	1.0
B	$20,000	20%	Plan	0.25	0.75	1.0	1.0	1.0
			Actual		0.7	1.0	1.0	1.0
C	$10,000	10%	Plan			0.25	0.75	1.0
			Actual			0.4	1.0	1.0
D	$40,000	40%	Plan				0.5	1.0
			Actual				0.4	1.0

* Activity weight = Activity cost / Total project cost

Table 11-2. Project Percent Complete

		Project Percent Complete at End of Week No.				
		1	**2**	**3**	**4**	**5**
Project Percent Complete:	Plan	0.15	0.35	0.525	0.775	1.0
	Actual	0.03	0.29	0.51	0.76	1.0

Figure 11-3.
Planned versus
Actual Progress

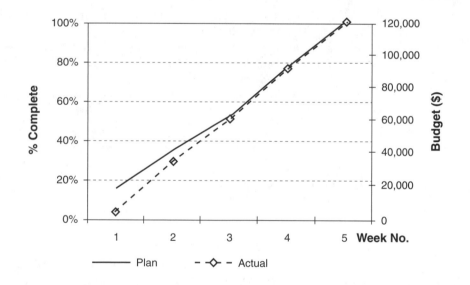

In General, **Earned Value = Actual Percent Complete × Budget.**
Thus, at the project level with n activities:

Earned Value = Budget of Actual Work

$$= \sum_{i=1}^{n} \textbf{Actual Percent Complete}_i \times \textbf{Budget}_i$$

Now, Earned Value at end of period 2 = 0.4 × $30,000 + 0.7 × $20,000
= $26,000

Another way to calculate this budget value is from the cumulative project progress in Table 11–2 and Figure 11–3, as follows:

Earned Value in period 2 only = (0.29 − 0.03) × $100,000 = $26,000

11.3   Cost and Schedule Control

The concepts discussed thus far provide a system for determining the percent complete of a single activity or a project as a whole. The next challenge is to analyze the results and to determine how well things are proceeding according to plan through a control system. Along the project, various reports should be prepared to determine those activities where expenses are excessive or delays are bound to occur. The objectives of a control system are:

1. To draw immediate attention to any activity that is proving to be uneconomic to the contractor, in order that corrective action can be taken to keep cost within acceptable bounds;
2. To analyze the construction progress in every period and determine how well things are proceeding according to the plan; and
3. To develop actual production rates of labor and equipment and actual percentages of material wastage to feedback estimating of future works.

The various techniques used for cost and schedule control are described in the following subsections.

11.3.1   S-Curve Method

In this method, we use the same calculations presented in Section 11.2.2 for comparing the actual versus the planned S-curves. However, the planned S-curve can be plotted as an envelope bounded by the early-start S-curve and the late-start S-curve, as shown in Figure 11–4. The shape and the width of the project's time-cost envelope will depend upon the relative amount of float each activity in the network has. Basically, a wide envelope indicates more flexibility than a narrow envelope.

Notice in Figure 11–4 that we compare actual expenditures to the planned costs (direct + indirect), not the budget. Also, it is possible draw an S-curve that is average of the early-start and the late-start S-curves and then use these curves for decision making. For example, if at any reporting period, the actual cost point is above the average S-curve, then we can assume that we have additional project expenses. One of the drawbacks of this method, however, is that it does not tell us if these extra expenses are caused by a fast execution of more work items than planned or simply because of higher unit rates paid to execute less work than planned. Therefore, while we can tell that the project exhibits a cost overrun, we have no indication on the amount of work for which these expenses were incurred.

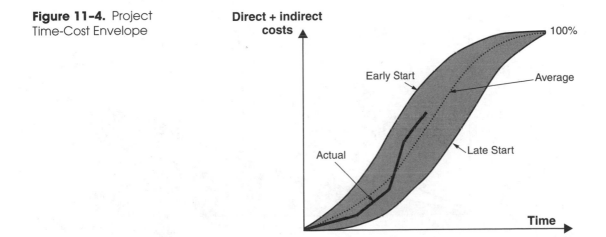

Figure 11-4. Project Time-Cost Envelope

11.3.2 Double S-Curve Method

To circumvent the drawback in the S-curve approach, a double S-curve approach can be used. In this approach, we plot actual versus planned costs (left-side y-axis) on the same plot with actual versus planned hours needed for the execution of the project (right-side y-axis), as shown in Figure 11–5.

In this case, we can not only view the cost progress but also the work hours (indicating the amount of work done). While the double S-curve approach is useful, particularly for projects in which a detailed estimate of the planned work hours is available (e.g., schedule of rates contracts), reading the progress from this plot can be misleading and requires extra care. For example, at time "Now" in Figure 11–5, it is possible to read the project as follows:

- The project exhibits a cost overrun equal to the distance between points "E" and "e."
- The project exhibits a slow work progress (schedule delay) indicated by the distance between points A and a.

Based on these progress evaluations, it is possible to conclude that the amount of cost overrun and the delay are not excessive and can be recovered in the remaining time till completion. However, this is a misleading picture of project performance and the reason is as follows:

- Point A shows the level of work done till time "Now";
- Using a horizontal line, point B shows the time at which the current level of work was supposed to be completed;
- Using a vertical line from point B, point C is the level of planned cost that correspond to the amount of work done;
- Using a horizontal line from point C, point D is the planned cost for the work done at time "Now"; and
- Recalculating the cost overrun of the project based on the amount of work done at time "Now" (the distance between points "E" and "D"), which is much larger than the cost overrun assumed earlier.

From that, we conclude that the two above techniques have their drawbacks and a more rigorous approach is still needed. This is discussed in the next subsection.

Figure 11-5.
Double S-Curve Plot

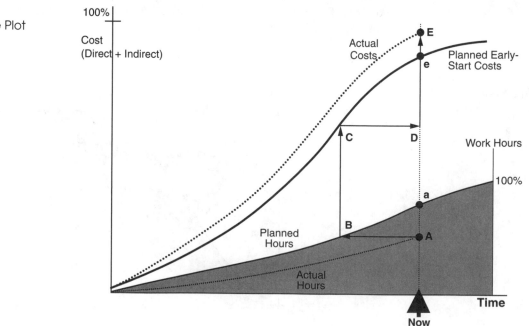

11.3.3 The Earned Value Technique

The Earned Value technique lends itself very well to the analysis of the cost and schedule performance in a project. It involves a combination of three measures that are needed for the analysis (Figure 11–6). The Earned Value system defines these terms as follows:

- *Budgeted Cost of Work Scheduled (BCWS):* measures *What is Planned* in terms of budget cost of the work that should take place (i.e., according to the baseline schedule of the work). Along the project, we can plot the BCWS S-curve by accumulating the budget cost on the schedule that shows the planned percent complete (similar to the example in section 11.3.2).
- *Budgeted Cost of Work Performed (BCWP) — Earned Value:* measures *What is Done* in terms of the budget cost of work that has actually been accomplished to date. We also plot the BCWP S-curve point by point after each reporting period. Here, we accumulate the budget cost on the schedule that shows the actual percent complete;
- *Actual Cost of Work Performed (ACWP):* measures *What is Paid* in terms of the actual cost of work that has actually been accomplished to date. We also plot the ACWP S-curve point by point after each reporting period. Here, we accumulate the actual expenditures on the schedule that shows the actual percent complete.

The significance of these three indicators is that they directly indicate the schedule and cost performances of the project at its different reporting period. This is illustrated as shown in Figure 11–7.

Now, applying the SPI and CPI performance indicators to the project illustrated in Figure 11–6, we can see that the project at time "Now" exhibits a schedule delay and a cost overrun. In our project control system, these provide warning signs and mandate corrective actions. In the next reporting period, new values for the BCWP and ACWP S-curves will be plotted and then used to calculate new SPI and CPI values to see if improvements are achieved in the project performance.

To facilitate the follow-up on project performance from one reporting period to the other, it is possible to draw a plot of the CPI versus SPI as shown in Figure 11–8. The figure connects the performance points in all periods, starting from the start of the project.

Figure 11-6.
Earned Value
Measures

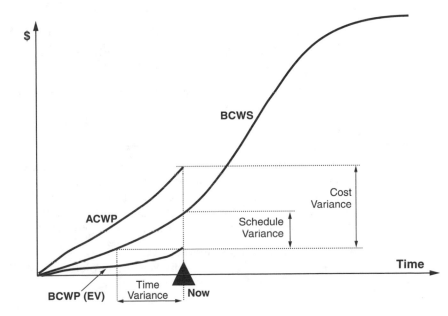

Figure 11-7.
Relationship
between Earned
Value Measures

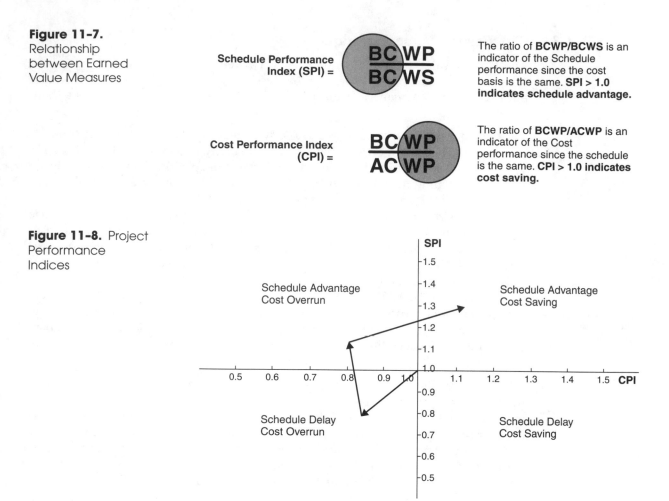

Schedule Performance
Index (SPI) =

$$\frac{BCWP}{BCWS}$$

The ratio of **BCWP/BCWS** is an indicator of the Schedule performance since the cost basis is the same. **SPI > 1.0 indicates schedule advantage.**

Cost Performance Index
(CPI) =

$$\frac{BCWP}{ACWP}$$

The ratio of **BCWP/ACWP** is an indicator of the Cost performance since the schedule is the same. **CPI > 1.0 indicates cost saving.**

Figure 11-8. Project
Performance
Indices

In addition to the SPI and the CPI, other performance indicators are:

- *Schedule Variance (SV):* difference between the actual cost (ACWP) and the Earned Value or the budget cost (BCWP).

$$SV = BCWP - BCWS; \quad \textbf{SV > 0 indicates Schedule Advantage}$$

- *Cost Variance (CV):* difference between the actual cost (ACWP) and the Earned Value or the budget cost (BCWP).

$$CV = BCWP - ACWP; \quad \textbf{CV > 0 indicates Cost Saving}$$

11.4   Forecasting

Along with progress measurement and performance evaluation, an important aspect of project control is to forecast the project completion cost at different stages of execution. One of the simple approaches for forecasting the Estimate at Completion (EAC) is by adjusting the Scheduled Budget (BCWS) according to the difference between the actual cost (ACWP) and budget cost (BCWP), as follows:

Estimate at completion (**EAC**)
$$= \textbf{BCWS} \text{ at completion} + (\textbf{ACWP} - \textbf{BCWP}) \text{ at present}$$

Graphically, the estimate for the actual costs from the present time till project completion is plotted parallel to the BCWS curve but shifted according to the difference between actual and budgeted costs of the works completed at present, as shown in Figure 11–9. It is noted that the end point represents the estimate at completion EAC costs. This EAC keeps changing as we update the progress from one reporting period to the other. The EAC value also can be adjusted further by adding possible additional costs such as:

- Outstanding commitments including changes issued.
- Known changes that are not yet issued.
- Allowance for unidentified changes.
- Claims received or anticipated and not yet settled.

Figure 11-9.
Estimate at Completion (EAC) on Earned Value Curves

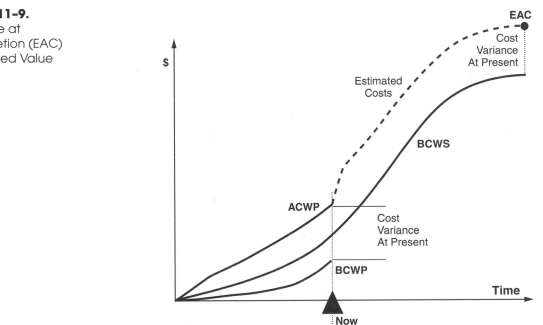

11.5   Schedule Updating

At any stage during construction, our plan becomes the baseline against which we compare actual progress. However, because changes during construction are imminent, soon the plan becomes unrealistic and needs to be updated to reflect the new circumstances. It is advisable to frequently update the plan at reasonable intervals. When we update the plan (for the following reasons), we will have a new baseline against which we compare actual progress.

Reasons for schedule updating:

- Changes in actual activity durations and network logic.
- Procurement delays.
- Sudden changes regarding the availability of craftsmen.
- Accidents.
- Strikes.
- Changes in owner requirements or in design.

Frequency of Schedule Updating:

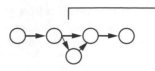

Depending on Network Shape

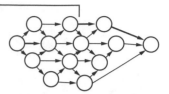

Linear networks (high percent
of all activities are critical)

Use fixed updating intervals
(monthly or shorter)

Fan-shaped networks (small
percent of all activities are critical)

Decreasing updating intervals
(large interval at beginning,
decreases towards end)

Schedule updating procedure:

- All completed activities become fixed in the revised plan.
- A new estimate of the amount of work remaining to be done should be made for each activity at the time of updating.
- The probable output of various resources should be assessed to revise the durations of future and proceeding activities.
- If the job is behind schedule, future activities may be crashed or new methods of construction introduced. Other remedial courses may include the redistribution of resources.
- Network analysis should be performed with an attempt to reschedule the work to obtain the cheapest overall solution to project constraints.

11.5.1 Evaluation of Work Changes and Delays

Work changes mean changes in the volume and duration of work to be performed from that envisaged at the start of the contract. Variation in the form of addition results in more or less cost and time to execute the changed item. On the other hand, work omissions mean less cost but not necessarily less time and may result in wasting resources. If the quantity of work in a critical activity is increased by $x\%$, for example, then the duration of the activity will be extended by $x\%$. The direct cost of the activity should be increased by the same ratio whereas the indirect cost of the contract might be increased for the extended period.

11.5.1.1 Types of Delays   Delays can be divided into the following categories:

Compensable delays: A delay is compensable to the contractor when it is caused by the owner (*o delay*). Examples include:

- Late possession of site;
- Faulty design;
- Incomplete drawings and specification;
- Changes in scope;
- Suspension of work;
- Differing site conditions;
- Late delivery of owner-supplied materials; and
- Owner failure to disclose information vital to the contractor.

The conditions of contract should allow the contractor to be entitled to a time extension and to monetary recompense for extra costs associated with these delays.

Nonexcusable delays: In this category, the contractor caused the delay (*c delay*). The contractor is entitled neither to time extensions nor to monetary recompense from the owner. He may pay liquidated damages according to the contract.

Excusable delays: These are occurrences over which neither the owner nor the contractor have any control (*n delay*). Examples include:

- Unforeseen future events (e.g., strikes);
- Impracticable work which the contractor can only do at excessive cost; and
- Events in that the contractor is blameless, such as material shortage beyond what was expected at the time of bidding.

The contractor should declare the excusable delays and can be entitled to a time extension.

Concurrent delays: Concurrent delays are two or more delays that occur at the same time and can be classified as follows:

1. Owner o delays and contractor c delays are concurrent;
2. Owner o delays, contractor c delays, and excusable n delays are concurrent;
3. Excusable n delays and contractor c delays are concurrent; and
4. Excusable n delays and owner o delays are concurrent.

When owner o delays and contractor c delays are concurrent (case 1), the contractor is allowed a time extension, with each party suffering its own losses (i.e., liquidated damages/compensation). The terms of the contract should declare the method of evaluation of such claims. On the other hand, when excusable delays are involved concurrently with other delays (cases 2, 3, and 4), the contractor is entitled to time extension if the delays are on the critical path. This protects him from any resulting liquidated damages.

11.5.1.2 Analysis of the As-Built Schedule   The *as-planned* schedule of a contract is its initial schedule. The *as-built* schedule will show the time status of the contract and the causes of all the time changes that happen. For comparison purposes and to facilitate the analysis of delays, both schedules are drawn as *time-scaled* diagrams.

The as-built schedule provides a compete record of the work as built. It shows all delays encountered and the actual starting and finishing dates of every activity. When compared with the initial schedule, it gives the date for the evaluation of each time delay encountered during construction. This schedule becomes the basis for analysis of the effect of different types of delays on the contractor's progress.

Step1: Identifying Primary Paths

If the as-built schedule contains more than one equally delayed critical path, each of them will be examined in turn to determine its net duration, which is the actual duration of this path under no changes or delays. This is:

Net Path Duration = Total path duration − all delay times lying on the path

Having examined all critical paths, we can determine the primary critical path(s) as those with the longest net duration. The project could not have been completed in less time than this, even if the delays had not occurred.

Step 2: Analysis of Primary Path(s)

If the as-built schedule contains one primary critical path, then the overall effects of all changes on the contract will be the difference between the path's actual duration and its net duration. The responsibility of each party for the delayed completion is then determined by the amount of delay days this party caused to the primary path. Liquidated damages, time extension amount, and compensation to the contractor are then determined.

If the schedule contains more than one primary critical path with the same net duration, then it may have concurrent delays. In this situation, analysis of the time-scaled as-built schedule is carried out as follows:

a. The number of days in which owner o delays and contractor c delays are concurrent on the different primary paths are determined.

b. The number of days of concurrent delays involving excusable n delays are determined.

c. Excluding the delays in 1 and 2 above, the number of days a contractor should be assessed for liquidated damages is the smallest number of days of c delays on all primary critical paths.

d. Excluding the delays in 1 and 2 above, the number of days a contractor should be reimbursed for additional overhead expense plus a time extension is the smallest number of days of owner o delays on all primary critical paths.

e. The number of days of excusable delays is the difference between the total delay duration and the summation of all the above four delays. These are part of the time extension given to the contractor.

Example

Consider the contract given in the Table 11–3. The delay report given in Table 11–4 was recorded for this contract. Determine how each party is responsible for the contract delayed completion.

Solution

The as-planned and as-built schedules are drawn below.

Step 1: Identifying Primary Paths

The two critical paths are B-E-H-J and A-C-F-I. Each of them has a net duration = 41 − 18 = 23 days, thus both are considered primary paths.

Step 2: Two Primary Paths

The total delay of 18 days can then be divided as follows:

a. Concurrent c and o delays   = 3 days (days No. 13, 14, and 16)

b. Concurrent with excusable   = 2 days (days No. 7 and 33)

c. Nonconcurrent inexcusable c delays   = 1 day
(Smallest of day 3 on Path B-E-H-J and days 2, 3, 12, 35, 36, and 39 on Path ACFI)

d. Nonconcurrent compensable o delays   = 2 days
(Smallest of days 4 and 15 on Path B-E-H-J and days 15, 24, 25, 32, and 40 on Path ACFI)

e. Nonconcurrent excusable = 18 − (3 + 2 +1 +2)   = 10 days

Accordingly, the contractor should be given a time extension of 17 days (a + b + d + e). He will pay liquidated damages for 4 days (a + c) and will be reimbursed for overheads of 5 days (a + d).

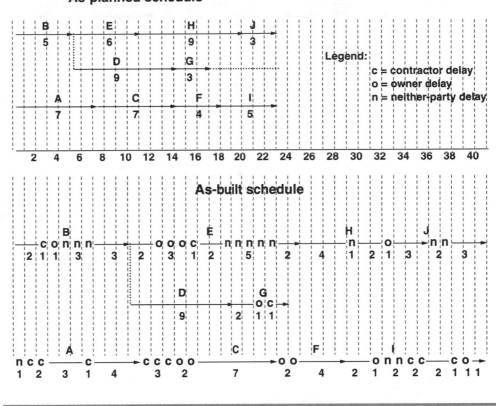

Table 11-3. Data of a Small Example

Activity	Predecessor	Duration (days)
A	—	7
B	—	5
C	A	7
D	B	9
E	B	6
F	C	4
G	D	3
H	E	9
I	F	5
J	H	3

Table 11-4. Recorded Delays for the Example

Delay No.	Category	Activity Affected	Effective Dates	Delay Time
1	Neither	A	1	1
2	Contractor	A	2–3	2
3	Contractor	A	7	1
4	Contractor	B	3	1
5	Owner	B	4	1
6	Neither	B	5–7	3
7	Contractor	C	12–14	3
8	Owner	C	15–16	2
9	Owner	E	13–15	3
10	Contractor	E	16	1
11	Neither	E	19–23	5
12	Owner	F	24–25	2
13	Owner	G	22	1
14	Contractor	G	23	1
15	Neither	H	30	1
16	Owner	H	33	1
17	Owner	I	32	1
18	Neither	I	33–34	2
19	Contractor	I	35–36	2
20	Contractor	I	39	1
21	Owner	I	40	1
22	Neither	J	37–38	2

11.6   Back to Our Case Study Project

Having won the bid for this project, we need to monitor project progress so that we can bring the project to a successful completion and secure our desired profitability level of the project.

In our project control, we will consider our finalized plan as our *baseline* for comparing actual performance. The finalized plan is the one we established in Chapter 10 (Figure 11–10 and Table 11–5).

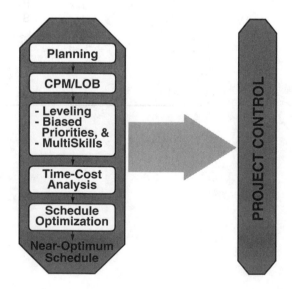

Figure 11-10. 28-Day Baseline Plan

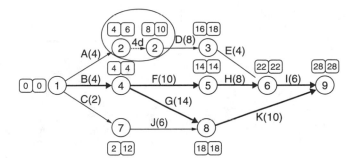

Table 11-5. Cost and Budget Data

Activity	Duration	Direct Cost	Indirect Cost (unbalanced bid)	Total Cost	Markup (5%)	Bid Price (budget value)
A	4	$2,000	$398	$2,398	$120	$2,518
B	4	$12,000	$1,707	$13,707	$685	$14,392
C	2	$4,000	$795	$4,795	$240	$5,034
D	8	$18,000	$1,778	$19,778	$989	$20,767
E	4	$20,000	$1,976	$21,976	$1,099	$23,075
F	10	$15,000	$1,783	$16,783	$839	$17,623
G	14	$12,400	$1,541	$13,941	$697	$14,638
H	8	$16,000	$1,758	$17,758	$888	$18,646
I	6	$10,000	$787	$10,787	$539	$11,326
J	6	$10,000	$787	$10,787	$539	$11,326
K	10	$8,000	$691	$8,691	$435	$9,126
Total Direct Cost =		**$127,400**	**Total Cost =**	**$141,400**	**Total Bid =**	**$148,470**

11.6.1 Using the Excel System

With our plan finalized and construction started, we can use the Progress sheet of the Excel system to apply project control. The steps followed are shown in Figures 11–11 to 11–14.

As shown in these figures, changes to the actual performance in the Progress sheet or to the baseline plan in the Schedule sheet updates our progress charts automatically and allows us to monitor performance at all stages of construction.

User input of start and
finish dates for payment report.

User inputs of actual
costs and daily accomplishments.

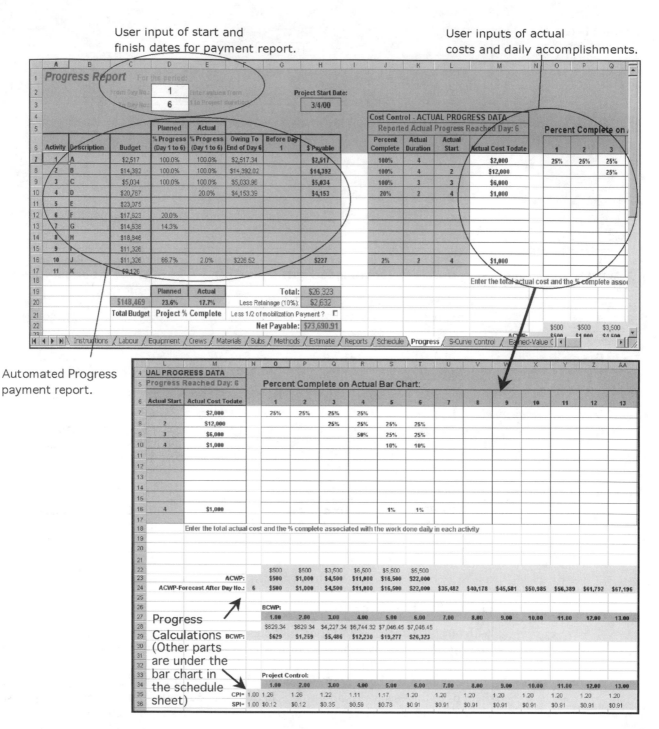

Automated Progress
payment report.

Progress
Calculations
(Other parts
are under the
bar chart in
the schedule
sheet)

Figure 11-11. Step 1: Input of Actual Progress Data Into the Progress Sheet

Construction reached day 6 and the progress made in each activity and actual costs are shown here. Between days 1 and 6, the project is 17.7% complete as opposed to the planned 23.6%.

306

Figure 11-12.
S-Curve Control

Now we can look at
the automated sheets
for project control.
Shown here is the S-
curve envelope of
early and late costs, as
well as actual
progress until day 6
and the estimate at
completion. Note here
that costs are the
direct plus indirect,
not the budget values.

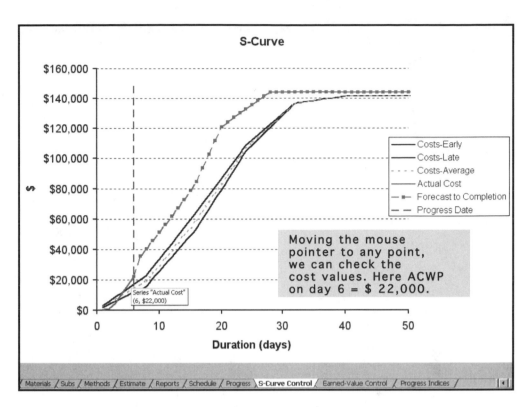

Figure 11-13.
Earned -Value
Control

Now, we look at the
automated Earned-
Value curves.

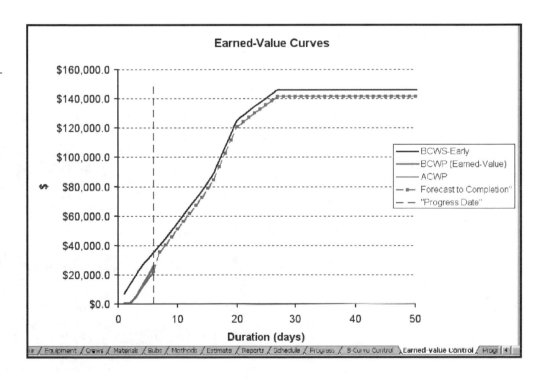

Figure 11-14.
Progress Indices

Automated chart for
monitoring the daily
schedule performance
index (SPI) versus the
daily cost
performance index
(CPI). Shown here is a
schedule delay but
also cost savings. The
trend also shows that
schedule delay is
decreasing.

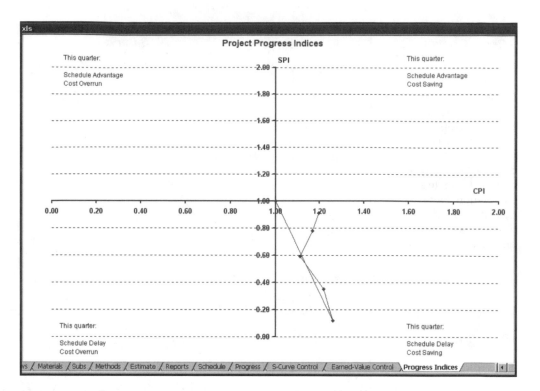

11.6.2 Using Microsoft Project

In addition to the project control charts in the Excel system, it is possible to export the
project data to Microsoft Project software to use its project control options. To do that,
we follow the steps in Figures 11–15 to 11–19.

Figure 11-15.
Exporting
Project Data to
Microsoft
Project

In the Schedule
sheet, we use the
Export button to
send the data of
the finalized
plan, and
optionally
performance
data, to Microsoft
Project.

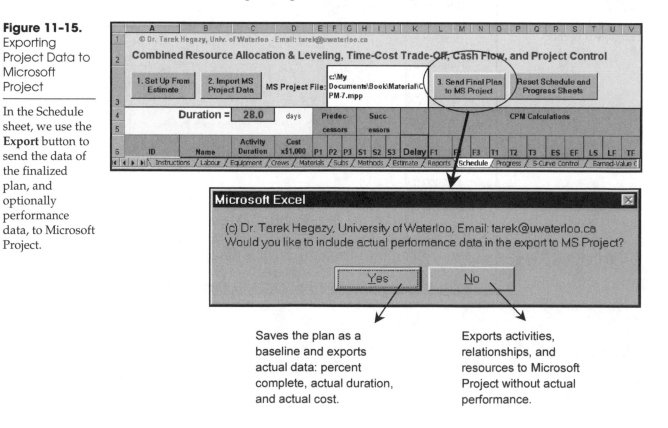

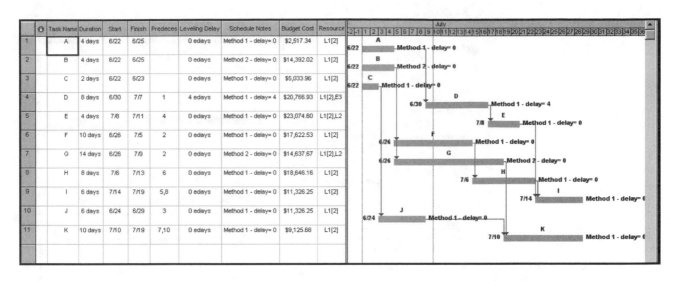

Figure 11-16. Gantt Chart of Exported Project

Shown here is the project generated when No is selected in Figure 11–15. The table shown here to the left of the Gantt chart view is the Entry table. In this option, actual performance data is not exported to Microsoft Project.

Tracking Table   Baseline Plan   Current Schedule with actual performance

	Task Name	Act. Start	Act. Finish	% Comp.	Act. Dur.	Rem. Dur.	Act. Cost	Act. Work
1	A	6/25	6/28	100%	4 days	0 days	$2,000.00	64 hrs
2	B	6/27	6/30	100%	4 days	0 days	$12,000.00	64 hrs
3	C	6/28	6/30	100%	3 days	0 days	$6,000.00	48 hrs
4	D	6/29	NA	20%	1.6 days	6.4 days	$1,000.00	38.4 hrs
5	E	NA	NA	0%	0 days	4 days	$0.00	0 hrs
6	F	NA	NA	0%	0 days	10 days	$0.00	0 hrs
7	G	NA	NA	0%	0 days	14 days	$0.00	0 hrs
8	H	NA	NA	0%	0 days	8 days	$0.00	0 hrs
9	I	NA	NA	0%	0 days	6 days	$0.00	0 hrs
10	J	6/29	NA	2%	0.12 days	5.88 days	$1,000.00	1.92 hrs
11	K	NA	NA	0%	0 days	10 days	$0.00	0 hrs

Figure 11-17. Gantt Chart of Exported Project

Shown here is the project generated when Yes is selected in Figure 11–15. In this option, actual performance data is exported to Microsoft Project. The plan in the Schedule sheet of Excel is saved as the baseline plan. The table shown here is the Tracking table whereas the view to the right is the Tracking Gantt view. Shown in this view is the current schedule (30 days) versus the baseline schedule (28 days). The reason for the current schedule being extended to 30 days is that actual performance, which had some delays, becomes a fixed part of the schedule. The question now is how to reoptimize the schedule to bring it within the deadline.

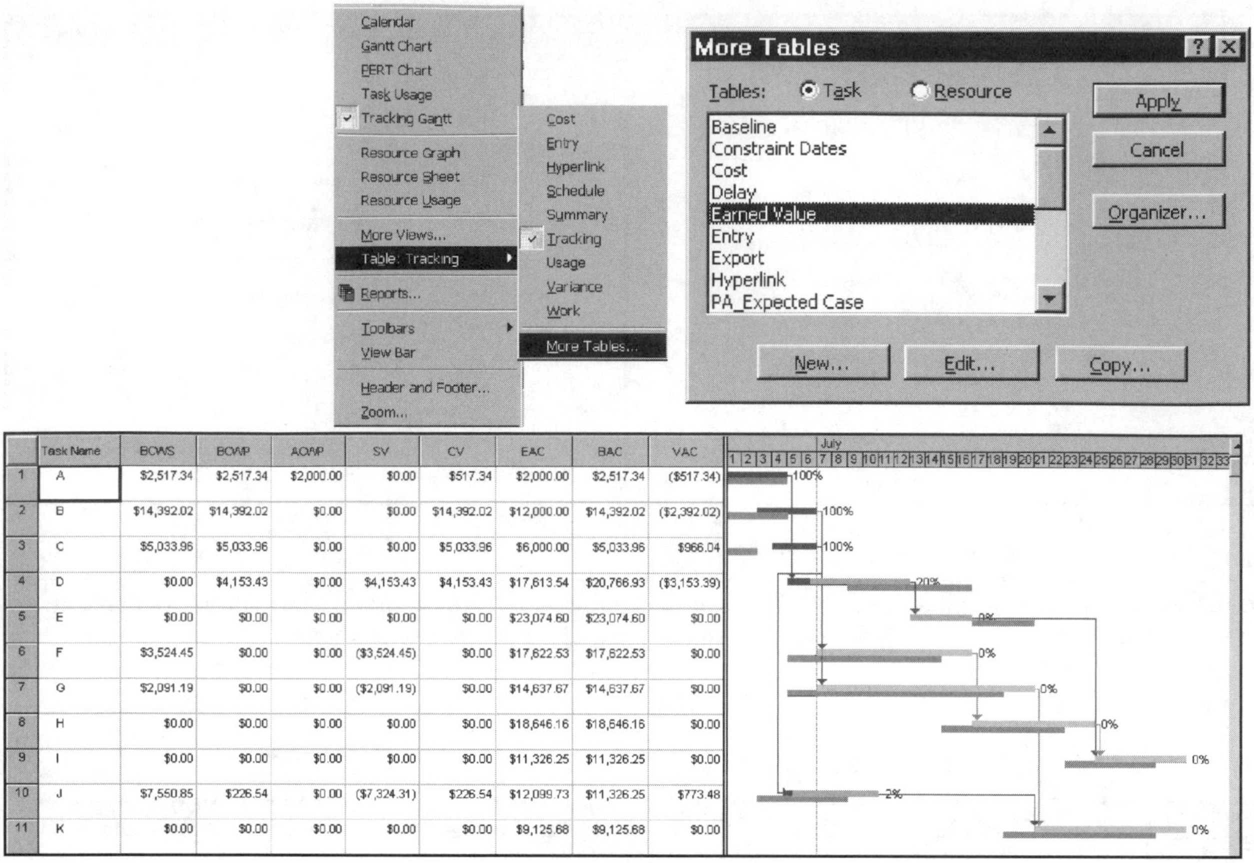

Figure 11-18. Viewing the Earned Value Table

	Task Name	BCWS	BCWP	ACWP	SV	CV	EAC	BAC	VAC
1	A	$2,517.34	$2,517.34	$2,000.00	$0.00	$517.34	$2,000.00	$2,517.34	($517.34)
2	B	$14,392.02	$14,392.02	$0.00	$0.00	$14,392.02	$12,000.00	$14,392.02	($2,392.02)
3	C	$5,033.96	$5,033.96	$0.00	$0.00	$5,033.96	$6,000.00	$5,033.96	$966.04
4	D	$0.00	$4,153.43	$0.00	$4,153.43	$4,153.43	$17,613.54	$20,766.93	($3,153.39)
5	E	$0.00	$0.00	$0.00	$0.00	$0.00	$23,074.60	$23,074.60	$0.00
6	F	$3,524.45	$0.00	$0.00	($3,524.45)	$0.00	$17,622.53	$17,622.53	$0.00
7	G	$2,091.19	$0.00	$0.00	($2,091.19)	$0.00	$14,637.67	$14,637.67	$0.00
8	H	$0.00	$0.00	$0.00	$0.00	$0.00	$18,646.16	$18,646.16	$0.00
9	I	$0.00	$0.00	$0.00	$0.00	$0.00	$11,326.25	$11,326.25	$0.00
10	J	$7,550.85	$226.54	$0.00	($7,324.31)	$226.54	$12,099.73	$11,326.25	$773.48
11	K	$0.00	$0.00	$0.00	$0.00	$0.00	$9,125.68	$9,125.68	$0.00

Figure 11-18. Viewing the Earned Value Table

Activating the Earned Value table shows the data as per the *status date* selected from the **Project-Project Information** menu option.

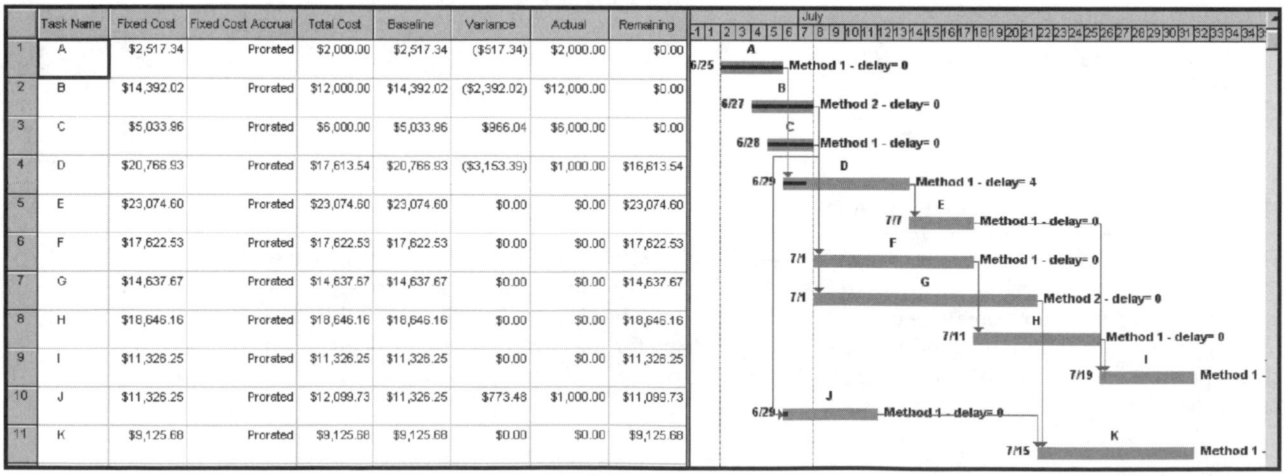

	Task Name	Fixed Cost	Fixed Cost Accrual	Total Cost	Baseline	Variance	Actual	Remaining
1	A	$2,517.34	Prorated	$2,000.00	$2,517.34	($517.34)	$2,000.00	$0.00
2	B	$14,392.02	Prorated	$12,000.00	$14,392.02	($2,392.02)	$12,000.00	$0.00
3	C	$5,033.96	Prorated	$6,000.00	$5,033.96	$966.04	$6,000.00	$0.00
4	D	$20,766.93	Prorated	$17,613.54	$20,766.93	($3,153.39)	$1,000.00	$16,613.54
5	E	$23,074.60	Prorated	$23,074.60	$23,074.60	$0.00	$0.00	$23,074.60
6	F	$17,622.53	Prorated	$17,622.53	$17,622.53	$0.00	$0.00	$17,622.53
7	G	$14,637.67	Prorated	$14,637.67	$14,637.67	$0.00	$0.00	$14,637.67
8	H	$18,646.16	Prorated	$18,646.16	$18,646.16	$0.00	$0.00	$18,646.16
9	I	$11,326.25	Prorated	$11,326.25	$11,326.25	$0.00	$0.00	$11,326.25
10	J	$11,326.25	Prorated	$12,099.73	$11,326.25	$773.48	$1,000.00	$11,099.73
11	K	$9,125.68	Prorated	$9,125.68	$9,125.68	$0.00	$0.00	$9,125.68

Figure 11-19. Other Project Control Views

Let's now activate the Cost table and the Gantt view. Shown here are the actual performance bars within the activity bars. Also, the Cost table shows a comparison of actual costs and baseline costs. All the data here are consistent with the calculations in the Excel system.

11.7 Critical Chain Project Management: A New Concept

Traditional project management concepts have been around since the 1950s, yet it is common that projects experience time and cost overruns. Critical Path-based project management was introduced as a cure for these problems with a goal of delivering projects within the original cost and time estimates. Today, Critical Path project management is a significant industry.

In 1997, Dr. Eliyahu Goldratt introduced a new approach for project management with the publication of his best-selling business novel, *Critical Chain*. The new concept is widely known as the Critical Chain Project Management (CCPM) concept. CCPM is beneficial and improves our understanding of the needs for successful management of projects. Let's have a look at the details.

11.7.1 Problems Addressed by the Critical Chain Concept

- **Estimating with Excessive Safety:** At the estimating stage, if a five-day task is sufficient, all estimators tend to add a hidden safety (contingency) into their estimates to account for any uncertainties. Although using a safety factor in a task estimate is not wrong, we need to understand the implications of this safety factor during actual performance.
- **Student Syndrome:** Given that the tasks have hidden safety, let's take a look at what happens when the task is actually performed. Similar to when students are given an assignment and, regardless of the length of time available, they tend to start only at the last minute. Therefore, the large safety gives a false feeling of security and leads to late starts, which consume the float and if any unexpected problems are encountered (often in construction), the task ends up with overruns;
- **Parkinson's Law:** Work expands to fit the allotted time. If a task is estimated to take 10 days, it usually does not take less. This adjustment of effort to fill the allotted time can come in a number of ways. People will simply adjust the level of effort to keep busy for the entire task schedule. Traditional project environments stress not being late, but they do not promote being early. This environment encourages hidden safety, the student syndrome, and Parkinson's Law effects.
- **Multitasking Problems:** Most of us work in a multiproject environment. We all have experiences of having to stop working on one task so that progress can be accomplished on another task in another project. Often, we wonder if all this jumping around makes sense because it comes with the penalties of reduced focus and loss of efficiency. The reason for this multitasking environment is that resources tend to migrate between projects in response to the latest, loudest customer demand in an attempt to keep as many customers satisfied as possible. This focus on showing progress on as many active projects as possible is the major cause of multitasking.

Let's consider the bad effects of multitasking in a simple multiproject example, as shown in Figure 11–20 on a case when four projects, A, B, C, and D each of which is estimated to take four weeks to complete.

- **No Reward for Early Finishes:** Our project management methods, including rewards and punishments, rarely reward early finishes. In fact, they often punish early finishes. If you finish a task earlier than planned, you might be accused of sandbagging your estimates instead of being rewarded for completing ahead of schedule. If you finish early and announce your results, you then encounter the next problem. The task that depends upon your completion might not be able to start early because the required resources are off doing something else. Remember that the project schedule gave a clear start date for the following task and the resources were allocated elsewhere based upon this schedule.

- When you integrate student syndrome, Parkinson's Law with the likelihood of no early finishes, you lose the effects of early finishes and only propagate late finishes in the schedule. In other words, the best you can do is to finish on time, not earlier.

Figure 11-20. Bad Effects of Multitasking

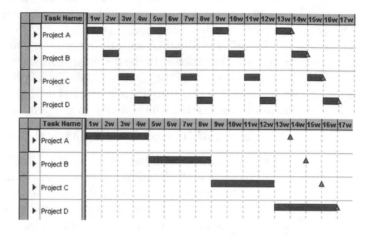

11.7.2   The Critical Chain Method

To address the problems in Section 11.7.1, the Critical Chain adopts the following steps:

1. **Scheduling backwards to reduce unnecessary dependencies:**   During the planning stage, you develop a plan backwards in time from a target end date for your project. One of the benefits of working backwards is that you are less likely to create unnecessary task dependencies. Additionally, because you start with the objectives and work back, you are also less likely to add tasks that do not add value to the objectives. This backward thinking approach, however, can be difficult and if you find it difficult to think this way, and many people do, do not do it.

2. **Task estimating with safety put aside:**   To be effective, Critical Chain task estimating requires a change in individual and organizational behavior. You want to remove the hidden safety in the task durations. Now, because this safety is hidden, you have to establish an organizational culture that removes the fear of exposing this safety and putting it aside. We are pooling this removed safety as a project resource as opposed to a hidden task-level resource. When you remove the safety from a task, the goal is to get a task estimate that has a *50% chance* of being met. When it is difficult to think in terms of probability, you should ask the team to provide estimates that are associated with three positive assumptions: (1) all the material and information needed for the task are on hand; (2) we are able to focus on the task without any interruptions; and (3) there will not be any surprises that cause additional work. If you use these assumptions, you will be off to a good start in deriving a 50% probability estimate. To compensate for the reduced safety, later we will insert buffers at key points in the project plan that will act as shock absorbers to protect the project end date against task duration increases.

3. **Scheduling as late as possible:**   In traditional Critical Path scheduling, your tasks are scheduled as soon as possible (ASAP) from the project start date. In Critical Chain planning, your tasks are scheduled as-late-as-possible (ALAP), based upon the target end date. This approach places the work as close as possible to the end of your schedule. One of the main benefits of this work delay is that you are not incurring costs earlier than necessary. One draw-

back of scheduling all work as late as possible is that all tasks become critical. An increase in duration of any task will push out the project end date by the increased amount. To circumvent that, in a later stage, we will insert buffers at key points in the project plan.

4. **Resolving resource conflicts:** Using backward resource leveling, resource conflicts are resolved. Traditional resource leveling techniques are applicable here.

5. **Identifying the Critical Chain:** The *Critical Chain* is the longest chain of tasks that consider both task dependencies and resource dependencies. This is different from the definition of the Critical Path, which is based upon task dependencies only. Critical Chain recognizes that a delay in resource availability can delay a schedule just as a delay in dependent tasks.

6. **Inserting buffer zones:** We have effectively removed the safety from our tasks based upon our estimating technique. Now we are going to form a pool of this safety and place it in shock-absorber buffers at key points in our project. When inserting buffers, we need to determine the size of the buffer. The two types of buffers (Figure 11–21) are:

   The *Project Buffer* is placed at the end of the project after the last Critical Chain task to protect the target end date against overruns in Critical Chain tasks. For our example, we will size this project buffer at 50% of the length of the Critical Chain. This buffer can be applied as an additional activity at the end of the project.

   The *Feeding Buffer*, on the other hand, is needed at the intersection between noncritical chains and the Critical Chain. This protects the Critical Chain against overruns on these feeding chains. In Figure 11–21, for example, activity B is a noncritical chain task that feeds into the Critical Chain activity 4. The size of the feeding buffer is 50% of the length of the feeding chain. To apply these buffers, we add an additional activity in front of each task that is a noncritical chain but has a Critical Chain successor.

7. **Relay race approach:** The relay race approach means that you must get your team to de-emphasize the task scheduled start and finish dates and concentrate, instead, on triggering their preparation and start on the preceding task's progress. In this manner, we capitalize on the early finishes of the preceding tasks. Importantly, once a task is started, the resources work as fast as possible towards completion without clocking themselves to the scheduled finish date. Using this relay race approach, when one task is getting close to completion, you must have the next task's resource on the track and ready to go as soon as possible after the preceding task completes. For subcontractors and suppliers, we need to establish a communication mechanism and incentive programs to frequently keep them informed of the status of their predecessor trades and the proper time they should start on site.

8. **Buffer management:** As in traditional project management, you update your schedule on a periodic basis by entering the completed duration on your tasks and updating the remaining duration with an estimate of the work needed to finish the task. In the Critical Chain concept, you do not worry when a particular task overruns its estimate. Instead, the concept simply watches the effect of many tasks on your buffers.

Figure 11-21.
Buffers

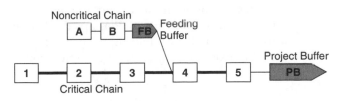

Buffer management is the key to tracking project performance in Critical Chain project management, rather than applying project control techniques such as variance analysis and Earned Value. The Critical Chain concept watches the buffers and acts depending upon how much of the buffer is penetrated by task schedule changes. It treats the buffer as if it were divided into three equally sized regions. The first third is the *green zone,* the second third is the *yellow zone,* and the final third is the *red zone.* If the penetration is in the green zone, no action is required. If the penetration enters the yellow zone, then you should assess the problem and think about possible courses of action. If the penetration enters the red zone, then you should act. Your action plans should involve ways to finish uncompleted tasks in the chain earlier or ways to accelerate future work in the chain to bring the buffer penetration back out of the red zone.

9. **Resource allocation decisions:** When faced with a resource conflict during the project, Critical Chain allocates the resource to the task with the goal of minimizing buffer penetration. This approach tries to optimize the use of resources towards the true highest priority goal: finishing the project early.

10. **Staggered multiprojects to prevent multitasking:** In the Critical Chain concept, you introduce new projects into your multiproject mix at a point that avoids conflict with key resources (called drum resources). This staggering of projects based upon key resource constraints is known as project synchronization. A capacity buffer is also inserted between the last use of the drum resource in the predecessor project and the first use of the drum resource in the successor project. This gap acts as a protection against delay due to the limited availability of the drum resource.

11.7.3 The Best of CPM and CCPM

Since its introduction, the Critical Chain Project Management (CCPM) concept has generated a lot of excitement about its use. Many papers have either extolled the benefits of the Critical Chain approach or advised restraint in adopting this theory. The various aspects of the CCPM approach have been met with varying degrees of acceptability. Some of the criticisms include:

- The assumption of dedicated resources to the tasks is not true in the real world.
- Multitasking, which is considered a problem in CCPM, can be viewed as a desirable management strategy for efficient use of resources, particularly with current trends of downsizing.
- The 50% estimates are too short and do not consider that resources have to develop a learning curve.
- Defining the Critical Chain and points at which feeding buffers should be placed is an excessive additional effort.
- Project buffer is advisable to use but feeding buffers reduce the total and free floats from noncritical tasks, thus giving a wrong indication of the impact of delays.
- Staggering multiprojects can lead to unnecessary delays.
- The dependence on buffer management and discarding the Earned Value concept leaves the CCPM without strong financial management.

Despite these criticisms, no doubt the CCPM concept is of great benefit to project managers and many successful implementations of the approach have been reported by various organizations. Perhaps the two most beneficial features of the CCPM are the change in the estimating culture and the use of project buffers, which can be used within existing project management techniques, and even on the Excel system discussed in this textbook. Other aspects need to be reflected upon by project managers to examine their suitability to the environment of the project and the organization.

11.7.3.1 Critical Chain Software   Commercial software systems that use the Critical Chain concept are now available. Two of the most well-known systems are Project Scheduler 8 (PS8) by Scitor corporation, which is full-fledged project management software, and ProChain add-in software for Microsoft Project (ProChain Solutions Inc.). Both software systems allow users to apply the CCPM concept with ease.

11.8   Golden Rules for Successful Construction

For the purpose of this text, the discussion on the Critical Chain and the EarnedValue concept, in addition to the following golden rules, provide us with the ingredients for successful project completion:

1. **Site organization:**   properly placing temporary facilities, access routes, and work areas improves the circulation on site and prevents accidents.
2. **Advance planning:**   planning does not end with the start of construction, it is a continuous task that helps you make proper decisions along the construction. Schedule updating and recording daily progress has to be the duty of dedicated staff for this task.
3. **Timely payments:**   accurate measurements of progress and on-time preparation of invoices prevents owner payment delays.
4. **Managing change orders:**   try to settle all change orders as they come up. Changes are like virtual pits for attracting surplus costs and schedule delays.
5. **Tracking trades' gaps:**   good aggressive project managers ensure that subcontractors all push the trades ahead of them while being pushed from those following. This keeps up the pace. When there are gaps between the trades, problems arise. Establish a system to monitor the gaps between the trades. Capitalize on the time saving by one trade and give incentive to its followers to start early. Establish a system for negotiation and communication with suppliers and subcontractors.
6. **Effective communication:**   keep all parties involved and informed of the progress and its requirements. Establish regular communication meetings and fully document all communication.
7. **Reducing work interruption:**   do not keep your resources moving and working partially on various projects at the same time. Multitasking can be disruptive to the crew's production, thus causing delays and extra cost.
8. **Documentation:**   establish a mechanism for permanent documentation of all aspects related to the project: photos, camcorders, time-lapse cameras, interim plans (network and bar chart), communications, minutes of meetings, progress reports, daily site reports, delivery slips, time sheets, site-utilized bar charts, site visits, and change orders. These can be useful in case of claims and disputes.

11.9   Summary

In this chapter, we dealt with the basics of project control and how to successfully complete the construction stage of the project. We learned the various techniques of evaluating the project progress and to evaluate its cost and time performance. We compared actual versus planned progress of work using the Earned Value technique, discussed schedule updating needs, estimated the cost at completion based on the actual progress of work, and we experimented with various software tools for project control.

11.10 Bibliography

Cass, D. (1991). Earned Value Graphics—New, Exciting, Innovative, 1991 AACE Transactions, AACE, pp. L.4.1–L.4.6.

Fish, J. (1991). Control in Design/Build, *Cost Engineering,* Vol. 33, No. 10. AACE, pp. 7–10.

Goldratt, E. (1997). *Critical Chain.* Great Barrington, MA: The North River Press.

Kim, J. (1990). An Object Oriented Database for Project Control, Transactions of the AFITEP 6th Annual Meeting, Paris.

Levine, H. (October 1999). "Shared Contingency: Exploring the Critical Chain" PM Network, PMI.

Martin, B. (1992). Aspects of Cost Control, *Cost Engineering,* Vol. 34, No. 6. AACE, pp. 19–23.

Rayburn, L. (1989). Productivity Database and Job Cost Control Using Microcomputers, *Journal of Construction Engineering and Management,* ASCE, Vol. 115, No. 4, ASCE, pp. 585–601.

Rizzo, T. (December 1999). "Operational Measurements for Product Development Organizations-Part 2" PM Network, PMI. Vol. 13, No. 12, pp. 31–35.

Sanvido, V., and Paulson, B. (1992). Site-Level Construction Information System, *Journal of Construction Engineering and Management,* ASCE, Vol. 118, No. 4, ASCE, pp. 701–715.

Wilkens, T. (July 2000). "Critical Path, or Chain, or Both?" PM Network, PMI. Vol. 14, No. 4, pp. 68–74.

11.11 Exercises

1. Draw the contract time-cost envelope. Discuss the relationship between the envelope and the actual cost-to-date curve.

2. The data of a small project are as follows. The indirect cost for this contract is $250/week and liquidated damages are $200/day.

Activity	Predecessors	Duration (weeks)
A	—	7
B	—	9
C	A	8
D	B	12
E	C, D	4
F	B	9
G	F	7
H	E, G	7

No.	Delay by	Activities Affected	Effective Delay Dates (week no.)
1	Owner	A	2–5
2	Contractor	C	14–16
3	Owner	C	21–23
4	Owner	D	15–18
5	Contractor	E	27–28
6	Neither	F	18–19
7	Neither	G	26–27
8	Owner	G	28–29

Given the delay report for this contract as shown, determine how each party is responsible for the contract delayed completion.

3. a. How can the engineer evaluate a claim where compensable and nonexcusable delays overlap on the contract primary Critical Paths?

b. Consider the following small contract and the recorded work changes and delays. Draw the as-built schedule and determine how each party is responsible for the contract delayed completion.

Activity	Predecessor	Duration (days)
A	—	8
B	A	12
C	—	5
D	C	10
E	—	7
F	C, E	15
G	B, D	8
H	F	2

No.	Delay by	Reason	Effective Dates	Affected Activity
1	Contractor	Equipment not on site	1–2	E
2	Owner	Redesign work in activity D	6–12	D
3	Owner	Design change (20% extra work)	—	F
4	Contractor	Late supply of materials	9–13	B
5	Owner	Late supply of drawings	10–12	F
6	Owner	Late inspection	25	B
7	Contractor	Equipment breakdown	25–26	F

4. The data for a small project is tabulated below.

Activity	Duration (days)	Depends upon
A	3	—
B	6	A
C	8	A
D	10	A
E	5	B, C
F	7	E
G	12	D, E
H	17	E
X	9	Y, Z
Y	3	H, D
Z	4	F, G

a. Construct a precedence network for this project and compute start and finish dates, total float, and free float for each activity. Also, indicate the Critical Path.

b. On day 12, the field scheduler gives you the following information and asks you to update the network and provide an accurate precedence diagram showing the updated schedule. The new diagram is to show start and finish dates and total float of each activity. Indicate the Critical Path, or paths. Information from field scheduler:

1. The project has been underway for 12 working days.
2. Some concrete forms broke during one pour, and activity B was delayed in completion by two days.

3. Activity D is now in progress but five days were lost waiting for better weather.

4. Activity A was completed on schedule.

5. Activity C was completed one day early.

6. The precast concrete supplier has been delayed; he can have the concrete on the job so that activity Y can begin on the morning of day 36.

In addition to the items provided by the field scheduler, your own office personnel have brought the following to your attention:

1. Activity H will not require 17 days, but seven days; the scheduling engineer discovered a 10-day error in the computations.

2. Activity Z, originally planned to last four days, is projected to take an additional two days because of a decrease in the labor force.

3. An error in log-in in the precedence diagram was discovered by the field engineer. He pointed out that activity Z must precede activity F instead of following it. Activity Z is still dependent on activity G and activity F is still dependent on activity E. All other activity dependencies remain as planned.

5. a. A cost control report of a certain contract gives the following figures as percentages of the total budgeted cost:

BCWP - 25% BCWS - 47% ACWP - 72%

Calculate the cost and schedule variances and comment on the status of the contract.

b. The application of a certain cost control system to a certain contract shows a that the use of materials exhibits an adverse variance (i.e., material wastage). Give three suggestions to the site manager in order to improve the situation.

6. A bar chart showing the *Plan* versus the anticipated *Actual* progress of a small project is shown below:

a. Plot the *BCWS* (S-curve).

b. On the same chart, draw the *ACWP* curve until current date (end of day 14).

c. Calculate the *EV* until the current time and plot it on the same chart.

d. Calculate the *CPI* and *SPI* values at the end of days 7 and 14. Plot these points and comment on the project progress.

e. What is your projection of the actual total project cost?

f. What is the anticipated actual cost of activity H?

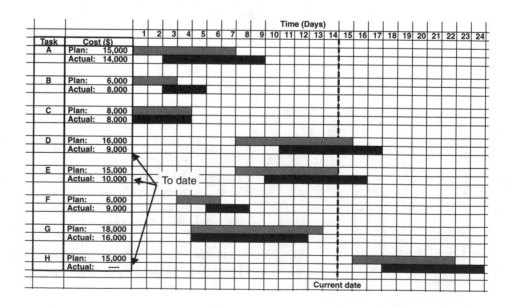

7. Replace the question marks by the appropriate answers:

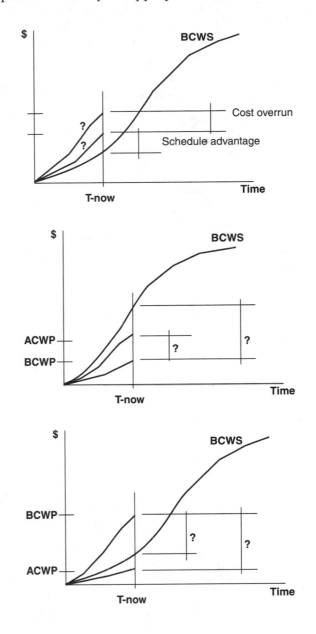

8. The table gives the activities involved in the first phase of the construction of an earth dam. The duration, predecessors, and budget costs of the activities are also listed. The project has a physical constraint: the river must be diverted (activity H) in January 2002 (time of low flow).

a. Choose a suitable date (week no. and month no.) for the start of the project, neglecting holidays.

b. Assume that the project starts on the date chosen in (a) above but the contractor encounters unexpected ground conditions during construction. This increases the duration required to drive the diversion tunnel (activities B and D) by 25%. How can the contractor deal with this situation to achieve minimum increase in contract cost?

c. Assuming that the budget of each activity is uniformly distributed over its duration, draw the contract time-cost envelope (early-start versus late-start), considering a four-week basis. Given that the actual cumulative cost at end of week 4 is $33,600 and at the end of week 8 is $85,000, draw the cost-to-date curve and comment on the progress of the project.

Activity	Duration (Weeks)	Predecessors	Budget Cost ($)
A. Establish site	6	—	50,400
B. Drive diversion tunnel east	12	A	84,420
C. Concrete diversion tunnel east	14	B	44,520
D. Drive diversion tunnel west	6	A	20,940
E. Concrete diversion tunnel west	8	D	25,440
F. Excavate forebay	3	A	15,000
G. Concrete forebay	6	F	12,000
H. Divert river	0	C,E,G	0

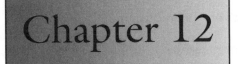

Chapter 12

SPECIAL TOPICS

After studying this chapter, you will be able to:

- Understand the effect of uncertainty on projects through the parade game.
- Use the PERT technique to consider the uncertainty in activity duration.
- Be familiar with the emerging concept of Enterprise-Wide Project Management.
- Be familiar with various technological trends including the Internet and its use in project management.

12.1 Effect of Uncertainty: A Classroom Game

To enhance our intuitive understanding of the impact of variability (e.g., uncertainty in duration estimates) on the outcome of a project, let's try out an experiment that can be carried out in a classroom setting with student participation. In this experiment, we will simulate a parade of trades in a building construction that form a single-line production system. Examples of building parades are (Tommelein et al., 1999):

- **Structural Parade:** e.g., erecting structural steel (steel erectors); placing and securing decking as well as welding shear studs (decking contractor); and placing rebar (rebar contractor); then pouring and finishing concrete (concrete contractor).
- **Overhead Work Parade:** e.g., installing an HVAC system (mechanical contractor); sprinkler system (fire protection contractor), emergency lighting (electrical contractor), and pipe (plumbing contractor).

A parade is considered as a production system. The subcontractors in a building parade can have daily variability in their production, representing the reliability in their production. This variability may jeopardize the succeeding trades' ability to perform because the output of one trade is prerequisite to the work done by the successor trades. Therefore, to enable the whole parade to expedite job completion and minimize waste, it is essential that work be released reliably between trades. The parade game illustrates the impact variability has on the production rates of trades that succeed one another.

Our game is a simplified version of the one presented in Tommelein et al. (1999). Each row of students represents a parade, with each student being one trade in the parade. Depending on the number of students in the class, we can have rows of equal sizes, e.g., five students each (Figure 12–1). Each parade is the same as the other and each trade, on average, produces the same production as the other (e.g., 4 units per day). The main difference is in the production variability, as follows:

Given four parades available (i.e., total of 20 students in the class), then:

- Each of the five trades in parade 1 produces exactly 4 units per day.
- Each of the five trades in parade 2 produces either 3 or 5 units per day.
- Each of the five trades in parade 3 produces either 2 or 6 units per day.
- Each of the five trades in parade 4 produces either 1 or 7 units per day.

As such, parade 1 has high production reliability whereas parade 4 has the highest variability in their production. Before playing the game, the materials we need to prepare are as follows:

- **Dice:** Each student will get one die that corresponds to the amount of production of its parade. All parade 1 trades, for example, will get dice with number 4 on all its six faces. Parade 2 trades will get dice with number 3 written on three faces and number 5 on the other three (called 3–5 dice), and so on. For that purpose blank dice are available commercially and also a 2-by-2 piece of lumber can be cut to make the dice.
- **Production Units:** Each parade will start with say 75, 100, or 150 (depending on the number of students) Popsicle sticks or cards that represent the units that have to be processed by each parade. As shown in Figure 12–1, all these units are put on one side before the game starts.
- **Production Plot:** Each parade will get an overhead transparent sheet with an empty grid so that the cumulative daily production can be plotted (Figure 12–2). This sheet is given to the last trade in each parade so that he or she can plot the amount of production made by his or her parade.
- **Colored Pens:** Along with the transparency sheet, each parade gets a transparency pen with a different color. Later at the end of the game, all transparency sheets can be put on top of each other on an overhead projector as to clearly show the results to the students.

Figure 12-1. Setup for the Parade Game

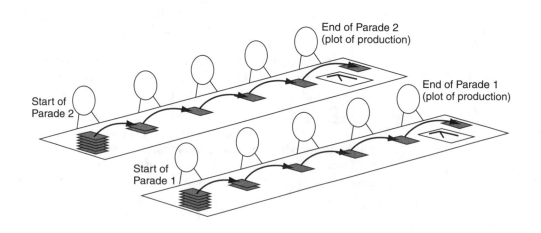

Figure 12-2. Blank Plot Sheet

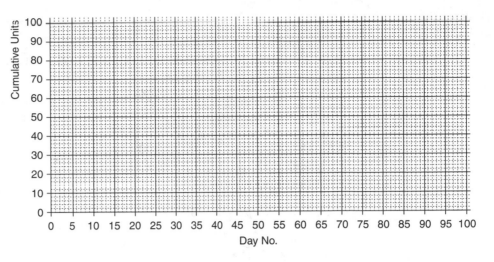

12.1 The Game

The essence of the game is that each member of the parade waits until his predecessor trade provides him with enough units of work on which he can progress. With high variability in trades' production, the amount one predecessor trade produces may be insufficient for the succeeding trade, thus causing delay in production. The parade game is played as follows:

- Students are arranged in their seats (in our case four rows of five students).
- The students of each parade get a die each, corresponding with their assumed variability. For example, each of the five students in parade 1 get one die with the number 4 on all faces, and so on.
- 100 Popsicle sticks are given to the first student of each parade (left most).
- One plot sheet and a colored pen are given to the last student (right most) of each parade.
- One additional student (or the instructor) acts as a day counter and loudly announces the counter number followed by a pause to allow the parades to finish their daily work.
- Day 1 in the project is announced and cycles of production start as follows:
  - Each student looks at his right side to see the amount of units (Popsicle sticks) available to him at the start of the day, call that U. On day 1, only the first trade has 100 available units.
  - Each student tosses his or her die and the uses the number as the production amount to be made by his trade on that day, call that P;
  - If a student (trade) finds enough units to work upon, i.e., $U >= P$, then he or she moves a number of units P from his or her right pile and places it to his or her left side (becomes ready in the following day for his successor trade). Partial daily production is not allowed (i.e., if $U < P$, no production is made).
  - Each time the end trade moves units to the end of the production line, he or she plots that amount cumulatively on the transparency sheet.
- If all parades move the 100 units to the end of the production line, the process stops, otherwise a day is incremented and the intermediate steps above are applied.
- At the end of the game, all transparency sheets are superimposed on an overhead projector and shown to the students. The expected result of the experiments is that project duration gets longer with increased production variability. Figure 12–3, for example, shows the results of an experiment in which 75 units took 18 cycles of a 4 dice (a die which has a 4 on all six faces) and 32 cycles of a 1–7 die (a die which has a 1 on 3 faces and a 7 on the other three faces). This demonstrates the effect of uncertainty on project duration.

Figure 12-3.
Sample Result of the
Parade Game

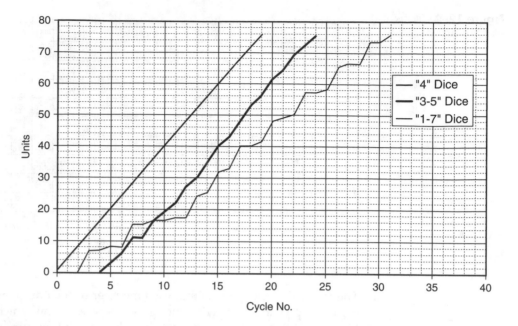

12.2 The PERT Approach for Project Risk Assessment

With uncertainty being demonstrated to have an effect on the project, let's introduce one of the well-known techniques for quantifying the impact of such uncertainty. The *program evaluation and review technique (PERT)* was developed by the late 1950s. The objective was to evaluate the risk in meeting the time goals of the execution of projects whose activities had some uncertainty in their duration estimates.

To represent the uncertainty in duration estimates, the PERT technique recognizes the probabilistic, rather than deterministic, nature of the operations involved in high-risk activities. Accordingly, the PERT technique incorporates three durations for each activity into its methodology. The three duration estimates are:

> **Optimistic duration (a):** estimated time (comparatively short) of executing the activity under very favorable working conditions. The probability of attaining this duration is about 0.01.

> **Pessimistic duration (b):** estimated time (comparatively long) of executing the activity under very unfavorable working conditions. The probability of attaining this duration is also about 0.01.

> **Most likely duration (m):** estimated time of executing the activity that is closest to the actual duration. This estimates lies in between the above two extremes.

These three estimates, rather than only one, express the time to accomplish an activity in terms of likelihood rather than for certain. Likelihood in turn can be expressed in terms of statistical probability and distribution curves representing the frequency of occurrence of various durations if the activity were to be performed a large number of times.

In PERT, the given estimates of times and the likelihood of occurrence are represented by a *beta curve,* as shown in Figure 12–4. However, with the three estimates of time for each activity, we cannot perform traditional CPM analysis to determine project duration. Therefore, we need to get a single weighted average duration for each activity. The formula for the expected duration, called expected elapsed time, (t_e) is as follows:

$$t_e = (a + 4\,m + b)\,/\,6$$

Figure 12–4. Beta Distribution of Activity Duration

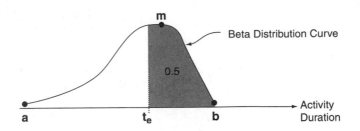

Beta Distribution Curve

The t_e value is a sort of an average with more weight given to the most likely time. As shown in Figure 12–4, the t_e point divides the area under the beta curve into two equal parts, meaning, the activity has a 50-50 chance of being accomplished earlier or later than t_e. Also, to represent the variability and level of uncertainty in the activity duration, the activity variance is calculated as follows:

$$\sigma t_e^2 = [(b - a) / 6]^2$$

In effect, the variance σt_e^2 is larger when optimistic and pessimistic estimates are far apart, representing high uncertainty in the activity duration estimate.

12.2.1 Step-by-Step Analysis

Now that we have one duration estimate value (t_e) calculated for each activity, let's discuss the probabilistic scheduling process using the PERT technique. Using an activity on arrow (AOA) representation of a project network, the process is as follows:

Step 1: Individual Activity Durations

a = optimistic duration (1 in 100 chance) = minimum duration

m = most frequent duration (most likely)

b = pessimistic duration (1 in 100 chance) = maximum duration

t_e = activity expected duration = $(a + 4 m + b)/6$

σt_e^2 = activity duration variance = $[(b - a)/6]^2$

Step 2: CPM Calculations

Using the activities' t_e durations, CPM calculations are performed following the forward and backward passes to determine the project duration (T_E). Activity floats and also calculated and critical activities are identified.

Step 3: Distribution of Project Duration

Because the probability is 0.5 that each activity will finish at its t_e durations, there is a probability of 0.5 for the entire project being finished at time T_E. However, the expected project duration does not follow a beta curve as did the activities comprising the project. Assuming that the project is executed a large number of times, the resulting population of project durations may be assumed normally distributed.

The normal distribution of project duration is defined by its mean (μ) and standard deviation (σ) values, determined as follows:

$$\mu_{T_E} = T_E = \Sigma\, t_e \qquad \text{of critical activities}$$

$$\sigma_{T_E} = \sqrt{\Sigma\sigma_{t_e}^2} \qquad \text{of critical activities}$$

Step 4: Analysis of Project Completion Probabilities

Using the project normal distribution, it is possible now to find the probability values associated with specific project duration. By scaling the project distribution to the standard normal distribution, we can obtain probabilities from standard probability tables and make conclusions, as follows:

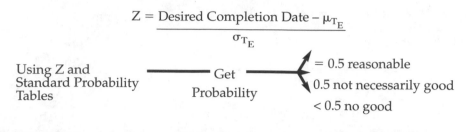

$$Z = \frac{\text{Desired Completion Date} - \mu_{T_E}}{\sigma_{T_E}}$$

Using Z and Standard Probability Tables ——— Get Probability

= 0.5 reasonable

0.5 not necessarily good

< 0.5 no good

Example:

Let's consider a simple example of a project network similar to the one we use for our case study but with three possible durations as shown in Figure 12–5. Calculate the probability of the project being completed in 30 days of less.

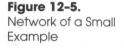

Figure 12–5.
Network of a Small Example

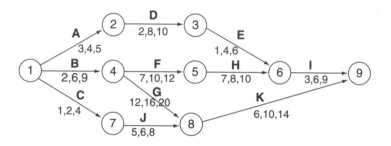

Solution:

Given:

Step 1: Activity Durations

Activity	a	m	b	t_e	σt_e^2
A	3	4	5	4.00	0.11
B	2	6	9	5.83	1.36
C	1	2	4	2.17	0.25
D	2	8	10	7.33	1.78
E	1	4	6	3.83	0.69
F	7	10	12	9.83	0.69
G	12	16	20	16.00	1.78
H	7	8	10	8.17	0.25
I	3	6	9	6.00	1.00
J	5	6	8	6.17	0.25
K	6	10	14	10.00	1.78

Step 2: CPM
Critical path is B-G-K.

Step 3: Project Duration Distribution

$$\mu_{T_E} = T_E = \Sigma\ t_e \text{ of critical activities} = 5.83 + 16.0 + 10 = 31.83 \text{ days}$$

$$\sigma_{T_E} = \sqrt{\Sigma\sigma_{t_e}^2} = \sqrt{1.36 + 1.78 + 1.78} = 2.217 \text{ days}$$

Step 4: Analysis of Project Completion Probability

Using the project normal distribution, it is possible now to find the probability of finishing the project in 30 days or less.

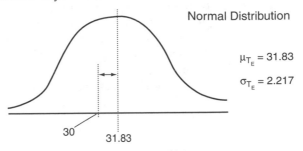

Normal Distribution

$\mu_{T_E} = 31.83$

$\sigma_{T_E} = 2.217$

30 31.83

Probability (Project duration <= 30 days): $Z = \dfrac{30 - 31.83}{2.217} = -0.8268$

From standard probability tables: Probability (<= 30 days) = 0.204 or 20.4%

Note:

The probability can be computed for achieving any other event in the project (e.g., event 5 which designates the end of activity F). Similar to what we did with project duration, we can assume a normal distribution for that event with (μ) and (σ) values calculated from all the tasks that lead to the event. Accordingly standard normal distribution tables can be used to determine the probabilities. For event 5:

$\mu_5 = \Sigma\, t_e$ activities leading to event 5 = 5.83 + 9.83 = 15.66 days; and

$\sigma_5 = \sqrt{\Sigma\sigma_{t_e}^2} = \sqrt{1.36 + 0.69} = 1.432$ days

---

12.2.2 Criticisms to PERT Technique

The PERT approach has been used for risk analysis in R&D projects. Many researchers, however, have reported several comments on its applicability, including:

- Requires three estimated durations for each activity, which requires time-consuming analysis of past projects.
- Assumes continuous probability distribution for activity durations. In various domains, including construction, only discrete durations are available.
- The assumption of the suitability of beta distributions for activity durations is debatable.
- It focuses on a single Critical Path and ignores close-to-critical paths.
- It assumes independent activity durations, whereas in practice, activity durations are correlated with one another.
- It ignores the risk that occurs at path convergence points, therefore, according to some, is suitable only for one-path schedules.

12.3 Monte Carlo Simulation for Project Risk Assessment

Monte Carlo simulation was introduced in an effort to overcome the limitations of PERT. The method basically uses randomly generated numbers to determine possible activity durations. The technique essentially generates various scenarios associated with the project, each involving a random set of durations for the project activities. Each of these scenarios is then used to produce a CPM-type deterministic schedule. At the end, we can analyze the results of all these scenarios to understand the resulting range of variability in project duration.

To generate the random project scenarios, the Monte Carlo simulation technique requires information about the duration of activities and their distributions, including discrete values. It is apparent that this technique requires numerous calculations. The number of activity duration sets may vary from 40 to 1000. The outcome of the technique is basically an estimate of expected time and variance of project completion time. Accordingly, the probability of meeting a particular completion date is determined and also the probability that a particular activity could become critical.

12.3.1   Step-by-Step Analysis

The following is a five-step procedure for performing Monte Carlo Simulation:

1. Determine the duration distribution of each activity. It is possible to use discrete values or to use the simplified assumption of a triangular distribution (Figure 12–6).

Figure 12-6.
Distribution of Activity Duration for Monte Carlo Simulation

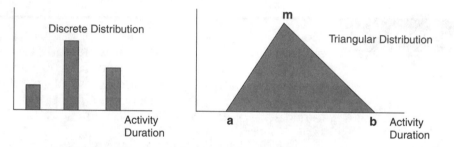

2. Generate one project scenario by randomly generating one possible duration for each activity in the project (based on its distribution). Perform CPM calculations for this scenario and determine the project duration.
3. Repeat step 2 for the number of desired simulations (scenarios) and then tabulate the results.
4. Project Duration Distribution: Calculate the mean (μ) and standard deviation (σ) values for the resulting project durations.
5. Using the (μ) and (σ) values, determine the probability of the project being completed on or before any given date similar to step 4 in PERT analysis.

Example:

Let's consider again the project network of Figure 12–5, which defines the uncertainty in terms of three estimated activity durations for each activity. Let's follow the five steps of Monte Carlo simulation for the example and then compare the results with the PERT analysis made earlier.

1. To enable a comparison with PERT analysis, let's consider the three estimates as discrete values for each activity.
2. Let's now generate 500 random scenarios of the project. We then calculate the CPM duration of each.
3. When can tabulate the results as shown in the example of Table 12–1.
4. Project Duration Distribution: We now calculate the mean (μ) and standard deviation (σ) of the 500 CPM durations at the bottom of Table 12–1. The results are as follows:

Mean (μ) = 35 days; and Standard Deviation (σ) = 7.45 days.

Table 12-1. Partial Monte Carlo Simulation Results

Activity	Scenario 1	Scenario 2	...	Scenario 500
A	3	4		5
B	2	9		2
C	1	2		8
D	8	8		1
E	4	12		7
F	10	16	...	12
G	16	7		12
H	8	10		9
I	9	8		6
J	8	5		8
K	14	10		6
CPM Duration	32	43		29

It is interesting to note that these values are larger than those estimated using PERT. These results point out to some of the frequently cited limitations of PERT, which result in underestimating the project duration.

5. Using the (μ) and (σ) values, we determine the probability of the project being completed in 30 days or less, as follows:

Probability (Project duration <= 30 days): $Z = \dfrac{30 - 35}{7.45} = -0.671$

From standard probability tables: Probability (<= 30 days) = 0.251 or 25.1%

12.4   Advanced Tools, Techniques, and Applications

In this section, some of the emerging new techniques, tools, and technologies are touched upon. Although the description here is brief, each of these topics, or other new ones, can be explored by the students in the form of a group course project. The project can be a search and summarization exercise and can end with student presentations. When the various groups present their work to the whole class, they bring additional up-to-date content and their combined knowledge complements the theoretical and quantitative aspects presented in this textbook.

12.4.1   Enterprise Project Management: A New Wave

With the turn of the millennium, many software vendors have put into the market project management software that is claimed to be usable by all parts of the "Enterprise." It ties scheduling, resource allocation, document management, timekeeping, financing, procurement, and reporting together into one integrated system. In the larger business community, such systems have been referred to as "ERP" or Enterprise Resource Planning systems. An Enterprise Resource Planning system is a packaged business software system that enables a company to manage the efficient and effective use of its resources (materials, plant, and equipment, etc). ERP systems have been used by large manufacturing, production, and larger corporations, and they cost millions of dollars in planning, customization, and training of users. The objectives of using such systems are to:

- Automate and integrate the majority of an organization's business processes.
- Share common data and practices across the entire enterprise.
- Produce and access information in a real-time environment.
- Tie all departments of a corporation together and facilitate the transfer of business information.
- Increase productivity, achieve a higher level of competitiveness, and ultimately attain larger market shares and profit margins.

With the increase in the number of corporations using ERP software, organizations are facing many challenges during the implementation, particularly with the large cultural changes required from users. In fact, the use of these systems is going through the second wave, which follows the "Go Live" step in their implementing. In this second wave, the focus is on addressing whether the promised benefits are attainable, the systems' impact on users' ability to adapt, and how to optimize the benefits gained from using such systems.

In a recent consulting report published by Deloitte Consulting (http://www.dc.com), various worldwide ERP implementations were analyzed through a survey among 230 respondents in 85 global companies. The report, "ERP's Second Wave: Maximizing the Value of Enterprise Applications and Processes", included a survey that was conducted between the summer of 1998 and spring of 1999. The ERP systems surveyed are *SAP, Oracle, Baan,* and *PeopleSoft.* Some of the findings in the report are shown in Figure 12–7. According to this report, full benefits of ERP implementation can be achieved through the following practices:

1. Focus on capabilities and benefits, not just going live.
2. Implementation does not end by go-live. ERP requires planning and program management practices throughout the program life cycle.
3. Companies should anticipate a temporary dip in performance after going live but substantial improvements will soon follow.
4. Achieve balanced people, process, and technology changes across all area.
5. Extend the ERP capabilities even further. Web-based ERP is an expected area.
6. Teach the organization to use new capabilities.
7. Build and leverage process expertise.
8. Promote post-implementation commonalties.
9. Assign clear ownership of benefits.
10. Define metrics and manage to them.

12.4.2 Simulation

Computer simulation is a powerful tool for accurate modeling of real-world construction systems to support planning, scheduling, and resource management. Since the introduction of the CYCLONE system for construction (discrete-event) simulation by Halpin in 1973, research in this domain has been growing increasingly. Over the years, several systems have been developed with various capabilities. Such tools are beneficial in modeling any cyclic process, such as the erection of steel elements in the various floors of a high-rise building, or earth-moving operations in which trucks are loaded with material, sent to dump area, and returned in a queue for another loading. These processes can have a lot of variability in the timing of each step, probability of process breakdowns, and various possible resource combinations.

With traditional simulation tools, the process of developing a simulation model requires the user to be familiar with specific terminology and the modeling schematics of particular software, in addition to the ability to write proprietary computer

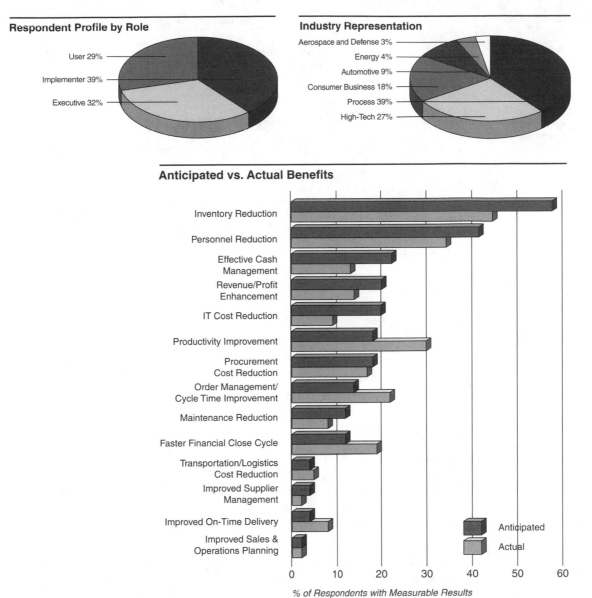

Figure 12-7. Analysis of ERP Implementations

code. This may not be suitable for many construction practitioners who are not familiar with the operational details needed for accurate simulation. Several researchers have, therefore, employed different ways to simplify the modeling process and to make it more attractive to practitioners. These include efforts to introduce simulation techniques imported from other domains such as Petri Nets, which were introduced by Wakefield and Sears in 1997. Still, however, Petri Nets still needs familiarity with new terminology.

One of the simple simulation tools available commercially that is remarkably easy to use is the Scitor Process software. It allows the user to draw a flowchart of any process, assign resources to the process steps, run the simulation, and then obtain various reports on productive times, idle times, and the production quantity produced at the various process steps. An example of a simple concrete placing operation is shown in Figure 12–8.

Figure 12-8. Model of a Simple Concrete-Placing Operation

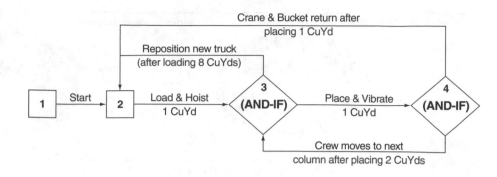

Using any simulation tool brings substantial benefits. This includes proper estimation of production rates, analysis of the impact of various resource combinations on production, analysis of the impact of uncertainty on production, and analysis of various reengineering decisions.

12.4.3 Artificial Intelligence Techniques

Artificial Intelligence (AI) is the area of computer science focusing on creating machines that can engage on behaviors that humans consider intelligent. The ability to create intelligent machines has intrigued humans since ancient times, and today with the advent of the computer and 50 years of research into AI programming techniques, the dream of smart machines is becoming a reality. Researchers are creating systems that can mimic human intelligence and preserve human experience.

In construction engineering and management, experience is crucial for decision making and problem solving. Thus, computer technologies that are capable of storing and re-using human experience are essential for developing practical decision support systems. The aspiration to work more productively and cope with increasing challenges has motivated many researchers in the academic arena to develop nontraditional problem-solving tools based on artificial intelligence. Examples of these tools are knowledge-based expert systems (KBES), artificial neural networks (ANNs), fuzzy logic systems, and genetic algorithms (GAs). A brief introduction to these tools and their application areas is as follows:

12.4.3.1 Knowledge-Based Expert Systems (KBES)   The primary goal of expert systems research is to store and preserve the knowledge of expert practitioners and make it available to decision makers at the time of need. When enough knowledge about specific subjects is acquired and stored in a computer, the Expert system mimics the human ability to make logical deductions based on this knowledge to come up with proper answers to problems.

KBES can assist supervisors and managers with situation assessment and long-range planning in many domains including business, science, engineering, and the military. Today's expert systems clients can choose from dozens of commercial software packages with easy-to-use interfaces. With many construction problems being solved based on experience and judgment, KBES can be applied to various areas including diagnostic problems such as determining the proper rehabilitation for cracked buildings, selection of proper foundation type for a large project, and decisions related to proper use of resources.

The key advantages of KBES is their method of representing and storing information and the manner in which they search through the knowledge to come up with solutions to problems. The knowledge storage and representation is mainly made in the form of IF-THEN rules that can be collected from various experts and stored separately from any processing mechanism. Let's, for example, represent some of the rules used to define the area of the batch plant needed on a construction site, as shown

Figure 12-9.
Knowledge
Representation and
the Backward
Chaining Process

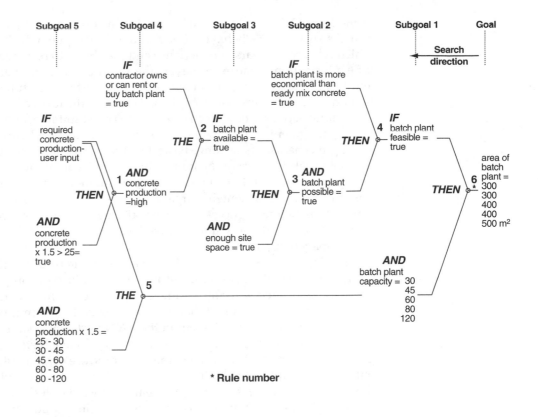

in Figure 12–9. This decision depends upon several factors including the quantity of concrete, site space, availability of cheaper alternatives, and potential reuse of the plant. This knowledge takes a hierarchical form suitable for rule-based representation. Also, the separation of the knowledge base from the processing mechanism simplifies the updating of the knowledge base.

During a consultation, a solution or conclusion to a problem is driven through an inference engine, which is a mechanism for searching the knowledge base for a solution. There are two common types of search: forward chaining and backward chaining. The forward chaining starts from the IF part and uses the available symptoms to activate one of the THEN parts that determine the conclusion or solution. The backward chaining, on the other hand, starts from the goal and searches the THEN part of the knowledge base. The mechanism works backward to determine its subgoals. Consider the chain of knowledge in Figure 12–9, for example, the goal to be determined (right side) is the area of the batch plant. Before a final conclusion is made, the subgoals have to be determined first. The process moves backward to evaluate the subgoals and their sub-subgoals following the knowledge chain. Following this process, the rules (numbered 1 to 6) are activated sequentially, and accordingly the area batch plant is determined. Because of its mechanism, one of the good features of a KBES is its ability to logically explain the conclusion reached by the system.

12.4.3.2 Artificial Neural Networks (ANNs) Many of the systems that engineers deal with exhibit dynamic, multivariate, and complex behaviors (e.g., wave forces, weather conditions, earthquake strengths, and material mechanics). Dealing with such systems has been a difficult task, and traditional tools, or even expert systems, have not been able to accurately predict and model the behavior of such systems as basis for design and analysis. Therefore, among the artificial intelligence tools, ANNs have been used for the modeling of such complex systems. Through their learn-by-example process, a neural network is able to automatically associate the causes with their related outcomes, without logical inferencing or explanation. After being trained, an ANN is able to quickly predict the outcomes of a completely new situation. As such, ANNs behave similar to the development of the human gut feeling, which is based on years of experience and the ability to recognize patterns even with little information. Some examples are the ability to recognize hand-written characters and to recognize the age of people from passport-size pictures. In these examples, human intelligence cannot be explained easily in the form of IF-THEN rules.

Neural networks have been suggested as most suitable for modeling problems involving judgment and analogy with previous situations, where a structured problem-solving mechanism is lacking. Basically, ANNs are computer programs simulating the biological structure of the human brain and its ability to learn from previous experiences and generate estimates for new situations. A typical ANN consists of a group of processing elements organized into a sequence of layers usually with full connections between successive layers through connection weights. Figure 12–10 shows the elements of a simple three-layer ANN, widely known as feed-forward backpropagation.

The input nodes accept the data that is presented to the network (representing model parameters) whereas the output nodes produce the outputs (representing the decisions associated with the parameters). The hidden nodes internally represent the relationships in the data and their number is usually determined in a trial-and-error manner. Each processing element in the ANN performs a simple sum product of its inputs by the corresponding weight value. Using some historical cases of known inputs and outputs, an ANN can be trained to produce correct outputs when presented only with the inputs. The training process, in fact, is a process of determining the optimum values for the ANN weights that produce the desired outputs. The calculations involved in ANN processing are discussed in a large number of references.

In recent years, the backpropagation type of ANN has been successfully used by many researchers to develop estimating models in construction. Examples of these models include estimating the cost of change orders, trenching productivity, and the structural behavior of concrete slabs.

12.4.3.3 Fuzzy Logic As many of the linguistic terms used by humans involve a degree of fuzziness and relative significance, it is desirable to address the impact of such fuzziness on the solutions made by experts for complex problems. To support the decisions under such fuzzy situations, the fuzzy logic technique of artificial intelligence is beneficial.

Figure 12–10.
Elements of a Three-Layer Neural Network

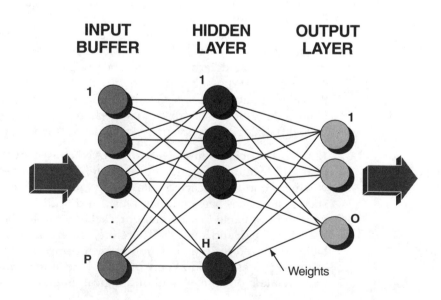

Figure 12-11.
Representing "Competition" as a Fuzzy Variable

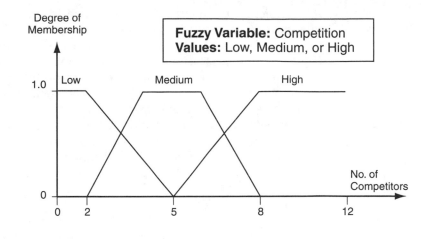

In fuzzy logic, each individual value for a given variable is not represented by a single number, rather, by a "Membership function" to represent the fuzziness involved. Looking at Figure 12-11, for example, when a contractor in a new bid considers that the level of competition to be "Medium," this means that the number of competitors can be between a range of 2 to 8 competitors. Using these membership functions, the technique applies rigorous mathematical formulation to determine a crisp value of the outcome or solution to a given problem.

No doubt that each of the artificial intelligence techniques presented here has its potential applications in construction engineering and management applications. Examples of application area being carried out by researchers and practitioners are: quality control, claims analysis, cost estimation, resources optimization, productivity assessment, diagnosis of problems, efficient material handling, risk assessment, and cause-effect analysis, among many others.

12.4.4 The Internet

The Internet has been regarded by many people as a revolution in communication and information technologies that is soon to change the manner in which everyday business is being conducted. Although the construction industry has been slow to adapt to almost all new technologies, the low cost and the many benefits of the Internet will prove to be very attractive to construction practitioners in formulating competitive business strategies. Contractors can use the Internet to coordinate among remote experts, advertise services cheaply to a broad base of customers, obtain information about out-of-town jobs, procure for cheaper materials and equipment, and find out who in the world has a solution to an urgent problem. Ultimately this means lower bids to submit, more jobs, global sophisticated appearance, and higher profits. With the industry's tighter project budgets and time constraints, information about new cheap materials, equipment, or techniques can mean higher job efficiency and productivity. The Internet, thus, becomes a key to reducing overhead cost and operating an efficient construction business.

Currently, and growing almost exponentially, thousands of commercial companies have connected to the Internet to offer online services to almost all countries in the world and almost 20 million computers. This is in addition to an increasing number of government agencies providing useful business information concerning trade, costs, and statistics. Some departments and cities have also taken the lead in advertising their online request for bidders, thus starting a change in the manner jobs can be obtained. It is expected that many processes will soon be redefined to make use of the wide reach and low cost of online communications, particularly with improved Internet security and confidentiality.

Physically, the Internet is a vast network connecting smaller networks of computers in many countries around the world, running on different platforms (e.g., workstations, microcomputers, mainframes) and using different operating systems (UNIX, Windows, Macintosh, DOS). To enable these computers to communicate, the Internet uses a Transmission Control Protocol/Internet Protocol (TCP/IP) to break the source information into packets and reassemble them at destination, bypassing operating system and platform barriers.

Access to the Internet is open for commercial users and individuals as it is for government, educational, and research organizations. The Internet is free, however for a fee, users can connect to a local service provider and save on their connection telephone bills. Among the Internet services, the World Wide Web (WWW) is the most interesting because of its multimedia nature and its user-friendly interface to the other Internet services.

As a general trend, the Internet will facilitate the replacement of current costly paper-based procedures with less-costly electronic means. Ultimately, with the introduction of new solutions to the Internet's security and confidentiality issues, the Internet can offer to a construction office a lot more than the telephone and the facsimile technologies are doing today.

The examples of Web-enabled devices and software applications are plenty. From cellular phones that can browse the World Wide Web to applications that can completely run from the remote server by the Web browser. Almost all the new versions of project management software such as Microsoft Project and Primavera have Web features. Other specialized software that provide Web-based project management services have also become available. Examples include BidCom, Framework, and Meridian. A listing of these software systems is provided in the appendix. With the new handheld gadgets and Web-enabled software, site-to-head-office communication is much facilitated so that reports are transmitted online and expert solutions are provided immediately to site professionals.

12.4.5 Advanced Applications

Based on the issues described in this chapter, among others, a wide spectrum of new and innovative technology and applications are being introduced by companies and research institutions. Although some of these applications are still under development, new improvements are being made daily and the near future will see a lot of these applications being mainstream. Some of the important technologies/applications include:

- Improving design productivity with the Internet.
- Virtual project extranets.
- Using 3D and video in design.
- Construction planning and management using 3D CAD models.
- e-Commerce and facilities management.
- Web-based GIS.
- Web-based design collaborative.
- Project-specific websites: Integrating the job site and the design office.
- Estimating and bidding on the Internet.
- Mobile and job site systems.
- Video conferencing.
- GIS/IT integration.
- Asset tracking.
- Mobile architecture: The impact of palm and wireless connectivity.
- Building the e-commerce infrastructure.
- Using your extranet to disseminate best practices.
- Surveying software.
- The paperless job site.
- Wireless construction management applications.

12.5 Summary

In this chapter, various special topics are presented. First, the techniques that deal with uncertainty in activity duration are discussed. Advanced tools and techniques are then introduced. The Internet is also presented as a fast growing approach for getting all business partners to collaborate for the purpose of reducing project cost. Various Web resources are included in Appendix A.

12.6 Bibliography

Ayre, R. & Willmott, D. (1995). "The Internet Means Business," *PC Magazine,* 14(9), pp. 195–203.

Eager, B. (1994). *"The Information Superhighway Illustrated,"* (Que Corporation).

Goldsborough, R. (1994). *"Straight Talk About The Information Superhighway."* Que Corporation.

Gonzalez-Quevedo, A. A., AbouRizk, S. M., Isley, D. T., and Halpin, D. W. (1993). "Comparison of Two Simulation Methodologies in Construction." *Journal Construction Engineering and Management,* ASCE, 119(3), pp. 573–589.

Hecht, A. (Dec. 1998). "A Web-Based Project Management Framework," PM Network, PMI.

Huang, R., Grigoriadis, A. M., and Halpin, D. W. (1994). "Simulation of Cable-stayed bridges using DISCO." *Proc., Winter Simulation Conf.,* Inst. of Electr. and Electronic Engrs., Piscataway, NJ, pp. 1130–1136.

Hulett, D. (Feb. 2000). "Project Schedule Risk Analysis: Monte Carlo Simulation or PERT?" PM Network, PMI. Vol. 14, No. 2, pp. 43–47.

Ioannou, P. G. (1989). *UM-CYCLONE User's Guide.* Dept. of Civ. Engrg. Univ. of Michigan, Ann Arbor, MI.

Schhuyler, J. (Jan. 2000). "Exploiting the Best of Critical Chain and Monte Carlo Simulation," PM Network, PMI. Vol. 14, No. 1, pp. 56–60.

Scitor Process V 3 (1999). Sunnyvale, CA: Scitor Corporation.

Tommelein, I., Riley, D., and Howell, G., (1999). "Parade Game: Impact of Work Flow Variability on Trade Performance," *Journal of Construction Engineering and Management,* ASCE, Vol. 125, No. 5, pp. 304–310.

Wakefield, R. R., and Sears, G. A. (1997). "Petri nets for simulating and modeling of construction systems." *Journal Construction Engineering and Management,* ASCE, 123(2), pp. 105–112.

12.7 Exercises

1. Conduct a Web search for information related to any of the topics described in this textbook. Report on the top interesting sites found.

2. Based on a Web search of various project management software, compare the capabilities of at least three Web-based software systems for integrated project management.

3. Student group projects: each group of two to four students uses one of the tools described under section 12.4, search the literature on state-of-the-art development and apply the technique to one case study purposes (can be obtained from the literature) for demonstration. Each group makes a 10-minute presentation of their findings.

WEB RESOURCES

The various websites provided in this section are by no means exhaustive. Everyday new web sites become available and new information is put on the Web. The following web sites serve as examples. Readers are encouraged to conduct a Web search using their desired keywords to obtain links to updated information.

Some Websites Related to Chapter 2: Project Acquisition

Website	Site Description
www.constructionplace.com or www.constructionplace.com/glossary.html	Various construction information, services, and glossary of terms
http://www.foulgerpratt.com/whycm.htm	Discussion on the benefits of project management
www.pubs.asce.org/contract.html	Sample contract forms
www.construction-pm.com or www.construction-pm.com/handbook.html#anchor31554	Construction project participants, project manager
www.dforeman.com	Foreman construction management, marginal subs
www.brtable.org/document.cfm/141	The business roundtable, contractual relations CICE Reports - "A-7 Contractual Arrangements"
www.new-technologies.org	Emerging construction technologies Emerging trends—construction technology
www.brtable.org or www.brtable.org/issue.cfm/1	The business roundtable, emerging trends—international projects—"Guide for Global Project Delivery" 04/23/99
www.regis-usa.com or www.regis-usa.com/psws.htm	Regis Communications, emerging trends—project-specific websites; Web-based project info. systems
www.usprojects.com or www.usprojects.com/customer/cnsprod/html/main.cfm	ConstructLink, emerging trends—project-specific websites; Web-based project info. systems
www.brtable.org or www.brtable.org/issue.cfm/1	The business roundtable, emerging trends—quality assurance CICE Reports—"Modern Management Systems"
www.brtable.org or www.brtable.org/issue.cfm/1	The business roundtable, emerging trends—quality assurance CICE Reports—"Improving Construction Safety Performance"

Some Websites Related to Chapter 2: Project Acquisition *(continued)*

Website	Site Description
www.brtable.org or www.brtable.org/issue.cfm/1	The business roundtable, project delivery method publications —"The Business Stake in Effective Project Systems" 09/16/99
http://138.25.138.94/signposts/articles/Generic/ Development/364.html	Signposts to Asia & the Pacific Project delivery method Build-Operate-Transfer (BOT)
www.fta.dot.gov/library/planning/prob/execsum.html	Federal Transit Administration, project delivery method, turnkey
www.dforeman.com/	Foreman construction management, project delivery method design/build
www.dig.bris.ac.uk/teaching/o_a_hf/pscales/pscales .htm	University of Bristol, project organizational structure, techniques that may be used in the management of large projects
www.dforeman.com/	Foreman construction management, types of contracts, contract baseline
www.dforeman.com/	Foreman construction management, types of contracts, contract-subcontract
http://www.aiaonline.com	The American Institute of Architects, Q&A discussion and case study projects
www.construction-on-line.co.uk	Information on various construction projects such as drawings, models, online pictures and site-related data.
www.copywriter.com/ab/constr.html	Connections to builders, contractors, construction managers, trade workers, architects, designers, engineers and vendors.
http://cic.vtt.fi/links/constrit.html	Network of construction IT centers
www.nationalcontractors.com/	Information on contractors nationally and internationally
www.4specs.com/	Directory of specified construction products divided by the CIC
www.nwbuildnet.com/nwbn/specifications.html	Building and construction specifications resource page
www.aecinfo.com	The e-market place for the global building industry
www.ncsbcs.org	Construction industry codes
www.nrc.ca	Canadian national research council, research in construction

Some Websites Related to Chapter 2: Data Management Tools

Website	Site Description
www.pcshowandtell.com or www.pcshowandtell.com/shows.asp?product= Excel_97	PC show and tell, video/audio demonstrations of Excel functions
www.microsoft.com	Microsoft Excel and Microsoft Project
www.primavera.com	Primavera, SureTrack, and Primavera P3 systems
www.wardsystems.com/genehunt.htm	GeneHunter software
www.palisade.com/html/trial_versions.html	Evolver software—download evaluation version

Some Websites Related to Chapters 3 and 5: Planning and Scheduling

Website	Site Description
www.byte.com/art/9702/sec15/art3.htm	BYTE, (Article) adding more PERT charting to Microsoft Project
www.people.virginia.edu/~av9y/ITC-PM-web/PM-planning-doc-july12.htm	Project planning processes
http://tiger.coe.missouri.edu/~perfsppt/Dbell/index.html	University of Missouri, Columbia PERT/GANTT and Critical Path review of Microsoft Project for Windows
www.byte.com/art/9504/sec12/art9.htm	BYTE, PERT/GANTT and Critical Path (article) comparing project management tools for Windows
www.scis.nova.edu/ or www.scis.nova.edu/~mcte/MCTE661/pert.html	Nova Southeastern University, PERT/GANTT and Critical Path descriptions of PERT charts, Gantt charts, and WBS
www.w3c2.com.au/steve/sd201/pert.htm	Optimum IS Solutions, PERT/GANTT and Critical Path example of PERT and Gantt charts
www.cs.cmu.edu/~SW_Managemnt/html/mod_2/mod_2_4.html	Carnegie Mellon, PERT/GANTT and Critical Path, making and using activity networks by Dr. James E. Tomayko
www.uwf.edu/coehelp/studentaccounts/rnew/perthome.html?ti2Xdw=www.uwf.edu/~coehelp/studentaccounts/rnew/perthome.html	University of West Florida, PERT/GANTT and Critical Path program evaluation and review technique
www.goalqpc.com/ www.goalqpc.com/RESEARCH/7mp.html	Goal/QPC, PERT/GANTT and Critical Path, the seven management and planning tools
www.dig.bris.ac.uk/ www.dig.bris.ac.uk/teaching/o_a_hf/pscales/pscales.htm	University of Bristol, PERT/GANTT and Critical Path, an overview of techniques that may be used in the management of large engineering projects
www.dforeman.com/	Foreman construction management, planning reconstruction

Some Websites Related to Chapter 4: Cost Estimation

Website	Site Description
www.rsmeans.com/	R.S. Means is North America's leading provider of construction cost data
www.mailbase.ac.uk/lists/construction-process	Discussion on construction processes
www.dcd.com/dcd.html	Design and cost magazine for engineers and contractors.
www.doc.gov	Bureau of Economic Analysis. Information on economic growth, inflation, regional development, etc.
www.CSInet.org	Construction specifications institute—MasterFormat
http://tacoma.wpi.edu/firsto//mainform1.htm	Detailed MasterFormat
www.rsmeans.com/means/demo/g2.html	G2 Estimator; An estimating software
www.build.com/	Building improvement network; Directory for building/home improvement products and info
www.icoste.org	The International Cost Engineering Council
http://www.copywriter.com/constr.htm	Connections to contractors, construction managers, trade workers, architects, designers, and vendors

Some Websites Related to Chapter 4: Cost Estimation *(continued)*

Website	Site Description
www.io.org/~estim8s/best-est.html	Best estimator software
www.dcd.com/d4cost.html	Design 4/cost. A square-foot cost-estimating software
www.umoncton.ca/cie/	Computers & ind. engineering. Int. journal for cost studies
www.aecinfo.com	AEC Info Center, useful prices for architects/constructors.

Some Websites Related to Chapter 6: Line of Balance

Website	Site Description
http://www.dcmc.hq.dla.mil/dcmc_o/oc/earnvalu/help/lob.htm	Origin of the line of balance in manufacturing
http://www.rdg.ac.uk/~kcshuwil/cme/edit161.htm	A study of controlling the activity interval time in LOB scheduling
http://www.umsl.edu/~jmartini/pomnotes/owebprocessdesign.htm	Design of repetitive processes

Some Websites Related to Chapter 7: Resource Allocation and Leveling

Website	Site Description
http://www.bham.ac.uk/planning/	The University of Birmingham, The Planning & Resource Allocation Section
http://officeupdate.microsoft.com/Articles/projht5.htm	Microsoft Project 98, using views to highlight the impacts of resource leveling
http://www.cisti.nrc.ca/cisti/journals/cjce/l99-028.html	A fuzzy optimal model for construction resource leveling scheduling
http://aug3.augsburg.edu/depts/infotech/project98/Features/Resource_Leveling.htm	Resource leveling
http://www.dcmc.hq.dla.mil/dcmc_o/oc/earnvalu/help/pert.htm	PERT and resource leveling
http://138.92.9.17/mtm630/resource_allocation.htm	Resource allocation
http://officeupdate.microsoft.com/articlelist/Projectarticles.htm	Microsoft Project 98 article lists

Some Websites Related to Chapter 8: TCT Analysis

Website	Site Description
http://www.engr.uiuc.edu/Publications/engineering_research/1996/gen1/gen1-11.html	Operations research, construction, time-cost, tradeoff optimization
http://www.engr.uiuc.edu/Publications/summary99/pg000136.htm	Construction, time-cost, tradeoff, optimization

Some Websites Related to Chapter 11: Project Control

Website	Site Description
www.prochain.com/faq.asp	ProChain Solutions, Inc—Innovations In Project Scheduling & Management
www.nnh.com/ev/pert2.html	NNH Enterprises, Earned Value Papers PERT/GANTT and Critical Path

Web sites of projects:
   www.bigdig.com/index.htm
   www.wpi.edu/~salazar/mqp
   www.wpi.edu/~salazar/holden
   www.anticruelty.org/thumbnail_gallery.htm
	
	Central Artery Project, Boston MA
	Brookfield Engineering Project, Middleborough MA
	Bullard Street School Project, Holden MA
	Construction thumbnail gallery for projects

www.nnh.com/ev/papers.html	NNH Enterprises—Papers on various constructio management issues: Earned Value, WBS, LOB

Some Websites Related to Chapter 12: Risk Analysis

Website	Site Description
http://gunsmoke.ecn.purdue.edu/CE597N/1997F/students/muhamad.abduh.1/project/	Purdue University, PERT tutorial on simulation of PERT networks

Some Websites Related to: General Project Management

Website	Site Description
www.pmi.org	Project Management Institute
www.synapse.net/~loday	Project Management Forum
www.bdcmag.com/	Building Design & Construction Magazine
www.4pm.com	Project Manager's Palette
www.asterlsk.co.uk/project/Pmgen.html	PM Cafe
www.pmforum.org/vendors/vendors.htm	Project management forum
www.pmboulevard.com	Project management boulevard
www.sn.no/ipma	International Project Management Association
www.eevl.ac.ul	Edinburgh Engineering virtual library
www.aiaonline.com	The American Institute of Architects. Q&A discussion and case study projects

Some Websites Related to: Web-Based Project Management

Website	Site Description
www.handilinks.com/index.php3/computers/software/project_management	Links to many project management software
www.pmboulevard.com	Internet portal for complete project management services with monthly subscription
www.constructionweblinks.com	More than 2,000 indexed online resources for the construction industry
www.web4engineers.com	Example projects
www.microframe.com	MicroFrame software
www.Bluelineonline.com	Blueline Online Web-based project management services
www.bidcom.com	Web-based project management services
www.planview.com	PlanView enterprise–wide project management
www.emergingsolutions.com	Web-based project management
www.grantlun.com	Web-based project management
http://www.meridian-marketing.com/ACCENT/nis_3.html	GraphicVUE project management system
www.Bbid.thebluebook.com	The Blue Book's Online Bid Management System
www.cincom.com/acquire	Acquire System: Bid Management Services Online
www.contractorsesource.com	Contractors E Source: Online system for acquiring subcontractors' quotes
www.e-builder.net	E-Builder: Internet–based project-specific sites for communication
www.account4.com	Web-based project control software
www.amsrealtime.com	AMS Realtime: Enterprise Project Management
www.webestimating.com	Web-based estimating system
www.callingwatson.com	Business-to-business service on environmental health and safety
www.mps-inc.com	Prolog website by Meridian Project Systems

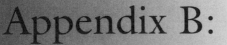

NEW CASE STUDY

The case study is to construct the infrastructure (water, sewer, and electricity facilities) for a new, small four-acre residential area. The objective is to conduct a cost estimate and a detailed schedule, select proper methods of construction, prepare a realistic bid, study the impact of seasonal productivity factors on project time and cost, and demonstrate the project control features.

Brainstorming

The project management team identified the main activities of the project, the supervisory personnel, and the logical relationships between activities as follows:

Activity No.	Type of Work	Activity Description	Predecessors	Supervisor
1		Clear site	ST	Ahmed
2		Survey & layout	1	Ahmed
3		Rough grade	2	Ahmed
4	CIVIL	Excavate for sewer	24	Ali
5		Excavate elec. manholes	3	Ali
6		Drill well	24	Ali
7		Water tank foundations	24	Hussen
8		Tank fabrication & erection	7	Hussen
9		Install manholes	5	Fawzy
10		Install electric duct	9	Fawzy
11		Erect overhead poles	3	Fawzy
12	ELECTRICAL	Overhead poles wiring	11	Sid
13		Duct wiring work	14,10,15	Sid
14		Transformer erection	9	Ziad
15		Bus bar erection	9	Ziad
16		Electric safety inspection	12,13	Ziad

(continued)

345

Activity No.	Type of Work	Activity Description	Predecessors	Supervisor
17		Connect piping	18, 20	Essam
18		Tank piping and valves	8	Essam
19	MECHANICAL	Install well pump	6	Essam
20		Underground water piping	19	Essam
21		Install sewer and backfill	4	Essam
22		Sewer inspection, test	21	Amr
23		Sanitary inspection, test	17	Amr
24		Milestone	3	

Planning:

Planning consists of:

- Construction of the Activity on Node (AON) and Activity on Arrow (AOA) diagrams.
- Defining the Work Breakdown Structure (WBS) and Organization Breakdown Structure (OBS) data.

In order to construct the AON and AOA diagrams, we need to calculate the activities' sequence steps from their dependency relationships. Notice that Start (ST) and Finish (FN) activities have been added (as discussed in Chapter 3).

Activity Dependency Table and Sequence Step Calculation

Activity No.	Activity Description	Immediately Preceding Activities (IPAs)	Sequence Step (SS)
ST	—	—	SS(ST) = 1
1	Clear site	ST	SS(1) = 2
2	Survey & layout	1	SS(2) = 3
3	Rough grade	2	SS(3) = 4
4	Excavate for sewer	24	SS(4) = 6
5	Excavate elec. manholes	3	SS(5) = 5
6	Drill well	24	SS(6) = 6
7	Water tank foundations	24	SS(7) = 6
8	Tank fabrication & erection	7	SS(8) = 7
9	Install manholes	5	SS(9) = 6
10	Install electric duct	9	SS(10) = 7
11	Erect overhead poles	3	SS(11) = 5
12	Overhead poles wiring	11	SS(12) = 6
13	Duct wiring work	14,10,15	SS(13) = 8
14	Transformer erection	9	SS(14) = 7
15	Bus bar erection	9	SS(15) = 7
16	Electric safety inspection	12,13	SS(16) = 9
17	Connect piping	18,20	SS(17) = 9

Activity Dependency Table and Sequence Step Calculation *(continued)*

Activity No.	Activity Description	Immediately Preceding Activities (IPAs)	Sequence Step (SS)
18	Tank piping and valves	8	SS(18) = 8
19	Install well pump	6	SS(19) = 7
20	Underground water piping	19	SS(20) = 8
21	Install sewer and backfill	4	SS(21) = 7
22	Sewer inspection, test	21	SS(22) = 8
23	Sanitary inspection, test	17	SS(23) = 10
24	Milestone	3	SS(24) = 5
FN	—	16, 22, 23	SS(FN) = 11

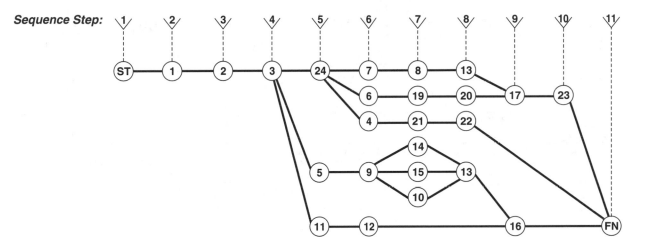

AON Network of the Case Study

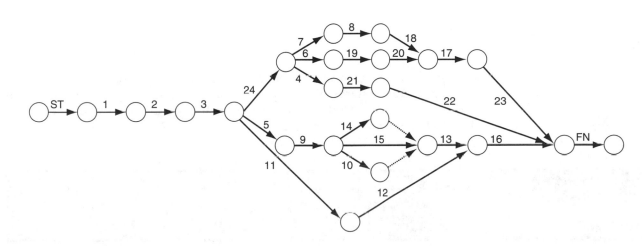

AOA Network of the Case Study

Work Breakdown Structure (WBS) and Organization Breakdown Structure (OBS) data:

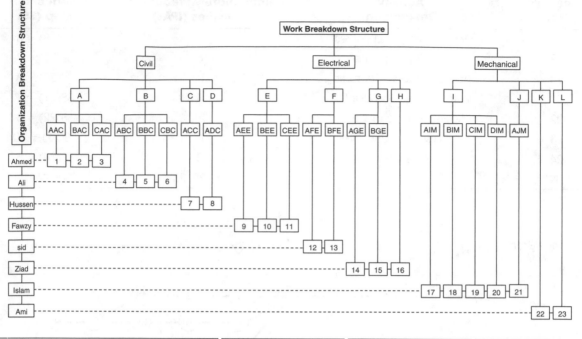

	WBS	Chart Key			
A	Site preparation		G	Transformer and bus bar erec.
B	Excavation		H	Electric safety inspection
C	Concreting		I	Sanitary water
D	Steel work		J	Sewer water
E	Electrical installations		K	Sewer inspection
F	Wiring work		L	Sanitary inspection

AAC	Clearing
BAC	Surveying
CAC	Grading
ABC	Excavation for sewer
BBC	Excavation for elec. manhole
CBC	Drill well
ACC	Water tank foundations
ADC	Tank fabrication & erection

AEE	Electrical manholes
BEE	Electrical ducts
CEE	Over head poles
AFE	Over head poles wiring work
BFE	Duct wiring work & cable pull
AGE	Transformer erection
BGE	Bus bar erection

AIM	Connect piping
BIM	Tank piping and valves
CIM	Install well pump
DIM	Under ground water piping
AJM	Install sewer and back fill

Resources Data

Let's now use our spreadsheet program and input the resource data that are needed for our project. We can start with a copy of the previous case study file but we change the data to our new case study file. Remember to use the **Reset** button in the Schedule sheet to remove the schedule data.

> **Note:** A spreadsheet file of this case study is included in the CD accompanying this book. The file is: **Case-Study-New.xls**. The various experiments made on this file are discussed in the following pages.

	A Code	B Description	C Rate/hr	D BasicRate
9	L51	Electrician	$47.5	$30.1
10	L81	Equip._Oper._Medium	$43.5	$27.6
11	L96	Labor_Foreman	$35.2	$22.3
12	L102	Laborer	$32.6	$20.7
13	L132	Plumber	$48.5	$30.7
14	L135	Plumber_Apprentice	$38.8	$24.6
15	L228	Welder	$45.4	$28.8

	A Code	B Description	C Rate/hr	D BasicRate
9	E135	Clamshell_Bucket_.38	$6.1	$5.6
10	E138	Clamshell_Bucket.76	$8.4	$7.6
11	E141	Concrete_Cart_.28	$6.8	$6.2
12	E228	Dozer_150_KW	$117.4	$106.8
13				
14				

Labour **Equipment** Crews Materials Subs Methods Estimate R

Labor and Equipment sheets

	J				
2	**Notes:**	1. A crew contains up to five labor and equipment resources;		L3	
3		2. Select LABOR or EQUIPMENT using the combo boxes		E1	
4		and then copy their codes from cells O2 or O3			
5		to resource fields **Res1** to **Res5**; and			
6		3. Shaded cells contain formulas that can be copied from one row to the other.			

	A Code	B Description	C Rate/d	NoR1	Res1	NoR2	Res2	NoR3	Res3	NoR4	Res4	NoR5	Res5
9	CRZ-26	Electrician	$1,282	2.00	L51	2.00	L102	1.00		1.00		1.00	
10	CRZ-28	Plumber	$1,220	1.00	L132	2.00	L102	1.00	L135	1.00		1.00	
11	CRZ-29	clearing crew	$1,549	1.00	E228	1.00	L81	1.00	L102	1.00		1.00	
12	CRZ-30	sewer excavation	$1,092	2.00	E138	1.00	L102	2.00	L81	1.00		1.00	
13	CRZ-31	sewer pipe install	$1,323	1.00	L132	1.00	L135	1.00	L228	1.00	L102	1.00	
14	CRZ-32	clearing crew (2)	$3,619	2.00	E228	2.00	L81	4.00	L102	1.00		1.00	
15	CRZ-33	manhole excav.	$658	1.00	E135	1.00	L81	1.00	L102	1.00		1.00	
16	CRZ-34	Duct works	$641	1.00	L51	1.00	L102	1.00		1.00		1.00	
17	CRZ-35	concreting crew	$1,173	3.00	L102	2.00	E141	1.00	L96	1.00		1.00	

Labour Equipment **Crews** Materials Subs Methods Estimate Reports Schedule Progr

Crews sheet

Materials sheet

	A	B	C	D	E	
1	Notes:	1. The "Avail" field can be used to link this table to other inventory sheets.				
2		2. An average 10% is added to the Basic$/Unit for overhead and profit.				
3		3. Material costs include delivery to the site. No sales tax included or allowance for was				
4						
5						
6						
7						
8	**Code**	**Description**	**Cost/Unit**	**Basic$/Unit**	**Unit**	**A**
9	M163-205-0400	Install circuit breakers 0.5MVA and bus bar	$286.0	260.00	Ea	
10	M157-610-3471	Sewer Pipe, isolation, fittings	$91.3	83.00	m	
11	M157-610-3472	Electrical duct	$11.0	10.00	m	
12	M157-610-3473	Electrical manhoples	$880.0	800.00	Ea	
13	M157-610-3474	electrical wires	$13.2	12.00	m	
14	M157-610-3475	Electrical poles	$242.0	220.00	Ea	
15	M157-610-3476	Transformer 0.5 MVA	$22,000.0	20,000.00	Ea	
16	M157-610-3477	Water pipe, isolation, fittings	$51.7	47.00	m	
17	M157-610-3478	Valves	$104.5	95.00	Ea	
18	M157-610-3480	pumps	$418.0	380.00	Ea	
19	M033-126-0350	Concrete material	$412.5	375.00	m3	
20	M160-230-3250	Electric wires (4 cm2)	$24.2	22.00	m	
21						

Tabs: Labour / Equipment / Crews / **Materials** / Subs / Methods / Estimate / Reports / Schedule / Pro

Materials sheet

Subcontractors sheet

	Code	Description	Cost/Unit	Sub-Contractor	SubCost/Unit	Unit
8						
9		**Electrical subcontractors**	$0.0			
10	S1-1	Electrical duct fixations	$35.2		$32.0	m
11	S1-2	Electrical pole supply&erection	$462.0		$420.0	Ea
12	S1-3	Electrical transformer and bus fitting	$14,520.0		$13,200.0	LSUM
13	S1-4	Poles wiring	$46.8		$42.5	m
14	S1-5	Duct wiring	$46.8		$42.5	m
15	S1-6	manholes installation	$2,750.0		$2,500.0	m
16	S30-00	Ontario Electricals	$0.0			
17	S30-01	Inspection main panel	$319.0		$290.0	ea
18			$0.0			
19		**Mechanical subcontractors**	$0.0			
20	S2-1	connect water pipes	$335.5		$305.0	ea
21	S2-2	sanitary water subcontractor	$93.5		$85.0	m
22	S2-3	sewer water subcontractor	$126.5		$115.0	m
23			$0.0			
24		**Civil subcontractors**	$0.0			
25	S3-01	steel work subcontractor	$0.0			
26	S3-02	concrete work subcontractor	$429.0		$390.0	m3
27	S3-03	excavation subcontractor	$4.1		$3.8	ea
28	S3-08	excavation subcontractor for manholes	$13.2		$12.0	ea
29	S3-04	survey work subcontractor	$550.0		$500.0	ea
30	S3-05	grading work subcontractor	$825.0		$750.0	ea
31	S3-06	drill well	$1,100.0		$1,000.0	ea
32	S3-07	drill well (1)	$1,375.0		$1,250.0	ea
33						
34		**Ontario Safety**	$0.0			
35	S26-01	Electrical Safety inspection	$605.0		$550.0	ea
36	S26-02	Sewer Safety inspection	$1,375.0		$1,250.0	ea
37	S26-03	Sanitary Safety inspection	$935.0		$850.0	ea
38	S26-04	Milestone	$0.0		$0.0	ea
39						
40		**Steel Work**				
41	S4-01	tank fabrication	$14,850.0		$13,500.0	ea
42	S4-02	tank fabrication	$18,700.0		$17,000.0	ea
43	S4-03	well pump & fittings	$1,980.0		$1,800.0	ea
44	S4-04	well pump & fittings (1)	$2,420.0		$2,200.0	ea
45						

Tabs: Instructions / Labour / Equipment / Crews / Materials / **Subs** / Methods / Estimate / Reports / Schedule / Progress /

Notes:

- Normal day is eight hours.
- Overtime hour has 90% productivity.
- The hourly rate of the first four overtime hours is 20% more than normal rate, afterwards 50%.
- All methods in the "Methods" sheet have initial seasonal productivity factors as 1.0 (last three columns).
- Notice that in the "Methods" sheet, various methods of construction are related to the same type of work. Example are rows 12, 13, & 14: the first uses a crew with normal hours, second uses same crew with overtime hours, and the third uses subcontractor.
- Material quantity in column "J" can be made = Total Production quantity in column "D" of the "Methods" sheet.

	Code	Description	Cost /d	TotPr /d	Unit Cost	Units	Crew	Sub	RegPr/d	MatQ/d	Material	Hrs/d	OTadj	MatCost	CrewCos	SubCost	WinPr	SprPr	FallPr
9	CSI-157-26	Electrical safety inspection	$605	1.00	$605	Ea		S26-01	1.000	1.00		8.00	8.00			605.00	1.00	1.00	1.00
10	CSI-021-108-0403	tank fabrication	$1,485	0.10	$14,850	lsum		S4-01	0.100	0.10		8.00	8.00			1,405.00	1.00	1.00	1.00
11	CSI-021-108-0404	tank fabrication (1)	$2,805	0.15	$18,700	lsum		S4-02	0.150	0.15		8.00	8.00			2,805.00	1.00	1.00	1.00
12	CSI-021-108-0405	water pipe installation and fitting	$5,356	80.00	$67		CRZ-28		80.000	80.000	M157-610-3	8.000	8.00	4,136.00	1,220.39		1.00	1.00	1.00
13	CSI-021-108-0416	water pipe installation and fitting (1)	$7,200	101.50	$71	m	CRZ-28		70.000	101.500	M157-610-3	12.000	12.80	5,247.55	1,952.63		1.00	1.00	1.00
14	CSI-021-108-0433	water pipe installation and fitting (2)	$14,025	150.00	$94	m		S2-2	150.000	150.00		8.00	8.00			14,025.00	1.00	1.00	1.00
15	CSI-021-108-0400	Clearing with dozer	$1,549	4,225.00	$0	m2	CRZ-29		4225.000			8.00	8.00		1,548.65		1.00	1.00	1.00
16	CSI-021-108-0426	Clearing with dozer (1)	$2,478	6,126.25	$0	m2	CRZ-29		4225.000			12.00	12.80		2,477.84		1.00	1.00	1.00
17	CSI-021-108-0412	Clearing with dozer (2)	$5,791	12,252.50	$0	m2	CRZ-32		8450.000			12.000	12.80		5,790.92		1.00	1.00	1.00
18	CSI-021-108-0435	Concrete for tank foundation	$3,218	7.50	$429	m3		S3-02	7.500	7.50		8.00	8.00			3,217.50	1.00	1.00	1.00
19	CSI-033-172-2650	Concrete for tank foundation (1)	$7,361	15.00	$491	m3	CRZ-35		15.000	15.00	M033-126-1	8.00	8.00	6,187.50	1,173.19		1.00	1.00	1.00
20	CSI-151-551-4420	connect water piping	$1,531	6.00	$255	Ea	CRZ-28		6.000	6.00	M157-610-3	8.00	8.00	310.20	1,220.39		1.00	1.00	1.00
21	CSI-021-108-0410	connect water piping (1)	$2,402	8.70	$276	Ea	CRZ-28		6.000	8.700	M157-610-3	12.000	12.80	449.79	1,952.63		1.00	1.00	1.00
22	CSI-021-108-0431	connect water piping (2)	$4,026	12.00	$336	Ea		S2-1	12.000	12.00		8.00	8.00			4,026.00	1.00	1.00	1.00
23	CSI-021-108-0402	Drill well	$1,100	1.00	$1,100			S3-06	1.000	1.00		8.00	8.00			1,100.00	1.00	1.00	1.00
24	CSI-021-108-0424	Drill well (1)	$1,684	1.23	$1,375	ea		S3-07	1.000	1.23		10.00	10.40			1,684.38	1.00	1.00	1.00
25	CSI-157-250-1600	Ductwork fittings	$1,081	40.00	$27	m	CRZ-34		40.000	40.00	M157-610-3	8.00	8.00	440.00	640.85		1.00	1.00	1.00
26	CSI-021-108-0422	Ductwork fittings (1)	$1,663	58.00	$29	m	CRZ-34		40.000	58.00	M157-610-3	12.00	12.80	638.00	1,025.36		1.00	1.00	1.00
27	CSI-021-108-0428	Ductwork fittings (2)	$4,216	119.77	$35	m		S1-1	82.600	119.77		12.00	12.80			4,215.90	1.00	1.00	1.00
28	CSI-157-29	dummy		100,000.00		ea		S26-04	100000.000	100000.00		8.00	8.00				1.00	1.00	1.00
29	CSI-021-108-0401	excavation for sewer	$1,092	280.00	$4	m3	CRZ-30		280.000			8.00	8.00		1,091.79		1.00	1.00	1.00
30	CSI-021-108-0420	excavation for sewer (1)	$1,747	435.00	$4	m3	CRZ-30		300.000			12.000	12.80		1,746.86		1.00	1.00	1.00
31	CSI-021-108-0411	excavation for sewer (2)	$2,273	551.00	$4			S3-03	360.000	551.000		12.000	12.80			2,272.88	1.00	1.00	1.00
32	CSI-022-238-0200	Excavation, manhole	$858	64.00	$10	m3	CRZ-33		64.000			8.00	8.00		658.00		1.00	1.00	1.00
33	CSI-021-108-0423	Excavation, manhole (1)	$1,053	92.80	$11	m3	CRZ-33		64.000			12.00	12.80		1,052.94		1.00	1.00	1.00
34	CSI-021-108-0421	Excavation, manhole (2)	$2,450	185.60	$13	m3		S3-08	128.000	185.60		12.00	12.80			2,449.92	1.00	1.00	1.00
35	CSI-021-108-0406	Fittings well pump	$1,980	1.00	$1,980	ea		S4-03	1.000	1.000		8.000	8.00			1,980.00	1.00	1.00	1.00
36	CSI-021-108-0425	Fittings well pump (1)	$5,929	2.45	$2,420	ea		S4-04	2.000	2.45		10.00	10.40			5,929.00	1.00	1.00	1.00
37	CSI-022-51	grading	$825	1.00	$825	acres		S3-05	1.000	1.00		8.00	8.00			825.00	1.00	1.00	1.00
38	CSI-163-205-0400	Install circuit breakers 0.5MVA and	$1,568	1.00	$1,568	Ea	CRZ-26		1.000	1.00	M163-205-0	8.00	8.00	286.00	1,281.70		1.00	1.00	1.00
39	CSI-021-108-0417	Install circuit breakers 0.5MVA and	$2,465	1.45	$1,700	Ea	CRZ-26		1.000	1.450	M163-205-0	12.000	12.80	414.70	2,050.71		1.00	1.00	1.00
40	CSI-021-108-0409	install transformer	$14,520	1.00	$14,520			S1-3	1.000	1.000		8.000	8.00			14,520.00	1.00	1.00	1.00
41	CSI-161-165-0020	Install wiring from breaker	$1,986	53.33	$37	m	CRZ-26		53.333	53.33	M157-610-3	8.00	8.00	704.00	1,281.70		1.00	1.00	1.00
42	CSI-021-108-0419	Install wiring from breaker (1)	$3,072	77.33	$40	m	CRZ-26		53.333	77.333	M157-610-3	12.000	12.80	1,020.80	2,050.71		1.00	1.00	1.00
43	CSI-021-108-0430	Install wiring from breaker (2)	$7,491	160.23	$47	m		S1-5	110.500	160.23		12.00	12.80			7,490.52	1.00	1.00	1.00
44	CSI-167-110-0005	manholes installion	$2,162	1.00	$2,162	Ea	CRZ-26		1.000	1.00	M157-610-3	8.00	8.00	880.00	1,281.70		1.00	1.00	1.00
45	CSI-021-108-0427	manholes installation (1)	$3,327	1.45	$2,294	Ea	CRZ-26		1.000	1.45	M157-610-3	12.00	12.80	1,276.00	2,050.71		1.00	1.00	1.00
46	CSI-021-108-0434	manholes installation (2)	$5,500	2.00	$2,750	Ea		S1-6	2.000	2.00		8.00	8.00			5,500.00	1.00	1.00	1.00
47	CSI-021-108-0408	Poles erection	$3,696	8.00	$462	ea		S1-2	8.000	8.000		8.000	8.00			3,696.00	1.00	1.00	1.00
48	CSI-160-230-3250	poles wiring	$3,218	80.00	$40	m	CRZ-26		80.000	80.00	M160-230-3	8.00	8.00	1,936.00	1,281.70		1.00	1.00	1.00
49	CSI-021-108-0418	poles wiring (1)	$4,858	116.00	$42	m	CRZ-26		80.000	116.000	M160-230-3	12.000	12.80	2,807.20	2,050.71		1.00	1.00	1.00
50	CSI-021-108-0429	poles wiring (2)	$9,338	199.74	$47	m		S1-4	137.750	199.74		12.00	12.80			9,337.73	1.00	1.00	1.00
51	CSI-157-28	Sanitary Safety inspection	$935	1.00	$935	Ea		S26-03	1.000	1.00		8.00	8.00			935.00	1.00	1.00	1.00
52	CSI-151-801-1040	Sewer pipe installation and backfill	$12,461	122.00	$102	m	CRZ-31		122.000	122.00	M157-610-3	8.00	8.00	11,138.60	1,322.78		1.00	1.00	1.00
53	CSI-021-108-0414	Sewer pipe installation and backfill	$15,355	145.00	$106	m	CRZ-31		100.000	145.000	M157-610-3	12.000	12.80	13,238.50	2,116.44		1.00	1.00	1.00
54	CSI-021-108-0432	Sewer pipe installation and backfill	$23,150	183.00	$127	m		S2-3	183.000	183.00		8.00	8.00			23,149.50	1.00	1.00	1.00
55	CSI-157-27	Sewer Safety inspection	$1,375	1.00	$1,375	Ea		S26-02	1.000	1.00		8.00	8.00			1,375.00	1.00	1.00	1.00
56	CSI-013-306-1100	Survey and Layout	$1,100	2.00	$550	acres		S3-04	2.000	2.00		8.00	8.00			1,100.00	1.00	1.00	1.00
57	CSI-151-181-5240	valve connections	$3,310	20.00	$166	Ea	CRZ-28		20.000	20.00	M157-610-3	8.00	8.00	2,090.00	1,220.39		1.00	1.00	1.00

Instructions / Labour / Equipment / Crews / Materials / Subs / **Methods** / Estimate / Reports / Schedule / Progress / S-Curve Control / Earned-Value Con

Methods sheet

The Estimate

In the Estimate sheet, we define the project activities and their data related to:

- The work breakdown structure (WBS) of the case study.
- The organization breakdown structure (OBS).
- The contract items and quantity of work associated with each activity.
- Up to three methods for constructing each activity.
- Specifying the three most critical resources and their daily limits.

After entering the data, automatic calculations are made for the cost, duration, and resource amounts for each activity, as a function of its selected method of construction (column O). Total cost and duration for each activity according to the selected method of construction shown in columns R and AH, respectively.

Indirect cost is considered as a fixed amount of $500/day in this case study.

The Estimate Sheet:

Note that initially, column O shows that method 1 (cheapest) is used in all activities. Also, observe the key resources and their limit specified on the top of the sheet.

WBS-OBS

Scheduling

After completing the Estimate sheet, we send data to Microsoft Project using the button on the Estimate sheet. In Microsoft Project, we add activity relationship (you can use the Predecessors column). Once done, the project duration is shown to be 35 days and the bar chart and PERT (network) diagrams of Microsoft Project are as follows:

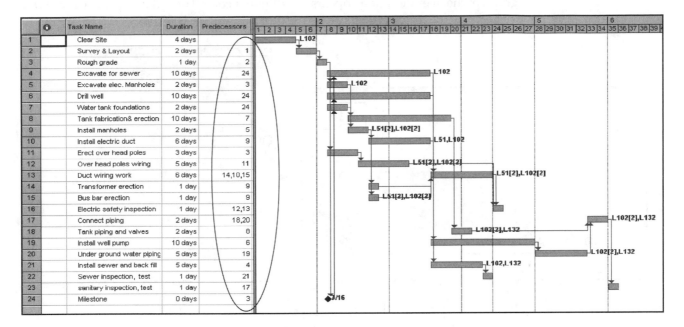

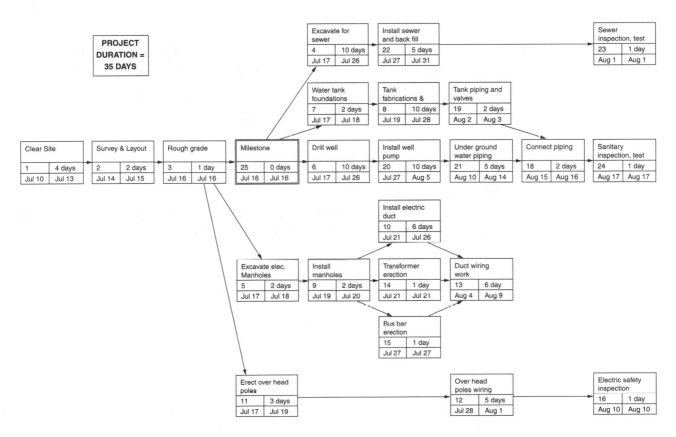

Dealing with Resource Limits in Microsoft Project

We assume the following resource limits: L102=3; L51=2; and L132=1

Viewing Overallocated Resources

With the resource limits specified in the Resource sheet, the view in the Resource graph of the overallocation appears in a different color. The following are the resource histograms for the three key resources (project duration is 35 days):

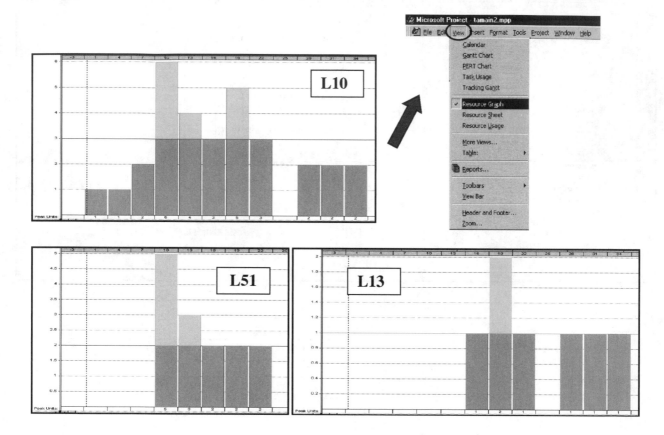

Resource Leveling

In order to allocate the overallocated resources in Microsoft Project we can use the **Resource Leveling** option from the **Tools** menu, as follows:

There are three
methods to leveling.
Try all.

1. Using resource leveling with the *Level Only Within Available Slack* option selected. This, however, did not relieve the overallocated resources.
2. Using resource leveling with the *Level Only Within Available Slac*k option *not* selected. Using the **Standard** leveling method, project duration extended to 39 days (bar chart shown in the following figure). Notice the leveling delay values.

3. Repeating step 2 with various trials in which we change the activity priority in Microsoft Project. The following table summarizes the priorities and the total project duration. According to these experiments, the Microsoft Project file of the last experiment was saved.

Resource Leveling with Random Priorities

No	Activity	Priorities	Priorities	Priorities
1	Clear site	Medium	Medium	Medium
2	Survey & layout	Medium	Medium	Medium
3	Rough grade	Medium	Medium	Medium
4	Excavate for sewer	Medium	Lowest	Lowest
5	Excavate elec. manholes	Medium	Medium	Medium
6	Drill well	Medium	Medium	Medium
7	Water tank foundations	Medium	Medium	Medium
8	Tank fabrication & erection	Medium	Medium	Medium
9	Install manholes	Medium	Medium	Medium
10	Install electric duct	Medium	Lowest	Lowest
11	Erect over head poles	Medium	Medium	Medium
12	Over head poles wiring	Medium	Medium	Medium
13	Duct wiring work	Medium	Medium	Medium
14	Transformer erection	Medium	Medium	Medium
15	Bus bar erection	Medium	Medium	Medium
16	Electric safety inspection	Medium	Medium	Medium
17	Connect piping	Medium	Highest	Highest
18	Tank piping and valves	Medium	Medium	Medium
19	Install well pump	Medium	Medium	Medium
20	Under ground water piping	Medium	Medium	Medium
21	Install sewer and back fill	Medium	Medium	Lowest
22	Sewer inspection, test	Medium	Medium	Medium
23	Sanitary inspection, test	Medium	Medium	Medium
24	Milestone	Medium	Medium	Medium
	Project Duration	**39**	**38**	**37**

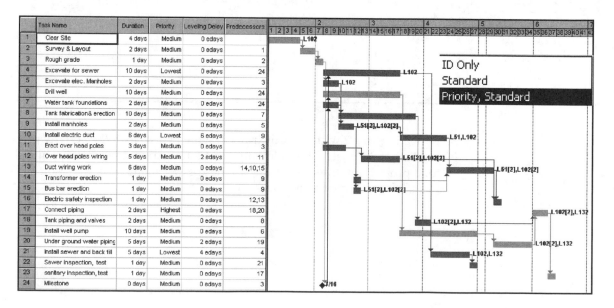

Best solution of Microsoft project with project duration = 37 days. Leveling option is **Priority-Standard.**

Importing Project Data to the Schedule Sheet

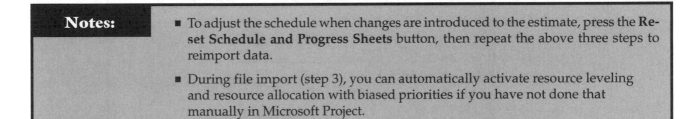

Step 1.
Select the Schedule sheet.

Step 2.
Click on the **Set Up From Estimate** button.

Step 3.
Click on the **Import MS Project Data** button.

Notes:

- To adjust the schedule when changes are introduced to the estimate, press the **Reset Schedule and Progress Sheets** button, then repeat the above three steps to reimport data.

- During file import (step 3), you can automatically activate resource leveling and resource allocation with biased priorities if you have not done that manually in Microsoft Project.

Overall Project Optimization Using Excel

We will use the Excel template and the Evolver Genetic Algorithm optimization software to conduct various experiments that attempt to optimize the project under various objectives and constraints.

- Experiment No. 1 Use Evolver to meet 32-day deadline.
- Experiment No. 2 Use Evolver to meet resource limits.
- Experiment No. 3 Use Evolver to meet 32-day deadline and resource limits.
- Experiment No. 4 Use Evolver to optimize all: meet 32-day deadline, meet resource limits, and minimize resource moments.
- Experiment No. 5 Repeat experiment 4 using the random improvements.
- Experiment No. 6 Use Solver to optimize bid unbalancing.

The six experiments are explained in the following figures:

Experiment No. 1: Meet a 32-Day Deadline Duration

Minimize: Total cost

Change: Index to construction methods

Constraints:
- Duration =< deadline duration
- Construction methods are integers.

Notes:
- Initial values for the variables (methods) are set as the shortest one (method 3). **Evolver** then minimizes total cost.
- This experiment executed under *unlimited resources*. Delay values are set to zeroes.

Results:

Project duration = 31.8 days.

Minimum cost = $259,136

Experiment No. 2: Meet Resource Limits of L102=3; L51=2; and L132=1

Minimize: Project duration

Change: Delay values in the delay column

Constraints:
- Resources =< available limits
- Delays are integer values.

Notes:
- Initial delay values are the best ones obtained from Microsoft Project with project duration = 37 days.
- This experiment executed under no deadline limit. Construction methods are all set to 1 (cheapest)

Results: Delay values remained the same and project duration = 37 days.

Experiment No. 3: Meet 32-Day Deadline; and Meet Resource Limits of: L102 = 4; L51 = 2; and L132 = 1

Minimize: Total cost

Change: Delay values in the delay column and methods of construction

Constraints:

- Duration =< deadline duration
- Construction methods are integers.
- Resources =< available limits
- Delays are integer values.

Notes:

- Initial delay values are the best ones obtained from Microsoft Project with project duration = 37 days. Then, we specify the method with minimum time (method 3) for all activities.

Results:

Project duration = 30.7 days.

Minimum cost = $266,801

Resources meet available limits.

Experiment No. 4: Meet 32-Day Deadline; Meet Resource Limits and Level Resource Profiles

Minimize: total cost

Change: Delay values in the delay column and methods of construction

Constraints:
- Duration =< deadline duration
- Construction methods are integers.
- Resources =< available limits
- Delays are integer values.
- Sum of all moments <= 2100

Notes:
- Initial delay and methods values are those obtained from experiment 3.

Results:

Project duration = 31.4 days.

Minimum cost = $266,260

Resources meet available limits.

	AJ	AK	AL	AM	AN	AO	AP
32	L102	4.0	4.0	158.4	1017.0		
33	L51	2.0	2.0	49.6	530.8		
34	L132	1.0	1.0	11.0	279.3	improved	
35		Avail.	Max.	Mx	My		
36		Limit	Used:	Flucc.	Utiliz.		Total Moment
37				Moment	Moment		2046.0

Experiment No. 5: Repeat Experiment 4 Using Random Improvements

Without using the Evolver software, we can now try to improve the whole schedule (i.e., repeating experiment 4) using the **Random Improvement** button on top of the Schedule sheet. Select the proper optimization objective (as shown below) and then let the program introduce random changes in both the delay column and the methods of construction column. Using one experiment with 100 trials, a good solution was obtained, as shown below.

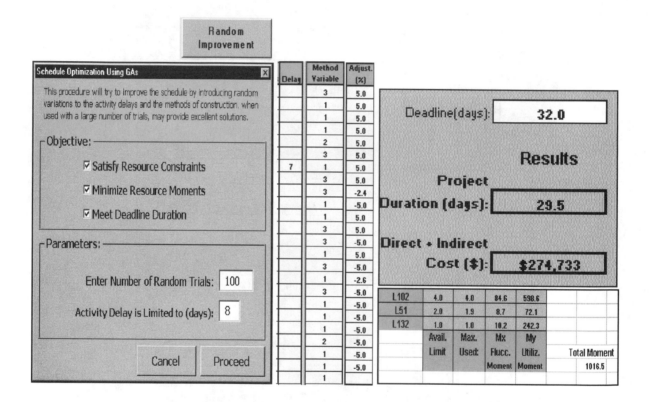

The result of applying random improvements to the variables, as shown here, duration is within deadline, resources are within limits, but cost is little high.

> **Note:** From the above five experiments, we can consider that experiment 4 is the one that determines for us a schedule that satisfies the deadline and resource limits while improving the resource profile of resources—all of this at the minimum cost.

Experiment No. 6: Use Solver to Optimize Bid Unbalancing

Now, let's try to optimize our bid proposal by improving the project cash flow through a bid unbalancing process, as follows:

Objective Function: Minimize the overdraft money (finance money, cell AG46).

Variables: Activities' adjustment column "AF", which leads to an increase or a decrease in the unit cost of the activities.

Initial Situation: Delays and construction methods are those of experiment 4. Adjustment values (variables) are zeroes.

Constraints:
- Variables are integers (-5 to 5) i.e., limit of $\pm 5\%$;
- Sum of the adjustment values $= 0$, i.e., total bid unchanged;
- Column "AJ" Total Budget $>= 0$, i.e., no negative budgets;
- Cell "AJ22" $>= 250$, i.e., example on how to fix the budget of one activity.

Note: Activity 24 is a milestone with no duration and no cost. Therefore, it is not part of the optimization.

Optimized Schedule

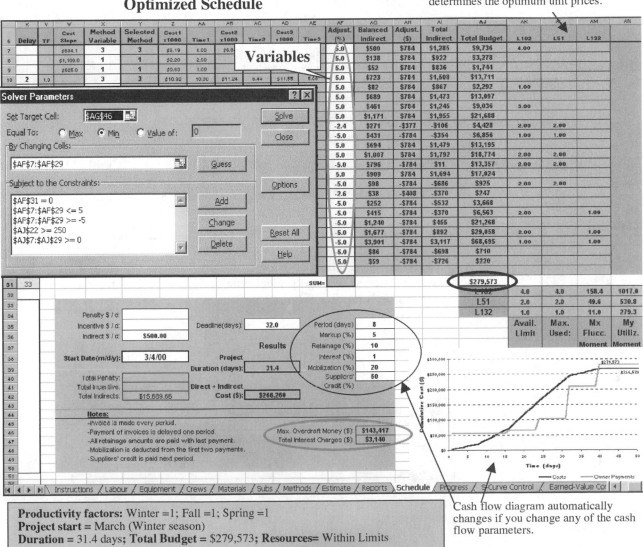

Activity Budget. Divided by the quantity determines the optimum unit prices.

Cash flow diagram automatically changes if you change any of the cash flow parameters.

Productivity factors: Winter =1; Fall =1; Spring =1
Project start = March (Winter season)
Duration = 31.4 days; **Total Budget** = $279,573; **Resources**= Within Limits

Bid Proposal Report

Once optimization is complete, a bid proposal for our case study becomes automatically ready in the Reports sheet. The report shows the unit prices associated with the work items in the project, to be submitted to the owner.

(a) Pivot Table Report For Bid Proposal.

Sum of TotalCost

Item	Desc.	Item_Q	Item_U	Unit Cost	Total
1.00	Clear Site	16900.00	m2	0.58	$9,736
2.00	Survey & Layout	4.00	acres	819.59	$3,278
3.00	Rough grade	1.00	acres	1744.20	$1,744
4.00	Excavate for sewer	2800.00	m3	4.90	$13,711
5.00	Excavate elec. Manholes	128.00	m3	17.91	$2,292
6.00	Drill well	10.00	Lsum	1309.69	$13,097
7.00	Water tank foundations	15.00	m3	602.42	$9,036
8.00	Tank fabrication& erection	1.00	unit	21688.17	$21,688
9.00	Install manholes	2.00	unit	2214.22	$4,428
10.00	Install electric duct	240.00	unit	28.57	$6,856
11.00	Erect over head poles	24.00	unit	549.80	$13,195
12.00	Over head poles wiring	400.00	unit	46.94	$18,774
13.00	Duct wiring work	320.00	unit	41.74	$13,357
14.00	Transformer erection	1.00	unit	17024.35	$17,024
15.00	Bus bar erection	1.00	unit	925.44	$925
16.00	Electric safety inspection	1.00	Lsum	246.70	$247
17.00	Connect piping	12.00	unit	305.69	$3,668
18.00	Tank piping and valves	40.00	Lsum	164.09	$6,563
19.00	Install well pump	3.00	unit	7089.36	$21,268
20.00	Under ground water piping	400.00	m	72.65	$29,058
21.00	Install sewer and back fill	610.00	m	112.61	$68,695
22.00	Sewer inspection, test	1.00	Lsum	710.44	$710
23.00	sanitary inspection, test	1.00	Lsum	219.52	$220
24.00	Milestone	1.00	Lsum	0.00	$0
Grand Total					**$279,573**

Crews / Materials / Subs / Methods / Estimate / **Reports** / Schedule / Progress

Effect of Productivity Factors on Project Time and Cost

Now, let's investigate the effect of using realistic productivity factors in the various methods of construction on total project time and cost. To add these seasonal productivity factors, let's modify the right part of the Methods sheet. We will use the three seasonal factors as follows:

Winter = 0.7

Fall = 0.9

Spring = 1.0

	Selection:									
CR-02	CR-02					Crew				
M2	M2					Material				
Excavation,	Excavation, manhole					Sub				

MatQ/d	Material	Hrs/d	OTadj	MatCost	CrewCost	SubCost	WinPro	SprPro	FallProd
1.00		8.00	8.00			605.00	0.70	1.00	0.85
0.10		8.00	8.00			1,485.00	0.70	1.00	0.85
0.15		8.00	8.00			2,805.00	0.70	1.00	0.85
80.000	M157-610-34	8.000	8.00	4,136.00	1,220.39		0.70	1.00	0.85
101.500	M157-610-34	12.000	12.80	5,247.55	1,952.63		0.70	1.00	0.85
150.00		8.00	8.00			14,025.00	0.70	1.00	0.85
		8.00	8.00		1,548.65		0.70	1.00	0.85

Crews / Materials / Subs / **Methods** / Estimate / Reports / Schedule / Progress / S-Curve C

Once the seasonal productivity factors are entered in one row and then copied to all methods, automatically all calculations are changed and the Schedule sheet reflects the modified cost, duration, and resources of all activities and for the whole project. Now, let's investigate one interesting feature, let's assume different project start times (in the Schedule sheet) and monitor project time, cost, and resources, as follows:

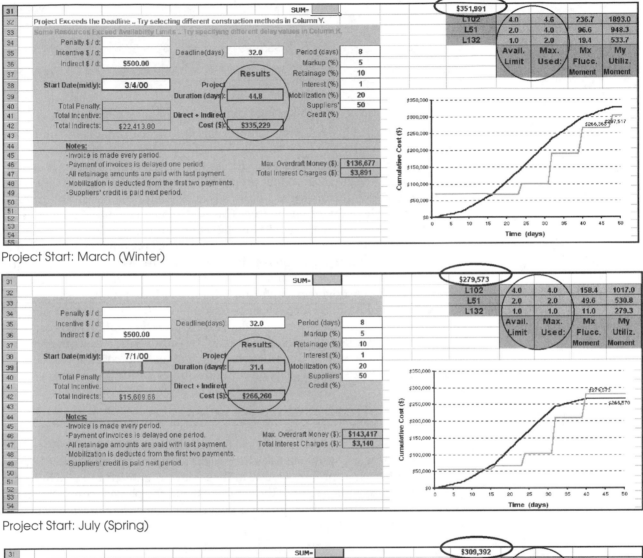

Project Start: March (Winter)

Project Start: July (Spring)

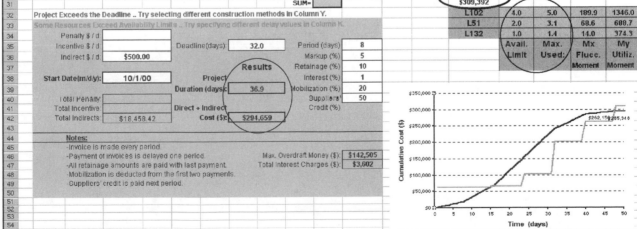

Project Start: Oct. (Fall)

The results are summarized in the following table:

	No Productivity Factors Winter = Spring = Fall = 1.0	Seasonal Productivity Factors Winter = 0.7; Spring = 1.0; Fall = 0.9		
Project Start	Any Month	March (Winter)	Spring (July)	October (Fall)
Project Duration	31.4	44.8 days	31.4 days	36.9 days
Total Budget	$279,573	$351,991	$279,573	$309,392
Resource Limit	Respected	Exceeded	Respected	Exceeded

From this table, we can see the following points:

- Productivity factors have a significant impact on project duration, cost, and resource use.
- The Excel template is a simple tool to address the impact of local weather conditions on project time and cost so that proper bid proposals can be made.
- With all productivity factors set as 1.0s, this is an assumption that all conditions are favourable, which might not be true. This is also means that the time of year in which the project is constructed has no effect on productivity.
- With seasonal productivity factors specified, the project becomes sensitive to the time of year in which construction is to be carried out. As seen in the table, winter resulted in much longer duration and substantial cost increase (25%). This means that a large cost overrun can result if improper bid is submitted.
- Using seasonal productivity factors can be used to investigate the impact of delaying some tasks to a different time of the year on project duration and cost.
- Using the Excel template, it is possible to redo the optimization experiments to select the proper methods of construction, delay values, and cost adjustment amount that minimize project cost and bring resources within their limits.

Progress Control

Assuming that a bid proposal was submitted for $279,573 and 31.4 days, let's use the control feature of the Excel system to track the project progress during the first 12 days of construction. The actual progress made in those days is entered in the white cells of the following figure, which refer to the actual cost and the percent complete on the actual bar chart. Accordingly, three progress curves become automatically available, as shown in the following figures.

Cost Control - ACTUAL PROGRESS DATA

Reported Actual Progress Reached Day: 14

	Percent Complete	Actual Duration	Actual Start	Actual Cost Todate
7	100%	3		$12,000
8	100%	4	1	$4,000
9	100%	2	3	$1,700
10	100%	8	6	$13,000
11	40%	2	4	$3,000
12	20%	2	4	$4,000
13	80%	2	4	$10,000
14	100%	3	9	$20,000
15				
16				
17	100%	4	6	$13,000
18	40%	2	10	$7,000

Percent Complete on Actual Bar Chart:

	1	2	3	4	5	6	7	8	9	10	11	12
7	50%	25%	25%									
8		40%	30%	20%	10%							
9				50%	50%							
10							15%	15%	15%	10%	20%	10%
11					20%	20%						
12					10%	10%						
13					40%	40%						
14										30%	30%	40%
17							25%	25%	25%	25%		
18											20%	20%

Actual Progress Data

Progress Report

For the period:

From Day No: **1** Enter values from
To Day No: **12** 1 to Project duration.

Project Start Date: **7/4/00**

Activity	Description	Budget	Planned % Progress (Day 1 to 12)	Actual % Progress (Day 1 to 12)	Owing To End of Day	Before Day 1	$ Payable
1	Clear Site	$9,736	100.0%	100.0%	$9,735.71		$9,736
2	Survey & Laye	$3,278	100.0%	100.0%	$3,278.35		$3,278
3	Rough grade	$1,744	100.0%	100.0%	$1,744.20		$1,744
4	Excavate for s	$13,711	100.0%	85.0%	$11,653.99		$11,654
5	Excavate elec	$2,292	100.0%	40.0%	$916.89		$917
6	Drill well	$13,097	76.2%	20.0%	$2,619.38		$2,619
7	Water tank fo	$9,036	100.0%	80.0%	$7,229.10		$7,229
8	Tank fabricati	$21,688	39.3%	100.0%	$21,688.17		$21,688
9	Install manho	$4,824					
10	Install electri	$6,856					
11	Erect over he	$13,195	100.0%	100.0%	$13,195.11		$13,195
12	Over head po	$18,774	52.4%	40.0%	$7,509.75		$7,510
13	Duct wiring w	$13,357					
14	Transformer	$17,024					
15	Bus bar erect	$925					
16	Electric safety	-$149					
17	Connect pipir	$3,668					
18	Tank piping a	$6,583					
19	Install well pu	$21,268					
20	Under ground	$29,058					
21	Install sewer	$68,695					
22	Sewer inspec	$710					
23	sanitary insp	$220					
24	Milestone		100.0%				

			Planned	Actual		Total:	$79,571
		$279,573	29.1%	28.5%	Less Retainage (10%):		$7,957
		Total Budget	Project % Complete		Less 1/2 of mobilization Payment ?	☐	
					Net Payable:		$71,613.59

Automated Progress payment report

Actual progress data and automated progress payment report

Note: Construction reached day 12. The progress made in each activity and actual costs are shown here. Between days 1 and 12, the project is 28.5% complete as opposed to the planned 29.1%

S- Curve Control

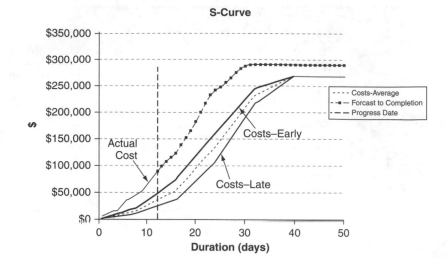

S-Curve

Legend:
- Costs-Average
- Forcast to Completion
- Progress Date

Labels: Actual Cost, Costs–Early, Costs–Late

Earned Value
Control

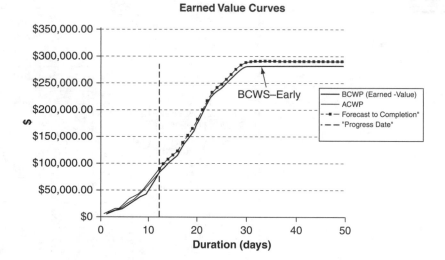

Earned Value Curves

Label: BCWS–Early

Legend:
- BCWP (Earned -Value)
- ACWP
- Forecast to Completion"
- "Progress Date"

Progress Indices

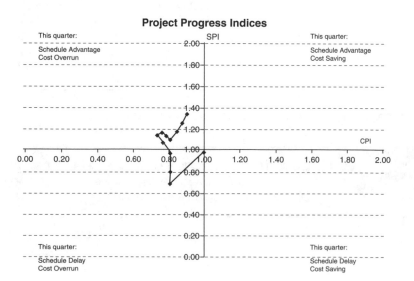

Project Progress Indices

This quarter:
Schedule Advantage
Cost Overrun

This quarter:
Schedule Advantage
Cost Saving

SPI

CPI

This quarter:
Schedule Delay
Cost Overrun

This quarter:
Schedule Delay
Cost Saving

EXERCISE PROJECTS

The following project cases are some exercises that can be solved either individually or by a group of students. In each project, students will have hands-on experience in developing an integrated framework for the planning, estimating, scheduling, resource management, cash flow optimization, and project control. Some of the resource data related to the exercises are included on the CD of this book as Excel files **Projectl.xls, Projectll.xls,** and **Projectlll.xls** for the three exercises, respectively.

Project 1

In this project, a two-level residential house is to be constructed. The following information is available for the project:

    a. The house plan is as follows:

    b. All civil work is supervised by Ahmed, electrical work, supervised by Majed and mechanical work, supervised by Samir.

c. The project consists of 35 activities as follows, with a detailed description below:

Item	Description	Tentative Predecessors	Quantity	Unit
1	Layout			
2	Excavate Foundation & Utility Trenches	1		
3	Forms, Footing	2		
4	Reinforcing, Light, Footing	3		
5	Placing Concrete, Direct Chute	4		
6	Removal of Forms, Footing	5		
7	Forms, Walls	6		
8	Reinforcing, Light, Walls	7		
9	Placing Concrete, Walls	8		
10	Removal of Form, Walls	9		
11	Insulation and Waterproofing of Foundation & Walls	6,10		
12	Back Fill	11		
13	Placing Concrete, Floor	12		
14	Wood Columns 100 mm × 150mm	13		
15	Stud Walls & Wooden	14		
16	Floor Joists & Cross Bridges	15		
17	Roof Trusses & Sheathing	14		
18	Subfloor 19-mm Thick	16		
19	Ductwork	17		
20	Exterior Walls Insulation	15,19		
21	Electrical System	18		
22	HVAC	20,21		
23	Install Plywood Underlay	18		
24	Install Stairs	14		
25	Plumbing Fixtures	23		
26	Window Installation	16		
27	Install Tiles & Ceramic	23,24		
28	Install Receptacles & Switches	21		
29	Doors Installation	26,27		
30	Drywall Installation	15		
31	Cabinets & Counters	29		
32	Exterior Brickwork	20,28		
33	Wall Painting	30,31		
34	Landscaping	32,33		
35	Final Inspection and Handing Over	25,34		

1. Layout: The excavation perimeter is to be located for foundations, strip footings, sewage pipe trenches, and drainage well point for the suction pump and weeping tile.
2. Excavate Foundation & Utility Trenches: Includes the removal of the excavated soil.
3. Forms, Footing: The foundations are to be located on the site with the exact dimensions.
4. Reinforcing, Light, Footing: Steel reinforcement to be laid inside the footing forms considering the proper concrete cover.
5. Placing Concrete, Direct Chute: After checking the soundness of the concrete forms, concrete to be poured inside the forms with suitable vibration.
6. Removal of Forms, Footing: twenty-four hours after the concrete has been poured and cured, the forms can be removed.
7. Forms, Walls: Forms for the 200-mm thick concrete walls are to be erected.
8. Reinforcing, Light, Walls: Steel reinforcement to be laid inside the wall forms considering the proper concrete cover.
9. Placing Concrete, Walls: After checking the soundness of the wall forms, concrete to be poured inside the forms with suitable vibration.
10. Removal of Form, Walls: twenty-four hours after the concrete has been poured and cured, the forms can be removed.
11. Insulation and Waterproofing of Foundation & Walls: After curing, the water/damp proofing can be applied, the material to be used is bituminous base material (EXPS IV). Fiberglass can then be used as an insulation material for the walls.
12. Back Fill: After the weeping tile is laid around the foundations covered with pea gravel and concrete curing is completed, backfill can take place with the specified amount of compaction (normally 95%) using a dozer with vibratory roller.
13. Placing Concrete, Floor: With special protection for all drainage pipes and columns/walls and the soil compacted properly, the concrete floor takes place.
14. Wood Columns 100 mm × 150 mm: These columns are to support the beams for the main floor and the roofing frames. These columns are to be supported on the footings and the surrounded walls. Steel columns may also be used.
15. Stud Walls & Wooden: These studs work as a support for the drywall from both sides. The studs are supported by the floor beams. The studs also determine the door and window locations.
16. Floor Joists & Cross Bridges: The distances between beams are to be divided by the joists to fit the plywood dimensions. These joists need cross bridges to support them against lateral forces in the transverse direction.
17. Roof Trusses & Sheathing: The top covering system to the second floor is to be supported on columns at the two sides of the building. The sheathing consists of plywood covered by waterproofing material.
18. Subfloor 19-mm Thick: This is to be laid on the floor joists to support the following flooring items.
19. Ductwork: Install the duct for heating and air-conditioning all around the two levels of the house.
20. Exterior Walls Insulation: All the walls around the building through the two levels have to be insulated.
21. Electrical System: This activity progresses along the construction of other activities, where the main electric circuit breaker is installed while the basement construction is being done, then the internal (walls, floors) wiring is installed during the construction of these items. After completing the installation of the drywalls, the on/off switches and their covering is to be installed.

22. HVAC: This activity also progresses along the construction of other activities because it is extended through the two levels of the house. Installing the needed ducts and vents for the HVAC system has to be completed before the interior drywalls have been installed.

23. Install Plywood Underlay: This activity is a predecessor to all the finishing activities.

24. Install Stairs.

25. Plumbing Fixtures: This activity also progresses along the construction of other activities because it serves the two levels of the house. The main discharge for the sewage system is always found at the basement floor. The plumbing pipes and water supply pipes/connections have to be installed before the installation of the drywalls.

26. Window Installation: Before the exterior or interior walls are finished, this activity has to take place.

27. Install Tiles & Ceramic: This activity applies to the washrooms and the kitchen and takes place after the installation of the subfloor.

28. Install Receptacles & Switches: This is the finishing stage of the electrical activity.

29. Doors Installation: The wall studs determine the location of the doors, which are installed in two stages: first is installing the door frames during the wall-studs installation, and the second is to install the doors after finishing the drywalls.

30. Drywall Installation: This activity comes after the installation of the wood studs and the door/window frames. The supervisor should make sure that all necessary services installed inside the walls are already completed and working efficiently, such as: duct work, water supply, sewage discharge pipes, electrical wires, HVAC ducts.

31. Cabinets & Counters: This is one of the finishing activities.

32. Exterior Brickwork: To be finished before landscaping.

33. Wall Painting: This activity takes place after most of the finishing activities and it consists of a primer and two coatings.

34. Landscaping: There are different choices for this activity, such as: concrete, asphalt, and grass, depending on the architectural design.

35. Final Inspection and Handing Over: This is the final and crucial activity before the house is ready for use.

    d. The developer has a system for keeping track of his labor, equipment, material, and subcontractor resource. The following resources are available to him with the hourly rates specified:

8	Code	Description	Rate/hr	BasicRate
9	L168	Sheet_Metal_Apprentice	$37.5	$23.8
10	L171	Sheet_Metal_Worker	$46.9	$29.7
11	L189	Steamfitter	$48.8	$30.9
12	L192	Steamfitter_Apprentice	$39.0	$24.7
13	L210	Tile_Layer	$40.5	$25.7
14	L78	Equip._Oper._Light	$40.6	$25.7
15	L15	Brick_Layer	$41.6	$26.4
16	L21	Brick_Layer_Helper	$32.2	$20.4
17	L24	Carpenter	$41.8	$26.5
18	L27	Carpenter_Foreman	$44.1	$27.9
19	L30	Carpenter_Helper	$30.9	$19.6
20	L33	Cement_Finisher	$39.1	$24.8
21	L36	Chief_of_Party	$40.6	$25.7
22	L51	Electrician	$47.5	$30.1
23	L72	Equip._Oiler	$36.1	$22.9
24	L75	Equip._Oper._Crane	$44.0	$27.9
25	L81	Equip._Oper._Medium	$43.5	$27.6
26	L93	Instrument_Man	$36.1	$22.9
27	L96	Labor_Foreman	$35.2	$22.3
28	L102	Laborer	$32.6	$20.7
29	L105	Lather	$40.2	$25.5
30	L117	Pianter_,ordinary	$37.4	$23.7
31	L126	Plaster	$38.9	$24.7
32	L129	Plaster_Helper	$32.5	$20.6
33	L132	Plumber	$48.5	$30.7
34	L135	Plumber_Apprentice	$38.8	$24.6
35	L150	Rodman/Chain_Man	$30.9	$19.6
36	L153	Roofer_Compistion	$36.4	$23.1
37	L162	Sheet_Metal_Worker	$46.9	$29.7

Instructions / Labour / Equipment / Crews / Materials / Subs / Met

8	Code	Description	Rate/hr	BasicRate
9	E150	Concrete_Pump_Small	$83.9	$76.3
10	E249	Dozer,55KW	$39.2	$35.6
11	E348	Gas_Engin_Vibrator	$10.3	$9.4
12	E402	Hyd._Crane_11mt	$59.5	$54.1
13	E456	Mixing_Machine_.17	$5.6	$5.1
14	E510	Power_tool	$4.2	$3.8
15	E567	Sand_blaster_accessories	$1.4	$1.3
16	E600	Tandem_Roller,4.5_metre_ton	$19.6	$17.8
17	E576	Sheepsft_Rolled_Towed	$16.0	$14.5
18	E423	hyd.Excavator,1.15m3	$97.8	$88.9

	A	B	C	D	E	F	G	H	I	J	K	L	M
8	Code	Description	Rate/d	NoR1	Res1	NoR2	Res2	NoR3	Res3	NoR4	Res4	NoR5	Res5
9	CRA-06	Crew CRA-06	$586	1.00	L36	1.00	L102	1.00		1.00		1.00	
10	CRB-10L	Crew CRB-10I	$792	1.00	L81	0.50	L102	1.00	E249	1.00		1.00	
11	CRB-10G	Crew CRB-10G	$561	1.00	L81	0.50	L102	1.00	E348	1.00		1.00	
12	CRB-10L	Crew CRB-10I	$792	1.00	L81	0.50	L102	1.00	E249	1.00		1.00	
13	CRB-12A	Crew CRB-12A	$696	1.00	L75	1.00	L102	1.00	E348	1.00		1.00	
14	CRB-37	Crew CRB-37	$1,733	1.00	L96	4.00	L102	1.00	L78	1.00	E348	1.00	
15	CRC-01	Crew CRC-01	$1,264	3.00	L24	1.00	L102	1.00		1.00		1.00	
16	CRC-02	Crew CRC-02	$1,951	1.00	L27	4.00	L24	1.00	L102	1.00		1.00	
17	CRC-06	Crew CRC-06	$1,839	1.00	L96	4.00	L102	1.00	L81	2.00	E348	1.00	
18	CRC-20	Crew CRC-20	$2,771	1.00	L96	5.00	L102	1.00	L81	2.00	E348	1.00	E150
19	CRD-01	Crew CRD-01	$591	1.00	L15	1.00	L21	1.00		1.00		1.00	
20	CRD-07	Crew CRD-07	$324	1.00	L210	1.00		1.00		1.00		1.00	
21	CRD-08	Crew CRD-08	$1,515	3.00	L15	2.00	L21	1.00		1.00		1.00	
22	CRF-02	Crew CRF-02	$736	2.00	L24	2.00	E510	1.00		1.00		1.00	
23	CRF-02A	Crew CRF-02A	$522	2.00	L102	1.00		1.00		1.00		1.00	
24	CRF-03	Crew CRF-03	$1,827	4.00	L81	1.00	L75	1.00	E348	2.00			
25	CRJ-02	Crew CRJ-02	$1,821	3.00	L126	2.00	L129	1.00	L105	1.00	E456	1.00	
26	CRL-02	Crew CRL-02	$581	1.00	L24	1.00	L30	1.00		1.00		1.00	
27	CRQ-01	Crew CRQ-01	$659	1.00	L81	1.00	L135	1.00		1.00		1.00	
28	CRQ-05	Crew CRQ-05	$739	1.00	L189	1.00	L81	1.00		1.00		1.00	
29	CRQ-09	Crew CRQ-09	$561	1.00	L102	1.00	L168	1.00		1.00		1.00	
30	CRQ-20	Crew CRQ-20	$1,055	1.00	L171	1.00	L168	1.00	L51	1.00		1.00	
31	CRZ-01	1 Laborer	$261	1.00	L102	1.00		1.00		1.00		1.00	
32	CRZ-02	1 Carpenter	$334	1.00	L24	1.00		1.00		1.00		1.00	
33	CRZ-03	2 Laborer	$522	2.00	L102	1.00		1.00		1.00		1.00	
34	CRZ-04	4 Rod-man	$1,044	4.00	L102	1.00		1.00		1.00		1.00	
35	CRZ-05	1 Chief_of_Party	$325	1.00	L36	1.00		1.00		1.00		1.00	
36	CRZ-06	1 Roofer_Compistion	$291	1.00	L153	1.00		1.00		1.00		1.00	
37	CRZ-07	1 Sheet_Metal_Worker	$375	1.00	L162	1.00		1.00		1.00		1.00	
38	CRZ-76	2 carp	$669	2.00	L24								
39	CRZ-77	1 TILF	$324	1.00	L210								
40	CRZ-78	1 PORD	$300	1.00	L117								
41	CRZ-26	Electrician	$380	1.00	L51								
42	CRZ-27	Sheet metal worker	$375	1.00	L162								
43	CRZ-28	Plumber	$388	1.00	L132								

Instructions / Labour / Equipment / Crews / Materials / Subs / Methods / Estimate / Reports / Sched

8		A	B	C	D	E
		Code	Description	Cost/Unit	SubCost/Unit	Unit
9		S31-01	Final inspection and handing over	$275.0	$250.0	ea
10		S76.02	Interior doors & frames	$1,573.0	$1,430.0	l.sum
11		S76.03	Windlws and frames	$6,930.0	$6,300.0	l.sum
12		S77.02	Kitchen cabinets & accessories	$2,864.9	$2,604.5	l.sum
13		S51.01	Excavation and levelling	$3.9	$3.5	ea
14		S53.01	Lawn preparation and final plan	$778.4	$707.7	ea
15		S54.03	Electric installation of Recpt	$67.8	$61.6	ea
16		S57.00	Mechanical works	$0.0		
17		S57.07	Plumbing fixtures (Washroom)	$4,730.0	$4,300.0	ea
18		S57.09	Form footings	$77.0	$70.0	ea
19		S51.03	Reinforcing light walls	$9,680.0	$8,800.0	ea
20		S51.04	Placing Concrete, Slab on grade	$163.9	$149.0	ea
21		S51.09	Exterior Walls Fiberglass Insulation	$6.9	$6.3	ea
22		S51.18	Exterior brick work	$115.0	$104.5	ea
23		S51.20	Dry wall instalation	$10.1	$9.2	ea
24		S51.22	wall color	$5.4	$4.9	ea
25		S51.24	Install 5/8' plywood underlay	$12.8	$11.6	ea
26		S51.32	Central air conditioning1	$3,426.5	$3,115.0	ea
27		S57.19	Form walls	$97.9	$89.0	ea
28		S51.44	Reinforcing light footing	$9,680.0	$8,800.0	ea
29		S51.45	Placing Concrete walls pump	$162.8	$148.0	ea
30		S51.46	Placing Concrete, Floor	$121.0	$110.0	ea
31		S51.55	Removal of form Walls	$3.2	$2.9	ea
32		S51.57	Plumbing fixtures (Washroom)	$4,803.7	$4,367.0	ea

Instructions / Labour / Equipment / Crews / Materials / Subs / Methods / Estimate

6	Code	Description	Cost/Unit	Basic$/Unit	Unit
7	M031-158-0010	Formwork, Plywood	$29.7	27.00	m2
8	M031-170-1000	End Forms	$2.3	2.13	m
9	M031-182-2000	Plywood, 1use in wall forms	$28.1	25.50	m2
10	M032-107-0500	#10M to #20M Reinforcing	$632.5	575.00	ton
11	M033-126-0350	31 Mpa Ready Mix Concrete	$89.1	81.00	m3
12	M061-908-0400	Wooden Roof Trusses, 13m to 18m span	$18.9	17.20	m2
13	M071-922-2100	Roof Deck Vapor Barrier	$1.0	0.91	m2
14	M072-116-0040	Fiberglass, 24 kg/m3, unfaced, 25mm thick, 0.	$2.7	2.48	m2
15	M072-118-0140	Fiberglass, kraft faced, 150mm thick, 3.3 m2.k	$3.2	2.91	m2
16	M072-118-0960	Fiberglass, kraft faced, 300mm thick, 6.7 m2.k	$7.6	6.90	m2
17	M061.160.01	Neumatic Nailed	$5.1	4.63	m2
18	M061.160.02	16 mm thick pneumatic nailed	$7.5	6.80	m2
19	M093.102.3000	Tiles,natural clay, random or uniform, thin set	$24.2	22.00	m2
20	M064.306.0400	Oak Treads 2438 mm	$715.0	650.00	flight
21	M092.608.0150	Drywall gypsum, nailed or screwed to stud	$1.8	1.61	m3
22	M099.224.0840	Paint 2 coats, smooth finish, roller	$0.8	0.75	m5
23	M061-118-0420	Wood columns 100mm*150mm	$396.0	360.00	m3
24	M061-164-0200	Plywood 19 mm thick	$7.2	6.55	m2
25	M042-184-0800	Exterior brick work	$28.6	26.00	m2
26	M061-114-2720	Floor joists 50*250 mm	$305.8	278.00	m3
27	M061-110-3500	Built-Up wood beam 50*100 mm	$385.0	350.00	m3
28	M157-125-1100	Central air conditioning	$2,530.0	2,300.00	Ea
29	M157-01	Plumbing fixtures (Washroom)	$2,970.0	2,700.00	Ea
30	M157-480-1020	Duct work access door	$16.2	14.70	Ea
31	M168-170-3250	Install recepticles & switches	$23.7	21.50	Ea
32	M163-245-0150	Connect meter board with main pannel	$429.0	390.00	Ea

Instructions / Labour / Equipment / Crews / Materials / Subs / Methods / Estimate / Reports / Schedule

e. The developer also keeps track of various methods to perform the activities:

Code	Description	Units	Crew	Sub	RegPr/d	MatQ/d	Material	Hrs/d
CSI-022-208-2043	Backfill from existing stockpile, no compaction	m3	**CRB-10L**		650.00	The daily		8.00
CSI-013-306-1100	Building layout, 2, person crew	day	CRA-06		1.00	material		8.00
CSI-064-76	Cabinets & counters	l.sum		S77.02	1.00	quantity		8.00
CSI-157-125-1100	Central air conditioning	Ea	CRQ-05		1.20	needed for	M157-125-1100	8.00
CSI-157-125-1103	Central air conditioning(2)	Ea	CRQ-05		1.20	each	M157-125-1100	12.00
CSI-157-125-1101	Central air conditioning(1)	Ea		S51.32	1.00	method is		8.00
CSI-092-608-0350	Drywall installation	m2	CRZ-76		89.65	always	M092.608.0150	8.00
CSI-092-608-0353	Drywall installation(1)	m2	CRZ-76		89.65	equal to	M092.608.0150	12.00
CSI-092-608-0351	Drywall installation(2)	m2		S51.20	89.65	the amount		8.00
CSI-157-480-1020	Duct work access door	Ea	CRZ-27		11.00	of daily	M157-480-1020	8.00
CSI-163-245-0150	Electric system	Ea	CRZ-26		1.00	production	M163-245-0150	8.00
CSI-022-238-0201	Excavation(1), backhoe = 57 m3/hr	m3		S51.01	500.00	of the crew		8.00
CSI-022-238-0202	Excavation(2), backhoe = 57 m3/hr	m3	CRB-12A		459.00	used.		12.00
CSI-022-238-0200	Excavation, backhoe = 57 m3/hr	m3	CRB-12A		459.00			8.00
CSI-042-184-0800	Exterior brick work	m2	CRD-08		19.97	In the	M042-184-0800	8.00
CSI-042-184-0801	Exterior brick work(1)	m2	CRD-08		19.97	Methods	M042-184-0800	12.00
CSI-042-184-0801	Exterior brick work(2)	m2		S51.18	19.97	sheet of		8.00
CSI-072-116-0041	Exterior walls fiberglass insulation	m2		S51.09	92.90	the Excel		8.00
CSI-072-116-0042	Exterior walls fiberglass insulation(1)	m2	CRZ-02		92.90	system,	M072-116-0040	12.00
CSI-170-31	Final inspection and handing over	Ea	S31-01		2.00	column D		8.00
CSI-061-114-2720	Floor joists 50 × 250 mm	m3	CRZ-02		3.52	calculates	M061-114-2720	8.00
CSI-031-158-0010	Forms, footing	m2	CRC-01		34.84	the total	M031-158-0010	8.00
CSI-031-158-0012	Forms, footing(1)	m2	CRC-01		34.84	production.	M031-158-0010	12.00
CSI-031-158-0011	Forms, footing(2)	m2		S57.09	34.84	You may		10.00
CSI-031-182-2000	Forms, walls	m2	CRC-02		34.37	use an	M031-182-2000	8.00
CSI-031-182-2002	Forms, walls(1)	m2		S57.19	34.37	equation		8.00
CSI-031-182-2001	Forms, walls(2)	m2	CRC-02		34.37	in this	M031-182-2000	12.00
CSI-093-102-3000	Install ceramic tiles (bath room)	m2	CRD-07		17.00	column,	M093.102.3000	8.00
CSI-061-168-0205	Install plywood underlay	m2	CRF-02A		161.00	therefore,	M061.160.02	8.00
CSI-061-168-0207	Install plywood underlay(1)	m2	CRF-02A		161.00	to refer to	M061.160.02	12.00
CSI-061-168-0206	Install plywood underlay(2)	m2		S51.24	161.00	column D.		8.00
CSI-064-306-0400	Install pref. stairs sections	flight	CRZ-76		3.00		M064.306.0400	8.00
CSI-168-170-3250	Install receptacles & switches	Ea	CRZ-26		10.00		M168-170-3250	8.00
CSI-168-170-323	Install receptacles & switches(1)	Ea	CRZ-26		10.00		M168-170-3250	12.00
CSI-168-170-324	Install receptacles & switches(2)	Ea		S54.03	10.00			8.00
CSI-072-118-0962	Insulation of foundation & walls	m2	CRZ-02		107.00		M072-118-0960	12.00
CSI-082-76	Int. doors frames installation	l.sum		S76.02	1.00			8.00
CSI-022-53	Landscaping	ea		S53.01	0.80			8.00
CSI-033-172-2650	Placing concrete, footings-direct chute, pumped	m3	CRC-20		115.00		M033-126-0350	8.00
CSI-033-172-4300	Placing concrete, slab on grade	m3	CRC-06		84.10		M033-126-0350	8.00
CSI-033-172-4301	Placing concrete, slab on grade	m3		S51.04	84.10			10.00
CSI-033-172-4301	Placing concrete, slab on grade(1)	m3	CRC-06		84.10		M033-126-0350	12.00
CSI-033-172-4302	Placing concrete, slab on grade(2)	m3		S51.46	84.10			8.00
CSI-033-172-4950	Placing concrete, walls, pumped	m3	CRC-20		46.46		M033-126-0350	8.00
CSI-033-172-4951	Placing concrete, walls, pumped(1)	m3	CRC-20		46.46		M033-126-0350	12.00
CSI-033-172-4952	Placing concrete, walls, pumped(2)	m3		S51.45	46.46			8.00
CSI-157-01	Plumbing fixtures (washroom)	Ea	CRQ-01		0.50		M157-01	8.00
CSI-157-07	Plumbing fixtures (washroom)(1)	Ea		S51.57	0.50			8.00
CSI-157-05	Plumbing fixtures (washroom)(2)	Ea	CRQ-01		0.50		M157-01	12.00